LANGUAGES OF NORTHERN PAKISTAN

Essays in Memory of Carla Radloff

LANGUAGES OF NORTHERN PAKISTAN

Essays in Memory of Carla Radloff

Editors
Joan L. G. Baart, Henrik Liljegren,
and Thomas E. Payne

Foreword by
Tariq Rahman

OXFORD
UNIVERSITY PRESS

OXFORD
UNIVERSITY PRESS

Oxford University Press is a department of the University of Oxford. It furthers the University's objective of excellence in research, scholarship, and education by publishing worldwide. Oxford is a registered trade mark of Oxford University Press in the UK and in certain other countries

Published in Pakistan by
Oxford University Press
No. 38, Sector 15, Korangi Industrial Area,
PO Box 8214, Karachi-74900, Pakistan

First Edition published in 2022

ISBN 978-0-19-940660-9

Typeset in Charis SIL
Printed on 68gsm Offset Paper

Printed by The Times Press (Pvt.) Ltd., Karachi

Acknowledgements
The Charis SIL Font is licensed under the SIL Open Font License,
Version 1.1 (http://scripts.sil.org/OFL)

Contents

Foreword

I think I met Carla Radloff in 1994 in Islamabad. Almost the first thing which struck me about her was her genuine courtesy, politeness, amiability, and gentle good manners. The SIL team of which she was a part was extremely courteous and respectful to local norms of behaviour but Carla—if I may use her first name, which I never did in our long association with her as my own norms of linguistic courtesy demanded that titles should be used—stood out even in that team. I also discovered that she was an excellent scholar when I had a chance to read and review her work on Shina. She was not only a descriptive linguist in the modern sense, but also a language activist concerned about the survival of the language. Thus, she did not content herself merely by writing a scholarly description of the language. She did more: she helped develop and standardize a writing system for the language, and worked with the community to publish folk tales and other materials in support of mother tongue-based education in the Gilgit area. She also helped young Pakistani language activists learn something about the basics of practical linguistics. This she did free of charge and with an endearing smile which was infectious and which must have made many people carry on learning despite the fact that there was not much encouragement of linguistics at the official level.

This volume in honour of Carla Radloff is the product of the hard work of its editors. It is a labour of love in memory of a person who deserves to be celebrated and remembered. Of course, since it is a scholar we are commemorating in addition to a really decent human being, it is befitting that most of the chapters are by scholars and about the subjects to which Carla dedicated her working life—the languages of northern Pakistan. We have in this volume gems by renowned scholars like Drs Georg Buddruss, Elena Bashir, Peter Hook, Ruth Laila Schmidt, Richard Strand, and Bertil Tikkanen. I could go on, but you can see the list of contributors and it will tell you what a prestigious work on the languages of the northern areas of Pakistan this is. In my view, it will be used both as a scholarly work, a kind of summation of achievement by several linguists working over many decades, as well as a token of a human engagement—a gift of human significance and courtesy.

This brings me to Carla Radloff as a human being again. As I said in the beginning, her most striking quality was politeness. And the editors of this volume follow that tradition by asking me to write these words. Academically speaking I do not deserve the honour since I am not what is considered a proper linguist. I am a historian of language—if you choose a favourable perspective on my work—and I do not even work on the languages of northern Pakistan. Yet the editors not only asked me to write these words, they also accommodated a chapter of mine on Urdu—the only one which the critics of the book will rightly dismiss as being irrelevant to the main theme—in their book. All I can say is 'Thank you', but I cannot thank Carla Radloff enough for being herself. That only teaches me the lesson that when one meets a good human being, one should be humble enough to thank them for entering one's life. I now thank her for being who she was on my behalf and that of Pakistan as a whole. She touched our lives and made them better and she has left a rich legacy of scholarly research. The volume you hold in your hands today is the least we can do for her. May it remain a landmark in the history of linguistics in Pakistan for the time to come.

Tariq Rahman

Preface

The mountainous northern parts of Pakistan, and their immediately surrounding regions in Kashmir and northeastern Afghanistan, are characterized by a rich diversity of cultures and languages. Some twenty-five different ethnolinguistic groups inhabit this area, famous for its gorgeous valleys and magnificent, sometimes unapproachable, mountains. Some of the local places and their inhabitants are widely known to the general public, such as Hunza and the Burusho people, Chitral and the Kalash people, and Skardu and the Balti people. Many other names are less familiar, such as the languages Chilisso, Domaaki, Gawri, Kalkoti, Ormuri, Palula, and Torwali.

With the arrival of modernization, such areas of abundant cultural and linguistic diversity have become highly endangered, and consequently the task of documenting and describing these languages and cultures is urgent. When a language dies without written records, all potential for enriching human experience embodied in the oral tradition and wisdom of that culture is lost forever. Many have argued that the loss of diversity that language extinction represents is a scientific and human tragedy. Though no language will survive unless speakers themselves want it to, linguistic research is an essential component of any program of language documentation and revitalization. The mere existence of a good dictionary and grammatical description confers a certain status on a language that may have previously been considered to be of little importance by speakers and non-speakers alike. Good linguistic research communicates to minority language speakers and to surrounding groups that the minority language has value and is worthy of respect. Furthermore, from a scientific perspective, good linguistic research contributes to an understanding of how the human mind is organized. The tension between universality and diversity of language constitutes the subject matter for the science of linguistics. The central questions are: 'How are all languages alike?' and 'What are the limits to their variation?' Needless to say, from this perspective, a corpus of reliable and usable data from as many languages as possible is essential. With every language that becomes extinct, the potential data source for this enterprise becomes narrower.

Larger-scale analysis and description of the languages in what is now northern Pakistan started in the early twentieth century with scholars such as Thomas Grahame Bailey, George Grierson, David L.R. Lorimer, and Georg Morgenstierne. In the second half of the century, the German linguist Georg Buddruss took the baton from Morgenstierne, and in turn inspired others to focus their attention on this area, including Hermann Berger, Ruth Laila Schmidt, and Elena Bashir.

Not all participants in this enterprise are or have been foreigners. Toward the end of the nineteenth century, Ghulam Muhammad Khan, a district inspector of schools in the Dera Ismail Khan district, composed the *Qawaid-e-Bargista*, which contains a grammar, a vocabulary, and a collection of short sentences and stories for the Ormuri language (also called Baraki) of Kaniguram in South Waziristan. This work served as the source for Grierson's description of Ormuri. Pakistani scholars who have contributed more recently to our knowledge of the languages of northern Pakistan include, among others, Said Alam Astori (linguistic and literary survey of the northern areas), N.A. Baloch (dialects of Kohistan), Muhammad Shahidullah (languages of the North-West Frontier), Muhammad Amin Zia (Shina grammar), Muhammad Shuja Namus (historical and comparative linguistics of Shina), Inayatullah Faizi (dialects of Khowar), Rozi Khan Burki (Ormuri), and Inamullah (Torwali). In the 1960s, Anwar S. Dil was prominently active as an editor of several volumes of papers by Pakistani linguists. From the 1990s onward, Dr Tariq Rahman, though in his own work more concerned with the sociology and politics of language than with linguistics proper, has been a strong supporter and effective advocate of linguistic work in Pakistan. Dr Khawaja Abdul Rehman is a recent and promising addition to the research community who has been publishing on languages of the Neelam Valley in particular.

Worldwide, there are probably between twenty and thirty professional linguists who devote a significant part of their time to studying and documenting the languages of northern Pakistan. The current volume is unique in bringing together—for the first time in history—a set of papers that represents the work of a very good number of these experts.

This volume, then, presents a cross section of current ongoing work focusing on languages of northern Pakistan. In bringing out this volume, our hope is that it will highlight these languages and draw additional linguists to their study. At the same time, we hope that the volume will highlight to the wider linguistic community the work that is already being done. Ultimately, we hope that through the affirmation of their languages, the ethnolinguistic communities themselves will be affirmed in their sense of self-worth.

Joan L.G. Baart
Henrik Liljegren
Thomas E. Payne

1

Burushaski: Some Areal-typological Comments on the Phonemics, Case Marking, and Complex Predicate Structure*

Gregory D.S. Anderson

1. INTRODUCTION AND OVERVIEW

Burushaski is an enigmatic isolate language spoken in the northern areas of Pakistan, primarily in the Hunza, Nager, and Yasin valleys.[1] In this study, a basic overview of the Burushaski phonemic system, case systems, and complex predicate structure is presented. In section 2, the phonemic system of Burushaski (its vocalism, consonantism, and suprasegmental phenomena) is discussed, and in sections 3 and 4, I introduce the case system and present its functions in the nominal system (3) and in complex sentence formation (4). In section 5, I briefly present the Burushaski system of complex predicates.

Burushaski stands at the meeting point of three large language families: Indo-European, Tibeto-Burman, and Altaic, and of three linguistic areas, viz. (Northern/Inner) Eurasia, South Asia, and the Himalayan zone. Burushaski speakers have interacted with numerous

* Thanks to an anonymous reviewer for many cogent and insightful critiques of an earlier draft of this paper without which the paper would be much worse. All errors of course remain the responsibility of the author.

[1] Some indeed assert a connection to a Macro-Caucasian phylum (e.g. Bleichsteiner 1930, Toporov 1971; cf. also Klimov and Edel'man 1995). Recently, Čašule (2012) rather argues in favour of an Indo-European genetic connection. Neither proposal is widely accepted, though Čašule's has garnered some support recently.

local language communities over the centuries, in particular with various Dardic and Indo-Aryan peoples, and with Balti speakers from the Tibeto-Burman family. Bilingualism among the Burusho is common, primarily in two Dardic Indo-European languages, Shina (Nager Burushaski speakers) and Khowar (the Burusho of Yasin Valley). Burushaski shares many features with Shina and Khowar. The inter-influencing could be due to borrowing or metatypy, or indeed both, at different points in history or simultaneously. Burushaski itself may have previously been spoken in a wider area than it is currently found: for example, in Dras, Baltistan, there is a group of people known as the Brokpa or Bruʃa; also, in Punyal, there are the so-called Burushken who are now Shina-speaking. Northern Shina varieties show especially close lexical connections to Nager Burushaski (Radloff 1992). In Gojal, Wakhi speakers often know Burushaski, but not vice versa (Backstrom 1992). In Hunza, especially in the village of Mominabad, the Indo-Aryan speaking Domaaki live in close contact with Burushaski speakers; virtually all Domaaki speakers are bilingual in Burushaski.

Data for this paper come from published sources on Hunza, Nager, and Srinagar Burushaski (e.g. Lorimer 1935–8; Berger 1998; Munshi 2006, 2010; Yoshioka 2012), as well as published and unpublished data collected by myself on the Yasin variety of Burushaski. The study is dedicated to the memory of our colleague Carla Radloff.

2. OVERVIEW OF THE BURUSHASKI PHONEMIC SYSTEM

Burushaski has a basic five vowel system, with two series of contrastive long vowels, alternatively bearing stress or higher pitch on the first or second mora respectively. This is realized as falling vs. rising tone restricted to long vowels only:

(1)	i		u	íi/î:	ií/ĭ:		úu/û:	uú/ŭ:
	e		o	ée/ê:	eé/ĕ:		óo/ô:	oó/ŏ:
		a				áa/â:	aá/ă:	

Varma (1941: 133) describes the suprasegmental or intonational contrasts of Burushaski long vowels as contrasting a rising and falling tone. Most modern investigators, however, e.g. Tiffou (1993), Berger

(1998), Morin (1989), Baart (2003), consider this to be a difference of moraic stress: that is, Burushaski long vowels may receive stress on either the first mora or the second, corresponding to Varma's falling and rising tones respectively. These tonal or length + moraic stress phenomena are phonemic in Burushaski. A lowered pitch on the second mora is sometimes heard with the initial mora prominent or rising tone forms.[2] Yasin Burushaski exhibits the same intonational phenomena as the standard Hunza/Nager varieties, although the moraic stress/tonal difference is less pronounced and may be in flux in the speech of Urdu-dominant male youth.

Three-way contrasts between short vs. first mora prominent/falling tone vs. second mora prominent/rising tone are not common in Burushaski but are found in a small number of lexical items. Such triplets include *bo* 'grain, seed, sperm/semen' vs. *bóo et-* 'low, bellow' vs. *boó* 'sit down, lower self' (cf. *nupáu* ~ *nupoón* in the converb form) or *don* 'large herd' vs. *dóon* (~*dóon ke*) 'still, yet, nevertheless' vs. *doón* 'woman's headscarf'; 'open' (Berger 1998-III: 121–2).[3] However, two-way contrasts between the falling tone/first mora prominent vs. rising tone/second mora prominent vowels are relatively common: *báak* 'punishment, torture' vs. *baák* 'generosity'. Similar 'tonal' systems can be found in other languages of northern Pakistan (Baart 2003) e.g. Gilgit Shina or Kalam Kohistani (Baart 2008). Burushaski is thus micro-areally typical and patterns with Shina in this manner.

---

[2] Note that diminutives are generally associated with this intonational pattern, e.g. *ʃon* 'blind' vs. *ʃoón* (*ʃŏ:n*) 'somewhat blind' or *ʈak* 'attached' vs. *ʈaák* (*ʈă:k*) 'somewhat attached'. Much remains to be done on Burushaski pitch, intonation, word- and phrase-level prosodies, and Burushaski experimental phonetics as a whole. Burushaski appears to be somewhat unusual in its system of contrastive tone and stress. In most derived or inflected forms the placement of stress in Burushaski is morpholexically, not phonologically, determined. Heavy syllables preferentially receive stress: *húnze* 'arrows', *ʂapík* 'bread', or *haɣúr* 'horse'. However, certain lexical items are pronounced with initial stress on a light syllable followed by a heavy syllable: *kʰápun* 'spoon'. Note that stress placement is at least minimally distinctive in Burushaski (i.e. of limited functional load), e.g. *báre* 'of the valley' vs. *baré* 'behold!' or *ɖuɖúr* 'apricot species' vs. *ɖúɖur* 'small hole'.

[3] Berger (1998) refers in its default interpretation to volume I (*Grammatik*). If a form comes from the other volumes, the citation is marked as 1998-II (*Texte*) or 1998-III (*Lexikon*) followed by the page number.

The consonantal inventory of Burushaski is characterized by a large number of coronal stops and affricates, phonemic retroflexion, phonemic aspiration on voiceless stops and affricates, and a uvular series of obstruents. In addition, the Hunza and Nager dialects of Burushaski possess a curious sound whose phonetic realizations vary from a retroflex, spirantized glide to a retroflex velarized spirant. This is symbolized {y.} in the standard transcription orthography, thus [j.] here. Tiffou (2004: 9) asserts that Hunza/Nager Burushaski is unique among the world's attested languages in possessing this phoneme. Note that it has been lost even in Yasin Burushaski and so it is diachronically unstable, as one might expect such a marked and unusual sound to be.

(2) The consonantal inventory of Burushaski

p	t	c	ʈ	tʃ	tʂ	k	q
pʰ	tʰ	cʰ	ʈʰ	tʃʰ	tʂʰ	kʰ	qʰ
b	d	z	ɖ	dʒ	dʐ	g	ɢ/ɣ/ʁ
(f)[4]		s		ʃ	ʂ	(x)	h
m	n					ŋ	
w				j	j.		
		l	r				

From a micro-areal perspective, the consonant inventory of Burushaski and Burushaski phonology in general (Morgenstierne 1942) share much in common with the immediately surrounding languages, in particular Shina and Khowar, but this could reflect Burushaski influence or substrata in these languages (or the reverse in principle as well) and thus these homologies could be of relatively recent origin.

Looking at proto-languages belonging to the South Asia region, it is clear that Burushaski shares little in common with the Proto-Dravidian phonemic system with its single stop series (Krishnamurti 2003). Burushaski also appears to share little in common with Proto-Munda as well (other than trivial details like *ɖ), insofar as Proto-Munda phonology can be inferred presently (e.g. Pinnow 1959). While the

[4] [f] and [x] occur only in loanwords, or as a variant of the aspirated stops [pʰ] and [qʰ] or [kʰ] respectively.

three stop series is of course reminiscent of Proto-Indo-European, the phonetic details of the Burushaski system do not parallel those of either Proto-Indo-European or Proto-Indo-Iranian as conventionally conceived. The retroflex affricate series and the uvulars unite Burushaski not only locally with nearby Dardic languages (Tikkanen 2008), but also farther afield across the Himalayas with various Tibeto-Burman languages currently spoken far to the east, e.g. Hruso Aka (author's field notes) of Arunachal Pradesh, India, with which it shares at least *ʈʂ*, *ɖʐ* (and *ʂ*) and *q[χ]* and *ɢʁ/ɣ*.

Unlike the nearby Balti language, consonant clusters at the beginning of words in Burushaski are extremely limited and furthermore, most of the words with initial clusters are loanwords, although some may not be, e.g. *praʈ man-* 'explode, detonate', *traŋ* 'half'. The clusters that may be found word-initially in Burushaski are mainly limited to unaspirated anterior stop + [r], that is *br-*, *pr-*, *dr-*, *gr-*, and *tr-* (*draá* 'jackass', *gra* 'mythical beast', etc.). The forms *tʰraq* 'cleft, tear' and *pʰraá* 'stone in ring' are among the very few examples of an initial aspirated stop + [r] cluster attested in Burushaski. Final clusters appear in indigenous vocabulary and are basically identical to those encountered word-medially; usually they consist of [l], [n], or [r], though sometimes [s] or [ʃ], followed by an obstruent, e.g. *gunc* 'day', *kʰask* 'girth', *manʈʂ* 'adze', *harʂ* 'plough', *tiʂk* 'dagger'. In the Hunza dialect these have sometimes been simplified; for example, Hunza *jas* 'sister' (plural *jás-caro*) vs. Yasin Burushaski *jast* (plural *jást-aru*).

3. THE BURUSHASKI CASE SYSTEM: NOMINAL MORPHOSYNTAX

Burushaski nouns are assigned to one of four lexical-grammatical noun classes. In addition to possessive prefixes, a singulative suffix, and a wide array of plural suffixes, a Burushaski noun stem may bear one of several structurally and semantically distinct sets of case forms, encoding grammatical, local–directional, and instrumental functions (see Appendix 1 for more details).

Burushaski makes use of a highly developed system of nominal case. Grammatical, local–directional, and instrumental cases each come in several subtypes. The ergative and genitive cases contrast only for class II or human female nouns; elsewhere, they are identical.[5] The range of other case forms actively used in Burushaski includes a set of three basic local–directional cases (dative–allative, ablative–elative, and the mostly archaic locative–essive), and a further set of complex local–directional cases, consisting of an initial complex case element and one of the three basic local–directional elements yielding such case forms as the superessive, superlative, superelative, inessive, illative, elative, adessive, allative, delative (> ABL), apudessive, apudlative, and apudelative. There are two instrumental cases (the *k*-instrumental and the *aŋe*-instrumental), as well as various lexicalized or lexically restricted local–directional and instrumental 'adverbial' case forms. Comitative, as well as a range of further complex local–directional functions, is expressed through the rich system of relational noun formations discussed below.

Nouns of classes I, III, and IV take the stem as the nominative–absolutive form, while class II nouns take the augment *-mo-/mu-*, an allomorph of the class II (genitive) inflectional marker. A brief sample paradigm of the four noun classes in the grammatical case forms as well as two common local-directional forms, the ablative and the allative, are given in (3).

(3)

	Class I	Class II	Class III	Class IV
<u>Case</u>	'man'	'woman'	'horse'	'sword'
NOM/ABS	*hir*	*gus*	*hayúr*	*yaténʈʂ*
ERG	*hír-e*	*gús-e*	*hayúr-e*	*yaténʈʂ-e*
GEN	*hír-e*	*gús-mo*	*hayúr-e*	*yaténʈʂ-e*
OBLQ (stem)	*hir-*	*gúsm-o-/-u-*	*hayúr-*	*yaténʈʂ-*
ALL	*hír-ar*	*gúsmu-r*[6]	*hayúr-ar*	*yaténʈʂ-ar*
ABL	*hír-cum*	*gúsmu-cum*	*hayúr-cum*	*yaténʈʂ-cum*

Some examples of the use of specific cases are offered below. In Yasin Burushaski, the locative takes the form *-ule* (6), while in Hunza and Nager Burushaski, the locative rather is *ulo* (5); the ergative is *e* in all three varieties.

[5] And indeed the older locative in -e appears to be etymologically the same case element as well.

[6] NB: the Nager ALL.II (class II dative form) has *gús-moore* 'to the woman' (Berger 1998: 60).

(4)	*ún-e*	*iskí-ulum*	*i-í-ar*	*dʐamé-e*
	you-ERG	three-ORD	I-son-ALL	bow-GEN
	káa	*hunc*	*j-u-úm-a*	
	with	arrow	I-give-AP-2	

'You gave his third son a bow and arrow.' (Tikkanen 1995: 488)

(5)	*ín-(e)*	*tʃái-ulo*	*bajú*	*n-ét-an-in*
	he-ERG	tea(GEN)-inside	salt	CV-do-CV-CV
	min-íʂ	*aj-ée-mai*	*bá-i*	
	drink-OPT/SUP	NEG-I-be.able.DUR	AUX-I	

'He can't drink tea with salt.' (Tikkanen 1995: 514)

(6)	*dasén-e*	*hir*	*párk-ule*	*dél-u*
	girl-ERG	man	park-LOC	hit-II

'The girl hit the man in the park.' (field notes, Yasin Burushaski dialect)

Burushaski shows a kind of tense/aspect/mood based split-ergative system that differs from, and is more complex than, that found in languages like Hindi. In Burushaski there is a cline of likelihood of ergative case use on agents from highest to lowest as follows: perfect/past > present > future, so it appears almost to reflect a[n incipient?] realis/irrealis mood opposition. Most complex is the distribution found in future forms (7) with second person agents. Compare (7) with (8) in this regard.

(7)	*un*	*in*	*mu-cútʃ-um-a*
	you	s/he	II-marry.DUR-AP-2

'You will marry her.' (Tiffou and Morin 1982: 88)

According to Berger (1998: 64), the distribution of the ergative case is as follows with respect to pronominal agents: first singular forms in the future and conditional almost never take ergative in Hunza Burushaski, but often do so in Nager Burushaski, while in second person singular and plural forms there is variation subject to as yet undetermined selectional factors, see example (8). Note that ergative almost never appears in transitive imperatives (or prohibitives). First plural agents are never marked for ergative in future and conditional forms across all dialects.

(8)	*ún(-e)*	*a-tʃ^{h}ítʃ-um-a*
	you-(ERG)	1-give.DUR-AP-2S

'You will give it to me.' (Berger 1998: 64)

In Yasin Burushaski, the ergative-absolutive distinction is apparently being lost with pronominal agents, having already been entirely lost for second singular agents.[7] There are thus clines found distinguishing the various dialects from each other as well as various person/number hierarchies operating intra-paradigmatically and inter-paradigmatically with respect to pronominal agents and the grammaticality of ergative-marked vs. absolutive-marked agents, especially in non-past formations.

Second singular agents in present tense forms may also appear optionally with or without ergative case marking (9–10) in Burushaski.

(9)	i.	*ún-e*	*in*	*mu-c^{h}útʃ-áa*	
		you-ERG	s/he	II-marry.DUR-2	

'You marry her.' (Tiffou and Morin 1982: 88)

ii.	*um-e*	*k^{h}ot*	*et-as*	*gu-may-am-a*
	you-ERG	this	do-INF	2-AUX.DUR-AP-Q

'Can you do this?' (Munshi 2006: 146) [Srinagar/Jammu and Kashmir dialect]

(10)	*dáa*	*uŋ*	*dʒe*	*ámul-ar*	*lip*	*a-tʃ-áa*
	again	you	I	where-ALL	throw	1-LIGHT.VERB.TR:IPFV-2

'... and where are you throwing me?' (Yoshioka 2012: 53, citing Tikkanen 1991: The frog as a bride, line 222)

[7] Thanks to the anonymous referee for drawing my attention to these facts.

Further, there is variation in ergative marking with third person subjects even in present tense forms that would typically trigger ergative case assignment in Burushaski.[8] Thus the conditions of the split-ergative patterning in Burushaski differ from those typically found in other South Asian or Himalayan ergative languages.

(11) *ín-(e)* *tʃái-ulo* *bajú* *n-ét-an-in*
s/he-ERG tea(GEN)-inside salt CV-do-CV-CV

min-íʂ *aj-ée-mai* *bá-i*
drink-OPT/SUP NEG-I-be.able.dur aux-i
'He can't drink tea with salt.' (Tikkanen 1995: 514)

Genitive case has a range of functions in Burushaski, and is structurally distinct from other cases insofar as it distinguishes class II nouns from all others. Functions of the genitive include the typical ones of possession (12–13), association (14), or origin (15):

(12) *dʒá-a* *a-ríiŋ*
I-GEN 1-hand
'my hand' (Anderson et al. 1998)

(13) *dasín-mo* *mó-miʂ*
girl-GEN.II II-finger
'the girl's finger' (Willson 1990: 5)

(14) *Híndi-e* *sis (~ ses)*
Hindi-GEN people
'the people of Hindi' (Lorimer 1935–38: 69)

[8] Note the Yasin Burushaski has neutralized the ergative vs. absolutive distinction in first and second singular pronouns. However, contra Silverstein (1976 et seqq.), this system appears to be an innovation and not an archaism in Yasin Burushaski: We can see that the first person singular form is based on the ergative (or genitive) form, while the second singular is based on the absolutive, viz. *dʒa* (not **dʒe*) and *on (un)* (not **one/*une*), if one compares Yasin with Hunza and Nager Burushaski.

(15)	*γéniʃ-e*	*salát*
	gold-GEN	moustache
	'golden moustache'	

The genitive is also the form that the semantic head noun takes in relational noun constructions (for more see below).

(16)	*híŋ-e*	*ulo*	*ke*	*sám-e*	*hóle*
	door-GEN	inside	and	smoke.hole-GEN	outside.LOC
	'in through the door, out through the smoke-hole' (Tiffou 1993: 47)				

Also, a semi-finite verb can be marked for genitive when appearing as the complement to a case marked nominal predicate, as in the following formation (17), as well as on the lexical predicate in the durative auxiliary verb constructions mentioned in section 5 below.

(17)	*gu-jeéc-as-e*	*armáan-ulo*
	2-see-INF-GEN	desire-LOC
	'(when) desiring to see you' (Lorimer 1935–38: 69)	

Burushaski makes use of a relatively expanded system of complex local–directional case forms. While the range of these contrasts pales in comparison with such case-exploded systems of Daghestanian languages like Lak or Tabassaran, at least twelve of these complex local cases are used commonly in Burushaski. Formally speaking, the Burushaski complex case forms consist of various specific, secondary local–directional elements (18) marking 'in-' (*ul*), 'apud-' (*al*), 'super-' (*aṭ*) and general locational/directional semantics (*c*), in combination with the three primary local–directional case formatives, viz. the locative–essive *-e*, elative (ablative) *-um*, and (al)lative *-ar* endings (19).[9]

(18)	*-ul-* in-	*-al-* ad-
	-c- general locational/directional	*-aṭ-* super-

[9] Note that the inessive/locative variant *-ule* is found in Yasin Burushaski, but *-ulo* in Hunza Burushaski.

(19) *-e* LOCAT-/ESS-IVE *-um* ABL-/EL-ATIVE *-ar* ALL-/LATIVE

(20) i. *ḍẓakún* *ún-al-e* *bi-m*
donkey you-AD-ESS be:III-PST:III
'The donkey was near you.' (Tiffou 1993: 103)

ii. *dasín* *háa-le* *hurúṭ-umo*
girl house-ADESS sit-PST:II
'The girl sat in/at the house.' (Willson 1990: 4)

(21) *é-ṣ-aṭ-um*
I-neck-SUPER-ABL
'from on his neck' (Tiffou 1993: 11)

Like many languages of Inner Asia (e.g. Turkic, Mongolic), Burushaski makes use of a complex system of 'relational' nouns. Relational nouns perform the same kind of function that many postpositions do, but are of a formally different type. These are nouns that either appear in a bound form (with obligatory person/number/class prefixes), or appear in an *izafet* construction, with the preceding noun in the genitive case. The relational nouns themselves may take primary local case endings (19) to mark complex case semantics.

(22) *-já(a)r(e)* 'in front of' *-jákal* 'in direction of' *-jántʃi* 'against'
-jóon 'over' *-tʃíaṭe/-ar* 'behind, after'
(Berger 1998: 97)

(23) *ṣéen* *gú-ldʒi* *wáʃi-a* *ke* *tilíaŋ-ar*
Shen 2-behind throw-DUR-2 if saddle-ALL

ɣaṣáp *é-tʃ-i*
snatch AUX.TR-DUR-I
'If you put a Shen (Shina) behind you (on a horse), he'll snatch the saddle.' (Tiffou 1993: 72)

As mentioned above, the complex local cases often have clear connections with relational nouns still active in the language. For example, compare the following 'super-' series of case forms with their corresponding adverbial/postpositional forms derived from the same relational noun stem that underlies the case elements.

(24) *jáṭ-e* 'above' cf. *-aṭe* SUPERESS
jáṭ-um 'from above, over-' cf. *-aṭum* SUPERABL 'super-'
jáṭ-ar 'to above' cf. *-aṭar* SUPERALL
< *jaṭ* 'over, above'
(Berger 1998: 92)

Other common relational noun forms include the following in (i) basic/locative/-essive, (ii) -ablative, and (iii) -lative forms:

(25)

i. Locative/ -Essive/Base	ii. -Ablative/ -Elative	iii. -Lative	Gloss
(dal)	*dál-um*	*dálar*	'up'
hol-e	*hól-um*	*(hol ne, hóle)*	'out'
úl-o	*úl-um*	*(úlo)*	'inside'
(íldʒi)	*íldʒ-um*	*íldʒi-n-ar*	'behind, after'
(q^ha(ṭ))	*q^háṭ-um*	*q^háṭ-ar*	'under'
(jar)	*jár-um*	*jár-ar (=Ng)* cf. (*jar ne* =Hz)	'before, earlier'

(Berger 1998: 93)

(26)

a-jáar-e	*q^hurk*	*$tʃ^h$oṭ*	*aj-e*
1-before-LOC	straw	piling.up	NEG-LIGHT.VERB.TRANS

'Don't pile up straw in front of me.' (Tiffou 1993: 82)

In order to mark possessive constructions of the 'X has Y' type, a construction is used with an adessive (*-ce*) or apudessive case (*-ale*) form of the possessor and unmarked possessum and a form of the copula ('be'). This type of formation in general terms may be found in many languages of Eurasia, but often with a locative case, rather than an adessive/apudessive case form as in Burushaski. The apudessive is the more normal construction (27 ii), but the adessive occurs in certain expressions as well (27 i).[10]

(27) i.

hín-mu-ce	*Gulzaazí*	*parí*	*mu-ík*	*bil-úm*
one-II.OBLQ-ADESS	Gulzaazi	fairy	II-name	be.IV-AP

'One (feminine) had the name Fairy Gulzaazi.' (Berger 1998: 75)

ii.

ín-ale	*maʃhúur*	*tumáq-an*	*bim*
he-APUDESS	excellent	weapon-SG	be.III:AP

'He had an excellent weapon.' (Berger 1998: 74)

One noteworthy aspect of the case system of Yasin Burushaski is that in conjoined structures, case marking shows a formally distinct pattern from verb agreement patterns in the same sentence. Thus, two conjoined nouns may both be inflected for case individually; however, only the closest conjunct can serve as the morphosyntactically activ(at)-e(d) referent and thus trigger verb agreement. Compare the following two examples (28–29) in this regard, where case is realized on both nouns in both sentences, but only 'local' object agreement on the verb is possible, i.e. there is only agreement with the rightmost conjunct, and the fact that the two NPs are conjoined is irrelevant. Thus a strict consideration of linear syntax determines the verb agreement pattern regardless of the case marking on the arguments involved, and the agreement pattern also does not reflect a hierarchically ordered set of features pertaining to animacy, class, or person, etc.

(28)

on	*kitáp*	*dʒá-ɣa*	*ka*	*hír-e*	*tʃʰí-a*
you	book(s)	I-ALL	and	man-OBLQ	give-2

'You gave the book(s) to me and the man.' (field notes, Yasin Burushaski)

(29)

on	*kitáp*	*hír-e*	*ka*	*dʒá-ɣa*	*a-tʃʰí-a*
you	book(s)	man-OBLQ	and	I-ALL	1-give-2

'You gave the book(s) to the man and me.' (field notes, Yasin Burushaski)

[10] Thanks to the anonymous reviewer for clarifying this issue for me.

Thus the system of case in Burushaski is more highly elaborated than is typically found in surrounding languages, and is more typical of Daghestanian languages, with which it may once have shared an older areal-typological relationship prior to the Indo-Iranian invasion of the subcontinent.

4. CASE IN BURUSHASKI INTERCLAUSAL SYNTAX

Like most other languages of the region, Burushaski is a fairly rigidly head-final language in its VP and S structure. In certain marked contexts of emphasis, topicalization, focus, etc. as well as in discourse-triggered afterthoughts and clarifications, an element may be found post-verbally in clause-final position. However, the predominance of verb-final sentences in both narrative and conversation is overwhelming. In many such SOV head-final languages across Eurasia, interclausal dependency is frequently marked by formations consisting of non-finite structures sentence medially followed by finite independent verbs in sentence-final position.

In terms of its complex or dependent clause structure, Burushaski reflects a wide array of formal means of combining clauses. Roughly speaking, there are finite and semi-finite or non-finite means of combining clauses in Burushaski. Non-finite strategies are likely the indigenous ones, and most (but not all) finite means are likely borrowed or calqued,[11] with various intermediate or partially calqued formations also attested. Non-finite means of subordination in Burushaski involve either what are known as 'converb' or 'adverbial subordination' formations. Inter-clausal dependency relations may also be encoded by case-marked verbal forms. Both formal means are commonly found in SOV languages in South Asia, and indeed are characteristic of the vast Trans-Eurasian areal complex, found as far afield as Evenki in northern Siberia. Many finite means of expressing subordination strategies in Burushaski reflect contact from local Indo-Iranian languages, e.g. in the form of a borrowed subordinator *kè*. The more common and likely indigenous means of combining clauses is to use various non-finite (or semi-finite) structures in the two formal subtypes mentioned above, but often subsumed together

[11] According to the anonymous reviewer '... *dáa* "and, again, then, more" appears to be indigenous'.

under a general heading of 'converb' formations (Tikkanen 1995—see Appendix 2 for more details).

A formation using the converb circumfix in *n-..(-n)* is one of the characteristic forms of Burushaski non-finite morphosyntax.[12] Its function is mostly to mark same subject clauses, temporally and logically preceding the following clause. Thus it is similar in function to so-called 'conjunctive participles' in Indo-Aryan languages or the converbs of various types found in Turkic languages, cf. Hapelsmath and König (eds.) (1995).

(30) *nu-ku-tʃí-n*
CV-2-give-CV
'having given it to you' (Tikkanen 1995: 492)

(31) *nu-mú-ic* *mu-jákal* *gáarc-im-i*
CV-II-see II-direction run-AP-I
'After he saw her, he ran towards her.' (Berger 1998: 164)

The other broadly conceived formal subtype of 'converb' subordination in Burushaski etymologically consists of a semi-finite form of the verb combined with one of several different case forms, in a system called 'case-marked clausal subordination' by Anderson (2002). The various subtypes of this system of case-marked clausal subordination in Burushaski are presented in subsequent examples.

Burushaski makes extensive use of case forms to encode interclausal relationships of various types. The ablative (*-cum*) is commonly found in Burushaski complex sentence formation attached to the aorist participial (or infinitival form) of the verb to mark temporally subordinate clauses of the 'after'-type.

(32) *in-é* *mi-ríiŋ-e* *wál-um-cum*
he-ERG 1PL-hand-LOC/GEN fall-AP-ABL
'after he fell into our hands' (Berger 1998: 75)

[12] Note the prefix part occurs in a slot that is mutually exclusive with the *d-* prefix in Burushaski that takes precedence over the converb prefix so the *n-* prefix does not occur with verbs lexically specified as containing the *d-* prefix.

Another common case used to create subordinate clauses in Burushaski is the dative case in *-ar*. This is frequently found attached to an aorist participle or an infinitive to express temporally subordinate clauses of the 'when'-type, as in (33) and (34), or conditional clauses, as in (35).

(33) *barén-a-m-ar*
look-1-AP-ALL
'when I looked' (Berger 1998: 190)

(34) *sén-as-ar*
say-INF-ALL
'when he said'

(35) *gáŋi-jar* *tóm-e* *sén-im-i* *ke* *'dʒáa* *a-rı́iŋ*
axe-ALL tree-ERG say-AP-III/IV comp I:gen 1-hand

gu-tʃʰí -j-a-m-ar *áa-skar-ʃ-aa'*
2-give-DUR-1-ST-ALL 1:AFF-cut-DUR-2(:Q)
'The tree said to the axe, "I give you my hand, will you cut it off?"' (Tiffou 1993: 99)

With a durative-marked stem, dative encodes purposive clauses (36 a–36 b).

(36) a. *sú-tʃ-ar*
bring-DUR-ALL
'in order to bring'
(Berger 1998: 140–1)

b. *maj-áar*
become.DUR-ALL
'in order to become'

The inessive case in *-ulo* in Burushaski may attach to either a participial or infinitival form of the verb to create temporally subordinate clauses of the 'when'-type as in (37) and (38).

(37) *du-ús-as-ulo*
D-come.out-INF-INESS
'when he came out' (Berger 1998: 190)

(38)	*ɣalíiz*	*báj-a-m-ulu*	*K^{h}udá-e-re*
	ill	be-1-PST/PRF-LOC	God-(GEN/OBLQ)-ALL
	duá	*ét-am*	
	prayer	AUX.TR-1.PST	

'When I was ill I prayed to God.' (Leitner 1889: 216)

On occasion, these are rather more properly rendered in English with a temporally subordinate clause of the 'after'-type (39).

(39) *d-íi-m-ulo*
D-IV-AP-INESS
'after it came (to her)' (Berger 1998: 190)

The mostly archaic locative (/genitive) case in *-e* (also grammaticalized as an ergative case marker in the modern language) similarly plays a role in Burushaski complex sentence formation. The primary function of this is to mark a subordinate clause in which the action is performed simultaneous to the action of the main clause, that is, 'while Vbing'. As such, it is hardly surprising that this case attaches to the durative or the pluractional (Tiffou and Patry 2008) form of the verb.

(40)	*k^{h}os*	*c^{h}igír-an-e*	*i-súmal*	*p^{h}íp^{h}il*
	this.III	goat-SG.ARTCL-ERG	III-tail	wag
	étʃ-um-e	*a-jár*	*man-ím-i*	
	AUX.TR-AP-LOC/GEN	1-side	become-AP-III	

'A goat went before me wagging its tail.' (Berger 1998: 171)

With the negative, the function often translates as 'without Vbing'; see (41). Not infrequently, the locative-marked durative form of the verb appears in a doubled construction as in (42).

(41)	*duró*	*aj-étʃ-um-e*
	work	NEG-do.DUR-AP-LOC/GEN

'without doing the work' (Berger 1998: 172)

(42) *ʂapík* *ʂíʈʂ-um-e* *ʂíʈʂ-um-e*
bread eat.DUR-AP-LOC/GEN eat.DUR-AP-LOC/GEN
'while eating his bread' (Berger 1998: 172)

The comitative case or relational noun construction, utilizing the relational noun *kaa(ʈ)* 'with, together', occurs with a durative or aorist participle or infinitive form of the verb in the genitive case. This marks an action either simultaneous to, or immediately preceding, the action of the main clause.

(43) *hér-um-e* *káa*
cry-AP-GEN COMIT
'on, after crying' (Tikkanen 1995: 493)

(44) *hér-as-e* *káa*
cry-INF-GEN COMIT
'on, after crying' (Tikkanen 1995: 493)

(45) *in* *ɣar* *étʃ-um-e* *káa* *girát-im-i*
he song AUX.TR.DUR-AP-GEN COMIT dance-AP-I
'He danced while singing.' (Berger 1998: 172)

That the *kaa(ʈ)* element of the comitative case construction is to be considered a relational noun rather than a postposition is shown by the fact that this element may itself take further local–directional case affixes.

(46) *d-ó-ʂqalt-as-e* *káaʈ-ar*
D-I/II.PL-arrive-INF-GEN COMIT-LAT
'after they arrived' (Berger 1998: 191)

Perhaps the single most characteristic and commonly used case in Burushaski complex sentence formation is the superessive case in *-aʈe*. Its primary function in the clausal subordination system is to form temporally subordinate clauses of the 'when'- or 'before'-type; see (47) and (48).

(47) *gu-ír-um-aṭe*
2-die-AP-SUPERESS
'when you die, before you die' (Tiffou 1993: 16)

(48) *laḍaí étʃ-um-aṭe*
fight AUX.TR.DUR-AP-SUPERESS
'when he fought' (Berger 1998: 171)

With the negative, this frequently corresponds to 'without having Vbed' as in (49); in other words, a past version of the locative-marked clause given in (41).

(49) *oó-ar-um-aṭe*
NEG-cry-AP-SUPERESS
'without crying, having cried' (Tikkanen 1995: 493)

Unlike other formations mentioned above, the superessive case may attach directly to a fully inflected (50–51) or semi-finite form of the verb (52).

(50) *barén-a b-á-ṭe*
see-1 AUX-1-SUPERESS
'when I saw' (Berger 1998: 140)

(51) *sén-a b-á-ṭe*
say-1 AUX-1-SUPERESS
'upon my having said' (Tikkanen 1995: 493)

(52) *ma ma-ír-áṭe dʒe taŋ a-máj-a-m*
y'all 2PL-die-SUPERESS I sad 1-become.DUR-1-AP
'When you all die I will be sad.' (Berger 1998: 140)

Functional overlap is considerable in the Burushaski system of case-marked clausal subordination: for example, according to Anderson (2002), temporally subordinate clauses of the 'after'-type can be expressed in at least *eighteen* formally different ways in various Burushaski texts![13]

At least one historically case-marked subordinate formation in Burushaski has been grammaticalized. This marks the conditional. The conditional synchronically occupies position +4 in the Burushaski verbal complex. It marks both irrealis and true conditions, and temporally subordinate clauses as well, the latter showing its formal and functional parallels and ties to the syntactic case-marked subordination strategies exemplified above. The conditional forms historically either incorporate (53) or consist of (54) an adessive case form.

(53) *a-mé* *b-ítʃance* *pʰíʈi* *a-t-áa-ɣurk-am,*
1-tooth be-CON pʰíʈi.bread/cake NEG-D-1-find-1-AP

pʰíʈi *b-ítʃance* *a-mé* *a-pí*
bread/cake be-CON 1-tooth NEG-be.III
'When I have teeth, I have no *pʰíʈi*.bread/cake; when I have *pʰíʈi*.bread/cake, I have no teeth.' (Tiffou 1993: 20)

(54) *á-jan-a-m-ce*
1-fall.asleep-1-AP-ADESS
'when I fell asleep' (Berger 1998: 191)

Analogues to Burushaski's system of case-marked clausal subordination may be found in various Himalayan languages like Limbu (Kiranti/Tibeto-Burman, Nepal; van Driem 1987) and in South Asian languages like Mundari (Kherwarian Munda/Austroasiatic, India; Osada 1992), Brahui (Dravidian, Pakistan/Iran; Bray 1986), or Odiya (Indic, India) to a limited extent (55), as in the following example of an ablative-marked subordinate clause.

---

13 Some are found only in same subject structures, some in different subject structures. A complete analysis of the range of forms and functions attested in Burushaski case-marked clausal subordination awaits the full-length study it merits.

(55) Odiya

Subhɔdra-ku	*pɔcar-iba-**ru***	*se*	*eɳu*	*teɳu*	*phand-i*
Subhodra-OBJ	ask-INF-**ABL**	she	so	so	invent-CV

michɔ	*kɔtha*	*kɔh-il-a*
lie	matter	say-PST-3SG

'When he asked Subodhra, she invented a false story and lied.' (Neukom and Patnaik 2003: 373)

However, more similar in the range of forms and functions seen in the Burushaski system of case-marked clausal subordination strategies are the systems found in northern Eurasian languages, in particular those of Central Asia and southern and (north)eastern Siberia. Thus, Burushaski is more reminiscent of such languages as Evenki (56–57)

(56) Evenki

bira	*dagadun*	*o:-**ri-du-v***
river	near	become-**PRTCPL-ALL-1**

so:t	*eduni-l-le-n*
very	blow.wind-INCH-NFUT-3

'When I found myself near the river, a strong wind began to blow.' (Nedjalkov 1997: 51)

(57) Evenki

min-duk	*pekture:vun-me*	*ga-**na-duk-in***
I-ABL	gun-ACC	take-**PRTCPL-ABL-3**

bega	*itten-e-n*
month	pass-NFUT-3

'A month had passed since he took my gun from me.' (Nedjalkov 1997: 51) or Turkic languages like Dolgan (58), Tuvan (59), or Xakas (60) than it is to most South Asian languages.

(58) Dolgan

min	*die-bit-ten*	*bar-**bɯʃut-tan***	*huruk*	*ɯl-a*	*ilik-pin*
I	house-1-ABL	go-**PRTCPL-ABL**	letter	get-CV	NEG.AUX-1

'Since I left my house, I haven't gotten any letters.' (Ubrjatova 1985: 162)

(59) Tuvan

men	*kel-**gen-im-de***	*aʒɯlda-ar men*
I	come-**PST.PRTCPL-1-LOC**	work-PRES/FUT 1

'When I come (here), I work.' (Anderson and Harrison 1999: 73)

(60) Xakas

naŋmur	*tʃaa-p*	*sɯx-**xan-da,***	*min*	*kil*	*pol-ba-a-m*
rain	precipitate-CV	INCH-**PST-LOC**	I	come	CAP-NEG-PST-1

'Because it (started to) rain(ed), I couldn't come.' (Anderson 1998: 78)

5. BURUSHASKI COMPLEX PREDICATE STRUCTURE

Burushaski makes extensive use of certain auxiliary and light verbs. The most common auxiliary verb in Burushaski conjugation is *b-/ba-* 'be'. Also, *huruţ* 'sit' is another frequently used auxiliary verb. Light verb usage in Burushaski involves *man-* 'become' for intransitive light verb constructions and *et-* 'do' for transitive ones. Auxiliary verb and light verb constructions are here understood in the sense of Anderson (2011).[14] Although many other verbs have auxiliary verb functions in the language, these will not be discussed in any detail here.

[14] Where auxiliary verbs are functional elements marking various TAME, etc. categories and light verbs serve to encode or instantiate valency and make predicative stems inflectable that are treated as non-verbal in a language. The complex mishmash category called vector verbs in South Asian linguistics should be replaced by serial, auxiliary, and light verbs, as appropriate.

The most common and important auxiliary verb in Burushaski is *b-/ba-* 'be'.[15] This appears in three of the six common tense(-aspect) forms, the imperfect and pluperfect.

(61)	*dʒe*	*á-jan-um*	or	(62)	*dʒe*	*á-jan-a-m*	*bá-ja-m*
	I	1-sleep-AP			I	1-sleep-1-AP	AUX-1-AP
	'I fell asleep.'				'I fell asleep.'		
	(Berger 1998: 133)						

Burushaski uses *et-* 'do, make' as the default element in transitive verb stem derivation in the language with nominal/infinitive stems, many borrowed from other languages. It thus has canonical light verb functions (Anderson 2011). This pattern of nominal or infinitive plus light verb 'do/make' or 'be(come)' is an areally common way of forming inflectable verb stems from borrowed or ideophonic elements seen in many South Asian and Central Asian languages, of various families, e.g. the Dravidian language Brahui (Bray 1908: 180) where the two light verbs are *kanning* 'do' and *manning* 'become', which function in an analogous manner to Burushaski *et* 'do' and *man-/maij-* 'become'.

(63) *q^hudáaj-e* *ún-ar* *gó-or* *ʃikáar* *manzúur* *ét-iʂ*
God-ERG you-ALL 2.OBLQ-ALL hunt grant TR.LV-OPT/SUP
'May God grant/provide you (with) a (lucky/successful) hunt.' (Berger 1998: 87)

(64) *hír-an* *i-mán-ʂ* *ke* *ɣaténtʂ-aʈe*
man-SG.ARTCL I-become-OPT/SUP subord sword-INS.C

j-áʈis *tʃaráp* *é-etʃ-i*
I-head slice.off I-AFF.TR.LV.DUR-III
'Would that he (cat) become a man, so that it may have his head cut off with a sword.' (Berger 1998: 163)

[15] It is also one possible source (reflecting a much earlier grammaticalization/fusing) for the *-m-* participle found in most finite verb forms.

Another common functional verb in Burushaski is the light verb (-) *man* 'become'. This is found with nominal stems in an intranstivizing or detransitivizing function (65–67).

(65) *i-ŋí* *burúm* *man-úm* *mapéer-an*
I-beard white be(come)-AP elder-SG.ARTCL
'an old man with a white beard' (Berger 1998: 166)

(66) *d-ée-ʂqal-tʃar* *asiír* *mán-um-o*
D-I-overtake-all near AUX.INTR-AP-II
'She came near to overtaking him.' (Bashir 1985: 15)

(67) *sihát* *q^{h}aráap* *maí-m-e* *d-í-ja*
health poor become-PRTCPL-GEN D.AUX<come>.IV:-NPST
'(His) health kept growing ever worse.' (Berger 1998: 172)

Preceded by a lexical verb in the optative/supine form, (-)*man* 'become' has been grammaticalized to form a (cap)abilitive, i.e. 'can, be able'. Note that an auxiliary meaning 'become' grammaticalized to a capabilitive is an areally common strategy.

(68) *mí-i-mo* *mí-u* *kaʃ* *ó-t-**iʂ***
we-GEN-POSS.ADJ 1PL-sons kill I.PL-AUX-**OPT/SUP**

*a-mée-**maij**-an*
NEG-**CAP.DUR**-1PL
'We won't be able to kill our own sons.' (Klimov and Edel'man 1970: 34)

Other commonly used auxiliary verb formations in Burushaski include three related formations consisting of the present participle in the genitive case plus the auxiliaries 'go' (69–70), 'sit' (71–72), or 'come' (73) to mark a durative aspect form.

(69) *ɣuró* ***giátʃum-e*** ***ní**-mie*
stones fall:**DUR.PRTCPL-GEN** **AUX**<go>-AOR:III.PL
'The stones kept falling.' (Berger 1998: 172)

(70) pʰu *balítʃum-e* ***ní**-mi*
fire burn:**DUR.PRTCPL-GEN** **AUX**$_{<\text{go}>}$-AOR:IV
'The fire kept burning.' (Berger 1998: 172)

(71) *in* ***jágutʃum-e*** ***hurúʈ**-umo*
she search:**DUR.PRTCPL-GEN** **AUX**$_{<\text{sit}>}$-AOR:II
'She kept searching for him.' (Berger 1998: 172)

(72) *harált* *d-i-áar**ʃum-e*** ***hurúʈ**-imi*
rain d-iv-rain:**DUR.PRTCPL-GEN** **AUX**$_{<\text{sit}>}$-AOR:IV
'It kept raining.' (Berger 1998: 172)

(73) *sihát* *qʰaráap* ***maím-e*** *díja*
health poor become:**DUR.PRTCPL-GEN** **AUX**$_{<\text{come}>}$:NPST
'(His) health keeps growing ever worse.' (Berger 1998: 172)

Broadly speaking, the morphosyntax of the Burushaski durative and capabilitive auxiliary constructions consists of a finite inflected auxiliary preceded by a nominalized form of a lexical verb.[16]

(74) *duwal-ʂ̨* ***a-mo**-mən-**ʊmo***
fly-**SUP** **NEG-II**-AUX-**II.PST**
'She was not able to fly.' (Lorimer 1935–38: 327)

Many South Asian languages show a similar auxiliary-headed pattern. Such languages include the Iranian-Baluchi language and Indic languages like Hindi.

[16] Light verb formations have uninflected elements followed by inflected light verbs in Burushaski. One exception is a formation that means 'help' where the logical object can be encoded as a prefix on the nominal element, e.g. *gu-mánc-e maj-áam* {gumәntsa maijam} [2-help-GEN AUX.DUR-1.AP] 'I shall help you.' (Lorimer 1935–38: 233).

(75) Baluchi

mən *svarəga* *koha* *ləgg-**əg-a*** ***bin***

I lunch mountain climb-**INF-DEF** **AUX:1**

'I shall be climbing the mountain at lunch(time).' (Bybee et al. 1994: 250–1, Barker and Mengal 1969: 233ff)

(76) Hindi

ghumta *hũ*

take.walk:**IPFV:MASC** AUX:1

'I take a walk.' (Kachru 1990: 482)

A number of Tibeto-Burman languages show similar auxiliary-headed structures with dependent-marked lexical verb followed by an inflected auxiliary that Burushaski shows in its durative or capabilitive AVCs. Such languages include Garo and Imphal Meithei of northeastern India, or Belhare of Nepal.

(77) Belhare

wa-si *ŋ-khatd-**att-i-n-na***

stroll-**SUP** NEG-go-**PST-1PL-NEG-EX**

'We didn't go for a stroll.' (Bickel 2003: 567)

(78) Impal Meithei

ə́j *tʃak* *tʃá-**bə*** *həw-**r-e***

I cooked.rice eat-**NMLZR** AUX-**PRF-ASS**

'I have started eating cooked rice.' (Chelliah 2003: 436)

(79) Garo

anga *reʔang-**na*** *manʔ-**ja***

I go.away-INF CAP-NEG

'I cannot go.' (Burling 2003: 398–9)

Table 1: Inflection in AVCs in selected Himalayan and South Asian languages

Hindi	AH+DEP	Indic
Baluchi	AH+DEP	Iranian
Burushaski	AH+DEP	Isolate
Meithei	AH+DEP	Tibeto-Burman
Garo	AH+DEP	Tibeto-Burman
Kham	AH+DEP	Tibeto-Burman
Belhare	AH+DEP	Kiranti Tibeto-Burman

KEY:
AH: AUX-headed; structure with fully inflected auxiliary, non-finite lexical verb
DEP: dependent; lexical verb appears in construction specific non-finite
Note: Table 1 is not supposed to be considered exhaustive or complete.

Looking at the morphosyntax of Burushaski negative inflection in complex verb forms that involve an auxiliary, a split inflectional pattern is found, where negative is marked on the lexical verb and not the auxiliary, and subject can be doubly marked as in (80).[17]

(80) ***oó-du-móo*** *b-**o-m***
NEG-D-II AUX-**II-AOR**
'She didn't come.' (Berger 1998-III: 198)

Doubled subject inflection is found in some Limbu auxiliary verb constructions and in large verbal complexes that derive from such forms in Camling.

[17] In this example, admittedly there appears to be no stem in this gloss, only the *d*-prefix. Basically, either one synchronically considers the stem to be Ø and for the *d*-prefix to be present as glossed here, or the other option is to consider the *d*-prefix to synchronically (also) be the stem that means 'come' in some forms, which it appears to have historically been at least, and thus gloss it as such in all relevant instances.

(81) Limbu

*sɛʔr-**u-ŋ*** *nɛtt-**u-ŋ***

kill-**3-1.PST** AUX-**3-1.PST**

'I was about to kill him.' (van Driem 1987: 125)

(82) Camling

*ca-**m**-pak-**u-m-ka***

eat-**1/2PL**-AUX-**3PAT-1/2PL-EX**

'We ate it up.' (Ebert 2003b: 542)

Limbu (84) and Camling (85) also both split negative inflection, as does their sister language Thulung (83), all three Himalayan languages belonging to the Tibeto-Burman Kiranti family.

(83) Thulung

***mi**-pe-thiŋa* *bu-ŋa*

NEG-eat-CV AUX-1

'I have not eaten.' (Ebert 2003a: 513)

(84) Limbu

***mɛn**-dee-ʔtee* *waa-ʔɛ*

NEG-SOW-CV AUX-1.NPST

'No, I haven't sown (it).' (Ebert 2003a: 513)

(85) Camling

***mi**-tim* *ŋas-i-e*

NEG-meet AUX-1PL-NPST

'We have not met.' (Ebert 2003a: 513)

The South Munda Remo (Bonda) language of Odisha, India has similar split negative forms as well (86).

(86) Remo (aka Bonda)

a-sap *ḍen-gi-t-iŋ*

NEG-come PROG-PST.I-NPST-1

'I have not been coming.' (author's field notes)

Table 2: Split Negative Inflection in AVCs in selected South Asian languages

Limbu		2x	Split NEG	Kiranti Tibeto-Burman
Camling	fSp/2x		Split NEG	Kiranti Tibeto-Burman
Thulung			Split NEG	Kiranti Tibeto-Burman
Remo			Split NEG	South Munda

KEY:

2x: doubled pattern; structure with fully inflected lexical verb

fSp[lit]/2x: split and doubled structure fused into single complex verb form

Split NEG: split inflectional pattern with negative on lexical verb

Note: Table 2 is not supposed to be considered exhaustive or complete.

Burushaski can have split object inflection in auxiliary structures as well, where objects appear on the transitive lexical verb and subject doubly encoded on both the auxiliary and the lexical verb.

(87) Burushaski

gó-sqaiy-a *b-**a***

2-kill.DUR-**1** AUX-**1**

'I am going to kill thee.' (Lorimer 1935–38: 219)

A somewhat similar formation may be found in Kinnauri, a Himalayan language spoken in Himachal Pradesh, India, though of course the object markers are prefixes in Burushaski, not suffixes as in Kinnauri. Also, Kinnauri shows a straight subject/object split formation, not a split/doubled formation with a second, redundant index of subject on the lexical verb, this latter pattern being the one found in Burushaski.

(88) Kinnauri (Tibeto-Burman, India)

khya-ci *du-**k***

see-**2** AUX-**1**

'I see you.' (Sharma 1988: 140)

Table 3: Split Subject/Object Inflection in AVCs in selected South Asian languages

Burushaski	Split/2x	Split O, 2x S	Isolate
Kinnauri	Split	Split S/O	Tibeto-Burman

KEY:

Split/2x: split and doubled structure: inflected auxiliary and lexical verb, but only some overlap

Split S/O: split inflectional pattern with object on lexical verb subject on auxiliary

Note: Table 3 is not supposed to be considered exhaustive or complete.

6. SUMMARY

Burushaski is a language isolate that reflects several layers or diachronic strata of influences. This can be seen in virtually all aspects of this language. Some features of Burushaski are widespread and some less so, and some highly localized or indeed potentially unique. Like many languages of Eurasia, Burushaski has a relatively strict preference for verb-final clauses. In addition, Burushaski shares some features with local languages of northern Pakistan, such as its tonal phenomena, with rising and falling tones realized on long vowels. Given its lack of close linguistic relatives, such a feature is hard to periodize in Burushaski. Some features of Burushaski find their analogues mainly in Daghestanian languages like Lak, e.g. four-way noun-class system and exploded case inventories, which might possibly reflect an archaic areal feature in Burushaski before Trans-Eurasian language features became dominant in the region. Other features it shares with distant Himalayan languages, again possibly reflecting a layer of continuity pre-dating the Indo-Iranian invasion of the region, such as morphological complexity of exponence of arguments in the inflection of verbs in complex predicate structures or phonemic uvulars. Yet other characteristic features of this intriguing isolate language are more typical of Central and Northern Asian languages, for example the expanded systems of case-marked clausal subordination. Still yet other features of Burushaski are common across contemporary South Asian languages, e.g. dependent-marked auxiliary structures and light verbs. Teasing apart the various diachronic layers and areal forces at play in Burushaski remains the subject of a more detailed future study.

ABBREVIATIONS

1 = First Person
2 = Second Person
2x = Doubled
3 = Third Person
ACC = Accusative
ADESS = Adessive
AFF = Affected
AH = AUX-headed
ALL = Allative
AOR = Aorist
APUDESS = Apudessive
ARTCL = Article
ASS = Assertive
AUX = Auxiliary
CAP = Capabilitive
CONT = Continuous
CV = Converb
D = D-prefix
DEF = Definite
DEP = Dependent
DUR = Durative
EMPH = Emphatic
ERG = Ergative
EX = Exclusive
F = Fused
FIN = Finite
FUT = Future
GEN = Genitive
HAB = Habitual
I = Class-I
II = Class-II
IMPFV = Imperfective
INCH = Inchoative
INCL = Inclusive
INF = Infinitive
ITR = Intransitive
LOC = Locative
LV = Light verb
M = Masculine
NEG = Negative
NFUT = Non-future
NMLZR = Nominalizer
NPST = Non-past
NPT = Non-preterite
Ø = Zero-marked
OBJ = Object
OBLQ = Oblique
OPT = Optative
ORD = Ordinal
PASS = Passive
PFV = Perfective
PL = Plural
PRF = Perfect
PROG = Progressive
PRTCPL = Participle
PST = Past
PT = Preterite
RDPL = Reduplication
REC = Reciprocal
SBJNCTV = Subjunctive
SG = Singular
SP/2X = Split/Doubled
SS = Same subject
SUBJ = Subject
SUP = Supine
SUPERESS = Superessive
T/A = Tense/Aspect
TAM = Tense/Aspect/Mood
TR = Transitive

APPENDIX 1

The four categories of inherent lexical noun-class in Burushaski constitute one of the most salient characteristics of the language's nominal system and also serve to distinguish the nominal system of Burushaski from those of surrounding languages. These classes are: class-I human male, class-II human female, class-III animals and many semantically inanimate nouns, and class-IV for the remainder (and majority) of inanimate nouns. In Lorimer and other traditional analyses of Burushaski, these are called hm, hf, x, and y, respectively. The particular noun class category is usually covertly expressed on the noun itself (except in oblique case forms of class-II nouns). Rather, class is generally marked through verb agreement (or lack thereof), and in some cases, through adjective and noun plural suffixes as well.

(i)	I: male human	II: female human
	hir 'man' (I)	*dasín* 'girl' (II)
	III: animate non-human, inanimate	IV: inanimate
	haɣúr 'horse'(III)	*ɣaténṭṣ* 'sword' (IV)

The most similar systems of noun categorization to the four-way system found in Burushaski are the systems found in certain Daghestanian languages such as Lak, but the formal expression of the two systems are not similar at all, just the semantic criteria for class-membership assignment.

The categories of person and class of an external possessor of a noun are marked by one of a set of four allomorphic prefix-series, differentiated by the 'grade' of the vowel and its stress/tonal quality. These prefixes occur obligatorily with a small, closed set of bound, inalienably possessed noun stems. The Burushaski person/class prefixes take the following shape:

	<u>A</u>	<u>A'</u>	<u>B</u>	<u>C</u>
1	*á-*	*a-*	*á-*	*áa-*
2	*gú-/-kú-*	*gu-*	*gó-/-kó-*	*góo-/-kóo-*
I	*í-*	*i-*	*é-*	*ée-*
II	*mú-*	*mu-*	*mó-*	*móo-*

III	*í-*	*i-*	*é-*	*ée-*
IV.SG/PL	*í-*	*i-*	*é-*	*ée-*
1PL	*mí-*	*mi-*	*mé-*	*mée-*
2PL	*má-*	*ma-*	*má-*	*máa-*
I/II/III.PL	*ú-*	*u-*	*ó-*	*óo-*

(Berger 1998: 91)

A	A'	B	C	
+	-	+	+	stress
+	+	-	-	high
-	-	-	+	long

TABLE A: PERSON/CLASS MARKERS

Examples include the following bound noun stems *´-ltʃin* 'eye' (stressed, type-Ai), *-mé* 'tooth' (unstressed, type-Aii), *-·s* 'heart' (type-B), *-: -ʂki* 'head' (also 'at/under the head, bedhead, pillow') (type-C) (Berger 1998: 44).

(ii)	*gú-ltʃin*	*gu-mé*	*gó-s*	*góo-ʂki*	2
	í-ltʃin	*i-mé*	*é-s*	*ée-ʂki*	I/III/IV
	mú-ltʃin	*mu-mé*	*mó-s*	*móo-ʂki*	II
	'eye'	'tooth'	'heart'	'head, (etc.)'	

Burushaski has an unusually high number of nominal plural suffixes, and the specific plural form is often a necessary part of the lexical entry of a nominal stem. Some plural suffixes are restricted to nouns of a particular noun class. Certain adjective stems require a particular plural suffix with nouns of a given class or group of classes, while with nouns of other classes, another, different plural suffix is required.

(iii)

SG			PL
hal	*hal-dʒó*		'fox'
dʒíip	*dʒíip-uc*		'jeeps'
ɣus	*ɣuʃ-ó(ŋo)*		'earthen clumps'
ʈʂonʈʂ	*ʈʂónʈʂ-iŋ*		'summit, peak'
-ɣárum	*-ɣárum-iŋ* ~	*ɣárim-iŋ*	'part'
gírkis	*gírkitʃ-o*		'rats'
ɣúrkun	*ɣúrkuj-o*		'frogs'
ɣúrkuc	*ɣúrkutʃ-o*		'frogs' Nager Burushaski
aʃaáto	*aʃaátu-tiŋ*		'weak(ling)'
ɣat-énʈʂ	*ɣat-áaŋ*		'swords'

Examples of double-plural marking or variant plural formations can be seen in (iv).

(iv)

tʃʰu	*tʃʰo-óŋu-miŋ* (NB)	'ears (of corn), spikes'
asqúr	*asqúr-iŋ* ~ *asqúr-iŋ-tʃiŋ*	'flowers'
kʰané-ŋ-itʃiŋ ~	*kʰané-ŋ-tʃaŋ* (NB)	'roasted grain/corn'
haɣúr	*haɣúr-a* ~ *haɣúr-iʃo* ~ *haɣúr-inc* (NB)	'horses'
nána	*nána-caro* ~ *nána-ku*	'uncles'

(Berger 1998: 43–4)

APPENDIX 2

There is an element explicitly called a converb that is formally a prefix *n-* in position -3 in the verbal template and also in a suffixal slot in position +4. Other non-finite formations have been considered manifestations of converbial subordination in Burushaski by Tikkanen (1995), but here such formations are called case-marked subordination patterns. Note that in Hunza Burushaski, there is no negative of the converb; a negative form of the *-m-* (aorist) participle is used:

(v) *aj-ét-um*

NEG-do-AP

'after not having done it' (Berger 1998: 165)

Certain stems have multiple marking of the CV; expressive repetition of the converb may also be found.

(vi)	*d-é-jal-in-in*	*n-íi-n-in-in-in*
	D-I-hear-CV-CV	CV-$\text{i}_{[:\text{go}]}$-CV-CV-CV-CV
	'after he heard'	'after he went' (Berger 1998: 133)

In narratives, the converb form often appears in such formations embedded within head-to-tail linkage, a narrative structuring device that consists of a nearly mechanical repetition of the finite verb of the preceding clause in a non-finite form at the beginning of the following clause; head-to-tail linkage is a relatively commonly used strategy in oral narratives in South Asian languages.

REFERENCES

Anderson, Gregory D. S. 2011. 'Auxiliary verb constructions (and other complex predicate types): a functional–constructional typology'. *Language and Linguistics Compass* 5.11: 795–828.

_______ 2002. 'Case marked clausal subordination in Burushaski complex sentence structure'. *Studies in Language* 26: 547–71.

_______ 1998. *Xakas*. München: Lincom Europa. (Languages of the World/ Materials 251).

_______ and Harrison, David K. 1999. *Tyvan*. München: Lincom Europa. (Languages of the World/Materials 257).

_______, Eggert, Randall H., Zide, Norman H., and Ramat, Fazal. 1998. *Yasin Burushaski Language Materials*. Chicago: University of Chicago Language Laboratories and Archives.

Baart, Joan L. G. 2008. 'The tones of Kalam Kohistani (Garwi, Bashkarik)'. In *Proceedings of the Third International Hindu Kush Cultural Conference*, edited by Israr-ud-Din. 263–82. Karachi: Oxford University Press.

_______ 2003. 'Tonal features in languages of northern Pakistan'. In *Pakistani Languages and Society: Problems and Prospects,* edited by Joan L. G. Baart and Ghulam Hyder Sindhi. 132–44. Islamabad: National Institute of Pakistan Studies and Summer Institute of Linguistics.

Backstrom, Peter C. 1992. 'Burushaski'. In *Sociolinguistic Survey of Northern Pakistan, Volume 2: Languages of the Northern Areas*, edited by Peter C. Backstrom and Carla F. Radloff. 29–54. Islamabad: National Institute of Pakistan Studies and Summer Institute of Linguistics.

Barker, Muhammad Abd-al-Rahman and Mengal, Aqil Khan. 1969. *A Course in Baluchi*. Montreal: McGill University, Institute of Islamic Studies.

Bashir, E. 1985. 'Toward a semantics of the Burushaski verb'. In *Proceedings of the Conference on Participant Roles: South Asia and Adjacent Areas,* edited by Arlene R. K. Zide, David Magier, and Eric Schiller. 1–32. Bloomington: Indiana University Linguistics Club.

Berger, Hermann. 1998. *Die Burushaski-Sprache von Hunza und Nager.* Teil 1: Grammatik. Teil II: Texte mit Übersetzungen. Teil III: Wörterbuch. (Neuindische Studien 13). Wiesbaden: Harrassowitz.

Bickel, Balthasar. 2003. 'Belhare'. In *The Sino-Tibetan Languages,* edited by Graham Thurgood and Randy J. LaPolla. 546–69. London: Routledge.

Bleichsteiner, Robert B. 1930. 'Die werschikisch-burischkische Sprache im Pamirgebiet und ihre Stellung zu den Japhetitensprachen des Kaukasus'. *Wiener Beiträge zur Kulturgeschichte und Linguistik* 1: 289–331.

Bray, Denys. 1986. *Brahui Language: Introduction and Grammar.* 26th ed. New Delhi: Asian Educational Services.

Burling, Robbins. 2003. 'Garo'. In *The Sino-Tibetan Languages,* edited by Graham Thurgood and Randy J. LaPolla. 387–400. London: Routledge.

Bybee, Joan, Perkins, Revere, and Pagliuca, William. 1994. *The Evolution of Grammar: Tense, Aspect, and Modality in the Languages of the World*. Chicago: University of Chicago Press.

Čašule, Ilija. 2012. 'Correlation of the Burushaski pronominal system with Indo-European and phonological and grammatical evidence for a genetic relationship'. *The Journal of Indo-European Studies* 40: 59–154.

Chelliah, Shobhana L. 2003. 'Meithei'. In *The Sino-Tibetan Languages*, edited by Graham Thurgood and Randy J. LaPolla. 427–38. London: Routledge.

Ebert, Karen H. 2003a. 'Kiranti languages: An overview'. In *The Sino-Tibetan Languages*, edited by Graham Thurgood and Randy J. LaPolla. 505–17. London: Routledge.

_______ 2003b. 'Camling'. In *The Sino-Tibetan Languages*, edited by Graham Thurgood and Randy J. LaPolla. 533–45. London: Routledge.

Kachru, Yamuna. 1990. 'Hindi–Urdu'. In *The World's Major Languages*, edited by Bernard Comrie. 470–89. Oxford: Oxford University Press.

Klimov, Georgij A. and Edel'man, Dzhoi I. 1995. 'K perspektivam rekonstruktsii istorii izolirovannogo jazyka. Na materiale jazyka burushaski [Some perspectives on reconstructing the history of a language isolate. Based on materials from Burushaski]'. *Voprosy Jazykoznanija* 5: 27–38.

_______ 1970. *Jazyk Burushaski*. Moscow: Akademija Nauk SSSR.

Krishnamurti, Bhadriraju. 2003. *The Dravidian Languages*. Cambridge: Cambridge University Press.

Lorimer, David L. R. 1935–38. *The Burushaski language*. I: Introduction and grammar; II: Texts and translation; III: Vocabularies and index. Oslo: Instituttet for sammenlignende kulturforskning.

Morgenstierne, Georg. 1942. 'Notes on Burushaski phonology'. *Norsk Tidsskrift for Sprogvidenskap* 13: 61–95.

Munshi, Sadaf. 2010. 'Contact-induced language change in a trilingual context: The case of Burushaski in Srinagar'. *Diachronica* 27: 32–72.

_______ 2006. *Jammu and Kashmir Burushaski: Language, Language Contact, and Change*. PhD dissertation. Austin: University of Texas at Austin.

Nedjalkov, Igor. 1997. *Evenki*. London: Routledge.

Neukom, Lukas and Patnaik, Manideepa. 2003. *A Grammar of Oriya*. Zürich: Universität Zürich. (Arbeiten des Seminars für Allgemeine Sprachwissenschaft 17).

Osada, Toshiki. 1992. *A Reference Grammar of Mundari*. Tokyo: Tokyo University of Foreign Studies.

Pinnow, Heinz-Jürgen. 1959. *Versuch einer historischen Lautlehre der Kharia-Sprache*. Wiesbaden: Harrassowitz.

Radloff, Carla F. 1992. 'The dialects of Shina'. In *Sociolinguistic Survey of Northern Pakistan. Volume 2: Languages of the Northern Areas*, edited by Peter C. Backstrom and Carla F. Radloff. 89–203. Islamabad: National Institute of Pakistan Studies and Summer Institute of Linguistics.

Sharma, Devi D. 1988. *A Descriptive Grammar of Kinnauri*. Delhi: Mittal Publications. (Studies in Tibeto-Himalayan Languages 1).

Silverstein, Michael. 1976. 'Hierarchy of features and ergativity'. In *Grammatical Categories in Australian Languages*, edited by Robert M. W. Dixon. 112–71. Canberra: Australian Institute of Aboriginal Studies.

Tiffou, Étienne. 2004. 'Avant-propos'. In *Bourouchaskiana: Actes du colloque sur le bourouchaski organisé à l'occasion du XXXVIème congrès international sur les études asiatiques et nord-africaines*, edited by É. Tiffou. 7–11. Louvain-La-Neuve: Peeters. (Bibliothèque des Cahiers de Linguistique de Louvain 113).

_______ 1993. *Hunza proverbs*. Calgary: University of Calgary Press.

_______ and Patry, Richard. 2008. 'Verbal plurality and the notion of multiple-event in Yasin Burushaski'. In *Proceedings of the Third International Hindu Kush Cultural Conference*, edited by Israr-ud-Din. 482–90. Karachi: Oxford University Press.

_______ and Morin, Yves-Charles. 1982. 'A note on split ergativity in Burushaski'. *Bulletin of the School of Oriental and African Studies* 45: 88–94.

Tikkanen, Bertil. 2008. 'Some areal phonological isoglosses in the transit zone between South and Central Asia'. In *Proceedings of the Third International Hindu Kush Cultural Conference*, edited by Israr-ud-Din. 250–62. Karachi: Oxford University Press.

_______ 1995. 'Burushaski converbs in their South and Central Asian areal context'. In *Converbs in Cross-Linguistic Perspective: Structure and Meaning of Adverbial Verb Forms, Adverbial Participles, Gerunds*, edited by Martin Haspelmath and Ekkehard König. 487–528. Berlin: Mouton de Gruyter.

_______ 1991. 'A Burushaski folktale, transcribed and translated: The frog as a bride, or, The three princes and the fairy princess Salaasír.' *Studia Orientalia* 67: 65–125.

Toporov, Vladimir N. 1971. 'Burushaski and Yeniseian languages: Some parallels'. In *Etudes de la phonologie, typologie et de la linguistique générale*, edited by Ivan Poldauf. 107–25. Prague: Editions de l'Academie Tchecoslovaque des Sciences. (Travaux Linguistiques de Prague 4).

Ubrjatova, Elizaveta I. 1985. *Jazyk noril'skikh dolgan* [The language of the Norilsk Dolgan]. Novosibirsk: Nauka.

Varma, Siddheshwar. 1941. 'Studies in Burushaski dialectology'. *Journal of Royal Asiatic Society of Bengal* 7: 133–73.

van Driem, George. 1987. *A Grammar of Limbu*. Berlin: Mouton de Gruyter.

Willson, Stephen R. 1990. *Verb Agreement and Case Marking in Burushaski*. MA Thesis. University of North Dakota.

Yoshioka, Noboru. 2012. *A Reference Grammar of Eastern Burushaski*. PhD dissertation. Tokyo: Tokyo University of Foreign Studies.

2

Two Types of Retroflex Harmony in Kalasha: Implications for Phonological Typology

Paul Arsenault and Alexei Kochetov

1. INTRODUCTION

Harmony is a phonological process by which a segment becomes more similar to, or identical to, another non-adjacent segment. Harmony systems can involve assimilation between consonants (taʈa → ʈaʈa), vowels (ta˞ka → ta˞ka˞), or both (ta˞na → ta˞ɳa˞). Recent cross-linguistic surveys have revealed that consonant harmony systems exhibit unique typological properties that set them apart from other types of long-distance assimilation, including most vowel and vowel-consonant harmony systems (Rose and Walker 2004, Hansson 2010). By way of explanation, these studies suggest that there are at least two mechanisms of assimilation at work in languages: feature/gesture agreement and feature/gesture extension (or *spreading*). Each mechanism has its own functional basis and gives rise to a unique set of typological properties. The properties that are most characteristic of consonant harmony are those that are said to arise from feature agreement. They include: (i) an inherent bias for regressive assimilation; (ii) transparency of intervening segments; and (iii) sensitivity to the similarity of interacting segments. Other types of assimilation, including most cases of vowel harmony, are typically attributed to gesture extension, which is not necessarily associated with these particular properties.

In this chapter we present a case study of retroflex assimilation in Kalasha, an Indo-Aryan language of northern Pakistan. We argue that the evidence from Kalasha provides compelling support for the typological distinction between feature agreement and gesture extension. Kalasha is uniquely suited to address this issue because it is one of the few languages known to exhibit two types of harmony involving the same feature: retroflex consonant harmony and retroflex vowel harmony. This unusual state of affairs is made possible by a typologically rare phonological inventory, in which retroflex stops, affricates, fricatives, and vowels are all contrasted with their non-retroflex counterparts. The two types of harmony in Kalasha are clearly distinct and each exhibits a different set of typological properties. The pattern of retroflex consonant harmony exhibits properties in keeping with most other consonant harmony systems: it is regressive, intervening segments are transparent, and it is highly sensitive to the similarity of interacting consonants. The pattern of retroflex vowel harmony, by comparison, is primarily progressive (but potentially bi-directional) and does not show clear evidence of similarity or transparency effects. The coexistence of these two types of retroflex harmony in the same language, each with a distinct set of typological properties, lends support to the hypothesis that two independent mechanisms of assimilation are at work.

The chapter is organized as follows. In section 2, we provide an overview of the two hypothesized mechanisms of assimilation—gesture extension and feature agreement—focusing on their functional grounding and associated typological properties. In section 3, we introduce Kalasha, and in sections 4 and 5, we review evidence of retroflex consonant harmony and retroflex vowel harmony in the language. In section 6, we compare the two harmony systems and discuss their implications for phonological typology. Finally, in section 7, we offer some concluding remarks.

2. MECHANISMS OF ASSIMILATION

Some form of assimilation can be found in most languages of the world, but not all patterns of assimilation are the same. A central problem for the field of phonology is to understand the typological variation in assimilation patterns and the mechanisms of assimilation responsible for them. At least two mechanisms have been proposed in the literature: gesture extension (or feature spreading) and feature agreement. In this section we provide a synopsis of these two mechanisms, focusing on their functional grounding and associated typological properties, as opposed to their formal representation in a given theoretical framework.

By most accounts, the mechanism responsible for local assimilation is gesture extension: an articulatory gesture is extended from one segment to another when the two are adjacent. The functional grounding of this mechanism is generally assumed to lie in low-level articulatory factors such as co-articulation or articulatory simplification. It is often easier to maintain an articulatory gesture over a span of contiguous segments than to implement a series of rapidly changing gestures. However, in cases of long-distance assimilation, such as vowel and consonant harmony, interacting segments are not adjacent in the normal sense and the assimilating gesture often appears to skip intervening segments. The apparent non-local nature of the interaction and the transparency of intervening segments demand explanation.

Under the hypothesis that local and long-distance assimilation are both products of gesture extension, the apparent non-local nature of assimilation in harmony systems has been explained by defining locality relative to some representational unit other than the segment. For example, in autosegmental analyses, locality has been defined with respect to autosegmental tiers (e.g. Clements 1980, Poser 1982, Shaw 1991). Alternatively, it has been argued that gesture extension does operate under strict segmental adjacency and that transparency effects are an illusion. According to this view, gesture extension targets, or *permeates*, all segments in a contiguous string. If a gesture has little or no audible effect on a segment, then that segment may be perceived as transparent to assimilation. For example, most vocalic gestures can be maintained through intervening consonants with no noticeable effect, thereby creating the illusion of transparency in vowel harmony systems (Gafos 1999). Moreover, it has been argued that coronal gestures such as retroflexion are particularly susceptible to this illusion. In most languages, the orientation of the tongue tip is irrelevant in the production of vowels and non-coronal (labial and dorsal) consonants. As a result, retroflexion can permeate those segments without notice (Gafos 1999; Ní Chiosáin and Padgett 1997, 2001).

Recent typological surveys of consonant harmony have challenged the assumption that all assimilation is the product of a single mechanism. Consonant harmony can involve the assimilation of coronal, laryngeal, nasal, liquid, and dorsal features/gestures (Hansson 2010, Rose and Walker 2004, Rose 2011). Not all of these harmony systems are amenable to the explanation offered for coronal harmonies because some exhibit transparency effects even when the assimilating feature/gesture is relevant for intervening segments (e.g. nasality). Moreover, these surveys reveal that consonant harmony systems tend to exhibit a recurring set of typological properties: (i) an inherent bias toward regressive assimilation (wherever direction is not determined by morphological constituency); (ii) transparency of intervening segments; and (iii) sensitivity to the similarity of interacting segments. This trend sets consonant harmony apart from most cases of local assimilation and vowel harmony. In these other systems, assimilation is often unconstrained by similarity so that any segment capable of accommodating the relevant gesture is liable to participate. In addition, it is not uncommon for intervening segments to undergo assimilation or block it, and the direction of assimilation is typically determined by independent factors, such as stem control, dominance, or the distribution of perceptual cues.

The uniqueness of consonant harmony has led some to hypothesize that it is the product of a different mechanism of assimilation, known as feature agreement. The distinction between agreement and gesture extension is represented schematically in (1). Whereas gesture extension involves the spreading of a feature/gesture over a contiguous span of segments, as in (1 a), feature agreement involves the repetition of a feature/gesture on non-contiguous segments, as in (1 b). A basic premise of agreement is that similarity can form the basis for non-local interactions. Similar non-adjacent segments can assimilate to one another without regard for intervening segments. Thus, intervening segments in (1 b) are truly transparent; they are skipped by the harmony feature, not permeated by it, as in (1 a).

(1) Gesture extension vs feature agreement

a. Extension (spreading) b. Agreement

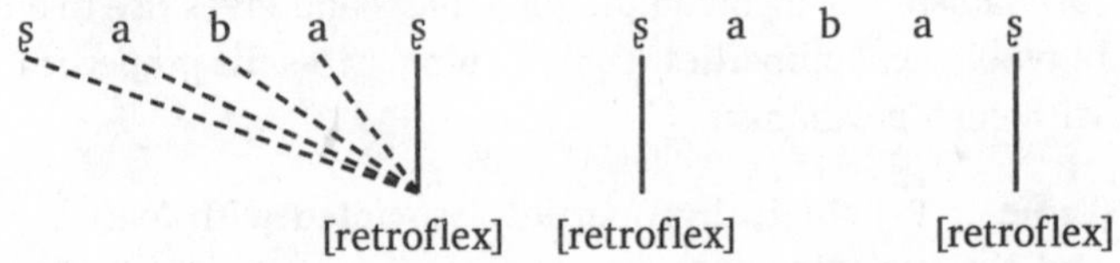

While gesture extension is grounded in low-level articulatory factors, feature agreement is grounded in higher-level cognitive functions pertaining to speech planning. In speech production, near-identical sounds can interfere with one another, producing familiar slips of the tongue, as when the English phrase [s]*ubjects* [ʃ]*ow* is mispronounced as [ʃ]*ubjects* [ʃ]*ow*. Such errors are common cross-linguistically and exhibit typological affinities with consonant harmony systems: (i) the direction of assimilation is predominantly regressive; (ii) intervening segments are ignored; and (iii) assimilation applies to segments that are highly similar (Rose and Walker 2004, Hansson 2010). The parallel between consonant harmony and similarity-induced speech errors suggests that the two share the same functional grounding.

Similarity-induced interactions have been explained in terms of spreading activation models of language production. In these models, the activation of a phonological feature or gesture entails the activation of associated processing nodes. When two consonants in a word are highly similar, there is significant overlap in the nodes that are activated. This creates the potential for interference between similar segments in language production (see Rose and Walker 2004, Hansson 2010, and the sources cited therein). The trend toward regressive (anticipatory) assimilation has been attributed to the functional requirements of serial order production. Three functional requirements are recognized: (i) a *turn-on* function, in which the system must activate the present; (ii) a *turn-off* function, in which it must deactivate the past; and (iii) a *prime* function, in which it must prepare to activate the future. The prime and turn-on functions are largely concurrent. As present elements are being activated and implemented, future elements are being planned. Thus, the planning of future activations can interfere with present activations, resulting in regressive assimilation (Dell et al. 1997, Hansson 2010).

In summary, there may be two distinct mechanisms of assimilation at work in languages: feature agreement and gesture extension. Each mechanism has its own functional basis and gives rise to a unique set of typological properties. Table 1 summarizes the properties associated with each mechanism.

Table 1: Typological properties associated with feature agreement and gesture extension

	Feature Agreement	Gesture Extension (Spreading)
Direction	Bias for regressive assimilation	No inherent/default directional bias
Opacity	Intervening segments are transparent and do not undergo assimilation	Intervening segments may be undergoers, opaque blockers, or both
Similarity	Interacting segments share a high degree of similarity	Interacting segments are not necessarily similar

It remains possible that the set of typological properties associated with consonant harmony might be generated by gesture extension. This is especially true in the case of retroflex consonant harmony because retroflexion is often irrelevant for vowels and non-coronal consonants. As a result, it can permeate them with little or no audible effect, creating the illusion of long-distance assimilation and transparency. In the remainder of this paper we present a case study of retroflex assimilation in Kalasha. The evidence from Kalasha supports the typological distinction between long-distance agreement and gesture extension, and suggests that (at least in this case) retroflex consonant harmony is the product of the former, not the latter.

3. THE KALASHA LANGUAGE

Kalasha is an Indo-Aryan language of the so-called Dardic subgroup spoken by about 5,000 people in Chitral District of Khyber Pakhtunkhwa (formerly North West Frontier) province in northern Pakistan (Heegård Petersen 2006, Lewis et al. 2013). The phonemic inventory of Kalasha is typologically rare in at least two ways. First of all, like most Dardic languages, Kalasha has a rich inventory of coronal obstruents that includes retroflex stops, affricates, and fricatives. The consonant phonemes of Kalasha are listed in Table 2.

Table 2: Consonant phonemes of Kalasha (Trail and Cooper 1999, Heegård and Mørch 2004)

Labial	Dental	Alveolar	Retroflex	Palatal	Velar	Glottal
p	t		ʈ		k	
pʰ	tʰ		ʈʰ		kʰ	
b	d		ɖ		g	
bʰ	dʰ		ɖʰ		gʰ	
	ʦ		ʈʂ	ʨ		
	ʦʰ		ʈʂʰ	ʨʰ		
	ʣ		ɖʐ	ʥ		
				ʥʰ		
	s		ʂ	ɕ		h
	z		ʐ	ʑ		
m	n		(ɳ)		ŋ	
	ɫ	l				
		r	(ɽ)			
w				j		

All dialects of Kalasha distinguish retroflex stops, affricates, and fricatives from their dental counterparts and, in the case of sibilants, also from their palatal counterparts.[1] Cross-linguistically, only about 9 per cent of the world's languages have a distinctive series of retroflex stops. Fewer have retroflex fricatives and/or affricates (about 5 per cent), and fewer still have both retroflex stops and retroflex fricatives or affricates (about 1 per cent). Of the 451 languages in the 1992 version of the *UCLA Phonological Segment Inventory Database* (UPSID), only one (0.2 per cent) has a three-way distinction between retroflex stops, affricates, and fricatives (Maddieson and Precoda 1992).[2] Even in the context of South Asia, where retroflexion is an areal feature

[1] Throughout this chapter we use the term sibilant to refer to the class of coronal affricates and fricatives, as distinct from un-affricated stops.

[2] The statistics cited here are based on the 1992 version of the *UCLA Phonological Segment Inventory Database* (UPSID; Maddieson and Precoda 1992), which includes a genetically diverse sample of 451 languages. Burushaski is the only language in

affecting most languages (Ramanujan and Masica 1969, Bhat 1973), systems containing retroflex stops, affricates, and fricatives are limited to a handful of Dardic languages in northern Pakistan (which includes Kalasha) and the isolate Burushaski.[3] Some dialects of Kalasha may also distinguish the retroflex sonorants /ɳ/ and /ɽ/ (Heegård and Mørch 2004). However, neither of these phonemes is distinguished in Trail and Cooper's (1999) Kalasha dictionary, which is the principal source of data for our study. Thus, they are not considered in the following discussions.

A second and even more intriguing aspect of the Kalasha sound system is the full set of retroflex vowels found in some dialects. Kalasha distinguishes five basic vowel qualities, each with an oral and nasal counterpart. In western dialects, each oral and nasal vowel also has retroflex and non-retroflex counterparts. The retroflex vowels are articulated with the tongue tip turned up and possibly with some bunching of the tongue body (Heegård and Mørch 2004). The vowel phonemes of Kalasha are listed in Table 3.

Table 3: Vowel phonemes of Kalasha (Trail and Cooper 1999, Heegård and Mørch 2004)

Front		Central		Back	
i	ĩ			u	ũ
i˞	ĩ˞			u˞	ũ˞
e	ẽ			o	õ
e˞	ẽ˞			o˞	õ˞
		a	ã		
		a˞	ã˞		

UPSID reported to have a three-way contrast between retroflex stops, affricates, and fricatives. No Dardic languages are included in the UPSID database.

[3] Dardic languages reported to contrast retroflex stops, affricates, and fricatives include: Dameli, Gawarbati, Kalam Kohistani, Kalasha, Kanyawali, Khowar, Indus Kohistani, Palula, Sawi, Shina, Shumashti, Torwali (all in Bashir 2003), and Dumāki (Lorimer 1939). Dardic languages that have retroflex stops but lack retroflex affricates and/or fricatives include: Brokskat, Grangali, Pashai, Tirahi (all in Bashir 2003), Kashmiri (Wali and Koul 1997), and Kundal Shahi (Rehman and Baart 2005). Beyond Dardic and Burushaski the only languages we know of with a three-way contrast between retroflex stops, affricates, and fricatives are the Yawelmani and Koyeti dialects of Yokuts in California (Gamble 1975, Bhat 1973).

Some degree of phonetic retroflexion is expected on vowels in any language with retroflex consonants, particularly as a result of co-articulation in VC transitions where C is a retroflex consonant. However, a phonological opposition between retroflex and non-retroflex vowels is extremely rare, occurring in less than 1 per cent of the world's languages. Kalasha is one of the few languages in the world (and the only Dardic language) reported to have retroflex vowel phonemes.[4]

Kalasha's retroflex consonant inventory and its retroflex vowel inventory are both typologically rare. As a result, Kalasha may well be the only language in the world with a three-way contrast between retroflex stops, affricates, and fricatives on the one hand, and a full set of retroflex vowels on the other. The uniqueness of Kalasha's phonemic inventory has given rise to another typological rarity. Kalasha exhibits two independent patterns of retroflex harmony, one affecting consonants and another primarily affecting vowels. In the following sections we review and compare the details of these harmony systems.

4. RETROFLEX CONSONANT HARMONY

Consonant harmony can manifest itself in one of two ways in a language. If it applies across morpheme boundaries, it can produce alternations. For instance, a coronal consonant in an affix might alternate between retroflex and non-retroflex articulations in accordance with the consonants of the root (e.g. /s-as/ → [sas], but /s-aʂ/ → [ʂaʂ]). However, if consonant harmony is limited to the domain of the root (or morpheme) itself, then it will not produce

[4] 4 out of 451 (0.9 per cent) of the languages in UPSID are reported to have retroflex vowel phonemes. They are Mandarin, Gelao, and Naxi (all in China) and Tarascan (in Mexico). Other reported cases that we know of include Badaga (South Dravidian; Emeneau 1939), Serrano (Uto-Aztecan; Bhat 1973), Yurok (Algic; Robins 1958), and the Tibeto-Burman languages Qiang (LaPolla 2003) and Sulong (Namkung 1996). Heegård and Mørch (2004) report retroflex vowels in Kati and Waigali, two Nuristani languages that border Kalasha on the west. However, the phonemic status of these vowels and their relation to the vowels of Kalasha remain unclear. Di Carlo (2009) suggests that retroflex vowels in Kalasha and Nuristani might form an isogloss corresponding to a former Hindu Kush linguistic area.

alternations. Instead, it will manifest itself only as a static co-occurrence restriction on consonants within roots, commonly known as a Morpheme Structure Constraint (MSC). Kalasha has a retroflex consonant harmony system of the latter kind. We present synchronic evidence of this system in section 4.1 and diachronic evidence of its development in section 4.2. In section 4.3, we discuss the typological properties of the system evident in the data.

4.1 Synchronic Co-occurrence Restrictions on Coronal Obstruents

From a synchronic point of view, retroflex consonant harmony in Kalasha is manifested as a co-occurrence restriction on coronal obstruents within roots. These restrictions have been documented in Arsenault and Kochetov (2011) and Arsenault (2012), where they are supported by statistical evidence calculated on the basis of data in Trail and Cooper's (1999) Kalasha dictionary. Here we summarize the generalizations that emerge from these studies without delving into the statistics that lay behind them. Readers who are interested in statistical support for the generalizations made here should consult the aforementioned studies.

Several generalizations can be made about the co-occurrence of coronal obstruents in Kalasha roots. First of all, roots containing two coronal obstruents with the same manner of articulation are subject to retroflex consonant harmony; the obstruents must agree with respect to retroflexion or non-retroflexion. For example, if a root contains two coronal stops then both are either dental, as in (2 a), or retroflex, as in (2 b). Roots containing a combination of dental and retroflex stops are systematically avoided, as indicated in (2 c). Similarly, roots containing two affricates or two fricatives tend to show a three-way coronal place harmony: dentals co-occur with other dentals, as in (3 a) and (4 a); palatals co-occur with palatals, as in (3 b) and (4 b); and retroflexes with retroflexes, as in (3 c) and (4 c). However, roots containing two sibilants with the same manner of articulation that disagree in retroflexion are avoided, as indicated in (3 d) and (4 d). Roots containing dental and palatal sibilants with the same manner are very rare.

(2) Retroflex consonant harmony between stops

a.	da˞ u tatu	'festival of beans'	dodak hik	'to wait'
	tʰedi	'now'	dʰenta	'mountain (of rock)'
	dit	'half full'	dond	'bull'
b.	ʈoʈ	'apron'	ɖinʈa	'efficient'
	ʈʰeʈ karik	'to scatter'	ɖonɖ	'double bride-price'
	ɖuɖ-ik	'to sleep'	ɖunɖulaʈ	'village of Dundulet'

c. *t…ʈ, *ʈ…t, *t…ɖ, *ɖ…t, *d…ɖ, *ɖ…d, etc. (rare or unattested)

(3) Retroflex/coronal consonant harmony between affricates

a.	tsẽtsaw	'squirrel'	tsurtsun-ik	'to become weak'
b.	ʨʰaʨi hik	'to take care of'	ʥaʥ	'hair, fur'
	ʨunʥo˞ ik	'magpie'	ʥinʥu	'thorn tree'
c.	ʈʂʰiʈʂ-ik	'to learn'	ɖʐaʈʂ	'spirit beings'
	ʈʂʰãʈʂ-ik	'to pierce'	ʈʂãɖʐa	'pinewood torch'

d. *ts…ʈʂ, *ʈʂ…ts, *ʨ…ʈʂ, *ʈʂ…ʨ, etc. (rare or unattested)

(4) Retroflex/coronal consonant harmony between fricatives

a.	sastir-ik	'to roof a house'	sazu djek	'to have a cold'
	sos	'insides (intestines)'	ispres	'mother-in-law'
b.	ɕiɕoa	'handsome'	ʑoɕi	'Spring festival'
	ɕãɕ	'fishhook'	iɕpaɕur	'father-in-law'
c.	ʂiʂ	'head, top'	ʂuʂ-ik	'to dry'
	ʂiɫeʂ	'glue'	iʂpoʂi	'nephew, niece'

d. *s…ʂ, *ʂ…s, *ɕ…ʂ, *ʂ…ɕ, etc. (rare or unattested)

Secondly, roots containing an affricate and a fricative are also subject to retroflex consonant harmony provided the affricate in question is not palatal. For example, retroflex affricates co-occur almost exclusively with retroflex fricatives and hardly at all with dental or palatal fricatives, as illustrated in (5). Similarly, dental affricates tend to co-occur with dental fricatives as opposed to palatal or retroflex fricatives. However, palatal affricates are exceptional. They co-occur with fricatives of any kind, as illustrated in (6). Statistically, palatal affricates occur less frequently with palatal fricatives than with any other kind, suggesting that affricate–fricative pairs containing palatal affricates might be subject to a gradient form of dissimilation. Whatever the case may be, it is clear that palatal affricates are *not subject to retroflex consonant harmony* when they co-occur with retroflex fricatives. The exceptional behaviour of palatal affricates produces an asymmetry in affricate–fricative pairs: palatal affricates co-occur with retroflex fricatives (/tɕ…ʂ/, /ʂ…tɕ/, etc.), but retroflex affricates do not co-occur with palatal fricatives (*/ʈʂ…ɕ/, */ɕ…ʈʂ/, etc.).[5]

(5) Harmony between retroflex affricates and fricatives

a.	ʈʂaʂa	'cottage cheese'	ʂanɖʐu-ik	'to wrinkle'
	ʈʂaʂku	'kind of evergreen tree'	ʐaʈʂg^{ɦ}ur	'half-lame'
b.	*ʈʂ…s, *s…ʈʂ, *ʈʂ…ɕ, *ɕ…ʈʂ, etc. (rare or unattested)			

(6) No harmony between palatal affricates and fricatives

a.	tɕaspan	'clever'	sutɕ	'ritually pure'
	dʑis	'time, occurrence'	zetɕi djek	'to become hungry'
b.	tɕeɕmak	'eye glasses'	tɕ^{h}uɕej	'Shoo! (said to goats)'
	tɕiʑ	'grass ornament'	ɕadʑuan	'the Shajuan clan of Rumbur'
c.	tɕaʂ(ʈ)	'lunch'	ʂatɕ	'temporary shelter'
	dʑoʂ-ik	'to consider'	ʂindʑ-ik	'to win someone back'

Finally, roots containing stop–sibilant pairs are not subject to retroflex consonant harmony, regardless of whether the sibilants in question

[5] This asymmetry sets Kalasha apart from Indus Kohistani, another Dardic language with an otherwise identical pattern of retroflex consonant harmony. In Indus Kohistani, palatal affricates are subject to retroflex consonant harmony whenever they co-occur with retroflex sibilants of any kind, whether affricate or fricative. Compare Kalasha /tɕuʂ-ik/ 'to suck' with Indus Kohistani /ʈʂoːʂ-áṽ/ 'to suck (out)', both of which are cognate with Old Indo-Aryan /tɕuːʂ-/ 'to drink, suck up or out'. Whereas Indus Kohistani has subjected this root to retroflex consonant harmony, Kalasha has not (Arsenault 2012).

are affricates or fricatives. For example, dental stops co-occur freely with retroflex affricates and fricatives, as illustrated in (7 a). Similarly, retroflex stops co-occur freely with dental affricates and fricatives, as illustrated in (7 b), and with palatal affricates and fricatives, as illustrated in (7 c). Retroflex stop–fricative pairs are rare, as indicated in (7 d), and retroflex stop–affricate pairs may be unattested. The only example we can find in Trail and Cooper's (1999) Kalasha dictionary is /gaʈniwaʈʂ/ 'disordered', which may be morphologically complex. The avoidance of retroflex stop–sibilant pairs may reflect one of two phonological processes. For one thing, stop–sibilant pairs might be subject to retroflex dissimilation. In this case, a sequence such as /ʈʂ…ʈ/ would be avoided in favour of one that disagrees for retroflexion, such as /tɕ…ʈ/ or /ʈʂ…t/. Alternatively, stop–sibilant pairs that agree in retroflexion might be subject to assimilation of manner. In this case, a sequence such as /ʈʂ…ʈ/ would be avoided in favour of one that agrees for manner (and retroflexion), such as /ʈ…ʈ/ or /ʈʂ…ʈʂ/. Unfortunately, we know of no evidence favouring one of these hypotheses over the other. What is clear and most important for our purposes is the fact that stop–sibilant pairs are not subject to retroflex consonant harmony, unlike stop–stop and most sibilant–sibilant pairs.

(7) No retroflex consonant harmony between stops and sibilants (affricates–fricatives)

a. Dental stops with retroflex sibilants

diʈʂ	'period of abstinence'	ʈʂʰet	'cultivated field'
tuʂ	'straw, chaff'	ʂit	'tight-fitting'

b. Retroflex stops with dental sibilants

tsaʈẽg-ik	'to move, shake'	ʈrits	'(kind of) bird'
saʈuk	'apple sauce'	ʈosu djek	'to peck'

c. Retroflex stops with palatal sibilants

tɕuʈ-ik	'to touch'	ʈõtɕuk	'active'
ɕoʈʰa	'a growth'	ɖʰuɕak	'a dance'

d. Retroflex stops with retroflex sibilants (rare)

ʂaʈ-ik	'to adhere'	ʈʰriʂ-ʈʰrõʂ-ek	'to make a suspicious sound'

In summary, Kalasha exhibits a system of retroflex consonant harmony within roots. Coronal obstruents within a root must agree for retroflexion whenever they share the same manner of articulation. In fact, Kalasha approaches a three-way coronal harmony favouring agreement for retroflex, palatal, and dental places of articulation in affricate–affricate and fricative–fricative combinations. Without alternations, however, it can be difficult or even impossible to establish all of the typological properties of a consonant harmony system. For instance, static co-occurrence restrictions tell us little about the direction of assimilation or the triggers and targets of assimilation. Given a sequence such as [ʈ...ʈ] we cannot say whether it is the product of regressive assimilation (/t...ʈ/ → [ʈ...ʈ]) or progressive assimilation (/ʈ...t/ → [ʈ...ʈ]), or whether it is the product of place assimilation or something else, such as assimilation of manner (/ʈʂ...ʈ/ → [ʈ...ʈ]). Under these circumstances the typological properties of a harmony system can often be established on the basis of historical-comparative evidence. Root-internal co-occurrence restrictions are often the product of the same assimilatory processes that drive alternations, only applied diachronically as opposed to synchronically. Where alternations are lacking, cognates from a historically prior form of the language, or from closely related languages or dialects, often reveal patterns of diachronic assimilation that shed light on the typological properties of the harmony system. In the following subsection we present historical-comparative evidence that sheds further light on retroflex consonant harmony in Kalasha.

4.2 HISTORICAL-COMPARATIVE EVIDENCE OF CONSONANT HARMONY

Within the Indo-Aryan language family, three broad diachronic periods are typically recognized: Old Indo-Aryan (OIA), represented by Vedic and Classical Sanskrit (c. 1500 BCE–600 BCE); Middle Indo-Aryan (MIA), represented by Pāli and Prakrit (c. 600 BCE–1000 CE); and New Indo-Aryan (NIA), represented by Kalasha and other contemporary Indo-Aryan languages (c. 1000 CE–present; Masica 1991). The diachronic development of retroflex consonant harmony can be traced by comparing Kalasha roots with cognates in OIA

Sanskrit. The consonant phonemes of Classical Sanskrit are shown in Table 4.

Table 4: Consonant phonemes of Sanskrit (Whitney 1993 [1889], Cardona 2003)

Labial	Dental	Retroflex	Palatal	Velar	Glottal
p	t	ʈ	tɕ	k	
pʰ	tʰ	ʈʰ	tɕʰ	kʰ	
b	d	ɖ	dʑ	g	
bʰ	dʰ	ɖʰ	dʑʰ	gʰ	
	s	ʂ	ɕ		ɦ
m	n	ɳ	ɲ	ŋ	
	l				
	r				
v			j		

Like most NIA languages, Kalasha has preserved the OIA contrast between dental and retroflex stops and palatal affricates. Dardic languages like Kalasha have also preserved the OIA contrast between dental, retroflex, and palatal fricatives, which was otherwise neutralized to /s/ or /ɕ/ in the MIA period (Masica 1991). Moreover, most Dardic languages have also developed a new series of retroflex affricates, primarily as reflexes of OIA /kʂ/ clusters (e.g. Kalasha /ʈʂʰir/ 'milk' < OIA /kʂiːra/, Kalasha /paʈʂ/ 'wing' < OIA /pakʂa/). Some Dardic languages have also developed retroflex affricates and fricatives from OIA /Cr/ clusters in which C was a labial or dental consonant. In Kalasha, OIA /Cr/ clusters show up sporadically as retroflex affricates or fricatives (possibly as a result of dialect variation or borrowings from other Dardic languages) but are otherwise preserved.

Old Indo-Aryan did not exhibit the co-occurrence restriction on coronal obstruents observed in Kalasha. In OIA, retroflex consonants were avoided in word-initial position. As a result, OIA roots containing two non-adjacent coronal obstruents were generally limited to two types: either both obstruents were non-retroflex (e.g. /t…t/) or the first was non-retroflex and the second retroflex (e.g. /t…ʈ/). Roots containing two retroflex obstruents (e.g. /ʈ…ʈ/) or a retroflex obstruent followed by a non-retroflex obstruent (e.g. /ʈ…t/) were rare at best in OIA.

A comparison of Kalasha roots with their OIA cognates reveals that consonant harmony in Kalasha is the product of regressive assimilation in roots containing a dental or palatal obstruent followed by a non-adjacent retroflex obstruent with the same manner of articulation (Morgenstierne 1973, Arsenault and Kochetov 2011, Arsenault 2012). Consider the examples in (8). Here and elsewhere, reference numbers in the rightmost column refer to etymological groups in Turner's (1962–66) *Comparative Dictionary of Indo-Aryan Languages* (CDIAL).[6]

(8) Retroflex consonant harmony between obstruents of the same manner in Kalasha

		Kalasha		OIA	CDIAL
a.	'dry and hard'	ɖaɖe		da:rɖ^{h}ya-	6302
b.	'pinewood torch'	ʈʂãɖʐa	*ʨanɖʐa	ʨandra	4661
	'spirit beings'	ɖʐaʈʂ	*ʥaʈʂ-	jakʂa	10395
c.	'ornate headband'	ʂuʂut(r)		*suʂu:tra-	13536
	'nephew'	iʂpoʂi	*spaʂi-	svasri:ja-	13918
	'head'	ʂiʂ		ɕi:rʂa-	12497
	'to dry'	ʂuʂik		ɕuʂjati	12559
	'dry, dried'	ʂuʂʈa		*ɕuʂʈa-	12555
	'precipice'	bruʂiʂ		*b^{h}rãɕiʂʈ^{h}a-	9645
	'glue'	ʂiɫeʂ	*ɕile:ʂp	ɕle:ʂman	12744

The examples in (8) demonstrate that retroflex consonant harmony has applied regressively between obstruents of the same manner class. Roots containing two retroflex stops are abundant in Kalasha but it is difficult to identify OIA cognates for most of them. Nevertheless, the single example in (8 a) is consistent with the pattern found in other NIA languages where the first can be traced to an OIA dental stop and the second to a retroflex stop that was part of a homorganic consonant cluster, in this case /-rɖ^{h}-/ (Arsenault 2012). The examples

[6] The OIA word forms may or may not be the precise ones from which the corresponding Kalasha words have developed in every case. The point is only to show that there are OIA cognates with non-retroflex obstruents where Kalasha has retroflexes.

in (8 b) provide evidence that retroflex affricates triggered harmony in other affricates. In the case of Kalasha /ʈʂãɖʐa/ 'pinewood torch' (< OIA /tɕandra/ 'shining'), retroflex /ɖʐ/ developed from OIA /dr/ and subsequently triggered harmony in the preceding palatal affricate (i.e. /tɕandra/ > */tɕanɖʐa/ > /ʈʂãɖʐa/). Kalasha /ɖʐaʈʂ/ 'spirit beings' derives straightforwardly from OIA /jakʂa/ 'supernatural being' by means of two other well-attested sound changes: /j/ > /dʑ/ and /kʂ/ > /ʈʂ/. The combination of these two developments would have produced a disharmonic sequence of two affricates, which was then subject to retroflex consonant harmony (i.e. /jakʂ/ > */dʑaʈʂ/ > /ɖʐaʈʂ/).[7] The examples in (8 c) are the product of retroflex consonant harmony between two fricatives. They demonstrate that both dental and palatal fricatives were potential targets and that intervening consonants did not block consonant harmony (e.g. /svasri:-/ > */spaʂi-/ > /iʂpoʂi/).

Recall that Kalasha exhibits an asymmetry when it comes to the co-occurrence of affricates and fricatives. This too is supported by historical-comparative data, as shown in (9) and (10).

(9) Retroflex affricates trigger harmony in palatal fricatives

	Kalasha		OIA	CDIAL
'to learn'	ʈʂʰiʈʂ-ik	*ɕiʈʂ-	ɕikʂate:	12430
'dried fruit'	ʈʂuʈʂʰik	*ɕuʈʂ-	*ɕukʂa- (<ɕuʂka-)	12508

(10) Retroflex fricatives do not trigger harmony in palatal affricates

		Kalasha	OIA	CDIAL
a.	'to suck'	tɕuʂ-ik	tɕu:ʂati	4898
	'to like'	dʑuʂ-ik	dʑo:ʂati	5271
	'thumb, big toe'	dʑeʂʈ a· ŋgu	dʑje:ʂʈʰa	5286
b.	'to stand'	tɕiʂʈ-ik	tiʂʈʰati	5837
	'bitter'	tɕiʂʈaka	tr̥ʂʈa	5938
	'hand span'	dʑiʂ(ʈ)	diʂʈi	6343
	'female spirit'	dʑeʂʈak	de:ʂʈri:	6556

[7] Cf. Morgenstierne (1973: 191) who suggests that /ɖʐ/ in Kalasha /ɖʐaʈʂ/ is 'probably an assimilated variant of dʑ'.

The examples in (9) demonstrate that retroflex affricates triggered harmony in preceding non-retroflex fricatives. Interestingly, the fricatives have also become affricates in these examples but it is not clear whether this reflects assimilation of manner or simple variation between affricates and fricatives, which is relatively common in Dardic. Note that affricate–fricative sequences that agree in retroflexion are not necessarily avoided or subject to assimilation of manner in Kalasha; see examples in (5). The examples in (10) demonstrate that retroflex fricatives have not triggered harmony in palatal affricates regardless of whether the affricates in question were inherited from OIA, as in (10 a), or whether they result from the palatalization of OIA dental stops, as in (10 b).

The synchronic evidence suggests that retroflex consonant harmony does not hold between stops and sibilants of any kind. The examples in (11) confirm that retroflex affricates and fricatives have not triggered harmony in dental stops, while those in (12) confirm that retroflex stops have not triggered harmony in non-retroflex sibilants.

(11) Retroflex sibilants do not trigger harmony in non-retroflex stops

	Kalasha	**OIA**	**CDIAL**
'grapes'	draʈʂ	dra:kʂa:-	6628
'right hand'	drãʈʂɯ˞ i	dakʂiɳa-	6119
'chaff'	tuʂ	tuʂa-	5892
'yesterday'	doʂ	doʂa:-	6590

(12) Retroflex stops do not trigger harmony in non-retroflex sibilants

	Kalasha	**OIA**	**CDIAL**
'to sting, to bite'	ʨunɖ-ik	ʨuɳʈati	4857
'lizard'	ɕanɖerak	ɕaraɳɖa-	13248

The diachronic evidence reviewed here affirms and sheds further light on the synchronic co-occurrence restrictions reviewed in the preceding section. In the following subsection we turn our attention to the typological properties of retroflex consonant harmony that can be inferred from the combined synchronic and diachronic evidence.

4.3 Typological properties of retroflex consonant harmony in Kalasha

Having reviewed both the synchronic and diachronic evidence concerning retroflex consonant harmony in Kalasha, we are now in a better position to discuss its typological properties. Here we focus our attention on the three typological parameters that are said to be most relevant for distinguishing consonant harmony from other assimilation patterns: the direction of assimilation, the transparency of intervening segments, and the similarity of interacting segments.

4.3.1 Directionality

If nothing else, the direction of assimilation in Kalasha's system of consonant harmony is regressive. All historical-comparative data points to regressive assimilation in which dental and palatal obstruents have become retroflex when followed by a retroflex obstruent with the same manner of articulation (e.g. /t…ʈ/ → [ʈ…ʈ]). However, the issue of directionality is complicated by the fact that Kalasha avoids not only dental–retroflex and palatal–retroflex configurations with the same manner articulation (/t…ʈ/, /s…ʂ/, /ɕ…ʂ/, etc.) but also their inverted counterparts (/ʈ…t/, /ʂ…s/, /ʂ…ɕ/, etc.). On the one hand, the general absence of these retroflex–dental and retroflex–palatal configurations might be attributed to the fact that OIA avoided word-initial retroflex consonants. Essentially, there were no configurations of this kind in OIA for Kalasha to inherit. On the other hand, however, Kalasha has developed word-initial retroflex obstruents independent of consonant harmony. Thus, in addition to retroflex–retroflex stop configurations (e.g. /ʈoʈ/ 'apron'), Kalasha has introduced retroflex–labial and retroflex–velar stop configurations (e.g. /ʈap/ 'suddenly', /ʈak/ 'stingy'). In light of this, the avoidance of retroflex–dental stop configurations (*/ʈ…t/) is significant and suggests the possibility of a bi-directional co-occurrence restriction. Nevertheless, the evidence remains inconclusive because the absence of retroflex–dental stop configurations could just as easily reflect regressive dental assimilation (*/ʈ…t/ → [t…t]) as progressive retroflex assimilation (*/ʈ…t/ → [ʈ…ʈ]) or some other phonological process. In the absence of historical-comparative evidence to support progressive assimilation we can only say that Kalasha has systematically avoided introducing retroflex–dental stop configurations (*/ʈ...t/) while subjecting inherited dental–retroflex configurations to regressive retroflex assimilation (*/t...ʈ/ → [ʈ...ʈ]). Anything beyond this is speculative. We conclude that retroflex consonant harmony in Kalasha is primarily (if not exclusively) regressive.

4.3.2 Transparency/Opacity

In Kalasha's consonant harmony system, the trigger and target of assimilation are separated minimally by a vowel and potentially by some combination of consonants and vowels. The segments that intervene between the trigger and target appear to be transparent; they are neither targeted by retroflex assimilation, nor do they block it.

Recall that coronal features/gestures such as retroflexion are typically non-distinctive, and therefore irrelevant, for vowels and non-coronal consonants in most languages of the world. On the basis of this, it has been argued that they are uniquely able to permeate vowels and non-coronal consonants with little or no audible effect, thereby creating the illusion of transparency. Kalasha, however, is one of the few languages in the world in which retroflexion is phonologically relevant for vowels. Significantly, Kalasha vowels are not recorded as retroflex when they occur between the trigger and target of assimilation in consonant harmony domains. There are no examples of phonemic retroflex vowels occurring between retroflex consonants in Trail and Cooper's (1999) Kalasha dictionary. The complete absence of retroflex vowels in these environments could indicate that the contrast is neutralized in consonant harmony domains. Even so, it remains significant that the contrast is neutralized in favour of non-retroflex vowels. If retroflexion were to target or permeate all intervening segments, we might expect neutralization to favour retroflex vowels in harmony domains.

The non-retroflex quality of vowels in consonant harmony domains is supported by phonetic data. Evidence from a limited number of field recordings that we examined indicates that vowels in retroflex consonant harmony domains exhibit a degree of retroflex co-articulation but remain notably distinct from phonemic retroflex vowels. The primary cue to retroflexion is a lowering of F3 (Ladefoged and Maddieson 1996). In words such as /ɖʐaʈʂ/ 'spirit beings', the F3 of the vowel begins relatively high and then drops sharply in the second half of the vowel's duration. This dynamic F3 pattern is typical of retroflex co-articulation, which tends to be more prominent before retroflex consonants (i.e. in VC transitions) than after them (i.e. in CV transitions; Hamann 2003). A different pattern can be observed in phonemic retroflex vowels, which exhibit a stable low F3 throughout their duration.[8] It is not surprising, therefore, that linguists and Kalasha speakers have regarded the vowels in consonant harmony domains as non-retroflex, and recorded them as such in phonemic transcriptions. We conclude that the transcriptions are appropriate, and that Kalasha vowels are indeed transparent to retroflex consonant harmony.

Intervening labial and velar consonants do not block retroflex consonant harmony (e.g. /iʂpoʂi/ 'nephew', /ʂiŋgiʂ/ 'spinach-like vegetable'), but without instrumental evidence it is impossible to say whether they are targeted or permeated by retroflexion. Similarly, intervening coronal consonants do not appear to block consonant harmony, although most of them remain ambiguous with respect to their status as targets of retroflexion. For instance, coronal nasals are always homorganic before stops. Thus, local assimilation is independently expected to produce a retroflex nasal in words like /ɖinʈa/ [ɖiɳʈa] 'efficient' and we cannot attribute the retroflex nasal in words of this type to consonant harmony. The liquid /r/ is independently prone to some degree of phonetic retroflexion cross-linguistically, which is why it is a common diachronic source of retroflexion in many languages (Bhat 1973, Hamann 2003), including Kalasha. Thus, it is not a reliable indicator of transparency or opacity in retroflex harmony domains. In many languages, retroflexion entails a degree of tongue retraction comparable to velarization (Hamann 2003). However, examples of both velarized and non-velarized laterals can be found in consonant harmony domains (e.g. /ʂiɫeʂ/ 'glue', /ɖuɳɖulaʈ/ 'village of Dundulet'). Thus, even if some relation could

[8] These phonetic observations are consistent with the auditory impressions of those who have worked extensively on the language. For instance, Ron Trail informs us that vowels in consonant harmony domains 'probably have a trace of retroflexion from the surrounding consonants, but do not share the tight retroflexed quality that we have noted with the retroflexed vowels' (personal communication).

be established between retroflexion and velarization in Kalasha, there would be no indication that intervening laterals are targeted by retroflex consonant harmony.

The only *potential* case of blocking involves roots of the type /t…ʂʈ/, in which a fricative intervenes between two coronal stops. Evidence bearing on this issue is sparse because there are few Kalasha roots containing the relevant sequences. Consider the data in (13), which lists the relevant Kalasha words alongside cognates from OIA and two related Dardic languages, Palula and Indus Kohistani (IK), both of which exhibit retroflex consonant harmony systems comparable to that of Kalasha (Arsenault 2012).[9]

(13) No harmony between stops in /t…ʂʈ/ and /d…ʂʈ/ sequences

		Kalasha	Palula	IK	OIA	CDIAL
a.	'visible, seen'	drẽʂʈ, drẽʂ	d^{h}riʂʈu		dr̩ʂʈa	6518
	'written cure'	draʂʈaw			??	??
b.	'bitter'	ʧiʂʈaka	tríʂʈu	ʧìʈ^{hi}	tr̩ʂʈa-	5938
	'to stand'	ʧiʂʈik			tiʂʈ^{h}ati	5837
	'hand span'	ʤiʂʈ, ʤiʂ	diʂʈ	ɖí:ʈ^{hi}, díʈ^{h}	diʂʈi	6343
	'female spirit'	ʤeʂʈak			de:ʂʈri:	6556

The examples in (13 a) suggest that retroflex stops have not triggered harmony in preceding dental stops when the sibilant /ʂ/ intervenes. These examples also contain an intervening /r/. The examples in (13 b) contained /t…ʂʈ/ or /d…ʂʈ/ sequences in OIA. However, in these cases the initial dental stops have been palatalized in Kalasha. There is reason to believe that neither palatalization nor the presence of /r/ are necessarily responsible for the lack of harmony in (13). Evidence for this can be found in the various cognates of 'hand span' in (13 b). The Palula cognate /diʂʈ/ is disharmonic despite the fact that it has neither palatalization nor /r/. Unlike Kalasha and Palula, Indus Kohistani has not preserved /ʂ/ in OIA /ʂʈ/ clusters. It is precisely the absence of /ʂ/ in the Indus Kohistani cognate that paves the way for (variable) harmony between the stops (OIA /diʂʈi/ > MIA */diʈʈ^{h}-/ > IK /díʈ^{h}/ ~ /ɖí:ʈ^{hi}/ 'span of hand'). Thus, the limited evidence

[9] Palula cognates were supplied by Henrik Liljegren. Indus Kohistani cognates are from Zoller (2005).

available suggests that harmony does not apply between coronal stops whenever /ʂ/ intervenes. However, this does not necessarily entail that /ʂ/ is opaque to retroflex consonant harmony in Kalasha. Recall that stop–sibilant (and palatal affricate–fricative) combinations are inclined toward dissimilation. If so, then the examples in (13) simply reflect the same trend. In each case, the initial stop is in closer proximity to /ʂ/ than to the following retroflex stop. Thus, a dissimilatory restriction on stop–sibilant pairs would take precedence over an assimilatory restriction on co-occurring stops in these cases.

In sum, the weight of evidence indicates that intervening segments are transparent to retroflex consonant harmony. The vowels that occur between the trigger and target of assimilation are not regarded as retroflex despite the fact that retroflexion is phonologically relevant for vowels in Kalasha. There is no indication that intervening consonants serve as targets or blockers of assimilation. The only potential case of blocking can be attributed to an independent dissimilatory co-occurrence restriction.

4.3.3 Similarity Effects

Perhaps the most striking property of consonant harmony in Kalasha is its unmistakable similarity effect. In Kalasha, retroflex consonant harmony holds only between obstruents that share the same manner of articulation. It applies to co-occurring stops or co-occurring sibilants but not mixed pairs of stops and sibilants, despite the fact that retroflexion is contrastive in both manner classes. This is significant because previously documented cases of retroflex consonant harmony tend to be ambiguous on this point, as shown in Table 5.

Table 5: Cases of retroflex consonant harmony reported in Rose and Walker (2004) and Hansson (2010) classified as sibilant or non-sibilant harmony

	Language (Genetic Affiliation)	**Retroflex Consonant Harmony**	
		Non-Sibilant	**Sibilant**
a.	Malto (Dravidian)	✓	–
	Javanese (Austronesian)	✓	–
	Pohnpeian (Austronesian)	✓	–
	Gaagudju (Australian)	✓	–
	Gooniyandi (Australian)	✓	–
	Mayali (Australian)	✓	–
	Murrinh-Patha (Australian)	✓	–
b.	Benchnon Gimira (Omotic, Afro-Asiatic)	–	✓
	Capanahua (Panoan)	–	✓
	Kinyarwanda (Bantu)	–	✓
	Komi-Permyak (Finno-Ugric)	–	✓
	Nebaj Ixil (Mayan)	–	✓
	Rumsen (Costanoan, Penutian)	–	✓
	Wanka Quechua (Quechuan)	–	✓

Table 5 lists all cases of retroflex consonant harmony (outside of the Dardic group) reported in recent surveys by Rose and Walker (2004) and Hansson (2010). All of the languages in the upper half of the table, identified as group (a), exhibit retroflex consonant harmony between non-sibilant coronals. In most cases the harmonizing segments are stops, although in the Australian languages they may include sonorants. All of the languages in the lower half of the table, identified as group (b), exhibit retroflex consonant harmony between coronal sibilants (affricates and/or fricatives). No language in Table 5 exhibits consonant harmony between sibilant and non-sibilant coronals. This might be interpreted as a similarity effect in which consonant harmony is sensitive to the distinction between sibilant and non-sibilant classes. However, data from the languages in Table 5 is ambiguous on this point because all of the languages in group (a) lack retroflex sibilants altogether while those in group (b) lack non-sibilant retroflex stops. Thus, with few exceptions, the class of segments participating in retroflex harmony is coextensive with the class of segments that is contrastive for retroflexion in each language. Under these conditions it is impossible to say whether consonant harmony is conditioned by similarity or whether it simply operates over all segments that are contrastive for retroflexion. Dardic languages, such as Kalasha, are unique in having retroflex stops and sibilants. Thus, they are uniquely situated to reveal similarity effects respecting these classes.

The similarity effect in Kalasha's consonant harmony system stands out all the more clearly when it is compared with co-occurrence restrictions on adjacent coronal obstruents. In Kalasha, morpheme-internal consonant clusters consisting of two coronal obstruents are limited to sequences of fricative + stop. These clusters show agreement for retroflexion or non-retroflexion without regard for similarity along the sibilant vs non-sibilant dimension. Representative examples are shown in (14).

(14) Assimilatory co-occurrence restrictions in fricative+plosive clusters

a.	post	'skin'	iston	'udder'
	asta	'also, too'	nast	'nose'
b.	paɕt	'ribs'	ɕuruɕtju	'thoroughness'
	piɕtjak	'behind'	paɕtari	'power'
c.	piʂʈ	'upper back'	iʂʈep karik	'to suffocate'
	aʂʈ(a)	'eight'	uʂʈ	'lip'
d.	*sʈ, *ʂt, *ɕʈ (no retroflexes with non-retroflexes)			

Kalasha overwhelmingly prefers fricative + stop clusters consisting of homorganic dental consonants (/st/), as in (14 a), or retroflex consonants (/ʂʈ/), as in (14 c). Palatal fricatives and dental stops can also co-occur in some clusters (/ɕt(j)/, as shown in (14 b). However, examples of this kind are less frequent. Moreover, the dental stops in these sequences are often followed by a palatal glide or high front vowel, suggesting that they might be somewhat palatalized. Whatever the case may be, it is clear that the language systematically avoids fricative + stop clusters that disagree in retroflexion, including */sʈ/, */ʂt/, and */ɕʈ/. The restriction on adjacent obstruents in (14) stands in sharp contrast to the restriction on non-adjacent obstruents. Unlike consonant harmony, local assimilation in Kalasha is not sensitive to the distinction between sibilant and non-sibilant obstruents.

Kalasha may show further sensitivity to similarity within the sibilant class. Palatal affricates behave somewhat like stops when they co-occur with fricatives. Like stop–fricative pairs, palatal affricate–fricative pairs show a gradient form of dissimilation: palatal–dental and palatal–retroflex configurations are more frequent than palatal–palatal configurations. At the same time, palatal affricates are subject to assimilation when they co-occur with other affricates: palatal–palatal configurations are more frequent than palatal–dental and palatal–retroflex configurations. Thus, palatal affricates appear to be sensitive to the distinction between affricates and fricatives. However, retroflex affricates are not sensitive to this distinction. They harmonize with sibilants of any kind, whether affricates or fricatives (e.g. /ɖʐaʈʂ/ 'spirit beings', ʂanɖʐu-ik 'to wrinkle').

In summary, synchronic and diachronic evidence from Kalasha reveal a system of retroflex consonant harmony in which the direction of assimilation is primarily (if not exclusively) regressive, intervening segments are transparent, and interaction between segments is conditioned by similarity. In what follows, we contrast this system with a second type of retroflex harmony in Kalasha.

5. Retroflex vowel harmony

The system of retroflex consonant harmony described above can be contrasted with the pattern of retroflex vowel harmony described by Heegård and Mørch (2004). Little is known about retroflex vowel harmony in Kalasha. Nevertheless, the few details that can be gleaned from the available data suggest an independent system with a different set of typological properties.

As discussed above, western dialects of Kalasha have a full set of retroflex vowels. These vowels have developed historically from the coalescence of (non-retroflex) vowels with intervocalic retroflex consonants (Heegård and Mørch 2004; cf. Di Carlo 2009). The intervocalic retroflex stops of OIA have been subject to various forms of lenition over time. They tend to show up as retroflex liquids, such as /ɽ/ and /ɭ/, in most NIA languages. In Kalasha the process of lenition has been carried one step further. The intervocalic retroflex stops of OIA have been lost altogether in some dialects. Where this has taken place, the feature of retroflexion has been preserved on the preceding vowel, thereby creating retroflex vowel phonemes. Representative examples from the Rumbur and Bumburet dialects are listed in (15). The examples in (15 a) contain retroflex vowels that have developed through the loss of an intervocalic oral stop. In cases where the lost consonant was a nasal stop, both nasalization and retroflexion are preserved on the vowel, as shown in (15 b).

(15) Diachronic origins of retroflex vowels in Kalasha (Heegård and Mørch 2004)

		Kalasha (Rum./Bum.dialects)	OIA	CDIAL
a.	'kind of cheese'	kila˞	kila:ʈa-	3181
	'bent'	ko˞ ho˞ k	kuʈi(ka)-	3230
	'blind'	ʂe˞ a	*çre:ɖa-	12717
	'little child'	ku˞ a˞ k	*kuɖa-	3245
b.	'palm of hand'	pẽ˞	pa:ɳi-	8045
	'beads'	mã˞ (h)ĩ˞ k	maɳi-	9731
	'arrowhead'	bõ˞	ba:ɳa-	9203
	'pillar'	tʰũ˞	stʰu:ɳa:-	13774

Some dialects of Kalasha still preserve OIA intervocalic retroflex consonants in some form. For instance, the Birir dialect tends to preserve them as /ɽ/ before /i/. Elsewhere, Birir has merged them with preceding vowels, like other western dialects. Compare the examples from Birir with those from the Rumbur and Bumburet dialects in (16).

(16) Dialectal variation in Kalasha (Heegård and Mørch 2004)

	Rum./Bum.	Birir	OIA	CDIAL
'apricot'	aʐa˞ i	aʐaɽi	a:ʂa:ɖʰi:ja	1474
'beads'	mã˞ (h)ĩ˞ k	mãɽik	maɳi-	9731
'goat's hair coat'	gũ˞ i	gũɽi	go:ɳi:	4275
'harvest walnuts'	ʈʂʰõ˞ ik	ʈʂʰõɽik	*kʂaɳati	3643

Given that retroflexion in vowels derives historically from consonants, it is reasonable to assume that the feature or gesture that distinguishes retroflex vowels from their non-retroflex counterparts is the same feature or gesture that distinguishes retroflex consonants. Even so, retroflex vowels do not appear to participate in the system of retroflex consonant harmony described above. Earlier we saw that vowels do not serve as targets of assimilation in retroflex consonant harmony domains. Similarly, the examples in (17) demonstrate that retroflex vowels do not trigger regressive assimilation in preceding dental or palatal obstruents, even in cases where the vowel in question reflects a lost retroflex obstruent; e.g. /ud^{h}ũ˞ / 'dust' < */udd^{h}u:ɖi-/ in (17 a).

(17) Retroflex vowels do not trigger regressive assimilation in dental and palatal obstruents

		Kalasha		OIA	CDIAL
a.	'post, column'	t^{h}ũ˞		st^{h}u:ɳa:-	13774
	'dust'	ud^{h}ũ˞		*udd^{h}u:ɖi-	2025
b.	'nil, zero'	tsũ˞	*su:ɳa-	su:na, ɕu:nja-	12567
	'braid, plait'	tɕu˞ i		tɕu:ɖa-	4883
c.	'gold'	sũ˞ a		suvarɳa-	13519
	'reed, arrow'	ɕa˞		ɕara-	12324

While retroflex vowels do not participate in consonant harmony, they do participate in a harmony system of their own, which can be described as retroflex vowel harmony (or possibly retroflex vowel-consonant harmony). In their study of retroflex vowels in Kalasha, Heegård and Mørch (2004) observe that retroflexion can assimilate from one vowel to another, at least optionally. This optional assimilation gives rise to variation of the type illustrated in (18).

(18) Retroflex vowel harmony in Kalasha (Heegård and Mørch 2004)

a.	/pĩ˞ ik/	[pĩ˞ ik] ~ [pĩ˞ i˞ k]	'to squeeze'
	/tʃa˞ ha˞ ka/	[tʃa˞ ha˞ ka] ~ [tʃa˞ ha˞ ka˞]	'maize bread'
	/a˞ ngu/	[a˞ ŋgu] ~ [a˞ ŋgu˞]	'finger'
	/sirã˞ /	[sirã˞] ~ [si˞ rã˞]	'wind'
b.	/a˞ in/	[a˞ in] ~ [a˞ i˞ ɳ]	'millet'

The few examples in (18) give us little to work with. Nevertheless, the picture they paint suggests a harmony system that is quite distinct from the system of retroflex consonant harmony. First of all, assimilation in (18) is predominantly progressive, although regressive assimilation also appears to be possible, as suggested by /sirã˞/ [sirã˞] ~ [si˞rã˞] 'wind'. Thus, with respect to directionality, retroflex vowel harmony in Kalasha is predominantly progressive but potentially bi-directional. Secondly, assimilation in (18) appears to respect strict locality. No vowels are skipped, and even though some intervening consonants appear to be transparent, they are most likely permeated by the retroflex feature or gesture. Evidence for this comes from examples like (18 b), where assimilation targets a coronal nasal /n/ that lies in its path, producing variation between [n] and [ɳ]. Finally, assimilation in (18) shows no clear evidence of similarity effects. All vowels participate in the pattern regardless of tongue height, backness, lip rounding, or nasalization. Moreover, as the example in (18 b) shows, both vowels and consonants can serve as potential targets.

6. IMPLICATIONS FOR PHONOLOGICAL TYPOLOGY

Having reviewed the basic facts concerning consonant and vowel harmony in Kalasha, we can now compare the two patterns and discuss their implications for phonological typology. Table 6 provides a summary of each pattern with reference to the three typological parameters introduced at the outset of the chapter: direction of assimilation, transparency/opacity of intervening segments, and similarity of interacting segments.

Table 6: Typological properties of two retroflex harmony systems in Kalasha

	Retroflex Consonant Harmony	Retroflex Vowel Harmony
Direction	Predominantly (if not exclusively) regressive	Predominantly progressive but potentially bi-directional
Opacity	Intervening segments are transparent and not targeted by retroflexion	Intervening segments appear to be targeted/ permeated by retroflexion
Similarity	Interacting segments share a high degree of similarity	Interacting segments are not necessarily similar

The two types of retroflex harmony in Kalasha are clearly distinct. They do not appear to interact with one another and each exhibits a different set of typological properties. Retroflex consonant harmony in Kalasha exhibits properties that are characteristic of most consonant harmony systems cross-linguistically. By comparing Table 6 with Table 1 in section 2, we can see that these are precisely the properties that are said to arise from feature agreement: (i) a regressive bias; (ii) transparency of intervening segments; and (iii) similarity of interacting segments. In contrast to this, retroflex vowel harmony in Kalasha exhibits properties that are more in keeping with gesture extension: (i) no inherent directional bias; (ii) intervening segments are targeted or permeated by the assimilating feature; and (iii) interacting segments are not necessarily constrained by similarity. The coexistence of two types of retroflex harmony in the same language, each with a different set of typological properties, lends support to the hypothesis that two independent mechanisms of assimilation are at work. We conclude that retroflex consonant harmony is the product of feature agreement in Kalasha while retroflex vowel harmony is the product of gesture extension.

Recall that coronal features such as retroflexion are said to be unique. Unlike most other consonant features, they can permeate vowels and non-coronal consonants with little or no audible effect. Thus, while there is considerable evidence that some consonant harmony systems are best explained in terms of feature agreement, unambiguous evidence concerning retroflex consonant harmony is hard to find. Kalasha, with its striking similarity effect and transparent non-retroflex vowels, provides what is probably the strongest case for retroflex consonant harmony arising from feature agreement. The point is not that all retroflex consonant harmony systems must be the product of feature agreement (nor that all vowel harmony systems must be the product of gesture extension), but only that retroflex consonant harmony systems *can* (and we would argue, *should*) be understood in terms of feature agreement when, like Kalasha, they exhibit the appropriate typological properties.

A good example of a retroflex harmony system involving consonants that does not exhibit properties in keeping with feature agreement is Sanskrit n-retroflexion. In Sanskrit, dental /n/ is realized as retroflex /ɳ/ when it occurs after an adjacent or non-adjacent /ʂ/ or /r/, e.g.

/tɕakʂ-aːna-/ → /tɕakʂ-aːɳa-/ 'see (middle participle)'. This rule is well-documented and widely discussed elsewhere (Whitney 1993 [1889], Schein and Steriade 1986, Hansson 2010, among others). We will not delve into a lengthy description here. Suffice it to say that, although it is one of the most cited examples of retroflex consonant harmony in the literature, it does not exhibit typological properties consistent with most other consonant harmony systems, a point argued convincingly by Hansson (2010). Among other things, Sanskrit n-retroflexion exhibits the following properties: (i) it is progressive; (ii) intervening vowels and non-coronal consonants appear to be transparent, but intervening coronals block assimilation, e.g. /kʂub^{h}-aːɳa-/ 'quake (middle participle)', but /kʂved-aːna-/ 'hum (middle participle)'; and (iii) interacting segments are not constrained by similarity, e.g. /ʂ/ targets a following /n/, but not a following /s/. By all accounts (including those that otherwise advocate feature agreement), Sanskrit n-retroflexion is the product of feature/gesture extension (Whitney 1993 [1889], Allen 1951, Gafos 1999, Ní Chiosáin and Padgett 1997, Hansson 2010). It is worth noting that retroflex vowel harmony in Kalasha bears a strong typological resemblance to Sanskrit n-retroflexion. This is consistent with the conclusion that it too is the product of gesture extension.

7. CONCLUSION

In conclusion, Kalasha's phonological system is typologically rare and has much to teach us. Not only is Kalasha unique in having retroflex stops, affricates, fricatives, and vowels, but it may also be the only language in the world with two independent retroflex harmony systems: retroflex consonant harmony and retroflex vowel harmony. The differences between these two harmony systems, and their independence of one another, are best explained if each is the product of a different mechanism of assimilation with its own functional grounding and associated typological properties. In Kalasha, retroflex consonant harmony exhibits properties consistent with feature agreement while retroflex vowel harmony exhibits properties consistent with gesture extension. The coexistence of these two harmony systems in the same language, each with a distinct set of typological properties, lends support to the hypothesis that more than one mechanism of assimilation is at work in human language. Moreover, the evidence from Kalasha affirms that retroflex consonant harmony can arise through similarity-induced feature agreement much like other types of consonant harmony.

APPENDIX: ACOUSTIC ANALYSIS OF SELECTED KALASHA VOWELS

This analysis is based on sound files from ‘Examples of Kalasha vowels. Recordings by Ida E. Mørch, Jørgen Rischel, and Jan Heegård’ (2008).

The vowel [a] in /ɖʐaʈʂ/ in (1 a) is considerably affected by the adjacent retroflex consonants. This is seen in its much lower F3 compared to F3 for [a] in /ʥatɕ/ in (1 b). Lower F3 is characteristic of retroflexion. Notably, however, F3 of /ɖʐaʈʂ/ varies substantially across the duration of the vowel, being higher in the first-half (up to 2,650 Hz) than in the second-half (down to 2,000 Hz). This is indicative of coarticulatory effects, as F3 tends to be lower before a retroflex consonant than after it (e.g. Hamann 2003). If the vowel were contrastively retroflex, we would expect F3 to be relatively stable and low throughout the vowel duration.

(1) ɖʐ[a]ʈʂ ‘religious spirit’ and ʥ[a]tɕ ‘hair (on body), fur’ (Male speaker AK)

a. b.

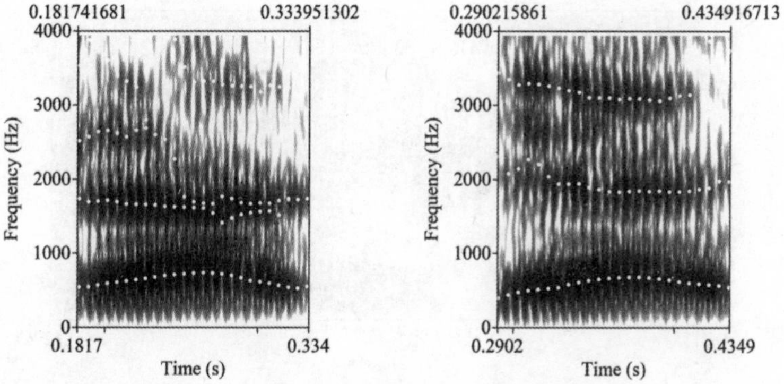

This is what we observe in the word /ga˞/ in (2 a), where F3 of [a˞] is low throughout the duration of the vowel (below 2,400 Hz), being very close to F2. Compare this to the quite high F3 (around 2,900 Hz) of [a] in /kałek/ in (2 b), produced by the same speaker. Finally, (3) shows another example of two retroflex vowels in /e˞hẽ˞/, produced by a different speaker. F3 stays low (below 2,300 Hz) throughout the word almost merging with F2, which reflects a strong degree of retroflexion.

(2) g[a˞] 'throat' and k[a]łek 'jaw, chin' (Male speaker MI)

a. b.

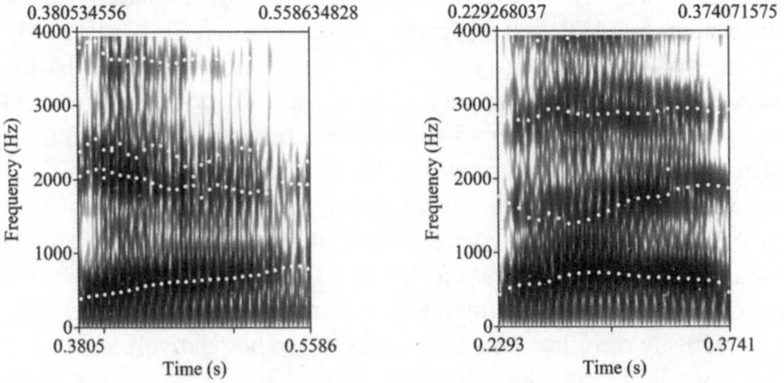

(3) [e˞ hẽ˞] 'Ayun (name of Chitrali/Khowar village, "Ayun" is Khowar)' (Male speaker IK)

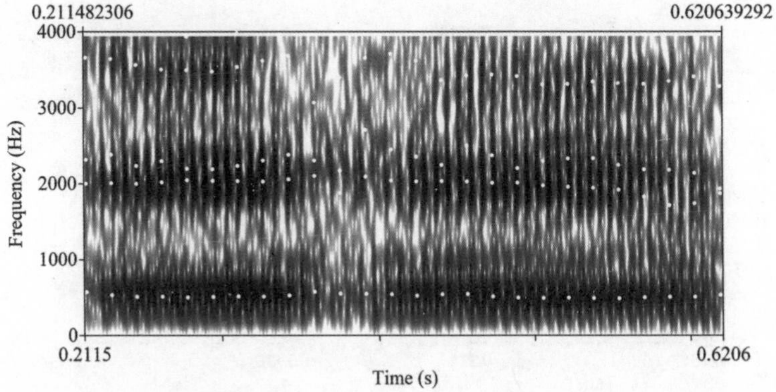

ACKNOWLEDGEMENTS

We would like to thank Ron Trail, Greg Cooper, Jan Heegård, Ida Mørch, and Pierpaolo Di Carlo for contributing data to our study and discussing many of the issues addressed in this paper with us. Any errors or omissions are our own.

REFERENCES

Allen, W. S. 1951. 'Some prosodic aspects of retroflexion and aspiration in Sanskrit'. *Bulletin of the School of Oriental and African Studies, University of London* 13.4: 939–46.

Arsenault, Paul. 2012. *Retroflex Consonant Harmony in South Asia*. PhD dissertation. Toronto: University of Toronto.

______ and Kochetov, Alexei. 2011. 'Retroflex harmony in Kalasha: Agreement or spreading?' In *Proceedings of the North East Linguistic Society 39*, edited by Suzi Lima, Kevin Mullin, and Brian Smith. 55–66. Amherst: GLSA.

Bashir, Elena. 2003. 'Dardic'. In *The Indo-Aryan Languages*, edited by George Cardona and Dhanesh Jain. 818–94. New York and London: Routledge.

Bhat, D. N. S. 1973. 'Retroflexion: An Areal Feature'. *Working Papers on Language Universals* 13: 27–67.

Cardona, George. 2003. 'Sanskrit'. In *The Indo-Aryan Languages*, edited by George Cardona and Dhanesh Jain. 104–60. London and New York: Routledge.

Clements, G. N. 1980. *Vowel Harmony in Nonlinear Generative Phonology: An Autosegmental Model*. Indiana: Indiana University Linguistics Club.

Dell, Gary S., Burger, Lisa K., and Svec, William R. 1997. 'Language production and serial order: A functional analysis and a model'. *Psychological Review* 104.1: 123–47.

Di Carlo, Pierpaolo. 2009. *I Kalasha del Hindu-Kush: Ricerche linguistiche e antropologiche* [The Kalasha of the Hindu-Kush: Linguistic and anthropological research]. Dissertation. Florence: University of Florence.

Emeneau, M. B. 1939. 'The vowels of the Badaga language'. *Language* 15.1: 43–7.

Gafos, Adamantios I. 1999. *The Articulatory Basis of Locality in Phonology*. New York and London: Garland Publishing.

Gamble, Geoffrey. 1975. 'Consonant symbolism in Yokuts'. *International Journal of American Linguistics* 41:4: 306–9.

Hamann, Silke. 2003. *The Phonetics and Phonology of Retroflexes*. Utrecht: LOT (Landelijke Onderzoekschool Taalwetenschap).

Hansson, Gunnar Ólafur. 2010. *Consonant Harmony: Long-Distance Interaction in Phonology*. Berkeley: University of California Press.

Ladefoged, Peter and Maddieson, Ian. 1996. *The Sounds of the World's Languages*. Oxford: Blackwell Publishers.

LaPolla, Randy J. 2003. 'Qiang'. In *The Sino-Tibetan Languages*, edited by Graham Thurgood and Randy J. LaPolla. 573–87. London and New York: Routledge.

Lewis, M. Paul, Simons, Gary F., and Fennig, Charles D. (eds.). 2013. *Ethnologue: Languages of the World*. 17th ed. Dallas, Texas: SIL International. <http://www.ethnologue.com> accessed 12 March 2014.

Lorimer, D. L. R. 1939. *The Dumāki Language*. Nijmegen: Dekker and Van de Vegt N. V.

Maddieson, Ian and Precoda, Kristin. 1992. *UPSID and PHONEME* (version 1.1). Los Angeles: University of California.

Masica, Colin P. 1991. *The Indo-Aryan Languages*. Cambridge: Cambridge University Press.

Morgenstierne, Georg. 1973. *Indo-Iranian Frontier Languages, Vol. 4, The Kalasha Language.* Oslo: Universitetsforlaget.

Namkung, Ju (ed.). 1996. *Phonological Inventories of Tibeto-Burman Languages.* Berkeley, CA: Center for Southeast Asia Studies, University of California at Berkeley.

Ní Chiosáin, Máire and Padgett, Jaye. 2001. 'Markedness, segment realization, and locality in spreading'. In *Segmental Phonology in Optimality Theory: Constraints and Representations*, edited by Linda Lombardi. 118–56. Cambridge: Cambridge University Press.

———. 1997. *Markedness, Segment Realisation, and Locality in Spreading.* Report No. LRC-97-01. Santa Cruz, CA: Linguistics Research Center, UCSC.

Petersen, Jan Heegård. 2006. *Local Case-Marking in Kalasha.* PhD dissertation. Copenhagen: University of Copenhagen.

———. and Mørch, Ida Elisabeth. 2004. 'Retroflex vowels and other peculiarities in the Kalasha sound system'. In *Himalayan Languages, Past and Present*, edited by Anju Saxena. 57–76. Berlin and New York: Mouton de Gruyter.

Poser, William. J. 1982. 'Phonological representations and action-at-a-distance'. In *The Structure of Phonological Representations, Part II*, edited by Harry van der Hulst and Norval Smith. 121–58. Dordrecht: Foris Publications.

Ramanujan, A. K. and Masica, Colin. 1969. 'Toward a phonological typology of the Indian linguistic area'. In *Current Trends in Linguistics, Volume 5: Linguistics in South Asia*, edited by Thomas A. Sebeok. 543–77. Paris: Mouton.

Rehman, Khawaja A. and Baart, Joan L. G. 2005. 'A first look at the language of Kundal Shahi in Azad Kashmir'. *SIL Electronic Working Papers 2005-008.* <http://www.sil.org/resources/publications/entry/7866> accessed 12 March 2014.

Robins, R. H. 1958. *The Yurok Language: Grammar, Texts, Lexicon.* Berkeley and Los Angeles: University of California Press.

Rose, Sharon. 2011. 'Long-distance assimilation of consonants'. In *The Blackwell Companion to Phonology*, edited by Marc van Oostendorp, Colin J. Ewen, Elizabeth Hume, and Keren Rice. 1811–37. Oxford: Wiley-Blackwell.

——— and Walker, Rachel. 2004. 'A typology of consonant agreement as correspondence'. *Language* 80.3: 475–531.

Schein, Barry and Steriade, Donca. 1986. 'On geminates'. *Linguistic Inquiry* 17.4: 691–744.

Shaw, Patricia A. 1991. 'Consonant harmony systems: The special status of coronal harmony'. In *The Special Status of Coronals: Internal and External Evidence*, edited by Carole Paradis and Jean-François Prunet. 125–57. San Diego: Academic Press.

Trail, Ronald L. and Cooper, Gregory R. 1999. *Kalasha Dictionary—with English and Urdu.* Islamabad: National Institute of Pakistan Studies, Quaid-i-Azam University, and Summer Institute of Linguistics.

Turner, Ralph Lilley. 1962–1966. *A Comparative Dictionary of Indo-Aryan Languages.* London: Oxford University Press. <http://dsal.uchicago.edu/dictionaries/soas/> accessed 12 March 2014.

Wali, Kashi and Koul, Omkar N. 1997. *Kashmiri: A Cognitive-Descriptive Grammar.* London and New York: Routledge.

Whitney, William Dwight. 1993 [1889]. *Sanskrit Grammar Including both the Classical Language and the Older Dialects of Veda and Brahmana*. 2nd ed. Cambridge, MA: Harvard University Press.

Zoller, Claus Peter. 2005. *A Grammar and Dictionary of Indus Kohistani, Volume 1: Dictionary.* Berlin and New York: Mouton de Gruyter.

3

Pronominal Clitics in the Logar Dialect of Ormuri

Joan L.G. Baart and Jeremy Hawbaker

1. INTRODUCTION

In this contribution, we explore the occurrence and use of pronominal clitics in the Logar dialect of Ormuri. Ormuri is an endangered Iranian language, traditionally spoken in two distinct locations: in the town of Kaniguram in South Waziristan, Pakistan, and in the Logar province of Afghanistan.[1]

Ormuri has a set of full, independent personal pronouns, as well as a set of demonstrative pronouns. As is common in Iranian languages,[2] Ormuri also has a set of pronominal clitics, that can be used in the role of direct object, indirect object, possessor, and as the subject of a transitive clause.[3] Ormuri pronominal clitics share the following characteristics that distinguish them from regular, independent pronouns: (i) Pronominal clitics do not bear lexical stress, nor can they be contrastively stressed; (ii) A pronominal clitic requires a host to its left (so it never occurs clause-initially); (iii) A pronominal clitic cannot be coordinated with another pronoun; and (iv) There is a

[1] This chapter is an abridged and revised version of Jeremy Hawbaker's MA thesis (Hawbaker 2014). For a more extensive presentation and discussion of the results of this study, the reader is referred to that work.

[2] See, among others, Dabir-Moghaddam (2008), Korn (2009), Windfuhr (2009: 23), Barjasteh Delforooz and Levinsohn (2014).

[3] In addition there are a few highly exceptional cases where a pronominal clitic occurs as the subject of a non-ergative clause; see 3.3 ahead.

strong tendency for Ormuri pronominal clitics to occur in the position immediately after the first phrasal constituent of the clause.

Of course, the first three characteristics in this list merely describe part of what it means to be a clitic, and more specifically an enclitic (a clitic that follows its host), while the fourth characteristic (a preference for the second position in the clause) is true of clitics in many languages around the world (Spencer and Luis 2012: 24–8).

In Ormuri, the use of a pronominal clitic is not obligatory in any context, as far as we have seen. This raises the question: When, exactly, is a pronominal clitic used, rather than a noun, an independent pronoun, or zero anaphora, to refer to an entity in the situation that is being talked about? Section 3 below describes grammatical constraints on the contexts in which pronominal clitics can occur, and in section 4 we share a few preliminary results of our study of discourse factors that influence the choice between a pronominal clitic and other referring expressions. For the discourse study we used the methodology for studying participant reference laid out in Dooley and Levinsohn (2001).

The data that we had at our disposal for this study were fifty-one texts recorded, transcribed, and translated by V.A. Efimov in 1971 and 1978–79 (Efimov 2011) and four texts recorded, transcribed, and translated by Charles M. Kieffer in the 1970s (unpublished). Unfortunately, we did not have access to the audio recordings of the texts, so we were limited to working with the phonemic transcriptions by Efimov and Kieffer. Our study focused on the Logar dialect; therefore, our conclusions may not apply without modification to the Kaniguram dialect.

2. LANGUAGE, LOCATION, SPEAKERS

The first known reference to the Ormuri[4] language and people, also known by the name of *Baraki*, is found in the *Baburnama*, the memoirs of Zahir-ud-Din Muhammad Babur (1483–1530), founder of the Mughal Empire. Until very recently, speakers of Ormuri have been

[4] ISO 639-3 code [oru]. The classification of Ormuri, either as a Western Iranian language or, alternatively, as an Eastern Iranian language, remains controversial, cf. Morgenstierne (1926: 27–36), Efimov ([1986] 2011: 3–7), Kieffer (1989: 451–3), Lecoq (1989: 247).

living in two locations on opposite sides of the Pakistan–Afghanistan border: in the town of Kaniguram in South Waziristan (Pakistan), and also around Baraki-Barak in the Logar province of Afghanistan. The two communities are 160 kilometres apart as the crow flies and the international border that separates them is sensitive; hence they have not been in close contact for centuries, and speakers from either place find it difficult to understand the other dialect.

In Afghanistan, the language is in serious trouble. As a matter of fact, when Georg Morgenstierne visited Afghanistan in 1924, he concluded—based on reports by people who knew the Logar Valley well—that Logar Ormuri was rapidly being superseded by Persian and Pashto, and that hardly anyone spoke the language anymore (Morgenstierne 1929: 14–15). Unfortunately, due to an invasion of rebel tribes into the Logar Valley, it was impossible for Morgenstierne to travel to Baraki-Barak at that time and check out the language situation in person.

Judging from the information that Morgenstierne was able to gather in 1924, one would not expect there to be a single native speaker of Logar Ormuri left in the current day and age, more than ninety years after his first visit to the country. However, unbeknownst to Morgenstierne, the language had been holding out, not in Baraki-Barak, the administrative headquarters of the Logar province and the ancestral city of the Ormur in Afghanistan, but rather in some of the *qala*, the fortified farms outside of the town of Baraki-Barak. The survival of the language on those farms was discovered in 1961 by Charles M. Kieffer (cf. 1977: 73–4).

Kieffer, who lived and worked in Afghanistan between 1957 and 1981, and was affiliated with the *Délégation archéologique française en afghanistan,*[5] had a keen interest in the common people of Afghanistan and their languages. When the Swiss linguist Georges Redard came to Afghanistan in 1961 to launch the work on the *Atlas linguistique de l'afghanistan,*[6] he noted that Kieffer was fluent in several local languages and would use them with the cook and the gardener and others. So he recruited Kieffer for his project and assigned him to the task of clarifying the fate of the Ormuri language.

---

[5] 'French Archaeological Mission to Afghanistan'.

[6] 'Linguistic Atlas of Afghanistan'. Redard passed away in 2005; the work on the publication of the atlas remains unfinished till the present day.

Kieffer went to conduct research in Baraki-Barak and its surroundings and returned with the astounding report that he had found actual speakers of Ormuri. Later that year, Georg Morgenstierne came to visit Afghanistan, and Kieffer took both Redard and Morgenstierne in his car to Logar where the men visited one of the farms. Upon hearing people speak Ormuri, the language he had believed to be all but dead in 1924, Morgenstierne was moved to tears (C.M. Kieffer, personal communication of 26 February 2014).[7]

In an article published in 1972, Kieffer estimated the remaining number of speakers of Logar Ormuri to be fewer than fifty, for the most part adult men or old people (p. 116). This was further updated in Kieffer (1989: 447), where he stated that he was not aware of more than a dozen people who still actively spoke Logar Ormuri. The Russian linguist V.A. Efimov, who conducted fieldwork on Ormuri in the Logar Valley in the summer of 1971, more optimistically estimated a number of one hundred or two hundred people who still spoke their mother tongue actively (Efimov 2011: 1).

According to information gleaned very recently by our colleague Dennis Coyle from a conversation he had with Dr Khalilullah Ormur at the Academy of Sciences of Afghanistan (Dr Ormur is himself a native speaker of Ormuri), there may still be as many as five hundred active speakers in Afghanistan, spread out over twelve or more villages in the Baraki-Barak district of Logar Province (D.W. Coyle, personal communication of 9 February 2015).

In Pakistan, the Kaniguram dialect of Ormuri is still viable, with the number of speakers estimated to be between six thousand and ten thousand.

3. THE GRAMMAR OF ORMURI PRONOMINAL CLITICS

3.1 The inventory of Ormuri pronominal clitics

The Ormuri system of pronominal clitics distinguishes person (first, second, and third) as well as number (singular and plural). There exist two areas of syncretism in this system: (i) The clitics indicating

[7] Dr Charles M. Kieffer passed away on 4 February 2015, in his home in Cernay, France, at the age of 91 years.

third person singular and third person plural share the same form; and (ii) The clitics indicating first and second person plural share the same form.

The forms of the pronominal clitics are listed in Table 1. In the table, the two areas of syncretism are shaded.

Table 1: Ormuri pronominal clitics

	Singular	Plural
1st	=(a)m	=(a)n
2nd	=(a)t	=(a)n
3rd	=(w)a	=(w)a

The table also shows that each clitic has two variant forms: the initial segment can be a vowel or a consonant. If the preceding word ends in a consonant, then the vowel-initial form of the clitic is selected. If the preceding word ends in a vowel, then the consonant-initial form of the clitic is selected. In the examples below (1–3), the boundary between a clitic and its host is indicated by an equals sign, as per linguistic convention. For additional ease of identification, we also underline the pronominal clitics in the examples.

(1) *ku* *mun=a* *dek*
obj me=PC.3 saw
'He/they saw me.'

(2) *kufo=t* *dek?*
that.one.OBJ=PC.2SG saw
'Did you see him?'

(3) *na,* *nak=am* *dek*
no not=PC.1SG saw
'No, I did not see him.'

For comparison, the independent personal and demonstrative pronouns of Ormuri are listed in Table 2.

Table 2: Ormuri personal and demonstrative pronouns

	Singular	Plural
1st	*az, mun*	*måx*
2nd	*tu*	*tos*
3rd	*a, afo*	*ain, afoin*

There is only one case distinction in the Ormuri personal pronoun system, which is that between *az* (1sg nominative) and *mun* (1sg oblique).[8] The demonstrative pronouns *a* (proximal) and *afo* (distal) and their plural counterparts *ain* and *afoin* can be used as third person pronouns. Some example sentences involving pronouns (underlined) are shown below (4–6).

(4)

az	*pa*	*zabån*	*ta*	*ormuṛi*	*poy*	*sam*
I	by	language	of	Ormuri	understanding	am

'I understand the Ormuri language.'

(5)

az	*ku*	*ahmad*	*dek*
I	OBJ	Ahmad	saw

'I saw Ahmad.'

(6)

afo	*ku*	*mun*	*dek*
that.one	OBJ	me	saw

'He saw me.'

Ormuri pronominal clitics may function in a clause as direct object, indirect object, possessor, and as the subject of a past tense transitive verb. Examples of pronominal clitics in a subject role are seen above (1–3). The following examples (7–8) illustrate pronominal clitics in the role of object. Both examples feature the third person clitic *=(w)a*.

[8] Note that contrary to the common pattern in Iranian languages, when serving as the agent of a past tense transitive verb, the nominative form *az* is selected, and not the oblique form *mun*, as seen in (5).

(7)

måya=wa=b	*ken*
leaven=PC.3=PROG	we.make

'We ferment it.'

(8)

tsaraqam=a=b	*biže*	*saṛay?*
how=PC.3=PROG	cooks	man

'How does a man cook it?'

The text corpus does not contain examples of pronominal clitics functioning as indirect object. However, in the main text of his monograph, Efimov provides a couple of (possibly elicited) illustrations of such use, quoted here (9–10). Both examples involve the first person clitic *=(a)m.*

(9)

tsa=m	*ka*	*poṭ*	*ne*	*nawešta*
what=PC.1SG	COMP	forehead	in	written

ye,	*be=b*	*nak*	*se*
is	other=PROG	not	it.becomes

'What is written for me on my forehead will not become different.' (Efimov 2011: 151)

(10)

afo=m=bu	*pa*	*kår*	*se*
that.one=PC.1SG=PROG	by	use	it.becomes

'It is useful for me.' (Efimov 2011: 151)

3.2 Position in the clause and clitic doubling

In the role of possessor, a pronominal clitic normally follows the noun phrase that it modifies, as in (11) and (12).

(11)

a	*dim=am=bu*	*zut*	*dumi*
the	stomach=PC.1SG=PROG	much	it.hurts

'My stomach hurts a lot.'

(12)

az	*ku*	*marzå=wa*	*dek*
I	obj	brother=PC.3	saw

'I saw his brother.'

If the possessed noun occurs in a postpositional phrase, the possessor clitic will normally occur after the postposition, as in (13) where the second instance of the pronominal clitic *=m* (indicating first person singular) modifies the noun *påy* 'feet' to produce the meaning 'my feet', while being separated from the noun by the postposition *ne* 'in/on'. The meaning of the entire phrase *påy ne=m* is 'on my feet'.

(13)

alhamdolelå	*ka*	*ditse=m*	*påy*
Praise.God	that	shoes=PC.1SG	feet
ne=m	*nak*	*da*	*buk*
on=PC.1SG	not	emph	were

'Praise God that my shoes were not on my feet!'

Efimov (2011: 151) cites two examples where a possessor clitic precedes its possessed noun; see (14) and (15).

(14)

kere	*kår*	*ne=m*	*zle*	*poxok*	*šuk*
this.OBJ	work	in=PC.1SG	heart	baked	Became

'In this matter my heart is baked.' (i.e. 'I am fed up with this.')

(15)

xronoki	*di=m*	*zle*	*altsok*
hunger	from=PC.1SG	heart	left

'My heart is gone due to hunger.' (i.e. 'I am dying of hunger.')

Such cases are exceptional, though. The normal pattern is for a possessor clitic to follow the noun that it modifies. Moreover, the examples in (14) and (15) could also be interpreted as involving indirect object usage: 'In this matter the heart is baked for me.' and 'Due to hunger the heart is gone for me.'

Pronominal clitics indicating core arguments (subjects and direct objects) normally occur in the second position in the clause, i.e. after the first phrasal constituent, as is the case in examples above (1–3,

7–10). Our text corpus contains a total of 573 occurrences of subject and object clitics. Of these, 493 (86 per cent) occur in the second position of the clause. Of the remaining 80 subject and object clitics, 64 occur in the third position (after the second phrasal constituent), and 16 occur even further to the right.

A majority of the cases in which a core argument clitic does not occur in the second position in the clause involve clitic doubling. In Ormuri, a pronominal clitic may 'double' an overt noun phrase occurring earlier within the same clause. In such cases, the noun phrase and the clitic are coreferential (i.e. they refer to the same participant in the event or situation that is being talked about) and function in the same role in the clause (either subject or object). The noun phrase itself may be lexical, or it may be a personal or demonstrative pronoun. An example of clitic doubling involving a subject argument is presented in (16). In the example we have put square brackets around the first and the second constituent of the clause. The third person clitic *=a* is coreferential with *askari* 'the soldiers', as indicated by the subscripted letter *i* on both elements.

(16)	*[askari]*$_i$	*[afo*	*nafar]=a*$_i$	*algostok*
	soldiers	that	person=PC.3	took.away

'The soldiers took that man away.'

Example (17) presents a case where the clitic (=*t*) is doubling a preceding pronoun rather than a lexical noun phrase.

(17)	*[tu]*$_i$	*[sefatnåma]=t*$_i$	*nawešta*	*dåk*
	you	eulogy=PC.2SG	writing	did

'You wrote an eulogy.'

Example (18) illustrates the possibility of the clitic occurring still further away from the left edge of the clause; in this case it appears after the third phrasal constituent of the clause. Here the third person pronominal clitic *=a* is coreferential with *bådår=at* 'your boss'.

(18)	*[ko*	*tu*	*ki]*	*[bådår=at]*$_i$	*[a*	*šay]=a*$_i$	*daršuk*
	obj	you	to	boss=PC.2SG	some	thing=PC.3	gave

'Your boss gave something to you.'

Example (19) illustrates the case where a pronominal clitic (=*a*) doubles an object argument (*kere maska* 'this butter') rather than a subject.

(19)	*[kere*	*maska]$_i$*	*[pa*	*dest]=a$_i$=b*	*ṭol*	*ke*
	this.OBJ	butter	by	hand=PC.3=PROG	collect	they.do

'They collect the butter by hand.'

In Ormuri, the pronominal clitic never attaches directly to the coreferential noun phrase. There has to be at least one intervening constituent, as is the case in (16), (17), and (19).

In our text corpus, a total of 44 out of 573 occurrences of core argument clitics involve clitic doubling constructions.[9]

In some closely related languages, similar cases of clitic doubling have been analysed in terms of left-dislocation, where one of the arguments of the clause is moved to the front of the sentence while a copy of it (in the form of a pronominal clitic) is left in its original position. An example from Persian, adapted from Mahootian (2005: 124) is shown in (20). Here, the third person pronominal clitic *(h)eš* is coreferential with the sentence-initial phrase *doxtar-i* 'the girl'.

(20)	*[doxtar-i]$_i$*	*ke*	*hæmkelasi-m-e*	*be=heš$_i$*
	girl-DEM	that	classmate-PC.1SG-is	to.PC.3SG
	telefon	*zæd-æm*		
	telephone	hit-1SG		

'The girl who is my classmate, I called her.'

Another example, this time from Parachi (adapted from Kieffer 2009: 308), is seen in (21).

(21)	*žū$_i$ -eka*	*nām=ē$_i$*	*air*	*bīn*
	one-GEN	name=PC.3SG	Air	was

[9] Clitic doubling (also described as redundant usage of a pronominal clitic) occurs in various related languages, too, such as Persian (see, for instance, Mahootian 2005: 124), Balochi (Dabir-Moghaddam 2008: 85–91), and Kurdish (Dabir-Moghaddam 2008: 96), and was already employed in Middle Iranian (Nyberg 1974: 282).

'Of someone, his name was Air.'

Example (20) is quoted in Mahootian's work in a section where she discusses 'means of indicating topic of a sentence'. Indeed, left-dislocation is a common strategy in the languages of the world to indicate topic (Givón 2001: 229).

Kieffer calls the example in (21) a 'focused construction' without further clarification. As a minimum, the use of the term 'focus' suggests that in his view the way the pronominal clitic is used in this sentence is connected with the pragmatic status of one or more of its constituents.

Under an analysis of Ormuri clitic doubling in terms of left-dislocation and topic marking, an apt translation of example (19) above would be: 'As for the butter, they collect it by hand.' Such an analysis may be worthy of further exploration. Due to limitations of space and time we will not pursue that here, except to note that there are some *prima facie* challenges to a left-dislocation and topic marking analysis. Example (18) above constitutes one challenge, because under a left-dislocation analysis one would have to say that in (18) not one but two constituents have been moved to the front of the sentence, viz. *ko tu ki* 'to you' as well as *bådår=at* 'your boss'. A further challenge is that there are many examples in our text corpus where a pronominal clitic refers to a noun phrase that does not represent known or accessible information and does not involve reactivation of a participant that was on the scene before. In other words, there are many examples of sentences with clitic doubling that do not look like typical cases of topicalization. The example in (22), for instance, is the opening sentence of a story and both the subject and the object represent brand-new information. The clitic *=a* is coreferential with the initial noun phrase.

(22)	*[še*	*saṛay=ye*	*badsurat]*$_i$	*[še*	*zarka=ye*
	one	man=EZAFE	ugly	one	woman=EZAFE

	šersurat]=a$_i$	*dornok*
	pretty=PC.3	had

'A certain ugly man had a pretty wife.'

Our conclusions so far with regard to the position in the clause of pronominal clitics can be summarized as follows: (i) Ormuri pronominal clitics are by and large restricted to the second position in the clause, i.e. the position immediately after the first phrasal constituent; (ii) Exception 1: in a possessive function, pronominal clitics occur with the noun they modify; and (iii) Exception 2: in a subject or object role, when they double a noun phrase occurring earlier in the clause, pronominal clitics occur in the third position or later, leaving at least one other phrase in between the clitic and the doubled noun phrase.[10]

3.3 Tense and Transitivity Constraints on Pronominal Clitics

Ormuri pronominal clitics that function as subjects occur in different kinds of clauses from clitics that function as objects: subject clitics primarily occur in past tense transitive clauses, while object clitics only occur in present tense transitive clauses.

There are 435 occurrences of subject clitics in our text corpus. Their distribution relative to the tense and transitivity of the clause in which they occur is displayed in Table 3.

Table 3: Subject clitic distribution

Transitivity	Tense	Count	Percent of total
transitive	past	425	98
	present	3	1
intransitive	past	7	1
	present	0	0

Table 3 clearly shows that subject clitics occur primarily in the past tense with transitive verbs. An exception is listed in (23) where the 1SG pronominal clitic appears as the subject of an intransitive verb.

[10] The position in the clause of Ormuri agent clitics seems to agree fairly well with the Agent Clitic Placement Rule proposed by Dabir-Moghaddam (2008: 88, 98–9): '[…] agent clitics in the past TAM-forms appear on the first (phrasal) constituent of the verb phrase / VP domain actually found in the clause.'

This happens in only 7 out of 435 cases and is clearly not the standard use of a subject clitic.

(23)	*ta*	*taqi*	*ta*	*qala*	*ne=m̲*	*tawallod*	*šuk*
	of	Taqi	of	fort	in=PC.1SG	born	Became

‘I was born in the fort of Taki.’

Equally unusual are cases where a subject clitic occurs together with subject-agreement marking on the verb. Examples are seen in (24) and (25), which have been taken from the text of Efimov’s monograph.

(24)	*ku*	*marzå=m̲=a̲*	*dek-in*
	obj	brother=PC.1SG=PC.3	saw-3PL

‘They saw my brother.’

(25)	*ku*	*marzå=t̲=a̲*	*dek-in*
	OBJ	brother=PC.2SG=PC.3	saw-3PL

‘They saw your brother.’

This kind of co-occurrence of a pronominal clitic and a coreferential verb ending is highly marked in Ormuri as well as in related languages. Efimov explains this co-occurrence of clitics and verbal agreement as a way chosen by some Ormuri speakers to give the clitic a plural-only meaning. He writes that ‘[…] this occurs when the logical subject is the enclitic third person pronoun *=(w)a*, which is the same in the singular and the plural, and, to express a plural, the speaker uses a transitive verb in the past tense with the ending *-in*, which is uncharacteristic, but is used optionally (as an alternative to the zero ending) with intransitive verbs in the past tense’ (Efimov 2011: 199).

The text corpus contains 138 occurrences of object clitics. Without exception, all of these occur in present tense transitive clauses. An example (in addition to the ones given earlier in this chapter) of a pronominal clitic functioning as an object is given in (26).

(26)	*čangål=a̲=b*	*ke*
	smooth=PC.3=PROG	they.make

‘They stir it (lit. they make it smooth).’

Ignoring the handful of anomalous cases discussed above, the generalization can be made that core argument clitics in Ormuri occur either in the present tense in an object role, or in the past tense in a subject role. In Table 4 we compare this distribution with the distribution of verbal agreement markers. In the table, 'A' stands for 'Agent' (of a transitive verb), 'S' for 'Subject' (of an intransitive verb), and 'O' for 'Object'. Furthermore, we use 'Agr' for 'Agreement' and 'PC' for 'Pronominal Clitic'.

Table 4: Complementary distribution of clitics and agreement

	A	S	O
Present	Agr	Agr	PC
Past	PC	Agr	(Agr)

It is clear from the table that pronominal clitics (when occurring in a core argument role) and verbal agreement markers are in complementary distribution; they do not occur together in the same role within the same clause.

Another way to say this is that Ormuri pronominal clitics do not occur in syntactic functions where they would control agreement on the verb. In Ormuri transitive clauses, agreement on the verb is controlled by the subject in clauses with a present tense verb. Agreement on the verb is controlled by the object in clauses with a past tense verb. (This is overt in the Kaniguram dialect only; in the Logar dialect, the personal endings on past tense verbs have been dropped.) In intransitive clauses, agreement on the verb is controlled by the subject. The argument that controls agreement on the verb cannot be encoded as a pronominal clitic, nor can it be referred to by a pronominal clitic (in clitic doubling constructions).

Even though the systems of case marking and agreement have undergone major erosion in Logar Ormuri, Table 4 above still shows different types of argument alignment between the present tense and the past tense. In the present tense we see accusative alignment: A and S have similar marking in the sense that they can be referred to by personal endings on the verb, as against O, which can be referred to by a pronominal clitic but not by verbal agreement. On the other hand, we see features of an ergative configuration in the past tense: S and O have similar marking in that they cannot be referred to by a pronominal clitic, as against A which can be referred to by a clitic.

4. PATTERNS OF PARTICIPANT REFERENCE

The question that we would like to explore in this final section of the chapter concerns the use of pronominal clitics vis-à-vis other types of referring expressions that are available in the language: full noun phrases, independent pronouns, personal endings on the verb (agreement), and zero anaphora. The question is, given the availability of multiple ways to encode a reference to an entity in the discourse world, when is a pronominal clitic used for that purpose, and when are other kinds of referring expressions used?

We have seen above that the distribution of subject and object clitics in Ormuri is constrained by tense and transitivity: we do not find pronominal clitics functioning as the subject of a present tense verb and neither do we find pronominal clitics functioning as the object of a past tense verb. Moreover, pronominal clitics are never coreferential with an agreement marker on the verb: pronominal clitics and agreement markers are in complementary distribution in that respect. That leaves us with three types of referring expressions that can occur in the same kind of contexts where pronominal clitics can occur: full noun phrases, independent pronouns, and zero encoding. In addition there is the possibility of clitic doubling, where one and the same argument may be referred to by a noun phrase as well as a pronominal clitic within the same clause.

The analysis method that we used is based on Dooley and Levinsohn's methodology for analysing participant reference patterns, also known as the Default/Marked method (2001: 127–34). A number of contexts are distinguished in this methodology, and the assumption is that for each of these contexts there is a default encoding pattern that holds when there is no great discontinuity or surprise, etc. Special, marked, cases come into play when there are discontinuities, surprises, or other complexities. The different contexts relevant for subjects that are distinguished by this method are listed in (27).

(27) S1 The subject is the same as in the previous clause or sentence.

S2 The subject was the addressee of a speech reported in the previous sentence.

S3 The subject was involved in the previous sentence in a non-subject role other than in a closed conversation.

S4 Other changes of subject than those covered by S2 and S3.

Likewise, the authors suggest a set of relevant contexts for non-subjects, presented in (28).

(28) N1 The referent occupies the same non-subject role as in the previous clause or sentence.

N2 The addressee of a reported speech was the subject (speaker) of a speech reported in the previous sentence.

N3 The referent was involved in the previous sentence in a different role from that covered by N2.

N4 Other non-subject references than those covered by N1–N3.

In addition they use the label *INTRO* for participants (whether subject or non-subject) that are being introduced or activated for the first time.

For the purpose of this analysis, we went through all the texts in our corpus and identified the context in which each reference to a participant occurs.[11] The results for subject contexts (in past tense transitive clauses only) are presented in Table 5. In each column the type of referring expression with the highest count is shaded.

Table 5: Distribution of subject encodings in past tense transitive clauses

Context: Encoding:	INTRO	S1	S2	S3	S4	Total
Zero	1	83	10	2	6	102
Pronominal clitic	3	280	11	14	20	328
Pronoun	2	11	27	7	9	56
Noun phrase	27	28	88	26	35	204
Clitic doubling	8	5	8	5	7	33
Total	41	407	144	54	77	723

[11] In this analysis, content from closed conversations has not been included as per Dooley and Levinsohn's (2001: 128) recommendation, as this content is embedded in the overall structure of the narrative and is not relevant to referential tracking.

As is seen in the table, the default encoding for a subject argument in a context, where the referent is being introduced or activated for the first time, is a noun phrase.

The default encoding for a subject argument in the S1 context (the subject is the same as in the previous clause or sentence) is a pronominal clitic.[12] In (29) we present a piece of dialogue that illustrates the use of a clitic in this context.

(29)

dawlatmand	*kere*	*kår*	*di*	*zot*
rich.man	this.OBJ	matter	from	very

qår	*šuk*	*aw*	*pox̌tǝna=wa*	*dåk*
angry	became	and	question=PC.3	did

'The rich man became very angry at this and asked:'

While in the S1 context the clitic encoding is by far the most popular, a zero encoding is a possibility as well and occurs in about 20 per cent of the cases. An example is provided in (30).

(30)

zot	*xox*	*šuk*	*o*	*ɣok*	*ka*	...
very	happy	became	and	said	that	...

'He became very happy and said ...'

In the remaining contexts, the noun phrase encoding is clearly the most frequently chosen option. It is interesting to see that independent pronouns are used rather sparingly as an encoding for subject arguments. Clitic doubling is an option in each of these contexts, but never a popular one.

The results for object contexts (in present tense transitive clauses) are presented in Table 6. Once again, the referring expression with the highest count is shaded in each column.

[12] This result meshes well with Barjasteh Delforooz and Levinsohn's (2014: 207–8) characterization of the pronominal clitic in Balochi of Sistan as a cohesive and associative device that indicates referent continuity (ongoing involvement of the referent in the expected role).

Table 6: Distribution of object encodings in present tense transitive clauses

Context: Encoding:	INTRO	N1	N2	N3	N4	Total
Zero	0	36	5	6	2	49
Pronominal clitic	3	81	0	12	4	100
Pronoun	2	44	0	24	12	82
Noun phrase	101	35	0	17	42	195
Clitic doubling	2	0	0	2	1	5
Total	108	196	5	61	61	431

As was the case for the subject encodings, noun phrases and pronominal clitics are used more frequently than independent pronouns and zero anaphora in these contexts. Clitics here, too, are the most popular choice in cases where an argument continues in the same role that it had in the previous clause. Noun phrases are used for the introduction of a new participant in an object role. As a choice for the encoding of objects, independent pronouns are slightly more popular than they are as a choice for encoding subjects. Clitic doubling encodings for object arguments are rare.

In all, what we see is that pronominal clitics are used prolifically for the encoding of ergative subject and object arguments. They are the default choice in same-subject contexts (the subject is the same as in the previous clause) as well as in same-object contexts. As compared to the clitics, free pronouns are used rather sparingly. Noun phrases are the encoding of choice when a new referent is to be introduced, but they occur frequently in other contexts as well.

5. CONCLUSION

In this chapter, we presented a description of the system of pronominal clitics in the Logar dialect of Ormuri, an Iranian language of Afghanistan and Pakistan. Among other things, the chapter identified grammatical constraints on the occurrence of pronominal clitics in Ormuri clauses: in present tense clauses, an object argument, but not a subject argument, can be encoded as a pronominal clitic. In past tense clauses on the other hand, the subject argument of a transitive verb, but not an object argument, can be encoded as a pronominal clitic. This asymmetrical distribution of pronominal clitics in past tense and present tense clauses is undoubtedly a remnant of a more elaborate tense-based split-ergative system that must have existed in the past, and which still exists in the Kaniguram dialect in Pakistan.

The chapter also explored discourse factors that influence when a pronominal clitic is used to refer to an entity in the situation that is being talked about, rather than a noun, an independent pronoun, or zero anaphora. Among other things, it was found that clitics are strongly preferred in contexts where they encode a reference to a participant that continues in the same grammatical role that it had in the previous clause or sentence.

The system of pronominal clitics in Logar Ormuri is similar to, albeit not identical to, the systems found in related languages, including Balochi, Parachi, Persian, and Pashto.

ABBREVIATIONS

1 = first person
2 = second person
3 = third person
A = Agent
Agr = Agreement
COMP = complementizer
DEM = demonstrative
EMPH = emphasis marker
GEN = Genitive
O = Object
OBJ = object marker
PC = pronominal clitic
PROG = Progressive
S = Subject
SG = Singular

REFERENCES

Dabir-Moghaddam, Mohammad. 2008. 'On agent clitics in Balochi in comparison with other Iranian languages'. In *The Baloch and Others: Linguistic, Historical and Socio-Political Perspectives on Pluralism in Balochistan,* edited by Carina Jahani, Agnes Korn, and Paul Titus. 83–100. Wiesbaden: Reichert Verlag.

Delforooz, Behrooz Barjasteh and Levinsohn, Stephen H. 2014. 'The Third Person Singular Pronominal Clitic in Balochi of Sistan: A Progress Report'. *Studia Iranica* 43: 203–20.

Dooley, Robert A. and Levinsohn, Stephen H. 2001. *Analyzing Discourse: A Manual of Basic Concepts*. Dallas, TX: SIL International, Global Publishing. <http://www.sil.org/resources/archives/3547> accessed 6 October 2016.

Efimov, V. A. 2011. *The Ormuri Language in Past and Present.* Islamabad, Pakistan: Forum for Language Iniatives. (FLI Language and Culture Series No. 6). [Originally published in 1986 as Jazyk ormuri v sinxronnom i istoričeskom osveščenii. Moskva: Izdatel'stvo 'Nauka', Glavnaja redakcija vostočnoj literatury. English translation edited by Joan L. G. Baart].

Givón, Talmy. 2001. *Syntax: An Introduction, Vol. 2*. Philadelphia: John Benjamins Publishing Company.

Hawbaker, Jeremy. 2014. *The Pronominal Clitics of Logar Ormuri*. MA thesis. Grand Forks, North Dakota: University of North Dakota. <http://arts-sciences.und.edu/summer-institute-of-linguistics/theses/_files/docs/2014-hawbaker-jeremy.pdf> accessed 6 October 2016.

Kieffer, Charles M. 2009. 'Parachi'. In *The Iranian Languages,* edited by Gernot Windfuhr. 693–720. New York: Routledge.

———. 2003. *Grammaire de l'ōrmuṛī de Baraki-Barak (Lōgar, Afghanistan).* Wiesbaden: Ludwig Reichert. (Beiträge zur Iranistik No. 22).

———. 1989. 'Le parâči, l'ôrmuṛi et le groupe des langues iraniennes du Sud-Est'. In *Compendium Linguarum Iranicarum,* edited by Rüdiger Schmitt. 445–55. Wiesbaden: Ludwig Reichert.

———. 1977. 'The approaching end of the relict South-Eastern Iranian languages Ormuri and Parači'. *International Journal of the Sociology of Language* 12: 71–100.

———. 1972. 'Le multilinguisme des Ormuṛs de Baraki-Barak (Afghanistan)'. *Studia Iranica* 1: 115–26.

Korn, Agnes. 2009. 'Western Iranian pronominal clitics'. *Orientalia Suecana* 58: 159–71.

Lecoq, P. 1989. 'Le classement des langues irano-aryennes occidentales'. In *Études irano-aryennes offertes à Gilbert Lazard,* edited by C. H. Fouchécour and P. Gignoux. 247–64. Paris: Association pour lавancement des études iraniennes. (Cahiers de Studia Iranica No. 7).

Mahootian, Shahrzad. 2005. *Persian*. London: Taylor & Francis.

Morgenstierne, Georg. 1929. 'Ormuri'. In *Parachi and Ormuri*. Vol. 1 of Indo-Iranian frontier languages. 307–413. Oslo: The Institute for Comparative Research in Human Culture.

———. 1926. *Report on a Linguistic Mission to Afghanistan*. Oslo: H. Aschehoug & Company.

Nyberg, H. S. 1974. *A Manual of Pahlavi, Vol. 2*. Wiesbaden: Harrassowitz.

Spencer, Andrew and Luís, Ana R. 2012. *Clitics: An Introduction*. Cambridge: Cambridge University Press.

Windfuhr, Gernot. 2009. 'Dialectology and topics'. In *The Iranian Languages*, edited by Gernot Windfuhr. 5–42. New York: Routledge.

4

A Life Story in the Shina of Gurez

Elena Bashir and Peter E. Hook

1. INTRODUCTION

We thank the editors of this volume for the opportunity to participate in this tribute to Carla Radloff, who was one of the foremost scholars of Shina in the late twentieth and early twenty-first centuries. Elena Bashir knew her as a valued colleague and friend. This oral text is offered as a modest contribution to Shina dialect studies. The text was recorded by the authors in August 1987 in Muzaffarabad, Pakistan-administered Kashmir; Urdu was the medium of communication during our recording sessions[1]. It represents the Shina of Mr Abdul Ghaffar, who was born in village Taobat (Taubat, Towbat) about 40 years prior to the time of recording. This village is located in the Gurez Valley in today's (i.e. 2015) Neelum District, about 200 kilometres northeast of Muzaffarabad, and had, according to Mr Ghaffar, about 400 inhabitants (in 1987). Mr Ghaffar left village Taobat at the age of about five years and in 1987 was living in village Ranjāṭa in Muzaffarabad District. According to him, the Gurez Valley used to be part of the main pack trail route between the Kashmir Valley and Gilgit, and this trade route remained open until 1965. In the northeastern part of Neelum District, Shina and Kashmiri are the

[1] The field work on which this article is based was conducted in the summer of 1987 as part of the linguistics component of the Multi-disciplinary Study of Pakistani Folk Culture under the joint auspices of the University of Pennsylvania and the Lok Virsa Institute in Islamabad. The project, coordinated by Wilma Heston and William Hanaway (University of Pennsylvania) and by Uxi Mufti and Adam Nayyar (Lok Virsa), was supported with a grant from the Smithsonian Institution, Washington DC, which we gratefully acknowledge.

major languages, and this text shows strong evidence of Kashmiri influence on Mr Ghaffar's speech. It is also possible that this influence was enhanced because Mr Ghaffar spent most of his childhood and all of his youth living with a Kashmiri speaker in Karachi and Rawalpindi, where he learned and used Urdu, and most probably also Pashto and Panjabi. He also spent a year in Lahore, where he would have heard Panjabi daily. Mr Ghaffar's language thus typifies the speech of a multilingual, urban working man in contemporary Pakistan: a first language overlaid with influences from several contact languages.[2]

The transcription used here is a broad phonetic representation of the sounds occurring in this text. The language of this text shows (some) pitch accent phenomena.[3] Where we have heard a distinctive pitch on the tape, we have represented it using the scheme originally proposed by Berger for Burushaski (1960) and since adopted by Buddruss (1996), Radloff (1999), and Schmidt (2000 and elsewhere) for Shina. In this analysis, long vowels are represented as bimoraic. Length is represented by doubling the vowel symbol; for example, *aa* represents a phonetically long *a*. For high-falling pitch, stress is indicated on the first mora, while with low-rising pitch, stress is marked on the second mora. Thus *aá* has low-rising pitch, while *áa* has high-falling pitch. Long vowels for which we have not heard pitch or where it is uncertain are left unmarked. Nasalization is represented by a tilde <~> above the vowel, and when a tense appears to contrast with a lax vowel, the tense variety is represented by a lower-case letter and the lax variety by a small upper-case letter: thus <i> represents a tense high front vowel and <ɪ> a lax high front vowel. Palatalization is indicated by a superscripted <y> following the palatalized consonant. This inventory and representation of vowel sounds makes no claim about the phonemic status of length in this variety of Shina.

[2] Ahmed (2014) is a sociolinguistic study of language-use patterns of speakers of Gurezi Shina in India.

[3] Radloff (1999: Chapters 4 and 5) discusses pitch accent in Gilgit Shina. Schmidt and Kohistani (1998, 2008) discuss it in Kohistani Shina, and Schmidt and Kaul (2010: 196) treat it in the dialects of Astor and Gures. Baart (2003) classifies the 18 tonal languages he identifies in northern Pakistan into three types: a Shina type, a Panjabi type, and a Kalami type.

The consonant and vowel sounds represented are charted below.

Vowels

	Front	Central	Back
High			
tense	i	ɨ	u
lax	I		U
Mid			
tense	e	ə	o
lax	E		O
Low	æ		a

Consonants

	Labial	Dental	Palatal	Retroflex	Velar	Post-velar	Glottal
Stops							
voiceless unaspirated	p	t		ṭ	k	q[4]	
aspirated	p^h	t^h		$ṭ^h$	k^h		
voiced	b	d		ḍ	g		
Affricates							
voiceless unaspirated			č	c̣			
aspirated			$č^h$	$c̣^h$			
voiced			j	j̣			
Fricatives							
voiceless		s	š	ṣ	x		
voiced		z	ž	ẓ	γ		h

Consonants

	Labial	Dental	Palatal	Retroflex	Velar	Post-velar	Glottal
Nasals	m	n					
Laterals		l					
Flaps		r		ṛ			
Semivowels	w		y				

2. The text: Life story of Abdul Ghaffar

(1) *myũũ* *nʊm* *h-ũũ* *ábdal* *ɣafáar.*
my[SgM] name be-Prs3SgM[5] Abdul Ghaffar
My name is Abdul Ghaffar.

(2) *mo* *b-ʊ́l-os* *ṭáubaṭ* *pædáa.*
I[Nom] become-PstSgM-1SgM Towbat born
I was born in Towbat.

(3) *mo* *ás-l-os*[6] *čʊn* *sád-õ*
I[Nom] be-Pst-1SgM small there-Abl

---

[4] The uvular stop [q] appears in this text in only one word, qurɨl 'attached, stuck'. With regard to /q/ in Shina, Schmidt (2010) does not note it for Gurezi Shina, but finds it fairly robustly present in Kohistani Shina (Schmidt and Kohistani 2008: 20).

[5] Abbreviations used in this paper follow the Leipzig Glossing Conventions, except for the following: AG = agentive, CP = conjunctive participle, EMPH = emphatic

kʰat-ós	*mo*	*tom*	*ẓ̌á-[v]a-sĩ́ĩ.*
came.out-1SgM	I[Nom]	REFL	brother-OBL-with

(When) I was small I left there with my brother,

(4)

áa-l-os	*pɪnḍií-j.*
come-Pst-1SgM	Pindi-Loc

(and) came to Rawalpindi.

(5)

pɪnḍií-j-ũ	*garmy-ɨl*[7]	*ma-ṭ*	*ek*	*manuuẓ*
Pindi-Loc-Abl	meet-Pst3SgM	I-Dat	one	man

koe[8]	*kašuur*	*as-Úl.*
who	Kashmiri	be-Pst3SgM

In Pindi I met a man who was a Kashmiri.

---

[6] as-l-os < as-Ul-os

[7] <*garmy-Ul?* In the past tense of intransitives, the masculine third Sg affix is *u*, reflected to the left of the *-l*-marker of past tense used with many intransitives (by the same kind of metathesis seen in Kashmiri phonology?).

[8] In Gurezi (as in some other dialects of Shina) the relative pronoun does not begin with *j-*, as it does in many other Indo-Aryan languages, but rather with *k-*, the characteristic sign of the interrogative. The preferred strategy in most forms of Shina for relativization is the use of a prenominal participle: Hook (1996). Bashir (2003: 882) discusses relative clauses in Shina consisting of a prenominal finite clause, without any resumptive pronominal element in the main clause, as in (a).

(a)

ráloo	*ẓiík_cʰineé*	*ĩç*	*beéyey*	*jéel-e-waar*	*géi*
from.there	boldly*	bear	stay(Fut3Sg)	jungle-Obl-toward	go(Pst3sgF)

'From there she went boldly to the jungle where the bear lived.' (Radloff and Shakil 1998: 132)

* This idiom consists of the noun *ẓiík*, having a meaning associated with 'pulling, stretching, spreading' and the conjunctive participle of the verb *cʰin-* 'to cut down'.

(6)

ses^{y}	*čhar-ów*	*ma*	*akók-ɨj*[9].
he[Ag]	keep-Pst3SgM	I[Nom]	self-Loc

He kept me with himself.[10]

(7)

sɨɨ-ṭ	*na*	*as-ɨl*	*auláad-ak*^{h}
he-Dat	Neg	be-PstSgF	offspring-one

He didn't have any children,

jɪŋ	*tE*	*rej-ów*[11]	*ma-ṭ*	*taáliím-gɨ.*
any	and	read.Caus-Pst3SgM	me-Dat	education-also

and also educated me.

(8)

p^{h}*áto*	*g-yeés*	*be*	*karaačií.*
then	go-PstlPlM	we	Karachi

Then we went to Karachi.

(9)

káafyii	*kunií*	*barẓ-õõ-ṭ*[12]	*dar-l-ós*
quite.a.few	19	year-OblPl-Dat	remain-Pst-1SgM

mə	*karačií.*
I[Nom]	Karachi

I stayed in Karachi quite a long time, about nineteen years.

---

[9] This locative suffix is subject to word-final devoicing, and is often heard as [č] after a short vowel in an unstressed final syllable, as in (6). Compare the [j] heard in (12), following a long vowel in a stressed final syllable.

[10] This text displays proximal and distal third person personal pronouns. See Schmidt (2000) for a discussion of parameters in the pronominal and deictic systems of the Palas (Kohistan) and Tilel (Gurez) Shina dialects.

[11] < *raz-ay-ow*? Bailey (1924: 265) gives *razonu* 'to read (aloud)'. In Eastern Shina *raz-* means 'say'. Similarly, in Khowar, the verb *reék* means both 'say', and 'read', just as *paṛhnā* means both 'recite' and 'read' in Urdu. Thus, *rej-ów I* can be understood as 'caused to study', i.e. 'got me educated'. This semantic development reflects the ancient tradition of orally imparted education in South Asia..

[12] Or, possibly, *barẓ-on.*

(10)	*tᴇ*	*ses^{y}-ɨ́ĩ*	*t^{h}-ey-ów*
	and	he[Ag]-Emph	do-Caus-Pst3SgM
	ma-ṭ	*káš-gɨ.*	
	me-Dat	marriage-also	

And he also arranged a marriage for me.

(11)	*p^{h}atoó …*	*sɨ*	*ás-ᴜl*	*jar*	*manuuẓ,*
	then …	he[Nom]	be-Pst3SgM	old	man
	sɨ	*m-úu.*			
	he[Nom]	die-Pst3SgM			

Then … he was an old man—he died.

(12)	*sád-õ*	*áal-os*	*mə*	*p^{h}áto*	*pɪnḍií-j.*
	there-Abl	came-1SgM	I[Nom]	then	Pindi-Loc

From there I then came back to Pindi.

(13)	*sás-ĩĩ*	*mir-iín-jõ*[13]	*p^{h}ató*	*pol^{y}*
	he.Obl-Gen.F	die-Inf-Abl	then	fall-Pst3SgF
	ma-ṭ	*pɪnḍií-j*	*uúiín^{y}.*[14]	
	I-Dat	Pindi-Loc	come[Inf.F]	

After his death I had to come to Pindi.

---

[13] The structure of this complex postposition [*j*(Loc) + *õ*(Abl) = 'from'] has a parallel in Marathi's *–t-un*:

(b)	*tyā-hun*	*tyā-t-un*	*tyā-var-un*	*tyā-pās-un*
	that-Abl	that-in-Abl	that-on-Abl	that-near-Abl
	'than that'	'from in that'	'from on that'	'from near that'

as well as in Urdu's *un-se* 'from them', *un-mẽ-se* 'from among them', *un-ke-pās-se* 'from near them', etc.

[14] This infinitive is feminine. Is feminine the default gender for infinitives in Gurezi? The infinitives in sentences (13), (21), and (70) are feminine. While it

(14)	*pɪnḍií-j*	*áa-l-os*	*mə*	*wáah*	*fœkṭrií-j.*
	Pindi-Loc	come-Pst-1SgM	I[Nom]	Wah	factory-Loc

In Pindi I came to the Wah Factory.

(15)	*wáah*	*fœkṭrií-j*	*dar-l-ós*	*ekʰ-dúu*	*barẓ-ũũ-ṭ.*
	Wah	factory-Loc	stay-Pst-1SgM	one-two	year-OblPl-Dat

I stayed in the Wah Factory for about one or two years.

(16)	*pʰáto*	*g-áas*	*mə*	*laáhɔ́r.*
	then	went-1SgM	I[Nom]	Lahore

Then I went to Lahore.

(17)	*ekʰ*	*barẓ-É-ṭ*	*dar-l-ós*	*laáhɔ́r.*
	one	year-OblSg-Dat	stay-Pst-1SgM	Lahore

I stayed in Lahore for one year.

(18)	*krÚm-akʰ*	*na*	*ṣat*	*jɪŋ.*
	work-one	Neg	attach.Pst3SgM	any

(But) I didn't get a single job.

---

appears that the infinitive in (21) could be feminine because it agrees with its feminine direct object *gaaṛii*, the feminine infinitive *tʰiinʸ* does not agree with its apparent masculine direct object *krum*. Could this be because in *krum thiinʸ* 'to work' the noun has become more incorporated? The apparently masculine infinitive in sentence (41) is a puzzle. Does it agree with its masculine direct object *yokʰ* 'what'? Feminine does seem to be the default gender for infinitives in some of the other dialects of Shina. Contrast (c) and (d) from Gilgiti Shina:

(c)	*j̣ig-u*	*mušaa*	*zaruuri*	*han*
	tall-SgM	man(M)	needed	is.M

'We need a tall man.'

(d)	*j̣ig-u*	*mušaa*	*layòoiky*	*zaruuri*	*hany*
	tall-SgM	man(M)	obtain. Inf	needed	is.F

'We need to find a tall man.' (Hook and Zia 2005: section 5)

(19) *sád-õ* *áa-l-os* *mə* *báṛa* *waápás*
there-Abl come-Pst-1SgM I[Nom] again back
wáah *fækṭrií-j.*
Wah Factory-Loc
From there I came back again to the Wah Factory.

(20) *kúl^{y}.bɪl* *sat* *barẓ-õõ-ṭ* *bǽṭ^{h}-os* *mə*
altogether seven year-OblPl-Dat sat-1SgM I[Nom]
wah *fækṭrií-j.*
Wah Factory-Loc
Altogether I stayed at the Wah Factory for seven years.

(21) *tE …* *wáah fækṭrií-j* *sõč-áas* *mii*
and … W. F.-Loc think-Pst1SgM I[Ag]
gáṛii *čal-v-iín^{y}.*
vehicle move-Caus-InfSgF
And … (while) in the Wah Factory I thought of driving a vehicle.

(22)	*tE*	*sad*	*t^{h}-Úm-l-os*	*mɨ*	*zi-ĩ*	*krUm*
	and	there	do-Fut-Pst-1SgM[15]	I[Nom][16]	this-Emph	work

And I was doing this very work there.

[15] *th-Um-l-os* (< *thUm* + *asUlos*) functions in the Shina system of tense, mood, and aspect like Urdu's past imperfect *kartā thā*. But unlike the past imperfect in Urdu, this form is composed of what in other contexts is the simple future or subjunctive (*-um*, etc.) plus the past tense of 'be'. Compare Bailey's (1924: 279) description of Kohistani Shina: 'The imperfect may also be formed by combining the future with the past of the verb substantive.' Bailey also reports this formation for Gurezi Shina (Bailey 1924: 254), shown here as (e).

(e)	*mõõ-s*	*aṭ-im*	*as-ul-os*
	I-Ag	bring-Sbjv1Sg	be-PstM-1Sg

'I was bringing; I used to bring.'

Similar word-internal use of a finite form is found in Hindi's *jaa-ũ-g-ā* go-1SgSbjv-Fut-SgM 'I will go'.

A similar construction, called the 'past imperfective' is found in Palula, the archaic variety of Shina spoken in southern Chitral (see Liljegren 2008: 220–1).

Both Shina's *-Um*, etc. and Urdu's *-ũ*, etc. are the modern reflexes of the OIA present active conjugation, which was known to Sanskrit grammarians as *laṭ*, the traditional abbreviation for the set of suffixes used to form the present indicative tenses of the Sanskrit verb. These endings are the morphological ancestors of the subjunctive in Urdu as well as the habitual past in Marathi and some other NIA languages. This formation can be also found in contemporary rural Hindi, as in (f).

(f)	*din*	*bhar*	*aisī*	*patangẽ*	*uṛāyā*	*kar-ū*
	day	full	such	kites	fly.Pfv.Ppl.Sg.M	do-Sbjv.1Sg

t^{h}ā	*ki*	*bhūkh*	*piyās*	*talak*	*sab*
be.Pst.Sg.M	that	hunger	thirst	even	all

vis-ī	*ke_sāth*	*uṛ_jāyā*	*kar-e*	*t^{h}ī*
it-Emph	with	fly.away.Pfv.Ppl.Sg.M	do-Sbjv.3Sg	be.PstSg.F

'All day I would fly such kites that even hunger and thirst would fly away along with them.' (Nagar 2007: 101)

[16] On the tape, this sounds more like the nominative form *mɨ* than the agentive *mii*.

(23)	*jæk-ĩĩ*	*gáaṛii*	*čal-v-úm-l-os.*
	someone(else)-GenSgF	vehicle	move-Caus-1Sg-Pst-1SgM

(At first) I was driving someone else's vehicle.

(24)	*p*^{h}*áto*	*gín*^{y}*-áas*	*mii*	*tem*^{y}[17]	*gáaṛií.*
	then	take-Pst1SgM	I[Ag]	Refl[FSg]	vehicle(F)

Then I bought my own vehicle.

(25)	*ek*	*č*^{h}*ak*^{h}	*b-ʊl*	*ma-ṭ*	*sad*	*æksɪḍÉnṭ.*
	one	day	become-Pst3SgM	I-Dat	there	accident

One day I had an accident there.

(26)	*ek*^{h}	*manúuẓ*	*áa-l*	*mĩĩ*	*gáaṛií*	*khœr*^{y}*.*[18]
	one	man	come-Pst3SgM	my[FSg]	vehicle	under

A man came under my vehicle (i.e. was run over).

(27)	*tE*	…	*sɪpíiḍ*	*ás-il*	*ma-ṭ*	*teéz.*
	and[19]	…	speed	be-Pst3SgF	I-Dat	fast

And I was driving fast (lit. my speed was fast).

(28)	*sɨ*	*áa-l*	*mʊṣn-ũṹ.*
	he[Nom]	come-Pst3gM	in.front.of-Abl

He came (from) in front of me.

---

[17] *toóm* + *i* (SgF) > *tem*^{y}.

[18] According to Abdul Ghaffar, *k*^{h}*aer*^{y} means 'a little bit down, inside', as opposed to *k*^{h}*ar*, which means 'a long way down'. *k*^{h}*ar* + *i*(diminutive) > *k*^{h}*aer*^{y} can be compared with *toóm* + *i* (SgF) > *tem*^{y}. (cf. fn.17 above). The form *k*^{h}*ari* 'below' occurs in Bailey's texts (1924: 238, 251).

[19] The long pause following *tE* indicates that it is used here as a hesitation/filler form.

(29)	*sarkáarii*	*mUláazîm*	*as-Úl,*	*maálíi*
	Government	employee	be-Pst3SgM	gardener

	as-Úl	*mágar*	*ás-Ul*	*jar.*
	be- Pst3SgM	but	be-Pst3SgM	old

He was a government employee, a gardener, but he was old.

(30)	*sɨɨ-ṭ*	*d-áas*	*mii*	*harán.*
	he-Dat	give-Pst1SgM	I[Ag]	horn

I sounded the horn (lit. I gave him the horn.)

(31)	*sɨ*	*k^hat*	*mÚtve-ṭ.*
	he[Nom]	exit.Pst3SgM	other.side-Dat

He went off to the other side.

(32)	*baṛa*	*áa-l*	*p^hir-ií*	*mU*	*mUç^{h}oó-ṭ.*
	again	come-Pst3SgM	turn-CP	I[Nom]	in.front.of-Dat

Again he came in front of me (having turned) back.

(33)	*ṣáayt*	*sɨ-ṭ*	*gáaṛií.*
	attach.PstFSg	he-Dat	vehicle

The vehicle hit him.

(34)	*áa-l*	*sɨ*	*gáaṛií*	*k^hær^y.*
	come-Pst3SgM	he[Nom]	vehicle	under

He came under the vehicle.

(35)	*tE*	…	*mə́-sĩĩ*	*as-ál*	*dúu-çə*	*manúuẓ*	*baṛá.*
	and	…	me-with	were-3Pl	two-three	men	also

There were two or three more men with me (in the vehicle).

(36)	*sa*	*wáat*	*kʰæʳʸ.*
	they[Nom]	arrived.3pl	down

They got down.

(37)	*míi*	*ça …*[20]	*mɨ*	*wáat-os*	*kʰæʳʸ.*
	I[Ag]	sa …	I[Nom]	arrive-Pst1SgM	down

I (also) got down.

(38)	*míi*	*çak-áas*	*kᴇ*	*sɨ*	*nə*
	I[Ag]	see-Pst1SgM	that	he[Nom]	Neg
	ás-ᴜl	*sad*	*jɪŋ.*		
	be-Pst3SgM	there	at.all		

I saw that he wasn't there at all.

(39)	*báar.hal*	*tʰ-áas*	*míi*	*pʰᴜṭʰ.*
	anyhow	do-Pst1SgM	I[Ag]	glance

Anyway, I looked around.

(40)	*sɨ*	*ás-ᴜl*	*gaáṛií*	*kʰæʳʸ.*
	he[Nom]	be-Pst3SgM	vehicle	under

He was underneath the vehicle.

(41)	*koe sí*	*siĩ*	*ás-ᴜl*	*mᴜt*	*manúuẓ*	*sesʸ*
	who he[Nom]	with	was-3SgM	other	man	he[Ag]
	ræj-ów	*zɨɨ-ṭ*	*yokʰ*	*tʰ-óono*	*če.*	
	say-Pst3SgM	he-Dat	what	do-InfMSg	now	

The other man who was with him said, 'What to do with him now?

[20] False start, followed by next sentence in narrative, *mɨ…*

(42)	*phat-tʰ-aa*	*anʸ-eé*	*zɨ*	*múu*	*h-ũũ.*
	release-do-Pst2Sg	here-Emph.	he[Nom]	dead.SgM	be-Prs3SgM

(If) you leave (him) right here he is dead.'

(43)	*míi*	*rœy-áas*	*ná zɨ*	*na*
	I[Ag]	say-Pst1Sg	no he[Nom]	Neg

pʰat-tʰ-ʊm	*mə*	*jɪŋ.*
release-do-Fut1SgM	I[NOM]	at.all

I said, 'No, I certainly won't leave him here.

(44)	*tE*	...	*zɨ*	*hár-ɨm*	*mə*	*haspatáal.*
	and	...	he[Nom]	take-Fut1Sg	I[Nom]	hospital

And I will take him to the hospital'.[21]

(45)	*pʰatoó*	*hunṭ-iy-áas*	*mii*	*sɨ*	*gáaṛií*	*sád-ũ.*
	then	lift-Caus-Pst1SgM	I[Ag]	that	vehicle	there-Abl

Then I got the vehicle lifted from there.

[21] Note the nominative of third person direct object in (43) and (44), which may reflect the influence of Kashmiri's person hierarchy in which a first person subject conditions the nominative of a third person object. Contrast the nominative *tsi* in (g) with the dative *tsye* in (h):

(g)	*tsi*	*chus-ath*	*bi*	*sooz-aan*	[Kashmiri]
	you.Nom	am-2sgNomDirObj	I.Nom	send-ing	

'I am sending you (somewhere).'

(h)	*tsye*	*chu-y*	*su*	*sooz-aan*	[Kashmiri]
	you.Dat	is-2sgDatDirObj	he.Nom	send-ing	

'He is sending you (somewhere).'

See further discussion in Section 3.2.

(46)	*kʰal-áas*	*sɨ*	*kʰǽrʸ-ũ.*
	set.free-Pst1SgM	he[Nom]	under-Abl [22]
	həə~[23] *cʰær-gyée-s,*	*gáaṛií-j,*	
	climb.Caus-Pst-1SgM	vehicle-Loc	

I freed him from under (the vehicle), lifted him into the vehicle,

(47)	*hary-áas*	*mii*	*haspatáal.*
	take-Pst1SgM	I[Ag]	hospital

(and) took him to the hospital.

(48)	*haspatáal*	*hary-ií*[24] …	*sɨɨ-ṭ*	*g-ów-s-Ul*[25]
	hospital	take-CP …	he-Dat	go-Pst3SgM-be-Pst3SgM
	léel	*kʰazy-ií*	*báskɨ.*	
	blood[M]	come.out-CP	much	

Taking him to the hospital … he had lost a lot of blood.

---

[22] <*chœr-gyee-s*. Is the *g* a trace of the Gilgit Shina type past tense transitive form in *g*? The raising of the stem vowel from *char* to *chœr* implies a high vowel in the following affix. (Cf. fn. 15 and fn. 16). See also (49), *razgyée*.

[23] This is a hesitation form. Note the sequence of three verb-initial clauses, which ends with a distinct sentence ending falling contour. See grammatical notes below on verb-initial clauses.

[24] The use of the CP *haryií* in this sentence appears exceptional in that its agent-subject is not the same as that of the matrix clause. However, there is a long pause between this CP phrase and the next sentence. Thus this appears to be another false start, after which the narrative resumes.

[25] According to our informant, Abdul Ghaffar, the form *gówsUl* is a shortening of *gow asUlo*, which corresponds to Urdu *gayā thā*. The form *gowsul kʰazyií* is, then, a compound verb analogous to the Urdu *nikal gayā thā*. In this variety of Gurezi Shina, however, it is now the fused past perfect component *gow-sUl* (and not just the former auxiliary *asUl*) that occupies the clause-second position reserved for finite forms. See Hook and Koul (1992) on compound verbs in Kashmiri.

(49)	*ḍáakṭar-ĩĩ*	*raz-gyée*	*kE*	*zɨɨ-ṭ*	*h-ũũ*
	doctor-Ag.Pl	say-Pst3Pl	that	he-Dat	be-Prs3SgM

	léel	*bakáar.*
	blood	necessary

The doctors said that he needed blood.

(50)	*léel*	*na*	*lyed*	*sad*	*jɪŋ.*
	blood	Neg	be.found-Pst3SgM	there	any

No blood was available there.

(51)	*pʰató*	*d-áas*	*mii*	*sɨɨ-ṭ*	*toóm*	*léel.*
	then	give-Pst1SgM	I[Ag]	he-Dat	ReflSgM	blood

Then I gave him my own blood.

(52)	*sɨ-sǘũ*	*grʊp*	*my-ǘũ*	*grʊp*
	his-GenSgM	group[M]	my-GenSgM	group

	áa-l	*bráabar.*
	come-Pst3SgM	same

His group turned out to be the same as mine.

(53)	*léel*	*d-əə́*	*pʰató*	*g-áas*	*mə*	*matalab*
	blood	give-CP	then	go-Pst1SgM	I[Nom]	meaning[26]

	sad	*tʰáan-val-uun-ṭ*	*tʰ-áas*	*rapóṭ.*
	there	police.station-people-OblPl-Dat	do-Pst1SgM	report

Having given blood, then I went—I mean—I (went) there to the police (and) made a report.

[26] The word *matalab* 'meaning' is from Urdu. In Gurezi (as in Urdu) it can be used as a filler or hesitation form.

(54)

sɨ-g	*áa-l*
he[Nom]-also	come-PstSgM

He also came.

(55)

tE	…	*p^{h}ató*	*g-áas*	*mə*	*t^{h}áana-j.*
and	…	then	go-Pst1SgM	I[Nom]	police.station-Loc

And then I went to the police station.

(56)

t^{h}áana-j	*rapórṭ*	*t^h-əə́*	*áa-l-os*
police.station-Loc	report	do-CP	come-Pst-1SgM

mə	*zamáant-ij*	*gooẓ.*
I[Nom]	bail-Loc	home[OBL]

Having made my report in the police station, I came home on bail.

(57)

pható	*čál-v-ij-uly*[27]	*keés.*
then	move-Caus-Pass-Pst-3SgM	case

Then a case was started.

(58)

keés	*báskɨ*	*káal-aṭ*	*nə*	*čál-v-ij-Ul*[28]
case	much	time-Dat	Neg	move-Caus-Pass-Pst-3SgM

The case didn't move ahead for a long time.

(59)

sɨɨ-ṭ	*d-áas*	*mii*	*p^{h}ató*	*čáar*	*sáas*	*rUpáay.*
he-Dat	give-Pst1SgM	I[Ag]	then	four	thousand	rupees

Then I gave him four thousand rupees.

---

[27] Palatalization is audible on this word in sentence (57), but not in (58).

[28] Bailey (1924: 49) notes that the passive affix *-iž* is never added to a verb causativized with *-ar*. Perhaps this passivized form indicates that the derived stem *calv-*, though a transitive derived from *cal-* 'move', is regarded by speakers as a basic transitive.

(60)

čáar sáas	*rʊpáay*	*d-ow*	*sɨ*
four thousand	rupees	give-Pst3SgM	that

manúuẓ-ĩĩ	*kʸœs-ĩĩ*	*mɨ*	*gáaṛíi*
man-Ag	who-GenSgF	I[Nom]	vehicle

čəl-v-Úm-l-os	*tE*	…	*sɨɨ-ṭ*[29]	*ta*	*kháríč.*
move-Caus-Fut-Pst-1SgM	and	…	he-Dat	Top	expenses

The man whose vehicle I was driving gave him the four thousand rupees, and … (he said), '(Here are) expenses for him'.

(61)

pʰatoó	…	*takríiban*	*ayEÉl-aṭ*	*dar-l-ós*
then	…	about	one.year-Dat	stay-Pst-1SgM

ma	*sad.*
I[Nom]	there

Then … I stayed there for about one year.

(62)

sád-õ[31]	…	*sád-ɨg*	*na*	*quryɨ-l*[32]
there-Abl	…	there-also	Neg	attach-Pst.3SgM

ma-ṭ	*hyúu*	*jɪŋ.*
I-Dat	heart	at.all

(But) I didn't like it there at all.

(63)

pʰató	*áa-l-os*	*mʊ*	*mʊzáffarabáad.*
then	come-Pst-1SgM	I[Nom]	Muzaffarabad

Then I came to Muzaffarabad.

---

29 Bailey (1924: 211) gives the dative postposition as *-ṭa* or *-ṭe*. Schmidt (2010: 200) has *-(V)ṭ* for the dative singular and *-őṭ* for the dative plural, and the present text has *-ṭ* postvocalically and *-Vṭ* after consonant-final words.

30 False start; continued correctly after pause.

31 This word is a puzzle. However, compare Khowar *qiír* 'a type of sticky black substance; a hunting falcon'.

(64)	*mᴜzáffarabáad*	*hú-n-os*	*mɨ*	*čey*	*an^{y}-éy.*
	Muzaffarabad	be-Prs-1SgM	I[Nom]	now	here-Emph

Now I am right here in Muzaffarabad.

(65)	*ayáal-gɨ*	*h-ũũ*	*ma-ṭ*	*sáat^{y}.*
	family-also	be-Prs3SgM	I-Dat	with

My family[33] also is here with me.

(66)	*kaš*	*t^{h}-áa-n-os*[34]	*mii*	*čikaár-õ.*
	marriage	do-Pst-Prs-1SgM	I[Ag]	Cikar-Abl

I have married (someone) from Chikar.[35]

(67)	*tᴇ*	*če*	*t^{h}-ᴜm-n-os*[36]	*an^{y}*	*vákat*	*páas.*
	and	now	do-Sbjv-Prs-1SgM	here	time	pass

And now I am spending my time here.

(68)	*kot*	*čál-v-ᴜm-n-os*	*mə*
	now	move-Caus-Sbjv-Prs-1SgM	I[Nom]
	án^{y}-gi	*gáaṛií.*	
	here-also	vehicle	

Now I drive a vehicle here also.

---

32 *ayáal* 'family', i.e. 'wife and dependants'. Cf. Khowar *aẓγáal* 'wife (honorific)' < Turkic, also Turkish *ayal* 'family'.

33 The form *t^{h}-aa-n-os* <*t^{h}-aas hu-n-os* yielding a present perfect sense.

34 Chikar is a town about 20 miles southeast of Muzaffarabad, in Pakistan-administered Kashmir.

35 Like the composite form discussed in fn. 15, it includes the reflex of the OIA *laṭ* as a word-internal finite element. Compare also the older Urdu *karū̃ hū̃* 'I would/used to do', as in the following ghazal (1216) from Mir Taqi Mir:

misrah koī koī kabhū mauzū̃ karū̃ hū̃ mãĩ

'Occasionally I would compose (such) a verse (that) …'

<http://www.columbia.edu/itc/mealac/pritchett/00garden/xradindex_n/n_men.html>

(69) *tE* … *ẓə-ĩĩ́*[37] *krUm* *h-ũũ* *mágar* *ma*
and … this-Emph work be-Prs3SgM but I[Nom]

hú-n-os … *talíimyáafta-g* *hú-n-os.*[38]
be-Prs-1SgM … educated-also be-Prs-1SgM
And … this is the work (I have), but I am also educated.

(70) *tE* … *báarhal* *krUm* *jéek* *na* *jéek* *pey*[39]
and … anyway work some not some fall.Sbjv

h-ũũ *t^h-iín^y.*
be.Prs3SgM do-Inf
Anyhow, one has to do some work or the other.

(71) *sɨs-ĩĩ* *káary-ũ* *tal^{y}íim* *h-ĩĩ* *tem^y*
this[Obl]-Emph reason-Abl education be-Prs3SgF own.F

diš-íj *tE* *krUm* *h-ũũ* *tem^y* *diš-íj.*
place-Loc and work be-Prs3SgM own.F place-Loc
For this reason, education is in its own place, and work is in its own place.

(72) *wU* *saláam* *xUdáa hafíz*
and salaam Khuda hafiz
And now salaam. May God protect you.

---

36 This is the only occurrence of *ẓi* 'this' in this text. Elsewhere in the text there are multiple occurrences of forms with initial /z/ in proximal deictic meanings; this occurrence of *ẓi* could be a mishearing. However Schmidt and Kaul (2010: 7) give robust forms in /ẓ/ for the visible or known third person personal pronouns 'he/she/it/they' in the Tileli variant of Guresi Shina..

37 It appears that here the speaker paused, then started his sentence again omitting the subject *ma* 'I'..

38 *pey* is a future form of *pōnu̧* 'to fall' (Bailey 1924: 258), indicating obligation. For example, *aso-ṭ pey sad bujiin* 'We will have to go there.'

3. GRAMMATICAL NOTES

3.1 WORD ORDER

The variety of Gurezi Shina in this text, while quite different from Kashmiri in morphology, corresponds quite closely to it in word order. In the text, out of some 88 clauses of all types which include a verb, all but four obey the Kashmiri constraints (Hook 1976): 72 independent (matrix) clauses have V2 order; the sole interrogative clause (third clause in (41)) has V3 order; and of the three relative clauses (second clause in (5), first clause in (41), and second clause in (60)) two ((5) and (60)) are verb-final. The third instance of a relative clause (41) is V3 if the relative pronoun is counted, V2 if it is not. Nine main clauses are verb-initial ((4), (7), (29), (33–34), (42), (46 [2]–47)). Compare *Hatim's Tales* (Grierson 1923), where many main clauses which express tightly sequenced action in a narrative are verb-initial.[39] A final residue of four clauses do not straightforwardly observe the Kashmiri rules.[40] The first of these is (52), which appears to be V3, but if the two initial phrases could be considered to be a compound subject, then V2. The second exception is (58), which is verb-final. The first clause in (71) is V2 if it is recognized that when an adverb has scope over conjoined main clauses it does not hold a position in either of them: *s-isīĩ karyũ talyiim hīĩ temy dišij te krum hũũ temy dišij* 'For this reason, education has its place and work has its place.' The final exception is the second clause of (42), which is verb-final. Following closely on the first, verb-initial clause of (42), this verb-final clause is an instance of chiasmus, which enhances the force of the initial verb-initial conditional clause. Another instance of chiasmus is found in (29), where a verb-final clause is followed immediately by a verb-initial clause.

In this text, *p^hato(o)* '(and) then' appears in three different functions. (i)) Most frequently it is an adverb, occurring sentence initially to introduce a clause and sequence the action it describes in the narrative, as in (8), (16), (24), (45), (51), (55), (57), and (63). In all of these sentences *p^hato* counts as a sentence constituent and the word order

[39] The negative particle is counted as part of the verb. Introductory *tE* 'and', the conjunction *m+agar* 'but', and the complementizer *kE* do not count toward establishing word order patterns.

[40] The sentences separately provided by Mr Ghaffar upon elicitation consistently show V2 word order.

is straightforwardly V2. It occurs as a sentence-medial adverb in (12) and (59); (ii) In sentences (11) and (61), in both of which initial *pʰatoó* both has a long final vowel and is followed by a considerable pause, *pʰatoó* functions as a hesitation form or filler; and (iii) In one instance (13), it unambiguously functions as a postposition: *sás-ĩ mir-iín-j-õ pʰató* 'after his death', where the postposition follows the ablative-marked noun phrase.[41] In (53), *léel dəə́ pʰató gáas mə* 'After giving blood I went ...', however, the situation is less clear. If it is possible for a conjunctive participial clause to be followed by a postposition, then this is a second instance of *pʰató* used as a postposition, and the word order is straightforwardly V2. If, on the other hand, the conjunctive participle *léel dəə́* is counted as the first constituent, it may count as a sentence adverbial having scope over the entire sentence, and the sentence is V2 by that argument.

This word order pattern is different from the situation in the Shina of the Tilel Valley (a side valley in Gurez) as described in Schmidt and Kaul (2010: 9), where, 'Despite its proximity to, and influence from, Kashmiri, there is no trace of verbs occurring in second position in the sentence. The verb always occurs in final position (SOV).' The Gurezi text in Wilson and Grierson (1899) also shows no trace of V2 word order. However, in Bailey's brief Gurezi text on 'The Death of the Gilgit Raja' (1924: 251), of seventeen clauses, six have V2, seven have V2 = V-final, one has V3, one has V1, and two have V-final order.[42] The Gurezi translation of the Parable of the Prodigal Son in the *Linguistic Survey of India* (Grierson 1919: 182) has three instances of V2-order sentences. One of them is: *žu manuž* ***ho*** *uniāl* 'That man **became** hungry.'

3.2 Case Marking and Adjective Agreement

Comparison of our text with information in Schmidt and Kaul (2010), yields an interesting difference. Schmidt and Kaul (2010) identify six

[41] Bailey (1924: 157) gives *phatú* 'behind, after, afterwards' as both adverb and postposition.

[42] A similar text on 'The Death of the Raja' (Bailey 1924: 238), has a similar pattern of word order distribution, but it is not clear whether this text represents Kohistani or Gurezi Shina.

noun cases: nominative (unmarked), agent (*-s[ə]*), genitive (*-õ* [m] *–ĩ* [f]), dative (*-ṭ*), ablative (*-jõ*), and locative (*-j*). They find that one paradigm, that of the word for 'bread', bears traces of a second agent case, and that transitive verbs take the first agent case, in *-sV*, in all tenses. Our text shows the following case forms: ablative in *-jũ* ((5) and (13)) and in *-õ/ũ* ((3), (12), (19), (28), (45–46), (62), (66), and (71)), in all of which the ablative ending follows a consonant; feminine genitive forms in *-ĩ(ĩ)* appear in (13), (23), and (71), and masculine forms in *-uũ* in (1) and (52). Dative forms are in *-(V)ṭ*, locative forms in *-j*. Our text shows the following agentive forms: *mii* (first person singular), *ses*ʸ (third person singular pronoun), and an agentive form in *-ĩĩ* in sentences (49) with a plural subject and (60) with a singular subject. Such a form is not mentioned in Schmidt and Kaul (2010), but it may correspond to the *-ĕĩ* mentioned by Bailey as used with past tenses of transitive verbs (1924: 211).

Regarding the marking of agents of transitive verbs, Schmidt and Kaul (2010: 199) say: 'Transitive verbs take the first agent case in *-sV -s -es* in all tenses.' However, in a footnote, (p. 4, fn. 6) they say: 'The Guresi, Drasi and Kohistani dialects have two agent cases, one marking subjects of imperfective transitive verbs (*sV* ~ *-s* ~ *-es*), the other marking subjects of perfective transitive verbs (*-e* ~ *-i*, *-o*).'[43]

Two agentive markers, Agentive I[mperfective] and Agentive P[erfective] are also reported for Gurezi Shina by Ahmed (2019: 30). In our text, the Agentive P appears in (49) and (60); however, the Agentive I does not appear. We are not claiming that it does not occur in Mr Ghaffar's speech, only that we do not find it in this text.

In Gurezi Shina, as in most varieties of Shina described so far (Palula, Gilgiti, Gultari, Drasi, and Kohistani, but not Sawi), the finite verb agrees in person and number with the clausal subject regardless of whether the subject is in the nominative or in the ergative. This distinguishes Gurezi and its immediate cousins from Kashmiri, Urdu, Panjabi, and other Indo-Aryan languages of the plains; as well as from Iranian Pashto and Balochi. Compare the Gurezi example (49)

[43] Bailey (1924: 211) says: '... the instrumental or agent, which has two distinct forms, one ending in *-ĕĩ* for use in the past tenses of transitive verbs, and the other in *-sŭ* used with all other parts of transitive verbs.' He (1924: 222 ff.) calls them Agent I and Agent II. Hook (1996: 135) discusses this 'dual ergativity' in eastern varieties of Shina (Guresi, Kohistani, Drasi, and Brokskat).

reproduced here, with its Urdu equivalent (a), in which the verb is (default) third person singular with an ergative subject 'doctors'.

49.	*ḍáakṭar-ĩĩ*	*raz-gyée*	*kE*	*zĩĩ-ṭ*	*h-ũũ*
	doctor-Ag.PI	**say-Pst3PI**	that	him-Dat	be-Prs3SgM
	léel	*bakáar*			
	blood	necessary			

'The doctors said that he needs blood.'

a.	*ḍākṭarõ-ne*	*kahā*	*ki*	*us-ko*
	doctor-OBL.PI-ERG	**say-Pst3Sg**	that	him-Dat
	xūn.kī	*zarūrat*	*hai*	
	blood's	necessary	is	

'The doctors said that he needs blood.'

With regard to direct object marking, the sample of Gurezi in this paper differs from the variety described in Ahmed (2019) in not marking animate direct objects with an accusative or "objective" case marker. Animate direct objects in this sample always get the (or direct) case. Other varieties of Shina (such as Gultari) differ in this. See example (b), in which the direct object Kesar takes the accusative marker *-aa*.

b.	*raaCh-ojaa*	*kesar-**aa***	*gii*	*wat-ye*
	guardian(angels)-ErgPl	kesar-**Acc**	taking	came-Mpl

'The guardian angels brought Kesar.' (Hook 1996: 152)

It should be noted that the appearance of nominative case on personal pronoun direct objects in Gurezi, as in (44) reproduced here for convenience, has nothing to do with a person hierarchy such as the one found in neighbouring Kashmiri where, in case the direct object pronoun is further down than the subject on the person hierarchy, the absent accusative/dative case is marked on the finite verb as in (c):

44.	*z-i*	*hár-im*	*mə*	*haspatáal*
	he[Nom]	take-Fut1Sg	I[Nom]	hospital

‘I will take him to the hospital.’

c.	*su*	*ny-ima-**n***	*bi*	*aspataal*
	he[Nom]	take-1stFut-**3rdSgAcc**	I[Nom]	hospital

‘I will take him to the hospital.’

Our text shows the adjective agreement described in Schmidt (2004: 48) for Gurezi, in which ‘the possessive singular agrees with the noun it modifies, like an adjective.’ For Example, *toómléel*(m)in(51)vs.*Tem*ˇ *gáaṛií* (24). Schmidt feels that ‘this probably reflects contact with Kashmiri, in which the possessive suffix inflects to agree with the possessed noun (Wali and Koul 1997: 330).’

3.3 Glossary

This glossary of words and forms appearing in the text is arranged in alphabetical order following the order of the Roman letters used in the transliterated forms. Dental consonants precede retroflex. Conjugated forms of verbs are listed separately if they are not transparently related to the verb root, as well as under the main entry for the verb root.

a

as- ‘be’ Past tense: *as-l-o* (2SgM) ‘you were’, *as-il* (3SgF) ‘she/it was’, *as-ᴜl* (3SgM) ‘he/it was’, *as-al* (3PlM) ‘they were’, *as-l-os* (1SgM) ‘I was’

áal, áalos ‘came’ (Pst < *uiiny* ‘to come’)

akók ‘self’s’, *akók-ij* = Ur. *apne paas*

*-ak*ʰ ‘one’ suffixal indefinite marker

anʸ, anʸ-ey/anʸ-ee ‘here’, ‘here-Emph’

auláad ‘child, offspring’ (< Ur.)

ayáal ‘family’ M (< Turkish)

ayᴇᴇl ‘one year’

æ

æksiḍɛnṭ 'accident' (< Eng.)

b

b- 'become'
bakáar 'needed'
báar háal/hal 'anyway, anyhow' (< Ur.)
barẓ 'year', *barẓ-õõ/barẓ-ŨŨ* 'years (OblPl)'
baṛa(a) 'again'
báskɨ 'much, a lot'
bæṭʰ- 'sit', *bæṭʰos* 'I sat' (Pst1SgM)
be 'we'
bráabər 'same'
bʊ-l 'became' (3SgM), *bu-l-os* 'I became' (Pst < *b-* 'to become')

č

čáar 'four'
čal- 'move'
čal-v-iin 'to drive' (Inf) (Derived transitive of *čal-* 'move'). Forms observed are: *čal-v-um-n-os* 'I drive' (PrsDur1SgM), *čal-v-Um-l-os* 'I was driving/used to drive' (PstDur1SgM), (< *čalvum* + *as-l-os*), *čal-v-iij-Ul(y)* 'was started' (Caus-Pass-Pst3SgM(?))
če(y) 'now'
čUn 'small'

čʰ

čʰakh 'day' (cf. Tib. *žag* 'day')
čʰar- 'to climb' Forms observed: *čʰær-g-yees* 'I lifted up' (Pst1SgM) (Caus. < *čʰar-* 'to ascend, climb'

ç̣

ç̣a 'three'
ç̣ak- 'see, look at', *ç̣ak-aas* 'I looked' (Pst1SgM)

ç^h

ç^har- 'put, keep', *ç^har-ow* 'kept' (Pst3SgM)

d

d- 'give', *d-áas* 'I gave' (Pst1SgM), *daá* 'having given' (CP), *d-ow* 'he gave' (Pst3SgM)
dar- 'to stay, remain', *dar-l-os* 'I stayed' (Pst1SgM). < Ir. **dar-* 'to hold, keep [v.t.]; to dwell [v.i.] (Cheung 2007: 57), probably through Persian and/or Pashto (cf. Pashto *daredal* 'to stay, remain')
diš 'place' F
duu 'two'

ḍ

ḍáakṭar-ĩĩ 'doctors-Ag' (*ḍáakṭar* + AgPl)

g

garmy- 'meet', *garm-im* 'I will meet' (Fut1Sg), *garmy-i-l* 'met'(Pst3SgM)
gá(a)ṛii 'vehicle' F (< Urdu)
g- 'go (past stem), *g-aas* 'I went' (1SgM), *g-yées* 'they went' 3pm, *gowsÚl* (< *g-ow as-ul-(o)* (= Ur. *gayā thā*) 'had gone'
-g(ɨ)- 'also' (= Ur. *bhī*)
gin^y- 'take, buy', *giny-aas* 'I bought' (Pst1SgM)
gooẓ 'house'
grʊp 'group' (i.e. blood type) (< Eng.)

h

h- 'be, become', *h-ĩĩ^y* 'is' (Prs3SgF), *hũũ* 'is' (Prs3SgM)
har^y- 'take', *har-im* 'I will take' (Fut1SgM), *hary-áas* 'I took' (Pst1SgM), *hary-ií* 'having taken' (CP)
harán 'horn' (< Eng.)
haspatáal 'hospital' (< Eng.)
hʊnṭ-iy-áas 'I got something lifted' (Pst1SgM of Caus. of 'lift')
hyuu 'heart'

i

-ĩĩ l. emphatic enclitic (cf. Ur. *hī*); 2. 3rd person agentive case ending.

j

-(V)j locative case ending: 'to, in'
jar 'old'
jæk-ĩĩ 'someone else's' (GenFSg of *jæk* 'someone')
jéek na jéek 'some or the other'
jɪŋ/jiŋ 'some, any; at all'

k

kaf^{y}ii 'quite a lot'(< Ur.)
káaryũ 'for', e.g. *sɨsĩĩ karyũ* 'for this reason'
kal(a) 'time'
kaš 'marriage' M
kašuur 'Kashmiri (person)' M
*k*E conjunction: 'that'
keés '(legal) case' (< Eng.)
koe 'who REL', *kyæs-ĩĩ* 'whose'(FSg) REL
kot 'now'
*kr*U*m* 'work' M
kúl^y.bil 'altogether'
kunii 'nineteen'

k^h

k^hal-aas 'I set free' (Pst1SgM)
k^hæry 'under, beneath' postposition governing Nom. 'a little bit down, inside', as opposed to *k^har* '(far) down'
k^har '(far) down'
k^harič 'expenses' (< Ur.)
k^hazy- 'come out, leave', *k^hat* 'he came out' (Pst3SgM), *k^hat-os* 'I came out' (Pst1SgM), *k^hazy-ii* 'having come out' (CP)

l

léel 'blood' M
lʸed 'was found' (Pst3SgM)

m

mə 'I (Nom)' with postpositions *mʊçʰo-ṭ* 'in front of', and *sĩĩtʸ* 'with'; also appears as *mɨ/mo,ma*
mii 'I (Ag)'
m-ĩĩ 'I (GenFSg), *my-ũũ* 'I (GenMSg)'
mágar 'but' (< Ur.)
manú(u)ẓ 'man' M
matalab 'meaning' (< Ur.) used as filler word, hesitation form
miriinʸ 'death' Inf. of 'die'
mɨ 'I' (see also *mə* and *mo*)
mo 'I' (see also *mə* and *m*)
mʊçʰoṭ Postp. 'in front of'
mʊláazɪm 'employee' (< Ur.)
mʊṣnũũ 'from in front of' (*mʊšn* + *Abl*) (= Ur. *sāmne se*)
mʊt 'other'
mʊ́tve 'one side'
múu 1. 'he died' (Pst3SgM); 2. 'dead' (MSg)

n

na 'not', Neg
nə 'not', Neg
nʊm 'name' M

p

paas tʰ- 'pass (time)'(< Eng.)
pædá(a) 'born' (*pædaa h-* 'to be born') (< Ur.)
pey < 'fall' indicates obligation; *polʸ* 'had to' (lit. Pst 3SgF of '(be)fall') (= Ur. *paṛī*); *pey* 'will have to'
pɪnḍi 'Rawalpindi'

p^h

p^{h}at t^{h}iin^y 'to abandon, leave' (lit. to do release)
p^{h}ato(o) 'then, afterwards, so'
p^{h}irií 'back' (This is the conjunctive participle of *p^{h}ir-* 'turn'.)
p^{h}uṭ^h 'glance'

q

quryi-l 'became attached' (cf. Ur. *lagā*) (Pst3SgM)

r

rapOṬ /rapaurṭ 'report' (< Eng.)
raz^y- 'to say, read'; *ræj-ow* 'he said' (Pst3SgM); *raz-gyee* (Pst3Pl); *ráay-aas* (=*raaj-aas*) 'I said' (Pst1SgM); *rej-ow* 'he educated' (lit. 'he caused to read' < Caus. of *raz^y-*)
rUpáay 'rupee(s)'

s

sa 'they (distal)' 3Pl demonstrative pronoun
sáas 'thousand'
sɨ(ɨ) 1. 'he Nom (distal)'; 2. 'that'(adj.), *ses(y)* 'he (Ag) (distal)', *sesyĩĩ* 'he' (Ag, Emph?), *sĩsũũ/sasũũ* 'his' (MSg)
sad 'there'
sáat^y 'with'
sat 'seven'
sɨɨt 'with' (< Kashmiri)
sĩ/sĩy 'with'
sIpiiḍ 'speed' F (< Eng.)
sõč- 'think', *sõčáas* 'I thought' (Pst1SgM)

ṣ

ṣat 'attached to' (Pst3SgM), < *ṣōnu̯-* 'to attach to' (Bailey 1924: 253). Cf. Gilgit Sh. *ṣačóik^y* v.i. 'to stick to', *ṣoik^y* v.t. 'to fix, apply, hit' (cf. Ur. *lagā*)

t

takriiban ‘about, approximately’ (< Ur.)
taliim ‘education’ F (< Ur.). *taliimyaafta* ‘educated’
tE ‘and’ (probably < Pj.)
tem^y*/tam*^{y} ‘self’s’ (FSg), *toóm* ‘self’s’ (MSg)
teez ‘fast’ (< Ur.)

t^h

t^h*aana* ‘police station’ (< Ur.)
t^h*an-val-uun* ‘policemen, constables’ (*t*^{h}*aana* + *valaa* + OblPl)
t^h*-* ‘do’, *t*^{h}*iin* ‘to do’ (Inf), *t*^{h}*-aa* ‘having done’ (CP), *t*^{h}*-ey-ow* ‘he caused to do’ (Caus-Pst3SgM), *t*^{h}*-aas* ‘I did’ (Pst1SgM), *t*^{h}*-Um* ‘I will do’ (Fut 1SgM), *t*^{h}*-Um-n-us* ‘I am doing/do’ (PrsDur1SgM), *t*^{h}*-Um-l-os* ‘I was doing/used to do’ (PstDur1SgM), *t*^{h}*-aa-n-os* ‘I have done’ (PrsPerf1SgM)

ṭ

-(V)ṭ Dative case ending ‘to’, ‘for’

u

-ũ/-õ Ablative case ending
-ũ(ũ) Genitive case ending (MSg)
uuiin^y ‘to come’ (Inf) Forms attested in this text: *áa-l* ‘he came’ (Pst3SgM), *áa-l-os* ‘I came’ (Pst1SgM)

w/v

waapás ‘back’ (< Ur.)
wáat ‘he got down’ (Pst3SgM), *wáat-os* ‘I got down’ (Pst1SgM)
vákat ‘time’ (< Ur.)
wU ‘and’ (< Prs/Ar.)

y

*yok*ʰ ‘what’

z

zamáanat ‘bail’ (< Ur.), *zamáant-ɪj* ‘on bail’ (*zamáanat* + loc.)
zã̄y ‘this’ (demonst. adj.)
zi-y ‘this’ (demonst. adj.)
z() ‘he (proximal)’
zĩy ‘this very’

ẓ̌

ẓ̌a ‘brother’, *ẓ̌a-va* (Obl)

REFERENCES

Ahmed, Musavir. 2014. 'Language use patterns and ethnolinguistic vitality of the Shina speaking Gurezi immigrants'. *International Journal of the Sociology of Language* 230: 1–17.

Ahmed, Musavir. 2019. *A Descriptive Grammar of Gurezi Shina.* SIL Language and Culture Documentation and Description, 40. SIL Digital Resources.

Bailey, T. Grahame. 1924. *Grammar of the Shina (Ṣiṇā) Language*. London: Royal Asiatic Society.

Bashir, Elena. 2003. 'Dardic'. In *The Indo-Aryan Languages*, edited by George Cardona and Dhanesh Jain. 818–94. London: Routledge.

Baart, Joan L. G. 2003. 'Tonal features in languages of northern Pakistan'. In *Pakistani Languages and Society: Problems and Prospects*, edited by Joan L. G. Baart and Ghulam Hyder Sindhi. 132–44. Islamabad: National Institute of Pakistan Studies and Summer Institute of Linguistics.

Berger, Hermann. 1960. 'Bericht über sprachliche und volkskundliche Forschungen im Hunzatal'. *Anthropos* 55: 657–64.

Buddruss, Georg. 1996. 'Shina-Rätsel'. In *Nānāvidhaikatā. Festschrift für Hermann Berger*, edited by Dieter B. Kapp. 29–54. Wiesbaden: Harrassowitz.

Cheung, Johnny. 2007. *Etymological Dictionary of the Iranian Verb*. Leiden and Boston: Brill. (Leiden Indo-European Etymological Dictionary Series, 2).

Grierson, George A. 1923. *Hatim's Tales*. London: J. Murray.

——— 1919. *Linguistic Survey of India, Volume VIII, Part II. Specimens of the Dardic or Piśācha languages (including Kāshmīrī)*. Calcutta: Superintendent, Government Printing, India.

Hook, Peter Edwin. 1996. 'Kesar of Layul: A Central Asian epic in the Shina of Gultari'. In *Studies in Pakistani Popular Culture*, edited by William Hanaway and Wilma Heston. 121–83. Lahore: Sang-e-Meel and Lok Virsa.

——— 1976. 'Is Kashmiri an SVO language?' *Indian Linguistics* 37.2: 133–42.

——— and Zia, Muhammad Amin. 2005. 'Searching for the goddess: A study of sensory and other impersonal causative expressions in the Shina of Gilgit'. In *Yearbook of South Asian Languages and Linguistics 2005*, edited by Rajendra Singh. 165–88. Berlin: Mouton de Gruyter.

——— and Koul, O. N. 1992. 'On the compound verb in Kashmiri'. *International Journal of Dravidian Linguistics* 21.1: 1–16.

Liljegren, Henrik. 2008. *Towards a Grammatical Description of Palula: An Indo-Aryan Language of the Hindu Kush*. Stockholm: Department of Linguistics, Stockholm University.

Nagar, Amritlal. 2007. *Seth Banke Mal*. Delhi: Rajpal & Sons.

Radloff, Carla F. 1999. *Aspects of the Sound System of Gilgiti Shina*. Islamabad: National Institute of Pakistan Studies and Summer Institute of Linguistics.

——— with Shakil, Shakil Ahmad. 1998. *Folktales in the Shina of Gilgit (Text, Gammatical Analysis and Commentary)*. Islamabad: National Institute of Pakistan Studies and Summer Institute of Linguistics.

Schmidt, Ruth Laila. 2004. 'A grammatical comparison of Shina dialects'. In *Himalayan Languages: Past and Present*, edited by Anju Saxena. 33–55. Berlin: Mouton de Gruyter.

_______ 2000. 'Typology of Shina pronouns'. *Berliner Indologische Studien* 13/14: 201–13.

_______ and Kaul, Vijay. 2010. 'A grammatical sketch of Guresi Shina'. In *Anantaṁ Śāstram: Indological and Linguistic Studies in Honour of Bertil Tikkanen*, edited by Klaus Karttunen. 195–214. Helsinki: Finnish Oriental Society. (Studia Orientalia 208).

_______ and Kohistani, Razwal. 2008. *A Grammar of the Shina Language of Indus Kohistan*. Wiesbaden: Harrassowitz. (Beiträge zur Kenntnis südasiatischer Sprachen und Literaturen 17).

_______ and Kohistani, Razwal. 1998. 'Páalus /kostyṍ/ Shina revisited'. *Acta Orientalia* 59: 106–49.

Wali, Kashi and Koul, Omkar N. 1997. *Kashmiri: A Cognitive-Descriptive Grammar.* London and New York: Routledge.

Wilson, J. and Grierson, George A. 1899. 'On the Gurezi Dialect of Shina'. *The Indian Antiquary* 28: 93–102.

5

Recent Developments in Wakhi Orthography

Fazal Amin Beg, John Mock, and Mir Ali Wakhani

1. INTRODUCTION

Wakhi,[1] like other modern Pamiri languages,[2] exists largely as a spoken language. But for many years, the community of scholars, researchers, poets, and other literary persons, both native and non-native, has been attempting to bring the language into a written form.

The earliest known efforts to write Wakhi were those of British colonial officers, who assembled vocabulary lists of, what was to them, a new language (Burnes 1834, Hayward 1871, Yule 1872). Robert Barklay Shaw, who served as the British Officer on Special Duty in Kashgar in 1874–75, published the first sketch of Wakhi grammar (Shaw 1876). Shaw's romanized transcriptions, although phonemically inaccurate, served as the basis for the monumental Linguistic Survey of India (Grierson 1921).

European linguists investigated Wakhi (Sköld et al. 1936, Klimchitsky 1936, Lorimer 1958), with Georg Morgenstierne making the most detailed study (Morgenstierne 1938). Soviet scholars working in Central Asia (now Tajikistan) contributed substantially to linguistic knowledge and documentation of Wakhi (Pakhalina 1975, 1983, 1987; Sokolova 1953, 1981), including the comprehensive two-volume work

---

[1] Wakhi people refer to themselves as (wa)x̌ ik, to their language as (wa)x̌ ikwor, and to Wakhan as wux̌, sharing a common root for the ethnonym, glossonym, and toponym.

[2] See Mock in this volume for more about Pamiri languages and Wakhi's areal position.

of Grünberg and Steblin-Kamensky (1976). To transcribe Wakhi, these scholars used a Latin-based transcription system (discussed below) that is employed widely among students of Iranian languages.

Wakhi has contrasting pairs of voiceless and voiced retroflex consonants (ṭ ḍ, č̣ ǰ̣, ṣ̌ ẓ̌), apparently borrowed from a non-Indo-Aryan substrate that is likely Burushaski (Edelman and Dodykhudoeva 2009: 779–80). Wakhi has a rich set of fricatives (f v, θ δ, s z, ṣ̌ ẓ̌ , x̌ γ̌, x γ), in which the development of velar and uvular fricatives (x̌ γ̌, x γ) is shared with most of the Eastern Iranian languages (Wendtland 2009: 184).

The thirty-five Wakhi consonants are the same in all four countries. The absence of the glottal fricative /h/ is a shared characteristic of Pamiri languages (Edelman and Dodykhudoeva 2009). Although Beg (2004) and Wakhani (2009) list it as a phoneme in Hunza and Wakhan Wakhi, it occurs only in Arabic and Persian loan words in Wakhan and in Gojal (Pakistan) and also as an unstable breathiness or glide at the beginning of some words with an initial vowel: ʉp / hʉp 'seven', ayem / hayem 'this' (Steblin-Kamensky 1999: 24–5).

Wakhi vowels also show regional variation. The Tajikistan and Wakhan mid-central vowel /ə/ has undergone sound change in Gojal to a mid-front vowel [ɛ], particularly in stressed syllables (Peter Backstrom: personal communication). In unstressed syllables it is still pronounced as /ə/.[3] Hence, in Gojal this phoneme is often represented as [e], which is easier for most Gojal Wakhi people to recognize and write.

The diversity of Wakhi phonemes and the diversity of the sociolinguistic context in each of the four countries have engendered a diversity of transcription systems, as discussed below.

Recent linguistic publications on Wakhi (Kieffer 1978; Gao 1985; Buddruss 1986; Payne 1989; Backstrom 1992; Reinhold 1992, 2006; Mock 1998; Steblin-Kamensky 1999; Pakhalina and Lashkarbekov 2000; Bashir 2009) have utilized Latin-based transcription systems (see Table 1). Interestingly, these transcription systems prompted Wakhi intellectuals and artists to write their language, a development that accompanies a resurgence of vitality for the language (Reinhold 1992, Mock 1998, Müller et al. 2008).

[3] Examples from Wakhan and Gojal: /kənd/ /kend/ 'woman, wife', /təy/ /tey/ 'is', /sərk/ /serk/ 'apricot pit', /rəč̣ən/ /reč̣ən/ 'we leave' (Mock: field notes).

Table 1: Consonant phonemes—Latin-based 'Iranian' system

	Labial	Dental	Alveolar	Retroflex	Palatal	Velar	Post-velar
Stop (voiceless)	p		t	ṭ		k	q
Stop (voiced)	b		d	ḍ		g	
Affricate (vl.)			c	č̣	č		
Affricate (vd.)			ʒ	ǰ̣	ǰ		
Fricative (vl.)	f	θ	s	ṣ̌	š	x̌	x
Fricative (vd.)	v	δ	z	ẓ̌	ž	γ̌	γ
Flap			r				
Lateral			l				
Nasal	m		n				
Semi-vowel	w		y				(h)

Vowel phonemes—Latin-based 'Iranian' system

Wakhan and Tajikistan	i,		ʉ,	ə,	o,	u
Gojal	i,	e,	ʉ,	a,	o,	u

In Pakistan, the efforts of Wakhi intellectuals to write their language began with the Gojal Isma'iliya Students Union's (1980) small booklet that presented a list of Wakhi letters in Perso-Arabic script accompanied by a grammatical sketch and a glossary, written in Urdu. Haqiqat Ali, who worked with Buddruss in northern Pakistan, was the first Wakhi intellectual to publish a primer for writing Wakhi using the Latin-based system (Ali 1980). Ahmed Jami Sakhi (2000) subsequently brought out a Wakhi primer and history of Wakhi language studies, written in Urdu. Jami commented that 'ordinary readers find it [Haqiqat Ali's Latin-based script] impossible to understand.' Jami adapted the Perso-Arabic script for Wakhi (see Table 2).

Table 2: Ahmed Jami Sakhi system—Consonant phonemes

	Labial	Dental	Alveolar	Retroflex	Palatal	Velar	Post-velar
Stop (voiceless)	پ		ت ط	ٹ		ک	ق
Stop (voiced)	ب		د	ڈ		گ	
Affricate (vl.)			ڎ	ڄ	چ		
Affricate (vd.)			ڗ	ژ	ج		
Fricative (vl.)	ف	ٿ	س ص ث	ڜ	ش	خ	خ
Fricative (vd.)	ڤ	ڎ	ذ ز ض ظ	ژ	ڃ	ڠ	غ
Flap			ر				
Lateral			ل				
Nasal	م		ن				
Semi-vowel`	و		ی ے				ہ ح ھ

Vowel phonemes—Ahmed Jami Sakhi system

ی		ۇ	ا	و	ۇ
i	e	ʉ	a	o	u

In Tajikistan, Boghshoh Lashkarbekov, a native Wakhi scholar, published Wakhi songs and poems in modified Cyrillic script along with a table correlating Cyrillic characters with the Latin-based characters for Wakhi phonemes employed by the Soviet scholars[4] (Lashkarbekov 1972). The poet and scholar Aziz Mirboboev, however, chose to use only the Latin-based transcription system to publish several poems in Wakhi (Reinhold 1992). Lashkarbekov's subsequent publications (Pakhalina and Lashkarbekov 2000) also utilized the Latin-based system.

When initially introduced in Afghanistan, the Latin-based system attracted Wakhi schoolteachers who had some knowledge of European alphabets, but their students and Wakhi poets and musicians found it confusingly unfamiliar and obtuse (Beg and Mock 2005: field notes). Subsequent efforts focused on developing a Perso-Arabic script to write Wakhi, employing a script similar to that used for Pashto, which shares some phonology with Wakhi. Literacy primers for first and second grade students developed by Mir Ali Wakhani in conjunction with the Ministry of Education and published by the Ministry of Education (Wakhani 2009) are now used in government schools in Wakhan (see Table 3).

The Wakhi community, residing in four countries, is subject to the respective national policies on minority languages. In each country, the national language dominates the educational and cultural spheres, a fact which, to a certain extent, might be expected to threaten Wakhi language survival. In this respect, the development of Wakhi literacy functions as a strategy to buffer the effect of national language policy and hegemony. Wakhi writers have responded to literacy in the national language acquired through the respective educational systems by adapting their literacy skills in the respective scripts to write Wakhi. For example, in Tajikistan, Wakhi speakers look to the Cyrillic script for their national and inter-regional languages (Tajik and Russian). It therefore becomes easy for them to adapt Cyrillic for writing Wakhi. In Afghanistan and Pakistan, Wakhi speakers look to Perso-Arabic script, which is used for writing in Farsi, Pashto, and Urdu, and is readily adapted to Wakhi. In China, a major part of socialization for the Wakhi community is mainly in Uyghur and Mandarin Chinese, although

[4] Edelman and Dodykhudoeva (2009: 775) present a chart of Cyrillic and Latin characters for transcribing Pamiri languages.

Table 3: Mir Ali system—Consonant phonemes

	Labial	Dental	Alveolar	Retroflex	Palatal	Velar	Post-velar
Stop (voiceless)	پ		ت ط	ٹ		ک	ق
Stop (voiced)	ب		د	ڈ		گ	
Affricate (vl.)			څ	ڇ	چ		
Affricate (vd.)			ځ	ڄ	ج		
Fricative (vl.)	ف	ٿ	س ص ث	ڜ	ش	ښ	خ
Fricative (vd.)	ڤ	ذ	ز ض ظ	ڙ	ژ	ڔ	غ
Flap			ر				
Lateral			ل				
Nasal	م		ن				
Semi-vowel	و		ی				ہ ھ

Vowel phonemes—Mir Ali system

ی	ۏ	ا	و	ۇ
i	ʉ	ə	o	u

English has also been introduced in some educational institutions (Beg 2004). Uyghur language is written mainly in Perso-Arabic script, and limited efforts have focused on that script (Beg 2004).

Historically, writing systems for Iranian languages have been 'generally determined by the dominant religion' (Windfuhr 1989). However, twentieth century advances in transportation, communication, and information technologies and a concurrent increase in globalization have altered this paradigm.

In this globalized world, small languages are increasingly vulnerable. An appropriate, logical, and acceptable writing system for unwritten languages with a small population, such as Wakhi, is therefore imperative.

In such circumstances, a key question arises: could there be any effective writing system that may create a uniformity among the Wakhi community and stimulate them towards intellectual productivity and literary contributions in an integrated way? It is a generally accepted fact that one can better express oneself in one's own mother tongue. An affirmative answer to this question requires an enabling environment in the local community. For instance, any writing system must be easy to learn, easy to understand, and easy to transmit to the present and coming generations, and the entire community must receive it with pride. Equally essential is cooperation for language preservation and promotion with local civil society organizations, educational institutions, and government agencies.

The writing systems developed so far for Wakhi are based either on the Latin-based Iranian transcription system produced by international linguists, the Cyrillic alphabet produced by Soviet and Tajik scholars, or the Perso-Arabic *alif-bey* systems produced by native intellectuals. To what extent these three writing systems are adopted and accepted by native speakers remains a question due to the factors that are determinative of an enabling environment for literacy. These include the prevalent educational system and script medium used for instruction, the ease of association of written symbols with the spoken/heard phonemes of the language, and whether a single writing system adequately represents the phonemes of Wakhi as spoken in all four nations.

The Latin-based Iranian system adequately represents Wakhi phonemes and allows for accuracy in representing regional variation, such as /ə/ in Tajikistan and Wakhan, and [ɛ] or /e/ in Gojal, as discussed above. This transcription system is a modified form of standard 'Indic' transcription using a subscript dot to indicate retroflex consonants and a superscript caron (ˇ) to indicate palatalization. The system uses several Greek characters to indicate phonemes not found in the 'Indic' system and a Cyrillic character / ы / for one non-Indic vowel. Some Wakhi writers continue to use the Cyrillic vowel character ы, but most have replaced it with the IPA character ʉ.[5]

The Latin-based Iranian transcription system is very productive for the international community of linguists and the scientific studies of languages. However, based on the authors' collective experience of more than two decades in reading, writing, and documenting Wakhi in the Latin-based system, what we have observed is that for students, professionals, poets, amateur learners, and intellectuals, this system has not been attractive and effective for their creative work and literary ventures. Many symbols remain either alien or confusing to Wakhi people not formally trained in this system. That is why a majority of the interested native community opted to write Wakhi using their own idiosyncratic transcription method in Perso-Arabic script.

The Perso-Arabic writing system is well known to Wakhi people in Pakistan and Afghanistan. Unlike the Latin-based system, however, there is no universal agreement on the sound values of each symbol. For example, Mir Ali has used the Pashto characters for the retroflex consonants rather than the Urdu characters. This is to be expected in Afghanistan, where Pashto is a national language. The officials at the Ministry of Education were quite insistent on this point. However, their choice of ذ for the voiced interdental fricative /δ/ is based on

[5] The Cyrillic symbol /ы/ represents a sound in the Russian language which is very similar to that represented by the IPA symbol [ʉ], except that it is produced with the lips in a flat or spread position, rather than a somewhat rounded or pursed position. The IPA symbol /ʉ/ has four advantages for use in writing Gojal Wakhi, as compared to using /ы/: (i) It more accurately represents the sound of this vowel in the Gojal dialect; (ii) The IPA symbol /ʉ/ is more widely recognized internationally than /ы/;(iii) /ʉ/ belongs to the same alphabetic family (Latin) as the other five vowel symbols currently being used for Wakhi in both Tajikistan and Pakistan; and (iv) For those unfamiliar with the Cyrillic script, /ы/ can be confusing because it may appear to be two separate symbols rather than one (Peter Backstrom: personal communication)

the Arabic pronunciation of this letter. Persian, Pashto, and Urdu all render the sound of this letter as /z/, and loan words into Wakhi from those languages that use ذ may result in confusion. The 'Jami' system avoids this by using two dots over the letter to distinguish it from the normal Urdu-Persian pronunciation /z/. However, the 'Jami' system does not distinguish between /ʉ/ and /u/, and uses standard Urdu diacritic marks to indicate short vowels and to distinguish /i/ and /e/. The Mir Ali system also does not fully distinguish vowels. This is not a major obstacle for general use by Wakhi speakers, who recognize the words readily enough, but for non-native speakers, the lack of precision can raise difficulties.

The Latin-based system, despite the difficulty of learning the characters, has found increasing acceptance among Wakhi poets and intellectuals in northern Pakistan. In part, this is indicative of the internationalization of Gilgit-Baltistan as compared to Wakhi population areas in other countries. Access to Gilgit-Baltistan is comparatively good and there is a long history of international research and scholarship in the region. Hence, the Latin-based system has a comparative advantage as a widely used and understood system for representing the unwritten languages of Gilgit-Baltistan.

An additional reason why the Latin-based system has been generally well-received by Wakhi intellectuals is in large part because it resembles English. English is today regarded as an international language and has been spreading and taking root throughout the world. It is established in the countries where the Wakhi community dwells (Pakistan, Afghanistan, Tajikistan, and China). The native Wakhi community in Pakistan is greatly exposed to and prefers English medium education for their children, as it is like an 'international passport' and is an effective language of science and technology. Importantly, English medium education is emphasized by the spiritual leader of the global Wakhi community, His Highness the Aga Khan. All Wakhi community members, wherever they live, are devout Shia Ismailis and followers of Prince Karim Aga Khan. Some people therefore become excited and theologize the language and the people as 'Ismaili language and cultural community'. This shows that there is also a religious perspective of the Wakhi community that motivates learning English and educating their children in English medium.

As previously mentioned, technology has an increasingly significant influence on the development of Wakhi literacy. The Internet has enabled technologically savvy users, and especially the younger generation, to chat with each other through romanized text messages. More interesting are the text messages on mobile cellular phones in which the local Wakhi community writes their messages, whether in Wakhi, Urdu, or Dari, more flexibly in an English-based transcription system than in Perso-Arabic. These indicators show the actual trends and motivations of the local community members, particularly the youngsters, who are the heirs to the heritages of their language and culture.

Several software- and font-based solutions have been developed to make Wakhi easier to write on the computer. One software-based solution using Latin-based characters is the Keyman© Software Package[6] for Wakhi language. The software is available for purchase and can be used with the freely available fonts[7] Doulos SIL and Charis SIL. Peter C. Backstrom developed a Wakhi package that assigns specific keys to specific characters. However, Wakhi users find this system difficult to use. It must be purchased, it occasionally crashes, and it requires the user to learn to use the unfamiliar symbols of the Latin-based Iranian system.

Another Latin-based 'Indic' font package that is Unicode compliant and works on both Windows and Macintosh operating systems is IndUni-T, developed by John Smith.[8] It contains all characters necessary to transcribe all languages of northern Pakistan, Afghanistan, and Tajikistan. Although available for free, it still requires familiarity with the 'Indic' transcription system.

---

6 Keyman is a proprietary keyboarding software engine with fonts for over 1,000 languages developed by Tavultesoft Pty Ltd. The fonts Charis and Doulos were developed by SIL.

7 Charis SIL and Doulos SIL are Unicode compliant fonts available free at: <http://scripts.sil.org/cms/scripts/page.php?site_id=nrsi&id=ipahome>

8 IndUni-T is available online at: <http://bombay.indology.info/software/fonts/induni/>

In this situation, Dr Boghshoh Lashkarbekov,[9] a native Wakhi of Tajik Badakhshan, came up with a creative contribution for the Wakhi communities of all nations by proposing an English-based writing system (see Table 4).

Table 4: Consonant phonemes—'Boghshoh' system

	Labial	Dental	Alveolar	Retroflex	Palatal	Velar	Post-velar
Stop (voiceless)	p		t	t̃		k	q
Stop (voiced)	b		d	d̃		g	
Affricate (vl.)			c	c̃ h	ch		
Affricate (vd.)			z̃	j̃	j		
Fricative (vl.)	f	th	s	s̃ h	sh	x̃	x
Fricative (vd.)	v	dh	z	z̃ h	zh	g̃ h	gh
Flap			r				
Lateral			l				
Nasal	m		n				
Semi-vowel	w		y				(h)

Vowel phonemes—'Boghshoh' system

Wakhan and Tajikistan	i,		ũ,	ə,	o,	u
Gojal	i,	e,	ũ,	a,	o,	u

[9] Dr Lashkarbekov sadly passed away on 2 February 2014. He was a senior researcher at the Institute of Linguistics of the Russian Academy of Sciences in Moscow.

He introduced a simplified orthography that uses a superscript *tilde/ madha* (˜) to indicate all consonants and vowels that were indicated by a subscript dot or superscript caron in the 'Indic' orthography, and uses an additional 'h' to indicate aspiration and some frication. This system simplifies the marking of consonants and is readily understood by most educated Wakhi.

This English-based writing system has several benefits. It does not require any special software or font to be installed on one's computer; rather the normal keys used for English are used with the addition of creating a shortcut for one symbol, the Spanish *tilde*/Arabic *madha* < ˜ > that is superscribed on top of some English letters to indicate contrastive Wakhi sounds. This symbol is readily assigned to a 'shortcut' key. Writing Wakhi on a computer is thus like writing in English language.

Lashkarbekov's creative work is based on English language orthography. All Wakhi phonemes are nicely accommodated within it. Contrastive phonemes that do not exist in English (such as retroflex consonants, velar fricatives, and the vowel /ы/ /ʉ/) are indicated through the *tilde/madha* sign < ˜ > and the grapheme <h> is used to indicate phonemic aspiration. This was greatly appreciated and taken up by the native speakers, especially the youth in Gilgit, Islamabad, and Karachi.

A Karachi-based student forum, the Gojal Ismaili Students Association (GISAK), organized a brief orientation session on the Wakhi language and its writing system in October 2013. It was interesting to note that the sixty-two participants were very enthusiastic in learning and quickly absorbing the writing system because they knew the English language. They needed to memorize only the *tilde/madha* symbol < ˜ > put as a cap on top of the letters that have their closest relations with them, such as <ch> with <c̃h>, <d> with <d̃>, <x> with <x̃>, <u> with <ũ>, etc.

Although the assignment of the superscript *madha/tilde* < ˜ > is arbitrary, it is a convenient and readily understood symbol to indicate Wakhi phonemes not found in standard English. Of course, it could be replaced by any other superscript symbol. However, some of the available symbols already have an assigned value in existing transcription systems, such as the symbols < ˘ >, < ˆ >, and <ˇ>. Some Wakhi people have asked if the Arabic *madha* symbol is inappropriate, as it has significance in Perso-Arabic script. However, the *madha* sign itself has no specific concept or meaning but rather is just an indicator that shows change or shift of sound from the regular unmarked letters.

There are some drawbacks to writing Wakhi with the shortcut key on the computer. In most word processing systems there is no difficulty, but other applications, such as spreadsheets, email, or web presentation software, lack a shortcut key and do not easily allow insertion of symbols and special characters. This situation therefore poses a challenge to writing Wakhi in other programmes and necessitates that we compromise and write in word processing programmes and then import or copy the text into spreadsheets, email, or web presentation software.

The current development in the Wakhi writing system, based on English orthography, may not be ideal for all Wakhi speakers who want to write their language, but in view of the absence of any other consensus-based and unified writing system for the language, this new system may be a significant step towards a unified and uniform script that is more practicable and easier to understand and write with. No special software and no special fonts are required to be installed first in order to write Wakhi. The English orthography-based Wakhi script is very simple. Users only need to assign a shortcut key to the Arabic *madah*/Spanish *tilde* key < ˜ > on the computer keyboard and start working in Wakhi using any Roman font.

Finally, we appreciate and request reader feedback on these questions. Whether you may be a language specialist or a language speaker, we call for an open discussion as to what needs to be done to bring further improvement in unifying and standardizing the Wakhi Pamiri writing system. This question is equally relevant to other Pamiri languages[10] and to their development and survival in the twenty-first century.

---

[10] Recent email correspondence with Shughni speakers in Tajikistan demonstrates that there is interest in developing a single writing system that can be used with all of the 'Pamiri' languages.

ACKNOWLEDGEMENTS

The Christensen Fund of Palo Alto and San Francisco generously provided funding to support research in Wakhan by John Mock and Fazal Amin Beg, travel to Gojal by Mir Ali Wakhani, research in Tajikistan by John Mock, and collaborative work by all three authors in Islamabad. The American Institute of Pakistan Studies provided office space, computer facilities, and tea for the team in Islamabad. In Kabul, the American Institute of Afghanistan Studies provided logistic assistance and support. We thank Peter Backstrom for his helpful discussions on issues of phonology and orthography.

REFERENCES

Ali, Haqiqat. 1980. *Wakhi Language: Xikwor zik book*. Passu (Gojal): Wakhi Culture Association.

Backstrom, Peter C. 1992. 'Wakhi'. In *Sociolinguistic Survey of Northern Pakistan, vol. 2: Languages of the Northern Areas*, edited by Peter C. Backstrom and Carla F. Radloff. 57–74. Islamabad: National Institute of Pakistan Studies and Summer Institute of Linguistics.

Bashir, Elena. 2009. 'Wakhi'. In *The Iranian Languages*, edited by Gernot Windfuhr. 825–62. London: Routledge.

Beg, Fazal Amin. 2004. *Kinship and Marriage among the Wakhis in the Tashkurgan Tajik Autonomous County of Xinjiang Region, China*. MA thesis. Peshawar: University of Peshawar.

Burnes, Alexander. 1834. *Travels into Bokhara*. London: John Murray.

Buddruss, Georg. 1986. 'Wakhi-Sprichwörter aus Hunza'. In *Studia Grammatica Iranica: Festschrift für Helmut Humbach*, edited by Rüdiger Schmitt and Prods O. Skjaervø. 27–44. München: R. Kitzinger.

Edelman, D. (Joy) I. and Dodykhudoeva, Leila R. 2009. 'Pamir languages'. In *The Iranian Languages*, edited by Gernot Windfuhr. 773–86. London: Routledge.

Gao, Erqiang. 1985. *Tajikeyu jianzhi* [Concise Grammar of (Sariquli and Wakhi) Tajik]. Beijing: Minzu Chubanshe.

Gojal Ismailia Students Union. 1980. *Wast Eshiya' men Wakhi log aur zaban* [Wakhi People and Language in West Asia]. Karachi: Gojal Ismailia Students Union.

Grierson, George A. 1921. 'The Ghalchah Languages'. In *Specimens of Languages of the Eranian Family*, edited by George A. Grierson. 455–548. Calcutta: Superintendent of Government Printing, India. (Linguistic Survey of India, vol. 10).

Grünberg, Alexander L. and Steblin-Kamensky, Ivan M. 1976. *Jazyki vostočnogo gindukuša: vaxanskij jazyk*. Moscow: Nauka.

Hayward, George. 1871. 'Appendices to Mr. Hayward's letters: Dialects of Wakhán, Shighnán, and Roshán'. *Journal of the Royal Geographical Society* 41: 29–30. London: John Murray.

Kieffer, Charles M. 1978. 'Einführung in die Wakhi-Sprache and Glossar'. In *Grosser Pamir: Österreichisches Forschungsunternehmen 1975 in den Wakhan-Pamir/ Afghanistan*, edited by Roger Senarclens de Grancy and Robert Kostka. 345–74. Graz: Akademische Druck- und Verlagsanstalt.

Klimčitskij, S. I. 1936. 'Vaxanskije teksty'. In *Trudy Akademia Nauka SSSR, Tadžikskij filial*. 75–112. Moscow: Nauka.

Lashkarbekov, Bogsho. 1972. 'Baze namunahoi nazmi Vakhoni [Some examples of verses of Wakhan]'. In *Zabonhoi Pomiri va folklor* [Pamir Languages and Folklore], edited by Dodkhudo Koramshoev and Svetlana V. Khushenova. 143–9. Dushanbe: Instituti Zabon va Adabieti ba nom Rudaki [Rudaki Institute of Language and Literature].

Lorimer, David. L. R. 1958. *The Wakhi Language*. London: School of Oriental and African Studies.

Mock, John. 1998. *The Discursive Construction of Reality in the Wakhi Community of Northern Pakistan*. PhD dissertation. Berkeley: University of California.

Morgenstierne, Georg. 1938. *Iranian Pamir languages: Yidgha-Munji, Sanglechi-Ishkashmi and Wakhi*. Oslo: H. Aschehoug & Co.

Müller, Katja, Abbess, Elisabeth, Tiessen, Calvin, and Tiessen, Gabriela. 2008. *Language Vitality and Development among the Wakhi People of Tajikistan*. <http://www-01.sil.org/silesr/2008/silesr2008-011.pdf> accessed 7 October 2016.

Pakhalina, Tatiana N. 1987. *Vaxanskij jazyk: Osnovy iranskogo jazykoznanija* [Wakhi language: Foundations of Iranian linguistics]. Moscow: Nauka.

_______ 1983. *Issledovanie po sravnitel'no-istoričeskoi fonetike pamirskix jazykov* [Investigation of the Comparative History of the Phonetics of the Pamir Languages]. Moscow: Nauka.

_______ 1975. *Vaxanskii jazyk* [Wakhan language]. Moscow: Nauka.

_______ and Lashkarbekov, Boghshoh. 2000. Vaxanskii iazyk [The Wakhi language]. In *Iazyki mira* (Iranskie iazyki 3). 174–86. Moscow: Indrik.

Payne, John. 1989. 'Pamir Languages'. In *Compendium linguarum Iranicarum*, edited by Rüdiger Schmitt. 417–44. Wiesbaden: Ludwig Reichert Verlag.

Reinhold, Beate. 2006. *Neue Entwicklungen in der Wakhi-sprache von Gojal (Nordpakistan): Bildung, Migration und Mehrsprachigkeit.* Wiesbaden: Otto Harrassowitz. (Iranica 10).

_______ 1992. 'Seven Wakhi poems'. *Journal of the Royal Asiatic Society* 2.1: 202–11.

Sakhi, Ahmed Jami. 2000. *Wakhi zaban tarikh ke aa'ine men ma' qa'idah* [Wakhi language in the mirror of history with primer]. Gilgit: Farman Printing Press.

Shaw, Robert B. 1876. 'On the Ghalchah languages (Wakhí and Sarikolí)'. *Journal of the Asiatic Society of Bengal* 45.1: 139–278. Calcutta: Lewis.

Sköld, Hannes, Smith, Helmer, Jarring, Gunnar, and Morgenstierne, Georg. 1936. *Materialien zu den Iranischen Pamirsprachen*. Lund: C. W. K. Gleerup.

Sokolova, Valentina S. 1981. 'K istorii vokalizma vaxanskogo iazyka [On the history of the vocalism of the Wakhi language].' In *Iranskoe iazykoznanie: Ežegodnik 1980*, edited by Mikhail N. Bogolübov, Alexander L. Grünberg, Valentin A. Efimov, and Vera S. Rastorgueva (eds.). 37–47. Moscow: Nauka.

_______ 1953. *Očerki po fonetike iranskixiazykov* [Essays on the phonetics of the Iranian languages]. Moscow: Nauka.

Steblin-Kamensky, Ivan M. 1999. Ètimologičeskij *slovar› vaxanskogo jazyka* [Etymological dictionary of the Wakhi Language]. Saint Petersburg: Saint Petersburg State University.

Wakhani, Mir Ali. 2009. *Xhikwor.* 2 vols. Kabul: Ministry of Education, Islamic Republic of Afghanistan.

Wendtland, Antje. 2009. 'The position of the Pamir languages within East Iranian'. *Orientalia Suecana* 58: 172–88.

Windfuhr, Gernot. 1989. 'New Iranian languages: Overview'. In *Compendium Linguarum Iranicarum*, edited by Rüdiger Schmitt. 246–50. Wiesbaden, Ludwig Reichert Verlag.

Yule, Henry. 1872. 'Papers connected with the upper Oxus region'. *Journal of the Royal Geographical Society* 42: 438–75. London: John Murray.

6

The Parable of the Prodigal Son in Shina and Ḍomaakí

Georg Buddruss

1. INTRODUCTION

Sir George Grierson's monumental multivolume *Linguistic Survey of India* includes translations into hundreds of languages of the *Parable of the Prodigal Son* (Luke 15: 11–32). In the introductory volume, Grierson gave his reasons why this text was selected as a linguistic specimen: among other arguments such as the beauty of the text, the parable would avoid Indian prejudices, and it contained a wealth of grammatical forms (1927: 17–19).

In the Shina language of Gilgit two specimens were collected in 1898 and 1899. The second one, by Khan Sahib Abdul Hakim Khan, is the better one, though it contains mistakes and is written in a phonologically quite underdifferentiated form. It was published in Grierson (1919). The third version of the parable is that by T. Grahame Bailey, included in his Shina grammar (1924: 106–9), which is quite satisfactory from a linguistic point of view. My Shina teacher, Mohammad Amin Zia, however, with whom I studied Bailey's text in Gilgit in 1982, was not quite satisfied with it and suggested formulating what he considered to be a better version, nearer to his language of the 1980s. It was this latter text that was read out by me several times to my Ḍomaaki informants, Habibullah Jan and some of his friends, who were present at our meetings.

Our first knowledge of the Ḍomaakí language came from Lorimer (1939). This work has merits of its own, though the author confesses that his material 'contains deficiencies, half hints, obscurities and uncertainties' (p. 16). Lorimer had only a short time for his work with a single informant. Their common medium was Burushaski (p. 15).

My own field studies of Ḍomaakí in Gilgit were begun in 1982 and continued in 1983. I collected vocabularies, grammatical details, and a number of texts: a lengthy life history and several folk tales. I read the texts in a university class with students, but unfortunately did not find the time to publish them completely, up till now.

After my visits to Gilgit, the Ḍomaakí studies have been fortunately intensified by two scholars, Bertil Tikkanen and Matthias Weinreich. Tikkanen's article on case syntax (2011) and Weinreich's various writings (1999, 2008, 2011), the last being his grammar sketch in Russian, bear witness to the great progress since Lorimer's time.[1]

The *Linguistic Survey of India* has no specimen of Ḍomaakí, as Grierson did not have Ḍomaakí materials at his disposal. Therefore I suggested getting Mohammad Amin Zia's text translated by speakers of Ḍomaakí, to which they happily agreed. That means the Ḍomaakí translation is not from English but from Shina. To write the texts in an interlinear form was rather difficult, as the Ḍomaakí version often differed from the Shina, especially in word order. The English translation tries to be as literal as possible. Regarding the terminology of the cases, I follow Tikkanen (2011). Long vowels, as now widely accepted for Burushaski and Shina, are written as two vowels (vv) with an accent either on the first or the second mora (v́v, vv́). Information on the contemporary vocabulary of Gilgit Shina can be obtained from the glossaries in the writings of Carla Radloff (1992, 1999), Degener (2008), and Buddruss and Degener (2012). Also recommended is Mohammad Amin Zia's Shina–Urdu word list (2010).

[1] Weinreich quotes a Ḍomaakí grammar sketch written in Japanese which I have not seen (Yoshioka 2006).

2. TEXT

Sh.	1. *ek mušáakei*	*du dáarye asél.*	2. *čúno puç-se maáleṭ reégo:*
D.	1. *ek maníšiki*	*dui peé čhéeka.*	2. *čuná puçán piíšu munín:*
E.	1. one man-GEN-SG	two son-NOM-PL be-PRET-3PL	2. small son-ERG father-DAT speak-PRET-3SG

Sh.	3. *'waá* [2] *baábo,*	*thei ẓabé-ǰo*	*ǰéek báaguk*
D.	3. *'bée bába,*	*teé*[3] *daulatásmo mášu*	*kís-ek baagúk*
E.	3. oh-INTJ father-VOC	your property-ABL I-DAT	what-SGL part-SGL

Sh.	*ašíiǰen*	*to,*	*oó maṭ de!'*
D.	*aaná (diṣqaltina*[4]*) čha*	*ta,*	*hei mášu de!'*
E.	come (be available)-PRES/INF is	PART[5]	that I-DAT give-IPV

Sh.	4. *maálus toóm ẓap*		*dáarya-maǰaá samareégu.*
D.	4. *piín apanéi daulat*	*apanéi*	*peéċ maǰána bagaín.*
E.	4. father-ERG own property	own	son-OBL-PL between divide-PRET-3SG

---

[2] Also pronounced *wáa*.

[3] Some speakers say *tée*.

[4] Bur. *d-ṣqalt-* German 'zukommen' (Berger 1998: 410).

[5] *ta* here forming a subordinate clause. Tikkanen glosses 'too, even'.

Sh. 5. *tonée bóde déezi* *neé gyées akí* *čúno púç-se*
D. 5. *noó*[6] *buútek gúċa* *ni gié čhéeka* *čuná puçán*
E. 5. then many-NOM-PL/much-SGL day-NOM-PL not go-PLQ-3PL self-PART small son-ERG

Sh. *toóm buṭi* *ǰéek* *siŋaleé* *duúr kúyekeṭ ǰaṣ búlu.*
D. *apanéi* *kis čháal* *gaṭi irí* *dúur*[7] *díšikišu ǰaṣ huyá.*
E. own all-f. what all collect-CP/together-do-CP far country-SGL-DAT start become-PRET-3SG

Sh. 6. *eé kúyer gyeé ros* *toóm ẓap* *kháče koómo maǰaá*
D. 6. *háai dišášu ǰaií* *apanéi daulát čháak* *ačaagé kamémei*
E. 6. this country-LOC/DAT go-CP he-ERG own property all bad-PL work-INEILL in

Sh. *çhaweégo.* 7. *ros har ǰéek çhawíite-ǰo* *phatú*
D. *xarč irín.* 7. *heyán har číis-ek zaayá irnásmo* *iċhuúna*
E. squander/spend-PRET-3SG 7. he-ERG every what/thing-SGL squandered/ruined making-ABL after

Sh. *eé kúyer* *ǰudá koóner wátu*
D. *háai mulkášu* *baḍí çhámaka*[8] *a(a)í*
E. this country-LOC/DAT very/big-f. famine-SGL come-PRET-3SG-m.f.

[6] Tikkanen *nóo* 'and'.

[7] Note difference in accent (Buddruss 1984: 17).

[8] Bur. *çham.*

Sh.	8.		*ro bodo*	*garíib búlu*	
D.	8. *e buút ašituuná* [9]	*yaaní*		*γaríib huyá*	
E.	8. he very become-weak-PRET	that-is	he very	poor become-PRET-3SG.	

Sh.	*tonée eé kúyei*	*ek manúẓeke-keč*		*gou.*
D.	*noó hei múlkei*	*ek bandáakis páa*	*e*	*gi(y)á.*
E.	then this country-GEN	a man-SGL near-to	he	went.

Sh.	9. *oó manúẓus*	*toóm khúuki čaroóikyei kóomer*	*ro*	*ṣeégu.*
D.	9. *hei bandán e*	*apanéi khúuka čaarinái kramás*		*lain.*
E.	9. this man-ERG him	own pig-PL graze-INF-GEN work-LOC/OBL	him	engage-PRET-3SG

Sh.	10. *keéi phoṭí khúkis kháanes*	*eéi phoṭí ros*	*khoóiky hawás*
D.	10. *kóone wáṭera*[10] *khúukee kháaŋ(y)e čheéka ta, eyán*	*eŋ*	*kháanai rai*
E.	10. which-PL pod-PL pig-ERG-PL eat-IPF-3PL PART he-ERG	these	eat-INF-GEN wish

Sh.	*thées*	*magám réseṭ*	*eéi ga*	*khoóiky neé déenes.*
D.	*irín*	*magám*	*eŋ kuli éšu*	*khaanášu ni déeŋ(y)e čhéeka.*
E.	do-IMPF/PRET-3SG	but he-DAT	they even.too at-least	him-DAT eat-INF-DAT not give-IPF-3PL

---

[9] *ašituuniná* 'to become weak'.

[10] Cf. Bur. *waṭhariŋ* (Berger 1998: 466). Greek *ek tōn keratíōn,* Vulgata *de siliquis* 'St. John's bread, carob'.

Sh.	11. *ané haalát*	*pašií réseṭ*	*hóoš áali*	*tonée*
D.	11. *háai haalát*	*dekhí ései*	*hóoš aayá*	*noó*
E.	11. this-f. situation	see-CP he-DAT/GEN	sense come-PRET-3SGf.m.	then

Sh.	*ros*	*guneégu*	*ki*	*'mei baábei aál kačáakak maristaní*
D.	*eyán*	*sambá irín*	*ta*	*meé bábei eét katéyek maristána*
E.	he-ERG	thinking make-PRET-3SG	that	my father-GEN-SG there how-many-SGL slave-NOM-PL

Sh.	*uníijenen!*	*ma nen*	*uyáno miríimus.*
D.	*pariḍoó ǰáaŋe če!*	*u tháa*	*bucháa maráa chíis.*
E.	be-nourished-PRES-3PL	I here	hungry die-PRES-1SG

Sh.	12. *ma*	*haṣphát*	*hun*	*beé*	*toóm baábe kač*
D.	12. *u hei čoq*		*hart*[11]	*huṭí*	*apanéi piís páa*
E.	12. I this manner	jumping	up	become-CP/rise-CP	own father-OBL near-to

Sh.	*búǰam*	*tonée réseṭ*	*ráam:*	13. *'ma xudáa ga tu*	*muc̣hoó*
D.	*ǰáas*	*noó éšu*	*munáas:*	13. *'u xudáa wo tus*	*minéeni*
E.	go-FUT-1Sg	then he-DAT	say-FUT-1SG:	13. I God and you-OBL	before/under

---

[11] Cf. Bur. *hart man-* 'to jump up'.

Sh.	*bódo gunaagáar bigás,*	*ma ané háaler nuš ki*	*thei puç*
D.	*buút gunaagáar huís,*	*u*	*teé puç*
E.	much sinner become-PRET-1SG	I this-f. position-LOC am-not that	your son

Sh.		*kalíǰam.*		
D.	*aṣáai haalatánaaná*		*ganinás*	*yoṣk náa.*
E.	that condition-INEILL	be-counted-FUT-1SG	count-INF-OBL	worthy not.

Sh.	14.	*ma*	*toóm maristanó*	*maǰaá*	*kalí!'*
D.	14.	*mas*	*teé maristanémei*		*gan!'*
E.	14.	I-OBL	your slave-INEILL	in	count-IPV

Sh.	15.	*aní moórye*	*akóoṣ*	*púç-se toóm*	*híier guneégu.*
D.	15.	*aṣeŋ čáγaaŋa*	*hei*	*puçán apanéi*	*yanaaná katín.*
E.	15.	this word.thing-PL	with-himself	that son-ERG own	heart-INFILL think-PRET-3SG

Sh.	16.	*axirkáar*		*toóm maále keč*	*uçháto.*
D.	16.		*ho pačí mušás*	*apanéi piís páa*	*diṣqaltá.*
E.	16.	at-last	then after at-the-end-OBL	own father-OBL near-to	arrive-PRET-3SG

Sh.	17.	*ro*	*duúr*	*wayoóiky pašií akí*
D.	17.		*dúurano íi heyéi piín puç apanés diri*	*aaná dekhí*
E.	17.	him	far-ELA PART his father-ERG son himself towards	come-INF see-CP PART

Sh.	*maálei*		*híier*	*ǰúuk*	*ačíti.*
D.		*ései*	*kunuwána*	*ǰúuka*	*pereeṭhí.*[12]
E.	father-GEN	his	heart-LOC interior-INEILL	compassion	enter-PRET-3SG-f.

Sh.	18. *maálo hun beé*	*puçéi*	*bóċeṭ* [13]		*gou,*
D.	18. *píya ċak*[14] *huṭí*	*puçéi*	*hot*	*giḍaanášu*	*gi(y)á,*
E.	18. father up become/get-up-CP	son-GEN	kiss-DAT hand	seek-INF-DAT	go-PRET-3SG

Sh.	*tonée*	*rése sā̃ ãti ṣaá*	*búlu.*	
D.	*noó*			*puçás baγúu*[15] *irín.*
E.	then	him with embracing	become-PRET-3SG	son-OBL embracing make.do-PRET-3SG

Sh.	19. *púç-se reégu:*	*'waá baábo,*	*ma xudáa ga tu muçhoó bódo gunaagáar bigánus tonée*
D.	19. *puçán munín:*	*waá bába,*	*u xudáa wo tus minéeni buút gunaagáar huí čhíis*
E.	19. son-ERG say-PRET-3SG	o father	I God and you-OBL before much sinner become-PF-1Sg then

---

[12] Inf. *pereešiná*.

[13] In this idiomatic expression 'to welcome a guest', Sh. has *bóċeṭ* 'for a kiss' with short *o*, otherwise *bóoċi*, DAT *bóoċyeṭ* 'kiss' with long *oo*. In D. a guest is honoured by 'seeking his hand' (to kiss it).

[14] *ċak* imitative interjection, cf. Bur. *ċak étas* 'to finish'.

[15] Bur. *baγú* 'double armful'.

Sh.		*ané háaler*	*ma*	*thei puç kalijoóiky*		*yáṣki nuš.*
D.	*heyásmo*	*aṣáai haalatánaaná*		*teé puç*	*apóon u ganinás*	*yoṣk náa.*
E.	this-ABL	this-f. condition-INEILL	I	your son be-counted-INF	myself I count	worthy am-not

Sh.	20. *maálus*	*ṣadaróṭ reégu:*	*búǰaa, míṣṭe-ǰo míṣṭe çhúile waleé*
D.	20. *piín apanéi*	*ṣádareču munín:*	*ǰóo, šoonásmo šoonée khaṭúa(a)re aaní*
E.	20. father-ERG own	servant-DAT-PL say-PRET-3SG:	go-IPV-PL good-ABL good clothes bring-CP

Sh.	*anéseṭ banareé*	21. *hagúyer*	*yáṣki barónuk*	*wiaráa*
D.	*aṣeyás luwaá,*	21. *agulís*	*yoṣk boróndok*	*iraá!*
E.	him-DAT/OBL put-on-CP/IPV-PL	21. finger-LOC/OBL-SG	precious ring-SGL	make-IPV-PL

Sh.	*tonée páawor*	*zaréi peizáare banaráa!*
D.		*sanéi kapšáaŋaare*[16] *luwaá!*
E.	then foot-LOC-PL	gold-GEN shoe-PL put-on-IPV-PL

Sh.	22. *dámši thíto bačhárak*	*waleé*	*haláal tháa!*	*to ho*	*bes khyeé*
D.	22. *dámši irá bačhárek*	*aaní*	*khaš irá!*	*ho*	*amé khaí*
E.	22. selected done-PTC calf-SGL	bring-CP	slaughter-IPV-PL	then	we-ERG eat-CP

[16] Bur. Pl ending *-aare* called by Tikkanen (2011: 211) 'limited/indefinite plural', Sg. Bur. *kafša* ← Persian.

Sh. *šuriyaár thóon,* *kye to* *mei anú puç múuwus,* *aš dugúnyo*
D. *šurayaár irám* *kǰe to* *meé aṣéi puç muyá čhááko,* *oče dubaará*
E. celebration do-FUT-1PL because my this son die-PLQ-3SG today again

Sh. *ǰíino búlun.›* 23. *anéše-ǰo phatú ris* *šuriyaár*
D. *ǰinuná čha.’* 23. *heyásmo pačí eŋ(y)ée* *šurayaár*
E. living become-PF-3SG become-alive-PERF-3SG 23. this-ABL after they celebration

Sh. *thoóiky ṣaáte.*
D. *irnái káaro lagé.*
E. do-INF-GEN for-the-sake-of begin-PRET-3PL

Sh. 24. *eé khéen* *anú mušáai* *baṛo puç-se çhéeçer* *kom thées.*
D. 24. *háai waqtána* *hei manišéi* *baḍá puçán çheeçána* *krom iréga čhááko.*
E. 24. this time-INEILL this man-GEN big son-ERG field-INEILL work do-IPF-3SG

Sh. 25. *goṭe-waary* *woyóoǰa* *šuriyaréi maṣáalek* *uthále boóiky*
D. 25. *garášu* *aanée-belek* *qhoši čhátaare*[17]
E. 25. house-towards house-DAT while-coming celebrating/rejoicing voices high.loud-PL become-INF

[17] *čhato, čhaataare* (cf. fn. 17) ‘voices, sounds’, plural of *čhot* (etymologically Gandhari *čhadda*; see Buddruss 1983: 5–19).

Sh. *parúdo.* 26. *ros* *ek* *ṣadáreket̤* *khóoǰan theégu*
D. *hai* *parudá.* 26. *eyán* *naukáriki poo*
E. he hear-PRET-3SG 26. he-ERG one servant-SGL-DAT/GEN from question do-PRET-3SG

Sh. *ki* *'ne* *jéek bílin?'*
D. *munaín:* *ki huyá čha?*
E. ask-PRET-3SG that this-f. what-SGL become-PERF-3SG-f.m.

Sh. 27. *ṣadár-se reégu:* *'thei* *ẓáa wátun* *tonée thei maálus*
D. 27. *maristanán munín:* *teé* *naṭhá* *biráaya aayá čha* *noó teé piín*
E. 27. servant/slave-ERG say-PRET-3SG your lost brother come-PF-3SG then your father-ERG

Sh. *dámši thitu bačhárak mareé* *khyeé pií* *šuriyaár* *théen.'*
D. *dámši irá bačhárek khaš iraí* *khaí piyí* *šurayaár* *iréŋye če.'*
E. select made calf-SGL kill-CP eat-CP drink-CP celebration do-PRES-3SG do-PRES-3PL

Sh. 28. *báṛo puç ané čága paruǰií róoṣ búlu* *toneé goṭéṭ buǰoóiky rak*
D. 28. *baḍá puç aṣéi čáɣaa paruǰí róoša huyá* *noó garášu ǰaanai rai*
E. 28. big son this story hear-CP angry become-PRET-3SG and house-DAT go-INF-GEN wish

Sh. *neé theégu.* 29. *maálus darú weií puç manačaroóiky lamiígu.*
D. *ni irín.* 29. *píya baár aí puç ismilaarinášu*[18] *lomín.*
E. not make-PRET-3SG 29. father-ERG/NOM out come-CP son appease-INF-DAT begin-PRET-3SG

Sh. 30. *báṛo púç-se reégu: 'çaké mas kačáakak bariṣo-ǰo*
D. 30. *baḍá puçán munín: 'ĩsil*[19] *u katéi barišásmo*
E. 30. big son-ERG say-PRET-3SG look-IMPV I-ERG how-much-SGL year-PL/SG-ABL

Sh. *thei kom-káar thámus,*
D. *teé kom iráa chíis,*
E. your work do-PRES-1SG

Sh. 31. *mágar tus ek čhak ga maṭ čháalak*
D. 31. *ek héešik kuli tu mášu eka čhaalíika kuli*
E. 31. but you-ERG one time-SGL at-least you day also I-DAT one kid-SGL at-least

Sh. *neé digáa ki mas toóm yáar-pháaṭo sấ ãti šuriyaár thámsik.*
D. *ni deníi táa ki u meé yáar-báaras kóoṭ šurayaár irásaka.*
E. not give-PRET-2SG that I-ERG my friends-OBL with celebration could-make-IRR.

[18] Bur. *d-smil-* (Berger 1998: 287).
[19] Bur. *-sal* (Berger 1998: 372).

Sh.	32.	*keé khéen*	*thei anú puç áalo to,*	*koós thei ẓap*
D.	32. *kabé*		*teé aṣéi puç*	*kónun teé daulát*
E.	32. when	which time	your this son come-PRET-3SG when	who-ERG property

Sh.	*koóinga*	*gaányo phatú*	*ç̣haweégun*	*tus*
D.	*čháak*	*gaániċ*	*xarč irín čháaka ta aayáaka*	
E.	somewhere	all prostitute-PL-OBL after	waste-PERF/spend-PLQ PART when-came	you-ERG

Sh.	*rései káari dámši thíto baċhárek máari theéga.'*
D.	*ései káaro damši irá baċháriki máari iríi.'*
E.	for his sake select calf-SGL-GEN offer.tribute make-PRET-2SG

Sh.	33. *maálus toóm puçéṭ reégu:*	*'waá puç çaké!*	*tu haméeš ma sã́ ãti*	*akí*
D.	33. *piín apanéi puçášu munín:*	*'bée púuç*[20]	*tu hamíiš mas kóoṭ*	
E.	33. father-ERG own son-DAT say-PRET-3SG	oh son-VOC look	you always me-OBL with	self-PART

Sh.	*hanú mei ẓap-daulát*	*háni-k*	*búṭi thei hin.*	35. *thei anú ẓáa*
D.	*čháai meé ẓap-daulát čháak*		*buṭí teé čhíi*	35. *teé aṣéi biráaya*
E.	be-PRES-2SG my property all	is-SGL	all your be-PRES-3SGf.	35. your this brother

[20] Vocative with long vowel.

Sh.	*kačáak mudát barišána*	*našií aš goṭéṭ áalun*	*gooyá múuwus*
D.	*katéi*	*naší oče garášu aayá čha*	*gooyá muyá čháaka,*
E.	how-much time year-INEILI	be-lost-CP today house-DAT	come-PF as-it-were die-PLQ-3SG

Sh.	*ǰíinu bulún*	
D.	*noó*	*ǰinuuná ċha (= ǰinoó giá čha)*
E.	then alive become-PF-3SG	become-alive-PF (alive has-gone)

Sh. *eé gye šuriyaár thoóiky yupóoṣ hain.*
D. *heyásmo šurayaár irná munaasíp čha.*
E. therefore-ABL celebration make-INF right.fitting be-3SGf./m.

3. Free Translation

1. A man had two sons. 2. The younger son said to his father: 3. 'Father, give me the part of your property that is coming (Ḍomaakí: has to come) to me!' 4. The father divided his property between his sons. 5. And many days had not passed, when the younger son, having gathered all his property, went to a far country. 6. Having gone to this country, he squandered all his property in bad works. 7. After he had squandered everything, a severe famine came to that country. 8. He became very weak, that is: he became very poor, and he went to a man of this country. 9. This man engaged him in the work of grazing his pigs. 10. He wished to eat the pods the pigs were eating, but even these they did not give him to eat. 11. Having seen this situation, he came to his senses and thought: How many slaves are nourished in my father's house! I am here dying of hunger. 12. I will jump up and go to my father and will say to him: 13. 'Before God and you, I became a sinner. I am not in a condition that I may be counted your son. 14. Count me among your slaves!' 15. These words the son thought in his heart. 16. Finally, after that, he arrived at his father's. 17. After he had seen from far his son coming towards him, compassion came into his father's heart. 18. The father rose and went to welcome his son and embraced him. 19. The son said: 'Father, I have become a sinner before God and you, and in this condition I am not worthy to be counted your son.' 20. The father said to his servants: 'Go, bring the very best clothes and put them on him. 21. Put a precious ring on his finger and shoes of gold on his feet.' 22. Bring a select calf and slaughter it. Then we will eat and celebrate, because this—my son—had died, but today he has become alive again.' 23. After this, they began to celebrate. 24. At this time this man's older son was working in the field. 25. While coming home, he heard the loud sounds of celebration (rejoicing). 26. He asked a servant: 'What has happened?' 27. The servant said: 'Your lost brother has come and your father has killed a select calf. They ate and drank and are celebrating.' 28. The older son, having heard this story, became angry and did not want to go into the house. 29. The father, having come out, began to appease the son. 30. The older son said: 'Look, for how many years I work for you. 31. But not even one day you have given me at least a kid that I might celebrate with my friends. 32. When this son came, who has wasted your property with harlots, you paid him the tribute of a select calf.' 33. The father

said to his son: 'My son, look, you are always with me. 34. All that is mine is yours. 35. Your brother had been lost for many years, but today he came home. He had died as it were and has become alive. 36. Therefore it is fitting to celebrate.'

ABBREVIATIONS

ABL = ablative
Bur. = Burushaski
CP = conjunctive participle
DAT = dative
D. = Ḍomaakí
E. = English
ELA = elative
ERG = ergative
f./F = feminine
FUT = future
GEN = genitive
INEILL = inessive–illative
INF = infinitive
IPF = imperfect
IPV = imperative
IRR = irrealis
LOC = locative
m. = masculine
NOM = nominative
OBL = oblique
PART = particle
PF = perfect
PL = plural
PLQ = pluperfect
PRES = present
PRET = preterite
PTC = participle
SG = singular
SGL = marked singular, indefinite
Sh. = Shina
VOC = vocative

REFERENCES

Bailey, T. Grahame. 1924. *Grammar of the Shina (Ṣiṇā) Language*. London: Royal Asiatic Society.

Berger, Hermann. 1998. *Die Burushaski-Sprache von Hunza und Nager. III: Wörterbuch*. Wiesbaden: Harrassowitz.

Buddruss, Georg. 1984. 'Ḍomaakí-Nachträge zum Atlas der Dardsprachen'. *Münchener Studien zur Sprachwissenschaft* 43: 9–24.

_______ 1983. 'Ḍomaaki čhot "Ton", mit Beiträgen zur historischen Lautlehre'. *Münchener Studien zur Sprachwissenschaft* 42: 5–21.

_______ and Degener, Almuth. 2012. *The Meeting Place: Radio Features in the Shina Language of Gilgit by Mohammad Amin Zia*. Wiesbaden: Harrassowitz.

Degener, Almuth. 2008. *Shina-Texte aus Gilgit (Nord-Pakistan)*. Wiesbaden: Harrassowitz.

Grierson, George A. (ed.). 1927. *Introductory* (Linguistic survey of India, vol. 1, part 1). Calcutta: Superintendent of Government Printing, India.

——— (ed.). 1919. *Specimens of the Dardic or Piśāchā Languages (Including Kāshmīrī)* (Linguistic survey of India, vol. 8, part 2). Calcutta: Superintendent of Government Printing, India.

Lorimer, David L. R. 1939. *The Ḍumāki Language*. Nijmegen: Dekker & van de Vegt.

Radloff, Carla F. 1999. *Aspects of the Sound System of Gilgiti Shina*. (Studies in Languages of Northern Pakistan, Vol. 4). Islamabad: National Institute of Pakistan Studies and Summer Institute of Linguistics.

——— 1992. 'The dialects of Shina'. In *Sociolinguistic Survey of Northern Pakistan, Vol. 2: Northern Areas*, edited by Peter C. Backstrom and Carla F. Radloff. 100–203. Islamabad: National Institute of Pakistan Studies and Summer Institute of Linguistics.

Tikkanen, Bertil. 2011. 'Domaki Noun Inflection and Case Syntax'. In *Pūrvāparaprajñābhinandanam: East and West, Past and Present (Indological and Other Essays in Honour of Klaus Karttunen)*, edited by Bertil Tikkanen and Albion M. Butters. 205–28. Helsinki: Finnish Oriental Society.

Weinreich, Matthias. 2011. 'Domaaki jazyk'. In *Jazyki mira: novye indoarijskie jazyki* [Russian: The Domaaki Language, Languages of the World: New Indo-Aryan Languages], edited by Tatiana I. Oranskaia, Yulia V. Mazurova, Andrej A. Kibrik, Leonid I. Kulikov, and Aleksandr Y. Rusakov. 166–94. Moscow: Academia.

——— 2008. 'Two Varieties of Ḍomaakí'. *Zeitschrift der Deutschen Morgenländischen Gesellschaft* 158: 299–316.

——— 1999. 'Der Ḍomaakí-Dialekt von Nager'. *Studien zur Indologie und Iranistik* 22: 203–14.

Yoshioka, Noburu. 2006. '[Japanese: A linguistic outline and phonological sketch of Domaaki]'. In *Corpus Analysis and Linguistic Theory in Linguistic Studies*, edited by Y. Tsuruga, T. Miyake, Y. Kawaguchi, and T. Takagaki (Working Papers in Linguistic Informatics 11). 327–56. Tokyo: Tokyo University of Foreign Studies.

Zia, Mohammad Amin. 2010. *Ṣinaá-Urdu luγat*. Gilgit.

7

Shina Poems of Mourning

Almuth Degener

1. INTRODUCTION

1.1 HISTORICAL BACKGROUND[1]

The background of the poems of mourning is a historical event of over 1,300 years ago in a small place situated in present day Iraq. After the death of his elder brother in 670 and the death of the caliph Mu'āwiya in April 680, Ḥusayn, son of 'Alī and grandson of the Prophet Muḥammad (PBUH), set off from Madinah in autumn 680 with a small group of supporters to put forward his claim for succession to the caliphate which, according to Shia interpretation, had been usurped by the Umayyads. Prevented from getting to Kufa, where he had expected to be supported by the inhabitants amongst whom 'Alī and his descendants enjoyed great popularity, he was obliged to set up camp at the desert spot of Karbalā. In order to force Ḥusayn to give in and pledge allegiance to the Umayyad ruler Yazīd ibn Mu'āwiya, access to the River Euphrates was cut off by the enemy troops. As a result, Ḥusayn's small party, among them women and children, spent several days without water. On 10 Muḥarram in 61 AH/680 CE, Ḥusayn, after asking his followers to leave because there was no chance of survival, prepared for the final battle. The desperate

1 For transcription of Arabic names in the English text and the Persian titles, the Library of Congress system has been used <http://www.loc.gov/catdir/cpso/romanization/persian.pdf> with a slight modification concerning the final -h: *nawḥa, sīna* instead of *nawḥah, sīnah*. Transcription of Shina follows the same system as in Buddruss and Degener (2012). Alternative readings or pronunciations noted by G. Buddruss are given in parentheses ( ). Angled brackets < > surround a part that is missing in the text and needs to be emended.

fight against the superior forces of the Umayyads ended with himself and all his followers being killed. Among the victims were his son 'Alī Akbar, his nephew Qāsim, his half-brother al-'Abbās, and the baby 'Alī Aṣghar. The martyrs' heads were cut off, perched on spears, and taken to the Umayyad capital Damascus. The survivors, women, children, and 'Alī Zayn al-'Ābidīn, who had been prevented from fighting due to sickness, were taken prisoner and sent to Damascus. The tragedy of Karbalā is the central narrative of Shia identity. The annual highlight of mourning the Karbalā martyrs is in the month of Muḥarram, with its climax on the tenth day, the day of 'Āshūrā. In fact, the importance of Karbalā lies not so much in the historical events, but in the meaning they have had for Shia collective memory,[2] and it is not limited to a particular time period. As a much quoted saying states: *kullu yaumin 'āšūrā, kullu 'arḍin karbalā* 'Every day is 'Āshūrā, every place is Karbalā'.

1.2 Source

In 1980, G. Buddruss spent some time in Gilgit to collect material about the beginnings of Shina as a literary language. It was in the context of this research that he was given a tattered copy of a collection of poems. The cover and front page of the book were missing, but Buddruss was told that the author was Ākhund Mihrbān (1892–1957), a fairly wealthy man who enjoyed considerable social prestige. Working as an *ākhund* 'cleric' for the community, he had also run a private school where Islamic subjects, among them Islamic mysticism, were taught. The school was in existence in 1980, and the students would still memorize and recite Ākhund Mihrbān's poetry. The booklet Buddruss was given contained Ākhund Mihrbān's collected poems, published on the initiative of his sons (Mihrbān 1963). For the purpose of writing his Shina poems, Ākhund Mihrbān had invented a system to transcribe Shina in a modified form of the Urdu script.[3] M. Amin Zia helped Buddruss to prepare a transcription and rough translation of the poems which he kindly let me use for the sake of this paper.

---

[2] On the significance of the Karbalā narrative in South Asia, see Hyder (2006).

[3] On attempts to write the Shina language, see Buddruss (1983: 235–6), where Ākhund Mihrbān's *Guldasta-i Mihrbān* is mentioned.

1.3 Genre

Typical Karbalā related literary genres are *marsiya, soz, salām*, and *nawḥa*, all of them calling to mind the Karbalā tragedy and performed to stipulate, express, and formalize both the lectors' and the audience's emotions which are expressed by speaking about the events that took place at Karbalā whilst weeping, sobbing, and performing *mātam* i.e. beating their chest with their hands. The poems published in this paper present a variety of Karbalā poetry composed for the Shina speaking Shia community of Gilgit. The Karbalā poems published in the *Guldasta-i Mihrbān* were referred to as *marsiya*. In a wider sense they belong to the *marsiya* genre, elegies of usually considerable length and often written in an elaborate style, which may be performed in full length but of which only shorter passages are often recited in a *majlis* 'commemorative assembly' (Bard 2000: 326). In a narrower sense, however, they are of the *nawḥa* type, 'a dirge or threnody that can have various poetical structures, recited in tune. Nauhas can be recited solo or in a chorus. However, unlike other genres, they are usually accompanied by rhythmic chest beating (*mātam* or *sīna zanī*), another sign of mourning' (Hyder 2006: 45–6). The *nawḥa* genre is commonly performed in regional languages in Pakistan.[4] The recitation of a *nawḥa* with the appropriate tunes, intonation, rhythm, and pathos is an art highly valued among Shias. Of the seven Shina poems, nos. 3, 6, and 7 are explicitly called *nawḥa*, while nos. 4 and 5 are said to be a *xaṭāb* 'speech, preaching', and there is no explicit mention of the genre of nos. 1 and 2. Another classificatory denomination with respect to genre is the title of no. 3 *nawḥa-i sīna-zanī-yi zabān-i ḥāl-i janāb-i Zaynab. zabān-i ḥāl* constitutes a type of poetry describing the emotional state of the speaker in the face of a particular situation. Although the word appears only in no. 3, the other poems are not much different in content. What distinguishes no. 3 is its form with a third person frame for Zaynab's speech. This, however, is not due to its belonging to the *zabān-i ḥāl* type, which is defined semantically.

Out of the twelve poems of G. Buddruss' collection, seven represent the words of one of the women of Karbalā. Thus they claim to be

[4] Abbas (2005: 160, fn. 26) 'In Pakistan, *nowhehs* are sung in languages such as Pashto, Balti, Sindhi, Siraiki, Baluchi, and regional dialects according to the speech communities.' For Balti, cf. Söhnen-Thieme (2007).

women's expressions of grief, although the poet is of course a man. Some women do write *marsiyas* (and related literature) themselves.[5] It is not known whether there are any women writers in the *marsiya* or *nawḥa* genre in the Shina language but given the fact that composing poetry in Shina is far less widespread than in Urdu, it seems rather unlikely.

Karbalā elegies are easy to find on YouTube and in social networks nowadays, and beside a considerable number of Burushaski *nawḥas*, a few may be found in Shina[6] which give an impression of a contemporary performance. The scope of this paper, however, is determined by its only available source, G. Buddruss' transliteration.

1.4 Female roles

The women who act as speakers of the *nawḥa* poems are Zaynab (Ḥusayn's sister), his wives Laylā and Rubāb, and his daughter Sakīna. Ḥusayn's wives, following the common South Asian Muslim code of conduct, do not address their husband directly neither do they speak about him or their emotions towards him. The subject of their dirges is their child. In Laylā's case this is her son 'Alī Akbar, whom she had wished to see as a bridegroom and a protector of her old age rather than being killed in battle. The historical Laylā may actually not have been alive when her husband and son were killed. The essential point about the *nawḥa* is not the historical truth but the possibility it offers the participants of the performance to identify themselves with the mother bewailing her dead son. This is encouraged by the form of most of the poems which, with a first person speaker and the present tense, make the performer as well as the audience feel they are directly involved in the Karbalā events. Rubāb's son is 'Ali 'Asghar who was only a few months old when he was killed. Rubāb recalls the baby's suffering, and expresses her own grief which is due to her role as a mother: she cannot give him milk due to her dried-out breasts, and she has to leave him unburied because she is deported with the other female prisoners.

---

[5] See Bard (2000).

[6] E.g. <http://www.youtube.com/watch?v=E81d5ONcMno>

Zaynab, one of the most important characters of the Karbalā narrative, is the speaker of nos. 1, 3, 4, and 6. She is the sister of Ḥusayn to whom nos. 3 and 4 are addressed, and the half-sister of 'Abbās to whom no. 6 is addressed. In no. 6, Zaynab's emotions are expressed only indirectly. The speaker's personality fades into the background; instead she mentions several other members of the family who are in some way or other affected by 'Abbās' death (Ḥusayn, Sakīna, 'Alī Akbar, and 'Alī 'Asghar). Her relationship towards Ḥusayn, on the other hand, is that of an affectionate (no. 1 *Huséen-e naazaníin* 'delicate/beloved Ḥusayn') and consoling companion (no. 3 'Not befitting you is a place in blood; get up and sit in (your) sister Zaynab's lap'), who suffers from his deplorable state as a headless corpse left uncovered on the battleground. In no. 1 she implores her father, Imam 'Alī (as a quasi-divine character transcending time and space—in fact he is long dead) to bury Ḥusayn. Here as elsewhere Zaynab's suffering is caused less by physical pain than by the hard fate of her relatives and by the degrading treatment suffered by the hands of the enemies. Above all, the fact that the women were stripped of their veils when they were brought to Damascus is felt to be deeply disgraceful. This is a topic in no. 3 ('Until today my camel-litter (was) hidden, (now) I go about bareheaded, a female slave of Syria'), no. 4 ('to walk together with the prisoners, bareheaded, shall be my share'), and most dramatically in no. 1 which is addressed to her mother, Fāṭima al-Zahrā ('They took me ... to the court of Yazid, while I was without a veil; seek ..., an old sheet, I will cover my hair in front of the infidels!'). The rough treatment of women and children is a consequence of the martyrdom of the male members of the family, for, as the poet states in no. 3, 'a brotherless sister is considered as contemptible', because she has nobody to protect her from unseemly behaviour. So Zaynab's role as a sister includes that she is in need of her brother's protection. Male and female roles are neatly divided up in no. 4: to be deprived of her veil, to be deported as prisoner, and to be unable to help the orphans is Zaynab's part of the suffering; to be killed and have his head paraded on a spear (all the while reciting the Qur'ān) is Ḥusayn's part. This gender role division with a remarkable parallelism of brother's and sister's roles can also be observed in no. 1 where Ḥusayn's being without a shroud is reported to Zaynab's father, while Zaynab's being without a veil is reported to her mother.

At the same time the division serves to stress Zaynab's importance as a direct counterpart of her brother and thus almost equivalent to the king of martyrs, Imam Ḥusayn.

No. 5 is spoken by Ḥusayn's daughter Sakīna who is often the topic of Karbalā literature, represented as a young girl who was very dear to her father. Like Zaynab in no. 6, Sakīna does not lament her own suffering but is concerned about the male members of the family. As for her father, the role she assigns to herself is to take care of the corpse and prepare it for burial, the burial itself would have been a male task. When she speaks about the prisoners, it is her brother Zayn al-ʿĀbidīn, the only male adult who is taken to Damascus, whose ill treatment she laments.

1.5 Form and Style

The length of the poems varies from 14 to 22 lines, organized into stanzas based on either a tristich or a distich division. The poems divided into units of three lines all have a refrain, while those divided into units of two do not. Semantically, there is a structure of 3 or 6 lines noticeable in two of the couplet type poems.

a) units of 3 lines:

No. 2: four units of 3 lines, rhyming aaa, bbb, ccc, ddd, eee, each followed by the refrain;

No. 5: units of 3 lines, rhyming aaa, bbb, etc., the refrain following after semantically coherent groups of 3, 6, 3, 3 lines;

No. 6: five units of 3 lines (aaa, bbb, etc.), each followed by the refrain.

b) couplets:

No 1: three semantic units of 6 lines each, defined as couplets by the rhyme scheme aa, bb, cc in units 2 and 3, but not unit 1, spoken by Zaynab, followed by 4 lines spoken by Mihrbān, with a different rhyme scheme abba;

No. 7: four semantic units of three verses each, with the rhyme scheme of a ghazal (aa, ba, ca, da, etc.);

No. 3: seven couplets, 1, 4, and 7 spoken by the poet, and 2, 3, 5, 6 of approximately the same rhyme (aa aa, bb bb) in 2/3 and 5/6;

No. 4: ten couplets, all except the first with the same rhyme (aa, bb, bb, bb, etc.).

As for rhyme, there seems to be considerable freedom in its use. In No. 1, while in stanzas 2 and 3 the rhyme scheme is aa, bb, cc, the first stanza shows the endings *dáaseṭ* - *bubáaṭe* - *áinaṭ* - *Huséenaa* - *kafán the* - *dáfan the* where a rhyme is impossible to make out in the first two couplets. No. 2 rhymes *ban* – *kafán* – *dubám*, no. 5 *darám* – *walám* – *tharám*. In nos. 3 and 5, the rhyme seems to suggest that no difference is made between *-ei/ -ee, -ei/ -i*, short and long vowels: no. 5 *the* – *thareé* – *thareé, ṭak tharéi* - *ṣak tharéi* - *ṣak thareé*; no. 3 *mei* - *bádi* – *Alíi* – *Alíi.* No. 6, while otherwise having the rhyme scheme aaa, bbb, has *Huséin* - *ṣiṣoón* - *pawoón* in the second stanza. If *ein/ oon* are here accepted as rhyming, then *-e/aa* could be imagined to be likewise equal in the context of rhyming, accordingly the rhyme scheme in no. 3 *máse* - *súmeǰaa* - *léeleǰaa* - *sayéi* might actually not be a b b a, but a a a a, and there is no irregularity in *thigáa* – *thigáa* – *bigyé* in the first stanza of no. 5.

The poems use word endings which are uncommon in spoken Shina. In the locative (singular) we often find *-ru* for common *-r* and *-ǰaa* for *-ǰa*, e.g. *Karbaláaru, qatlgáaru, múunyeru, tanúureru*, and *nušéǰaa, náašeǰaa, súmeǰaa, léeleǰaa, niizáǰaa*. In the dative, likewise, common *-ṭ* is often replaced by *-ṭe*, e.g. *bubáaṭe, Madiináaṭe, Mustafáaṭe, birgyeéṭe/birgaáṭe*. This ending is also preserved in common Gilgiti Shina *ǰáaṭe* 'where(to)', formally a dative of *ǰáa* 'where'. In no. 1 there is an accusative *Huséenaa* instead of *Huséen*, in no. 3 the ergative of the personal pronoun *máse* for common *mas*, in no. 6 the optative *bóot* appears as *bóotaa*. The extended endings seem to be used for metrical reasons. In no. 6, for example, the use of *bóotaa* and *qatlgáaru* (pronounced *qatalgaaru*) leads to an equal length of 11 syllables throughout the poem (except the refrain which has 15 syllables and *Alíi Asɣarér táliṣ léeler ṣak bugú* 12 syllables). Apparently no line with more syllables than usual in a particular poem has an extended form. But then why did the poet not use the extended form *ṹũṭeǰáa* in no. 5 *páaye bẽ́ ye nán ṹũṭeǰ ṭak thareé* to make it 11 syllables as the other lines of this stanza? While Shina prosody seems to be based on qualitative rather than quantitative metre, for a valid statement it would be necessary to analyse the poems with their corresponding tunes when they are actually performed.

The 11 syllable line, with variants of 10 to 12 syllables, is common. It is found in nos. 1, 2, 5, and 6. No. 7 uses verse units of 9 to 11 syllables in the first hemistich and 10 in the second. Another fairly common pattern, used for the refrains of nos. 2, 5, and 6, is the 15 syllable line, with a caesura after 8 syllables.

All poems are composed with a first person speaker. In one case (no. 3) the poet introduces the speaker in third person before she starts with her own words from the second verse. The same poem contains two other verses, one in the middle and one at the end, which are apparently spoken by the poet himself. The last verse of no. 1 also seems to be spoken by the poet. All the other poems are in first person throughout, even when the subject shifts from the characters of Karbalā to the poet himself. His name, Mihrbān, is mentioned in five poems, in order to invoke the blessing and intercession of the Ahl-e Bayt (the family of the Prophet [PBUH]).

The language of some of the poems is highly Persianized, in particular nos. 1 and 4 where the Persian Izafa construction is extensively used in epithets of the Karbalā characters: no. 1) *Huséen-e naazaníin* 'beloved Husayn', *šáah-e mardáan* 'king of men', *núur-e áinaṭ* 'light of (my) eye', *fíkr-e kafán* 'thought of a shroud'; no. 4) *e šah-e tišná-ǰigár zīná-e šams u qamár* 'Oh king of thirsty liver, ladder to Sun and Moon', *šéer-e xudáa-e laxt-e ǰigár* 'Lion of God, piece of (my) liver', *Abbáas-e ǰawáan* 'young 'Abbās'; no. 3) *núur-e ain* 'light of (my) eye', *áal-e nabíi* 'family of the Prophet' (PBUH). No. 1 uses the Persian prepositional phrase *az qóom-e kaafár* 'from the tribe of infidels', and no. 4 uses the Persian conjunction *u/o* (common also in Urdu) in *sidr o kafúur u kafán* '*sidr*, camphor, and shroud'. The speaker of nos. 1, 3, and 4 is Zaynab who is famous for her eloquence. However, this may not be the reason why these poems use more Persian elements than the others, for Zaynab is also the speaker of no. 6. All poems, except for nos. 1 and 2, have a title that is purely Persian.

2. MOURNING POEMS

2.1 ZAYNAB ADDRESSES HER PARENTS AND HER GRANDFATHER

The first three stanzas are understood to be spoken by Zaynab, the daughter of ‘Alī and Fāṭima, the granddaughter of Prophet Muḥammad (PBUH). She sends the ‘wind of sighs’ from Karbalā to her father (stanza 1), her mother (stanza 2), and her grandfather (stanza 3). The fourth stanza is an invocation by the poet asking Imam ‘Alī to intercede on his behalf. In fact, Zaynab's parents and grandfather all died years before the events of Karbalā happened. To include them in Karbalā poems is common, suggesting that the members of the Prophet's (PBUH) family (Ahl-e Bayt) are not subject to the constraints of time and space.

1. *khabár har hḗ ẽṣei ṍõši Naǰáf*
dáaseṭ khabár de šáah-e mardáan
mei bubáaṭe adée ra ‘Karbaláaru
núur-e áinaṭ pareégyen bee-kafán
tanháa Huséenaa wála waá ǰiíl
bubáa, fíkr-e kafán the! waá
Huséen-e naazaníin húun the,
dáfan the!’

1. Take, O wind of sighs, to the
desert of Najaf[7] the message, give
the message to the king of men,
to my father. Say thus: ‘In Karbalā
they slew the light of (my) eyes,
without a shroud, alone, Ḥusayn.
O, (my) life, father, take care of a
shroud!
O lift up the beloved Ḥusayn,
bury him!’

2. *khabár har hḗ ẽṣei ṍõši Baaqíi*
dáaseṭ khabár de mei zizí Zahráa,
yatíimeṭ ‘“hariígye thei çaloó
Zainváb raróoža waá Yazíidei
maǰliséṭ bulqá nušéeǰaa uḍoór the
ǰiíl zizí ek próoni čadár sátar tham
toóm ǰakúr az qóom-e kaafár.’

2. Take the message, O wind of
sighs, to the desert of Baqī‘,[8] give
the message to my mother Zahrā,
to the orphan: ‘They took (me),
your lamp Zaynab, while they
made (me) cry, oh, to the court of
Yazīd, while I was without a veil.
Seek, (O) my life, (O) mother, an
old sheet, I will cover my hair in
front of the infidels.’

---

[7] Imam ‘Alī was buried in Najaf, where the shrine erected over his tomb is one of the most important places of pilgrimage for Shia Muslims.

[8] *Jannat al-baqī‘*, a cemetery at Madinah where several relatives of the Prophet (PBUH) are buried, among them Fāṭima al-Zahrā, although the exact location of her grave is unknown.

3. *khabár har hẽ́ẽṣei ṍõši Madiináaṭe khabár de mei ṣiṣéi táaǰ Mustafáaṭe. 'ç̣aké, waá ǰiíl bapó, tus Karbaláaru pareégyen nauǰawáan qatlgáaru hariígye thei ǰamáat nana-paá lúṭe theé Yazíidei maǰliséṭ Šáamei báde theé.'*

3. Take the message, O wind of sighs, to Madinah, give the message to the crown of my head, to Muṣṭafā:[9] 'Look, you, O (my) life, (my) grandfather, in Karbalā they slew the youth in the place of martyrdom.[10] They took your wives,[11] having made (them) barefoot, bareheaded, to the court of Yazīd, having made (them) prisoners of Syria.'

4. *búǰaa ǰukaáṭe hẽ́ ẽṣe Karbaláa-waar buyát tháa mei imáameṭ ċhos xudáa kaary 'miroóikyer mei ṣiṣoón wa toóm xudáa kaary ç̣aké tus, ǰiíl palám mas toóm xudáa-waar.'*

4. Go, painful sighs, towards Karbalā!
Beseech my imam, for the sake of God:
'Come, while (I) die, to my bedside, for the sake of your God! Look, I will commit (my) life to my God.'

2.2 Laylā mourns her son 'Alī Akbar[12]

The speaker is Laylā who is the mother of Ḥusayn's son 'Alī Akbar; her name is explicitly mentioned in a variant of stanza 2. According to tradition he was a beautiful young man closely resembling the Prophet (PBUH). In Shia iconography he is usually represented as a beardless youth. He is said to have asked his father's permission to go into battle and to have been the first of the Hashimite clan to be killed. The Persian loanword *ǰawáan* 'youth' of the refrain also has the connotation 'warrior'. The poem stresses 'Alī Akbar's youth, and

---

[9] Muṣṭafā 'the chosen one' is commonly used for the Prophet Muḥammad (PBUH).

[10] *Qatlgáah* 'place of execution' has been translated as 'place of martyrdom', in accordance with the Shia interpretation and the context.

[11] The poet refers not to the Prophet's (PBUH) wives but those of his descendants and their companions who were present at Karbalā.

[12] Guldasta-i Mihrbān: S. 11.

his role as a son who had been expected to support his mother. When Ḥusayn set out from Madinah to fight against the Umayyad ruler, there was a rumour that he was leaving the town to arrange the marriage of his son ‘Alī Akbar. This is the tradition alluded to in the words of his mother who stresses that he should be covered with bridal clothes instead of a shroud.

1. *Alíi Akbár dušmanóo birgyeéṭe gáa zizí názur, ma ph at theé tu ǰáaṭe gáa? ac̣híiyei c̣aloó, traŋ ǰilé-ǰo sā̃́ ãty gáa*	1. ‘Alī Akbar, you went into battle against the enemies (of Islam). (May I, your) mother (be an) offering (to you). Where did you go, leaving me? Light of (my) eye, you went away with half my life.
Ali Akbár, ǰawáan asóo, mei ǰiléi aaráam asóo	‘Alī Akbar, you were a youth, you were the comfort of my life.
2. *Ali Akbár, čhuút beé bo, mei ǰiíl bodoó zizí wátin,*[13] *ḍuúŋa beéi, ac̣híiyei c̣aloó zizís tharám Ali Akbár hilalóo*	2. ‘Alī Akbar, go slowly, (may) my life be a sacrifice (for you)! (Your) mother has come, stay a short while, light of (my) eye! I, (your) mother, shall make ‘Alī Akbar a bridegroom.
Ali Akbár, ǰawáan asóo, mei ǰiléi aaráam asóo	‘Ali Akbar, you were a youth, you were the comfort of my life.
3. *Ali Akbár, hilaléeke c̣híile ban! yáṣki nuš nuú yar theé banoóiky kafán. zizí qurbáan ané γam timoóiky dubám.*[14]	3. ‘Alī Akbar, put on (your) bridal clothes! Surely it is not proper to put on the shroud early. (May I, your) mother, (be a) sacrifice (for you). I shall not be able to bear this grief![15]

---

[13] Var.: *Lailá wátis* ‘I, Laylā, have come.’

[14] Var.: *xudáayaa mas ne ǰūk tiimoóiky dubám.*

[15] Var.: O God, I shall not be able to bear this pain!

Ali Akbár, ǰawáan asóo, mei ǰiléi aaráam asóo.	'Alī Akbar, you were a youth, you were the comfort of my life.
4. *Ali Akbár ráatyeṭ aaráam neé thigís 'báṛo beé zizíiyeṭ madád dei' thigís aš Ali Akbar nayií beekás bigís*	4. 'Alī Akbar, I did not rest at night 'After he has grown up, he will be a help to (his) mother,' I said. Today, after having lost 'Alī Akbar, I have become destitute.
Ali Akbár, ǰawáan asóo, mei ǰiléi aaráam asóo	'Alī Akbar, you were a youth, you were the comfort of my life.

2.3 Zaynab Mourns over the Corpse of Her Brother Ḥusayn[16]

Zaynab is introduced in the third person in verse 1. Verses 2–8 are Zaynab's own words, apparently uttered at the side of the dead body of her brother, Imam Ḥusayn. After deploring his sad state, lying unburied in the desert, she points out that the loss of a protecting brother has made her helpless in face of the disgrace suffered from the enemies.

nawḥa-i sīna-zanī-yi zabān-i ḥāl-i janāb-i Zaynab	*nawḥa (accompanying) breast beating (as) an expression of the state of Lady Zaynab*
1. *wáti sa ẓawéi náašeǰaa tíri weéi hat khalíini Zainád-se*	1. The sister approached (her) brother's corpse. Having circumambulated him, Zaynab swings around (her) hands.[17]

[16] Guldasta-i Mihrbān: 23–4.

[17] Swinging around the hands in a circle is a typical greeting used exclusively by women. This gesture has to be distinguished from the raised hands which are often shown in religious paintings showing the Karbalā events to signify grief and despair.

2. *'ǰéek pašiígis ǰiíl ẓáa aš máse (= mas)* *paášamis léel ga súmeǰaa (= súmeǰ)*	2. 'What did I see today, (my) life, (my) brother? I see (you) in blood and dust.
3. *'yáṣki nuš thei diš léeleǰaa* *hun beé beéi múunyeru Zaináb sayéi*	3. 'Not befitting you is a place in blood. Get up and sit in (your) sister Zaynab's lap!
4. *'hai hai muškíl dunyáater* *ẓáa nuš sa hain x(w)aar-nazár*	4. 'Alas! (how) difficult (it is) in the world: a brotherless sister is considered as contemptible.
5. *'ǰap asoósaŋe (?) zampáan mei* *búǰamis lúṭi beé Šáamei bádi*	5. 'Until today my camel-litter (was) hidden (now) I go about bareheaded, a female slave of Syria.
6. *'ǰáaṭe gau thei ẓáa Abáas Alíi* *nuš ṣiṣoón núur-e ain Akbar Alíi*	6. 'Where did your brother 'Abbās 'Alī[18] go? The light of (your) eyes, (your son) Akbar 'Alī,[19] is not at your bedside.
7. *'hai hai afsóos dunyáater* *maǰlisér lúṭe waleégye áal-e nabíi!'*	7. 'Ah! Woe (is me)! in the world. Bareheaded they took the Family of the Prophet (PBUH) to the meeting!'

2.4 Zaynab addresses her brother Ḥusayn[20]

This poem is composed as an address of Zaynab to her brother, Imam Ḥusayn. The structure of this poem is a division of a female vs a male share of the suffering of Karbalā throughout. The events referred to

[18] On 'Abbās ibn 'Alī, see no. 6.

[19] On 'Alī Akbar, see no. 2.

[20] Guldasta-i Mihrbān: 17–19.

are the killings of Karbalā, the prisoners' transport to Damascus, and the treatment of the dead heroes' corpses by the enemies. The poem ends with an invocation to intercede on behalf of the poet, again with a male/female division.

khaṭāb-i janāb-i Zaynab bā birādar	*Lady Zaynab's address to her brother*
1. *e šah-e tišná-ǰigár zīná-e šams u qamár* *ẓáa ga sas ɣam samaróon šéer-e xudáa-e laxt-e ǰigár*	1. Oh king of thirsty liver,[21] ladder[22] to Sun and Moon, as brother and sister we'll divide up (our) grief, O Lion of God,[23] piece of (my) liver!
2. *šuh(a)dáa thei hissá bóot, báde hanék mei hissá bóot* *qatlgáah thei hissá bóot, Šáamei safár mei hissá bóot*	2. The martyrs shall be your share—those who are prisoners, shall be my share. The place of martyrdom shall be your share, the journey to Syria shall be my share.
3. *sidr o kafúur u kafán, ɣusl o dafán thei hissá bóot,* *yatíimis ã́ã́ ṣe birií róoǰa yayoóiky mei hissá bóot*	3. *Sidr*, camphor, and shroud, corpse-laving and burial shall be your share, the orphans walking, while they weep, shedding tears, shall be my share.

21 The Persian compound *tišna-jigar* 'thirsty-livered' would normally be understood metaphorically as 'longing, full of desire' (Lughat'nāma-i Dihkhudā, <http://www.loghatnaameh.org> accessed 8 October 2013). Here, however, it alludes to the thirst suffered by Ḥusayn and his followers in the desert of Karbalā.

22 The exact meaning of 'ladder of Sun and Moon' is obscure. Perhaps *zīnat* 'ornament' instead of *zīna* 'ladder'?

23 *šer-i khudā* is usually used as an epithet of 'Alī rather than Ḥusayn.

4. *Qaasim o Akbar o Abbáas-e ǰawáan thei hissá bóot,* *Úmm-e Kulsúum ga Šuhrbáan ga Rubáab mei hissá bóot*	4. 'Qāsim, Akbar, and young 'Abbās shall be your share, Umm Kulsum,[24] Shuhrbān (Shahrbānu),[25] and Rubāb[26] shall be my share.
5. *Xulíiei tanúureru dáaleǰ saroóiky thei hissá bóot,* *yatíimis babáa thóoǰa nir neé waloóiky mei hissá bóot.*	5. To put (your head) to sleep on ashes in Khuli's oven[27] shall be your share, while the orphans call out 'Father!', not to give sleep to them, shall be my share.
6. *Xulíiei niizáǰaa*[28] *suurá rayoóiky thei hissá bóot,* *ṣiṣéru doón nušéǰaa*[29] *ā̃ā́ ṣe biroóiky mei hissá bóot.*	6. On Khuli's spear to recite a surah[30] shall be your share, to shed tears on (= about?) the absence of a headscarf shall be my share.

[24] Umm Kulsūm was the child of 'Alī and Fāṭima, and Zaynab's as well as Ḥusayn's sister.

[25] Shahrbānū was Imam Ḥusayn's wife, of Iranian origin. She was the mother of 'Alī Zayn al-'Ābidīn.

[26] Rubāb was Imam Ḥusayn's wife. She was the mother of the baby 'Alī 'Asghar; see no. 7.

[27] Khuli (or: Khawlī) ibn Yazīd was one of the fighters of the Umayyad army. When the martyrs' heads were pierced on lances and taken to the Umayyad capital Damascus, he is said to have taken Imam Ḥusayn's head to his home and put it inside the oven in his kitchen. He was denounced by his wife, arrested, and killed.

[28] *niizáǰ*

[29] *nušéǰ*

[30] According to tradition, Imam Ḥusayn's head, pierced on a lance on the way to Syria, recited verses from the Qur'ān.

7. *niizá*[31] *čurúuǰo súmeǰ diǰoóiky thei hissá bóot,*
súmeǰo hun theé aṭeé sum khaṣ tharoóiky mei hissá bóot.

7. To fall to the ground from the spearhead shall be your share,
to lift (your head) up from the ground, to bring it, and to have the earth wiped off shall be my share.

8. *ṣiṣóǰo yar beé yayoóiky pon pašaroóiky thei hissá bóot,*
lúṭi beé báde ginií sã́ãty yayoóiky mei hissá bóot.

8. To walk in front of the heads, to lead the way shall be your share,
to walk together with the prisoners, bareheaded, shall be my share.

9. *Yazíidei daróoc̣ejaa dun beé bayoóiky thei hissá bóot,*
šaŋaáli hatéǰ ginií hun beé bayoóiky mei hissá bóot.

9. To stay hanging on Yazīd's gate shall be your share,
to stand up with my hands in chains[32] shall be my share.

10. *Mehrbáan gunaahgár*[33] *áfu bičhoóiky thei hissá bóot,*
babáai xidmatéru šafáa bičhoóiky mei hissá bóot.

10. To intercede[34] for Mihrbān the sinner shall be your share,
to intercede with (our) father ('Alī)[35] for (Mihrbān's) health shall be my share.

2.5 SAKĪNA MOURNS HER FATHER ḤUSAYN[36]

The speaker of this poem is Sakīna, Ḥusayn's young daughter, and one of the favourite characters of the Karbalā narrative,[37] who speaks

[31] *niizáai.*

[32] Lit.: chain on hand.

[33] *gunaahgár*<ei>.

[34] Lit.: beg for forgiveness.

[35] Lit.: beg in the service of the father.

[36] Guldasta-i Mihrbān: 13–14.

[37] See Burney Abbas (2005).

to her father in a *khatāb* 'speech' as does Zaynab in no. 4. In the refrain she calls herself *beekas* 'without anybody', without a friend or relative to support her. Above all, however, the subject of the poem is the fate of her father, whose beheaded body is lying uncovered in the dust, and her half-brother 'Alī Zayn al-'Ābidīn (son of Ḥusayn and Shahrbānu), the only male member of the Holy Family to survive the battle of Karbalā because he was sick and could not go out to fight. He was taken prisoner and taken to Damascus with the women and children, while the heads of the martyred male members of the family were paraded on spears.

khaṭāb-i janāb-i Sakīna	*Speech of Lady Sakīna*
1. *ma fidáa geéš! ṣiṣ ḍiméǰo ǰéek thigáa?* *c̣híilo hun theé léel ga súmer phat thigáa.* *thei bubáa ga dáadeǰo laš neé bigyé*	1. May I be (your) ransom![38] What did you do (with your) head (severed) from (your) body? Having taken off the garment you left it in blood and dust. They were not remorseful towards your father and grandfather.
Sakíina thei yatíim hanís, ẓáa nayeé beekás hanís.	I, Sakīna, am your orphan. Having lost (also my) brother, I am without a friend.
2. *dáaseǰo tu hun theé haroóiky ma dubám* *γusl theé*[39] *kafán theé khaṭoóiky ma dubám.* *xudáaya mas ané γam timoóiky dubám*	2. I'll not be able to pick you up from the desert and take you away, I'll not be able to bathe you, make a shroud and bury you. O God, I'll not be able to bear this grief!

[38] Expression of devotedness.

[39] M. Amin Zia suggested to emend *deé* or *thareé* for *theé*.

3. *ãã̃ ṣe wií ga thei ḍiméi tam darám.* *sidr kaafúur γúsleṭ koóiñ gyeé walám?* *ḍúŋ beéi to thei ḍiméṭ kafán tharám.*	3. I'll bathe your body in tears.[40] Where shall I go and fetch sidr and camphor for washing (the corpse before burial)? Stay on a while, then I shall have the shroud made for your body.
Sakíina thei yatíim hanís, ẓáa nayeé beekás hanís.	I, Sakīna, am your orphan. Having lost (also my) brother, I am without a friend.
4. *kakáa Zainul-Ibáade-waar phúṭak (phuúṭak) the!* *ṣakér gon*[41] *wií aṭeégye lúṭo thareé* *páaye bẽ́ ye náni ṹũṭeǰ ṭak thareé.*	4. Give (my) brother Zayn al-'Ibād[42] a (quick) glance! Having tied (a rope) around (his) neck,[43] they brought him, having made him bareheaded, having tied up both (his) feet on a bare female camel.[44]
Sakíina thei yatíim hanís, ẓáa nayeé beekás hanís.	I, Sakīna, am your orphan. Having lost (also my) brother, I am without a friend.

[40] Lit.: having thrown tears also I'll bathe your body.

[41] Otherwise: *goṇ*.

[42] = Zayn al 'Ābidīn. *Kakáa* means 'younger brother'. However, as Sakīna is definitely younger than Zayn al 'Ābidīn, over here this can only mean: 'brother'.

[43] Lit.: on the nape of neck.

[44] One of the hardships imposed on the prisoners was that they were mounted on camels without saddles.

5. *Mehrbáan-se hẽ́ ẽṣei*[45] *sayṍ ṭak tharéi*	5. Mihrbān will tie up (in a bundle) the supplies of sighs.
ãā́ ṣei múuse bẽ́ ye açhíiyor ṣak tharéi	He will fill both eyes with floods of tears.
wáanu (wáan) tu-waar γam gye híio ṣak thareé	He comes towards you, having filled (his) heart with grief.
Sakíina thei yatíim hanís, ẓáa nayeé beekás hanís.	I, Sakīna, am your orphan. Having lost (also my) brother, I am without a friend.'

2.6 ZAYNAB MOURNS HER HALF-BROTHER 'ABBĀS[46]

This poem is a *nawḥa* for Ḥaẓrat 'Abbās, *ḥaẓrat* is a honorific title. The speaker is 'Abbās' half-sister Zaynab. 'Abbās, the son of 'Alī, is known as a great warrior and revered for his loyalty to his half-brother Ḥusayn. He is commonly called the bannerholder (Persian *'alamdār*). In the refrain he is called *qamar banī Hāshim* 'the moon of the Hashemites', another title which according to tradition was conferred upon him by his father 'Alī. The third stanza refers to the circumstances of his death. Since the way to the Euphrates had been blocked by the enemies, the followers of Ḥusayn suffered from lack of water. On 10 Muḥarram, 'Abbās went to the Euphrates to get some water for the children, especially for Ḥusayn's daughter Sakīna, who was very fond of him. He managed to get down to the river, filled a water skin, and started to ride back towards the camp. On the way he was attacked, both his arms were cut off, and he fell off his horse, fatally wounded.

---

[45] Written *ḥyṣe*, better **hẽ́ ẽṣo*.

[46] Guldasta-i Mihrbān: 12.

nawḥa-i ḥaẓ rat ʻAbbās(-i) ʻalamdār	*nawḥa for Haẓ rat ʻAbbās the bannerholder*
1. *Alíi Abbáas thei ǰiléǰo ma fidáa* *thei ǰawaaníiei núureǰo thei sa fidáa* *thei čaráaṭi neé timíiǰin, e xudáa*	1. ʻAlī ʻAbbās, I (wish to be) the ransom for your life your sister (wants to be) the ransom for the light of your youth. The separation from you is unbearable,[47] O God!
Alíi Abbáas ǰawáan asóo, *Haašimíiyoo yúun asóo.*	ʻAlī ʻAbbās, you were a youth, you were the moon of the Hashemites.
2. *Alíi Abbáas, thei γamér thei ẓáa Huséin* *ḍáakye phuṭeé ronaál théeno thei ṣiṣoón.* *xudáayaa, mei qábur bóotaa (bóot) thei pawoón,*	2. ʻAlī ʻAbbās, your brother Ḥusayn, in (his) grief, (with his) back broken,[48] is lamenting at your bedside. O God, may my grave be at your feet!
Alíi Abbáas ǰawáan asóo, *Haašimíiyoo yúun asóo.*	ʻAlī ʻAbbās, you were a youth, you were the moon of the Hashemites.
3. *Alíi Abbáas, Sakíina-se zóof walíin* *ʻFuráateǰo wei waléiʼ theé tu çakíin.* *ʻçaloó bubáa loóko wa!ʼ theé hat khalíin,*	3. ʻAlī ʻAbbās, Sakīna is about to faint (with thirst).[49] Saying, ʻHe will fetch water from the Euphratesʼ, she is looking out for you. Saying, ʻ(My) light, father, come quicklyʼ, she swings (her) hand around.[50]
Alíi Abbáas ǰawáan asóo, *Haašimíiyoo yúun asóo.*	ʻAlī ʻAbbās, you were a youth, you were the moon of the Hashemites.

4. Alíi Akbár qatlgáaru phat bugú
Alíi Asγarér táliṣ léeler ṣak bugú
dáarye nayeé maálo beekás phat bugú

4. 'Alī Akbar stayed behind in the place of martyrdom,[51]
'Alī 'Asghar's[52] nappies were covered in blood.
Having lost (his) sons, (Ḥusayn as their) father stayed behind destitute.

Alíi Abbáas ǰawáan asóo,
Haašimíiyoo yúun asóo.

'Alī 'Abbās, you were a youth, you were the moon of the Hashemites.

5. Alíi Abbáas, thei γuláam Mehrbáan hanú
thei sumúle šáakoǰo qurbáan hanú
bẽ́ ẽye phyóoloǰ bóoče doóiky armáan hanú

5. 'Alī 'Abbās, your slave is Mihrbān:
he is a sacrifice[53] for your holy arms,
he longs to kiss both (your) shoulders.

Alíi Abbáas ǰawáan asóo,
Haašimíiyoo yúun asóo.

'Alī 'Abbās, you were a youth, you were the moon of the Hashemites.

2.7 Rubāb mourns her son 'Alī 'Asghar

This poem is about Imam Ḥusayn's baby son 'Abd Allāh, called 'Alī 'Asghar, addressed to him by his mother Rubāb. His tender age made him suffer even more than the others from thirst. 'Alī 'Asghar was

---

47 Lit.: on the nape of neck.

48 This is a reference to an utterance attributed to Ḥusayn: "Abbas, your death is like the breaking of my back.'

49 Lit.: fetches weakness.

50 Apparently she calls her uncle 'father' and waves her hands in a circle as a greeting.

51 'Alī Akbar is understood to have been the first of the Ahl-e Bayt to have been martyred.

52 On 'Alī 'Asghar, see no. 7. 'Alī Akbar and 'Alī 'Asghar are Ḥusayn's sons, while 'Alī 'Abbās (= 'Abbās ibn 'Alī) is his half-brother.

53 Expression of devotedness.

killed in his father's arms, his neck pierced by an arrow from the bow of Ḥarmala (or Ḥurmala) ibn Kahil. When the prisoners were deported to Damascus, he had to be left in the desert, but was later buried with his father Ḥusayn and his brother 'Alī Akbar in Karbalā.

nauḥa-e ma'sūm Ali Asγar

nawḥa for the innocent 'Alī 'Asghar

1. *zizí bodoó geéš yaa Alíi Asγár*
ṓõṭye šaweégaa,[54] *yaa Alíi Asγár*

1. May I, (your) mother, become (lit.: go) (your) sacrifice, O 'Alī 'Asghar!
You made your lips parched, O 'Alī 'Asghar!

2. *mei ċhágei bulbúl Hormaláai kóon gye aċhíi nileégaa, yaa Alíi Asγár*

2. Nightingale of my garden, by Hormala's arrow
you closed (your) eyes, O 'Alī 'Asghar!

3. *'Hormaláai kóon ṣóṭej poóun'*
theé ṓõṭye pieégaa, yaa Alíi Asγár

3. Saying, 'Hormala's arrow has fallen on (my) neck',
you pressed (your) lips together, O 'Alī 'Asghar!

4. *Hormaláai kóonei naṭhukéi dud*
pií tus nir waleégaa, yaa Alíi Asγár

4. Having drunk the milk of Hormala's arrow shaft,
you fell asleep,[55] O 'Alī 'Asghar!

5. *agúyei nóoro gye ḍuḍúro kar the! dud doóiky dubaális, yaa Alíi Asγár*

5. Scratch (my) nipple with your fingernail!
I was unable to give you milk, O 'Alī 'Asghar!

6. *ḍuḍú<ror> dud weéi čúče šilaáde*
ǰúuk neé timíiǰei, yaa Alíi Asγár.

6. After milk had come into (my) nipples, (my) breasts hurt,
the pain is unbearable,[56] O 'Alī 'Asghar!

7. *dušmanéi sĩ́ o ṹũṭe waleégye*
bádi haroóikyeṭ, yaa Alíi Asγár

7. They brought camels of the enemy's armies
to take away the female prisoner, O 'Alī 'Asghar!

8. *afsúus afsúus dáasei múunyeǰaa*[57]
ḍiŋ neé beé phat bée, yaa Alíi Asγár

8. Alas! Alas! in the desert's lap
you will be left unburied, O 'Alī 'Asghar!

9. *šáamei badéyer khée the lafaá dam*
tu dáaser phat theé, yaa Alíi Asγár

9. How shall I go into Syria's captivity,
having left you in the desert, O 'Alī 'Asghar!

10. *mei qáburei ṣiṣoón páṭuk quráan ra*
ronáale thóoǰa, yaa Alíi Asγár

10. By the side of my grave recite a leaf (from) the Qur'an,
weeping, O 'Alī 'Asghar!

11. *'innaa lilaahi wa innā ilaihi (rāje'ūn)'*
róoǰa[58] *be yaátes, yaa Alíi Asγár*

11. 'We are from God, and to Him (we return)'[59]
saying (this), we went, O 'Alī 'Asghar!

12. *mahšaréi dáaser Mehrbáane káary*
hun beé buyát the, yaa Alíi Asγár

12. In the desert of the assembly (of the resurrected on the Day of Judgement)
get up for Mihrbān and pray[60] (for him), O'Alī 'Asghar!

---

[54] Buddruss and Bailey always have short *-ga* in the second singular preterite, Radloff (e.g. 1998) has *-gaa*.

[55] Lit.: you fetched sleep

[56] Lit.: will not be tolerated.

[57] = múunyeǰ.

[58] corr. *rayóoǰa* 'saying' which is semantically more plausible, but *róoǰa* 'weeping' seems to agree better with the metre.

[59] Ar. *innā lillāhi wa innā ilayhi rāji'ūn* (Qur'ān: 2.156).

[60] Lit.: plead.

3. Glossary

a

Abbáas n. pr.
Abáas Alíi n. pr.
açhíi f. eye. Gen. Sg. *açhíiyei*. Loc. Pl. *açhíiyor.*
adée adv. thus. *afsóos, afsúus* sorrow, woe.
áfu n. forgiveness, forgiving. [Ar. *'afw*].
agúi n. f. finger; Gen. Sg. *agúyei.*
Akbar n. pr.
áal-e nabíi Family of the Prophet (PBUH).[61] [Ar. Pers.].
Alíi Abbáas n. pr.
Alíi Akbár = Akbar Alíi n. pr.
Alíi Asγár n. pr. Loc. Ali Asγarér.
anú m., *ané* f. Dem. pron. this.
aaráam rest, respite, comfort. [Pers.].
armáan desire, longing. [Pers., cf. U. *armān honā* to wish].
as- Pret. stem of 'be' 2sg. m. *asóo.*
asoósaŋe The word is obscure. M. Amin Zia suggested *aš boósaŋ* 'until today'.
Aš adv. today.
ã̃ã́ şo n. m. tear. Gen. Sg. *ã̃ã́ şei*. Pl. *ã̃ã́ şe.*
aţ- vb. to bring. Abs. aţeé. Pret. 3pl. aţeégye.
az prep. from. [Pers.].

b

b- become. Abs. beé. Fut 2sg. *bée*. Opt. 3sg./pl. *bóot, bóotaa*. Pret. 1sg. f. bigís, 3sg. m. *bugú*, 3pl. *bigyé*. vb. noun *boósaŋ.*
babáa n. m. father, dad. Gen. Sg. *babáai.*
badéi n. bondage, slavery. Loc. Sg. *badéyer.*
bádo m., *bádi* f. prisoner, slave, exile. Pl. *báde.*
ban- trans. put on (clothes).
bap'o grandfather (used in kings' and Sayyid's families).

---

[61] Cf. *şall Allāhu ʿalaihi wa-ʾālihi* - SAWW) a formula (with several variants) used after the name of the Prophet Muhammad (PBUH).

baaqíi place name.
be we.
beéi- intr. sit, stay. Inf. *Bayoóiky.* Imp. 2sg. *beéi.*
bee-kafán shroudless. [Pers.].
beekás adj. helpless, without a friend, destitute, orphaned. [Pers.].
bḗ ye adj. both.
bich- vb. trans. to ask for, beg. Inf. *bičhoóiky.*
bir- vb. trans. to shed, pour. Inf. *biroóiky.* Abs. *birií.*
birgá f. battle. Dat. Sg. *birgyeéṭe.* [= Bur.].
bóoċi n. f. kiss. Pl. *bóoċe.*
bodoó n. sacrifice. [Bur. budoó].
bubáa n. m. father. Dat. Sg. *bubáaṭe.*
buǰ- vb. itr. to go. Pres. 1sg. f. *búǰamis.* Imp. Sg. *bo,* Pl. *búǰaa.* Abs. *gyeé.* Pret. 2sg. m. *gáa,* 3sg. m. *gau.* Voluntative *geéš.*
bulbúl n. nightingale. [Ar.].
bulqá n. veil. [Ar. *burqa*].
buy'at n. plea, request. [= Bur.]. *buyát th-* to plead, ask for.

c

ċhágo n. m. orchard, garden. Gen. Sg. *ċhágei.*
ċho you (Pl.). Erg. *ċhos.*
čadár n. f. sheet, cloth, veil.
čaráaṭi n. f. separation. [= Bur.].
čúčo n. m. Pl. *čúče* breasts.
čurúu n. m. tip, end. Abl. Sg. *čurúuǰo.*
čhuút adv. slowly, late.
ċak- vb. trans. look. Pres. 3sg. f. *ċakíin.* Imp. 2sg. *ċak'e.*
ċaloó n. m. torch, light, lamp.
ċhíilo n. m. gown, clothing. Pl. *ċhíile.*

d

d- vb. trans. to give. Inf. *doóiky.* Fut. 1sg. *dam.* Imp. Sg. *de.*
dáado n. m. grandfather. Abl. Sg. *dáadeǰo.*
dafán n. burial. *dáfan th-* bury. [← Ar. *dafn*].
dáal n. m. ashes. Loc. Sg. *dáaleǰ.*

dar- vb. trans. to cause to be given. Fut 1sg. *darám.*
daár n. m. son. Pl. *dáarye.*
daróoç n. gate, door of palace. Loc. Sg. *daróoçejaa.*
dáas n. wasteland, uncultivated land. Gen. Sg. *dáasei.* Dat. Sg. *dáaseṭ.* Abl. Sg. *dáaseǰo.* Loc. Sg. *dáaser.* [Bur. *das*].
diǰ- vb. itr. to fall. Inf. *diǰoóiky.*
diš n. f. place.
doón n. women's headscarf. [= Bur.].
dub- vb. intr. cannot, be unable to. Fut. 1sg. *dubám.* Pret. 1sg. f. *dubaális.*
dun b- vb. itr. to hang.
dunyáat n. f. world. Loc. Sg. *dunyáater.* [Bur. *duináat* ← Ar. *dunyā*].
dušmán n. m. enemy. Gen. Sg. *dušmanéi.* Gen. Pl. *dušmanóo.* [Pers.].
dud n. m. milk.
ḍáako n. m. back. Pl. *ḍáakye.*
ḍim n. m. body, self. Gen. Sg. *ḍiméi.* Abl. Sg. *ḍimeǰo.*
ḍiŋ b- vb. intr. to hide, be kept, be buried.
ḍuḍúro nipple. Loc. Pl. *ḍuḍúror.* [Bur. *ḍuḍuúro* bud, nipple, etc.].
ḍuúŋ(a) n. a short span of time. [= Bur.].

e

e interjection. [Pers.].
ek one, a.

f

fidáa n. ransom; devotedness. *fidáa buǰ-* to be devoted to sb. [Ar. *fidā'*].
fikr n. anxiety, thought. [Ar.]. *fíkr-e … th-* be concerned about, think of, provide for.
Furáat n. pr. Euphrates. Abl. *Furáateǰo.* [Ar. *furāt*].

g

ga and, also. *ge, gye* with.
gin- vb. trans. to take. Abs. *ginií* with.
gon n. f. knot. *gon wi-* to tie, to knot.

gunaahgár n. sinner. Gen. Sg. *gunaahgárei*. [Pers.].

γ

γam n. grief, sorrow. Loc. Sg. *γamér*. [Ar.].
γuláam n. m. slave, servant. [Ar.].
γusl n. bath, washing. [Ar.].

h

hai hai exclamation of grief. *hai hai afsos* id. [cf. U. *hāe afsos*].
hain vb. itr. to be. Pres. 3sg. f.
han- vb. itr., copula, to be. 1sg. f. *hanís*, 3sg. m. *hanú*, 3sg./pl. han, with indefinite suffix *hanék* 'those that are'.
har- vb. trans. to take away, take to .... Inf. *haroóiky*, Inf. Dat. *haroóikyeṭ*. Imp. Sg. *har*. Pret. 3. Pl. *hariígye*.
Haašimíi member of the Hashemite family. Gen. Pl. *Haašimíiyoo*.
hat n. m. hand. Loc. Sg. *hatéǰ*.
hḗẽṣ n. sigh. Gen. Sg. *hḗẽṣei*. Pl. *hḗ ẽṣe*. [cf. *hī́ĩṣ*, Bur. *hiṣ* sigh].
hilaléeko adj. marriage-, bridal. Pl. *hilaléeke*.
hilalóo n. m. bridegroom.
híio n. m. heart.
hissá part, portion, share. [Ar. *ḥiṣṣa*].
Hormaláa n. pr. Gen. Hormaláai.
hun b- to rise, get up. *hun th-, húun th-* to pick up, lift up.
Huséen n. pr. Huséenaa.

ǰ

ǰáa where. Dat. *ǰáaṭe* where-to, where.
ǰakúr hair.
ǰamáat Pl. family, wife. [Ar.-U. *jamā'at* group, assembly].
ǰap hidden.
ǰawáan n. m. youth, youngster. [Pers.].
ǰawaaníi n. f. youth. Gen. Sg. *ǰawaaníiei*. [Pers.].
ǰéek what.
ǰiíl f. life. Gen. Sg. *ǰiléi*. Abl. Sg. *ǰiléǰo*.
ǰúuk n. f. pain.
ǰukaáṭo adj. painful. Pl. *ǰukaáṭe*. [cf. *ǰúuk*].

k

kafán n. shroud. [← Arab.].
kafúur n. camphor. [Ar. *kāfūr*].
kakáa n. m. younger brother. [cf. *kaáko* elder brother].
kar th- vb. trans. to scratch, scrape. [Bur. *qar*].
Karbaláa place name. Loc. Sg. *Karbaláar(u).*
káary on behalf of, for the sake of.
kóon n. m. arrow. Gen. Sg. *kóonei.*
khabár news. [Ar. *xabar*].
khal- to swing around in a circle. Pres. 3sg. *khalíin, khalíini. hat khalíini* swings (her) hands around (as a greeting).
khaṣ th- vb. trans. to clean, wipe. *khaṣ thar-* to have cleaned.
khaṭoóiky vb. trans. to bury, conceal.
khée the adv. how. [*khée theé*].

l

lafaá gait, walking. *lafaá d-* to go.
Lailá n. pr.
laš n. f. shame. *laš b-* to be ashamed.
laxt-e ǰigár piece of liver (term of endearment). [Pers.].
léel n. m. blood. Loc. Sg. *léeleǰaa.* Loc. Sg. *léeler.*
loóko adj. adv. quick, soon.
lúṭo m., *lúṭi* f. bareheaded, shameless. Pl. *lúṭe.* [Bur. *lóṭo*].

m

ma pers. pron. 1sg. Erg. Sg. *mas, máse.*
Madiinaa place name. Dat. Sg. *Madiináaṭe.*
mahšár n. place of gathering for the resurrected on the Day of Judgement. Gen. Sg. *mahšaréi.* [Ar. *maḥšar*].
maǰlís n. assembly, council. Dat. Sg. *maǰliséṭ.* Loc. Sg. *maǰlisér.*
maálo n. m. father.
Mehrbáan n. pr. Obl. Sg. *Mehrbáane.*
mei my.
mir- vb. intr. to die. Inf. Loc. *miroóikyer.*
múuni n. f. lap. Loc. Sg. *múunyeǰ, múunyeǰaa, múunyeru.*

múus n. f. flood, mudflow. Pl. *múuse*. [Bur. *mos*].
Mustafáa pr. n. Dat. Sg. *Mustafáaṭe*.
muškíl adj. difficult. [Ar.].

n

nai- vb. trans. to lose, ruin. Abs. *nayií, nayeé*.
Naǰáf place name. *Naǰáf dáas* wasteland of Najaf.
náno m., *náni* f. adj. naked, bare.
nana-paá adj. barefoot. [*nana* naked, *páa* (!) foot].
náaš n. corpse. Loc. *náašeǰ, náašeǰaa*. [Ar. *na'š*].
naṭhúk n. arrow shaft. Gen. Sg. *naṭhukéi*.
naazaníin adj. delicate, lovely, beloved.
názur n. vow, offering, sacrifice. [Ar. *naẕr*].
neé not.
nil- vb. trans. to hide, close (eyes). Pret. 2sg. m. *nileégaa*.
nir n. f. sleep.
niizá n. lance, spear. Gen. Sg. *niizáai* Loc. Sg. *niizáǰ, niizáǰaa*. [Pers.].
nóoro n. m. fingernail.
núur n. light. Abl. Sg. *núureǰo*. [Ar.].
núur-e áin light of eye. Dat. Sg. *núur-e áinaṭ*. [← Ar. Pers. *nūr-e 'ain*].
nuš is not. Loc. Sg. *nušéǰ, nušéǰaa*.

o

o and [Pers.].
ő̃ši n. f. wind.
ő̃ṭo n. m. lip. Pl. *ő̃ṭye*.

p

p- vb. intr. to fall. Perf. 3sg. m. *poó(w)un*.
páa n. m. foot. Pl. *páaye*.
pal- vb. trans. hand over. Fut. 1sg. *palám*.
par- vb. trans. cause to fall, slay. Pret. 3pl. *pareégyen*.
paš- vb. trans. see. Pres. 1sg. f. *paášamis*. Pret. 1sg. f. *pašiígis*.
pašar- vb. trans. to cause to be seen, to show. Inf. *pašaroóiky*.

páṭo n. m. leaf. indef. *páṭuk*.
pawoón n. foot (end of bed).
pi- vb. trans. to drink. Abs. *pií*.
piy- vb. trans. to press together. Pret. 2sg. m. *pieégaa*.
pon n. f. path, way.
próono m., *próoni* f. adj. old.
phat b- vb. intr. to stay behind, be left behind. *phat th-* vb. trans. to leave, give up. [= Bur.].
phuṭ n. glance, look. Indef. *phúṭak*. [= Bur.].
phuṭ- vb. trans. to break. Abs. *phuṭeé*.
phyóolo n. m. shoulder. Loc. Pl. *phyóoloǰ*.

q

qábur n. grave. Gen. Sg. *qáburei*. [Ar. *qabr*].
qamár n. moon. [Ar.].
Qaasim n. pr.
qatlgáa(h) n. place of execution, place of murder. Loc. Sg. *qatlgáaru*. [Pers. *qatlgāh*].
qóom n. community, tribe, family. [Ar. *qaum*].
qóom-e kaafár n. people of infidels. [Pers. *qaum-e kāfir*].
quráan n. m. Qur'ān. [Ar.].
qurbáan n. sacrifice. [Ar.].

r

ra- vb. trans. to say, speak. Inf. *rayoóiky*. Imp. Sg. *ra*. vb. noun *rayóoǰa*.
rar- vb. trans. to cause to cry. adv. *raróoǰa*.
ro- vb. itr. to weep. vb. noun *róoǰa*.
ronáal n. weeping, lamentation. Pl. *ronáale*. *ronáal th-* to weep, lament.
Rubáab n. pr.

s

sa n. sister. Gen. Sg. *sayéi*. Erg. Sg. *sas*.
safár n. journey, travel. [Ar.].
Sakíina n. pr. Erg. Sakíina-se.

samar- vb. to divide. Fut. 1pl. *samaróon.*
sar- vb. tr. to put to sleep (*s-* to sleep). Inf. *saroóiky.*
sátar th- vb. to cover, veil. [Ar. *satr* covering].
sā̃́ ā̃ty postposition: with, together. *ǰiléǰo sā̃́ ā̃ty* with life.
sayṓ n. provisions for a journey.
sī̃́ ī̃ n. f. army. Obl. Pl. *sī̃́ o.*
sidr n. a precious bath essence.
sum n. m. earth, dust. Loc. Sg. *súmeǰ, súmeǰaa.* Loc. Sg. *súmer.* Abl. Sg. *súmeǰo.*
sumúlo m. adj. holy, noble. Pl. *sumúle.* [= Bur.].
suurá n. surah, chapter of the Qur'ān. [Ar.].
šafā n. recovery, health. [Ar.].
šah, šáah n. m. king. [Pers. *šāh, šah*].
šáah-e mardáan n. m. king of men. [Pers. *šāh-e mardān*].
šaáko n. arm. Abl. Pl. *šaákoǰo.*
Šáam Syria. Gen. Sg. *Šáamei.* [Ar.].
šams u qamár n. Sun and Moon. [Ar.-Pers.].
šaŋaáli n. f. chain.
šaw- vb. trans. to dry out, make parched. Pret. 2sg. m. *šaweégaa.*
šéer-e xudáa n. Lion of God.
šila- vb. intr. to hurt, be painful. Pret. 3pl. šilaáde.
šuh(a)dáa Pl. of *šahīd* n. martyr. [Ar.].
Šuhrbáan n. pr. [Pers. *Šahrbānū*].
ṣak n. m. nape of neck. Loc. Sg. *ṣakér.*
ṣak adj. full. ṣak thar- to fill. [Bur. *ṣek*].
ṣiṣ n. m. head. Gen. Sg. *ṣiṣéi.* Loc. Sg. *ṣiṣéru.* Abl. Pl. *ṣiṣóǰo.*
ṣiṣoón n. head end (of bed).
ṣóto n. m. neck. Loc. Sg. *ṣóṭeǰ.*

t

táaǰ n. crown. [← Pers.].
táliṣ nappy, diaper. [= Bur.].
tam dar- vb. trans. to bathe, wash (+ gen.). [Bur. *tam –dil-*].
tanháa adj. alone. [← Pers.].
tanúur n. oven, stove. Loc. Sg. *tanúureru.* [U. Ar.].
tim- vb. trans. to suffer, tolerate. Inf. *timoóiky.*
timiiǰ- vb. intr. (passive) to be suffered, tolerated. Fut. 3sg. *timíiǰei.*

tíri wa- to circumambulate, a religious shrine, or a holy person's grave.
tišná-ǰigár whose liver is thirsty. [Pers.].
toóm reflexive pronoun: own.
traŋ half. [= Bur.].
tu you, thou. Erg. Sg. *tus.*
th- vb. trans. do, make, say. Abs. *theé.* Imp. 2sg. *the,* 2pl. *tháa.* Fut. 1sg. *tham.* Pres. 3sg. m. *théeno.* Pret. 2sg. m. *thigáa.* Vb. n. *thóoǰa.*
thar- vb. trans. cause to be done. Inf. *tharoóiky.* Abs. *thareé.* Fut. 1sg. *tharám,* 3sg. *tharéi.*
thei your.
ṭak joined. *ṭak thar-* to bind, fasten, fix. [= Bur.].

u

uḍoór th- vb. trans. seek, look for. [Bur. *uḍóori*].
Úmm-e Kulsúum n. pr.
ṹũṭ n. f., n. m. camel. Loc. Sg. *ṹũṭeǰ.* Pl. *ṹũṭe.*

w

wa- vb. intr. come. Imp. Sg. *wa.* Pres. 3sg. m. *wáan, wáanu.* Pret. 1sg. f. *wátis,* 3sg. f. *wáti.* Perf. 3sg. f. *wátin.* Abs. *weéi.*
waá interjection.
wal- vb. trans. fetch, bring. Inf. *Waloóiky.* Fut. 3sg. *waléi.* Pres. 3sg. f. *walíin.* Pret. 2sg. m. *waleégaa,* 3pl. *waleégye.*
wála (= wa laá) interjection.
-waar postposition: towards, to.
wei n. m. water.
wi- vb. trans. to put, throw. Abs. *wií.*

x

xataab n. discourse, address, speech. [Ar. *xiṭāb*].
xidmát m. service. Loc. Sg. *xidmatéru.* [Ar. Pers., cf. Pers. *xidmat-e* in the presence of].
xudáa God. [Pers.]. Voc. *xudáaya(a)* O God!
Xulí n. pr. Gen. *Xulíiei.*

x[w]aar-nazár adj. whose sight is wretched, who is contemptible in the eyes of others. [Pers. *xwār* contemptible, wretched; Ar. *naẓar* 'look'].

y

yaa interjection. [Ar.].
yai- vb. itr. to go. Inf. yayoóiky. Pret. 1pl. *yaátes.*
yar beé adv. first, in front.
yáṣki adj. fitting, proper. [= Bur.].
yatíim n. orphan. Dat. Sg. *yatíimeṭ.* Erg. Pl. *yatíimis.* [Ar.].
Yazíid. pr. n. Gen. Sg. *Yazíidei.*
yúun n. f. moon.

z

Zahráa n. pr.
Zainâb n. pr. Erg. Zainâb-se.
Zain ul-Ibáad n. pr. Obl. Zain ul-Ibáade-waar.
zampáan n. camel-litter.
zīna n. stairs, ladder. See footnote on nos.4 and 1. [Pers.].
zizí n. f. Mother. Erg. Sg. *zizís.* [Berger, Bur. *zizí* used only at the court and in Sayyid families].
zóof n. weakness. [Ar. *żu'f*], or for *zaáp* fainting.
ẓáa n. m. brother. Gen. Sg. *ẓawéi.*

ABBREVIATIONS

Abl. = ablative
Abs. = absolutive
adj. = adjective
adv. = adverb
Agr = agreement
Ar. = Arabic
Bur. = Burushaski
Dem. pron. = demonstrative pronoun
Erg. = ergative
f. = feminine
Fut. = future
Gen. = genitive
Dat. = dative
Imp. = imperative
Inf. = infinitive
intrans. = intransitive
Loc. = locative
m. = masculine
n. = noun
n. pr. = proper name
Opt. = optative
Perf. = perfect
Pers. = Persian
Pl. = plural
Pres. = present
Pret. = preterite
Sg. = singular
trans. = transitive
U. = Urdu
vb. = verb(al)

REFERENCES

Abbas, Shemeem Burney. 2005. 'Sakineh, the narrator of Karbala: An ethnographic description of a women's majles ritual in Pakistan'. In *The Women of Karbala: Ritual Performance and Symbolic Discourses in Modern Shi'i Islam,* edited by Kamran Scot Aghaie. 141–60. Austin: University of Texas.

Bard, Amy. 2000. 'Value and vitality in a literary tradition: Female poets and the Urdu marsiya'. *The Annual of Urdu Studies* 15: 323–35.

Buddruss, Georg. 1983. 'Neue Schriftsprachen im Norden Pakistans: Einige Beobachtungen'. In *Schrift und Gedächtnis: Archäologie der literarischen Kommunikation*, edited by Aleida Assmann, Jan Assman, and Christoph Hardmeier. 231–44. München: Fink.

——— and Degener, Almuth. 2012. *The Meeting Place*. Wiesbaden: Harrassowitz. (Beiträge zur Indologie 46).

Hyder, Syed Akbar. 2006. *Reliving Karbala: Martyrdom in South Asian Memory.* Oxford: Oxford University Press.

Mihrbān, Ākhund. 1963. *Guldasta-i Mihrbān*. Lahore: Inṣāf Press.

Radloff, Carla F. and Shakil, Shakil Ahmad. 1998. *Folktales in the Shina of Gilgit: Text, Grammatical Analysis and Commentary.* Islamabad: National Institute of Pakistan Studies, and Summer Institute of Linguistics.

[Romanization of Persian] <http://www.loc.gov/catdir/cpso/romanization/persian.pdf> accessed 20 October 2013.

[Shina *nawḥa*] <http://www.youtube.com/watch?v=E81d5ONcMno> accessed 2 October 2013.

Söhnen-Thieme, Renate. 2007. 'Six Balti marsiyas'. In *Dimensions of South Asian Religion*, edited by Timothy Hugh Barrett. 35–65. London: The School of Oriental and African Studies. (SOAS Working Papers in the Study of Religion).

8

Ek akhabir sher ais—'There was an Old Lion': A Linguistic Analysis of a Kalasha Narrative as told by Sher John of Kraka, Mumoret

Jan Heegård and Nabaig

1. INTRODUCTION

This article is inspired by Carla Radloff and Shakil Ahmad Shakil's *Folktales in the Shina of Gilgit* (1998). With its detailed commentary on the grammar and discourse structure of a set of Shina of Gilgit folk tales,[1] this publication may serve as an example of an introduction to both the grammar and the oral literature of a primarily oral community in the Hindu Kush region. The present article presents in a similar fashion a piece of oral literature, a fable, from another Hindu Kush language, Kalasha. The article serves three purposes. First, it presents to the reader a piece of traditional oral literature from a speech community in the Hindu Kush region. Second, with the grammatical notes, it serves as an introduction to the grammar and to text-linguistic discourse strategies in this language. Third, and as a humble hope, it may serve as a small contribution to a broader understanding of the grammatical structures in the oral literature of the languages of the Hindu Kush.[2]

[1] We refer henceforward to this variety of Shina as 'Gilgit Shina'.

[2] The authors are grateful to Sher John of Kra'ka', Mumoret, for the narrative. We are also thankful to Taj Khan for various comments on the transcription of the narrative, and we are also very grateful to an anonymous reviewer for various

2. THE KALASHA AND THE KALASHA LANGUAGE

The Kalasha language is spoken by approximately 5,000 people, the Kalasha (see <www.endangeredlanguages.com> and <www.ethnologue.com>), in the multilingual Hindu Kush mountain range in north-west Pakistan (Chitral District, Khyber Pakhtunkhwa province). Today two main dialects can be identified, northern Kalasha in the valleys Rukmu, Mumuret, Biriu, and Jinjiret, and southern Kalasha, in the Utsun Valley.[3] Northern Kalasha can further be divided into a Rukmu-Mumuret variety and a Biriu-Jinjiret variety (Mørch 2000, Heegård Petersen 2006: I, 13). The narrator of the narrative below is a speaker of the Rukmu-Mumuret variety.

Traditionally the Kalasha people practise a polytheistic religion which is characterized by, for example, worshipping of gods at altars on the mountain sides, in village temples, or in houses. Sacrifice of goats, wine, bread, and walnuts over an open fire plays an important part in the worship. Needless to say, this makes the Kalasha stand out religiously and culturally from the surrounding Muslim community, which, due to the enforced Islamization in the north-west part of Pakistan, in later years has become more orthodox.[4]

In earlier times the Kalasha people were linguistically, and perhaps also culturally, more heterogeneous, and occupied a large area of the southern part of Chitral District, including the valleys Urtsun and Jinjiret, as well as hamlets and villages in the Shishi Kuh Valley and in the main Chitral Valley (Robertson 1896; Morgenstierne 1973; Cacopardo and Cacopardo 1991, 2001; Mørch 2002). In 1949, shortly after the independence of Pakistan, the Kalasha populations in these locations converted to Islam (Cacopardo and Cacopardo 1991, 2001). With this wave of conversion, the vitality of the Kalasha culture and religion, as well as of the different varieties of the Kalasha language, faced a serious threat through a strong rejection by converts of all cultural and religious elements that would connect people with the

comments and suggestions as to the analyses and translation of the Kalasha language. The authors take full responsibility for any errors and shortcomings.

[3] We use the Kalasha denominations for these and other Kalasha localities. The valleys Rukmu, Mumuret, Biriu, and Utsun are also known as Rumbur, Bumboret, Birir, and Urtsun.

[4] For ethnographic studies of the Kalasha, see, for example, Maggi (2001), Parkes (2001), A. S. Cacopardo (2006, 2008), Snoy (2008), and Fentz (2011).

'pagan' past. From a linguistic perspective, this wave of conversion was dramatic because the rejection of the religious and cultural heritage also included a language shift to Khowar, the lingua franca of the Chitral District. The linguistic consequence of this massive language shift is that we now have only very little knowledge about the dialects of Kalasha that were spoken in the places where conversion took place; the only exceptions were the valleys Jinjiret and Urtsun where the language was used up till the 1980s, but since then Khowar has gradually taken over as the language of daily life, and presumably, today, only old people can speak Kalasha fluently in these two valleys.[5]

Since the 1970s many Muslims from the neighbouring Kho tribe, the dominant Muslim tribe in Chitral, have settled in the three remaining 'Kalasha valleys'. In addition, a large number of the Kalasha have converted to Islam, and today Muslims, i.e. Khos, Nuristanis (settlers from neighbouring Nuristan in Afghanistan), and converts (*shekhs*) form a majority in each of the three valleys (Heegård and Khan forthcoming).

Although the approximate total number of the remaining Kalasha people of today (2015) is larger than the 2,000 to 3,000 that has been reported in earlier research,[6] the Kalasha are still exposed to considerable pressure from the surrounding Muslim communities, and individual conversions are frequent. Since language shift still goes hand in hand with religious conversion today, there are good reasons for considering Kalasha as an endangered language.

3. KALASHA ORAL LITERATURE

The oral literature of the Kalasha is rich, and known from other research and publications. It encompasses several genres, for example

---

[5] Cacopardo and Cacopardo (1991) give undocumented linguistic evaluations of the Kalasha language of these former Kalasha-speaking localities. Based on fieldwork in 1995–97 with 'rememberers' of the now extinct dialects and speakers of the Utsun, Jinjiret, Lawi, Kalkatak, and Suwir varieties, Heegaard Petersen and Mørch (1997: 62–5) give suggestions as to isoglosses between the Kalasha dialects. For reasons probably due to family relations, the people of the former Kalasha village Kalkatak in the main Chitral Valley shifted to Palula instead of Khowar, but today this village is mainly Khowar-speaking (Liljegren 2008).

[6] See, for example, Siiger (1956), Morgenstierne (1973), and Decker (1991).

fables, mythical legends, and heroic stories, and with the oral literature we may also include a variety of song genres, for example praise songs and lineage songs (see Parkes 1996, Di Carlo 2009). Previous linguistic and anthropological research has presented various examples of these genres. Morgenstierne's (1973) pioneer work contains some lexically glossed tales about legends and mythical persons from the religious world of the Kalasha, as well as songs and prayers from some of the religious festivals, collected by Morgenstierne himself in the 1920s, and by the Danish ethnographer Halfdan Siiger in 1947 (Siiger 1956, 1963). The British anthropologist Peter Parkes' unpublished PhD dissertation (1983) contains numerous lexically glossed stories, and Parkes (1996) analyses the importance of traditional songs for the ethnnic identity of the Kalasha. Cacopardo (2010) analyses religious songs from the winter solstice festival in Biriu. Di Carlo's works (2007, 2009, 2010) contain detailed grammatical glossing of songs from the *Pu'* festival 'wine-harvest festival' in Biriu, and Di Carlo (2010) analyses the pragmatic meanings of the combination of two topicalizing and contrastive particles *o* and *-ta* in a number of songs from the Biriu Valley. Finally, Heegård et al. (2015) is a collection of seven annotated texts with an introductory phonology and grammar.

With its grammatical commentary, the following narrative supplements these works by utilizing grammar in a discourse. As such, it can be seen as supplemental towards an understanding of text-linguistic structures in Kalasha.

4. TEXT AND COMMENTARY

4.1 THE NARRATIVE AND THE NARRATOR

The narrative *Ek akhabir sher ais* 'There was an old lion' is a traditional fable, with animal figures that behave and act partly as humans and partly as animals, a well-known genre from other cultures in the world. This genre is not the most frequent in the literature mentioned above (Morgenstierne (1973) presents two examples of this narrative type), but it makes up an important part of the oral literature of Kalasha, for example by being a type of narrative that is often told to children.

Typically the same fable is narrated in a way that is specific for the individual narrator. Although an illiterate shepherd, Sher John, the narrator of the fable in this article, is an esteemed storyteller and singer in the Kalasha community, and he is often invited to private houses to entertain. At the time of recording, 1997, he was around 30 to 35 years old. His narrative style is vivid and fascinating. He narrates in a clear voice, and an accurate articulation, with widespread use of mimic, gesture, and prosodic means such as creaky voice and variation in tempo. Although significant and characteristic, these prosodic and paralinguistic features are not represented in the transcription below.

4.2 The Transcription

The orthographic transcription of the narrative is based on a Kalasha orthography developed by the Australian linguist Greg Cooper and adopted at a conference in 1999 by Kalasha school teachers and village elders (Cooper 2005: in particular pp. 115–34, 2011; see also Heegård and Khan 2016). The orthography is strictly phonemic. In actual use, for instance by Kalasha people on Facebook or on web pages, there seems to be some sort of vacillation, in particular with regard to writing certain nominal suffixes as independent words or as word endings, the spelling of certain inflectional endings, in particular the third singular present tense and past tense endings, and the rendering of certain sentence particles as independent words or suffixes. In addition, one finds vacillation in representing the glides [ʊ̯] and [ɪ̯]. [ʊ̯] may be written <w> or <u>, [ɪ̯] may be written <y> or <i>. The confusion is caused by the de-syllabification of /u/ and /i/ after a preceding vowel, for example *kay* 'when' and *kai* 'done; doing' are both pronounced [kaɪ̯].

The present orthographic transcription follows Cooper (2005) by writing a nominal suffix together with the stem, by standardization of all verbal particles, and by systematization of glides that represent morphemes so that these are written with a vowel letter, hence [ʊ̯] with <u> and [ɪ̯] with <i>, and of glides that do not represent morphemes with a consonant letter, <w> and <y>, respectively. The present orthographic transcription differs from Cooper (2005), however, by using a hyphen between particles and the preceding phrase.

The phonemic transcription is based on the analysis in Heegård Petersen and Mørch (1997, 2004). It is in in many ways segmentally identical to the orthography, but there are a few phoneme–grapheme differences to be noticed. Nasalization of vowels is written with a superscript ~, and retroflex consonants and retroflexion of vowels, which is phonemic in Kalasha, is written with postscript apostrophe <'> in the orthography and with a postscript 'hook' /˞/ in the phonemic analysis. The apostrophe is also used to distinguish the dento-laminal and velarized lateral /ɫ̪/ from the alveolar (and potentially palatalized) /l/. For the sake of simplicity, the dento-laminal and velarized lateral is rendered as /ɫ/ in the phonemic transcription. The phoneme /ɽ/, represented by <r'>, is only relevant for the Biriu dialect. The digraphs <ts>, <dz>, <sh>, and <zh> represent the dental affricates /ts/ and /dz/ and the palatal sibilants /ɕ/ and /ʑ/. Aspirated phonemes are represented by digraphs with <h> as the second element, or, in the case of the dental and retroflex aspirated affricates, as trigraphs, <tsh> for /ts^{h}/ and /t's'h/ for /ʈʂ^{h}/. The orthography does not have specific letters for the sounds [ɳɲŋ], which occur only before retroflex, palatal, and velar stop consonants respectively. In the surface phonemic analysis applied in the text, these sounds are represented with ɳ, ɲ, and ŋ respectively.

Table 1 shows the Kalasha letters and their corresponding phonemes.

Table 1: Kalasha letters (in boldface) and corresponding phonemes (cf. Cooper 2005)[7]

a	a	**E**	e	**l**	l	**tsh**	tsʰ
ã	ã	**Ẽ**	ẽ	**l’**	ɫ̪	**t**	t
a’	a˞	**e’**	e˞	**m**	m	**th**	tʰ
ã’	ã˞	**ẽ’**	ẽ˞	**n**	n	**t’**	ʈ
b	b	**G**	g	**o**	o	**t’h**	ʈʰ
bh	bʰ	**Gh**	gʰ	**õ**	õ	**t’s’**	ʈʂ
c	tɕ	**H**	H	**o’**	o˞	**t’s’h**	ʈʂʰ
ch	tɕʰ	**I**	Ĩ	**õ’**	õ˞	**u**	u
c’	ʈʂ	**Ĩ**	Ĩ	**p**	p	**ũ**	ũ
c’h	ʈʂʰ	**i’**	i˞	**ph**	pʰ	**u’**	u˞
d	d	**ĩ’**	ĩ˞	**r**	r	**ũ’**	ũ˞
dh	dʰ	**J**	dʑ	**r’**	ɽ	**w**	w
dz	dz	**Jh**	dʑʰ	**s**	s	**y**	j
d’	ɖ	**j’**	ɖʐ	**sh**	ɕ	**z**	z
d’h	ɖʰ	**K**	K	**s’**	ʂ	**zh**	ʑ
		Kh	kʰ	**ts**	ts	**z’**	ʐ

[7] It is an ungoing discussion whether actually occurring aspirated sequences such as [mɦ], [nɦ], [lɦ], [ɫɦ], [rɦ], and [ʐɦ], and also [bɦ], [dɦ], [ɖɦ], [gɦ], and [dʑɦ] should be analysed as complex phonemes /mʰ/, /lʰ/, /bʰ/, /gʰ/, etc. as in Table 1, or whether they are realizations of a combination of, for example, /m/, /l/, /b/, /g/ with /h/.

4.3 GRAMMATICAL ANALYSIS AND ABBREVIATIONS

The grammatical analysis is based mainly on Bashir (1988, 1990, 2003) and Heegård (2006, 2014). The following abbreviations are used.

1P = first person plural
1S = first person singular
2S = second person singular
3P = third person plural
3S = third person singular
A = actual aspect (past, non-inferential)
ABL1 = ablative ending -(y)ei
ABL2 = ablative ending -ani
ABL3 = ablative ending -aw
ACC = accusative (pronouns)
ACROSS.EDGE = across-edge location (place adverbs)
AN = animate
AU = augment (prefix in past inflection)
AUX = auxiliary
COND = conditional (particle)
CONJ = conjunction
CP = conjunctive participle (a participle verb form used as a clausal adverbializer)
CS1 = primary causative suffix
CS2 = secondary causative suffix
CTR = contrastive particle
DIR = direct case
DI = distant (third person pronouns, demonstrative pronouns, and place adverbs)
EXCL = exclamation
IMPF = imperfective aspect
INAN = inanimate
INF = inferential aspect (past and perfect, not actual)

INFTV = infinitive
INSTR = instrumental case
IPV = imperative
LOC1 = locative ending -a
LOC2 = locative ending -una
LOC3 = locative ending -ai
NE = near (third person pronouns, demonstrative pronouns, and place adverbs)
NONSPEC = non-specific location (place adverbs)
NS = non-specific aspect
OBL = genitive-oblique case
P/F = present-future tense
PL = plural
PRS.PRF = present perfective
PST = past tense
PTC = participle (in a compound verb aspect form)
PURP = purpose particle -a
QUOT = quotative particle
REDUPL = reduplication
REM = remote (third person pronouns, demonstrative pronouns, and place adverbs)
S/P = singular/plural (zero morpheme)
SG = singular
SPEC = specific (aspect of verbals and location of place adverbs)
SUBJ = subjunctive particle
TOP = topicalizing particle

The following signs are used in the grammatical glossing:

Underscore:	combines words in fixed constructions
Hyphen:	shows morpheme combination (flexives)
Point:	indicates portmanteau morphemes
Square brackets:	square brackets are used
Equals sign:	shows combinations with morphemes that are enclitics

Grammatical analysis of *Ek akhabir sher ais*:

(1) *S'umberan, ne, s'umberan ek akhabir sher ais.*

ṣum'ber-an[8]	*ne=e*	*ṣum'ber-an*	*ek*[9]	*akha'bir*
before-INSTR	not=right	before-INSTR	an	old.AN[10]

ɕer	*'a-is*[11]
lion[DIR.S/P][12]	be.AN-PST.A.3S

[8] *S'umberan* 'in earlier times' is a lexicalization of *s'umber* 'before' and the unproductive instrumental *-an*. This time phrase initiates the narrative and sets it in a non-actual universe.

[9] *Ek* is a numeral, meaning '1', but it also has the function of introducing a discourse referent and as such it is translated with 'a' or 'an'. The discourse referent may be referred to later in a text anaphorically with a pronoun or a nominal phrase consisting of a demonstrative pronoun and the noun, or by the noun without any determiners. See Radloff and Shakil (1998: 23, 89) for a similar use of *ek* in Gilgit Shina.

[10] In the past tense and in the perfect aspect Kalasha distinguishes between 'actual' and 'inferential', or 'hearsay', verb forms. The inferential is often used when the speaker reports events or situations that s/he has not her-/himself experienced or for fictive events (Bashir 1988: 69–72). However, in this narrative the narrator chooses, it seems, not to use the inferential form *asta* 'be.PST.INF.3S/3P' as a means of setting the narrative in a fictive universe. This indicates that the inferential aspect does not necessarily 'carry the main burden of narration in storytelling' (Bashir 1988: 70).

Kalasha has two 'be' verbs, *shiik*, used with inanimate subjects, and *asik*, used with animate subjects. Both are used as auxiliaries in compound verb forms. *Asik* has in all its inflections a casual variant without *s*, for example *aik*. This intervocalic consonant elision is often seen in high frequency words. It is not marked explicitly in either the orthographic or the phonemic transcription.

[11] Kalasha adjectives are inflexible, unless they function as heads in nominal phrases. A set of core adjectives that denote inherent characteristics of a person, a thing, or entity, come in lexemically different pairs according to the animacy of the noun modified. The inanimate counterpart to *akhabir* 'old' is *l'az'na*.

[12] Kalasha nouns inflect in two syntactic cases, the direct (or 'nominative'), which has a zero-ending in the singular, and the genitive-oblique (henceforward referred to as the 'oblique', abbreviated OBL), which has the ending *-as* in the singular and the allomorphs *-an* and *-on* in the plural. Only few nouns that denote people of esteem take a plural suffix in the direct case. The direct case is used for the subject of verbs of all tenses and aspects and for the direct object for most verbs.

(2) *Akhabir sher lahaz ais, se.*

akhaˈbir	*çer*	*laˈhaz*	*ˈa-is*	*se*[13]
old.AN	lion[DIR.S/P]	ill	be.AN-PST.A.3S	3S.ABS.DIR[14]

(3) *Akhabir sher lahaz ais.*

akhaˈbir	*çer*	*laˈhaz*	*ˈa-is*
old.AN	lion[DIR.S/P]	ill	be.AN-PST.A.3S

A long time ago, right, a long time ago, there was an old lion. The old lion was ill, he. The old lion was ill.

The oblique case has a number of functions, including marking the object of verbs that denote an action directed to someone or something and marking the object of postpositions. See Heegård Petersen (2006: I: 53–61) and Heegård (2012, 2014) for analyses of the case endings in Kalasha.

[13] Kalasha is an SOV language. It is common in narratives to mention the subject or other verbal complements in post-clausal position, as a so-called afterthought expression. The construction is a means of clarifying or emphasizing the complement, and it may also function as a focus construction. See Radloff and Shakil (1998: 93) for a similar function in Gilgit Shina, and Perder (2013: 188–9) for the use of the afterthought expressions in Dameli.

[14] Third person personal pronouns distinguish between 'near', 'distal', and 'absent' and for each proximity category between three cases—direct, accusative, and oblique—and between singular and plural. These pronouns are identical to the demonstrative pronouns. See Bashir (2003: 852) and Heegård Petersen (2006: II, 9–10) for descriptions of these paradigms.

(4) *Khabar biko ek l'awak tara parau.*

kha'bar	*'biko*	*ek*	*ła'wak*	*ta'ra*	*pa'r-au*
and so[15]		a	fox[DIR.S/P]	there.ABS.SPEC[16]	go-PST.A.3S

And so a fox went there (where the lion was).

(5) *Tara pai amaau, tasa kai, sheras kai,*

ta'ra	*'pa-i*[17]	*a-'ma-au*	*'tasa*
there.ABS.SPEC	go-CP	AU-say-PST.A.3S	3S.ABS.OBL

'kai	*'ɕer-as*	*'kai*
to	lion-OBL.SG	to

---

[15] After having set the scene, the narrator now begins the unrolling of events, starting with the advent of the fox and initiated with a time phrase borrowed from Khowar, *khabar biko*. Radloff and Shakill (1998: 119, 126 *et passim*) notice a similar discourse strategy in Gilgit Shina. We follow here an interpretation suggested by an anonymous peer-reviewer who hypothesizes that *khabar biko* might reveal an 'English meaning more like *And then* or *And so* [functioning] as a discourse filler while the speaker gathers his/her thought'. We agree with the peer-reviewer that this may be a reasonable alternative interpretation and we apply it in this analysis, although, as also pointed out to us, it remains for future text-linguistic studies of Kalasha discourse to explore this idea.

[16] Kalasha place adverbs distinguish between 'near', 'distal', and 'absent'. For each of these proximity categories, the adverbs distinguish between 'specific' and 'non-specific' location. In the non-specific category the adverbs further distinguish between a location across or on the other side of an edge from the speaker's perspective and location that is not across an edge. See Heegård Petersen (2006: I, 178) and Heegård et al. (2015) for descriptions of the place adverb system.

[17] As a means of forming adverbial subordination, Kalasha makes extensive use of converb constructions where a present perfect verb form and possible complements function in the construction known as 'conjunct participle construction', 'CP', in South Asian languages (Masica 1991: 397–401). A sentence in Kalasha with a CP construction contains a finite verb as the matrix verb and one or more infinite verbs, formed with the perfective partiple *-i* or a suppletive participial form, according to the specific lexeme. The form of the CP verb is identical to the participial verb form that is used in perfect tenses (the grammatical glossing CP denotes the conjunctive function of the participle). The CP denotes what can be called perfective sequentiality of events or actions (Haspelmath 1995, Liljegren 2008: 233) and the specific semantics expressed may be instrumental, causal, anteriority (i.e. event(s) preceding main event in time), manner, or circumstance

(6) *'Eh sher sahib, batsha sahib,*

e	*çer*	*sa'hib*	*bat'ça*	*sa'hib*
Oh	lion[DIR.S/P]	sir	king[DIR.S/P]	Sir

(7) *tu lahaz aas,' aghõau.*

tu	*la'haz*	*'a-as*	*a-'ghõ-au*
2S.DIR	ill	be.AN-P/F.2S	AU-say-PST.A.3S

Having gone there, he said to him (the lion), to the lion, 'Oh, lion, sir, king-sir, you are ill,' he said.

(8) *'Tu bo akhabir,' aghõau.*

tu	*bo*	*akha'bir*	*a-'ghõ-au*
2S.DIR	much	old.AN	AU-say-PST.A.3S

'You are very old,' he said.

(9) *'Tay hatya warek-o kia dawai ne,' aghõau.*

taj	*'hatja*	*wa'reg=o*[18]	*'kia*	*da'wai*
2S.OBL	for	another[DIR]=TOP	what	medicine[DIR]

ne	*a-'ghõ-au*
not	AU-say-PST.A.3S

(Bashir 1988: 56–7). The literal translation into English is similar to 'having V-ed' or 'V-ing', but often a paraphrase is more obvious, for example with the conjunction 'and', or adverbializing 'by means of'. In narratives the main verb from the preceding sentence is often repeated in the following sentence as a conjunctive particle, and often, like here, with an adverbial phrase denoting a place or a time. The repetition of the preceding verb as a CP does not add new information but can be seen as a means of creating cohesion between succeeding events, and a literal translation into English often seems awkward or unnecessary. This phenomenon is known as a tail-head linkage (Coupe 2006), and it is reported for languages throughout the Hindu Kush region, see, for example, Radloff and Shakil (1998: 124, 150), Schmidt (2006), Liljegren (2008: 313 *et passim*), and Perder (2013: 189–90).

[18] The enclitic *-o* has several discourse functions, typically conveying contrast or adversation (Bashir 1988: 50–2, Di Carlo 2010: 149). Here it occurs in the

(10) *'Warek-o kia dawai ne shiu,' ghõi amaau.*

waˈreg=o	*ˈkia*	*daˈwai*	*ne*
another[DIR]=TOP	what	medicine[DIR]	not

ˈçi-u[19]	*ˈghõi*[20]	*a-ˈma-au*[21]
be.INAN-P/F.3S	QUOT	AU-say-PST.A.3S

'For you there is no medicine at all,' he said. 'No medicine at all,' he said.

(11) *'Biko tay hatya warek-o dawai ne shiu,'*

biˈko	*taj*	*ˈhatja*	*waˈreg-o*
because	2S.OBL	for	another[DIR]=TOP

daˈwai	*ne*	*ˈçi-u*
medicine[DIR]	not	be.INAN-P/F.3S

---

lexicalized phrase made up by *warek* 'another', *kia* 'what', and *ne* 'not', and adds contrastive emphasis to the negation.

[19] *Shiu* is the third person singular form of *shiik* 'be (ANIM)' rendered by Bashir (1988: 49), and the spelling also reflects the actual pronunciation. However, in the speech of many Kalasha one also hears *shiau*, also given by Trail and Cooper (1999: 285). It is unclear whether this is a genuine variation or whether *shiau* is formed by analogy from *aau* 'be.ANIM-P/F.3S'. Alternatively, as has been suggested to us by a native speaker, *shiu* is a fast speech variant of *shiau*.

[20] The particle *ghõi*, morphologically the perfective participle of *ghõik* 'speak, say', has various functions, according to Bashir (1988: 267–85, 309–21; 1996), comparable to other 'say' complementizers in other South Asian languages. In this sentence it functions as a complementizer for the utterance verb.

[21] A large number of verbs form the preterite forms with the prefix *a*-. Morgenstierne (1973: 229) considers this prefix as a relict of an old Indo-Aryan preterite formation, the so-called 'augment', glossed AU here.

(12) *aghõau, 'tu ek prus't' juhan shara.'*

a-ˈghõ-au	*tu*	*ek*	*pruʂʈ*	*ʥuˈhan*	*ˈɕara*
AU-say-PST.A.3S	2S.DIR	a	good	young	markhor[DIR.S/P]

'Because there is not medicine for you,' he said, 'you (have to eat) a young markhor('s brain).'[22]

(13) *'Sharaas mhasta pe ashi haw,*

ɕaˈra-as[23]	*ˈmhasta*	*pe*[24]	*aˈɕ-i*	*haw*
markhor-OBL.SG	brain[DIR.S/P]	if	eat.PST.A-PST.A.2S	when

(14) *Tu pak taza his,' ghõi amaau,*

tu	*pak*	*taˈza*	*h-is*
2S.DIR	completely	healthy	become-P/F.2S.NS

ˈghõi	*a-ˈma-au*
quot	AU-say-P/F.A.3S

(15) *l'awak, tasa kai, sheras kai.*

łaˈwak	*ˈtasa*	*ˈkai*	*ˈɕer-as*	*ˈkai*
fox[DIR.S/P]	3S.ABS.OBL	to	lion-OBL.SG	To

'If you eat a markhor's brain, then you will become completely healthy,' he said, the fox, to him, to the lion.

---

22 It seems as if the narrator, perhaps unintentionally, leaves out the verb phrase of this sentence.

23 *Shara* 'markhor' has the accent on the first syllable, but words with stems ending in *-a* shift their accent to the stem-final syllable when suffixed (Heegård (2012).

24 If-constructions are expressed by the conjunction *pe*, following the first constituent of the clause, and the subjunctive *haw*, in the final position of the clause. The main verb is in the past or perfect tense (Bashir 1988: 63–71).

(16) *Toa se amaau ki,*

ˈtoa	*se*	*a-ˈma-au*	*ki*[25]
then	3S.ABS.DIR	AU-say-PST.A.3S	CONJ

(17) *sher tasa kai amaau,*

çer	*ˈtasa*	*ˈkai*	*a-ˈma-au*
lion[DIR.S/P]	3S.ABS.OBL	to	AU-say-PST.A.3S

(18) *'Kura may hatya haliu, to?' ghõi amaau.*

ˈkura[26]	*maj*	*ˈhatja*	*haˈl-iu*[27]	*to*
who[DIR]	1S.OBL	For	bring-P/F.3S.NS	3S.ABS.ACC

ˈghõi	*a-ˈma-au*
QUOT	AU-say-PST.A.3S

Then he (the lion) said, the lion said to the him (the fox), 'Who will bring (him, the markhor) for me, it?' he said.

(19) *'A tay hatya halim,' ghõi amaau,*

a	*Taj*	*ˈhatja*	*haˈl-im*	*ˈghõi*	*a-ˈma-au*
1S.DIR	2S.OBL	for	bring-P/F.1S.NS	QUOT	AU-say-PST.A.3S

---

25 *Ki* is another sentential complementizer in Kalasha and it may be translated as 'that'. It is probably a recent borrowing from Persian, and it seems to have a more narrow range than *ghõi* (Bashir 1988: 295–8, 302–6, 321–4), occurring mainly with a 'say' verb or introducing purpose or reason clauses (with a non-realized but understood 'say' verb) (Bashir (1988: 322).

26 The pronoun *kura* 'who' has a direct form and an oblique form, *kaas*.

27 *Halik* 'bring (something animate)' also means 'give birth'. *Halik* is one of several verbs in Kalasha that distinguish lexemically between animate and inanimate variants. The inanimate counterpart to *halik* is *onik* 'bring (something inanimate)'.

(20) *l'awak, tasa kai. 'A tay hatya halim.'*

ła'wak	*'tasa*	*'kai*	*a*	*taj*
fox[DIR.S/P]	3S.ABS.OBL	to	1S.DIR	2S.OBL

'hatja	*ha'l-im*
for	bring-P/F.1S.NS

'I will bring (him, the markhor) for you,' he said, the fox, to him. 'I will bring (him, the markhor) for you. '

(21) *'Tu to gri sustek bhaas,' se aghõau.*

tu	*to*	*'gri-i*	*su'st-ek*
2S.DIR	3S.ABS.ACC	take-CP	defeat-INFTV

'bha-as[28]	*se*	*a-'ghõ-au*
be able-P/F.2S.NS	3S.ABS.DIR	AU-say-PST.A.3S

'Can you defeat (him), having caught (him)?' he said.

(22) *'Sustek bhaas-e?' aghõau haw,*

su'st-ek	*'bha-as=e*	*a-'ghõ-au*	*haw*
defeat-INFTV	be able-P/F.2S.NS=INTERR	AU-say-PST.A.3S	when

(23) *sher amaau ki, 'Bilkul a to sustem,'*

çer	*a-'ma-au*	*ki*	*'bilkul*
lion[DIR.S/P]	AU-say-PST.A.3S	CONJ	of course

a	*to*	*su'st-em*
1S.DIR	3S.ABS.ACC	defeat-P/F.1S.NS

[28] *Bhaik* 'be able to' takes an infinitival object, here *sustek* 'to defeat'.

(24) *ghõi amaau.*

ˈghõi	*a-ˈma-au*
QUOT	AU-say-PST.A.3S

When he (the fox) said, 'Can you defeat (him)?' the lion said, 'Of course I can defeat (him),' he said.

(25) *Shẽhẽ amaal'-aw, 'Tu nanga ne pe abhai haw?'*

ɕẽˈhẽ[29]	*a-ˈma-ał=aw*[30]	*tu*	*ˈnaŋga*
like this	AU-say-PST.A.3S=REDUPL	2S.DIR	perhaps

ne	*pe*	*a-ˈbha-i*	*haw*[31]
not	if	AU-be able-PST.A.2S	SUBJ

(26) *ghõi amaau, l'awak, tasa kai.*

ˈghõi	*a-ˈma-au*	*łaˈwak*	*ˈtasa*	*ˈkai*
QUOT	AU-say-PST.A.3S	fox[DIR.S/P]	3S.ABS.OBL	to

He said like this, 'Suppose you cannot defeat (him)?' he said, the fox, to him.

(27) *Se amaau ki, 'Ne, a bhaam.'*

se	*a-ˈma-au*	*ki*	*ne*	*a*	*ˈbha-am*
3S.ABS.DIR	AU-say-PST.A.3S	CONJ	not	1S.DIR	be able-P/F.1S.NS

He (the lion) said, 'No, I can.'

---

29 *Shẽhẽ* 'like this' has several variant forms, for example [ɕẽˈɦẽ], [ɕẽ], [ɕẽˈẽ], and [ɕeˈɦe].

30 The ending *aw/au* is sometimes reduplicated to *-awau*. As a morphonological rule a final [w] may become [ɫ̥] when followed by a suffix with an initial vowel.

31 *Haw*, the past actual root of *hik* 'become', may function as a conjunction with the meaning 'when', or as a subjunctive, expressing that a situation is hypothetical.

(28) *Toa l'awak parau, phato.*

ˈtoa	*ła'wak*	*paˈr-au*	*ˈphato*[32]
then	fox[DIR.S/P]	go-PST.A.3S	then

Then the fox left, after that.

(29) *L'awak pai parau, parau, parau.*

łaˈwak	*ˈpa-i*	*paˈr-au*	*paˈr-au*	*paˈr-au*[33]
fox[DIR.S/P]	go-CP	go-PST.A.3S	go-PST.A.3S	go-PST.A.3S

The fox going, (he) went, (and) went, (and) went.

(30) *Ek dhenta-senduna res'una parau, 'Ha!'*

ek	*dhenta.ˈsend-una*	*ˈreʐ-una*[34]	*paˈr-au*	*ha*[35]
a	mountain.side-LOC2	small path-LOC2	go-PST.A.3S	EXCL

He went to a certain difficult path on a mountain side, 'Hey!'

32 Kalasha has two adverbs that can be glossed 'then', *toa* and *phato*. Whereas *toa*, with the variant form *to*, seems to merely indicate a succession of events, *phato* indicates that a following event or situation has come about as an effect or a consequence of the preceding.

33 Repetition of motion verbs indicates that the activity is going on for a long time.

34 It is a characteristic feature of Kalasha morphophonology that word final unvoiced consonants can become voiced by suffixation, as in [ˈrɛʂ] > [ˈrɛʐuna]. Not all words show this voice alternation, for example [bat] 'stone' > [ˈbatuna] 'stone-LOC2' and [hãç] 'horse' > [ˈhãças] 'horse-OBL.SG'. It is not clear how the Kalasha orthography will deal with this morphologically conditioned variation, i.e. whether words should be written according to their underlying structure, *res'* and *res'una*, or their surface structure, *rez'* and *rez'una*.

35 With this interjection the narrator may address the audience or he may, as suggested by an anonymous peer-reviewer, express the narrator's echo of the fox's surprise at the sudden discovery of the markhor.

(31) *Res'una parau shara anday*[36] *niau.*

ˈreẓ -una	*paˈr-au*	*ˈɕara*
small path-LOC2	go-PST.A.3S	markhor[DIR.S/P]

anˈd-aj	*ni-ˈau*
here.NONSPEC-LOC3	appear-PST.A.3S

(When the fox) arrived at the path, a markhor appeared here.

(32) *Andai nii to l'awak jagai,*

anˈd-aj	*ˈni-i*	*to*
here.NONSPEC-LOC3	appear-CP	3S.ABS.ACC

łaˈwak	*dʑaˈga-i*[37]
fox[DIR.S/P]	look at-CP

(33) *kibaw-goni hawau, 'T'em,' ghõi acitau.*

kibaw=ˈgoni	*ˈhaw-au*	*ʈem*
something=-ish	become.PST-PST.A.3S	time[DIR]

ˈghõi	*a-ˈtɕit-au*
QUOT	AU-think-PST.A.3S

Having appeared here, and seeing the fox, something happened (to him, the markhor; he became worried).' (It's) time,' he thought.

---

[36] The narrator does not use expected *tal'ai* 'there.REM.NONSPEC' but instead a 'here'-adverb, accompanied with pointing gesture (according to first author's field notes), with the purpose of making the reported action more present and real to the audience.

[37] Succeeding CP constructions are used to 'squeeze' events together with a dramatizing function, and can be seen as a means of creating tension.

(34) *Toa se l'awak bo shaythan, se amaau ki,*

ˈtoa	*se*	*łaˈwak*	*bo*	*ɕajˈtan*
then	3S.ABS.DIR	fox[DIR.S/P]	very	mischievous

se	*a-ˈma-au*	*ki*
3S.ABS.DIR	AU-say-PST.A.3S	CONJ

(35) *'Sher sahib akhabir thi aau,*

ɕer	*saˈhib*	*akhaˈbir*	*thi_ˈa-au*
lion[DIR.S/P]	Mr	old.AN	become.PRS.PRF_AUX.AN-PRS.3S

(36) *sher sahib akhabir thi aau.'*

ɕer	*saˈhib*	*akhaˈbir*	*thi_ˈa-au*
lion[DIR.S/P]	Mr	old.AN	become.PRS.PRF_AUX.AN-PRS.3S

Then the fox (was) very mischievous, he said, 'Mr Lion has become old, Mr Lion has become old.'

(37) *'Onj-o nasiat kariu-dai.'*

ˈoɲʥ=o	*nasiˈat*	*ˈkar-iu=ˈdai*
now=TOP	advice[DIR.S/P]	do-P/F.3S=SPEC

(38) *'Bo shishoyak shishoyak mon del-dai.'*

bo	*ɕiˈɕojak*	*ɕiˈɕojak*[38]	*mon*	*ˈd-el=le*
very	beautiful	beautiful	word[DIR.S/P]	give-P/F.3S=SPEC

'Now (he) is giving advice (to animals in his kingdom). He speaks very beautiful words.'

---

[38] Repetition of an adjective is an often used as a means for emphasis or vehemence, or as expressing plurality. A similar function of adjective repetition in Gilgit Shina is observed by Radloff and Shakill (1998: 118).

(39) *'Saw thi ita tasa mon kõ' kai paron,*

saw	*thi*[39]	*ˈita*	*ˈtasa*
all[DIR]	be.CP	come.CP	3S.ABS.OBL

mon	*kõ˞ _ˈka-i*[40]	*paˈr-on*
word[DIR.S/P]	ear_do-CP	go-PST.A.3P

(40) *tu-o ne a, pre, tay kai asta del.'*

ˈtu=o	*ne*	*a*	*pre*
2S.DIR=TOP	not	come.PST.A.2S	go.IPV.1P

taj	*ˈkai*	*ˈasta*	*d-el*
2S.OBL	to	also	give-P/F.3S.NS

'Everybody came, heard his words, and went (away), but you did not come, come, he will give (advice) to you too.'

---

[39] The present particple *thi* 'being; becoming' is used in a number of non-verbal functions. With *saw* 'all', *saw thi*, literally 'all being', it emphasizes that a situation or event involves everybody.

[40] In South Asian linguistics a complex verb like *kõ' karik*, 'listen, hear' (literally 'ear do') is known as a conjunct verb (Masica 1991: 368–9), consisting of a a nominal element and a dummy verb, 'vector verb'. In Kalasha, the conjunct verb construction is a very productive way of creating verbs. The most frequently used vector verbs in Kalasha are *hik* 'become', which makes intransitive verbs, *karik* 'do', which makes transitive verbs, and *dek* 'give', which can make intransitive or transitive verbs. The nominal element may be an independent nominal, like *kõ'* 'ear' or *mon* 'word' in *mon dek* 'say, speak', or it may be nominal-like element that does not exist as an independent word (and it cannot take flexive or derivative affixes). Examples of the latter type in this text are *phan dek* 'lie', *apaw dek* 'live; stay'and *khir hik* 'deny' (see lines 44, 102, 126). Radloff and Shakil (1998: 34, 89, 151) observe a similar pattern in Gilgit Shina and they call these elements 'precategorical' since they do not follow the regular criteria for part of speech membership. We follow Radloff and Shakil by translating these elements with a derivative in '-ing' or '-ness'.

(41) *'Tu andena mocaw adrakai*

tu	*an'den-a*[41]	*'motç-aw*	*a'drak-ay*
2S.DIR	here.ACROSS.EDGE-LOC1	middle-ABL3	forest-LOC3

(42) *bo shishoyak ishnehari shara.'*

bo	*çi'çojak*	*içne'hari*	*'çara*
very	beautiful	thing	markhor[DIR.S/P]

'You, out of the whole forest, are the most beautiful thing, markhor (among the animals).'

(43) *'Tu to mon griik bhaas,' ghõi.*

tu	*to*	*mon*	*'gri-ik*	*'bha-as*	*'ghõi*
2S.DIR	3S.ABS.ACC	word	catch-INFTV	be able-P/F.2S.NS	QUOT

'You can understand his advice,'[42] (he) said.

(44) *To phan-dai aniau. Tara parau.*

to	*phan_'da-i*	*a-'ni-au*
3S.ABS.ACC	lying_give-CP	AU-take-PST.A.3S

ta'ra	*pa'r-au*
there.ABS.SPEC	go-PST.A.3S

Lying about this, he took him (to the king). He (the fox) went there.

---

[41] *Andena* is one of the non-specific adverbs that denotes location across an edge or on another side of a barrier from the speaker's perspective (see fn. 11). The 'across-edge' meaning is derived by a reduplication-like process where the first syllable is reduplicated and the root vowel replaced by *e*, cf. the root in *and-ai* 'here.NONSPEC-LOC3' (see Heegård Petersen 2006: I, 177–81). It is not quite clear what sort of edge or barrier is meant here, perhaps the jungle with its many trees is to be perceived as a location with 'edges' or barriers.

[42] Literally *to mon* means 'that word'.

(45) *Tara parau haw, 'Asa gehen khezas,'*

ta'ra	*pa'r-au*	*haw*	*'asa*
there.ABS.SPEC	go-PST.A.3S	when	3S.DI.OBL

ge'hen	*'khez-as*
direction[DIR.SG]	move-P/F.2S.NS

(46) *ghõi amaau, sharaas kai, l'awak.*

'ghõi	*a-'ma-au*	*ɕa'ra-as*	*'kai*	*ła'wak*
QUOT	AU-say-PST.A.3S	markhor-OBL.SG	to	fox[DIR.S/P]

When (he) went there, 'Move in his (the king's) direction,' (he) said, to the markhor, the fox.

(47) *'Asa kõ' karut'u, ne sangaau-dai.'*

'asa	*kõ*	*ka'ruʈu*	*ne*	*saŋ'ga-au='dai*
3S.DI.OBL	ear[DIR.S/P]	deaf	not	hear-P/F.3S=SPEC

(48) *'Asa sher akhabir, karut'u thi aau,'*

'asa	*ɕer*	*akha'bir*
3S.DI.DIR	lion[DIR.S/P]	old.AN

ka'ruʈu	*thi_'a-au*
deaf	become-PRS.PRF.A_AUX.AN.3S

(49) *ghõi amaau.*

'ghõi	*a-'ma-au*
QUOT	AU-say-PST.A.3S

'His ear is deaf, he cannot hear. That lion (is) old, (he) has become deaf,' he (the fox) said.

(50) *Toa lash thi s'oy parau haw,*

ˈtoa	*laɕ*	*thi*	*ʂoj*	*paˈr-au*	*haw*
then	slow	be.CP	near	go-PST.A.3S	when

(51) *shẽhẽ kai se sher dramut's' prau,*

ɕẽˈhẽ	*ˈka-i*[43]	*se*	*ɕer*	*draˈmutʂ_ˈpr-au*
like this	do-CP	3S.DI.DIR	lion[DIR.S/P]	claw_give.PST.A-PST.A.3S

(52) *tasa tap agriau haw pal'ais.*

ˈtasa	*tap*	*a-ˈgri-au*	*haw*	*paˈɬa-is*
3S.ABS.OBL	quick	AU-catch-PST.A.3S	when	escape-PST.A.3S

Then, when he slowly went near (to the king), doing like this the lion clawed, (but when he had almost) quickly caught him, he (the markhor) escaped.

(53) *Dramut's' dyai kõ' achinau,*

ˈdramutʂ_ˈdja-i	*kõ*	*a-ˈtɕhin-au*
claw_give-CP	ear[DIR.S/P]	AU-cut-PST.A-3S

(54) *sharaas kõ' achinau, shara pal'ai parau.*

ɕaˈra-as	*kõ*	*a-ˈtɕhin-au*
markhor-OBL.SG	ear[DIR.S/P]	AU-cut-PST.A.3S

ˈɕara	*paˈɬa-i*	*paˈr-au*
markhor[DIR.S/P]	escape-CP	go-PST.A.3S

Clawing (him) (he) cut the ears, (he) cut the markhor's ears, (and) the markhor escaping, went (away).

[43] The present participle *thi* 'being; becoming' functions here as an intransitive adverbializer, forming a manner adverbial implying that the state denoted by the adverbial has come about non-volitionally or without an active agent. In contrast, *kai*, as in *shẽhẽ kai* 'like this' in the following sentence, forms transitive adverbials that imply that the denoted manner has come about through a volitional act by someone.

(55) *Pal'ai parau haw l'awak tasa kai amaau ki,*

paˈła-i	*paˈr-au*	*haw*	*łaˈwak*	
escape-CP	go-PST.A.3S	when	fox[DIR.S/P]	
ˈtasa	*ˈkai*	*a-ˈma-au*	*ki*	
3S.DI.OBL	to	AU-say-PST.A.3S	CONJ	

As (the markhor) had escaped and gone (away), the fox said to him (the king),

(56) *'Onj-o ko bata iu, aya, tu ne abhai.'*

ˈoɲʥ=o	*ko*	*ˈbata*	*ˈi-u*
now=TOP	why	CTR	come-P/F.3S.NS
aˈja	*tu*	*ne*	*a-ˈbha-i*
here.NE.SPEC	2S.DIR	not	AU-be able-PST.A.2S

(57) *'Tu ne abhai.'*

tu	*ne*	*a-bha-i*
2S.DIR	not	AU-be able-PST.A.2S

'Now why would it come again, here, you didn't manage (to kill him).[44] You couldn't.'

(58) *Biko tasa kai amaau ki,*

biko	*ˈtasa*	*ˈkai*	*a-ˈma-au*	*ki*
and so	3S.ABS.OBL	to	AU-say-PST.A.3S	CONJ

[44] Although the meaning of this sentence is rendered by the present translation, the syntax is not quite obvious. The 'have to' meaning seems to come about through the contrastive particle *bata*. An alternative translation would be '*Why weren't you able (to kill him)? Now he has to come again.*' Following this, the question-part is interrupted by the sentence that expresses the consequence of the lion's not being able to kill the markhor.

(59) *'Onj-o a khẽ kai halim, to, se pal'ais.'*

ˈoɲʥ=o[45]	*a*	*khẽ*	*ˈka-i*	*haˈl-im*
now=TOP	1S.DIR	how	do-CP	bring-P/F.1S.NS

to	*se*	*paˈła-is*
3S.DI.ACC	3S.DIR.DI	escape-PST.A.3S

And so (he, the fox) said to him (the lion), 'Now how will I bring (him) here, him, he ran away?'

(60) *Toa sher amaau ki,*

ˈtoa	*ɕer*	*a-ˈma-au*	*ki*
then	lion[DIR.S/P]	AU-say-PST.A.3S	CONJ

(61) *'Pari, hali, onj-o pe hal'aw to sustem,*

paˈr-i	*haˈl-i*	*ˈonʥ=o*	*pe*
go-IPV.2S	bring-IPV.2S	now=TOP	if

ˈhał=aw	*to*	*suˈst-em*
when=REDUPL	3S.ABS.ACC	defeat-P/F.1S.NS

(62) *to shara sustem,' ghõi.*

To	*ˈɕara*	*suˈst-em*	*ˈghõi*
3S.ABS.ACC	markhor[DIR.S/P]	defeat-P/F.1S.NS	QUOT

Then the lion said, 'Go, bring (him), now I will be able to defeat him, I will defeat that markhor,' (he said).

(63) *To gheri ahut'au.*

to	*ˈgheri*	*a-ˈhuʈ-au*
3S.REM.ACC	again	AU-send away-PST.A.3S

He (the lion) sent him (the fox back) again.

---

45 The final -a in *onja* 'now' is elided when suffixed by the topicalizer *-o*.

(64) *Gheri ahut'au haw l'awak parau,*

ˈgheri	*a-ˈhuʈ-au*	*haw*	*ɬaˈwak*	*paˈr-au*
again	AU-send away-PST.A.3S	when	fox[DIR.S/P]	go-PST.A.3S

(65) *pai gudas thi tasa pis't'au azhal'au.*

ˈpa-i	*guˈdas*	*thi*	*ˈtasa*	*ˈpiʂʈaw*	*a-ˈʐaɬ-au*
go-CP	tired	be.CP	3S.ABS.OBL	behind	AU-arrive-PST.A.3S

When he sent (the fox away), the fox went (away), and having gone to a lot of trouble, (the fox) arrived behind the markhor.

(66) *Zhal'i se kahari hawau, 'Tay nashem, a.'*

ˈʐaɬ-i	*se*	*kahaˈri*	*ˈhaw-au*
arrive-CP	3S.ABS.DIR	angry	become.PST.A-PST.3S

taj	*naˈɕ-em*	*a*
2S.OBL	kill-P/F.1S.NS	1S.DIR

(When he, the fox) arrived, the markhor became angry, '(I) will kill you, I.'

(67) *'Tu may atra sheras s'at'awai z'uawaika*

tu	*maj*	*a'tra*	*'ɕer-as*
2S.DIR	1S.OBL	there.DI.SPEC	lion-OBL.SG

ʂaʈa'wai[46]	*ʐu-a'w-a-ik-a*[47]
by way of	eat-CS2-CS1-INFTV-PURP

(68) *niman ay, ha!' ghõi amaal'au.*

'ni-man_'a-i	*hah*
take-IMPF.PTC_AUX.AN-PST.2S	EXCL

'ghõi	*a-'ma-ał-au*
QUOT	AU-say-PST.A.3S-REDUPL

'You took me there so that the lion could eat me, ha!' he said.

(69) *'Ne, tay ne zhuiman ais.'*

ne	*taj*	*ne*	*ʐu-'iman_'a-is*
not	2S.OBL	not	eat-IMPF.PTC.A_AUX.AN-PRS.3S

(70) *'Tu galat ari pal'ai.'*

tu	*ga'lat*	*'ar-i*	*pa'ła-i*
2S.DIR	wrong	do.PST.A-2S	escape-CP

'No, he was not eating you,' (the fox said). 'You did wrong by running away.'

---

46 *S'at'awai* 'by way of' is a postposition marking the secondary agent in a double causative formation. It is a frozen form, the present participle of the intransitive *s'at'ik* 'stick to, adhere to, attach to' formed by the double transitive form of this verb: *s'at'- + aw + a + i* (see note below).

47 *Zhuawaik* is a double causative formation with the fox, *tu,* as the primary agent, the lion as the secondary agent, marked by *s'at'awai*, and the markhor as the patient. The formation is to be understood as such: The primary agent, the fox, causes the secondary agent, the lion, to bring about a transitive action, the eating, on the patient, the markhor. Causative formation and transitivity in Kalasha is analysed in detail by Bashir (1988: 155–217).

(71) *‘Se tay kay kõ’una kai mon diman ais.’*

se	*taj*	*ˈkai*	*ˈkõ˞ -una_ˈka-i*
3S.ABS.DIR	2S.OBL	to	ear-LOC2_do-CP

mon_ˈdi-man_ˈa-is
word_give-IMPF.PTC.A_AUX.AN-PST.3S
‘He was telling you something.’

(72) *‘Se ne sangaau, tu tasa s’oi ne para*

se	*ne*	*saŋˈga-au*	*tu*
3S.ABS.DIR	not	hear-P/F.3S.NS	2S.DIR

ˈtasa	*ʂoi*	*ne*	*paˈr-a*
3S.ABS.OBL	near	not	go-PST.A.2S

(73) *shẽhẽ kai, tay dramut’s’ak prau-e kõ’ achis,*

ɕeˈhe	*ˈka-i*	*taj*	*draˈmuʈʂak*
like	do-CP	2S.OBL	claw[DIR.S/P]

ˈpr-au=e	*kõ˞*	*a-ˈtɕhi-is*
give.PST.A-3S=as	ear[DIR.S/P]	AU-cut-PST.A.2S

(74) *ghõi amaau-e, se amaau ki,*

ˈghõi	*a-ˈma-au=e*	*se*	*a-ˈma-au*	*ki*
QUOT	AU-say-PST.A.3S=as	3S.ABS.DIR	AU-say-PST.A.3S	CONJ

(75) *‘Ne, se may zhu.’*

ne	*se*	*maj*	*ʐ-u*
not	3S.ABS.DIR	1S.OBL	eat-P/F.3S.NS

As he (the fox) said, ‘He cannot hear, you did not go near (to him), like this, as (he) scratched you, like this, (he) cut (your) ear,’ He (the markhor) said, ‘No, he (intended to, lit. will) eat me.’

(76) *'Ne zhu, pre,' gheri phan-dai,*

ne	*ʐ-u*	*pre*	*ˈgheri*	*phan_ˈda-i*
not	eat-P/F.3S.NS	go.IPV.1P	again	lying_give-CP

(77) *to shara halaw.*

to	*ˈɕara*	*haˈl-au*
3S.ABS.ACC	markhor[DIR.S/P]	bring-PST.A.3S

'(He) will not eat (you). Let's go (and try it out).' Lying again, he (the fox) brought the markhor (there).

(78) *Shara patiau.*

ˈɕara	*pati-ˈau*
markhor[DIR.S/P]	believe-PST.A.3S

The markhor trusted (the fox).

(79) *Aau, tara aau-e:*

ˈa-au	*taˈra*	*ˈa-au=e*
come.PST.A-3S	there.ABS.SPEC	come.PST.A-3S=AS

(80) *'Asa s'oy pari,' aghõau.*

ˈasa	*ʂoj*	*paˈr-i*	*a-ˈghõ-au*
3S.DI.OBL	near	go-IPV.2S	AU-say-PST.A.3S

As (he, the markhor) came there, 'Go near (to the king),' he (the fox) said.

(81) *Se sher-o shẽhẽ thi apaw prau*

se	*ˈɕer=o*	*ɕeˈhe*
3S.ABS.DIR	lion[DIR.S/P]=TOP	like this

thi	*aˈpaw_ˈpr-au*
be.CP	dwelling_give.PST.A-PST.A.3S

(82) *hũk asta ne kai.*

huŋk	*ˈasta*	*ne*	*ˈka-i*
sound[DIR.S/P]	indeed[48]	not	do-CP

The lion was sitting (quietly) like this, not saying anything at all.

(83) *'Tadaka pari, ' aghõau. Tadaka parau.*

tadaka[49]	*paˈr-i*	*a-ˈghõ-au*	*ˈtadaka*	*paˈr-au*
near	go-IPV.2S	AU-say-PST.A.3S	near	go-PST.A.3S

'Go quite near (to the lion),' (he) said. (He) went quite near.

(84) *Tadaka pai khabar biko thedi tasa kai amaau:*

ˈtadaka	*ˈpa-i*	*khaˈbar ˈbiko*	*theˈdi*	*ˈtasa*
near	go-CP	and so	now	3S.ABS.OBL

ˈkai	*a-ˈma-au*
to	AU-say-PST.A.3S

(85) *'Kia maas-dai, sher sahib?'*

ˈkia	*ˈma-as=ˈdai*	*ɕer*	*saˈhib*
what	say-P/F.2S=SPEC	lion[DIR.S/P]	Mr

Having gone near (to the lion), and so now (he, the markhor) said to him, 'What are you saying, Mr Lion?'

(86) *'Mon de, tay tada ita aam,'*

mon_d-e	*taj*	*ˈtad-a*	*ˈi-ta_ˈa-am*
word_give-IPV.2S	2S.OBL	near-LOC1	come-PRS.PERF.A_ AUX.AN-P/F.1S

[48] As an adverb, *asta* is polysemous, meaning, for example, 'also', 'indeed', more', 'very', 'ever' (Trail and Cooper 1999: 16). The adverb is homonymous to the suppletive past inferential verb form of be (animate), *asta*.

[49] *Tadaka* is a diminutive derivation with *-ka* on the postposition *tada*, itself formed by the bound noun root *tad-* and the locative suffix *-a*.

(87) *aghõau,shara tasa kai.*

a-ˈghõ-au	*ˈɕara*	*ˈtasa*	*ˈkai*
AU-say-PST.A.3S	markhor[DIR.S/P]	3S.ABS.OBL	to

'Say (something), I have come near to you,' he said, the markhor (said) to him.

(88) *Hũk na arau, sher,*

huŋk	*ne*	*ˈar-au*	*ɕer*
sound[DIR.S/P]	not	do.PST.A-PST.A.3S	lion[DIR.S/P]

(89) *chimcilit thi apaw prau.*

tɕhimtɕiˈlit_thi	*aˈpaw_ˈpr-au*
quiet_be.CP	dwelling_give.PST.A-PST.A.3S

(He) said nothing, the lion, he (just) sat (there), very quiet.

(90) *Gheri amaau ki, 'Kia maas-dai? '*

ˈgheri	*a-ˈma-au*	*ki*	*ˈkia*	*ˈma-as=ˈdai*
again	AU-say-PST.A.3S	CONJ	what	say-P/ F.3S=SPEC

Again (he, the markhor) said, 'What are you saying?'

(91) *'A tay tada ita aam,*

a	*taj*	*ˈtad-a*	*ˈi-ta_ˈa-am*
1S.DIR	2S.OBL	near-LOC1	come-PST.PERF.A_AUX.AN-PRS.1S

(92) *onj-o mon de,' ghõi.*

ˈoɲdʑ=o	*mon_d-e*	*ˈghõi*
now=TOP	word_ give-IPV.2S	QUOT

'I have come close to you, now speak,' (he said).

(93) *Shẽhẽ thi pai kõ'una az'al'au haw,*

ɕeˈhẽ	*thi*	*ˈpa-i*	*ˈkõ˞ -una*
like this	be.CP	go-CP	ear-LOC2

a-ˈʐał-au	*haw*
AU-reach-PST.A.3S	when

(94) *tap gri to taa sharaas ga'ani gri,*

tap	*ˈgri-i*	*to*	*ɕaˈra-as*
quickly	3S.ABS.ACC	3S.ABS.OBL	markhor-OBL.SG

ˈtasa	*ˈga˞ -ani*	*ˈgri-i*
3S.ABS.OBL	throat-ABL2	hold-CP

(95) *kat'ar kai to s'is' ahistau.*[50]

kaˈʈar_ˈka-i	*to*	*ʂiʂ*	*a-ˈhist-au*
knife_do-CP	3S.ABS.ACC	head[DIR.S/P]	AU-throw-PST.A.3S

Like this, when (he, the markhor) got near to (his, the lion's) ear, catching him quickly, catching the markhor's throat, (and) cutting his throat, (he, the lion) threw away the head (of the markhor).

(96) *Histi thedi l'ui pikas praw.*

ˈhist-i	*theˈdi*	*łui*	*ˈp-ik-as*	*ˈpr-au*
throw-CP	now	blood[DIR]	drink-INFTV-OBL.SG	give.PST.A-PST.A.3S

Having thrown away (the head), then (he, the lion) started drinking blood.

---

[50] Three CP's in a row, the first one forming a manner adverbial, signal a very dramatic chain of events, here the lion's rapid seizing of the markhor and cutting of its throat.

(97) *L'ui pi prus't' tatsiris.*

ˈɬui	*ˈpi-i*	*pru::ʂʈ*[51]	*taˈtsiris*
blood[DIR]	drink-CP	very well	Satisfied

Drinking blood, he became very full/satisfied.

(98) *L'awak-o to khuran thara dramut's'ak dyai*

ɬaˈwag=o	*to*	*ˈkhur-an*
fox[DIR.S/P]=TOP	then	leg-OBL.PL

ˈthara	*draˈmuʈʂak_ˈdja::-i*
upon	claw_give-CP

(99) *to mhasta chal'ai plik ashau*

to	*ˈmhasta*	*tɕhaˈɬa-i*
3s.abs.acc	brain[DIR.S/P]	take out-CP

plik	*ˈaɕ-au*
all	eat.PST.A-PST.A.3S

The fox, clawing at the legs, took out the brain (and) ate all of it.

(100) *Zhui-o desha pai nisi apaw prau,*

ˈʐu-i=o[52]	*ˈdeɕa*	*ˈpa-i*
eat-CP=TOP	far away	go-CP

niˈs-i	*aˈpaw_ˈpr-au*
sit-CP	dwelling_give.PST.A-PST.A.3S

---

[51] Vowel lengthening is often used in narratives as a means of emphasis, for example indicating a large or a very small volume of something, or that an activity has a prolonged duration. This way of expressing intensity or vehemence is also observed in Gilgit Shina (Radloff and Shakil 1998: 77). It is unclear how or if this vowel lengthening should be represented in the orthography.

[52] With a CP construction, the topicalizer *-o* emphasizes the sequentiality of the linked events (Bashir 1988: 51).

(101) *samlat shẽhẽkai drĩki-o.*

samlat	*ɕẽˈhẽ*	*ˈka-i*	*driŋk-i=o*
moustache[DIR.S/P]	like this	do-CP	clean-CP=TOP

After having eaten, (he, the fox) went (a little way) away and sat down, cleaning his moustache like this.

(102) *Desha pai nisi apaw prau haw,*

ˈdeɕa	*ˈpa-i*	*nis-i*	*aˈpaw_ˈpr-au*	*haw*
far away	go-CP	sit-CP	dwelling_give-PST.A-PST.A.3S	when

(103) *thedi prus't' l'ui pii tasiris, sher tasiri.*

theˈdi	*pru::ʂʈ*	*ˈɬui*	*ˈpi-i*
then now	well	blood[DIR]	drink-CP

taˈsir-is	*ɕer*	*taˈsiri*
full-PST.A.3S	lion[DIR.S/P]	full

When (he, the fox) going away (he) sat down, (then) now, after drinking the blood well, (he, the lion) was full, the lion being full.

(104) *Toa ger arau,*

ˈtoa	*ger_ˈar-au*
then	awareness_do.PST.A-PST.A.3S

(105) *ger kai tasa kai amaau ki,*

ger_ˈka-i	*ˈtasa*	*ˈkai*
awareness_do.PST.A-PST.A.3S	3S.ABS.OBL	to

a-ˈma-au	*ki*
AU-say-PST.A.3S	CONJ

Then he became aware (about the brain), having become aware, (he, the lion) said to him (the fox),[53]

(106) *Tara pai jiaw,*

taˈra	*ˈpa-i*	*dʑiˈa-u*
there.ABS.SPEC	go-CP	look-PST.A.3S

(107) *jiai, to s'is' bat-batay tyai,*

dʑiˈa-i	*to*	*ʂiʂ*
look-CP	3S.ABS.ACC	head[DIR.S/P]

bat-ˈbat-aj[54]	*ˈtja-i*
stone-REDUPL-LOC3	beat-CP

(108) *to s'is' bis'ai jiaw haw,*

to	*ʂiʂ*	*biˈʂa-i*
3S.ABS.ACC	head[DIR.S/P]	crack-CP

dʑiˈa-u	*haw*
look-PST.A.3S	when

(109) *mhasta ne shiu*

ˈmhasta	*ne*	*ˈɕi-u*
brain[DIR.S/P]	not	be.INAN-P/F.3S

(He) went there and looked, having looked, beating the head on some stones, (and) cracking the head, when he saw, there was no brain.

---

53 The narrator seems here to interrupt himself by first clarifying the lion's activity before the direct speech addressed to the fox.

54 This reduplication indicates dispersion of the entity denoted by the reduplicated noun (Heegård Petersen 2006: II, 48). The locative ending *-ai* indicates that the location is inexact or spread out. In contrast, the locative ending *-una* would indicate that the lion beat the head on a specific point on the rocks or on some specific rocks. Either way, the sentence would be odd with the dispersion denoted by the reduplication and the 'exact location' meaning of *-una*. See Heegård Petersen (2006: I, 99–171) and Heegård (2014) for analyses of the semantics of the local case endings.

(110) *To amaau ki,*

to	*a-ˈma-au*	*ki*
then	AU-say-PST.A.3S	CONJ

(111) *'Ey l'awak, to mhasta ko ashi,'*

ej	*ła'wak*	*to*	*ˈmhasta*
hey	fox[DIR.S/P]	3S.ABS.ACC	brain[DIR.S/P]

ko	*aˈɕ-i*
why	eat.PST.A-PST.A.2S

(112) *ghõi amaau, tasa kai.*

ˈghõi	*a-ˈma-au*	*ˈtasa*	*ˈkai*
QUOT	AU-say-PST.A.3S	3S.ABS.OBL	to

Then (he) said, 'Hey, fox, why did you eat the brai?' (he) said, to him.

(113) *Se amaau ki, 'Asa mhasta ne shial'a,*

se	*a-ˈma-au*	*ki*	*asa*[55]
3S.ABS.DIR	AU-say-PST.A.3S	CONJ	3S.DI.OBL

ˈmhasta	*ne*	*ɕi-ˈała*
brain[DIR.S/P]	not	be.INAN-PST.INF.3S

(114) *khali asta, asa.'*

khaˈli	*ˈasta*	*ˈasa*
empty	be.AN.PST.INF.3S	3S.DIR.DI

He (the fox) said, 'He had no brain, (he) was empty, he.'

[55] Kalasha does not have a 'have' verb. Possession is indicated with the possessor in the oblique case, the possessed item in the direct case, and with the verb congruent in number with the possessed item.

(115) *Sher tasa kai amaau ki,*

çer	*ˈtasa*	*ˈkai*	*a-ˈma-au*	*ki*
lion[DIR.S/P]	3S.ABS.OBL	to	AU-say-PST.A.3S	CONJ

(116) *'Mhasta ne thi-o khẽ thi kasiu-day, asa?'*

ˈmhasta	*ne*	*ˈthi=o*	*khẽ*	*thi*
brain[DIR.S/P]	not	be.CP=TOP	How	be.CP

ˈkas-iu=ˈdai	*ˈasa*
walk-P/F.3S=SPEC	3S.DI.DIR

The lion said to him (the fox), 'If there (was) no brain, how could (he) walk, he?'

(117) *'Al'a ko lawaas-day, tu?' ghõi amaau haw*

ˈała	*ko*	*laˈwa-as=ˈdai*	*tu*
3S.DI.ACC	why	lie-P/F.2=SPEC	2S.DIR

ˈghõi	*a-ˈma-au*	*haw*
QUOT	AU-say-PST.A.3S	when

(118) *L'awak tasa kai jawap arau,*

łaˈwak	*ˈtasa*	*ˈkai*	*ʥaˈwap_ˈar-au*
fox[DIR.S/P]	3S.ABS.OBL	to	answer_do.PST.A-PST.A.3S

(119) *l'awak tasa kai amaau ki,*

łaˈwak	*ˈtasa*	*ˈkai*	*a-ˈma-au*	*ki*
fox[DIR.S/P]	3S.ABS.OBL	to	AU-say-PST.A.3S	CONJ

(120) *'Asa mhasta ne shial'a, khali asta.'*

ˈasa	*ˈmhasta*	*ne*	*ɕi-ˈała*
3S.DI.OBL	brain[DIR.S/P]	not	be.INAN-PST.INF.3S

khaˈli	*ˈasta*[56]
empty	be.AN.PST.INF.3S

When (he) said (the lion), 'Why are you lying (about) this, you?' (then) the fox answered him, the fox said to him, 'He didn't have a brain, (he) was empty.'

(121) *'Asa mhasta pe ashis,*

ˈasa	*ˈmhasta*	*pe*	*ˈaɕ-is*
3S.DI.OBL	brain[DIR.S/P]	if	be.INAN.PST.A-3S

(122) *tu asa kõ'chini ai*

tu	*ˈasa*	*kõ˞*	*ˈtɕhin-i_ˈa-i*
2S.DIR	3S.DI.OBL	ear[DIR.S/P]	cut-PRS.PERF.A_AUX.AN-2S

(123) *asa gheri au dyapa-e?'*

ˈasa	*gheri*	*ˈa-u*	*ˈdjapa=e*
3S.DI.DIR	again	come.PST.A-3S	CTR=as

'If he had a brain, (he wouldn't have come here again, because) you cut his ear, (so) would he have come back?'[57]

---

56 This use of these two hearsay/inferential verb forms seems peculiar since it is in direct speech and it is not repeated in the two next lines where the past actual form *ashis* is used. However, the function of hearsay/inferential *asta* here may be that of expressing mirativity, a well-known potential co-effect of inferentiality morphemes (Delancey 1997).

57 The meaning of this sentence may be that if the markhor had had a brain, the lion would not have been able to cut the markhor's ears.

(124) *'Asa mhasta ne ashis,*

ˈasa	*ˈmhasta*	*ne*	*ˈaɕ-is*
3S.DI.OBL	brain[DIR.S/P]	not	be.INAN.PST.A-PST.A.3S

(125) *toa au,' ghõi.*

ˈtoa	*ˈa-u*	*ˈghõi*
then	come.PST.A-PST.A3S	QUOT

'He did not have a brain, so he came.'

(126) *Mon khir hawau, phato sher patiau.*

mon_khir_ˈhaw-au	*ˈphato*	*ɕer*	*pati-ˈau*
word_denying_become. PST.A-PST.A.3S	then	lion[DIR.S/P]	trust-PST.A.3S

(He, the fox) counter-argued (the lion's) accusation, consequently the lion trusted (him).

(127) *At's'ho'ĩk asta khul hawau.*

aˈʈʂhõ iŋk	*ˈasta*	*khul*	*ˈhaw-au*
story[DIR.S/P]	indeed	finish	become.PST.A-PST.A.3S

The story has also ended.

(128) *Phato kia bata may al'ei tharaw, hah!*[58]

ˈphato	*ˈkia*	*ˈbata*	*maj*
then	what	CTR	1S.OBL

aˈɬ-ei	*ˈthar-aw*	*hah*
there.NONSPEC.DI-ABL1	up-ABL3	EXCL

So what more will there be from my side? Ha!

[58] This sentence is difficult to translate literally and should be seen as a fixed construction, used as a ritualized way of ending a story.

CONCLUDING REMARKS

The above text analysis has shown how a typical narrative in the fable genre can be realized in an oral speech community in the Hindu Kush region. It is important to bear in mind that there can be different versions of the same fable. The version presented here undoubtedly has features that are typical for the narrator, Sher John, and other narrators are likely to frame the story differently with respect to grammatical style. We see it as a task for future documentation work and research to show in what aspects such narratives can vary, linguistically and content-wise, and as to how idiosyncratic narrative strategies are expressed.

The grammatical notes have pointed to certain characteristic elements of the Kalasha language and of the text-linguistic structure of a narrative in this language. By referring to the grammatical analyses in previous research we have shown how certain grammatical elements and categories are expressed in this particular discourse. In particular, we have noticed that the inferential aspect need not be the main verbal aspect in fiction, and that it seems to be a typical feature of this genre to omit a pronominal subject, an object, and/or the goal, the addressee, of an utterance verb from the clausal core and, instead, expressing these main syntactic constituents post-clausally, in a so-called afterthought expression. In addition, we have seen examples of how the conjunctive participle construction may be used to create cohesion and to emphasize a dramatic series of events.

Finally, by referring to a similar example of language documentation (Radloff and Shakil 1999), supplemented by the references to grammatical descriptions of other Hindu Kush languages, we have pointed to similarities and differences between narrative structures in speech communities in the Hindu Kush region, in particular Kalasha and Gilgit Shina. We hope that further comparative narrative research will provide interesting and new insight into how the languages of this region use grammars in discourse.

REFERENCES

Bashir, E. 2003. 'Dardic'. In *The Indo-Aryan Languages,* edited by George Cardona and Dhanesh Jain. 818–94. London: Routledge.

_______ 1996. 'Mosaic of tongues: Quotatives and complementizers in Northwest Indo-Aryan, Burushaski, and Balti'. In *Studies in Pakistani Popular Culture,* edited by William L. Hanaway and Wilma Heston. 187–286. Lahore: Sang-e-Meel Publishers and Lok Virsa Publishing House.

_______ 1989. 'Inferentiality in Khowar and Kalasha'. *Chicago Linguistic Society* 24: 47–59.

_______ 1988. *Topics in Kalasha Syntax: An Areal and Typological Perspective.* PhD dissertation. Michigan: Department of South Asian Languages, University of Michigan.

Cacopardo, Augusto S. 2010. 'Texts from the winter feasts of Kalasha'. *Acta Orientalia* 71: 187–242.

_______ and Cacopardo, Alberto M. 2001. *Gates of Peristan. History, Religion and Society in the Hindu Kush.* Rome. (Reports and Memoirs Series Minor, Vol. V).

_______ and Cacopardo, Alberto M. 1991. The other Kalasha: A survey of Kalashamun-speaking people in Southern Chitral. Parts I–II. *East and West* 41: 273–350.

Cooper, Gregory R. 2011. 'History is being written: Documenting, revitalizing and developing the Kalasha language'. In *Selected Papers from the International Conference on Language Documentation and Tradition—with a Special Interest in the Kalasha of the Hindu Kush Valleys, Himalayas,* edited by C. E. Everhard and E. Mela-Athanosopoulou. 85–8. Thessaloniki: School of English and Department of Theoretical and Applied Lingustics, Aristotle University of Thessaloniki.

_______ 2005. *Issues in the Development of a Writing System for the Kalasha Language.* PhD dissertation. Sydney: Macquarie University.

Coupe, A. R. 2006. 'Converbs'. In *Encyclopedia of Language and Linguistics,* edited by K. Brown. 145–52. Oxford: Elsevier.

Decker, K. D. 1991. 'Languages of Chitral'. *Sociolinguistic Survey of Northern Pakistan, vol. 5.* Islamabad: National Institute of Pakistan Studies and Summer Institute of Linguistics.

Delancey, S. 1997. 'Mirativity: The grammatical marking of unexpected information'. *Linguistic Typology* 1.1: 33–52.

Di Carlo, P. 2010. 'Take care of the poets! Verbal art performance as key factors in the preservation of Kalasha language and culture'. *Anthropological Linguistics* 52.2: 141–59.

_______ 2009. *I Kalasha del Hindu Kush. Ricerche linguistiche e antropologiche* [The Kalasha of the Hindu Kush. Linguistic and anthropological investigations]. Firenze: University of Firenze Press.

_______ 2007. 'The Prun Festival of the Birir Valley, Northern Pakistan, in 2006'. *East and West* 57.1–4: 45–100.

Fentz, M. 2011. *The Kalasha. Mountain People of the Hindu Kush.* Copenhagen: Rhodos.

Haspelmath, M. 1995. 'The converb as a cross-linguistically valid category'. In *Converbs in Cross-linguistic Perspective: Structure and Meaning of Adverbial Verb-Forms, Adverbial Participles, Gerunds*, edited by M. Haspelmath and E. König. 1–55. Berlin: Mouton de Gruyter. (Empirical Approaches to Language Typology 13).

Heegård Petersen, J. 2015. 'Kalasha texts—with introductory grammar'. *Acta Linguistica Hafniensia* 47.S1): 1–275.

——— 2014. 'Local case semantics in Kalasha'. *Journal of South Asian Languages and Linguistics* 1.2: 187–215.

——— 2012. 'Animacy, Vedic accent and Kalasha case allomorphy'. *Münchener Studien zur Sprachwissenschaft* 61.1: 55–80.

——— 2006. *Local Case-marking in Kalasha, Vol. I–II*. PhD dissertation. Copenhagen: University of Copenhagen.

——— and Khan, T. forthcoming. Dynamics of cultural survival of the Kalasha. In *In the Footsteps of Halfdan Siiger—Danish Research in Central Asia.*

——— and Mørch, I. E. 1997. *Retroflekse vokalers oprindelse i kalashamon i historisk og areallingvistisk perspektv. Variation i sprogbeskrivelsen: vokallængde i kalashamon* [The origin of retroflex vowels in Kalashamon in historical and areal-linguistic perspective. Variation in language description: Vowel length in Kalashamon]. MA thesis. Copenhagen: University of Copenhagen, Department of General and Applied Linguistics.

Liljegren, H. 2008. *Towards a Grammatical Description of Palula. An Indo-Aryan Language of the Hindu Kush*. PhD dissertation. Stockholm: Stockholm University.

Maggi, W. 2001. *Our Women Are Free. Gender and Ethnicity in the Hindukush*. Ann Arbor: The University of Michigan Press.

Masica, C. P. 1991. *The Indo-Aryan Languages*. Cambridge: Cambridge University Press.

Mørch, I. E. 2002. 'How fast will a language die when it is officially no longer spoken?' In *17th Scandinavian Conference of Linguistics II*, edited by C. E. Lindberg and S. Nordahl. 161–76. (Odense Working Papers in Language and Communication 19). Odense.

Morgenstierne, G. 1973. *The Kalasha Language*. Oslo: Universitetsforlaget. (Indo-Iranian Frontier Languages, Vol. 4).

Parkes, P. 1996. 'Kalasha oral literature and praise songs'. In *Proceedings from the Second International Hindu Kush Cultural Conference, Held in Chitral 1990*, edited by E. Bashir and Israr-ud-Din. 315–28. Karachi: Oxford University Press.

——— 1983. *Alliance and Elopement: Economy, Social Order, and Sexual Antagonism among the Kalasha (Kafirs) of Chitral*. PhD dissertation. Oxford: Oxford University.

Perder, Emil. 2013. *A Grammatical Description of Dameli*. PhD dissertation. Stockholm: Stockholm University.

Radloff, C. and Shakil, S. A. 1998. *Folktales in the Shina of Gilgit (Text, Grammatical Analysis and Commentary)*. Islamabad: National Institute of Pakistan Studies and Summer Institute of Linguistics. (Studies in Languages of Northern Pakistan 2).

Robertson, S. 1896. *The Kafirs of the Hindu Kush*. London.

Schmidt, R. L. 2006. 'A Nāga-Prince tale in Kohistan'. *Acta Orientalia* 67: 159–88.
Siiger, H. 1956. *Ethnological field-research in Chitral, Sikkim and Assam*. København. (Historisk-filologiske Meddelelser, Det Kongelige Danmarks Videnskabernes Selskab, Vol. 41).
Siiger, H. 1963. 'Shamanism among the Kalash Kafirs of Chitral'. *Folk* 5: 205–303.
Snoy, P. 2008. 'The rites of the winter solstice among the Kalash of Bumburet'. *Journal of Asian Civilizations* 26.1–2: 36–64.
Trail, R. and Cooper, G. *Kalasha Dictionary—with English and Urdu*. Islamabad: Summer Institute of Linguistics and National Institute of Pakistan Studies. (Studies in Languages of Northern Pakistan 7).

9

Gojri Tone and its Representation in Written Text

Wayne E. Losey

1. INTRODUCTION

1.1 GUJARS AND THE GOJRI LANGUAGE

Gojri, or Gujari, is the language of some one million or more Gujars (or *Gujjars*) living in the mountainous areas of northern Afghanistan, northern Pakistan, the disputed region of Kashmir, and northern India (Lewis, Simons, and Fennig 2015). The Gojri speakers, along with many more ethnic Gujars of the plains who no longer speak Gojri, are the descendants of the ancient Gurjaras whose origins are widely debated. Gojri-speaking Gujars include nomadic pastoralists who herd sheep and goats or dairy buffalo, settled agriculturalists, and semi-settled agriculturalists who practise seasonal transhumance.

The focus of this study is the Gojri of the Hazara region of Pakistan's Khyber Pakhtunkhwa Province (KPK), within which a Western and an Eastern dialect are distinguished. The highest concentrations of Western dialect speakers in Hazara reside in the Allai and Batagram *tehsils* of Batagram District, in Mansehra District, and Tor Ghar District (formerly Kala Dhaka, 'Black Mountain'). The highest concentration of Eastern dialect-speaking Gujars in Hazara lives north of Shinkiari in eastern Mansehra District within the area bounded on the west by the Siran River and on the east by the Kunhar River which runs through the Kaghan Valley.

1.2 History of research into Gojri

The earliest investigation into Gojri was made in the greater Murree area of extreme northern Punjab by Bailey, who initially published nine pages of Gojri description (1903: 3–11) and later contributed specimens from two Hazara locations to the 'Gujari' section of the *Linguistic Survey of India* (Grierson 1973: 925–81). The latter work, being comparative in nature, included skeletal grammars and text data from Gojri varieties spoken in Hazara, Swat, and Kashmir. A more substantial linguistic description, however, is Sharma's account of the sound system (1979) and grammar (1982) of the Gojri spoken in the Poonch district of Indian-administered Kashmir.

More recent scholarship has focused on the sociolinguistic situation. Hallberg and O'Leary (1992) published an extensive survey of the Gojri varieties spoken by settled and semi-settled Gujars in Pakistan and Pakistan-administered Kashmir. Hugoniot and Polster (1997) completed a similar survey of the 'Eastern Gujari' spoken by the *Dodhi* (from /dúd/ 'milk') or dairy buffalo-herding Gujars in Indian-administered Kashmir and the Indian states of Himachal Pradesh and Uttar Pradesh.

One question that has remained unanswered in the literature is the precise relationship between Gojri and *Bakarwali,* the speech of the Bakarwals, which is thought to be a form of Gojri (Sharma 1982: 2). Hallberg and O'Leary write:

> There are known to be landless Gujars continuing to pursue a nomadic herding lifestyle, particularly the Bakarwals in Azad Kashmir. The general opinion of settled Gujars in Azad Kashmir was that the Bakarwal Gujari was only slightly different from their own, the lifestyle being the main difference between the peoples. However no linguistic evidence has been collected to substantiate these opinions (1992: 108).

Interestingly, Grierson, who to my knowledge never used the term Bakarwal, had reported that *Ajri,* the speech of the sheep-herding *Ajars,* was a distinct subdialect but still nearly identical to the *Gujari* spoken by cow-herding Gujars in Swat (1973: 941, 948).

1.3 Overview of this chapter

In the remainder of this chapter I discuss the Gojri tone system and how tone can be represented in a practical orthography for the language. The segmental phonemes of Gojri are presented in section 2. Section 3 contains an impressionistic phonetic description of tonal contrasts in Gojri. An autosegmental-metrical analysis of Gojri tone and its interaction with stress is presented in section 4. Implications for writing tone in Gojri are discussed in section 5. To distinguish comparative data for the Western and Eastern speech types, represented by the Allaiwal and Kaghani dialects, respectively, I have shown unique Western forms in parentheses where not otherwise introduced. Wherever a Western form is shown in parentheses, the cognate shown immediately to the left or immediately above is uniquely Eastern. Unmarked forms are pronounced the same in both dialects.

2. PHONEMES

The consonant phonemes of Gojri are listed in Table 1 below, while the Gojri vowel phonemes are listed in Table 2 (oral vowels) and Table 3 (nasalized vowels).

Table 1: Gojri consonant phonemes

	Labial	Dental	Palatal	Retroflex	Velar	Glottal
Stop						
aspirated	ph	th		ṭh	kh	
voiceless	p	t		ṭ	k	
voiced	b	d		ḍ	g	
Affricate						
aspirated			čh			
voiceless			č			
voiced			ǰ			

Fricative						
voiceless	f	s	š		x	h
voiced		z			ɣ	
Nasal	m	n	ṇ			
Glide	w		y			
Flap		r		ṛ		
Lateral		l		ḷ		

Table 2: Gojri oral vowel phonemes

	Front	**Central**	**Back**
Close	ī		ū
	i		u
Close-mid	e		o
		a	
Open-mid	ɛ		ɔ
Open		ā	

Table 3: Gojri nasalized vowels phonemes

	Front	**Central**	**Back**
Close	ī̃		ū̃
Close-mid	ẽ		õ
Open-mid	ɛ̃		ɔ̃
Open		ā̃	

3. GOJRI TONE: PHONETIC CONTRASTS

Sharma describes a three-way tone or pitch contrast for Poonch Gojri (1979: 110–13; 1982: 12). This observation also holds for Kaghani and Allaiwal Gojri. The contrasting pitches consist of a level high pitch ('level tone' or 'mid tone') which is not marked in transcription, a high-falling pitch contour ('falling tone' or 'high tone') marked with an acute accent /´/ above the vowel in my phonemic transcription, and a low-rising pitch contour ('rising tone' or 'low tone') marked with a grave accent /`/ above the vowel.

The high-falling contour commences at an extra-high pitch relative to that of the level high pitch and glides to a mid pitch that is lower relative to that of the level high pitch. When another syllable follows the stressed syllable within the word, the stressed syllable will have the extra-high pitch, and the larger part of the fall to the mid pitch occurs on the following syllable. In my phonetic transcriptions, this is indicated by writing [´] on the stressed syllable and [`] on the following syllable, whereas a glide fully executed on the stressed syllable is indicated by [ˆ].

The low-rising contour commences at an extra-low pitch relative to that of the level high pitch and glides to a mid pitch that is lower than the level high pitch. When another syllable follows the stressed syllable within the word, the stressed syllable will have the extra-low pitch and the larger part of the rise to a mid pitch occurs on the following syllable. In phonetic transcriptions, this is indicated by [`] on the stressed syllable and [´] on the following syllable, whereas a glide fully executed on the stressed syllable is indicated by [ˇ].

Concomitant with the initial extra-low pitch of the low-rising contour is creaky voice, in which the vocal cords are more tense than in normal voicing and therefore produce a creaking sound. In many words of the Eastern dialect, the low-rising contour follows a voiceless initial plosive (as is also the case in Punjabi, see Masica 1991: 205). This voiceless plosive corresponds to a voiced plosive at the same point of articulation in the Western dialect, and to a breathy-voiced plosive at the same point of articulation in Urdu cognates. For example, the word 'horse' is /ˈkòṛɔ/ in Eastern, /ˈgòṛɔ/ in Western, /ˈkòṛā/ in Punjabi, and /ˈghoṛā/ in Urdu. For some words of this type, a level low pitch, higher than the 'extra-low' pitch of the low-rising contour but still marked [̀] phonetically, occurs with creaky voice on any syllables preceding a low-rising contour.

Both contour tones are extremely common, and there do not seem to be any general constraints on the kinds of consonants, vowels, or syllable patterns with which either may occur. In words with level high pitch, there is no conspicuous pitch rise or pitch fall; however, the pitch of the stressed syllable is somewhat higher than the mid pitch of the other, unstressed syllables, but lower than the 'extra-high' pitch of the high-falling contour.

Thus, there are at least five phonetic pitches in Gojri: 'extra-low', the initial pitch of the low-rising contour; 'low', the pitch occurring with creaky voice prior to the low-rising contour in some low-tone words; 'high', the pitch of stressed syllables in level-tone words; 'extra-high', the initial pitch of the high-falling contour; and 'mid', the pitch on which both of the gliding pitches terminate, and the pitch of unstressed syllables in level-tone words and of unstressed syllables preceding non-initial low-rising contours.

Contrasts between the three phonetic pitch melodies serve to differentiate lexical items such as those in (1), but do not function morphosyntactically.

(1) Contrasts of high-falling, level, and low-rising pitch melodies

/ˈsā́rɔ/ [ˈsá:rɔ̀]	(phonetic high-falling pitch)	masc. 'flat'
/ˈsārɔ/ [ˈsa:rɔ]	(phonetic level high pitch)	masc. 'entire'
/ˈsā̀rɔ/ [ˈsà:rɔ́]	(phonetic low-rising pitch)	'assistance'
/lā́/ [lâ:]	(phonetic high-falling pitch)	'take off [article of clothing]!'
/lā/ [la:]	(phonetic level high pitch)	'put on [article of clothing]!'
/lā̀l/ (/hìˈlāl/) [lǎ:l]	(phonetic low-rising pitch)	'slay!'
/čáṛ/ [čâṛ]	(phonetic high-falling pitch)	'climb!'
/čaṛ/ [čaṛ]	(phonetic level high pitch)	'bed bug'
/čàṛ/ (/ǰàṛ/) [čǎṛ]	(phonetic low-rising pitch)	'fall!' also 'cloud'

/bɛ́s/	[bɛ̂:s]	(phonetic high-falling pitch)	'argument'
/bɛs/	[bɛ:s]	(phonetic level high pitch)	'sit!'
/pès/ (/bès/)	[pě:s]	(phonetic low-rising pitch)	'apparel'

4. AN AUTOSEGMENTAL-METRICAL ANALYSIS

4.1 PRELIMINARY OBSERVATIONS

In Gojri words, lexical pitch is associated with the stressed syllable. The level tone occurs only on the stressed syllable. In polysyllabic words, the contour tones typically commence at their pitch targets on the stressed syllable and conclude at a mid pitch in any following syllable, often a gender-number agreement marker. In monosyllabic words, contour tones are realized within a single syllable, which in the absence of any other syllable is stressed by default.

Within a morpheme, the location of stress can be predicted by syllable weight. Syllable weight, in turn, is determined by the number of segments, or *moras* (μ), in the rhyme, where the rhyme of a syllable consists of the vowel nucleus plus any trailing consonants, and where a long vowel counts as two moras. Distinctions can therefore be made between light (where the rhyme consists of V), heavy (where the rhyme consists of VV or VC), and super heavy syllables (where the rhyme consists of VVC or VCC).

There have been several studies of stress placement in Hindi-Urdu (e.g. Dyrud 2001, Hussain 1997) which posit that if the final segment of a word is considered to be extra-metrical (not counted with respect to determination of syllable weight), then stress rules for Hindi-Urdu can be summarized as follows: the last heavy syllable in a word is stressed; if there is no heavy syllable (i.e. if the word consists of light syllables only), the penultimate syllable is stressed. These same stress assignment rules operate in Gojri. For example, the word /ǰisam/ [ˈǰɪsəm] 'body' is stressed on the first syllable because, once the word-final mora, [m], is excluded, what remains are two equally weighted CV syllables of which the penultimate is stressed. In the word /asˈmāṇ/ [ʌsˈma:ṇ] 'sky', the second syllable receives stress by the same assignment process. Segmented into syllables and moras, the word yields |as.maaṇ|. With or without the required exclusion of the final mora [ṇ], the second syllable is the last heavy syllable and therefore the one to receive stress. In morphologically complex words, morphological rules may supersede the normal stress placement rules. For example, in verb stems formed with the causative suffix, the suffix is always stressed, superseding stress placement based on syllable weight. Throughout this analysis I have included stress marking in the phonemic representations, despite the predictability of stress, so that the reader will not have to determine the location of stress for each example.

It is useful to think of the contour tones as combinations of two level tones, one 'high' and one 'low'. In abstract terms, the high-falling contour is thus a combination of a relatively high pitch, H, and a relatively low pitch, L. Phonetically, an underlying HL combination is realized as an extra-high pitch resolving in a mid pitch on a subsequent mora, and an underlying LH combination is realized as an extra-low pitch resolving in a mid pitch on a subsequent mora. I will assume that the presence of any H in a contour melody is by default, i.e. H is assigned to all stressed syllables. The presence of any L in a contour melody is lexical, i.e. it is part of the specification of the phonological form of a word in the lexicon. When a stressed syllable receives an H by default, and no underlying L is present in the word, the phonetic result is a level high pitch.

Diachronically, the genesis of this low pitch (L) in the lexicon is related to a word-initial /h/, or to the loss of aspiration, loss of /h/, or loss of /s/ at an earlier linguistic stage (cf. Masica 1991: 119–20). Such evolution is attested even by dialectical variants such as the Eastern /hàk-/ 'be able' and the older, Western (and Urdu) cognate /sak-/ 'be able'. Many of the older word forms are attested by Urdu cognates of Gojri words (cf. Masica's discussion of Punjabi tonogenesis 1991: 205). The location of lexical L in a root corresponds roughly to the location of the earlier segment that has disappeared. What determines whether the L is ultimately realized within a high-falling melody or a low-rising melody is its location with respect to the nucleus of the word's stressed syllable. If it precedes the stressed nucleus, the result is LH (low-rising). If it follows the stressed nucleus, the realization is HL (high-falling).

The clearest evidence of the existence of lexical L in Gojri and its participation in falling and rising tones is seen in a number of causative and non-causative pairs of verbs. For many verbal roots, the addition of the suffix /-ā/ yields a new causative verb stem. A classic example that holds for other area languages as well as for Gojri is the root /pak-/ [ˈpʌk-] 'ripen, be cooked' and its causative counterpart, /paˈkā-/ [pʌˈka:-] 'cook'. Since there is no lexical L associated with the root, only default H applies. As a result, the high pitch is realized on the stressed syllables of both forms and the mid pitch is realized on the unstressed first syllable of /paˈkā-/. However, when a lexical L is associated with the latter part of the verb root, its phonetic realization in all inflections of the root will be high-falling. Again, this is because H is assigned by default to the stressed monosyllabic root, the nucleus of which precedes lexical L in the vicinity of the coda; thus HL. Whenever the inherently stressed causative suffix is added to make a new stem, the stress shifts from the verb root to the causative suffix such that default H then follows lexical L; thus LH. Consider the examples in (2).

(2) Non-causative and causative manifestations of lexical low pitch (L)

Verb stem consisting of root (showing high-falling tone)		Verb stem consisting of root + causative suffix /ā/ (showing low-rising tone)	
/báṇ/	'become!'	/baˈṇā̀/	'make!'
/páṛ/	'read!'	/paˈṛā̀/	'teach!'
/bán/	'tie!'	/baˈnā̀/	'get someone to tie!'
/bád/	'grow!' also 'tie!'	/baˈdā̀/	'let grow!' also 'get someone to tie'
/láng/	'pass by!'	/lanˈgā̀/	'shoot!'
/sámj/	'understand!'	/samˈjā̀/	'explain!'
/káḍ/	'remove!'	/kaˈḍā̀/	'get someone to remove!'

It is on the basis of such examples that we can posit the existence of a lexical L in the vicinity of the root coda. This hypothesis is of course supported by the existence of aspiration at the root coda in many Urdu cognates. I assume that in Gojri, an L tone that is historically due to a de-aspirated voiced consonant, is underlyingly associated with the mora that immediately follows the de-aspirated consonant. Should there be no following mora—i.e. if the de-aspirated consonant is word-final—then L can be said to be 'floating' in the underlying form of the word.

The process described above, by which verb roots such as those in (2) alternately feature high-falling and low-rising melodies, is represented with greater precision in (3) and (4) for the root /báṇ/ 'become!'. In (3), a 'floating' L (circled) is shown as being part of the word's underlying form:

(3) The underlying form of /báṇ/ 'become!'

```
b  a  ṇ
   |  |
   μ  μ
         (L)
```

In the absence of a following mora, the floating L docks on the final mora of the root. Next, default H is associated with the remaining empty mora, creating the HL sequence shown in (4). The HL sequence then precipitates a high-falling melody commencing at an extra-high pitch on the first mora and resolving in a mid pitch on the second mora.

(4) The surface form of /báṇ/ 'become!'

```
b  a  ṇ
   |  |
   μ  μ
   |  |
   H  L
```

With the addition of the inherently stressed causative suffix /-ā/, floating lexical L docks on the mora immediately to the right of the de-aspirated consonant, as shown in (5). H is then assigned to the remaining mora of the stressed second syllable, creating an LH sequence. The underlying LH sequence precipitates a low-rising melody on the second syllable, which commences at an extra-low pitch on the first mora and resolves in a mid pitch on the second mora. Since there is no L or H in the unstressed syllable, the phonetic result is a mid pitch on that syllable.

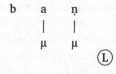

(5) The surface form of /baˈṇã̀/ 'make!' (stressed syllable in boldface)

```
b   a   ṇ   a   a
    |       |   |
    μ       μ   μ
            |   |
            L   H
```

Perhaps the most striking phonological difference between Eastern and Western varieties of Gojri is the variation in voicing which is concomitant with low-rising tone. The variation involves word-initial plosives at all five points of articulation (here and below, Western forms are shown in parentheses): /p/ (/b/), /t/ (/d/), /č/ (/ǰ/), /ṭ/ (/ḍ/), and /k/ (/g/). These are cognate with the Urdu initial voiced aspirates: /bh/, /dh/, /ǰh/, /ḍh/, and /gh/, respectively. Eastern forms reflect both the de-aspiration and devoicing of these older initial voiced aspirates, or 'breathy voiced stops' (Ladefoged and Maddieson 1996: 57–63). Western forms are also de-aspirated but remain voiced. For example, the Gojri word for 'horse', /ˈkòṛɔ/ (/ˈgòṛɔ/), is cognate with the Urdu /ˈghoṛā/. I have found that, in pronouncing words of this type in conversation with both Eastern and Western speakers, correct production of the low-rising tone, rather than correct voicing, is more critical to being understood. These segments remain voiced in both dialects in medial position (where they are rare), e.g. /uˈgã̀ṛī/ fem. 'naked', /kaˈḍã̀/ 'get [someone] to remove!'

Low-tone words attesting the East-West initial voicing distinction are shown in (6) for each of the five points of articulation.

(6) Low-tone words involving East-West initial voicing distinction

Articulation	East-West correspondences (Western forms are shown in parentheses)	
/p/ (/b/)	/ˈpã̀bī/ (/ˈbã̀bī/) 'brother's wife'	/ˈpã̀rū/ (/ˈbã̀rū/) 'sheep and goats'
/t/ (/d/)	/tàr/ (/dàr/) 'set down!'	/tìk/ (/dìk/) 'push!'
/ṭ/ (/ḍ/)	/ṭàk/ (/ḍàk/) 'cover!'	/ˈṭã̀kɔ/ (/ˈḍã̀kɔ/) 'mountain'

/č/ (/ǰ/)	/ˈčòṭɔ/ (/ˈǰòṭɔ/) 'male buffalo'	/ˈčȁnṭhī/ (/ˈǰȁnṭhī/) 'stick'
/k/ (/g/)	/kàl/ (/gàl/) 'pour!'	/kȁ/ (/gȁ/) 'grass'

For all words attesting the initial voicing distinction between dialects, I assume that L is linked with the mora immediately following the historically de-aspirated consonant. This is the place in the lexical structure that was previously characterized by the lowering of pitch following breathy voicing. The derivation of surface tone for such words is shown in (7) below.

When the first syllable of such a word is stressed, the assignment of H on the second mora creates an LH sequence. The LH sequence precipitates a low-rising melody that commences at an extra-low pitch on the first mora and resolves in a mid pitch on the second mora.

(7) Derivation for /ˈkòṛɔ/ (/ˈgòṛɔ/) 'horse'

a) Location of underlying L

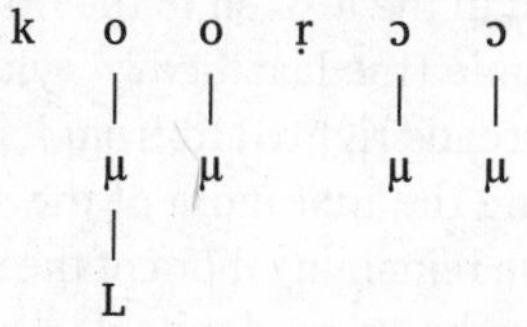

b) Results of H-assignment

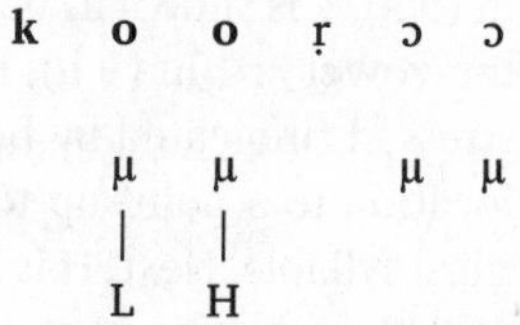

When such words are stressed on a subsequent syllable, the low-rising melody occurs on that syllable and a level low pitch occurs on all preceding syllables. Some examples are shown in (8).

(8) Cross-dialectal voice variation for words featuring non-initial low-rising tone

Eastern	E. Phonetic	Western	Gloss
/pìgēˈāṛ/	[pìgè:ˈǎ:ṛ]	/bìgī ˈāṛ/	'wolf'
/pùˈkam/	[pùˈkʌ̌m]	/bàˈkham/	'earthquake'
/pàˈṛās/	[pʌˈṛǎ:s]	/bàˈṛās/	'steam'
/pàˈṛāī/	[pʌˈṛǎ:y]	/bàˈṛāy/	'miller's share'
/pàˈtī ǰɔ/	[pʌˈtì:ǰɔ́]	/bàˈtī ǰɔ/	'nephew'
/dèˈāṛɔ/ or /tèˈāṛɔ/	[dē:ˈà:ṛɔ́]	/dȉˈāṛɔ/	'day'

The level low pitch preceding the low-rising contour is readily observed in the contrast between /pàˈṛās/ [pʌ̀ˈṛǎ:s] ‘steam’ and /paˈṛā̀/ [pʌˈṛǎ:] ‘teach!’.

The derivation for the surface tones of /pìgeˈāṛ/ (/bìgīˈāṛ) ‘wolf’ is shown in (9).

(9) Derivation for /pìgeˈāṛ/ (/bìgī ˈāṛ/) ‘wolf’ (L-spread indicated by diagonal lines)

a) Location of underlying L

b) Results of L-spread and H-assignment

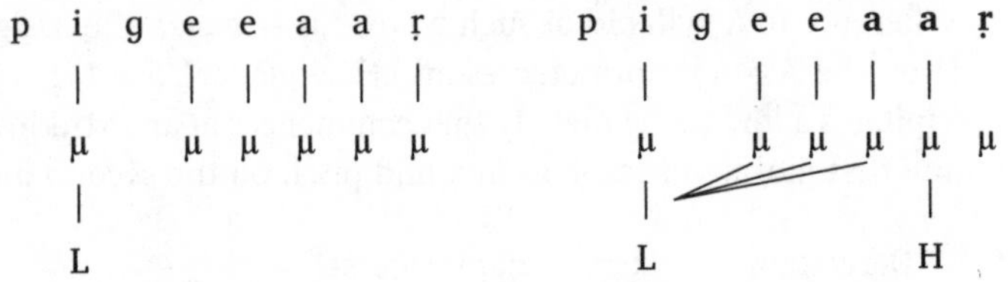

In (9 a), L is shown as being pre-linked in the lexicon to the first mora, the vowel /i/. In (9 b), the third syllable (the last ‘heavy’ syllable) is stressed (indicated by boldface). L spreads rightward from its lexical location to a point up to and including the first mora of the stressed third syllable. Next, H is assigned to the remaining mora of the stressed syllable, resulting in an LH sequence in the stressed syllable. On moras preceding the stressed syllable, the spread of L produces a plateau of level low pitch. In the stressed syllable, the LH sequence precipitates a low-rising surface melody which commences at an extra-low pitch on the first mora and resolves in a mid pitch on the second mora. For words like /pàˈtīǰɔ/ (/bàˈtīǰo/) ‘nephew’ and /dèˈāṛɔ/ (/dī̀ˈāṛɔ/) ‘day’, the stressed syllable is penultimate and so the low-rising melody resolves in the suffixal ultima, i.e. [pʌ̀ˈtì:ǰɔ́], [dè:ˈà:ṛɔ́].

4.2 OTHER LOW-TONE WORDS

In this section I describe low tone which is associated with initial /h/ and low tone related to the loss of medial /h/.

4.2.1 LOW TONE ASSOCIATED WITH INITIAL /h/

The voiceless glottal fricative /h/ is always associated with low tone on the following vowel. This is most readily observed in the grammatical monosyllables /hàm/ 'we', /hū̀~/ 'I', and the Eastern present auxiliaries /hɛ̀/ 'is' and /hɛ̀~/ 'are' (cf. Western /ɛ/ 'is/are'). Such words attest the linkage of lexical L with the mora following initial /h/. When a word beginning with /h/ is stressed on the first syllable, the frication is audible and the derivation of surface tone is identical to that shown for /ˈkòṛɔ/ (/ˈgòṛɔ/) 'horse' in (7).

However, when a word beginning with /h/ is stressed on a subsequent syllable, there is no friction, and level low pitch occurs with every syllable preceding the low-rising pitch contour commencing on the stressed syllable. The phonetic differences attending change of stress from the first syllable to a subsequent syllable are most clearly shown by comparison of causative and non-causative forms of verbs beginning with /h/. Some examples are shown in (10).

(10) Causative and non-causative pairs of verbs beginning with /h/

verb stem consisting of root verb	stem consisting of root + causative suffix /-ā/
/hàḷ/ [hʌ̌ḷ] 'shake!'	/hàˈḷā/ [ʌ̀ˈḷǎ:] trans. 'shake!'
/hàg/ [hʌ̌g] 'defecate!'	/hàˈgā̀/ [ʌ̀ˈgǎ:] 'get [someone] to defecate!'
/hàṭ/ [hʌ̌ṭ] 'move!'	/hàˈṭā̀/ [ʌ̀ˈṭǎ:] trans. 'move!'

Some examples with polysyllabic stems are given in (11). For all these words and the causative verbs in (10) above, the derivation of surface tone (via L-spread) is identical to that shown for /pìgeˈāṛ/ (/bìgīˈāṛ/) 'wolf' in (9).

(11) Words beginning with /h/ that are stressed on a non-initial syllable

/hàˈsāb/	[ʌ̀ˈsǎ:b]	‘account’ (cf. Urdu /hiˈsāb/)
/hàˈzār/	[ʌ̀ˈzǎ:r]	‘thousand’ (cf. Urdu /haˈzār/)
/hàˈmešā~/	[ʌ̀ˈmè:šá~]	‘always’ (cf. Urdu /haˈmešā/)
/hàmˈzoḷɔ/	[ʌ̀mˈzò:ḷɔ́]	‘age mate (masc.)’
/hàˈrīṛ/	[ʌ̀ˈrǐṛ]	‘a medicinal herb’

There is evidence suggesting that the unstressed, low pitch first syllables of words like those in (11) (which also lack a phonetic onset) are vulnerable to elision and loss. For example, some speakers pronounce /hàˈvā/ ‘wind’ as monosyllabic [vǎ:]. Such loss also accounts for the difference between the Eastern /lā̀l/ ‘slay!’ and the Western cognate /hìˈlāl/. The process is also attested by Western copular forms like /wɛ̀ gɔ/ ‘(he) will be’ (Eastern /ˈhòwɛ kɔ/), in which lexical L is all that survives of the verb stem /hò/ ‘be’ and presumably epenthetic /w/ has become word-initial (cf. Marwari /vheṇo/ ‘to be’, Masica 1991: 104). Likewise, the genitival first plural pronoun /ˈmā̀rɔ/ ‘our’ surely represents the loss of a weakened first syllable from an older form attested by the Urdu cognate, /haˈmārā/, with retention of the L tone which was associated with that syllable.

4.2.2 Low tone related to loss of medial /h/

A large number of Gojri words feature the low-rising pitch contour in a first syllable consisting of consonant + long vowel in which the consonant is constant cross-dialectically. These words are cognate with Urdu words in which /h/ occurs between a first-syllable short vowel and a second-syllable long vowel. Examples are listed in (12) below. The origin of the low tone for such words cannot be the de-aspiration of old initial voiced aspirates, since there is no East-West voicing variation for the initial consonant and the set of initial consonants is not limited to just stops. Rather, it appears that the historic erosion of medial /h/ and related loss of preceding short vowels has left a trace in the form of an L tone associated with the initial mora. The derivation of surface tones for such words is therefore identical to that noted for words like /ˈkòṛɔ/ (/ˈgòṛɔ/) ‘horse’ shown in (7).

(12) Low-tone words attesting loss of medial /h/ before long vowel

Gojri word	Gloss	Urdu cognate (or source in most cases)
/mā̀l/	'mahal, palace'	/maˈhāl/
/ˈkā̀ṇī/ (/ˈgā̀ṇī/)	'story'	/kaˈhānī/
/pā̀ṛ/	'mountain'	/paˈhāṛ/
/ǰā̀z/	'ship'	/ǰaˈhāz/
/ˈswā̀gā/	'ashes'	/suˈhāge/
/ˈmī̀ṇɔ/	'month'	/maˈhīnā/
/ˈbā̀dar/	'brave'	/baˈhādar/
/ǰā̀d/	'jihad'	/ǰiˈhād/
/ˈmā̀ǰar/	'refugee'	/muˈhāǰir/
/sā̀l/	'diarrhea'	/saˈhāl/
/lɔ̀r/	'Lahore'	/laˈhor/
/ˈbā̀nɔ/	'excuse'	/baˈhānā/

For a small number of words, stress falls on a non-initial syllable and surface tones attest a medial, rather than initial, lexical L. Examples include /dādeˈā̀ḷ/ [da:deˈǎ:ḷ] 'paternal relatives' (cf. /ˈdādɔ/ 'paternal grandfather' and /ˈāḷā/ (/ˈhā̀ḷā/) 'ones of …'), and /maleˈàp/ [mʌleˈǎp] 'worm'. For the latter example, it is not clear why stress and the low-rising tone occur on the short-vowel ultima.

4.3 OTHER HIGH-TONE WORDS

Whereas low tone almost always derives from initial lexical L, high tone derives from medial or final lexical L. The historical source of lexical L in such words is generally less transparent than it is for the various kinds of low-tone words described above.

In (13) a number of words are listed for which high tone is associated with the loss of aspiration in a non-initial voiced aspirate. The de-aspirated consonants remain voiced in both dialects. There are no Gojri words featuring a high-falling tone with a short vowel preceding a final voiceless consonant.

(13) High-tone words associated with de-aspiration of non-initial voiced aspirates

/dúd/	'milk'	cf. Urdu /dudh/
/ˈčɔ́drī/	'Choudhry'	cf. Urdu /ˈčɔdharī/, title taken by prominent Gujars
/kúǰ/	'some'	cf. Urdu /kučh/
/ˈbúḍī/	'old woman'	cf. Urdu /ˈbuṛhī/
/ˈdā́ṛī/	'beard'	cf. Urdu /ˈdāṛhī/
/rúṛ/	'roll!' (intransitive)	
/ˈkáṛī/	'boiled buttermilk'	

For cases involving monosyllabic words, L is floating in the underlying form of the word, and the derivation of surface tones is identical to that shown above for /báṇ/ 'become!' in (3) and (4). For cases involving two-syllable words, L is pre-linked in the lexicon with the mora following the de-aspirated consonant. Default H tone is then assigned to the single mora of the stressed first syllable, creating an HL sequence that is realized phonetically as a high-falling melody spread over the two syllables. The underlying and derived forms of /ˈbúḍī/ 'old woman' are shown in (14).

(14) Derivation for /ˈbúḍī/ 'old woman'

a) Location of underlying L b) Results of L-spread and H-assignment

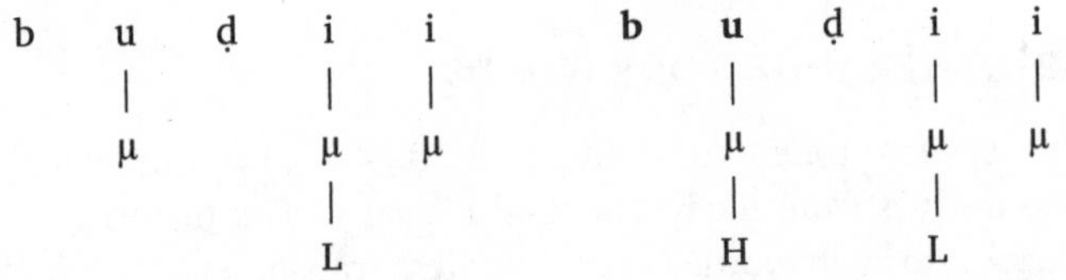

Almost all other indigenous high-tone words involve lexical L following a medial or final long vowel. The sources of lexical L include loss of /s/ (e.g. /bī́/ 'twenty' vs Urdu /bīs/) and loss of /h/ (e.g. /čā/ 'want' vs Urdu /čāh/). Many high-tone stems such as /gāk/ 'customer' (Urdu /ˈgāhuk/) represent the loss of medial /h/ after a long vowel along with loss of the following unstressed short-vowel syllable and subsequent association of L with the end of the long vowel. Some examples of high-tone words attesting medial or final L are shown in (15).

(15) Contrast between high-falling and level tonal melodies

/ˈḍóḷɔ/	'upper arm'	/ˈḍoḷɔ/	'large water pot'
/ˈsā́yɔ/	'rabbit'	/ˈsāyɔ/	'shadow'
/ˈmā́nǰī/	'one who tends buffalo'	/ˈmānǰī/	'bride's guests'
/mā́/	'second month of lunar calendar'	/mā/	'mother'
/ˈbóṭī/	'bride'	/ˈboṭī/	'piece of meat, kabob'
/čā́/	'want!'	/čā/	'lift!'
/zā́r/	'poison, saliva'	/zār/	'darling'
/bā́/	'arm'	/bā/ E.only	'water hole, dam'

The derivation of surface tone for such words is shown in (16) for /ˈbóṭī/ 'bride'.

(16) Derivation of /ˈbóṭī/ 'bride'

a) Location of underlying L b) Results of H-assignment

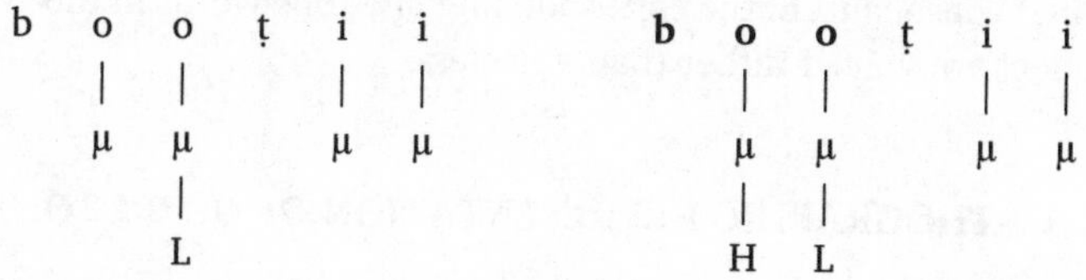

In (16 b), an HL sequence is created by the assignment of H to the first mora of the stressed syllable, the mora which immediately precedes lexical L. The HL sequence precipitates a high-falling melody which commences on the stressed syllable and resolves in the following suffixal syllable. For monosyllabic words like /bā́/ 'arm', the high-falling melody commences on the first mora and resolves on the second mora of the root vowel. I have not investigated the historical antecedents of lexical L for these words, nor is such information needed to determine the location of L within words.

4.4 LOW TONE CO-OCCURRING WITH ASPIRATION

For a few words such as those in (17), low tone co-occurs with aspiration. In my research to date, all instances noted involve the segment /th/.

(17) Co-occurrence of low tone and aspiration

/ˈthȁṇɔ/ [ˈtʰa:ṇɔ́]	‘to be found’
/ˈthȁrɔ/ [ˈtʰà:rɔ́:]	pl. ‘your’
/ˈthòṛī/ [ˈtʰò:ṛí:]	‘hammer’ (Eastern)
/maˈthȁǰ/ [məˈtʰă:ǰ]	‘deprivation, lack’, cf. Urdu /mɔˈtāǰ/

Only for the Eastern word /ˈthòṛī/ ‘hammer’ is the origin of lexical L transparent (from comparison with cognates retaining an initial /h/). Further research is likely to reveal the source of L for the other examples shown here. Words showing that low tone is not automatic with /th/ include /ˈthoṛī/ ‘a little (fem.)’ and /ˈthānɔ/ ‘police station’. Elsewhere, low tone and aspiration contrast. Some examples include /ṭànḍ/ ‘still water’ vs /ṭhanḍ/ ‘cold’, /kàl/ ‘pour!’ vs /khal/ ‘stop, wait!’, and /ˈčȁtī (ˈmārṇī)/ ‘(playing) peek-a-boo’ vs /ˈčhātī/ ‘chest, upper torso’. This contrast is limited to the Eastern dialect, since the initial consonants of the corresponding low-tone words in the Western dialect are voiced rather than voiceless.

5. ORTHOGRAPHIC REPRESENTATION OF GOJRI TONE

5.1 TONE MARKING IN ORTHOGRAPHY DESIGN

While the literature on tone marking is not extensive, empirical studies in African tonal languages by Bird and others he cites (1997) demonstrate that exhaustive marking of surface tone is detrimental to fluent reading, as is ‘zero marking’—ignoring tone altogether. The former extreme is born of the traditional compulsion to represent every phonemic contrast in the orthography, but often results in solutions that are cumbersome and notoriously difficult for mother tongue readers to master. The latter extreme rightly acknowledges the ability of readers to identify words based on contextual and other clues, but in many languages leaves readers to ‘stumble and guess unnecessarily' (Bird 1996, citing Nida 1964: 27). The compromise approach advocated by Bird (1996) on theoretical and experimental grounds involves representing the underlying or lexical tone elements while maintaining a constant word image, given that post-lexical spell-out is phonologically predictable and presumably automatic for linguistically naive mother tongue readers. Such an approach has the added advantage of tending to minimize dialect differences (Bird 1996: 25), and is even more promising for languages like Gojri in which the tone pattern of each word remains basically constant (i.e. is not very sensitive to phrasal influences).

A fourth approach would mark tone only when necessary for disambiguation, much as Urdu diacritics indicating vowel quality are normally employed only to distinguish ambiguous pairs. This would necessarily involve special tone diacritics, as optional writing of tone graphemes (letters) in a linear and cursive Perso-Arabic representation would largely preclude maintenance of fixed word images. Marking tone with diacritics would avoid this problem, allowing for optionality in books and complete tone marking in primary literacy materials. In my opinion, however, a diacritic-marking solution is inferior to that suggested by the correspondence of Gojri lexical L with Urdu /h/ and aspiration (with voiced consonants). Given the influence of Urdu and literate Gujars' familiarity with Urdu spellings, a representation that maintains fixed word images between Gojri and Urdu cognates has the greatest potential to facilitate transitional literacy and the acceptance of Gojri literature among Urdu-literate Gujars. The challenge then is to achieve a solution that utilizes Urdu-based spellings in a consistent representation of underlying rather than surface Gojri tonal facts.

5.2 Evaluation of conventions in use

In general, orthographic solutions have attempted, whether consciously or unconsciously, to represent Gojri tones as per the representation of their cognate segments in Urdu: by means of *do chashmi he,* ھ, denoting aspiration, and *choti he,* ہ, (rendered /nikī hè/ in Gojri) denoting the voiceless glottal fricative /h/. One common pattern is for literate Gujars to slavishly write Gojri in the same way they write Urdu, with no awareness of Gojri tonal phenomena. In writing of this type, tone is usually only represented, albeit accidentally, in tonal words that have known Urdu cognates. Tone is usually ignored in words that are uniquely Gojri, because writers are both unaware of tone and lacking any technique for transcribing it. Some literate Gujars intuitively identify tone as aspiration, and by analogy to known Gojri-Urdu cognate relationships will write this 'aspiration' on uniquely Gojri words. In my experience, the writing produced by both types of literates is highly idiosyncratic and inconsistent from one occurrence of a word to the next. High tones occurring with medial long vowels tend to get particularly ignored, since cognate relationships of such words with Urdu words are comparatively less transparent.

Among the few who are aware of tone and consciously reflect on how to write it, some, in keeping with the default tendency to write words the way they sound, attempt to represent all of the surface tonal contrasts. The difficulty with writing surface tones lies in determining which of the two Urdu letters should represent which tonal pattern in a given context. The problem is exacerbated by the fact that even for Urdu their employment has only recently been standardized, with *do chashmi he* now prescribed for all aspiration and *choti he* for all instances of /h/ (Mathews 1999: xxvi). It should be evident from the variety of tone phenomena described above, however, particularly from that shown in section 4.1, that the traditional ideal of consistently representing one toneme with one grapheme while maintaining constant shape of lexical roots is not achievable for Gojri (e.g. the addition of the causative suffix turns a high tone verbal root into a low-tone stem). Furthermore, since the mapping of Gojri toneme to Urdu phoneme/grapheme is not one-to-one, at some point a surface representation must compromise in favour of either the Urdu spellings or tonemic–graphemic correspondence.

5.2.1 Writing of low tone occurring with initial /h/

If there is any 'given' or non-negotiable convention which can be taken as a starting point for either an underlying or surface approach to tone marking (aside from leaving the level tone unmarked), it is the representation of word-initial low-rising tones, concomitant with /h/ in monosyllables, with *choti he*. This decision is largely unconscious and is based on the spelling of Urdu cognates. The practice is nearly universal in Gojri writing. Since initial /h/ in Gojri monosyllables is always followed by the low-rising tone, this decision would tentatively associate *choti he* with lexical L. Thus, the first person pronouns and present auxiliaries, together the highest frequency words involving tone of any kind, remain constant between the two languages:

(18) Uniform spellings for Gojri and Urdu first person pronouns and present auxiliaries

Gojri /hàm/ [hʌ̌m] 'we'	Urdu /ham/ [hʌm] 'we' ہَم
Gojri /hṻ~/ [hǔ:~] 'I' also 'am' (Eastern only)	Urdu /hū~/ [hu:~] 'am' ہُوں
Gojri /hɔ̀/ [hɔ̌:] 2pl. 'are' (Eastern only)	Urdu /ho/ [ho:] 2pl. 'are' ہو
Gojri /hɛ̀/ [hɛ̌:]([ɛ:]) 'is'	Urdu /hai/ [hɛ:] 'is' ہے
Gojri /hɛ̀~/ [hɛ̌:~]'are' (Eastern only)	Urdu /he~/ [he:~] 'are' ہیں

5.2.2 SURFACE APPROACH TO LOW TONE RELATED TO LOSS OF INITIAL ASPIRATION

The association of *choti he* with low tone leads next to an evaluation of its suitability for writing low tones resulting from the de-aspiration of initial voiced aspirates, e.g. writing /kȁ/ (/gȁ/) 'grass' as کہا. The impetus behind this convention is the desire to represent the initial consonant as de-voiced, per its Eastern pronunciation, while avoiding the intolerable ambiguity with voiceless aspirated segments that would result from using *do chashmi he* for the following low-tone vowel. (For example, /kȁ/ (/gȁ/) 'grass' and /khā/ 'eat!' would both be written as کھا.)

Unfortunately this approach has its own problems. First and most obviously, since the segments in question remain voiced in the Western dialect, the use of *choti he* in these contexts unnecessarily precludes the possibility of a single representation for both dialects. This problem by itself may not be of great concern to Eastern writers, who are seldom if ever exposed to Western speech. It can be demonstrated, however, that the approach is problematic even for the Eastern phonology because it creates unnecessary ambiguity between certain low-rising and high-falling pairs of tonal words; for example /kȁ/ (/gȁ/) 'grass' is written as کہا, while /kã́~/ 'we say' is written as کہاں. Such ambiguity is particularly evident wherever low-rising and high-falling tones contrast within syllables featuring short (or written as short, as in the case of /ɛ/) vowels. A few such ambiguous examples are shown in (19).

(19) Ambiguous Eastern low-tone/high-tone pairs

/kàṭ/	'few'	کہٹ
/ˈkɛ́tɔ/	'he (doesn't) say'	کہتو
/ˈkàṇī/	fem. 'many'	کہٹی
/ˈkɛ́ṇī/	fem. 'to say'	کہٹی
/ˈpàlā/	masc. pl. 'excellent'	پہلا
/ˈpɛ́lā~/	'before'	پہلاں
/ˈtùnī/	'navel'	تُہنی
/ˈtúmat/	'slander'	تُہمت

Granted, such ambiguities are few in number and would scarcely present any difficulty for Gujar literates, but the larger pattern they represent could be a serious challenge for new readers. The ambiguity issues from the fact that all Gujar writers have continued writing the verbs /kɛ́-/ 'say' and /rɛ́-/ 'stay' as per their Urdu spellings, i.e. with the initial consonant joined to *choti he*, but without writing the vowel /ɛ/ (Urdu /ah/, approximating but shorter than /ai/ + /h/). By itself, representing the Gojri segment /ɛ́/ with *choti he* is good, since morphophonemic changes alter /ɛ́/ in a majority of contexts anyway, and this practice allows the lexical roots to remain constant in writing before any suffixed vowel. Furthermore, it also maintains a constant word shape between the two languages. For example, Urdu /raˈho/ and Gojri /rɔ́/, 'stay!' can both be represented by رہو; Urdu /kaˈho/ and Gojri /kɔ́/, 'say!' can both be represented by کہو.

This convention, however, together with using *choti he* for low tones resulting from the de-aspiration of initial voiced aspirates, perpetuates an ambiguous system in which, given the unusually high frequencies of /kɛ́-/ 'say' and /rɛ́-/ 'stay' in Gojri text (the latter being an important grammatical morpheme), the new reader has to memorize which instances of *choti he* indicate which type of tone. And of course the transitional reader must learn two spellings (Gojri and Urdu) for a great many pairs of cognates like those for 'mare': /ˈkòṛī/ کھوڑی and /ˈghoṛī/ گھوڑی (respectively). This disadvantage, along with the introduction of ambiguity between representations of high-tone and low-tone short vowels, constitutes compelling grounds to consider better orthographic solutions—even for the Eastern phonology.

5.2.3 Writing of /ɛ/

The preceding discussion, however, may be enough to establish a second orthographic 'given', namely, that the segment /ɛ́/—cognate with Urdu /ah/—is well represented by a *choti he* per the Urdu spelling convention (note: reducing ambiguity by writing the vowel /ɛ/ would preclude a morphophonemic representation, since /ɛ/ is always altered before vowel suffixes). This convention is followed in all Gojri writing. Some examples are shown in (20).

(20) /ɛ́/ written with *choti he* and no other vowel letter

/ˈrɛ́ṇɔ/	'to stay'	رہݨو
/ˈkɛ́ṇɔ/	'to say'	کہݨو
/lɛ́r/	'anger'	لہر
/bɛ́ṇ/	'sister'	بہݨ
/ˈmɛ́ndī/	'henna'	مہندی
/bɛ́k/	'a roost'	بہک

Particularly from the perspective of surface tone marking, this practice may appear to contradict the first given, by which *choti he* is associated with initial low tones. Against any charge of ambiguity, however, is the fact that the distributions of initial and non-initial *choti he* are constrained such that no ambiguous spellings can be adduced. If the approach that marks only underlying lexical L is adopted, there is no contradiction between the two 'givens'. The former can be seen as marking lexical L initially, which after L-spread and the assignment of H on the second mora of the stressed syllable will invariably precipitate the low-rising pitch contour. The latter can be seen as marking lexical L root-finally (it is lexically linked with the second mora of /ɛ/), which after the assignment of H to the first mora of the stressed syllable (i.e. the root nucleus) will invariably precipitate the high-falling pitch contour. For the lexical tone-marking approach, then, *choti he* and *do chashmi he* do not represent two distinct tonemes; rather, they are allographs representing lexical L, and their distributions are constrained by Urdu spelling patterns rather than by surface tonal contrasts.

5.2.4 Iconic Approach to Low Tone Related to Loss of Initial Aspiration

Returning to the representation of low tones resulting from the de-aspiration of initial voiced aspirates, we now consider the remaining alternative, that of preserving the Urdu voiced aspirate spellings which consist of the voiced consonants joined to *do chashmi he*. For Eastern Gojri, such a solution is iconic rather than phonemic (cf. Bird 1996: 35), since the consonants are voiceless in initial position. It has been adopted for Punjabi (Parvez 1996: 47–54), the phonology of which is identical in this respect to that of Eastern Gojri. The leading proponents of this technique for Gojri have been the (Eastern-speaking) Gujar scholars associated with the Jammu and Kashmir Academy of Art, Culture, and Languages. In the introduction to their *Gojri Dictionary* (Iqbal 1985), the editors explain that they have utilized the Urdu orthography, and that the Urdu digraphs for initial /bh/, /dh/, /ḍh/, /ǰh/, and /gh/ are pronounced in Gojri (Eastern) as /p̀/, /t̀/, /ṭ̀/, /č̀/, and /k̀/, respectively. These scholars have applied this approach more or less consistently in their many Gojri publications. Its advantages should be clear by now, namely, that it offers a uniform representation for both dialects while maintaining a constant word image with Urdu and avoiding the ambiguities created by writing the consonants as voiceless (whether joined with *choti he* or *do chashmi he*). Consider the sample spellings in (21):

(21) Spellings for low-tone words related to loss of initial aspiration

Eastern	Western	gloss	iconic spelling	alternative phonemic spelling (E. only)
/ˈpȁnḍā/	(/ˈbȁnḍā/)	'pots and dishes'	بھانڈا	پہانڈا
/ˈčòṭɔ/	(/ˈǰòṭɔ/)	'male buffalo'	جھوٹو	چہوتو
/ˈtȁgɔ/	(/ˈdȁgɔ/)	'thread'	دھاگو	تہاگو
/ˈṭȁkɔ/	(/ˈḍȁkɔ/)	'mountain'	ڈھاکو	ٹہاکو
/ˈkòṛɔ/	(/ˈgòṛɔ/)	'horse'	گھوڑو	کہوڑو
/pìgeˈāṛ/	(/bìgīˈāṛ/)	'wolf'	بھگیاڑ	پِھگیہاڑ or پگیہاڑ
/pàˈṛās/	(/bàˈṛās/)	'steam'	بھَڑاس	پَہڑہاس or پڑہاس
/pàˈtīǰɔ/	(/bàˈtīǰo/)	'nephew'	بھَتِیجو	پَہتہِیجو or پَہتِیجو

In my experience, Eastern literates in Pakistan (who have never seen their language in print) often reject this iconic solution upon initial exposure. They feel it is contrary to their distinct pronunciation, and say that the Western dialect does not concern them. However, Eastern speakers need not think that the iconic solution is based on the low-prestige Western dialect, but rather on Urdu, the high-prestige language of wider communication for Muslim Gujars in all locations. Thus, when presented with the ambiguities created by the alternative and the considerations for Urdu transitional literacy, their impression becomes favourable. The counter-intuitive nature of this solution thus underscores the need for orthography promotion, and for orthographic explanation in the introductions to Gojri publications and literacy materials.

As for pedagogical method, the five segments in question, along with the five voiceless aspirates, must be taught iconically as digraphs, i.e. as single alphabetic units. For example, new Eastern readers in Pakistan readily learn to associate the /gh/ digraph گھ with the segment /k̀/ by looking at the horse pictured in their alphabet primer, /ˈkòṛɔ/. Similarly, they learn to associate the /kh/ digraph کھ with the segment /kh/ by looking at the pictured donkey, /ˈkhotɔ/. Eastern speakers already literate in Urdu need only a concise orthographic 'key', such as that contained in the *Gojri Dictionary* (Iqbal 1985), when transitioning to Gojri text.

To summarize, the problems with the phonemic solution are that it 'splits' the Eastern and Western dialects, complicates transitional literacy by precluding consistency of word images with Urdu, introduces ambiguities for short vowels even within the Eastern dialect, and at present enjoys comparatively little use. Furthermore, the phonemic solution is ill-equipped to represent the effects of L-spread on words like /pàˈtī̃jɔ/ (/bàˈtījɔ/) 'nephew' and /pàˈṛās/ (/bàˈṛās/) 'steam'. To be consistently phonemic, awkward spellings like those on the farthest right in (21) would be needed to indicate that the first unstressed syllables also bear low tone (and are tonally distinct from words like /naˈtī̃jɔ/ 'result' and /paˈṛā̀/ 'teach!'). The iconic solution, by representing lexical L only (via familiar Urdu-ized spellings), enables readers to correctly interpret low tone from the beginning of the word through to the low-rising pitch contour on the stressed syllable, based on their innate awareness of stress. Given intrinsic merits such as this and the pervasive influence of the Academy's publications, the adoption in Pakistan and Pakistan-administered Kashmir of the iconic solution promoted by the Academy represents the best opportunity for the broader Gojri movement to achieve a standard, internally consistent representation.

5.2.5 Writing of High-Tone Words (Other than /ɛ/-Type)

The remaining orthographic matters pertaining to tone have received relatively little attention to date, with writers typically defaulting to the Urdu spellings or, when words lack an Urdu cognate, often ignoring the tone entirely. This is probably because the remaining tonal phenomena occur less frequently and are more problematic than those considered thus far in this section. Sharma (1979: 151) proposes that the high toneme be represented by *do chashmi he* written immediately after the vowel bearing high tone. This, however, would put the *do chashmi he* immediately after a consonant whenever the vowel was short (or perceived as short), given the practice of not writing short vowels. This in turn would create many ambiguities with voiceless aspirates and low-tone segments, the latter rightly consisting of a (voiced) consonant followed by *do chashmi he*. Any related proposal (I know of none) for explicitly writing the short vowels and /ɛ́/ would be problematic in view of the widely accepted practice of ignoring them or of writing /έ/ simply as *choti he*. Representing the short vowels with the appropriate diacritics would not reduce the ambiguities created by Sharma's proposal, since the consonants would still get joined to *do chashmi he*.

An Urdu-ized solution to the writing of high-tone words is suggested by two different spelling patterns for Urdu cognates. Both patterns are used for Gojri high-tone words when the spellings of such words are known from Urdu. These patterns are not, however, consistently applied to uniquely Gojri words.

<u>Writing of high tone associated with loss of medial /h/</u>

The first and most common spelling pattern features *choti he* or *bari he*, ح, (in the Arabic loans 'gentleman' and 'wedding ceremony' below) written after the high-tone long vowel, as shown in (22). It corresponds to the words shown in (15) in section 4.3.

(22) High-tone words written with post-vocalic *he*, per spelling of Urdu cognates

Word	Gloss	Urdu(-ized) Spelling	Urdu Cognate
/sā́b/	'gentleman'	صاحب	/ˈsāhib/
/gā́k/	'customer'	گاہک	/ˈgāhuk/
/ˈsóṇī/	fem. 'beautiful'	سوہݨی	/ˈsohanī/
/mā́ir/ (/mā́r/)	'expert'	ماہر	/ˈmāhir/
/čā́/	'want!'	چاہ	/čāh/
/bādˈšā́/ (/bāˈčā́/)	'king'	بادشاہ	/bādˈšā/
/niˈkā́/	'wedding ceremony'	نِکاح	/niˈkā/
/ˈčū́ɔ/	'rat'	چُہو	/ˈčūhā/

Uncommon in Gojri are high-tone medial short vowels having Urdu cognates other than the kind shown below in (23). Words featuring high-tone medial short vowels but lacking such cognates can be written with *choti he* after the vowel diacritic, by extension of this pattern and the pattern noted earlier for /έ/, e.g. /ˈtúmat/ 'slander' تُہمت.

Writing of high-tone associated with de-aspiration

The second, lower-frequency spelling pattern features *do chashmi he* after a voiced consonant, as shown in (23).

(23) High-tone words written with final *do chashmi he*, per spelling of Urdu cognates

Word	Gloss	Urdu-ized Spelling	Urdu Cognate	(original spelling, if different)
/kúǰ/	'some'	کُجھ	/kuch/	(کُچھ)
/dúd/	'milk'	دُدھ	/dudh/	
/ˈdā́ṛī/	'beard'	داڑھی	/ˈdāṛhī/	
/ˈbúḍī/	'old woman'	بُڈھی	/ˈbuṛhī/	(بُڑھی)
/ˈčɔ́drī/	'Choudhry'	چوَدھری	/ˈčɔdharī/	
/páṛ/	'read!'	پَڑھ	/paṛh/	
/sámǰ/	'understand!'	سَمجھ	/ˈsamaǰh/	

The Urdu-ized spellings presented above for both patterns are superior to any surface spellings of high-tone words, despite variation in position and appearance. By representing the location of lexical L, whether by a post-vocalic *choti he* or final *do chashmi he*, such spellings clearly indicate the high-falling pitch contour to mother tongue readers. Furthermore, these spellings maintain a relatively constant word image between Gojri and Urdu. The greatest advantage to adopting both patterns for Gojri, however, is that writing *do chashmi he* after formerly aspirated voiced consonants maintains a constant word image for many non-causative and causative pairs of Gojri verbs like those in (24). Any surface representation (whether representing the high toneme everywhere with post-vocalic *do chashmi he* or, better, with post-vocalic *choti he* everywhere given its prior association via /kɛ́-/ 'say' and /rɛ́-/ 'stay') must resort to two surface spellings: one for the high-tone root and another for the low-tone causative. However, the Urdu-ized representation of lexical L by means of post-consonantal *do chashmi he* enables readers to interpret high tone and, alternately, low tone from a single spelling of the root.

Consider these examples:

(24) Spellings for high-tone root and low-tone causative pairs of verbs

Verb Pairs	Gloss	Urdu-ized Spellings	Alternate Surface Spellings
/páṛ/	'read!'	پَہڑ	پَڑھ or پَھڑ
/paˈṛā̀/	'teach!'	پَڑھا	پَڑہا
/láng/	'pass by!'	لَنگھ	لَہنگ or لَھنگ
/lanˈgā̀/	'shoot!'	لَنگھا	لَنگہا
/báṇ/	'become!'	بَنّھ	بَہنّ or بَھنّ
/baˈṇā̀/	'make!'	بَنّھا	بَنّہا
/ˈbáṛak/	intrans. 'boil!'	بَڑھک	بَہڑک or بَھڑک
/baṛˈkā̀/	trans. 'boil!'	بَڑھکا	بَڑکہا or بَڑکھا

The final pair in (24) is unique in that it shows the effect of L-spreading through an intervening root-final consonant and onto the stressed causative suffix. Only the Urdu-based representation allows for correct indication of surface tones while avoiding awkward spellings which all but completely obscure any relationship between the two stems. An analysis mistakenly linking lexical L with root-final /k/ rather than with /ṛ/ would lead to the spelling shown to the far right of the bottom line in (24), the final syllable of which is ambiguous with the aspirated level tone /khā/ 'eat!'

A similar pair of verbs are /pɔ́č/ 'arrive!' and /pɔˈčā̀/ 'deliver!' As indicated by its voicelessness, the root-final consonant has not been de-aspirated like those presented above. Rather, the root is a contraction of an older form attested by the Urdu cognate /paˈhunč/ 'arrive!' Writing lexical L with *choti he* after the vowel and before the final consonant accounts for L-spread through that consonant and onto the stressed causative suffix, while avoiding a spelling ambiguous with the aspirated level tone sequence /čhā/ (cf. /čhā~/ 'shade'). The spellings which correctly indicate surface tones are thus پَوہچ 'arrive!' and پَوہچا 'deliver!' Again, any other analysis and related spellings would complicate the interpretation of surface tones.

5.2.6 Writing of other low-tone words

Three remaining kinds of low-tone words warrant discussion, the first two involving a small number of words and the third constituting a much broader pattern.

Writing of polysyllabic words beginning with /h/

The tone and spelling issues related to words like /pàˈtīǰɔ/ (/bàˈtīǰɔ/) 'nephew' and /pàˈṛās/ (/bàˈṛās/) 'steam' are similar to those for words like /hàˈmešā~/ 'always'. The latter begin with /h/ but are stressed on a non-initial syllable, and like the former words bear low tone on all syllables preceding the stressed syllable, followed by a low-rising pitch on the stressed syllable. Most Gujar writers simply write these words with initial *choti he* (e.g. ہَمیشان /hàˈmešā~/ 'always'), per their familiarity with the spellings of Urdu cognates (e.g. ہَمیشہ /haˈmešā/ 'always'). This practice actually constitutes a 'shallow' orthographic solution and is often followed even by those normally advocating a phonetic approach to spelling. A surface representation would mark the low-rising tone where it is heard on the stressed syllable, and begin with a vowel since /h/ is not phonetically realized (e.g. آمہیشان [ʌˈmè:šá~] 'always', in which the first-syllable low tone still remains unwritten). A natural application of this approach would spell the intransitive verb /hàḷ/ [hăḷ] 'shake!' as ہَل, and its transitive (i.e. causative) counterpart /hàˈḷā/ [àˈḷă:] trans. 'shake!' as آلہا. Such spellings preclude a constant image of the Gojri root, as well as precluding a constant word image between Gojri and Urdu. The Urdu-ized practice of simply writing initial lexical L with initial *choti he* is the best solution for all words of this type.

Writing low tone in words featuring initial aspiration

Words in which low tone and aspiration co-occur are most commonly written with reference only to aspiration. Thus, /ˈthā̀rɔ/ [ˈtʰà:rɔ́:] pl. 'your' is spelled تھارو and /ˈthā̀ṇɔ/ [ˈtʰa:ṇɔ́] 'to be found' is spelled تھاݨو. An alternative phonemic approach representing both low tone and aspiration would yield double-*he* spellings for /thā̀rɔ/: تھہارو or تھھارو. It so happens that the first of these looks remarkably similar to its Urdu cognate, /tumhārā/ تمہارا, and is therefore attractive for pedagogical reasons. Ignoring the tone altogether is an acceptable solution for such words, since only a handful are truly indigenous and lack accepted

Urdu spellings. The interpretation of indigenous words like the two spelled above is greatly assisted by contextual clues (given the unique semantics of these two words).

Writing low tone not associated with loss of aspiration

This category includes all words with Urdu cognates featuring medial /h/ before a long vowel, as well as many which do not. The fact that Urdu medial /h/ corresponds to both Gojri high tone and low tone means that any phonemic spelling approach which values compatibility with Urdu is forced either to promote some spellings which are contrary to Urdu or to accept ambiguity in the interpretation of *choti he*. Since most Gojri words of the type corresponding to medial /h/ before a long vowel in Urdu are in fact Perso-Arabic loans whose spellings are well-known to literate Gujars, there is little warrant for promoting unique Gojri spellings (although diacritics representing Urdu first-syllable short vowels must be omitted for Gojri). Examples of such loans are shown in (25).

(25) Spellings of Perso-Arabic loans pronounced with low tone in Gojri

Word	Gloss	Urdu Pronunciation	Urdu Spelling
/mȁl/	'palace'	/maˈhāl/	مَحل (with *bari he*)
/ǰȁz/	'ship'	/ǰaˈhāz/	جَہاز
/ǰȁd/	'jihad'	/ǰiˈhād/	جِہاد
/ˈmȁǰar/	'refugee'	/muˈhāǰir/	مُہاجِر

Along with such borrowed spellings, some Gujar writers, including the editors of the Academy dictionary, have been writing indigenous words of this type using *do chashmi he* by analogy with Urdu-ized spellings for low tones resulting from de-aspiration. Others write all such words with *choti he*, consistent with their writing of low tones resulting from de-aspiration [by analogy with the spellings of loans like those in (25)]. Some common words for which such alternate spellings are used are shown in (26).

(26) Alternate spellings for indigenous low-tone words not related to de-aspiration

Word	Gloss	with *do chashmi he*	with *choti he*
/ˈmȁrɔ/	'our'	مھارو	مہارو
/mɛ̏s/	'dairy buffalo'	مھیَس	مہیَس
/maleˈàp/	'worm'	مَلیھَپ	مَلیہَپ
/lwȁ/	'get [someone] to remove [article of clothing]!'	لُوھا	لُہا
		cf. لاہ /lȁ́/ 'remove [article of clothing]!'	

In between the words which are clearly loans and those which are truly indigenous are many more words which are not thought of as loans (and which might be indigenous) but whose Urdu cognates do have known spellings. For a small number of words like /ˈkȁṇī/ (/ˈgȁṇī/) 'story' the Urdu medial-/h/ spelling کَہانی (/kaˈhānī/) might be abandoned in favour of گھانٓی, so that both dialects can be represented by a single form. Conversely, words beginning with any of the plosives /p/, /b/, /t/, /d/, /č/, /ǰ/, /ṭ/, /ḍ/, /k/, and /g/ but not showing the initial voicing variation between dialects should always be written with the Urdu spellings to avoid confusion about voicing, e.g. بہادر /ˈbȁdar/ 'brave' (Urdu /baˈhādar/) and پہاڑ /pȁṛ/ 'rocky crag' (Urdu /paˈhāṛ/ 'mountain'). For words beginning with any other consonant (i.e. any lacking a homorganic voiceless or voiced counterpart), there is no reason to promote a unique Gojri spelling (aside from unique Gojri endings), given the frequency of medial-/h/ loan spellings in the lexicon. In practice such words are typically written with Urdu spellings, but the *do chashmi he* spellings are also possible. Some examples of this variation are shown in (27).

(27) Alternate spellings for Gojri low-tone words cognate with Urdu medial-/h/ words

do chashmi he Spelling		Urdu Spelling (with *choti he*)	
/nȁ/ 'bathe!'	نھا	نُہا	/nuˈhā/
/ˈswȁgā/ 'ashes'	سُوھاگا	سُہاگو	/suˈhāgā/ 'ash'
/ˈmȉnā/ 'months'	مھینا	مہینہ	/maˈhīnā/ 'month'
/sȁl/ 'diarrhea'	سھال	سہال	/saˈhāl/

The remaining problem, then, is that there are two competing representations for unique Gojri low-tone words not resulting from de-aspiration. Since there are no low-tone roots featuring initial short vowels which are not the result of de-aspiration, neither *choti he* nor *do chashmi he* written before a long vowel create any ambiguities with high tone roots (assuming rejection of the ambiguous practice of writing *choti he* for low-tone short vowels associated with de-aspiration). This is because both letters accurately represent the pre-vocalic location of lexical L (whereas *choti he* represents post-vocalic lexical L in high-tone words, provided it is consistently written after any explicit vowel). Therefore, since both representations rightly represent lexical L unambiguously, and enjoy current use for large numbers of other Gojri words (assuming validation of the iconic representation for low tones resulting from de-aspiration), the spelling of uniquely indigenous words like those in (26) must be determined with reference to other criteria.

Two possible solutions are: (i) to simply spell all low-tone words of this type with *choti he*; or (ii) to spell with *do chashmi he* all such Gojri words for which transparent Urdu cognates are not found in modern Urdu dictionaries. Either solution is preferable to subjectively determining the spelling of each word on a case-by-case basis. The first solution may be preferable from the standpoint of maintaining constant word images between Gojri and Urdu, but its adoption is somewhat complicated by the proliferation of spellings like مھارو /mà̄rɔ/ 'our' in the Gojri literature of Indian-administered Kashmir. The second solution would afford an overall representation of low tone that is more uniform within Gojri itself, especially for text material that utilizes fewer non-indigenous words (i.e. it would strengthen rather than dilute the association of *do chashmi he* with the low toneme). Testing of both spelling patterns with new readers is needed to determine which potential ambiguity poses the greater problem: (i) the confusion of such *do chashmi he* spellings with spellings of words featuring initial voiceless aspiration; or (ii) the confusion of such *choti he* spellings with spellings of high-tone words, especially those involving stems ending in /έ/ and a long vowel suffix (e.g. کہاں /kā́~/ 'we say').

5.3 CONCLUSION

The evaluation presented above obviously reflects my own conviction that a tone representation which 'joins' the dialects and maximizes ease of transfer between Gojri and Urdu is better than a representation that 'splits' the dialects and promotes unique Gojri spellings. I have extensively documented the claim that a consistent one-to-one mapping of grapheme to toneme is impossible for any representation that values compatibility with Urdu. A surface representation for Gojri must admit high functional loads (and conflicting functions) for the letters *do chashmi he* and *choti he*, while still failing to represent all of the contrastive surface phenomena (most notably, any level low tone preceding a low-rising tone in words like /pìgeˈāṛ/ (/bìgīˈāṛ/) 'wolf').

The documentation demonstrates, however, that Urdu-based conventions in use by some Gujar writers approximate a consistent representation of underlying lexical L. In this view, *do chashmi he* and *choti he* are allographs of lexical L, and their distributions are dictated by Urdu spelling patterns rather than by surface contrasts. Such Urdu-based spellings correctly indicate the interpretation of surface tones while maintaining consistency of word image within Gojri and between Gojri and Urdu.

REFERENCES

Bailey, Thomas Grahame. 1903. *Studies in Northern Himalayan Dialects*. Calcutta: Baptist Mission Press.

Bird, Steven. 1997. *When Marking Tone Reduces Fluency: An Orthography Experiment in Cameroon*. University of Edinburgh, Human Communication Research Centre. (Research Paper 91).

Dyrud, Lars O. 2001. *Hindi-Urdu: Stress Accent or Non-Stress Accent?* MA thesis. University of North Dakota.

Grierson, George A. (ed). 1973 (c1903). *Linguistic Survey of India, Vol. IX*. Delhi: Motilal Banarsidass.

Hallberg, Calinda E. and O'Leary, Clare F. 1992. 'Dialect variation and multilingualism among Gujars in Pakistan'. In *Sociolinguistic Survey of Northern Pakistan Vol. 3*, edited by Calvin R. Rensch, Calinda E. Hallberg, and Clare F. O'Leary. Islamabad: National Institute of Pakistan Studies and Summer Institute of Linguistics.

Hugoniot, Ken, and Polster, Dietmar. 1997. *A Sociolinguistic Profile of Eastern Gujari*. (Unpublished manuscript).

Hussain, Sarmad. 1997. *Phonetic Correlates of Lexical Stress in Urdu.* PhD dissertation. Northwestern University.

Iqbal, Azim et al. (eds). 1985. *Gojri Dictionary.* Srinagar: Jammu and Kashmir Academy of Art, Culture, and Languages.

Ladefoged, Peter and Maddieson, Ian. 1996. *The Sounds of the World's Languages.* Oxford: Blackwell.

Lewis, M. Paul, Simons, Gary F., and Fennig, Charles D. (eds). 2015. *Ethnologue: Languages of the World, Eighteenth Edition.* Dallas, Texas: SIL International.

Losey, Wayne E. 2002. *Writing Gojri: Linguistic and Sociolinguistic Constraints on a Standardized Orthography for the Gujars of South Asia.* MA thesis. University of North Dakota.

Masica, Colin P. 1991. *The Indo-Aryan Languages.* Cambridge: Cambridge University Press.

Mathews, David and Dalvi, Mohamed Kasim. 1999. *Teach Yourself Urdu.* London: Hodder & Stoughton Ltd.

Nida, E. A. 1964. 'Practical limitations to a phonemic alphabet'. In *Orthography Studies: Articles on New Writing Systems,* edited by W. Smalley. 22–30. London: United Bible Societies.

Parvez, Aslam. 1996. *The Adaptation of the Perso-Arabic Script for Urdu, Panjabi and Sindhi.* New Delhi: Monumental Publishers.

Shackle, Christopher. 1979. 'Problems of classification in Pakistan Panjab'. *Transactions of the Philological Society* 77.1: 191–210. Oxford.

Sharma, Jagdish Chander. 1979. *Gojri Phonetic Reader.* Mysore: Central Institute of Indian Languages. (Phonetic Reader Series No. 19).

Sharma, Jagdish Chander. 1982. *Gojri Grammar.* Mysore: Central Institute of Indian Languages. (Grammar Series No. 9).

Thikri, M. Aslam Armani and Losey, Wayne E. 2001. *Gojri Alphabet Primer.* Abbottabad: Wayne E. Losey.

10

The Indus Kohistani Indefinite Specific Marker *=uk*

Beate Lubberger

1. INTRODUCTION

The Indus Kohistani[1] marker *=uk* is an enclitic[2] that attaches to the end of noun phrases to mark them as indefinite and specific.[3] Buddruss (1959: 13) in his description of an Indus Kohistani dialect spoken in Tangir is, to my knowledge, the first to mention this marker as a 'secondary *k*-suffix'. The entry in the Indus Kohistani dictionary (Zoller 2005: 90) is as follows:

> *-ṓk*^{h} a suffix denoting indefiniteness (indefinite article). K. *akh* 'indefinite article' (in postnominal position). The grammeme is also found in Shina (Masica 1991: 371). [...] Same construction also in Pers. *bādshāh-e* 'some king'. The locative suffix *-ḗ* can be additionally added: *bangalà-ōkē* 'in some bungalow or other'. Also with postp.: *ā̃ĩ bazī́, šāzādagī̃̀ gā̃̀ ak*^{h} *dhút-ōk-maz bhḕṭ-gē* [...] 'they go to the village of the princess and sit down in any corner' (from an oral tale). Cf. *kàlōk*^{h}.

---

[1] ISO 639–3 code [mvy].

[2] Clitics are defined as expressions that are like independent words meaningwise, but are phonologically dependent on and bound to the host they attach to. Enclitics are clitics that follow their host (Haspelmath 2002: 149–55).

[3] A noun that is marked as specific or referential refers to an 'individuated, bounded entity in the message world' (Payne 1997: 264) as in 'yesterday he saw a leopard'. The opposite would be non-specific or non-referential as in 'leopards are mammals' and 'I would like to see a leopard' where 'leopard' does not refer to a specific animal.

A similar marker =*ek* (=*k* when following a vowel) has been described in Gilgiti Shina (Radloff 1998, 1999), in Kohistani Shina (Schmidt and Kohistani 2008), and is found in Gultari, another Shina dialect (Hook 1996: 143). Furthermore, in a text of the Nuristani language Waigali, Buddruss (1987: 33) mentions the marker *eog* 'a certain' which consists of the numeral *e* 'one' plus the suffix -*og*, and which is used to introduce a certain custom that subsequently is the main topic of the text (see also Degener 1998).

As far as I know, an in-depth description of the Indus Kohistani marker =*uk* has not been undertaken so far. My aim in this paper is to provide a more detailed account of form and function of this marker. In section 2, I will show that =*uk* is neither suffix nor independent word but an enclitic, to be distinguished from another Indus Kohistani adjectivizer suffix -*úk*. In section 3, I will describe the function of =*uk* as an indefinite specific marker and, more specifically, as an indicator of entities introduced into the discourse for the first time. This will be followed by a brief description of other means of indicating indefiniteness in Indus Kohistani.

The Indus Kohistani data used in this paper are of the Pattan variety, belonging to the dialect spoken in settlements near the River Indus (Hallberg 1992: 93). The corpus includes folk stories, narratives of personal experiences, expository, and procedural texts recorded and transcribed between 2000 and 2014.[4] I am deeply indebted to my main language consultant for providing the data and for teaching and sharing with me her knowledge about her mother tongue.

2. FORM: =*UK* AS A NOUN PHRASE LEVEL ENCLITIC

Is the Indus Kohistani indefinite marker =*uk* a suffix, a clitic, or an independent word? In this section I argue, based on phonological, morphological, and syntactic evidence, that =*uk* is a phrase-level enclitic, its host being the noun phrase.

[4] The corpus used for this study includes 107 texts of varying length: the shortest ones consist of twenty sentences, the longest ones of 530 sentences. Average length is between one and two hundred sentences.

2.1 Phonological Evidence

Indus Kohistani is a pitch accent language; that is, every independent word carries one accent which is perceived as high (on short vowels), rising, or falling (on long vowels). Plural suffixes as well as case markers do not carry an inherent accent, nor does the indefinite marker *=uk*. The fact that *=uk* is accent-less is, however, not so much evidence for it being a suffix (some Indus Kohistani suffixes do have an inherent accent) as for it not being an independent word (see section 2.2). However, there is an accent shifting rule which applies when a suffix is added to a noun with a rising accent on its last syllable. This rule is blocked when the indefinite marker follows the noun. Table 1 illustrates the rule by showing a noun with a rising accent on the last syllable. As soon as a suffix is added, the accent on the last syllable of the stem will shift to the right, to the suffix. Rising accent is represented as *v́*, falling accent as *v̀*.

Table 1

(i)	gharimaáṣ	woman SG
(ii)	gharimaaṣ-á	women PL
(iii)	gharimaaṣ=ã̀ĩ	of woman GEN.F
(iv)	gharimaaṣ=eé	woman ERG

When the plural suffix follows, as in (ii), then the rising accent moves to the suffix. When the genitive case marker is added, as in (iii), then the accent shifts to the first mora of the suffix and is then perceived as a falling accent. When the ergative case marker follows, as seen in (iv), then the accent shifts to the second mora of the suffix and is perceived as a rising accent.

Table 2 shows the same noun, now with the indefinite marker *=uk*.

Table 2

(i)	gharimaáṣ =uk	woman.SG=INDEF
(ii)	gharimaaṣ-á =uk	women-PL=INDEF
(iii)	gharimaáṣ =uk=ãĩ	of woman=INDEF=GEN.F
(iv)	gharimaáṣ =uk=ee	woman=INDEF=ERG

In (ii), the stem accent shifts to the right, to the plural suffix. Adding the marker =*uk* does not influence this shifting rule. However, in (iii), where the indefinite marker comes in between the stem and the genitive marker, the stem accent no longer shifts to the right; =*uk* has blocked the shifting rule. The same blocking of accent shift happens when a noun is followed by both indefinite marker and ergative case marker, as seen in (iv). Thus, this blocking of the accent shifting rule shows that =*uk* is less integrated within the domain of the preceding word than the case markers.

To further illustrate the differences in prosodic integration of suffixes versus clitics, let us look at a suffix with an inherent accent, the diminutive indicator -*ṭuú*. In case this suffix is added to a noun, the noun stem accent will be deleted, as seen in example (1).

(1)	*tabàax*	bowl for kneading bread dough
	tabaax-ṭuú	small bowl for kneading bread dough

Note that in the diminutive form the stem accent has disappeared; the word accent is now on the suffix.

To recapitulate, Indus Kohistani suffixes may be accent-less in which case accent shifting rules apply, or they may have an inherent accent in which case the adding of the suffix causes the stem accent to be deleted. The marker =*uk* is different in that it is accent-less but the accent shifting rule does not apply; =*uk* does not show the same prosodic integration as do proper suffixes. I therefore argue that it is not a suffix.

2.2 Morphological evidence

In regard to its meaning, the marker =*uk* might be thought of as a separate word. However, it cannot stand on its own. The indefinite marker always requires a host to its left which also implies that it cannot occur clause-initially or after a pause. Further evidence for =*uk* not being an independent word is the fact that it does not carry an inherent accent or, in other words, it does not constitute a separate domain for word accent or stress (Haspelmath 2002: 151). I conclude that the indefinite marker =*uk* cannot be considered an independent word.

2.3 Syntactic evidence

Another reason for not classifying =*uk* as a suffix is that it does not only attach to nouns but to any element that happens to be the last within a noun phrase. Affixes, on the other hand, are much more restricted in that they have no such freedom of host selection; usually they can attach to one kind of stem only.

In Indus Kohistani, the rightmost element of a noun phrase usually is the head noun, and consequently the marker =*uk* often follows the head, as shown in example (2).

(2)	*ék*	*màaṣ=uk=ee*	*man-ágil*
	one	man=INDEF=ERG	say-PFV2

'A certain man said …' (More about sin no. 135)

In this example, the head noun 'a man' is marked for ergative case.[5] Case markers, too, are enclitics; they always follow the indefinite marker =*uk* where it is present.

There are instances, however, where the last element of a noun phrase happens to be something other than the head; in such a case, =*uk* also cliticizes to this last element. It is examples like (3) to (6), that show the nature of =*uk* as a phrasal enclitic.

In example (3) the noun phrase marked by =*uk* (in square brackets) is actually a noun modified by a relative clause.

(3)	*[tamàam*	*maxlùuk*	*ầãs=uk]*	*mẽ̀ẽ*	*kha-áthe*
	all	people	be.PST.M=INDEF	1SG.ERG	eat-PRS.PFV

'I have eaten all people that were there.' (Gulbagh 2 no. 234)

In this and the next example, the last element of the phrase that the indefinite marker cliticizes to is a form of the verb 'be'.

[5] Like the indefinite marker =*uk*, the Indus Kohistani case markers are not suffixes (as it may seem) but have to be analysed as phrasal clitics. They, too, cliticize to the end of a noun phrase. In respect to accent shifting, however, they differ from =*uk* as shown in section 2.1.

(4)

phát	*kareé*	*ã̃í*	*ǰhṹũ*
leaving	do.CV	3PL.PROX	downstream
màazãã	*baá*	*man*	*ầãs-e*
other.POSS.M	house	in	be.PST.M-PL.M
[ṣã̃í	*zànd*	*thé=uk]*	
3PL.DEM	alive	be.PRS.PL.M=INDEF	

'Having left (them) they were downstream, in another one's house, those ones that were alive.' (The torrent no. 137)

In the next two examples again, =*uk* cliticizes to the last element of a relative clause, the verb.

(5)

[ṣás	*gàaḍii*	*man*	*katiúk*	
DEM.OBL	car	in	how.many	
ầãs=uk]		*sã̃í*	*búṭ*	*mar-ígee*
be.PST.IPFV.M=INDEF		3PL.DIST	all	die-PFV2.F.SG

'All those who were inside the car died.' (elicited 26 October 2015)

Examples (5) and (6) are typical instances of a left-dislocated relative clause; again the marker =*uk* attaches to its last element, the verb.

(6)

[ṣás	*gàaḍii*	*če*	*kãã́*	*čala-ánt=uk]*
DEM.OBL	car	CONJ	who	drive-PRS.M=INDEF
so	*màaṣ-ãã*		*qasùur*	*thú*
3SG.DIST	man-GEN.M.SG		fault	be.PRS.M.SG

'It is the fault of the man who is driving the car.' (elicited 26 October 2015)

The evidence presented so far supports the analysis of the indefinite marker =*uk* as a phrase level enclitic whose host is a noun phrase.

2.4 Comparison between enclitic *=uk* and adjectivizer suffix *-uk*

There is another morpheme *-úk*, a true derivational suffix, that should be distinguished from the indefinite marker *=uk*. The Indus Kohistani adjectivizer suffix *-úk* attaches to nouns and adverbs that express concepts of time, thereby changing them into adjectives. In contrast to the clitic *=uk,* which is never accented, this adjectivizer suffix has an inherent accent that overrules the accent of the preceding stem. Table 3 shows examples of such adjectives.

Table 3

	Stem		**Adjective**	
(a)	*kàal*	'year'	*kaal-úk*	'yearly'
(b)	*dìis*	'day'	*diis-úk-i góli*	'midday meal'
(c)	*ràal*	'night'	*raal-úk ṭiímb*	'night time'
(d)	*sahár*	'early morning'	*sahar-úk-i čèey*	'early morning tea'
(e)	*basaánd*	'spring'	*basand-úk moosám*	'spring season'
(f)	*šáral*	'autumn'	*šaral-úk moosám*	'autumn season'
(g)	*oktá*	'in the morning, tomorrow'	*okt-úk wáxt*	'morning time'
(h)	*lawaár*	'beginning of dawn'	*lawaar-úk wáxt*	'beginning of dawn'
(i)	*poór*	'previous (year)'	*poor-úk zòṛ*	'last year's clothes'

The root accent of the nouns and adverbs is suppressed once the suffix *-úk* has been affixed. Such derived adjectives are marked for gender; in examples (b) and (d) the noun modified by the adjective is feminine, the adjective has therefore the feminine suffix *-i* following the adjectivizer suffix *-úk*.

Furthermore, Indus Kohistani has a set of symmetrical deictic adjectives that may take the suffix *-úk*, shown in Table 4.

Table 4

ṣati-ãấ (M), ṣati-ĩ́ (F)	'this (much), like this' (visible and nearby, in contrast to something else)
ati-ãấ (M), ati-ĩ́ (F)	'this (much), like this' (visible and further away)
tati-ãấ (M), tati-ĩ́ (F)	'that (much), like that' (out of sight)
kati-ãấ (M), kati-ĩ́ (F)	'how much'

The use of such deictic adjectives is illustrated in (7). The utterance has the character of an exclamation said about a child that the speaker had not seen for a while.

(7) hȉĩ ṣatĩĩ́ hu-úthi
now like.this become-PRS.PFV.F
'She has become this tall!' (field notes 1 March 2014)

The same set of adjectives can take the suffix *-úk*; the gender marker is then dropped, as presented in table 5. Here again, the accent on the suffix causes the stem accent to be deleted.

Table 5

ṣati-úk	'this much/many' (visible and nearby, in contrast to something else)
ati-úk	'this much/many' (visible and further away)
tati-úk	'that much/many' (out of sight)
kati-úk	'how much/many'
bee-kati-úk	'not known how much/many'

The use of these adjectives is exemplified in (8).

(8)

miı́	*gee*	*ati-úk*	*pèes*	*thé*
1SG.OBL	with	this.much	money	be.PRS.M.PL

má	*kati-úk*	*zikàat*	*dàm*
1SG	how.much	zakat	give.SUBJ.1SG

'I own this much money; how much zakat (tax) should I give?' (Beggars, ... no. 33)

In this example, *ati-úk* 'this much' points to a more or less exact amount of money; the speaker expects to be given as response an exact amount of the money to be paid.

If the speaker wants to convey that the quantity of an entity is an approximation then the indefinite marker =*uk* may follow the adjective, adding the meaning 'approximately, about', as shown in (9).

(9)

sãĩ́	*ati-úk=uk*	*ç̣hiír*	*di-ínt*
3PL.DIST	this.much-INDEF	milk	give-PRS.F

'They (buffalo cows) give about this much milk.' (Buffalo care no. 50)

To summarize, the suffix -*úk* described in this section should be treated as distinct from the indefinite marker =*uk*. The latter, an accent-less clitic, marks indefiniteness and specificity, or approximation; the former is—apart from having a different meaning—a true suffix that is inherently accented.

3. FUNCTION: THE DISCOURSE DEVICE =*UK*

In neighbouring languages, the Gilgiti Shina marker =*ek* (Radloff 1999: 103) and the Kohistani Shina marker -*ek* (Schmidt and Kohistani 2008: 75) have been described as indicators of indefiniteness that are used to introduce characters and entities into the discourse. This use as an introductory discourse device is also the main function of Indus Kohistani =*uk*. However, the marker =*uk* seems to indicate not only indefiniteness but also specificity. That is, an entity followed by =*uk* is marked as not identifiable (or definite) and also as specific, as 'a bounded, individuated entity in the message world' (Payne 1997: 264). In other words, if my analysis of =*uk* as a specific marker is correct, it cannot be used to indicate generic referents as in 'dogs are faithful', nor does it indicate a non-specific referent as in 'he wants to buy a flat (but has no specific flat in mind)'. In the corpus used for this study there are no instances of =*uk* being used to mark entities as generic. However, more work has to be done in identifying and differentiating indefinite specific and indefinite generic/non-specific Indus Kohistani noun phrases. For now, let me say that an analysis of =*uk* as an indefinite specific marker would agree with the observation made by Himmelmann (2001: 834) that specific articles may be used to introduce new participants into the universe of discourse.

3.1 =*UK* INTRODUCING PARTICIPANTS AND ENTITIES

In narrative texts, particularly in folk tales, the indefinite marker =*uk* is used as a discourse device to introduce characters, places, and other entities. The standard example is the introductory sentence of a folk tale as in (10).

(10)	*qasá*	*gài*	*gài*	*ék*	*baačàa=uk*	*ȁãs*
	story	go.PFV2.F	go.PFV2.F	one	king=INDEF	be.PST.M.SG

'Once upon a time there was a king.' (Prince and fairy no. 1)

The king introduced in this (first) sentence of a story is a new, unknown, not yet identified, but specific person (as opposed to a generic concept as in 'a king wears a crown'). When a person as in example (10) or a thing is mentioned for the first time, often both the indefinite marker and the numeral *ék* 'one' are used. With, as well as without, the numeral *ék*, the meaning of =*uk* is similar to 'a certain' in English.

In example (11), the entity being introduced is a place; again both the marker =*uk* and the numeral *ék* 'one' are used.

(11)	*só*	*ék*	*zaí=uk*	*gee*	*gèe*
	3SG.DIST	one	place=INDEF	to	go.PFV2.F
	khẽ	*qà=õ*	*bahuú*	*thú*	
	when	crow=GEN.PL	hut	be.PRS.M.SG	

'She went to a place where there was a crow's hut.' (Princess and crows no. 68)

New entities/characters may be marked by =*uk* only, as in example (12).

(12)	*màaṣ=uk*	*ii-galeé*	*mii=geé*	*man-álaas*
	man=INDEF	come-CV	1S.DAT	say-PST.PFV

'A man came and said to me, ...' (Dreams no. 87)

Each character, place, or other entity that is subsequently introduced to the hearer may be marked with =*uk*. For instance, in the story about the adventures of a prince (Gulbagh 2), consisting of 329 sentences, =*uk* is used 53 times: 23 times to introduce a new character, 24 times to introduce a new entity, place, or time; and six times =*uk* occurs in its function as a marker of approximation (see section 3.3). A few instances of it are shown in example (13).

(13)	No. 1	Once upon a time there was a king.=*uk*
	No. 12	When they went ahead there came an ascetic.=*uk*
	No. 13	When the ascetic=*uk* came he said to the king ...
	No. 44	But the king mistakenly also gave him the key to a room.=*uk*
	No. 60	... there was another king=*uk* ...
	No. 62	Suddenly a rabbit=*uk* came.
	No. 66	After travelling for a long time he came to a place=*uk*
	No. 69	He wrote a note=*uk* and threw it back ...
	No. 80	... there came a gate=*uk*

No. 84 There was a watchman=*uk* at the gate.

No. 188 One time=*uk* he was crossing the trench ...

(Gulbagh story 2)

Note that no. 13 is a repetition of the second clause of no. 12. One might wonder why the speaker uses the marker =*uk* in no. 13 although the referent of the marked noun phrase has already been introduced in no. 12. This is an instance of tail-head linkage common in oral narratives. Its usage here is simply to help the hearer to associate events (Levinsohn 2007: 47).

A comparison among folk stories, narratives of personal experiences, and non-narrative texts shows that =*uk* most frequently occurs in folk stories, less so in other narratives. This can be explained as follows: the teller of a folk story has to create a whole new 'story world' with all its characters, places, and props that are new to the hearer, hence the frequent use of =*uk*. In narratives of personal experiences, on the other hand, there are more characters and entities already identifiable by the hearer, so =*uk* is used less frequently. In particular, the introductory sentences of the corpus' seven folk stories all contain both the indefinite particle *ék* (see section 4) and the marker =*uk*, as seen in example (10) above. The same introductory sentence pattern can be found in other stories 'of olden times'. In the narratives about personal experiences or events that a speaker has heard of, the first character or entity introduced is not marked by =*uk*, for the reasons mentioned above.

Table 6 shows the occurrences of =*uk* in both narrative and non-narrative texts. The use of the indefinite marker has been grouped into three categories: (i) =*uk* introducing a character; (ii) =*uk* introducing other entities, places, or times; and (iii) =*uk* indicating approximation (see section 3.3). This table shows that =*uk* as an introducer of characters and other entities is more frequent in narrative texts than in non-narrative texts.

Table 6

	narrative texts	non-narrative texts
occurrences of =*uk* introducing characters	65	39
occurrences of =*uk* introducing other entities, places, times	65	6
occurrences of =*uk* indicating approximation	23	46

In non-narrative discourse the indefinite clitic =*uk* is used when the speaker wants to illustrate or exemplify a particular state of affairs or event. Take for instance a section from a text about forgiving. Here the speaker creates a story to illustrate one aspect of the importance of forgiving. In example (14) the first few sentences are translated. In the first sentence, 'a man' is followed by =*uk*; he is the main character of this particular section of the text and is subsequently referred to with pronouns.

(14) No. 25 Now suppose there is a man=*uk* who thinks, 'I have been alive until now; why should I die!'

No. 26 So he does not ask forgiveness from his parents; he does not give them the opportunity to forgive him.

No. 27 He does not ask forgiveness from his wife, he does not ask forgiveness from his parents and from his parents-in-law; so when this man suddenly dies he leaves behind his parents and his brother.

No. 28 Then he (the brother) will gather all the family members and will say, 'Do forgive him where he did not fulfill his duties towards you'.

No. 29 '(Otherwise) God will punish him until this time (when you forgive him)'. (Forgiving)

Throughout the non-narrative texts in the corpus such 'stories' are created to illustrate or explain a state of affairs or an event or procedure, and the main character in such mini-narratives is introduced with the indefinite marker =*uk*.

3.2 =*UK* INTRODUCING A SUBSET OF AN ALREADY KNOWN ENTITY

The indefinite marker =*uk* may co-occur with determiners such as possessive pronouns and demonstrative adjectives. In example (15) the noun phrase marked by =*uk* contains a possessive pronoun.

(15)	*bazií*	*sayằã*	*amìir=uk*	*ằãs*
	go.CV	3PL.DIST.POSS.Ma	leader=INDEF	be.PST.M

'There was a leader of theirs' (A tablighi story no. 4)

This utterance introduces a new participant into the discourse, the leader of a group of men. The group as a whole is already known to the hearer but not their leader, who is part of it.

Example (4), repeated here, shows the co-occurrence of the marker =*uk* and the demonstrative adjective 'these'.

(4)	*phát*	*kareé*	*ãĩ́*	*ǰhũṹ*	*màazãã*	*baá*
	leaving	do.CV	3PL.PROX	downstream	other.POSS.M	house
	man	*ằãs-e*	*ṣãĩ́*	*zànd*	*thé=uk*	
	in	be.PST.M-PL.M	3PL.DEM	alive	be.PRS.PL.M=INDEF	

'Having left (them) they were downstream, in another one's house, those ones that were alive.' (The torrent no. 137)

The text containing this example is about the people of one household whose house was destroyed by a landslide following torrential rains. As a family, they have been introduced at the beginning of the narrative, but now the speaker points out those of the household who survived the disaster. The noun phrase 'those who are alive' is marked by =*uk* as indefinite and specific in regard to the identity and number of the persons who constitute this sub-group; but at the same time the demonstrative *ṣãĩ́* 'these', here used as a tracking device (Himmelmann 1996), refers back to the family as a whole, a concept that is already activated in the mind of the hearer. So here again, =*uk* is used to introduce a subset of an already known set.

In example (16 a) the noun phrase marked by =*uk* contains both a possessive pronoun and a demonstrative. It is taken from a conversation during which the speaker told of her husband's ailment, quoting him.

(16) a.

mĩ̀ĩ	*ṣṹ*	*khuúr=uk*	*bhaaṣz-àant*
1SG.POSS	3SG.DEM	leg=INDEF	swell-PRS.M

'(He said,) "My leg is swollen."'

b.

daçhõ̀õ	*ṣṹ*	*khuúr*	*bhaaṣz-ií*
right	3SG.DEM	leg	swell-CV
khalài	*ho-ínt*		
inflated.goat.skin	become-PRS.F		

'"Having become swollen the right leg is becoming (like) an inflated goat skin."' (conversation 25 March 2013)

In (16 a) the quoted speaker mentions his leg for the first time but does not point out which one of his two legs is swollen. 'My leg' is specific but not identifiable as the right or the left one, hence the marker =*uk*. In the subsequent utterance in (16 b), the use of *daçhõ̀õ* 'right' then identifies the affected leg. So in (16 a), we find the same pattern as in the examples above: =*uk* indicates an indefinite but specific member of an already introduced whole set.

Example (17) has been elicited and can be said in the following context: Suppose one of the children has broken a dish but their mother does not know who exactly did it. So she might tell someone else about the incident in the following words.

(17)

mĩ̀ĩ	*ṣãĩ́*	*maasmá=uk=õõ*	*bhãã́*
1SG.POSS	3PL.DEM	child.PL=INDEF=OBL.PL	dish
šaar-áthe	*šeetã̀ã*	*thé*	
break-PRS.PFV	satan	be.PRS.PL.M	

'My children have broken the dish, they are naughty.' (elicited 22 February 2014)

Here again, the whole set, all the mother's children, is a concept already identifiable by the hearer. 'My children=*uk*' on the other hand refers to a specific subset of the children in the family, namely to the subset of dish breakers.

Based on the examples examined so far it seems that whenever the marker =*uk* co-occurs with other determiners, its function is to introduce an unidentified part or subset of an already identified/identifiable entity or group. However, the presence of other determiners is not necessary for this subset-of-a-given-set introduction. Example (18) is from a talk about food and meals. The food that has been cooked for a meal is a concept already present in the mind of the hearer when the speaker utters the following sentence.

(18)	*dharèel=uk*	*yaá*	*màal=ii*	*deént*
	remain.ADS.M=INDEF	or	cattle=DAT	give-PRS.M
	yaá	*kutsúr=õõ*	*galàant*	
	or	dog=OBL.PL	throw	

'What is left over (of the cooked food) we give to the cattle or to the dogs.' (Food no. 139)

The noun phrase marked by =*uk* in this example consists of an adjectival participle. Here, too, the indefinite marker is used to introduce an unidentified part of the already known entity 'cooked food', but no other determiner is present.

Introducing the unidentified subset of an already known set fits into the overall function of =*uk* as an introducer of participants or entities that appear in discourse for the first time.

3.3 =*UK* AS A MARKER OF APPROXIMATION

When =*uk* follows words expressing amounts of time or substances, the meaning is 'approximately' or 'more or less'. That is, the speaker is not sure about or does not want to express the exact amount of time or quantity. Table 7 presents a few of such terms with the marker =*uk*.

Table 7

biàal=uk	'a few days ago'
yũ̀ũ=uk	'about one month'

wáxt=uk man	'after some time'
geenṭá=uk	'about an hour'
piaalá=uk	'approximately a cup'
tsamtsàa=uk	'about a spoon(ful)'
áṛ=uk	'about half'
kiluú=uk	'approximately a kilo'
argáṭi=uk	'about half-finished'
ç̣àa tsòur=uk	'about three, four'
maydàar=uk	'about average'
dís dèš=uk huúgee	'about ten days ago'

In example (19), the indefinite marker modifies the quantifier *áṛ* 'half', rendering the meaning 'about one half of a bucket'.

(19) *ék* *baalṭìi* *pu-ìint* *kàl*
one bucket drink-PRS.F sometimes

áṛ-i=uk *baalṭìi* *pu-ìint*
half-F=INDEF bucket drink-PRS.F
'(Buffalo cows in the cold season) drink one bucket (of water), sometimes about half a bucket (of water).' (Buffalo care no. 24)

In this particular function, the marker =*uk* does not introduce a new character or entity into discourse, but adds a sense of vagueness to the quantity or quality expressed by its host.

4. MARKING (OF) INDEFINITENESS

In Indus Kohistani, marking of indefiniteness is not obligatory, neither is the indefinite marker =*uk* the only means to indicate indefiniteness. In section 3 we have seen that=*uk* may occur on its own or together with the numeral *ék* 'one'. In this section, I briefly look at two other strategies that may be used to mark indefiniteness: (i) the use of the numeral/indefinite particle *ek* on its own; and (ii) no marking at all.

To mark a noun phrase as indefinite, the numeral *ék* 'one' may occur on its own, illustrated in example (20).

(20)

hãã	*gí*	*wáxt=a*	*ék*	*màaṣ*	*bimàar*
and	what	time=OBL	one	man	ill

tsòo	*thú*	*meešwaál*	*hòo*
very.M	be.PRS.M.SG	man	become.SUBJ.3SG

gharimaáṣ	*hòo*	*ű*	*bimàar*
woman	become.SUBJ.3SG	3SG.PROX	ill

tsài	*thí*	*tèe*	*gatá*	*aś*
much.F	be.PRS.F	then	again	3SG.PROX.OBL

wáxt=a	*man*	*bé*	*xátam*	*kar-àant*
time=OBL	in	1PL	Quran-i-Khatam	do-PRS.M

'And if a person is very ill, may it be a man, may it be a woman, if she is very ill, then that time again we perform a recitation of the Quran.' (Prayer no. 41)

In example (20) the meaning of the numeral is not 'one' but that of an indefinite particle similar to the English indefinite article 'a'. The speaker of this utterance is not talking about a particular person but of anyone who might fall ill.

The next examples, (21) and (22), further illustrate the use of *ék* as an indefinite particle marking noun phrases that do not refer to a specific person.

(21)

gí	*wáxt*	*ék*	*màaṣ*	*mar-ìgaa*
what	time	one	man	die-PFV2.M.SG

mı̃ı̃	*baá*	*khun*	*yaá*	*mút=ãã*
1SG.POSS	house	in	or	other=GEN.M

baá	*khun*	*tèe*	*sàat*	*dìs*	*haár*
house	in	then	seven	days	until

só	*bȁã*	*xoraák*	*nií*	*kha-ṣát*
3SG.DIST	house.GEN.M	food	not	eat-FUT.M

'Suppose someone dies, in my house, or in another's house, then for seven days (the people of that household) will not eat food prepared in that house.' (Graves, graveyard no. 99)

(22)	*ék*	*ṣű̃*	*húm*	*ho-ínt*	*ék*	*màaṣ*	*mar-ígaa*
	one	3SG.DEM	also	become-PRS.F	one	man	die-PFV2.M.SG

'One (thing) that also happens is this: suppose a man died ...' (About inheriting no. 53)

The speaker, in both above utterances, has no particular person in mind; the term 'a man' is used in a non-specific sense.

In the corpus, most instances of *ék*—as an indefinite particle—occur in texts of an explanatory nature where the speaker does not narrate a particular event but rather talks about how something is done or happens in general. In these contexts, noun phrases preceded by *ék* often do not refer to a specific person or entity.

A possessive pronoun may occur in a noun phrase marked by *ék*. The following example (23) is the introductory sentence of a short personal experience narrative.

(23)	*zȁã*	*koostȁ ĩ*	*ék*	*màaṣ*	*gúzur*	*màaṣ*	*ȁãs*
	1PL.POSS.M	Kohistani	one	man	Gujjar	man	be.PST.M

'There was a man, one of us of Kohistan, a Gujjar...' (About seizures and fairies no. 68)

Another way to translate this utterance would be 'There was a man of ours, of Kohistan, a Gujjar.' Both meanings of *ék*, that of the numeral 'one' as well as that of indefiniteness, make sense in this context. Although here *ék* may indicate indefiniteness, the noun phrase it marks is by no means non-specific. The possessive pronoun clearly marks *ék màaṣ* 'one/a man' as referring to a particular person, who is part of a group already known to the hearer. Example (24) is another illustration of this use.

(24) *tsiṭ-ìl* *khẽ* *màz* *zȁã* *ék* *peɣambár* *ȁãs*
cut-PFV1 when inside 1PL.POSS.M one prophet be.PST.M

če *tasȉĩ* *nàa* *mii=geé* *ní* *e-ént*
CONJ 3SG.DIST.POSS name 1SG.DAT not come-PRS.M

'When (he) cut (the tree), there, inside, was a prophet of ours; I do not remember his name.' [or: ... one of our prophets ...] (Monkeys and leopards no. 31)

Here again, the noun 'prophet' is preceded by a possessive pronoun as well as *ék*; it refers to a specific person who is a hitherto unidentified member of the group of prophets, a concept the hearer is familiar with. This use of *ék* seems to be similar to that of =*uk* in 'unidentified-subset-of-an-identified-set' constructions described in section 3.2.

Examples (20) to (24) show that a noun phrase preceded by the indefinite particle *ék* may be non-specific or specific. It follows that the particle *ék*, like the clitic =*uk*, indicates indefiniteness but is neutral in respect to specificity.

Is there a way to distinguish the numeral *ék* from the indefinite particle *ék*? One possible difference between the two might be lack of an accent on the indefinite marker (the numeral *ék* is accented). However, data in the corpus for this study show no difference; both numeral and indefinite particle are accent-bearing.

Neither the indefinite particle *ék* nor the indefinite-specific enclitic =*uk* are high-frequency items, the former even less than the latter. The marking of Indus Kohistani indefinite noun phrases as such is not obligatory; this means that there is a fourth possibility concerning indefinite noun phrases: no marking at all.

In the Indus Kohistani folk story 'Princess and Crows', for instance, the very first character, a king, is introduced using the particle *ék* as well as the indefinite marker =*uk* (after the first episode he remains inactivated for the rest of the story). Later on, another participant, a herdsman, who appears in one episode only, is introduced by using =*uk* but not *ék*. In the same story, other characters are being mentioned for the first time without any marking for indefiniteness. For instance, the little bird in (25) is subsequently mentioned only one more time, thus suggesting that it is a very minor participant.

(25) *gatá bazíthi bazìl khẽ tsakluú i-íthu*
again go.PRS.PFV.F go.PFV1 when bird.DIM come-PRS.PFV.M.SG
'Again (they) went. When (they) had gone a little bird came.' (Princess and crows no. 59)

In example (26) the unmarked indefinite entity 'river' is a prop, a concept that is mentioned one more time.

(26) *ék zaí=uk gee gèe khẽ*
one place=INDEF to go.PFV2.PL when

muúṭhioon dariàab iínt
from.ahead river come.PRS.F.SG
'When they came to a certain place there was a river ahead.' (Princess and crows no. 18)

To conclude, indefiniteness in Indus Kohistani may be indicated by the indefinite specific marker =*uk*, by the indefinite particle *ék*, by both =*uk* and *ék* occurring in one noun phrase, or it may not be marked at all. Quite often a speaker expects the audience to identify the referent of a noun phrase without the help of clues such as definite or indefinite markers. As marking of indefiniteness is not obligatory, a next step would be to look at texts in more detail to determine what conditions the explicit marking for indefiniteness. This is, however, beyond the scope of this study.

5. Conclusion

The Indus Kohistani indefinite marker =*uk* is a phrasal enclitic that attaches to noun phrases. I have shown that =*uk* is not a suffix; an accent shifting role is blocked by the presence of the clitic; =*uk* may attach not only to one lexical category such as nouns but to any noun-phrase final element. If there are other phrasal clitics present, such as case markers, then =*uk* always precedes them. The marker =*uk* cannot be classified as an independent word either, as it always needs a host. Furthermore, it is phonologically dependent on its host as it has no accent on its own.

As to the function of *=uk*, I have shown that the marker indicates indefiniteness; I also strongly suspect it to be a marker of specificity, as *=uk* is not used to mark a noun phrase as generic.

Particularly in narrative discourse, the marker *=uk* is used as a discourse device to introduce characters or other entities that are new to the hearer. The indefinite marker *=uk* also indicates hitherto unidentified subsets that belong to an already introduced set. When attached to words expressing amounts of time or substances then *=uk* indicates approximation or, in other words, indefiniteness of the quantity or quality expressed.

In Indus Kohistani, marking of indefiniteness is not obligatory; an indefinite noun phrase may not be marked at all. When indefiniteness is indicated then there are three means to do so: the use of the indefinite marker *=uk* only, the use of the indefinite particle *ék* 'a' (otherwise the numeral 'one'), or the use of both of them together. I have also shown that contrary to *=uk*, the particle *ék* indicates indefiniteness but is neutral in respect to specificity, that is, noun phrases preceded by the particle *ék* may be indefinite specific or indefinite non-specific. The question when to use which of the four ways to indicate indefiniteness remains to be answered; this might be the topic of another study.

So far, only brief descriptions exist of the corresponding indefinite markers in Gilgiti Shina and Kohistani Shina. In this study I have presented a more detailed account of both form and function of the Indus Kohistani equivalent *=uk*. The material presented here will, I hope, increase our knowledge of one of the lesser studied languages of northern Pakistan, and of indefinite markers as such which, within NIA languages, are rather a rarity.

ABBREVIATIONS

ABL = ablative case marker
ADJ = adjective
ADS = adjectival derivative suffix
CONJ = conjunction
CV = converb
DAT = dative case marker
DEM = demonstrative, near and visible
DIM = diminutive
DIST = distant, not visible
IPFV = imperfective
INDEF = indefinite marker
M = masculine
OBL = oblique case marker
PFV = perfective
PFV1 = perfective 1
PFV2 = perfective 2
PL = plural
POSS = possessive

ERG = ergative case marker
F = feminine
FUT = future
GEN = genitive case marker
IMP = imperative
PROX = proximal, near and visible
PRS = present
PST = past
SG = singular
SUBJ = subjunctive

REFERENCES

Buddruss, G. 1959. 'Kanyawali: Proben eines Maiyã-Dialektes aus Tangir (Hindukusch)'. Cohiers Ferdinand de Saussure 41: 31-43. Geneva: Librarie Droz.

Buddruss, G. 1987. 'Ein Ordal der Waigal-Kafiren des Hindukusch'. *Cahiers Ferdinand de Saussure* 41: 31–43. Geneva: Librarie Droz.

Degener, Almuth. 1998. *Die Sprache von Nisheygram im afghanischen Hindukusch.* Wiesbaden: Harrassowitz Verlag.

Hallberg, Daniel G. 1992. 'The languages of Kohistan'. In *Sociolinguistic Survey of Northern Pakistan Vol. 1: Languages of Kohistan,* edited by Calvin R. Rensch, Sandra J. Decker, and Daniel G. Hallberg. Islamabad: National Institute of Pakistan Studies and Summer Institute of Linguistics.

Haspelmath, Martin. 2002. *Understanding morphology*. London: Arnold.

Himmelmann, Nikolaus P. 1996. 'Demonstratives in narrative discourse: a taxonomy of universal uses'. In *Studies in Anaphora,* edited by Barbara Fox. 205–54. Amsterdam/Philadelphia: John Benjamins Publishing Company.

Himmelmann, Nikolaus P. 2001. 'Articles'. In *Language Typology and Language Universals: an International Handbook,* edited by Martin Haspelmath, Ekkehard König, Wulf Oesterreicher, and Wolfgang Raible. 831–41. Volume 1. Berlin, New York: Walter de Gruyter.

Hook, Peter E. 1996. 'Kesar of Layul: A Central Asian Epic in the Shina of Gultari'. In *Studies in Pakistani Popular Culture,* edited by William L. Hanaway and Wilma Heston. 121–83. Lahore: Sang-e-Meel Publications and Lok Virsa Publishing House.

Levinsohn, Stephen H. 2007. *Self-Instruction Materials on Narrative Discourse Analysis.* SIL International.

Payne, Thomas E. 1997. *Describing Morphosyntax*. Cambridge: Cambridge University Press

Radloff, Carla F. with Shakil, Shakil Ahmad. 1998. *Folktales in the Shina of Gilgit: Text, Grammatical Analysis and Commentary.* Islamabad: National Institute of Pakistan Studies and Summer Institute of Linguistics. (Studies in Languages of Northern Pakistan 2).

Radloff, Carla F. 1999. *Aspects of the Sound System of Gilgiti Shina*. Islamabad: National Institute of Pakistan Studies and Summer Institute of Linguistics. (Studies in Languages of Northern Pakistan 4).

Schmidt, Ruth L. and Kohistani, Razwal. 2008. *A Grammar of the Shina Language of Indus Kohistan*. Wiesbaden: Otto Harrowitz.

Zoller, Claus Peter. 2005. *A Grammar and Dictionary of Indus Kohistani. Volume 1: Dictionary.* Berlin: Mouton de Gruyter.

11

Orality, Literacy, and Scholarship: Shifts in Gender, Genre, and Performance of Wakhi Oral Expression

John Mock

1. WAKHI PEOPLE

The Wakhi are an ethnic minority residing in contiguous high mountain valleys where Pakistan, Afghanistan, Tajikistan, and China meet, with a total population of approximately 50,000 (Kreutzmann 2003: 220, Payne 1989: 420). Their language, also called Wakhi,[1] is an East Iranian Pamir language (Bashir 2009). The Pamir language grouping is based more on geographical proximity than genetic proximity, as no single common ancestor is identifiable for the languages of the Pamir linguistic area or *sprachbund* (Wendtland 2009). Convergence between Wakhi and a neighbouring Indic language, Khowar, demonstrates persistent contact between Wakhi and Khowar from 'very ancient' times up to the present (Morgenstierne 1926: 81, 1973: 433–4; Bashir 2001: 3). Wakhi preserves archaic Iranian features (Morgenstierne 1975, Pakhalina 1975a), indicating that the Wakhi were 'the very earliest wave of Iranian settlers in the [Pamir] region' (Morgenstierne 1938: 435), which, along with historical and archaeological evidence, suggests that Wakhi people settled along the Panj River as early as the Iron Age, 1000–500 BCE (Payne 1996: 367, Mock 2013).

[1] Wakhi people refer to themselves as *(wa)x̌ ik*, to their language as *(wa)x̌ ikwor*, and to Wakhan as *wux̌*, sharing a common root for the ethnonym, glossonym, and toponym.

The traditional home of Wakhi people, the former principality of Wakhan, lies along both banks of the Panj River (upper Amu Darya), which forms the border between Badakhshan Province of Afghanistan and the Mountainous Badakhshan Autonomous Province of Tajikistan, and extends along its two upper tributaries, the Pamir River and the Sarhad River (Shahrani 1979: 4–5). From Wakhan, Wakhi people migrated over the passes into adjacent high altitude valleys into what are now northern Pakistan and China's Xinjiang. Geopolitical events of the nineteenth and twentieth century disbursed and fragmented the Wakhi population, with resulting degrees of segregation between the communities (Badenkov 1992: 281, Kreutzmann 2003: 234, Lorimer 1958: 8).

In Pakistan, Wakhi people live in Chitral District of the Khyber-Pakhtunkhwa Province (previously the North West Frontier Province, or NWFP), and Ghizar and Gilgit districts of the Gilgit-Baltistan administrative area (previously the Northern Areas of Pakistan). In Ghizar District, Wakhi communities are along the upper Ishqoman River, where Imit is the largest Wakhi village. In Gilgit District, Wakhi communities are along the upper Hunza River, in an area called Gojal, which is where the majority of Pakistan's Wakhi population resides.

Accessibility to Wakhi communities remains difficult even today. The most useful overview of Wakhi communities focuses on adaptations in livelihood to external geopolitical change (Kreutzmann 2003). The sole descriptive ethnography of Wakhi people (Shahrani 1979) was done prior to the 1979 closure of Afghanistan's Wakhan corridor. Although China's Xinjiang Province has remained largely restricted to Chinese researchers (Gao 1985), cross-border access granted to Wakhi people of northern Pakistan has enabled some Wakhi scholars to visit the Wakhi community in China (Beg 2004). Tajikistan presents its own set of political and geographic difficulties in accessing its Wakhi population area (Herbers 2001, Reinhold 1992). In Pakistan, the construction of the Karakoram Highway (KKH) in the 1970s provided access to the Wakhi-speaking communities there, which have been the focus of research in language (Backstrom 1992, Buddruss 1986, Buddruss and Wiehler-Schneider 1978, Gojal Ismailia Students Union 1980, Reinhold 2006), cultural geography (Butz 1996, Butz and Eyles 1997, Cook and Butz 2013, Kreutzmann 1996), and linguistic anthropology (Mock 1998). The 2010 landslide and resulting formation of the Attabad Lake submerged the KKH between Gojal and the rest of Pakistan, and significantly impacted access to the Wakhi population of Pakistan.

Initial scholarly research on the Wakhi language in the twentieth century identified Wakhi's unique areal position and issues of phonology (Lorimer 1958, Morgenstierne 1938). Soviet scholars working in the Tajik Soviet Socialist Republic completed more thorough studies of Wakhi (Sokolova 1953: 209–29; Pakhalina 1969, 1975b, 1983 1989; Grünberg and Steblin-Kamensky 1976, 1988). The comprehensive work of Alexander Grünberg and Ivan Steblin-Kamensky resolved most of the questions regarding Wakhi phonology and morphology (Grünberg and Steblin-Kamensky 1976). John Payne (1996) examined Wakhi in the context of the Pamir linguistic area, Peter Backstrom (1992) conducted a sociolinguistic survey, and Elena Bashir (2009) summarized Wakhi morphology. Grünberg and Steblin-Kamensky collected and published texts of Wakhi stories and songs in a phonemic Latin-based transcription that is widely employed among students of Iranian languages. These transcriptions have served as the basic resource for most linguistic analysis.[2]

2. WAKHI CULTURE TODAY

In Tajikistan and northern Pakistan, Wakhi language and culture is experiencing a resurgence. In Tajikistan, Pamiri people organize and celebrate an annual Roof of the World Festival, highlighting the cultural heritage of the entire Pamir ethnolinguistic area.[3] In Pakistan, the Wakhi-Tajik Cultural Association (WTCA), the Gojal Educational and Cultural Association (GECA), and the Pamir Welfare and Development Organization (PWDO) have organized to promote interest in Wakhi language and culture. They have been instrumental in producing: a Wakhi language radio program *Sadoi Bami Duniyo*

[2] See Mock 1998 for a substantial body of Wakhi transcriptions from Pakistan.

[3] The festival has drawn support from the public association Amesha Spenta, the Aga Khan Health Services (AKHS), German Agency for Technical Cooperation (GTZ), the Mountain Societies Development Support Programme (MSDSP) of the Aga Khan Foundation (AKF), De Pamiri Handicraft, the Christensen Fund, the Swiss Agency for Development and Cooperation (SDC), and the University of Central Asia (UCA).

(Voice of the Roof of the World) that is broadcast by Radio Pakistan from Gilgit; a magazine, *Wakhi Express*, dedicated to developing Wakhi literature; and an annual Silk Route Festival.[4]

The work of Grünberg and Steblin-Kamensky has played a significant role in the resurgent interest in poetry, song, music, and cultural heritage. Their transcriptions of Wakhi material have stimulated interest in both Tajikistan and Pakistan, where Wakhi poets have adopted a Latin-based system to write poetry (Reinhold 1992, K.K. Saka 2011). This has led to a fascinating situation in which the transmission and production of a culture's oral expressive forms are being altered by the work of the scholars who study the culture. The effects of technologies such as audio and video cassettes on oral expressive modes have long been a topic of interest to scholars of oral expressive traditions (Appadurai 1993, Heston 1993, Manuel 1993). But in the present case we are dealing with the effect of scholarship and a concomitant introduction of a new mode of literacy on an oral culture.[5] Composition and transmission of Wakhi oral expressive forms now incorporate the technology of writing in a phonetic, Latin-based transcription. Although the new generation of poets may write their compositions, they still perform orally, since many Wakhi people cannot read the new transcription. The reception and appreciation of poetry is still as words heard, not seen.

In Gojal, one of the more interesting results of all this is the appropriation and reworking of older poetic forms from Wakhan. Material recorded and transcribed from oral performance by Soviet scholars has been transmitted through their publications to Gojal, where it has been reworked and again performed for an appreciative audience. The alternation of transmission from oral to written and back to oral performance indicates a flexibility and adaptiveness in oral

[4] This festival has drawn support from Lok Virsa, Pakistan's National Institute for Folk Heritage, the Tourism Department of the Government of Gilgit-Baltistan, Serena Hotels, the Tour Operator Association Gilgit-Baltistan (TOAGB), Karakoram International University, Aga Khan Rural Support Program (AKRSP), Aga Khan Cultural Services Pakistan (AKCSP), the Worldwide Fund for Nature (WWF), and the Karakoram Area Development Organization (KADO).

[5] Ruth Schmidt and Razwal Kohistani have presented, however, a remarkable study of the effects of two different orthographies, Perso-Arabic script and Latin-based script, on the phonemic inventory of the Shina of Kohistan, Pakistan (Schmidt and Kohistani 1995).

expressive forms. This flexibility also argues against any conception of hard and fast boundaries between oral and literate cultures, or any insistence on 'pure' oral transmission and performance.[6] Within the Wakhi community, the written and oral modes of language use engage in what might be more aptly termed a dialogical interplay, in which the context of performance is a more salient characteristic than the mode of discourse.

3. WAKHI ORAL POETRY

In Gojal, poetry is a significant manifestation of the current resurgent interest in Wakhi culture. Many young and old men are actively composing and performing, encouraged by the enthusiastic reception Wakhi audiences give their work.[7] Their poetic genre of choice is the *bayd* or song, typically with a romantic theme.[8]

Bayd are songs that consist of rhymed stanzas, typically of either two or four lines. A common *bayd* feature is the repetition of the last

[6] The relationship between oral and literate discourse has been a central concern of scholarship. One of the main implications of literary studies of epic poetry (Havelock 1991, Lord 1991), along with work in anthropology (Goody 1987, Levi-Strauss 1966), and in cognition (Luria 1976), was the existence of a 'great divide' (Finnegan 1973) in human society brought about through literacy. Walter Ong extended these ideas into all areas of human existence, characterizing literacy and abstract thinking as dominating, but not replacing orality, a situation Ong refers to as 'residual orality' and 'secondary orality' (Ong 1982).

Linguistic and ethnographic approaches to the relationship of language and culture (Bauman 1977, Chafe 1982, Heath 1983, Hymes 1962, Tannen 1982), however, show that the distinction of a clear separation between oral and literate discourse is an inadequate description, and correct the Havelock-Goody-Ong assumption of a dynamic that favours literacy and posits a directionality moving from orality to literacy. Cross-cultural studies have identified the cultural bias underlying their assumption and show that such assumptions are not globally extendable to other cultures (Scollon and Scollon 1981, Scribner and Cole 1981). This implies that 'great divide' conceptions of orality and literacy are products of a particular way of thinking that is self-biased towards its own history.

[7] Wakhi poets in Gojal frequently publish online (in a Latin-based transcription system) at PamirTimes.net. *SGA Wakhi Express* has featured (in Latin-based transcription) the poetry of Bulbul Nazir, Saifuddin Saif, Ahmed Riaz Ahmed, Ali Quban, Afzal Karim, and other poets.

[8] *Bait* in Urdu or Persian means a stanza, a couplet. In Wakhi, *bayd* refers to sung poetry; hence 'song' is a better translation than 'stanza'.

line of a stanza as the first line of the subsequent stanza, thereby maintaining the rhyme scheme throughout. A refrain line, which is repeated at the end of each stanza, is also typical. The *bayd* genre has many subgenres, all of which are identifiable by performance context and identity of performer (Mock 1998: 105–6).

One unique Wakhi genre is called *bulbulik*, which means 'of the nightingale', or '(voice) of the nightingale'. *Bulbulik* is a distinctive Wakhi genre, unknown among other Pamir-Hindukush ethnic groups (Grünberg and Steblin-Kamensky 1988: 18).[9] The only previously known examples are from Tajikistan Wakhan, where young girls composed and sang *bulbulik* in the high pastures during the summer herding season. My research in Afghanistan Wakhan confirmed this context of composition and performance (Mock, unpublished field notes, 2004–07, 2010). The Soviet scholars characterized *bulbulik* as having an archaic three-line stanza with an *aba* rhyme pattern that takes as its main subject matter the pain of separation, usually from a lover, but also from family (Lashkarbekov 1972).[10]

Although Lashkarbekov (1972) reports collecting 280 *bulbulik* verses, his brief article presents just 14 examples. The largest published collection of *bulbulik* consists of 56 stanzas from Soviet Wakhan (now Tajikistan) (Grünberg and Steblin-Kamensky 1976: 25–30), which Jean Indoujien translated and republished (Grünberg and Steblin-Kamensky 1988: 25–30). An English translation of 37 of these *bulbulik* stanzas appeared in a small volume titled, *The Voice of the Nightingale: A Personal Account of the Wakhi Culture of Hunza*

---

[9] Benjamin Koen, however, notes that *bulbulik* is one of several similar Pamir folk genres which he terms laments. In his experience, the genre names are often used interchangeably for the same piece (Koen 2009: 120). The Wakhi genre is much more specific and Koen's description should be taken as a broad discussion of the entire Pamir region rather than a specific description of Wakhan Wakhi genres of performance. Professor Dilshod Rahimov, Chairman of the Department of Folklore at the Institute of Language and Literature of the Rudaki Academy of Science of the Republic of Tajikistan, confirms that *bulbulik* is distinctive to Wakhi culture (Rahimov 2010: pers. comm.).

[10] Lashkarbekov's brief article on *bulbulik* is important because he is a native Wakhi speaker who did graduate studies (PhD) in Moscow. His work carries probably the sharpest critical awareness of the genre.

(Felmy 1996: 86–91).[11] Although Wakhi people in Gojal had heard about *bulbulik*, I found no evidence that *bulbulik* were being heard or composed in Gojal. This raised the questions of whither the *bulbulik*, and why was it no longer composed in Gojal?

During fieldwork in 1996, I learned that *bulbulik* was still known by old Wakhi people in the Ishqoman Valley, which had received an influx of Wakhi migration from Wakhan in the late nineteenth century.[12] I began a correspondence with Hassan Raza Nizari, a teacher at the government high school in Imit, the largest Wakhi village in the Ishqoman Valley. He wrote to me that *bulbulik* could still be heard in Ishqoman, so I visited Imit and met with Hassan Raza, his uncle, and his younger cousin, who had recorded many *bulbulik* in their village. One recording was sung in unison by two women, and the other recording was of a single old man. We sat together and listened to the recordings and transcribed the words and made a rough translation of each stanza.

The structure of the *bulbulik* from Imit is similar to that presented by the Soviet scholars, with one significant difference: the third line of each stanza is repeated, with a vocative (equivalent of English 'O', or 'Hey') at the beginning of the repeated line and a lyrical syllable *-ey* at the end of the line, which, the Imit Wakhi told me, are additions for metrical weight (*vazan*). The previous description and presentation of *bulbulik* as a three-line genre does not include the dimension of performance found in the Imit examples; that is, the repetition of the third line with metrical additions. A substantial majority of the Imit *bulbulik* recordings follow the *aba* rhyme scheme that was identified by Lashkarbekov. However, two stanzas follow an *aaa* scheme, three have an *abc* pattern, and two have an *aab* pattern. Lashkarbekov noted that the *aaa* rhyme scheme marks these triplets as a different but related genre, and that this genre characteristically includes the

---

[11] Felmy presents English translations of the French translation of Grünberg and Steblin-Kamensky's Russian translation of the original Wakhi *bulbulik* from Tajikistan, but does not discuss the existence of *bulbulik* in Gojal.

[12] The last Mir of Wakhan, Ali Mardan Shah, along with much of the Wakhi population, fled Wakhan in 1883, eventually settling in Imit. Wakhi people in Imit state that their ancestors came with Ali Mardan, first to Yasin (via Broghil and the Darkot Pass), where they stayed for six years, and then to Imit.

phrase *wuz x̌ʉ dʉrer γ̌irem, x̌ʉ bʉlbʉler γ̌irem* (I circle for my pearl, I circle for my nightingale).

The Imit Wakhi people agreed with the Soviet characterization of composition and performance, in which young unmarried girls composed and sang *bulbulik* typically, but not exclusively, while in the summer pastures. The topic of the Imit *bulbulik*, like that of the Soviet collection, and according to my field research in Afghanistan Wakhan, is usually romantic love or heartbreak resulting from unrequited love. The imagery is that of the Pamir; hawks, partridge, ibex, hunting, herding, alpine wildflowers, and several items of women's dress. These items are still worn in the Afghan Pamir, but no longer worn in either Gojal or in Imit, and their names are not recognized by Wakhi men in Gojal. The internal evidence of *bulbulik's* archaic imagery, coupled with external evidence of cultural change in Gojal offered plausible reasons why *bulbulik* is no longer known in Gojal. Wakhi society in Gojal now differs considerably from Wakhi society in the Wakhan Pamir. Border formation, development, and education have reduced the homogeneity of the greater Wakhi community (Kreutzmann 1996). Aspects of the material and symbolic culture have been altered or replaced and social behaviour has changed. This change is exemplified in the response of one man in Shimshal, a Wakhi village in Gojal, when I asked him if young girls in his village sang *bulbulik*. He took offence at the idea that girls would behave so immodestly as to sing romantic and slightly risqué songs in public. Such behaviour would violate religiously sanctioned norms of female modesty which even one generation ago had not entered into Wakhi society.

The Imit Wakhi said that *bulbulik* was a famous genre in its time. I found 10 of the 46 stanzas from Imit to be identical to stanzas published by Grünberg and Steblin-Kamensky, indicating that *bulbulik* was indeed widely known.

Additionally, fourteen of the stanzas from Imit show only slight variations from stanzas published by Grünberg and Steblin-Kamensky. Interestingly, the variation typically occurs in the second line, which does not share the rhyme scheme of the first and third lines. That the variation is in the second, unrhymed line, points to the importance of rhyme as a memory device for singers of *bulbulik*. Five sets of stanzas from Imit were sung in the same order as they appear in the Soviet work, suggesting that the stanzas have a specific order in which the singers learned them.[13]

This brief comparative discussion of the 56 *bulbulik* stanzas from Wakhan and the 46 *bulbulik* stanzas from Imit[14] gives a clearer picture of *bulbulik* performance and composition, and raises new questions about performance and transmission, and the role of *bulbulik* in Wakhi society. This study also offers an explanation to the question of the famous *bulbulik* and sheds light on why the 'voice of the nightingale' is no longer heard in Gojal. Or is it? Let me add one more bit of information, which brings us back to the point of the effects of scholarship.

4. FROM *BULBULIK* TO *BAYD*

While attending a WTCA Cultural Festival in Gulmit village in Gojal, I heard Fazal ur Rahman (who performs under the name of *Shireen Sado* 'sweet voice'), an educated young man from the Chapursan Valley, sing a Wakhi *bayd* whose ten stanzas clearly were based upon the traditional *bayd* genre structure but incorporated *bulbulik* verses. The first three lines of the first three stanzas and the last stanza in Fazal ur Rahman's performance are identical with *bulbulik* stanzas published in the Soviet collection of Wakhi material from Wakhan. Stanzas four to nine, however, do not have an *aba* rhyme scheme, but rather follow the *aaa* pattern. However, all ten stanzas are found in the Grünberg and Steblin-Kamensky collection of triplets from Tajikistan, in which the triplets with *aaa* rhyme scheme are presented as stanzas in a longer song. Even more interesting is that each stanza of Fazal ur Rahman's song includes constant fourth, fifth, and sixth refrain

---

[13] Internal evidence of the *bulbulik* verses suggests that composition and performance may not have been exclusively by young girls, but that *bulbulik* may have been a social performance where girls sang a verse and boys sang an answering verse. This taunting-joking genre is well known. For example, verses 1, 3, and 7 seem to be a female voice, answered by a male voice in 2, 4, and 8. In verse 1, *kiltiča* is a men's vest and in verse 2, *pirhən* is a woman's blouse. In verse 7, binoculars (*dʉrbin*) are typically carried by men, not women, and in verse 8 *Gim Jon* is a woman's name. This and other aspects of *bulbulik* are the topic of a larger study that I will publish separately.

[14] For the full text of the 56 *bulbulik* stanzas, see Grünberg and Steblin-Kamensky 1986. For the 42 Imit *bulbulik* stanzas, see Mock 1998.

lines in addition to each traditional three-line stanza which are very similar to the 'refrain' line noted by Lashkarbekov for the *aaa* pattern triplets. What Fazal ur Rahman has done is to combine and modify several traditional Wakhi triplet genres to produce a folk song that is no longer a three-line *bulbulik* or related three-line song, but rather a folk song that Fazal ur Rahman identifies as a *bayd*. This shift in genre is indicated by the name ascribed to this *bayd* in Gojal. The *bayd* is now named for the refrain line, *barg e gʉler wuz ɣ̌irem*, and it is this line that the largely male audience sings along with, clapping their hands and moving rhythmically to the music and beat.

Bayd 'Barg e Gʉler Wuz Γ̌irem' as performed by Fazal ur Rahman *Shireen Sado*:

1.	Tem ti tani kiltiča ey	O the vest on your body
	Qəd e bast ce didɣ̌em	When I look at your shape
	Qadi basti mirbəča ey	Your look like a Mir's son
	Barg e gʉler wuz ɣ̌irem	I circle[15] for the rose petal
	Barg e gʉler wuz ɣ̌irem	I circle for the rose petal
	x̌ʉ bʉlbʉler wuz ɣ̌irem	I circle for my nightingale
2.	Tem ti tani pirhən ey	O the shirt on your body
	Koški ti wətan merim	Would that I die in your country
	Ya sarʉng mar go kəfən ey	Make my burial cloth from your shirt
	Barg e gʉler wuz ɣ̌irem	I circle for the rose petal
	Barg e gʉler wuz ɣ̌irem	I circle for the rose petal
	x̌ʉ bʉlbʉler wuz ɣ̌irem	I circle for my nightingale
3.	Ẓ̌ʉmaki be dem ti yorč ey	My moon is in your *yorch*[16]
	Har bor ki tow yod carem	Every time I think of you
	Cem tow yoden ṣ̌ʉw skorč ey	I am burned by your memory
	Barg e gʉler wuz ɣ̌irem	I circle for the rose petal
	Barg e gʉler wuz ɣ̌irem	I circle for the rose petal
	x̌ʉ bʉlbʉler wuz ɣ̌irem	I circle for my nightingale
4.	Tilo noqrayi nigin ey	O golden jewel O pearl
	Wuz banda e xʉδoyem	I am a creature of God
	Xizmatgorem wuz be tin ey	But I am also your servant
	Barg e gʉler wuz ɣ̌irem	I circle for the rose petal
	Barg e gʉler wuz ɣ̌irem	I circle for the rose petal
	x̌ʉ bʉlbʉler wuz ɣ̌irem	I circle for my nightingale

5. Ẓ̌ʉ petr rex̌ ki da Qoqən[17] ey
Da Qoqən yowen zəman
Nasti dʉr tər Wʉx̌ wətən ey
Barg e gʉler wuz γ̌ irem
Barg e gʉler wuz γ̌ irem
x̌ʉ bʉlbʉler wuz γ̌ irem

My son went to Qoqan
He has a child at Qoqan
There is no pearl in Wakhan
I circle for the rose petal
I circle for the rose petal
I circle for my nightingale

6. Ẓ̌ʉ petr rex̌ ki da Bijin ey
Sayli kert Čin et močin
Yow yombʉw də Xon xerjin ey
Barg e gʉler wuz γ̌ irem
Barg e gʉler wuz γ̌ irem
x̌ʉ bʉlbʉler wuz γ̌ irem

My son went to Beijing
He made a great journey
through China
His silver coins are on the king's
saddle bag
I circle for the rose petal
I circle for the rose petal
I circle for my nightingale

7. Ti kučeki Sarəsin[18] ey
Ti kafi tilo dʉrbin
Wəxti tʉk tuwep maž win ey
Barg e gʉler wuz γ̌ irem
Barg e gʉler wuz γ̌ irem
x̌ʉ bʉlbʉler wuz γ̌ irem

Your livestock are in the pasture
In your hand are the precious
binoculars
When I walk [outside] you will
see me
I circle for the rose petal
I circle for the rose petal
I circle for my nightingale

8. Dem ti bari piskəδʉw[19] ey
Gim Jon čizəreṣ̌ maẓ̌e bʉw
Yi loy be tu maẓ̌e qʉw ey
Barg e gʉler wuz γ̌ irem
Barg e gʉler wuz γ̌ irem
x̌ʉ bʉlbʉler wuz γ̌ irem

In your house are biting flies
Why does Gim Jan bother me?
Just call me one time
I circle for the rose petal
I circle for the rose petal
I circle for my nightingale

9. Yupkem dix̌t ska bʉland woδ ey
Noqəra dix̌te tər ẓ̌ʉ yod
Ẓ̌ʉ jigar vite bʉrbod ey
Barg e gʉler wuz γ̌ irem
Barg e gʉler wuz γ̌ irem
x̌ʉ bʉlbʉler wuz γ̌ irem

I let the water into the highest
channel
My beloved flooded into my
memory
And my heart was devastated
I circle for the rose petal
I circle for the rose petal
I circle for my nightingale

10.	Dem ti xunsari yimʉk ey ṣ̌ux qəsa be tu me x̌an Jʉwononišt tər yinʉk ey Barg e gʉler wuz γ̌ irem Barg e gʉler wuz γ̌ irem x̌ʉ bʉlbʉler wuz γ̌ irem	The brushwood is on your roof Don't speak loudly The [other] youths are sleeping I circle for the rose petal I circle for the rose petal I circle for my nightingale

The Soviet collection utilizing a phonetic Latin-based transcription of the original Wakhi was introduced to Gojal by foreign scholars conducting research in the Wakhi community. Many members of the WTCA have photocopies of this text. It seemed logical that the *bulbulik* from Wakhan had been transmitted to Gojal through this written medium and that the *bayd* sung by Fazal ur Rahman was an adaptation of the older Wakhan stanzas to a modern form with a refrain. The refrain was a feature of a *bulbulik*-related genre that had been described by Lashkarbekov, and which could have been introduced to Gojal by the small but continuous stream of Wakhi immigrants fleeing political instability in both Afghanistan and Tajikistan.

On a 2004 field trip, I visited Chapursan Valley and spent several days in Zood Khun, the highest Wakhi village in the valley. I stayed at the home of Alam Jan Daryo, a well-known Wakhi poet. One evening, Alam Jan called Fazal ur Rahman to his home, where they performed numerous Wakhi songs, with Fazal ur Rahman playing *rabob* and

---

15 'I circle' means 'to circumambulate' in respect or honour. This is a common politeness phrase in Wakhi.

16 *Yorch* is the floor area inside a traditional Pamir house. Most of the interior, the *raž*, is raised above the smaller *yorch*. In the roof is an opening to allow light and air in and smoke out, called the *ricn*. Moonlight would shine through the *ricn* and illuminate a small area of the interior.

17 *Qoqan* is Kokand, a city in the Ferghana Valley of modern Uzbekistan.

18 *Sarsin* means the place where *sars* (*Artemesia dracunculus*) grows.

19 These insects, *piskəðiu*, are probably what are called *piðʉw* 'biting midges' in Wakhan.

singing, and Alam Jan accompanying him rhythmically on *daf.*[20] One of the songs they performed, of course, was Fazal ur Rahman's now-famous *bayd: Barg e gʉler wuz ɣ̌ irem*. Alam Jan told me that he had composed the *bayd*, taking the *bulbulik* and *bulbulik*-like songs from the Soviet collection, adding the refrain lines, and setting it to music. Alam Jan and Fazal ur Rahman had also both traveled to Afghanistan Wakhan, where they met local artists who retained knowledge of Wakhi song genres, including *bulbulik* and the refrain lines of the *wuz x̌ʉ dʉrer ɣ̌ irem, x̌ʉ bʉlbʉler ɣ̌ irem* triplet with *aaa* rhyme scheme described by Lashkarbekov. Alam Jan's new composition, performed by Fazal ur Rehman, was indeed derived from written transcriptions made by Soviet-era scholars and from visits to Afghanistan, across officially closed, but unofficially open, borders.

Transmission and circulation of oral expressive forms that largely ceased in the twentieth century is once again occurring, substantially promoted through the medium of published research by non-Wakhi scholars, and is being adapted to live performance in Gojal. The recreation and adaptation of traditional Wakhi material from Wakhan within the more modern context of Wakhi culture in Gojal is strong evidence of the vitality of Wakhi poetry. It is also evidence of the effects of educational and socio-economic change on oral expressive forms (Appadurai, Korom, and Mills 1993, Flueckiger 1996). Through incorporation and innovation, the once-famous Wakhi *bulbulik* genre has found a new audience and a new lease on life in Gojal. Its adoption by male performers is indicative of changing social norms. It is no longer appropriate for young girls to sing picaresque songs in Gojal, which is increasingly becoming integrated into the norms of Pakistani society. The assimilation of the female performance genre of *bulbulik* into the male performance genre of *bayd* offers an example of shifting genre boundaries and corresponding social change.

[20] Traditional Wakhi instruments: *rabob* is a fretless four-string instrument, and a forerunner of the modern *sarod*. Notes are fingered and the strings are picked or strummed. *Daf* is a wide but shallow single-head drum that is open at one end (similar to a large modern tambourine but without the cymbals).

REFERENCES

Appadurai, Arjun, Korom, F. J., and Mills, M. 1993. *Gender, Genre, and Power in South Asian Expressive Traditions*. Philadelphia: University of Pennsylvania Press.

Backstrom, Peter C. 1992. 'Wakhi'. In *Sociolinguistic Survey of Northern Pakistan, Vol. 2, Languages of the Northern Areas*, edited by Peter C. Backstrom and Carla F. Radloff. 57–74. Islamabad: National Institute of Pakistan Studies and Summer Institute of Linguistics.

Badenkov, Yuri. 1992. 'Mountains of the Former Soviet Union'. In *The State of the World's Mountains: A Global Report*, edited by P. B. Stone. 257–97. London: Zed Books.

Bashir, Elena. 2009. 'Wakhi'. In *The Iranian Languages*, edited by Gernot Windfuhr. 825–62. London: Routledge.

———— 2001. 'Khowar-Wakhi contact relationship'. In *Tohfa-e Dil: Festschrift Helmut Nespital*, edited by D. Lonne. 3–17. Reinbeck bei Hamburg: Wetzler.

Bauman R. 1977. *Verbal Art as Performance*. Rowley MA: Newberry House.

Beg, Fazal Amin. 2004. *Kinship and Marriage among the Wakhis in the Tashkurgan Tajik Autonomous County of Xinjiang Region, China*. MPhil thesis. Area Study Centre (Russia, China & Central Asia). Pakistan: University of Peshawar.

Buddruss, Georg. 1986. 'Wakhi Sprichwörter aus Hunza'. In *Studia Grammatica Iranica: Festschrift für Helmut Humbach*, edited by R. Schmitt and Prods O. Skjaervø. 27–44. München: R. Kitzinger.

———— and Wiehler-Schneider, S. 1978. 'Wakhi-Lieder aus Hunza'. In *Jahrbuch für Musikalische Volks-und Völkerkunde* 9: 89–110.

Butz, David. 1996. 'Sustaining Indigenous Communities: Symbolic and Instrumental Dimensions of Pastoral Resource Use in Shimshal, Northern Pakistan'. *The Canadian Geographer* 40.1: 36–53.

———— and Eyles, J. 1997. 'Reconceptualizing Senses of Place: Social Relations, Ideology and Ecology'. *Geografiska Annaler* 79.1: 1–25.

Chafe, Wallace. 1982. 'Integration and Involvement in Speaking, Writing and Literature'. In *Spoken and Written Language: Exploring Orality and Literacy*, edited by D. Tannen. 33–53. Norwood NJ: ABLEX.

Cook, Nancy and Butz, D. 2013. 'The Atta Abad Landslide and everyday mobility in Gojal, Northern Pakistan'. *Mountain Research and Development* 33.4: 372–80.

Felmy, Sabine. 1996. *The Voice of the Nightingale: A Personal Account of the Wakhi Culture in Hunza*. Karachi, Pakistan: Oxford University Press.

Finnegan, Ruth. 1973. *Modes of Thought: Essays on Thinking and Non-Western Societies*. London: Faber.

Flueckiger, Joyce B. 1996. *Gender and Genre in the Folklore of Middle India*. Ithaca, NY: Cornell University Press.

Gao, Erqiang. 1985. *Tajikeyu Jianzhi [Concise Grammar of (Sariquli and Wakhi) Tajik]*. Beijing: Minzu Chubanshe.

Gojal Ismailia Students Union. 1980. *Wast Eshiya' men Wakhi Log aur Zaban [Wakhi People and Language in West Asia]*. Karachi: Gojal Isma'iliyah Students Union.

Goody, J. 1987. *The Interface Between the Written and the Oral*. Cambridge: Cambridge University Press.

Grünberg, Alexander L. and Steblin-Kamensky, Ivan M. 1988. *La Langue Wakhi*. Paris: Maison des Sciences de l'Homme.

——— 1976. *Iaziki Vostochnogo Hindukusha: Vakhanski Iazik*. Moscow: Nauka.

Havelock, E. 1991. 'The oral–literate equation: a formula for the modern mind'. In *Literacy and Orality*, edited by D. R. Olsen and N. Torrance. 11–27. Cambridge: Cambridge University Press.

Heath, Shirley. 1983. *Way with Words*. Cambridge MA: Harvard University Press.

Herbers, Hiltrud. 2001. 'Transformation in the Tajik Pamirs: Gornyi-Badakhshan—an example of successful restructuring?' *Central Asian Survey* 20.3: 367–81.

Heston, Wilma. 1993. 'Footpath Poets of Peshawar'. In *Gender, Genre, and Power in South Asian Expressive Traditions*, edited by Arjun Appadurai, F. J. Korom, and M. A. Mills. 305–45. Philadelphia: University of Pennsylvania Press.

Hymes, Dell. 1962. 'The Ethnography of Speaking'. *Anthropology and Human Behavior* 13.53: 11–74.

Koen, Benjamin D. 2009. *Beyond the Roof of the World: Music, Prayer, and Healing in the Pamir Mountains*. Oxford; New York: Oxford University Press.

Kreutzmann, Hermann. 2003. 'Ethnic Minorities and Marginality in the Pamirian Knot: Survival of Wakhi and Kirghiz in a Harsh Environment and Global Contexts'. *The Geographical Journal* 169.3: 215–35.

——— 1996. *Ethnizität im Entwicklungsprozeß—Die Wakhi in Hochasien [Ethnicity in development—Minority Studies in the Wakhi settlement regions of High Asia]*. Berlin: Dietrich Reimer Verlag.

Lashkarbekov, Bogsho. 1972. 'Baze Namunahoi Nazmi Vakhoni' [Some Examples of Verses of Wakhan]. In *Zabonhoi Pomiri va Folklor* [Pamir Languages and Folklore], edited by Dodkhudo Koramshoev and Svetlana V. Khushenova. 143–9. Dushanbe: Instituti Zabon va Adabieti ba nom Rudaki [Rudaki Institute of Language and Literature].

Levi-Strauss, Claude. 1966. *The Savage Mind*. Chicago: Chicago University Press.

Lord, A. 1991. *Epic Singers and Oral Traditions*. Ithaca: Cornell University Press.

Lorimer, David L. R. 1958.*The Wakhi Language*. London: School of Oriental and African Studies.

Luria, A. R. 1976. *Cognitive Development and its Social Foundations*. Cambridge: Cambridge University Press

Manuel, Peter. 1993. 'The Popularization and Transformation of the Light-Classical Urdu *Ghazal*-Song'. In *Gender, Genre, and Power in South Asian Expressive Traditions*, edited by Arjun Appadurai, F. J. Korom and M. A. Mills. 347–61. Philadelphia: University of Pennsylvania Press.

Mock, John. 2013. 'New Discoveries of Rock Art from Afghanistan's Wakhan Corridor and Pamir: A Preliminary Study.' *The Silk Road* 11 (Fall 2013): 36–53; Plates III–IV. Saratoga (CA): Silkroad Foundation.

——— 1998. *The Discursive Construction of Reality in the Wakhi Community of Northern Pakistan*. PhD dissertation. Berkeley: Department of South and Southeast Asian Studies, University of California.

Morgenstierne, Georg. 1975. 'Ancient Contacts Between N.E. Iranian and Indo-Aryan?' In *Mélanges Linguistiques Offerts À Émile Benveniste,* edited by Georges Redard, Hansjakob Seiler et al. 431–4. Paris: Société de Linguistique de Paris.

_______ 1973. 'Iranian Elements in Khowar'. In *Irano-Dardica,* edited by Georg Morgenstierne. 241–55. Wiesbaden: Dr Ludwig Reichert. (Beiträge zur Iranistik Vol. 5).

_______ 1938. *Iranian Pamir Languages (Yidgha-Munji, Sanglechi-Ishkashmi and Wakhi).* Oslo: H. Aschehoug.

_______ 1926. *Report on a Linguistic Mission to Afghanistan.* Oslo: H. Aschehoug & Co.

Ong, Walter. 1982. *Orality and Literacy: The Technologizing of the Word.* London: Methuen.

Pakhalina, Tatiana N. 1989. *Sravnitel'no Istoricheskaia Morfologiia Pamirskikh Iazykov [Comparative Historical Morphology of Pamir Languages].* Moskva: Nauka.

_______ 1983. *Issledovanie po Sravnitel'no Istoricheskoi Fonetike Pamirskikh Iazykov [Investigation of the Comparative History of the Phonetics of the Pamir Languages].* Moskva: Nauka.

_______ 1975a. 'Éléments Indo-Aryan dans les Langues Iraniennes Orientales'. In *Mélanges Linguistiques Offerts À Émile Benveniste*, edited by Georges Redard et al. 441–5. Paris: Société de Linguistique de Paris.

_______ 1975b. *Vakhanskii Iazyk [Wakhan Language].* Moskva: Nauka.

_______ 1969. *Pamirskie Iazyki [Pamir Languages].* Moskva, Nauka.

Payne, John. 1996. 'Tajikistan and the Tajiks'. In *The Nationalities Question in the Post-Soviet States,* edited by G. Smith. 367–84. London: Longman.

_______ 1989. 'Pamir Languages'. In *Compendium Linguarum Iranicarum,* edited by R. Schmitt. 417–44. Wiesbaden: Dr Ludwig Reichert.

Reinhold, Beate. 2006. 'Neue Entwicklungen in der Wakhi-sprache von Gojal (Nordpakistan)'. *Iranica* 10. Wiesbaden: Harrassowitz.

_______ 1992. 'Seven Wakhi Poems'. *Journal of the Royal Asiatic Society* 2.1: 202–11.

Saka, Karim Khan. 2011. *SGA Wakhi Express* 2. Aliabad (Gilgit-Baltistan): Shadow Girls Academy.

Scollon, Ronald and Scollon, Suzanne B. 1981. *Narrative, Literacy and Face in Interethnic Communication.* Norwood NJ: ABLEX.

Scribner, S. and Cole, M. 1981. *The Psychology of Learning.* Cambridge MA: Harvard University Press.

Shahrani, M. Nazif Mohib. 1979. *The Kirghiz and Wakhi of Afghanistan: Adaption to Closed Frontiers.* Seattle: University of Washington Press.

Sokolova, Tatiana S. 1953. *Ocherki Po Fonetike Iranskikh Iazykov.* Moskva: Izdatlstvo Akademii Nauk.

Tannen, Deborah. 1982. *Spoken and Written Language: Exploring Orality and Literacy.* Norwood NJ: ABLEX.

Wendtland, Antje. 2009. 'The Position of the Pamir Languages within East Iranian'. *Orientalia Suecana* LVIII: 172–88.

12

Ergativity and Gilgiti Shina

Carla F. Radloff[1] and Henrik Liljegren[2]

1. INTRODUCTION

The Shina of Gilgit follows two systems of alignment simultaneously: a nominative–accusative alignment for verb agreement and an ergative–absolutive alignment for case marking.[3] The verb agrees with the subject (transitive and intransitive alike) in person, number, and gender in all tenses. At the same time, the subject of a transitive verb is always overtly marked for ergative case, while the subject of an intransitive verb and the object of a transitive verb always occur in the absolutive (or zero-marked) case. Thus, Gilgiti Shina manifests a particular type of split system for organizing grammatical relations, which is also seen in other parts of the world.

While it is intriguing that ergative case marking is not confined to any one tense or aspect category in Gilgiti Shina, still more interesting is the fact that ergative case marking also occurs in subordinate clauses headed by a non-finite transitive verb, even when the main clause verb is intransitive. Many other Indo-Aryan languages in the surrounding

---

[1] Special thanks to Shakil Ahmad Shakil of Gilgit, a mother tongue speaker of Shina, and a research colleague of Carla Radloff, for his patient input over the years. Thanks also to Thomas E. Payne for his substantial input to the first version of this paper.

[2] Henrik Liljegren contributed with input to Carla Radloff in drafting the paper, encouraging her to publish it, and successive to her demise, edited and carefully rewrote it as part of the project Language contact and relatedness in the Hindu Kush region, supported by the Swedish Research Council (421-2014-631).

[3] In the following text, ergative–absolutive alignment is simply referred to as ergative, and nominative–accusative alignment as accusative.

region display a split-ergative system of a different kind, namely one similar to the aspectually conditioned split manifested by, e.g. Urdu. Other Shina dialects manifest ergativity much the same as Gilgiti, but use different ergative markers/forms for imperfective as opposed to perfective aspect, while Gilgiti Shina uses the same ergative marker regardless of aspect. It therefore seems that ergativity in Gilgiti Shina is firmly grounded in transitivity as specified in the verb lexicon, rather than one being sensitive to discourse semantics or pragmatic factors. These and other aspects of the split ergative system of Gilgiti Shina are described in the paper.

The language variety and its geographical and linguistic setting is introduced in Section 2; the split system for organizing grammatical relations is described in detail in Section 3; the ergative systems of surrounding and related languages are briefly examined in Section 4. In sections 5 to 8, examples from texts are used to illustrate different characteristics of Gilgiti Shina's ergative system: the presence of ergative case in all tenses and on all forms (Section 5), the ergative case marker and the noun phrase (Section 6), how any transitive element prompts ergative case (Section 7), and the structural grounding of ergativity in Gilgiti Shina shown through its interaction with complex predicates (Section 8). These findings are summarized in Section 9.

2. GILGIT AND THE SHINA LANGUAGE

Gilgiti Shina is spoken in the northern, mountainous region of Pakistan in the watershed of the Gilgit River, particularly around Gilgit town, the centre for trade, education, and government for the political division now called Gilgit-Baltistan.[4] Burushaski, Balti, and Wakhi are some of the other widely spoken languages within this division. Other major varieties of Shina are spoken in the Astor Valley, in parts of Baltistan, and south along the Indus River, including Chilas and Kohistan.

There are also enclaves of relatively divergent Shina varieties (locally not referred to as 'Shina', and normally regarded as languages in their own right) spread out in far-flung parts of this mountainous region: Palula (in Chitral), Kalkoti (in Dir Kohistan),

[4] It was previously called the Northern Areas.

Sawi (in Afghanistan's Kunar Valley), Ushojo (in Swat Kohistan), Kundal Shahi (in Azad Jammu and Kashmir), and Brokskat (in Indian-administered Kashmir). Estimates of the total population of speakers of all varieties of Shina vary from some 500,000 (Radloff 1992) to over a million (Kohistani and Schmidt 2006). Shina is in its turn part of the primarily geographically-based, so-called '*Dardic*' grouping of Indo-Aryan languages which includes the majority of the languages spoken in northern Pakistan, such as Khowar, Kalasha, Gawri (also known as Kalam/Dir Kohistani), Torwali, Indus Kohistani, Bateri, and Dameli. Kashmiri to the east (primarily in Indian-administered territories) and the Pashai varieties to the west (in Afghanistan) are also normally included in this grouping.[5]

The Gilgiti examples in this paper are primarily drawn from a text corpus gathered (by Carla Radloff) over a period of twenty years, largely with the patient cooperation of Shakil Ahmad Shakil, mother tongue speaker of Gilgiti Shina, language consultant and researcher.[6] Bailey (1924) wrote the first extensive grammar of Gilgiti Shina. Buddruss (1993, 1996) has extensively studied Gilgiti Shina along with Zia (1986). Schmidt and Kohistani (2008) describe the grammar of Kohistani Shina, spoken in valleys on the east side of the Indus in Kohistan. Degener (2008) includes a brief grammatical description of Gilgiti Shina. Radloff and Shakil (1998), an annotated text collection, includes features of grammatical description in the form of footnotes.

3. ALIGNMENT SPLITS

Because Gilgiti Shina consistently uses case marking to differentiate between a transitive subject on the one hand, and an intransitive subject and a direct object on the other, we define it as *ergative or ergatively*

[5] Other 'Dardic' languages, with smaller numbers of speakers, in adjacent areas of Afghanistan include Gawarbati, Shumashti, Grangali-Ningalami, Tirahi, Wotapuri; some of these languages have a small number of speakers in Pakistan. Very small language groups such as Chilisso and Gowro in Kohistan are also included in this grouping. See Bashir (2003) and Strand (2001) for further discussions concerning the designation Dardic.

[6] A few additional contrasting examples were provided by Amir Haider Bagoro. Unless otherwise indicated with the name of a particular language or variety, the examples are of Gilgiti Shina.

aligned. However, while many accusative languages (such as English) are consistently or almost exclusively accusative, morphologically ergative languages tend to manifest accusative alignment in one or more of their subsystems, resulting in a split system for organizing grammatical relations (Dryer 2007: 253, Farrell 2005: 46, Dixon 1994: 94–7). In Shina, we find an accusative alignment in the area of verb agreement. Thus, Gilgiti Shina shows an alignment split between case marking and verb agreement (or between 'free' and 'bound' marking, to use Dixon's terminology), a particular split type observed in individual languages in various parts of the world.[7]

To explore this split system, it is helpful to represent the core syntactic roles of grammatical relations as A, S, and O,[8] where: *A* is the subject of a transitive verb or (using a semantics-based definition) the most agent-like argument in a two-argument predicate; *S* is the subject of an intransitive verb or the sole argument of a one-argument predicate; and *O* is the object of a transitive verb, the other, more patient-like (alternatively, less agent-like), argument of a two-argument predicate.

Case marking in Gilgiti Shina follows an ergative alignment {A}{S, O} where *A* normally is overtly marked for ergative case (with the suffix *-se)*, while *S* and *O* occur in the zero-marked absolutive case. *Verb agreement*, on the other hand, follows an accusative alignment {S, A}{O} where *S* or *A* fill the subject role in a sentence and the verb always agrees with this subject in person, number, and gender.[9] O never triggers verb agreement in Gilgiti Shina.

[7] Twelve (or about 6 per cent) of the 188 languages that were used in Siewierska's (2011) typological study of alignment in verbal marking sample as well as in Comrie's (2013) study of case marking alignment belong to this type (representing as disparate locations as Australia, North America, the Caucasus, Greenland, and Southeast Asia). This stands in contrast to the non-existence of the reverse combination (accusative case marking and ergative verb agreement) in the same sample.

[8] These abbreviations for universal syntactic relations were introduced by Dixon (1979, 1987, 2010, 1994) and are used commonly, e.g. Farrell (2005), Bickel (2010), Payne (2006: 216ff). Comrie (1978, 2013) favours A, S, and P, which have also been used extensively; cf. Croft (2003), Dryer (2007: 252). For copula constructions, we use Dixon's (2010: 100) abbreviations CS (copula subject) and CC (copula complement).

[9] In the most common variety of Gilgiti Shina, gender differentiation in verb agreement suffixes is not present in future tense or with plural reference.

The simplified examples below (1–4) have these roles marked. The *S* in (1) is *baál* 'boy'; the intransitive verb (labelled V_i) *yaáyan* 'he walks' agrees with it in the masculine singular. The S in (2), *muláay* 'girl', on the other hand, triggers feminine singular verb agreement. Example (3) has a transitive verb (V_t) *pían* 'he drinks', which agrees with the *A*, *baál* 'boy', because it is masculine and singular. The *A* is marked for ergative case with the marker *-se*. Example (3) also has an *O*, *ča* 'tea', a feminine noun (F) that is the object of the transitive verb *pían* 'he drinks'. The corresponding transitive clause with a feminine A, (4), shows verbal agreement in the feminine singular. Neither the *S* nor the *O* has any overt case marking; they are in the absolutive case. The *S* or *A* and the verb agree, never the verb with the O argument (whether animate or inanimate, human or non-human, pronominal or nominal, as will be evident in the examples to follow; see Section 5 in particular).[10]

(1) *baál* *yaáy-an*
boy walk-MSG.PRS
S $\mathbf{V_i}$
'The boy walks.' (Elicited data)

(2) *muláay* *yaáy-in*
girl walk-FSG.PRS
S $\mathbf{V_i}$
'The girl walks.' (Elicited data)

(3) *baál-se* *ča* *pí-an*
boy-**ERG** tea(F) drink-MSG.PRS
A **O** $\mathbf{V_t}$
'The boy drinks tea.' (Elicited data)

[10] For explanation of transcription conventions and a list of abbreviations, please see the relevant sections preceding the references.

(4)

muláay-se	*ča*	*pí-in*
girl-**ERG**	tea(F)	drink-FSG.PRS
A	**O**	**V_t**

'The girl drinks tea.' (Elicited data)

Gilgiti Shina has one ergative marker, *-se,* which is used in both imperfective and perfective aspects. This *-se* has an allomorph *-s*, which is phonologically conditioned; *se* occurs when the word it attaches to ends in a consonant, and the allomorph *-s* occurs when the word it attaches to ends in a vowel. In (5), *baál* 'boy' ends in a consonant, so *se* is used; in (6), *maálo* 'father' ends in a vowel, so *-s* is used. Here the verb is shown in both present and past tense to highlight the fact that agreement is not affected by tense, nor is the form of the ergative marker. And again, the masculine *A*s and the verbs agree, not the feminine *O*.

(5)

baál-se	*ṭíki*	*wal-éen/wal-eég-u*
boy-**ERG**	bread(F)	bring-MSG.PRS/bring-PFV-3MSG
A	**O**	**V_t**

'The boy brings/brought the bread.' (Elicited data)

(6)

maálo-s	*ṭíki*	*wal-éen/wal-eég-u*
father-**ERG**	bread(F)	bring-MSG.PRS/bring-PFV-3MSG
A	**O**	**V_t**

'The father brings/brought the bread.' (Elicited data)

This split system for organizing grammatical relations can be presented in diagram form to further highlight its characteristics. Gilgiti Shina follows an ergative alignment for *case marking.* This is illustrated in Figure 1, where *A* is circled separately because it is always marked for ergative case, and *S* and *O* are circled together because they are always zero-marked, that is, occurring in absolutive case.

Figure 1: Gilgiti Shina Case Marking: Ergative–Absolutive

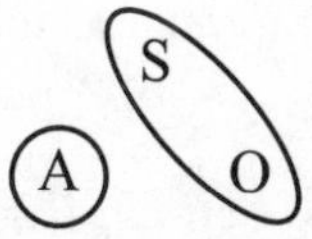

Gilgiti Shina follows an accusative alignment for *verb agreement*. Figure 2 illustrates this—*A* and *S* are in the same circle to show they behave similarly in triggering verb agreement. *O* is circled separately because it behaves differently, never agreeing with the verb.

Figure 2: Gilgiti Shina Verb Agreement: Nominative–Accusative

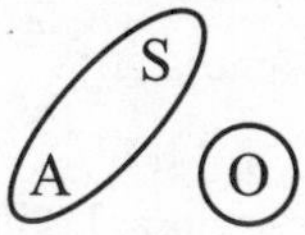

4. COMPARISON WITH RELATED AND SURROUNDING LANGUAGES

Gilgiti Shina has long been known to be a language with ergative features. Bailey (1924: 60) observed that the 'agent' (i.e. ergative) case 'is used with every part of the active voice of trans. verbs', separating it from the 'nominative' case used with intransitive verbs (1924: 57). Gilgiti Shina's consistent split between ergative alignment for case marking and accusative alignment for verb agreement contrasts in various ways with the alignment features found in most of the other languages of the surrounding region and beyond.

Urdu (Indo-Aryan) and Pashto (Iranian), two dominant languages of wider communication in northern Pakistan, both manifest split systems in which case marking as well as verb agreement are ergatively aligned in some of their tense-aspect categories, while in other tense-aspect categories alignment is entirely accusative (Schmidt 1999: 7, 22, 73). In Urdu, the dividing line is aspectual. In the perfective, as in example (7), the verb agrees with O in gender and number, and A is marked with a clitical element *nē* (which is preceded by an oblique form of the noun or pronoun, except for the first and second person pronouns), while in the imperfective, the verb agrees with A which then occurs in its basic (i.e. nominative) form, as can be seen in (8).

(7) Urdu

*ahmad=**nē***	*sārē*	*samōsē*	*khā-**ē***	***haĩ***
Ahmad=**ERG**	all	samosa.PL	eat-**MPL**	**are**
A	**O**		$\mathbf{V_t}$	

'Ahmad has eaten all the samosas (a kind of pastry).' (Schmidt 1999: 73)

(8) Urdu

ahmad	*sārē*	*samōsē*	*khā*	*rah-**ā***	***hai***
Ahmad	all	samosa.PL	eat	CONT-**MSG**	**is**
A	**O**		$\mathbf{V_t}$		

'Ahmad is eating all the samosas.' (Elicited data)

In Pashto, the verb agrees with O in person, number, and (for 3 person) gender in past tenses, as in (10), regardless of aspectual distinctions, whereas in present tenses (9), verb agreement is with A. In the past, A occurs in the 'oblique' (as in (10)), a non-nominative multiple-use case category (Robson and Tegey 2010: 730).

(9) Pashto

xədza	*ṭikray*	*akhl-**i***
woman	scarf(M)	buy.PRS.IPFV-**3SG**
A	**O**	$\mathbf{V_t}$

'The woman is buying the scarf.' (Robson and Tegey 2010: 756)

(10) Pashto

xədze	*ṭikray*	*akhist-ə*
woman.**OBL**	scarf(M)	buy.PST.IPFV-**3MSG**
A	**O**	$\mathbf{V_t}$

'The woman was buying the scarf.' (Robson and Tegey 2010: 756)

Indo-Aryan languages other than Shina but native to the region itself, display a somewhat surprising variety as far as alignment features are concerned (Liljegren 2014). While many of them, such as Kashmiri (Koul 2003: 919), Gawri (Baart 1999: 134–7), Torwali (Lunsford 2001: 95–7), Indus Kohistani (Lubberger 2014: 207–10), and Pashai (Morgenstierne 1973: 64–94, Lehr 2014: 145), manifest an aspectual split-ergativity similar to that of Urdu, at least two languages behave similar to Gilgiti Shina in their consistent accusative verb agreement patterns. In Gawarbati (11), as well as in neighbouring Dameli (Perder 2013: 59–60, 110–12), both spoken in the Kunar-Chitral Valley, A is ergatively case-marked (albeit in the perfective only) while still triggering verb agreement (in perfective and imperfective alike).

(11) Gawarbati

doos	***tui***	*čir*	*bikin-**uu**-a*
yesterday	you.**ERG**	milk	sell-**2SG**-Q
	A	**O**	**V_t**

'Did you sell milk yesterday?' (Questionnaire data)

Another group of Indo-Aryan, represented by Khowar and Kalasha, both spoken in Chitral, are entirely accusative, that is, not ergative in any of their subsystems (Bashir 2003: 849–50). A occurs in Khowar in the nominative case across all tense-aspect categories and triggers verb agreement,[11] as can be seen in examples (12) to (14).[12]

[11] Khowar past and non-past take different sets of agreement suffixes (Bashir 2003: 847).

[12] It is not entirely clear whether the suffix *-an* is to be interpreted as an instance of 'indigenous' oblique plural marking (which in fact assumes a definite or specific reading of the direct object: 'he is writing the letters') or an extended use of a formally identical (nominative) plural marker 'imported' from Persian (Bashir 2007: 226–8).

(12) Khowar

hase	*xat-**an***	*niveš-**ir***
3SG.REM.NOM	letter-**OBL**.PL	write.PRS.NS.ACT-**3SG**
A	**O**	**V_t**

'He is writing the letters.' (Questionnaire data)

(13) Khowar

hase	*xat-**an***	*nivešit-**ai***
3SG.REM.NOM	letter-**OBL**.PL	write.PST.ACT-**3SG**
A	**O**	**V_t**

'He wrote the letters.' (Questionnaire data)

(14) Khowar

hase	*obrit-**ai***
3SG.REM.NOM	die.PST.ACT-**3SG**
S	**V_i**

'It died.' (Questionnaire data)

Many Shina varieties other than Gilgiti (also referred to as Northern Shina, cf. Radloff 1992: 100) are equally ergative in all tense-aspect categories but have different ergative markers for the perfective and the imperfective aspect (Schmidt 2004: 49–50). Among them are Eastern Shina (Hook and Koul 2004: 213), Kohistani Shina (Schmidt and Kohistani 2008: 51–7), and the divergent, and to other Shina-speakers mostly unintelligible, variety spoken in Ladakh, named Brokskat (Sharma 1998: 63). Schmidt and Kohistani (2008: 51–3) observe that, for instance, Kohistani Shina has markers *-e* ~ *-i*, *-o*, and plural *-ǰi*, in the perfective (15), and a marker *-sa or –s* in the imperfective (16).

(15) Kohistani Shina

*bal-ó-**ǰi***	*láa*	*móẓ-i*	*khoǰ-eég-**a***
child-OBL.PL-**ERG.PFV**.PL	many	matter-PL	ask-PFV-**3PL**
A	**O**		$\mathbf{V_t}$

'The children asked a lot of questions.' (Schmidt and Kohistani 2008: 167)

(16) Kohistani Shina

bal-í-s	*láa*	*móẓ-i*	*khoǰ-ée-n-**an***
child-PL-**ERG.IPFV**	many	matter-PL	ask-IPFV-PRS-**3PL**
A	**O**		$\mathbf{V_t}$

'Children ask a lot of questions.' (Schmidt and Kohistani 2008: 167)

A similar distribution and similar-sounding forms are found in the other varieties, and it seems plausible that the use of the former set has a long history in these and other Indo-Aryan varieties, whereas the presence of the latter represents a more recent development in Shina (Schmidt 2004: 51). Already Bailey (1924: 211) hinted at a Western Tibetan origin of the suffix *-sa/-s*, a hypothesis reiterated and supported by modern-day Shina scholars (Hook and Koul 2004: 213–14, Schmidt and Kohistani 2008: 51–2).

The use of an s-ergative in Gilgiti in all aspects is therefore most likely the result of the 'new' imperfective ergative case being extended into the perfective, thus pushing the 'old' marker out of use, a course of development further evidenced by comparing Bailey's (1924: 211) almost century-old statement that Guresi, a sub-variety of Eastern Shina, kept these two sets of case markers distinct for different tense-aspect categories, with those of Schmidt (2004: 51) and Schmidt and Kaul (2010), who note that Guresi now use the same s-marker in both imperfective and perfective, and that the 'old' perfective ergative case has almost completely disappeared in nouns but survives with some pronouns.

A few other Shina varieties, mostly those spoken in small enclaves further to the west, show no traces whatsoever of ergativity outside of the perfective realm, probably because they split off geographically from the main Shina speaking population well before the expansion of the Tibetan-derived ergative marker. Their systems are evidently more similar to what we saw for Pashto, Urdu, and a number of other Indo-Aryan languages. For instance, Palula, an 'archaic' Shina variety spoken in southern Chitral, manifests this type of aspectual split, whereby verb agreement is ergative in the perfective, as in (17), and accusative in the non-perfective, as in (18).[13]

(17) Palula

míi	*preṣ-í*	*ma*	*bhuuǰ-óol-**u***
my	mother.in.law-**OBL**	I.NOM	wake.up-PFV-**MSG**
A		**O**	**V_t**

'My mother-in-law woke me up.' (Corpus data)

(18) Palula

ma	*tu*	*the*	*ǰinaazeé*	*aṭ-**úum***
I.NOM	you.NOM	to	corpse.PL	bring-**1SG**
A			**O**	**V_t**

'I will bring you the corpses.' (Corpus data)

Similar patterns have been observed in Sawi (Buddruss 1967: 33, 40, 51–2), Kalkoti (Liljegren 2013: 148), and Kundal Shahi (Rehman 2011: 221–2).

Gilgiti Shina's close neighbours to the north and east are the isolate Burushaski and Western Tibeto-Burman Balti. Both of these languages manifest ergativity. Interestingly, Burushaski nominal ergativity applies, just as in Gilgiti Shina, regardless of tense or aspect distinctions (Berger 1998: 64–6). Another similarity is that the same verbal agreement suffixes apply to A and S alike. In addition to A agreement in person, number, and noun class, the verb agrees with the zero-marked O (and S) by a prefix whose form also varies according to person, number, and noun class (Berger 1998: 177–8), as can be seen from (19) to (21).[14]

[13] For further details, see Liljegren (2014: 150–1, 2016: 291–8).

[14] Burushaski has a four-gender system: (i) human feminine; (ii) human masculine; (iii) animals and a few inanimate entities (typically countable); and (iv) abstract

(19) Burushaski

hír	*i-írim-i*
man	3SG.HM-die.PST-3SG.HM
S	**V_i**

'The man died.' (Berger 1998: 178)

(20) Burushaski

hír-e	*gus*	***mu-yeétsim-i***
man-**ERG**	woman	3SG.HF-see.PST-3SG.HM
A	**O**	**V_t**

'The man saw the woman.' (Berger 1998: 178)

(21) Burushaski

*šaapiya-**a***	*ha-a*	*duro*	*e-ču=b-**o***
Shapia-**ERG**	home-GEN	work	3SG.Y-do=COP-3SG.HF
A		**O**	**V_t**

'Shapia does the work of the home.' (Munshi n.d.: 37)

In Balti we find, again, case marking patterns (and even the forms themselves, as mentioned above) similar to those of Gilgiti Shina. An ergative case suffix *-si* (or *-isi*) occurs with A, while S or O remain zero-marked, almost regardless of tense-aspect categories (Bielmeier 1985: 138). Balti verbs, on the other hand, do not agree with any of their arguments (Jones 2009: 30). However, on closer inspection, it is evident that marking of the A argument is subject to variation. Bielmeier (1985: 141–2) exemplifies how noun phrases in syntactically and lexically near-identical clauses alternate between ergative case marking and (absolutive) zero-marking, probably due to fine semantic and highly contextual differences. Read (1934: 7) also notes that speakers occasionally drop the ergative suffix, especially in present tense, and Zeisler (2004: 628–33) points out that even S arguments

entities, fluids, and the rest of the inanimate entities (typically non-countable). These four are by tradition abbreviated as HF, HM, X, and Y, respectively (Berger 1998: 33–8, Willson 1999: 5).

can receive ergative marking in West Tibetan varieties. The latter observations point us in the direction of considering A marking here as a device associated with a high degree of agentivity or control.

5. ERGATIVE CASE IN ALL TENSES AND ON ALL FORMS

Gilgiti Shina is equally ergative in all tense and aspect categories, and the same ergative and absolutive case markings apply to nouns, pronouns, verbal nouns, or substantivized adjectives. Similarly, verb agreement remains with the S or A arguments throughout the entire paradigm. In (22) to (27) a variety of examples help illustrate some of these facts (the ergative marker and subject agreement markers are given in boldface).[15]

(22)	*ǰag-**se***	*tu*	*neé*	*paáš-**an***
	people-**ERG**	you	not	see-FUT.**3PL**
	A	**O**		**V_t**
	magám	*tu-**s***	*púur-e*	*paáš-**ee***
	but	you-**ERG**	all-PL	see-FUT.**2SG**
		A	**O**	**V_t**

'People will not see you but you will see everything.' (Husan 35.2)

(23)	*tu-**s***	*súu~ço*	*r-**áanoo**,*	*mor*
	you-**ERG**	true	say-PRS.**2MSG**	matter(M)
	A	**O**	**V_t**	**CS**
	anú	*akií*	*han*	
	this	EMPH	be.PRS.3MSG	
	CC		**V_c**	

'You speak the truth, the matter is exactly this.' (Road Accident 2.6)

[15] All examples are taken from the text corpus. References to the name and line of texts in the database are in parentheses in the free translation line.

(24)

aáǰi-s	*re*	*tušáar*	*pharang-eég-i*
mother-**ERG**	she	much	investigate-PFV-PST.**3FSG**
A	**O**		**V_t**

'Mother really questioned her.' (Husan 48.6)

(25)

súu~ço	*be-s*	*tsho*	*bódi*	*dam-ar-eég-**enes***
true	we-**ERG**	you.all	much	trouble-CAUS-PFV-PRF.**1PL**
	A	**O**		**V_t**

'Truly we have caused you both much trouble.' (Husan 87.2)

(26)

máazak	*gá-**us***	*ek*	*čhak*
a.month(M)	go-PPRF.**3MSG**	one	day
S	**V_i**		

ma-s	*çhúilak*	*duǰ-**ámisis***
I-**ERG**	some.clothes	wash-PST.IPFV.**1FSG**
A	**O**	

'A month had passed, one day I was washing some clothes ...' (HBP 3.1)

(27)

púure-s	*gáṭi beé*	*naṭ*	*d-**áa***
all-**ERG**	together	dance	give-IMP.**2PL**
A		**O**	**V_t**

'Everyone dance together!' (Distant 171.1)

Pronouns as *A* and in ergative case forms are seen in examples (22), (23), (25), and (26). They are all regularly formed by adding the ergative suffix *-s* to the absolutive form of the pronoun: *ma* 'I.ABS' vs *ma-s* 'I.ERG', *tu* 'you.ABS' vs *tu-s* 'you.ERG', etc. The adjective or quantifier *púure* 'all' functions substantively and heads a noun phrase in example (27) where it functions as an *A* argument; it is therefore marked with ergative case. Pronouns as *O* and in the absolutive case are seen in examples (22), (24), and (25): tu 'you', re 'she', and tsho 'you all', respectively. Substantivized quantifiers/adjectives in the

O slot are zero-marked for case (i.e. in the absolutive) in examples (22) and (23). Verbal nouns that occur as *A*, and subsequently ergatively marked, can be seen in examples (35) and (36) below.

The transitive verb in example (22) is in future tense, example (23) is present tense, example (24) past tense, example (25) (present) perfect, example (26) past imperfective, and example (27) is imperative. Further below, the transitive verb in example (36) is in pluperfect.

6. ERGATIVE CASE AND THE NOUN PHRASE

In Gilgiti Shina, the ergative marker *-se* is suffixed to the head of the *A* noun phrase and to the last member of an A consisting of a noun compound.[16] Examples are drawn from texts to illustrate these characteristics; the noun phrase serving as the A argument in each is enclosed in square brackets. The examples (28) to (31) show the ergative marker suffixed to the last member of a compound *A,* and it is the noun phrase as a whole that is marked for ergativity in the transitive clause. Notice also that because the *A* is consistently marked for ergativity, word order does not affect meaning (other than perhaps pragmatically); this is highlighted in examples (30) and (31), where A in contrast to the basic word order AOV immediately precedes the verb without any intervening or explicit direct object, and further below in example (46).

(28)	*[hopóti*	*ga*	*hopóto]-s*	*toóm*
	Hopoti	and	Hopoto-**ERG**	own
	[A			**]**

dadidáadeṭ	***bódo***	***kom***	***th-éenes***
to.grandparents	much	work	do-PST.IPFV.**3PL**
		O	**V_t**

'Hopoti and Hopoto used to do a lot of work for their grandparents.' (Hopoti 71.1)

[16] Gilgiti Shina is generally head-final or left-branching: the direct object precedes the verb (OV), adjectives precede the nouns they modify, and postpositions, not prepositions, are used.

(29)

[hiiroošimáa	*ga*	*gaáyiḍ]-se*	*rinóṭ*
Hiroshima	and	guide-**ERG**	to.them
[A		**]**	

tambuwí-ṣ-oók	*paš-ar-eég-e*
tents-connect-INF	see-CAUS-PFV-PST.**3PL**
O	$\mathbf{V_t}$

'Hiroshima and the guide showed them (how) to set up the tents.' (Hiroshima 106.1)

(30)

manganíi-riwáaǰ	*[ṣiín*	*ga*	*yéṣkun]-se*
engagement-custom	Shin	and	Yeshkun-**ERG**
O	**[A**		**]**

ga	*th-éenen*
also	do-PRS.**3PL**
	$\mathbf{V_t}$

'Shins and Yeshkuns also do (follow) the custom of engagement.' (Views 7.1)

(31)

rinóǰ	*[uyanaár*	*ga*	*wayaál]-se*
on.them	hunger(F)	and	thirst(F)-**ERG**
	[A		**]**

bódi	*kúri*	*wal-eég-i*
much	greatly	bring-PFV-PST.**3FSG**[17]
		$\mathbf{V_t}$

'Hunger and thirst very greatly affected them.' (Speech 8.2)

The *A* subjects in examples (32) to (36) below are all complex noun phrases, set apart by square brackets. Again we see that the noun

[17] The two abstract nouns, 'hunger' and 'thirst', are obviously treated as singular as far as verb agreement is concerned.

phrase as a whole is marked for ergativity whenever in the same clause as a transitive verb. The A, 'birth' in example (32) is modified by the genitive phrase 'firstborn son's', while the A in (33) 'heart' is modified by the possessive adjective 'my', and 'girl' is modified by the phrase *húsan-baanóo háai kayíili* 'wise like Husan Bano'. That in (34) is a relative clause, and in both (35) and (36) the head of the noun phrase is a verbal noun.

(32)	*[čamiáako*	*puçéy*	*ǰaát]-se*	*kunú*	*d-ar-**íin***
	firstborn	son.GEN	birth-**ERG**	illness	give-CAUS-PRS.**3FSG**
	[A			**]O**	**V_t**

'(Her) firstborn son's birth causes this illness.' (Finess 1.188)

(33)	*[mey*	*hío]-s*	*yárešo*	*r-**áas**,*
	my	heart-**ERG**	from.before	say-PST.IPFV.**3MSG**
	[A		**]**	**V_t**

[húsan-baanóo	*háai*	*kayíili*	*muláayak]-se*
Husan-Banoo	like	wise	a.girl-**ERG**
[A			**]**

ayéek	*th-**ey**-aa*
like.that	do-FUT.**3SG**-Q
O	**V_t**

'From before my heart was saying, "Will a wise girl like Husan Banoo do like that?"' (Husan 76.3)

(34)	*[kíčaner*	*han*	*gées]-se*	*hagáar*	*lam-iíg-**un***
	in.kitchen	he.is	gas-**ERG**	fire	catch-PFV-PRF.**3MSG**
	[A			**]O**	**V_t**

'The gas which is in (has filled) the kitchen has caught fire.' (Fire 3.5)

(35)

[anú	*kóoṭey*	*čheé~ye*	*réseṭ*	*neé*
this	fort.GEN	keys	to.him	not
[A				

doók]-se	*luúkga*	*tor*	*th-ar-eég-**u***
give-INF-**ERG**	even.more	perturb	do-CAUS-PFV-PST.**3MSG**[18]
]			V_t

'(His) not giving him this fort's keys made (him) even more perturbed.' (Husan 16.3)

(36)

[baráamey	*lilimér*	*uçhač-oók]-se*	*résey*
Beraam.GEN	in.Lilim	arrive-INF-**ERG**	her
[A			]

ǰilér	*ǰiíl*	*ač-ar-eég-**iš***
in.life	life	enter-CAUS-PFV-PPRF.**3FSG**
	O	V_t

'Beraam's arriving in Lilim had inserted life in her life (invigorated her).' (Husan 70.4)

7. ANY TRANSITIVE VERBAL ELEMENT TRIGGERS ERGATIVE CASE

Ergative marking is so robust in Gilgiti Shina that even non-finite transitive verbal elements prompt the ergative case, no matter if an intransitive element intervenes, no matter if the finite verb is intransitive, and no matter if the transitive element is even left implicit.

In each of the examples (37) to (39), an intransitive action—in participle form—occurs before the transitive action. Nevertheless, in each case the *A* argument is marked for ergative case because of the transitive finite verb that it agrees with. In example (37) the

[18] It is not clear why the verb here shows masculine singular agreement, since there is feminine singular agreement with the infinitive in (36), and Shina infinitives have earlier been analysed as being feminine (Hook and Zia 2005: 175–6).

A argument *hagáar* 'fire' is marked ergatively because of the transitive finite main verb (V_t), *dáy* 'burn', not the intervening intransitive converb (V_i) *geé* 'having gone'. A similar case is seen in (38), with the intervening intransitive converb *beé* 'having become', and in (39), with the intervening intransitive converb *uçhačií* 'having arrived'.

(37)

hagáar-se	*g-eé*	*kóṇo*	*day-iíg-**u***
fire-**ERG**	go-CV	thorn	burn-PFV-PST.**3MSG**
A	**(V_i)**	**O**	**V_t**

'The fire went and burned the thorn.' (Blackberry 2.9)

(38)

baráam-se	*lang*	*b-eé*	*résey*
Beraam-**ERG**	sideward	become-CV	his
A		**(V_i)**	

čoṭ	*ṭhis*	*th-ar-eég-**u***
blow	mistake	do-CAUS-PFV-PST.**3MSG**
	O	**V_t**

'Beraam moved to the side and made him miss his blow.' (Beraam 11.1)

(39)

*deéw-**se***	*arú*	*uçhač-ií*	*akií*
giant-**ERG**	inside	arrive-CV	EMPH
A		**(V_i)**	

húung	*d-eé*	*réseṭ*	*ra-iíg-**u***
oath	give-CV	to.him	speak-PFV-PST.**3MSG**
(O	**V_t)**		**V_t**

'The giant arrived inside and swore and spoke to him.' (Husan 17.6)

More interestingly, the reverse is true in examples (40) to (44), where the intransitive main verb (e.g. *bigí in (40)*) agrees with A, yet in each example that subject is marked with ergative case (*čúni muláay-se*) because of an intervening non-finite transitive verb form (e.g. *dujeé*).

In examples (40) and (42), the transitive elements are converbs,[19] and in (41) a present participle. In (43) and (44), it is a transitive infinitive which triggers ergative case marking, despite the fact that the main, finite verb 'became' is intransitive. Baart has made a similar observation about Kohistani Gawri (Baart 1999: 140–2), spoken in the same general region, although it may be less pervasive in that language than in Gilgiti Shina (Joan Baart, pc).

(40)	*[čúni*	*muláay]-se*	*mukh*	*duǰ-eé*
	small	girl-**ERG**	face(M)	wash-CV
	([A		**]O**	**V_t)**

	lam	*b-ig-í*
	bright	become-PFV-PST.**3FSG**
		V_i

'The little girl washed (her) face and she became bright (clean and shiny).' (September 1997 1.43)

(41)	*tu-s*	*nu*	*ç̣ak-óoǰo*	***beéy***
	you-**ERG**	he	look-PRSPTC	remain.IMP.**2SG**
	(A	**O**	**V_t)**	**V_i**

'You keep on looking at him! (Lit: While looking at him you remain!)' (Distant 230:4)

(42)	*[hiroošimáa*	*ga*	*pon pašáaro*	*hunzúǰo*
	Hiroshima	and	guide	Hunza.person
	([A			

	rahíim]-se	*morkál*	*th-eé*	*ẓas-b-óon*
	Rahim-**ERG**	discuss	do/say-CV	depart-become-FUT.1PL
		]O	**V_t)**	**(V_i)**

[19] Converbs are also referred to as conjunctive participles in the South Asian linguistic tradition.

th-eé	*guči-íl-**e***
do/say-CV	agree-PFV-PST.**3PL**
(V_t)	**V_i**

'Hiroshima and the guide from Hunza, Rahim, discussed and agreed to depart.' (Hiroshima 5.1)

(43)	*kuyoóč-**se***	*šazadá*	*uḍar-oók*	*šor*	*b-ig-é*
	subjects-**ERG**	prince	search-INF	dispersed	become-PFV-PST.**3PL**
	(A	**O**	**V_t)**		**V_i**

'The subjects dispersed to search (for) the prince.' (Gorpachin 6.3)

(44)	*[darunóo*	*wátek*	*riwáaǰe]-s*	*aséy*
	from.outside	those.coming	customs-**ERG**	our
	([A			**]**

abašóo,	*aséy*	*gunaníi,*	*aséy*
of.difficulties	our	of.thoughts	our

taáto šidáley	*surúp*	*th-oók*	*dub-**éen***
of.climate	consideration	do-INF	be.unable-FUT.**3PL**
	O	**V_t)**	**V_i**

'Customs which come from outside will be unable to take into consideration our difficulties, our thoughts, our climate.' (Views 34.1)

Examples (45) and (46) illustrate how even an unstated or implicit transitive predicate may trigger ergative case marking. In (45) the left out verb would be *thíin* 'she says'. The riddle is more rhythmic without the stated verb, and is understood even without the verb.[20] In (46), the second part of the sentence has left out the verb, but the compound A argument (noted by square brackets) is still marked with *-se* because of its co-reference with the preceding ergatively marked noun phrase, which is the A of transitive *phuṭéenan* 'they break'.

---

[20] Buddruss (1996: 31) presents a somewhat different version of this riddle, with the verb included.

(45)

ek-se	*ma*	*mililiíli,*	*ek-se*	*ma*	*mililiíli*
one-**ERG**	I	beautiful	one-**ERG**	I	beautiful
A			**A**		

yúun-se	*ma*	*mililiíli,*	*súuri-s*	*ma*	*mililiíli*
moon-**ERG**	I	beautiful	sun-**ERG**	I	beautiful
A			**A**		

'Riddle: One (says) I (am) beautiful, one (says) I (am) beautiful = The Moon (says) I (am) beautiful, the Sun (says) I (am) beautiful.' (Finess 1.10)

(46)

ruzá	*[dúu*	*čhíizi]-s*	*phuṭ-éenan,*	*[ṣuṣuríie*
fasting	two	things-**ERG**	break-PRS.3PL	back.bitings
O	**[A**		**]** $\mathbf{V_t}$	**[A**

th-oók	*ga*	*čóṭe*	*wi-oók]-se*
do/say-INF	and	lies	put-INF-**ERG**
			]

'Two things break (ruin the benefit of) the fast: back-biting and lying.' (A Speech 3.3)

8. ERGATIVITY AND COMPLEX PREDICATES

That ergativity in Gilgiti Shina is grounded in syntactic structure and lexical specification, rather than in semantics or pragmatics, is illustrated through a type of complex predicate, in South Asian linguistic literature often referred to as a *conjunct verb*. A conjunct verb consists of a non-verbal element (usually a noun or an adjective) and a verbal element which jointly function as the predicate of a clause.[21]

---

[21] The verbal element, drawn form a closed set of verbs with a generic semantic content, such as 'do', 'give', 'become', is referred to as a *verbalizer* (Masica 1991: 368, Liljegren 2016: 241) or an *operator verb* (Schmidt and Kohistani 2008: 206). Liljegren (2010) presents an in-depth study of complex verbs, building upon their instance in Palula.

In examples (47) to (49), the complex predicate consists of the transitive verb *thé* 'do' and a non-verbal element (that is, a noun or an adjective), with the latter filling the *O* slot. However, in these sentences, an overall recipient of the action is also involved, but since the *O* argument role is already 'filled', the recipient occurs in an *oblique* form, either in the genitive or in the dative case. In (47), the complex predicate is enclosed in square brackets. The formal direct object of the transitive verb *thé* 'do' is filled by the noun element of this complex predicate, *ma* 'kiss' (in the absolutive case). 'Ghazanfar', the recipient of the overall action 'kiss', is not the grammatical *O*, and must therefore be marked obliquely, here with genitive case. Similarly, the recipients of the overall actions in (48) and (49) occur in the dative case, showing their non-core argument status. The grammatical *O* is part of the complex predicate (marked with square brackets). As a contrast, in (50), two S arguments show agreement with their complex predicates whose verbal elements are intransitive.

(47)	*taárik-se*	*gazanfaréy*	*[ma*	*th-**éen**]*
	Tariq-**ERG**	Ghazanfar.GEN	kiss	do-PRS.**3MSG**
	A		**O**	**V_t**

'Tariq kisses Ghazanfar.' (Finess 1.64)

(48)	*muláay-se*	*haṇeǰéṭ*	*[khoš*	*th-**íin**-aa]*
	girl-**ERG**	to.eggs	happy	do-PRS.**3FSG**-Q
	A		**O**	**V_t**

'Does the girl like eggs?' (2 & 3Tape 39.1)

(49)	*samaláar*	*čháaṇo-s*	*amiruláaṭ*
	in.wrestling	Chaano-**ERG**	to.Amirullah
		A	

[šat	*th-eég-**u**]*
power	do-PFV-PST.**3MSG**
O	**V_t**

'Chaano beat Amirullah in wrestling.' (Apr 97 107.1)

(50)

afšáa~ey	*hatéǰo*	*ǰag*	*[taṣ*
Afshan.GEN	from.hand	jug(F)	slipping
		S	
*b-íl-**i**]*	*wey*	*[čúur*	*b-úl-**u**]*
be-PFV-PST.**3FSG**	water(M)	spilling	be-PFV-PST.**3MSG**
V_i	**S**		**V_i**

'The jug slipped from Afshan's hand (and) the water spilled.' (Finess 1.164)

Complex predicates with transitive verbal elements also help illustrate that transitivity is lexically specified in Gilgiti Shina. The complex predicates in examples (51) to (54) are marked with square brackets. Those including a transitive verb trigger ergative marking on the subject of the sentence even though their translation equivalents in English are not necessarily transitive: 'crawling' in (51), 'running' in (52), 'flying' in (53), and 'lying down' in (54).

(51)

baál-se	*[dol*	*d-**éen**]*
boy-**ERG**	crawling	give-PRS.**3MSG**
A	**O**	**V_t**

'The (baby) boy crawls (lit. gives crawling).' (Finess 1.21)

(52)

re-s	*[hay*	*th-eé]*	*w-eéy*
she-**ERG**	running	do-CV	come-CV
A	**(O**	**V_t)**	**(V_i)**
rinóṭ	*[krum*	*b-ig-**í**]*	
to.them	Embraced	become-PFV-PST.**3FSG**	
		V_i	

'She ran (lit. did running), came, and embraced (lit. became embraced to) them.' (Hopoti 9.7)

(53)	*gorphaçín-se*	*[thar*	*d-eé]*	*lúkak*	*satér*
	Gorpachin-**ERG**	flight	give-CV	a.bit	in.time
	A	**(O**	**V_t)**		

akií	*ají*	*šazadáakač*	*uçhá-t-i*
EMPH	above	near.prince	arrive-PFV-PST.**3FSG**
			V_i

'Gorpachin flew (lit. gave flight) and in just a short while arrived up near the prince.' (Gorpachin 35.4)

(54)	*ma-s*	*aán*	*[gaál*	*d-eé]*	***hánus***
	I-**ERG**	here	lying.down	give-CV	be.PRS.**1MSG**
	A		**(O**	**V_t)**	**V_c**

'I have just lain down (lit. am giving lying down) here.' (Jan 09 Notes 150)

SUMMARY

Gilgiti Shina manifests a split system for organizing grammatical relations, where case marking is ergatively aligned and verb agreement is nominative–accusatively aligned. This means that the *A* argument of a transitive verb is always marked for ergative case, while the subject, whether A or S, will always trigger verb agreement. The S and O arguments are consistently zero-marked (i.e. occurring in their most basic forms). This sets Gilgiti Shina apart from many of the other Indo-Aryan languages of this region, which apply ergative case marking only in some of their past or perfective forms; a subset of those languages also manifest verbal agreement with O in the same tense-aspect categories. Gilgiti Shina also differs from some of its closest linguistic relatives within the Shina cluster in its use of a single ergative marker (*-se* or *-s*) for perfective and imperfective paradigms alike. On the other hand, Gilgiti Shina shares some of its distinctive alignment features with two neighbouring, yet unrelated, languages. The language isolate Burushaski manifests identical ergative case marking regardless of tense or aspect, and shows consistent verb agreement with A and S. The West Tibetan language Balti also manifests ergative case marking on A arguments (although it seems to be context sensitive and subject to a certain degree of variation related to pragmatic or semantic factors), using a marker *-si* or *-isi* (corresponding in form and function to markers in a number of Tibetan languages, one of which has been suggested as the source of the Gilgiti Shina ergative marker).

Gilgiti Shina is consistently ergative in all tenses as far as case marking is concerned. The ergative marker *-se* attaches to the last member of the *A* noun phrase, no matter if compound. The same ergative and absolutive case markings apply equally to nouns, pronouns, verbal nouns, or substantivized adjectives. Ergative marking is very robust, such that a transitive element triggers the ergative case even if the main verb is intransitive, even if intransitive forms intervene before a transitive main verb, even though the overall sense may not necessarily be transitive, and even in cases where the transitive verb itself might remain unstated. Complex predicates help to highlight the fact that the display of ergativity in Gilgiti Shina is grounded in syntactic structure and in lexically specified transitivity rather than in semantic or pragmatic factors.

ON TRANSCRIPTION

Vowel length is shown by geminate vowels, *aa*. The accented vowel manifests a higher pitch and is marked with an acute accent´, either on a short vowel: *á* (a higher pitch), on the first mora (part) of a long vowel: *áa* (falling from the high pitch), or on the second mora of a long vowel: *aá* (rising to the high pitch), following Berger (1960) and Buddruss (1993, 1996). By convention, the accent is often not marked on monosyllabic words. Nasalized vowels are shown by tilde ~ after the vowel: *a~*, *áa~*, *aá~*, following an *Orientalist* system of transcription described by Masica (1991: xvi). In that same vein, retroflex consonants are marked with a dot below: *ç, ḍ, ṇ, ṛ, ṣ, ṭ, ẓ*. The velar nasal *ŋ* is represented by *ng*. Morpheme breaks are shown by hyphens: *th-eég-u* 'do-PFV-PST.3MSG'. If more than one word is required to gloss a single morpheme, the words of the gloss are separated by full stops, *awaáǰ-in* 'be.necessary-PRS.3FSG'. Where the grammatical analysis of a word is not in focus, the non-separated morphemes are indicated in the gloss by a full stop: e.g. *rinóṭ* 'by.them'.

ABBREVIATIONS

A = Subject of transitive verb
ACT = Actual
CAUS = Causative
CC = Copula complement
CS = Copula subject
CV = Converb
EMPH = Emphasis
ERG = Ergative
F = Feminine
FUT = Future
GEN = Genitive
HF = Human feminine
HM = Human masculine
IMP = Imperative
INF = Infinitive
IPFV = Imperfective

M = Masculine
NOM = Nominative
NS = Non-specific
O = Direct object of transitive verb
OBL = Oblique
PFV = Perfective
PL = Plural
PPRF = Pluperfect
PRF = Perfect
PRS = Present
PRSPTC = PRESENT PARTICIPLE
PST = Past
Q = QUESTION
REM = REMOTE
S = Subject of intransitive verb
SG = Singular
V_I = Intransitive verb
V_T = Transitive verb
Y = Y class (typically non-human, non-countable noun)
1 = First person
2 = Second person
3 = Third person

REFERENCES

Baart, Joan L. G. 1999. *A Sketch of Kalam Kohistani Grammar.* Islamabad: National Institute of Pakistan Studies and Summer Institute of Linguistics.

Bailey, Thomas Grahame. 1924. *Grammar of the Shina (Sina) Language; Consisting of a Full Grammar, with Texts and Vocabularies of the Main or Gilgiti Dialect and Briefer Grammars (with Vocabularies and Texts) of the Kohistani, Guresi, and Drasi Dialects.* London: Royal Asiatic Society.

Bashir, Elena. 2007. 'Contact-Induced Change in Khowar.' In *New Perspectives on Pakistan: Visions for the Future,* edited by Heather Bolton and Saeed Shafqat. 205–38. Oxford: Oxford University Press.

_______ 2003. 'Dardic'. In *The Indo-Aryan Languages,* edited by George Cardona and Danesh Jain. 818–94. London: Routledge.

Berger, Hermann. 1998. *Die Burushaski-Sprache von Hunza Und Nager 1. Grammatik.* Neuindische Studien, Bd. 13. Wiesbaden: Harrassowitz.

_______ 1960. 'Bericht Über Sprachliche Und Volkskundliche Forschungen Im Hunzatal. ' *Anthropos* 55: 657–64.

Bickel, Balthasar. 2010. 'Grammatical Relations Typology'. In *The Oxford Handbook of Linguistic Typology,* edited by Jae Jung Song. 399–444. Oxford: Oxford University Press.

Bielmeier, Roland. 1985. *Das Märchen Vom Prinzen Čobzań: Eine Tibetische Erzählung Aus Baltistan: Text, Übersetzung, Grammatik Und Westtibetisch Vergleichendes Glossar.* Sankt Augustin: VGH Wissenschaftsverlag. (Beiträge Zur Tibetischen Erzählforschung, Bd. 6).

Buddruss, Georg. 1996. 'Shina-Rätsel'. In *Nānāvidhaikatā: Festschrift Für Hermann Berger*, edited by Dieter B. Kapp. 29–54. Wiesbaden: Harrassowitz Verlag.

——— 1993. 'On artificial glaciers in the Gilgit Karakorum.' In *Studien zur Indologie und Iranistik, Band 18*, edited by Georg Buddruss, Oskar von Hinüber, Hanns-Peter Schmidt, Albrecht Wetzler, and Michael Witzel. 77–90. Reinbek: Dr Inge Wezler. Verlag für Orientalistische Fachpublikationen.

——— 1967. *Die Sprache Von Sau in Ostafghanistan: Beiträge Zur Kenntnis Des Dardischen Phalûra.* Münchener Studien Zur Sprachwissenschaft, Beiheft [Supplement] M. Munich: Kitzinger in Kommission.

Comrie, Bernard. 2013. 'Alignment of Case Marking of Full Noun Phrases'. In *The World Atlas of Language Structures Online*, edited by Matthew S. Dryer and Martin Haspelmath. Leipzig: Max Planck Institute for Evolutionary Anthropology. <http://wals.info/chapter/98>.

——— 1978. 'Ergativity'. In *Syntactic Typology: Studies in the Phenomenology of Language*, edited by Winfred P. Lehmann. 329–94. Austin: University of Texas Press.

Croft, William. 2003. *Typology and Universals.* 2nd ed. Cambridge; New York: Cambridge University Press.

Degener, Almuth. 2008. *Shina-Texte aus Gilgit (Nord-Pakistan): Sprichwörter und Materialien zum Volksglauben, gesammelt von Mohammad Amin Zia.* Wiesbaden: Harrassowitz.

Dixon, Robert M. W. 2010. *Basic Linguistic Theory: Volume 1, Methodology.* Vol. 1. 3 vols. Oxford: Oxford University Press.

——— 1994. *Ergativity.* Cambridge: Cambridge University Press.

——— 1987. 'Studies in Ergativity: Introduction'. *Lingua* 71.1–4: 1–16. doi:10.1016/0024-3841(87)90065-9.

——— 1979. 'Ergativity'. *Language* 55.1: 59–138. doi:10.2307/412519.

Dryer, Matthew S. 2007. 'Clause Types'. In *Language Typology and Syntactic Description: Volume 1, Clause Structure*, edited by Timothy Shopen. 224–75. 2nd ed. Cambridge University Press.

Farrell, Patrick. 2005. *Grammatical Relations.* Oxford Surveys in Syntax and Morphology. Oxford: Oxford University Press.

Hook, Peter E. and Koul, Omkar N. 2004. 'Case as Agreement: Non-Nominative Subjects in Eastern Shina, Non-Dative Objects in Kashmiri and Poguli, and Labile Subjects in Kashmiri and Gujarai Intransitive Inceptives'. In *Non-Nominative Subjects. Vol. 1*, edited by Peri Bhaskararao and K. V. Subbarao. 213–25. Amsterdam; Philadelphia: John Benjamins Publishing Company.

Hook, Peter E. and Zia, Muhammad Amin. 2005. 'Searching for the Goddess: A Study of Sensory and Other Impersonal Causative Expressions in the Shina of Gilgit'. *The Yearbook of South Asian Languages and Linguistics* 2005: 165–88.

Jones, Eunice. 2009. *Evidentiality and Mirativity in Balti*. MA thesis. London: School of Oriental and African Studies, University of London.

Kohistani, Razwal and Schmidt, Ruth Laila. 2006. 'Shina in Contemporary Pakistan'. In *Lesser-Known Languages of South Asia, Status and Policies, Case Studies and Applications of Information Technology*, edited by Anju Saxena and Lars Borin. 137–60. Berlin; Boston: De Gruyter Mouton.

Koul, Omkar N. 2003. 'Kashmiri'. In *The Indo-Aryan Languages*, edited by George Cardona and Danesh Jain. 895–952. London: Routledge.

Lehr, Rachel. 2014. 'A Descriptive Grammar of Pashai: The Language and Speech Community of Darrai Nur'. PhD dissertation. Chicago: University of Chicago.

Liljegren, Henrik. 2016. 'A grammar of Palula'. *Studies in Diversity Linguistics* 8. Berlin: Language Science Press.

——— 2014. 'A Survey of Alignment Features in the Greater Hindukush with Special References to Indo-Aryan'. In *On Diversity and Complexity of Languages Spoken in Europe and North and Central Asia*, edited by Pirkko Suihkonen and Lindsay J. Whaley. 133–74. Amsterdam: John Benjamins Publishing Company. (Studies in Language Companion Series 164).

——— 2013. 'Notes on Kalkoti: A Shina Language with Strong Kohistani Influences'. *Linguistic Discovery* 11.1: 129–60. doi:10.1349/PS1.1537-0852.A.423.

——— 2010. 'Where Have All the Verbs Gone? On Verb Stretching and Semi-Words in Indo-Aryan Palula'. *Himalayan Linguistics* 9.1: 51–79.

Lubberger, Beate. 2014. *A Description and Analysis of Four Metarepresentation Markers of Indus Kohistani*. MA thesis. Grand Forks, North Dakota: University of North Dakota.

Lunsford, Wayne A. 2001. '*An Overview of Linguistic Structures in Torwali, a Language of Northern Pakistan*'. MA thesis. Texas: University of Texas at Arlington.

Masica, Colin P. 1991. *The Indo-Aryan Languages*. Cambridge; New York: Cambridge University Press.

Morgenstierne, Georg. 1973. *Indo-Iranian Frontier Languages. Vol. 3, The Pashai Language, 1, Grammar.* Instituttet for Sammenlignende Kulturforskning. Serie B, Skrifter, 0332-6217; 40:3:1. Oslo: Universitets-forleget.

Munshi, Sadaf. n.d. *A Grammatical Sketch of Hunza Burushaski*. Unpublished manuscript. <http://www.ltc.unt.edu/~sadafmunshi/Burushaski/language/grammatical_sketch.pdf>.

Payne, Thomas. 2006. *Exploring Language Structure: A Student's Guide*. Student edition. Cambridge, UK; New York: Cambridge University Press.

Perder, Emil. 2013. *A Grammatical Description of Dameli*. PhD dissertation. Stockholm: Stockholm University.

Radloff, Carla F. 1992. 'The Dialects of Shina'. In *Sociolinguistic Survey of Northern Pakistan Vol. 2: Languages of the Northern Areas*, edited by Peter C. Backstrom and Carla F. Radloff. 89–203, 301–408. Islamabad: National Institute of Pakistani Studies and Summer Institute of Linguistics.

——— and Shakil, Shakil Ahmad. 1998. *Folktales in the Shina of Gilgit: Text, Grammatical Analysis and Commentary.* Islamabad: National Institute of Pakistan Studies and Summer Institute of Linguistics.

Read, Alfred F. C. 1934. *Balti Grammar.* London: James G. Forlong Fund.

Rehman, Khawaja A. 2011. 'Ergativity in Kundal Shahi, Kashmiri and Hindko'. In *Himalayan Languages and Linguistics: Studies in Phonology, Semantics, Morphology and Syntax,* edited by Mark Turin and Bettina Zeisler. Leiden: Brill Academic Publishers.

Robson, Barbara and Tegey, Habibullah. 2010. 'Pashto'. In *The Iranian Languages,* edited by Gernot Windfuhr. 721–72. London; New York: Routledge.

Schmidt, Ruth Laila. 2004. 'A Grammatical Comparison of Shina Dialects'. In *Himalayan Languages: Past and Present,* edited by Anju Saxena. Berlin: Walter de Gruyter.

——— 1999. *Urdu, an Essential Grammar.* London; New York: Routledge.

——— and Kaul, Vijay Kumar. 2010. 'A grammatical sketch of Guresi Shina'. In *Anantam Sastram: Indological and Linguistic Studies in Honour of Bertil Tikkanen,* edited by Klaus Karttunen. 195–214. Studia Orientalia 108. Helsinki: Finnish Oriental Society.

——— and Kohistani, Razwal. 2008. *A Grammar of the Shina Language of Indus Kohistan.* Wiesbaden: Harrassowitz. (Beiträge Zur Kenntnis Südasiatischer Sprachen and Literaturen 17).

Sharma, Devidatta. 1998. *Tribal Languages of Ladakh. Part One: A Concise Grammar and Dictionary of Brok-Skad.* New Delhi: Mittal Publications. (Studies in Tibeto-Himalayan Languages 6).

Siewierska, Anna. 2011. 'Alignment of Verbal Person Marking'. In *The World Atlas of Language Structures Online,* edited by Matthew S. Dryer and Martin Haspelmath. Munich: Max Planck Digital Library. <http://wals.info/chapter/100>.

Strand, Richard F. 2001. 'The Tongues of Peristân. Appendix 1'. In *Gates of Peristan: History, Religion and Society in the Hindu Kush,* edited by Alberto M. Cacopardo and Augusto S. Cacopardo. 251–7. Rome: IsIAO. (Reports and Memoirs 5).

Willson, Stephen R. 1999. *Basic Burushaski Vocabulary.* Islamabad: National Institute of Pakistan Studies and Summer Institute of Linguistics.

Zeisler, Bettina. 2004. *Relative Tense and Aspectual Values in Tibetan Languages: A Comparative Study.* Berlin: Mouton de Gruyter.

Zia, Muhammad Amin. 1986. *Shina Primer and Grammar (in Urdu and Shina).* Gilgit: Zia Publications.

13

Gilgiti Shina Voice, Valence, and the Detransitivizer *-íij*[1]

Carla F. Radloff and Thomas E. Payne[2]

1. INTRODUCTION

The term 'valence' (or 'valency') in linguistics can refer to a semantic notion or a grammatical notion (Comrie 1989: 174). Semantic valence refers to the number of required participants in a conceptual 'scene'. For example, a scene describable as EATING must have two participants—an 'eater' and an 'eaten thing.' Without both those participants an event cannot felicitously be described as 'eating.' Therefore an event of eating has a semantic valence of two. However, an event describable as JUMPING requires only one participant, therefore it has a semantic valence of one. Syntactic valence, on the other hand, is a property of verbs or clauses and refers to the number of core arguments expressed in a particular grammatical construction. For example, a clause such

[1] Gilgiti Shina is spoken in the northern, mountainous area of Pakistan in the watershed of the Gilgit River particularly around Gilgit town. It is a major language in the political division of Pakistan now called Gilgit-Baltistan, along with the Burushaski, Balti, and Wakhi languages. Other major varieties of Shina are spoken in Astore, in parts of Baltistan, and along the Indus River, including Chilas and Kohistan. Gilgit town is the centre for trade, education, and government for Gilgit-Baltistan. Estimates of the total population of Shina speakers vary from some 500,000 (Radloff 1992) to over a million (Kohistani & Schmidt 2006). Shina belongs to the Dardic branch of Indo-Aryan. See Schmidt & Kohistani (2008) for a description of the grammar of Kohistani Shina, spoken in valleys on the east side of Indus Kohistan.

[2] Special thanks to Shakil Ahmad Shakil of Gilgit, a mother tongue speaker of Shina, for his input over the years.

as 'I already ate' has only one core argument, 'I', therefore it has a syntactic valence of one. The scene it evokes, however, still has two participants—I must have eaten something. However, speakers may omit reference to the eaten thing if it is not relevant to the particular communicative task at hand. We can say then that the construction 'I already ate' is a valence decreased construction in that it expresses a situation with a semantic valence of two using a construction with a syntactic valence of one. In contrast to English, many languages require special verbal morphology in order to register this mismatch between semantic and grammatical valence. Valence decreasing and increasing constructions have been discussed extensively in the typological literature, e.g. by Comrie 1989, Payne 1997, Dixon and Aikhenvald 2000, and others. In this paper we will assume this literature as background.

Gilgiti Shina has two primary derivational suffixes that adjust the valence of a verb—a valence increasing suffix *-aré*, 'CAUS', and a general 'detransitivizing' (i.e. valence decreasing) suffix *-íij* 'DTR'. These derivational suffixes attach directly to a verb root to form a new stem.[3] The new stem formed with *-aré* 'CAUS' is always a 'post-accenting' transitive stem; while the new stem formed with *-íij* 'DTR' is always an accented intransitive stem.[4]

As we will see below, the detransitivising suffix seems to have a different, inchoative, function when appearing on certain stative verbs. However we consider 'detransitivizing' to be the basic, or overarching, function of this suffix for two reasons. First, it is very

---

[3] See *Radloff and Shakil (1998: 183–8)* for a detailed description of the formation of a finite verb. In Radloff and Shakil (1998: 116), this -íij 'dtr' suffix was referred to as 'pass', the passive marker (see also Bailey 1924, Buddruss 1993, Degener 2008, etc.). The term *detransitive* is adopted here to highlight the wide variety of functions this suffix fulfils, including passives.

[4] Gilgiti Shina verbs can be classified as accented or post-accenting. These two types are differentiated by the final sound of the stem—stems ending with a consonant or accented *á* or *í* are accented stems and retain their accent when inflected. Stems ending in accented mid-vowels *é* or *ó* are post-accenting stems, since they lose the final vowel when inflected, leaving the accent to fall on the syllable following the stem. The form of inflectional suffixes is influenced by the accented or post-accenting nature of the stem. Grammatically transitive and intransitive verb stems can be either accented or post-accenting. Inflections and their morphophonemic processes are treated more fully in Radloff 1999: 89–107.

productive in the detransitivizing function, occurring with almost any grammatically transitive verb that involves an AGENT acting on an UNDERGOER. Its grammatical effect in such cases is to eliminate one of the arguments. In many cases it also affects the *Aktionsart* of the situation by converting an action-process into a process (terms from Chafe 1970, adapted from Vendler 1957). Second, this suffix is not as productive on intransitive verbs, occurring only with a relatively small number of verbs that describe semantic states. However, as we will see, there is semantic overlap between these functions in that with both types of verbs the detransitivizer creates a stem that describes a process. In other words, this is not a case of homophony—two suffixes that have the same phonological form but entirely different meanings, but rather polysemy, one suffix that has different effects depending on the construction in which it appears.

Although the functions of the suffix *-íiǰ* differ depending on the stem on which it appears, its structural shape and behaviour are identical in all contexts. For this reason, in the following sections we will first describe the structure of detransitive verbs of all types (section 2), and then the main functions of *-íiǰ* with transitive (section 3.1) and intransitive stems (section 3.2). Finally in section 4 we describe the deployment of detransitive constructions in the voice system of Gilgiti Shina.

2. STRUCTURE OF DETRANSITIVE VERBS

Because the detransitivising suffix *-íiǰ* 'DTR' carries its own inherent accent, the resulting stem is accented. In *imperfective aspect*, for example, the accent remains on the stem when the tense agreement markers are added, as exemplified in (1). The transitive verb *taré* 'cross' shows the inflection patterns.[5]

(1) Formation of imperfective aspect, using *taríiǰ* 'be crossed' and *-an* 'PRES3sm'

Stem	+	**Tense Agreement**	=	**Finite form**
taríiǰ	+	*-an*	=	*taríiǰan*

[5] *taré* 'cross', a transitive verb, occurs in all these forms in the database.

A few example verb stems and their detransitivized forms inflected for imperfective aspect are given in (2), using a variety of tense agreement markers. Notice that normal morphophonemic changes (including loss of stem accent, shortening of stem long vowel, coalescing of final mid-vowel, assimilation of final *í*) happen to each verb stem as it joins with *-íiǰ*.[6]

(2)

Stem	Gloss	Detransitive Imperfective	Gloss
Sané	'build'	*saníiǰ-anan*	'they are built'
Phayé	'break'	*phayíiǰ-as*	'he was being broken'
Paáš	'see'	*pašíiǰ-ee*	'you will be seen'
Laáy	'find'	*layíiǰ-ey*	's/he will be found'
Chibí	'keep'	*čhibíiǰ-anet*	'you all are kept'
Kurí	'strengthen'	*kuríiǰ-amus*	'I am strengthened'

In *perfective aspect*, a perfective valence marker is joined to the detransitivized verb stem, and then a perfective tense agreement marker. Detransitivized stems formed with *-íiǰ* take the valence markers *-d* and *-íl* in perfective aspect.[7] The essential parts of such a verb in perfective aspect are illustrated in (3), again using *taré* 'cross'.

(3) Formation of perfective aspect, using *taríiǰ* 'be crossed', valence markers, and *–u* 'SIMP3sm'

Stem +	Valence-Perfective	+	Tense Agreement	= Finite form	Gloss
Taríiǰ +	*-d*	+	*-u*	= *taríidu*	'it was crossed'
Taríiǰ +	*-íl*	+	*-u*	= *tariílu*	'he crossed (intransitive)'

Regular morphophonemic processes occur when these perfective valence markers are suffixed to the detransitivized stem, just as with any other accented stem—the final consonant of the stem is dropped when the valence marker is added. Thus, *-íiǰ* becomes *-íi* and joins

---

[6] Morphophonemic changes are fully described in Radloff (1999).

[7] Perfective valence markers are abbreviated 'PFI' for intransitive and 'PFT' for transitive.

with *-d* to become *-íid, taríidu.* On the other hand, *-íl* has an inherent accent, so not only does *-íiǰ* lose its final consonant in that case, but also its accent and the long vowel. Thus, *-íiǰ* becomes *-i* and joins with *-íl* to become *-iíl, tariílu.* These processes are summarized in (4).

(4)	*-íiǰ +-d*	→	*-íi +-d*	→	*-íid*		
	-íiǰ +-íl	→	*-ii+-íl*	→	*-i+-íl*	→	*-iíl*

A few examples of detransitivized verbs in perfective aspect are shown in (5).

(5)

Stem	Gloss	Detransitive Perfective	Gloss
saníiǰ	'be built'	*saníi-d-e*	'they were built'
phayíiǰ	'be broken'	*phayíi-d-u*	'he was broken'
pašíiǰ	'be seen'	*pašíi-d-iee*	'you were seen'
layíiǰ	'be found'	*layíi-d-i*	'she was found'
chibíiǰ	'be kept'	*čhibíi-d-et*	'you all were kept'
kuríiǰ	'be strengthened'	*kuri-íl-is*	'I strengthened (intrans.)'

3. FUNCTIONS OF DETRANSITIVIZATION

As noted above, the effect of the detransitivizing process on the meaning of semantically transitive and intransitive verbs is varied. The effect on semantically transitive stems will be examined first, then the effect on semantically intransitive stems.

3.1 DETRANSITIVIZATION AND TRANSITIVE VERBS

When a Gilgiti Shina speaker uses the detransitivizer *-íiǰ* 'DTR' to reduce the valence of a given transitive verb, the apparent intent is to change the perspective of that verb within the context of the sentence. The verb is *detransitivized,* that is, one or the other of its arguments is downplayed, thereby bringing increased attention to the other argument.[8] This could apply either to the central participant of

[8] *Downplay, upgrade,* and *perspectivize* are terms used by linguists to describe such processes; see, for example, Fillmore 1977, Payne 1997: 219ff.

the action (the subject of the active verb) or the other main participant of the action (the object of the active verb). If the central participant is downplayed it is either put into an oblique role with a postposition or not mentioned at all. At the same time the other participant (sometimes referred to in a general way as the UNDERGOER) is upgraded to subject and it is in the unmarked absolutive case. In this occurrence, the detransitive suffix is interpreted as expressing passive voice.

Alternatively, if the UNDERGOER is downplayed, it is then put into an oblique role with a postposition or not mentioned, and the upgraded participant appears in the absolutive case. The resulting structure can then be understood as antipassive voice.

Further, if the UNDERGOER is upgraded to subject (in the absolutive case) but with no outside controller/agent implied, the use of the *-íiǰ* suffix in this case can be interpreted as expressing middle voice. This upgraded UNDERGOER can also be understood to be controlling the action.

In addition, some uses of the *-íiǰ* suffix remain ambiguous between passive or middle voice. In such cases there may be an unnamed controller off the scene (passive), or the UNDERGOER as subject both controls and undergoes the action (middle). Since it is not necessary or even possible to conclude one way or the other, the interpretation remains ambiguous. Examples with the same verb in different contexts will help illustrate the phenomenon that the detransitivizer *-íiǰ* is one form that has various functions, depending on the intent of the speaker.

In addition to these grammaticalized effects involving the argument structure of the clause, the detransitivizer often changes the *Aktionsart* (inherent aspect) of the situation from an action process to a simple process (Chafe 1970). For example, a middle construction is a construction in which an UNDERGOER undergoes a processural change, quite independently of any distinct act on the part of an AGENT. This secondary effect of detransitivization is relevant to the extended usage of the detransitivizer with inherently intransitive verbs, as described in section 3.2.

Example (6) presents an underived transitive verb in future tense, *taróon* 'we will cross'. The subject of that transitive verb, *be-s* 'we-ERG', appropriately carries the ergative marker. The UNDERGOER (object) is in the unmarked absolutive case, *gamúk* 'glacier'.

(6) *be-s*   *keé*   *khéen*   *gamúk*   **tar-óon?**
     we-ERG   which   time   glacier   cross-FUT1p

'What time will we cross the glacier?' (Hiroshima 12.8)

In (7) the perspective of this transitive verb has changed—the
UNDERGOER of the action, *ẓingáati* 'ravines', is now subject of the
verb. *taré* 'cross' has been *detransitivized* with *-íiǰ* 'DTR' (in bold) and is
in perfective aspect with *-d* as the perfective valence marker—*taríide*
'they were crossed'. This UNDERGOER as subject is in the unmarked
absolutive case (not ergative) because the verb is now intransitive.
The AGENT—which is *be* 'we', gleaned from the context—has been
downplayed to the extent it is no longer mentioned. If it were, it would
be marked with a postposition such as *-ǰo* 'from', as in *asóo-ǰo* 'us-from'.

(7) *šong-beé*   *ri*   *ẓingáat-i*   *tar-íi-d-e*
     care-become.CONJP   those   ravine-PL   cross-**DTR**-PFI-SIMP3p

'Carefully those ravines were crossed.' (May1998 1.57)

In example (8) the perspective of the detransitivized verb is again
different. Here the centrality of the AGENT has been enhanced by
downplaying the UNDERGOER; no mention is made of what exactly
was crossed. The subject is in absolutive case and the *-íiǰ* on the verb
accomplishes the detransitivization.

(8) *ek_ek_beé*   *be*   *púur-e*   *tar-i-íl-es*
     one.by.one   we   all-PL   cross-**DTR**-PFI-SIMP1p

'One by one we all crossed.' (Hiroshima 16.8)

In imperfective aspect all the detransitivized verbs are formed
identically with *-íiǰ*, regardless of the speaker's intent. In perfective
aspect, however, in addition to *-íiǰ*, the choice of perfective valence
marker appears to give some indication of the speaker's intent. In
general, perfective valence markers are lexically determined for
intransitive verbs.[9] For these detransitivized verb stems formed with

---

[9] Schmidt (2002) cites Turner who states that the variety of perfective valence
markers for intransitive verbs comes from Middle Indian consonant groupings
occurring in the early form of the verbs.

-íij̆, however, an utterance interpreted as passive voice will always use the perfective valence marker *-d*. Utterances interpreted as middle or antipassive voice will often use *-íl*, but also *-d*. Because the perfective valence marker *-d* can be used when expressing passive, middle, or antipassive voice, the choice of perfective valence marker by the speaker is not consistently predictable. The speaker chooses which argument to upgrade or downplay when using the detransitivizer *-íij̆*; the actual voice manifested is a matter of interpretation.

Example (7), above, then, is interpreted as expressing *passive* voice, since the UNDERGOER (the former object of the verb) is upgraded to subject of the verb (while still undergoing the action), and the AGENT, the former subject of the transitive verb, is downplayed by not being mentioned. This is how passive voice is recognized—the subject is the UNDERGOER of the action of the verb, and the more gentive participant is downplayed.

Example (8) (also above), on the other hand, is interpreted as expressing *antipassive* voice, since the centrality of the agentive participant is enhanced by downplaying the UNDERGOER, not mentioning it in this case. The stem *taríij̆* is intransitive, and the upgraded AGENT is now the subject in absolutive case, doing the action which is no longer transitive in form. This is how antipassive voice is recognized.

Example (9) (below) is interpreted as expressing *middle* voice. The transitive verb *palé* 'spread' has been detransitivized through joining with *-íij̆*. The subject, *burgalíik* 'some clouds', of the now-intransitive verb undergoes the process of *spreading*. Here there is no thought of an AGENT somewhere offstage controlling things; the clouds are spreading, both undergoing and controlling the process. This is the difference between this example (9) and the passive example in (7) :in the earlier example the sense is passive, since there are unseen AGENTs controlling the crossing of the ravines. Here there is no controller other than the clouds themselves; it is middle voice.

(9)	*buúr_báyaj̆o*	*kíṇ-e*	*burgalíik*	*pal-**íij̆**-anas.*
	from.sunset	black-PL	some.clouds	spread-**DTR**-PIMFV3p

'Since the setting of the sun some black clouds were spreading.' (Rainy 2.6)

In section 4, additional detransitivized examples are given; some can be interpreted as expressing passive voice, some antipassive or middle voice, and some remain ambiguous in their interpretation. The function of *-íiǰ* is accomplished, however, no matter what the interpretation of the ensuing voice: the transitive verb has been detransitivized and its perspective changed.

3.2 Detransitivization and Intransitive Verbs

Perhaps surprisingly, *-íiǰ* occurs with some intransitive verbs. A class of *stative* intransitive stems joins with the detransitivizer *-íiǰ* 'DTR' to form new stems that can be labeled *inchoative* verbs. The function of *-íiǰ* in this case is not grammatical detransitivization, since the single argument is not eliminated. Rather, the subject of such a stative verb might be said to be *in* a certain state of being, whereas the subject of its inchoative counterpart *enters into* that state of being. In other words, the stative verb describes a semantic state, whereas the inchoative counterpart describes a process. Though the detransitivizing *-íiǰ* 'DTR' marker is the same as that which appears on transitive verbs, and the verb forms are structured in the same fashion, the meaning and effect of *-íiǰ* on an intransitive verb are totally different. The detransitivizing function is basic because it is much more productive than the inchoative use. The inchoative function only occurs in a subset of stative verbs, whereas the canonical detransitive function occurs with pretty much any grammatically transitive verb.

Example stative–inchoative pairs from the database are given in (10). [10]

(10)

Stative Stem	Gloss	Inchoative Stem	Gloss
galató	'be tangled'	*galatíiǰ*	'become tangled'
baskó	'be excess'	*baskíiǰ*	'become excess'
banaló	'be numb'	*banalíiǰ*	'become numb'
agayó	'be greedy'	*agayíiǰ*	'become greedy'

[10] These verb pairs are a relatively stable feature of Gilgiti Shina; Bailey (1924: 64) highlights such pairs, noting the form with *-íiǰ* is 'passive in form', but not a 'true passive'.

(10)

Stative Stem	Gloss	Inchoative Stem	Gloss
čhutó	'be late'	čhutíiǰ	'become late'
haliẓó	'be pale'	haliẓíiǰ	'become pale'
báaš	'be played'	bašíiǰ	'sound, ring'
noóṭh	'be amused'	noṭhíiǰ	'become amused'
saár	'move on'	saríiǰ	'begin to move', 'get going'

A constellation of features characterizes these stative–inchoative verb pairs: (i) the inchoative form is used in perfective or imperfective aspects, while the stative form only appears in imperfective aspect[11]; (ii) in perfective aspect the inchoative form almost exclusively uses -íl as the perfective valence marker; (iii) for many such verbs, the stative form is rarely, if ever, used; and (iv) some of these pairs have a transitive counterpart, while others use causative formations to express transitivity.

It must be borne in mind that the change in meaning indicated in the examples above in (10) is only an approximation. Any overt shift in meaning with the change from stative to inchoative is not easy to grasp. The term *inchoative*—entering into a state—has been chosen to reflect what appears to be the overarching function that works out in various ways in different contexts. Nevertheless, much understanding of these 'detransitivized intransitives' can be gleaned from exploring how they are used. The following paragraphs examine some characteristic trends.[12]

---

[11] One could surmise that in the perfective, the inchoative form is used since the completed result of being and becoming is realized, the subject is in that state, fully entered. This could be explained the other way around—the inchoative verbs express a process that results in a change of state. Such processes can be completed, therefore perfective aspect can be applied to inchoative verbs. Stative verbs, on the other hand, do not imply a process that can be completed. Therefore, perfective aspect cannot be applied to bare stative verbs (thanks to Joan Baart p.c., for this observation).

[12] As might be observed, a few verbs are included in this class of intransitives that are not stative in their meaning, *per se*, yet their counterparts with -íiǰ could be said to express the process of entering into a state. For example, the counterpart of *saár-an* 'he moves on' could be said to imply 'entering into movement'—*saríiǰ-an* 'he begins to move, gets going'. With a few other verb pairs it is difficult to discern

Basic Intransitive–Inchoative Verb Pairs

Intransitive verbs that have inchoative counterparts with *-íiǰ* do not occur in perfective aspect. The vast majority of these verbs describe states or properties, though there are a few that describe intransitive actions (see below). Another characteristic of intransitive verbs that occur with *-íiǰ* is that in perfective aspect the preferred valence marker is *-íl*. Four example verb pairs in (11) to (14) illustrate these characteristics: the first two pairs, (11 a and b) and (12 a and b), show stative verbs with their inchoative imperfective counterparts, and then their common inchoative perfective forms. The third example pair (13 a and b) illustrates a stative verb which always occurs with the detransitivizer *-íiǰ* in perfective aspect, but no imperfective inchoative counterpart has been noted. Finally the pair in (14) illustrate a verb appearing in the stative imperfective, present tense (14 a), and two instances of the same root in the inchoative perfective and stative imperfective, future tense (14 b):

(11) a. Stative imperfective

páae	***banal-éen***	*theé*	*khirí*	*beyoók*	*ar_bámis*
feet	be.numb-FUT3p	(thinking)	down	to.sit	afraid.become.PRES1sf

'I'm afraid to sit on the floor because my feet will numb up.' (August 99 1.10)

b. Inchoative imperfective

mey	*páae*	***banal-íiǰ-an***
my	feet	be.numb-**DTR**-FUT3p

'My feet will become numb.' (August 99 1.10)

---

a difference in meaning, as with *baášan* versus *bašíiǰan*, where both carry the meaning 'it is played, it sounds', unless the form with *-íiǰ* gives more of a middle or reflexive sense. These 'quasi-stative' pairs are the minority, however; the vast majority portray a state of being as is shown.

(12) a. Common inchoative perfective

ẓakalé	*neé,*	*mey*	*gáaṇ*	***banal-i-íl-in***
pull.IMP2s	not	my	leg	be.numb-**DTR**-PFI-NEARP3sf

'Don't pull (on me), my leg has become numb (fallen asleep).' (Distant 3.44)

b. Stative imperfective

gaṛíi	*maṣoó*	***kač-éen***
watch.of	sound	be.near-PRES3sm

'The sound of the watch is near.' (August 99 1.15)

(13) a. Inchoative imperfective

šudáarioo	*maṣoó*	*ga*	*háhaa*	***kač-íij-in***
children.of	sound	and	laughter	be.near-**DTR**-PRES3sf

'The children's sound and laughter draws near.' (Distant 5.18)

b. Common inchoative perfective

qurbáanay	*eétay*	*déezi*	*ga*	***kač-i-íl-es***
sacrifice.of	Eid.of	days	also	be.near-**DTR**-PFI-REMP3p

'The days of Qurbaani Eid (festival) had also drawn near.' (Chaagun 2.2)

(14) a. Stative imperfective

phaṛáki	*bam*	*theé*	***bij-ámis***
bald.F	become-FUT1s	(thinking)	be.afraid-PRES1sf

'I'm afraid I'll become bald.' (Finess 1.185)

b. Inchoative perfective and stative imperfective

khudáaǰo	*naá*	***biǰ-i-íl-u***	*to*	*ǰagóǰo*	*ǰéek*	***biǰ-éy?***
God.from	not	be.afraid-**DTR**-PFI-SIMP3sm	so	people. from	what	be.afraid-FUT3s

'If he did not become afraid from (of) God, what (how much) will he fear from (of) people?' (Finess 1.140)

The examples in (15) show the verb ***saár*** 'to move on' and its perfective detransitive forms. This is one of the few intransitive action verbs that occur with *-íiǰ*. In the database, three of the four occurrences of this verb in perfective aspect use the perfective valence marker *-íl*. Interestingly, though, the perfective valence marker *-d* is used once on this verb and that in the same paragraph of a text where *-íl* is also used on another occurrence of the same verb. Although it is difficult for a Shina speaker to articulate why one form is chosen over another, that is, what nuance of meaning is intended, the vast majority of perfective inchoative forms used the *-íl* marker as opposed to *-d*. Example (15 b) illustrates the occasional use of perfective valence marker *-d* on an intransitive action verb:

(15) a. Imperfective

muçhoóṭ	***saár-on-aa***
ahead	move.on-FUT1p-Q

'Shall we move ahead?' (April 1997 1.14)

b. Perfective inceptive

ro	*thuriám*	*theé*	*muçhoóṭ*	***sar-íi-d-us***	*akií*	…
he	loose.FUT1s	(intent)	ahead	move.on-**DTR**-PFI-REMP3sm	emph	

'Just as (Tephuur) had (begun to) move to loose him …' (Beraam 10.2)

c. Perfective inceptive

tephúur	*se*	*múti*	*ẓa~w*	*tham*	*theé*
Tephuur	ERG	other	blow	do.FUT1s	say.CONJP

muçhoóṭ	***sar-i-íl-us***	*akií*	*akií…*
ahead	move.on-dtr-pfi-remp	3sm	emph

'Just as Tephuur had (begun to) move ahead to give another blow …' (Beraam 10.5)

INCHOATIVE VERBS WITH RARELY USED STATIVE COUNTERPART

As introduced above, some concepts appear to be better expressed with an inchoative verb form, since no stative counterpart for them has been observed.[13] While this group of verbs is not large, still it is interesting that they always seem to be used with the detransitivizer *-íij* and appear to express entering into a state. Examples of such verbs are presented in (16). A characteristic of these verbs is that in perfective aspect they always occur with *-íl* as the valence marker.

(16) a.

wey	***čuruw-i-íl-u***	*to*	*bawí*	*ají*	*phat_th-óon*
water	drain-**DTR**-PFI-SIMP3sm	so	utensil-PL	above	leave.do-FUT1p

'When the water becomes drained (drains off) we'll put the dishes up.' (Feb 03 1.1)

b.

á~špo	*ga*	*dóoney*	*pon,*	*á~špo*	***ṣum-íij-an***	*dóono-s*	*tar-éen*
horse	and	ox.of	path	horse	tire-**DTR**-PRES3sm	OX-ERG	cross-PRES3sm

'Horse and ox's path (the Milky Way): the horse grows tired, the ox crosses it.' (April 1997 1.17)

c.

ek	*čhak*	*čalbuǰií*	*čal*	*baráam*	*batháariǰo*	***uth-i-íl-u***
one	day	morning	early	Beraam	bedding.from	rise-**DTR**-PFI-SIMP3sm

'One day, early in the morning, Beraam rose up from bed.' (Revised Husan 16.4)

[13] Stative forms of these verbs can be elicited, but have not been observed in actual use.

d. *čayná* *çhíilo* *loóko* ***murguṭ-íiǰ-an***
China cloth quick wrinkle-**DTR**-PRES3sm
'Chinese cloth quickly becomes wrinkled.' (Finess 1.105)

e. *paár_beé* *akií* *hagáarek* ***gum-íiǰ-as***
over.there.being EMPH a.fire smoulder-**DTR**-PIMFV3sm
'Just over there a fire was smouldering.' (Blackberry 1.12)

INCHOATIVE VERBS DERIVED FROM ADJECTIVES

Many inchoative verbs generally do not appear in stative form in the database, but appear to be derived from adjectives. A sampling of such verbs is presented in (17), and examples of their use follow in (18).

(17) Inchoative stems that appear to be derived from adjectives

Adjective	Gloss	Inchoative Stem	Gloss
ẓígo	'long'	*ẓigíiǰ*	'lengthen'
ašaáto	'thin'	*ašatíiǰ*	'grow thin'
yúlo	'different'	*yulíiǰ*	'become separate'
uyáno	'hungry'	*uyaníiǰ*	'become hungry'
káči	'near'	*kačíiǰ*	'draw near'
Níilo	'green, unripe'	*nilíiǰ*	'sprout up'
šatiílo	'strong'	*satíiǰ*	'become victorious'
básko	'more'	*baskíiǰ*	'become excess'
halíẓo	'yellow'	*haliẓíiǰ*	'become pale'
čhuút	'late'	*čhutíiǰ*	'become late'
agáao	'greedy'	*agayíiǰ*	'become greedy'
duúr	'far'	*duríiǰ*	'become distant'

Apparent adjective-derived inchoative verbs in context:

(18) a. *ané* *báali* *ṭak* *theé*
this rope fasten do-CONJP

khíṭe	*wátoo*	*to*	*re*
downwards	come-PFI-SIMP2sm	so	it

akoṣaá	***ẓig-iǰ-ií***	*to …*
itself	long-**DTR**-CONJP	so

'When you tie this rope and come down the rope itself lengthens and so ….' (Revised Husan 26.3)

b.

sókoti	*theé*	*theé*	*básko_ga*	***ašat-i-íl-u***
worries	do-CONJP	do-CONJP	even.more	thin-**DTR**-PFI-SIMP3sm

'He kept worrying over it and became even thinner.' (Bald Son 5.1)

c.

khéenekeǰo	*siríṣ*	***yul-i-íl-i***	*to*	*ho…*
after.some.time	joint.family	separate-**DTR**-PFI-SIMP3sf	so	then

'If after some time the joint family becomes separated, so then …' (Engagement 5.8)

d.

kutúri	*bódi*	***uyan-i-íl-iš***
bitch	very-fem	hungry-**DTR**-PFI-REMP3sm

'The mother dog had become very hungry.' (Hopoti 7.5)

e.

šudáarioo	*maṣoó*	*ga*	*háhaa*	***kač-íiǰ-in***
children.of	sound	and	laughter	near-**DTR**-PRES3sf

'The sound and laughing of the children draws near.' (Distant 5.18)

f.

ṣingáayasaa~t	*akií*	*kóṇok*	*ga*	***nil-íi-d-us***
bush-with	EMPH	thorn-INDEF	also	green-**DTR**-PFI-REMP3sm

'Just near the blackberry bush a thorn had sprouted (lit: 'become green').' (Blackberry 1.7)

g. *buláar* *koó* ***šat-i-íl-e***
polo-in who victorious-**DTR**-PFI-SIMP3p
'Who was victorious in polo? (i.e. who won?)' (April 1997)

h. *áẓeǰ* *beé* *tom* ***bask-íiǰ-an***
rain.on be-CONJP plants excessive-**DTR**-FUT3p
'Because of the rains plants will become excessive (grow a lot).' (August 99 1.7)

i. *aš_balá* *wey_ǰuláap* *kayáakek* *bask-i-íl-un*
nowadays diarrhea as.much.as excessive-**DTR**-PFI-NEARP3sm

ayáakek *yar* *neé* *asúu*
so.much before not he.was
'Nowadays, as much as (infectious) diarrhea has become excessive, before it was not so.' (Children's 1.1)

3.3 Transitive/Causative Counterparts to Inchoative Verbs

Occasionally an inchoative verb needs to be expressed in a transitive sense. Generally the causative[14] is used for this purpose, though some inchoative verbs have unmarked transitive counterparts. The examples below have causative counterparts: (19 a) shows an inchoative verb and (19 b) its causative counterpart; (20 a) shows an intransitive verb, (20 b) its perfective inchoative form, and (20 c) its causative counterpart.

(19) a. *dúu* *sáal* *geé* *ri*
two year go.CONJP those

[14] The suffix *-aré* 'CAUS' is joined to the verb stem to form the causative. The resulting stem is post-accenting.

ẓáare	***manoç-i-íl-e***
brothers	reconcile-**DTR**-PFI-SIMP3p

'After two years those brothers became reconciled ....' (August 99 1.11)

b.	*sarbisá-s*	*ho*	*ro*	***manoç-ar-eég-i***
	Sarbisa-ERG	then	he	reconcile-**CAUS**-PFT-SIMP3sf

'Then Sarbisa made him reconcile (to her demands).' (Beraam 12.6)

(20)	a.	*šú~ek*	*khéenek*	*résey*	*phatú*	***çoóṭ-an***
		dog.INDEF	some.time	it.of	behind	run.about-PRES3sm

'A dog runs after it for a while.' (Distant 3.22)

b.	*á~špok*	*šuwaáraṇer*	*huṇé_kheré*	***çoṭ-i-íl-u***
	horse.INDEF	in.polo.ground	back.forth	run.about-**DTR**-PFI-SIMP3sm

'A horse ran back and forth in the polo ground.' (Revised Husan 5.5)

c.	*akheér*	*baráam*	*šazadá-s*	*akií*	*ro*	***çoṭ-ar-eég-u***
	finally	Beraam	prince-ERG	self	he	run.about-**CAUS**-PFT-SIMP3sm

'Finally Prince Beraam himself made him run (chased him).' (Revised Husan 5.9)

The intransitive verbs in (21) and (22) have transitive counterparts, with no causative marker: the verb in (21 a) has both an inchoative (21 b) and transitive (21 c) counterpart. Similarly, the verb in (22) also has an inchoative form (though, like the other non-stative verbs in this section, it does not have a clear inchoative meaning) shown in (22 a), and a transitive counterpart (22 b):

(21) a. Intransitive

duúr	*dáṇik*	*ga*	***báaš-in***
far	some.music	also	be.played-PRES3sf

'Far away some music also is playing.' (Distant 7.32)

b. Inchoative imperfective

ṭelíi	***baš-íij-in***
bell	be.played-**DTR**-PRES3sf

'The bell sounds (rings).' (August 99 1.16)

c. Transitive

wakáar	*se*	*tarúy*	*míṣṭi*	***baš-éen***
Waqar	ERG	flute	good	play-PRES3sm

'Waqar plays the flute nicely.' (Finess 1.122)

(22) a. Inchoative perfective

ǰaháaz	*se*	*tharí*	*deé*	*deé*	***biṣam-i-íl-i***
plane	ERG	flights	having. given	having. given	land-**DTR**-PFI-SIMP3sf

'The plane flew and flew and then landed.' (August 99 1.21)

b. Transitive

ro-s	*ǰaháaz*	***biṣam-eég-u***
he-ERG	plane	land-PFT-SIMP3sm

'He landed the plane.' (November 1997 1.4)

In summary, when the detransitivizer *-íij* is suffixed to a particular, lexically determined sub-class of intransitive verbs, the meaning usually shifts to entering into a state, or beginning an action. These derived stems are here called inchoative verbs, since inchoative means 'entering into' or 'beginning' a state. Such verbs require the detransitivizer in order to appear in perfective aspect. This makes semantic sense, since a state is inherently imperfective, and therefore is incompatible with perfective aspect, which implies the completion of a process. Some of these verbs appear to occur only in the inchoative form with -*íij̃*, while still others appear to be derived from adjectives.

4. EXPRESSIONS OF VOICE THROUGH DETRANSITIVATION

As established above, there are no specific structural characteristics that distinguish passive from antipassive and middle voice in Gilgiti Shina—they are all expressed by the one verb suffix -*íij̃* 'DTR'. In imperfective aspect they are all formed identically with -*íij̃*. In perfective aspect, however, the choice of valence marker appears to give some indication of the speaker's intent. An utterance interpreted as passive voice will always use the perfective valence marker -*d*. Utterances interpreted as middle or antipassive voice will often use -*íl*, but may also use -*d*.

4.1 PASSIVE VOICE

The interpretation of passive voice is most clearly made when the downplayed participant is mentioned in an oblique role. In the following examples, the downplayed participant appears with a postposition and the other argument has been upgraded to subject of the detransitivized verb. In example (23) the downplayed participants are marked with the dative -*ṭ*, which is the most common way to include an EXPERIENCER or RECIPIENT in a passive construction. In (24) other postpositions are used for this purpose, and in (25) the downplayed participant (an AGENT in these examples) is not mentioned at all. In all of the following examples, the postpositions and the detransitivizer are shown in boldface.

EXPERIENCERS/RECIPIENTS downplayed with -*ṭ* 'DAT':

(23) a. *tsho*   *maṭ*   *burduúme*   *paš-íij̃-anet*
       you.all   I.DAT   blurry.PL   see-**DTR**-PRES2p
       'You all are seen as blurry to me.' (Finess 1.132)

b.	*muláayoṭ*	*résay*	*anú*	*mor*	*ajóonok*	*paš-**íi**-d-u*
	girls.DAT	his	this	word	strange	see-**DTR**-PFI-SIMP3sm

'To the girls his word (talk) was seen (as) strange (appeared strange).' (Chaagun 16.6)

c.	*ninóǰo*	*maṭ*	*ayáakak*	*ga*	*neé*	*haš-**íiǰ**-in*
	these.from	I.DAT	this.much.INDEF	even	not	gain-**DTR**-PRES3sf

'From these even this much is not obtained (by) me.' (Chaagun 13.5)

d.	*aš*	*may*	*damiǰaraáy*	*khariín*	*maṭ*	*lay-**íi**-d-i*
	today	my	trouble.of	worth	I.DAT	find-**DTR**-PFI-SIMP3sf

'Today the worth of my trouble (labour) is received to (by) me.' (Chaagun 5.7)

Less frequently, interpretations of passive voice occur with postpositions *-ǰ* 'on' or *-ǰo* 'from' on the central participant, as in the examples in (24).

(24)	a.	*ne*	*pon*	***máaǰo***	*neé*	*tar-**íiǰ**-in.*
		this.f	path	I.**from**	not	cross-**DTR**-PRES3sf

'This path (journey) cannot be crossed (completed) from (by) me.' (Distant 7.12)

b.	*ané*	*pon*	*ṭekṭaróǰ*	*wa~ṣ-**íi**-d-in*
	this.f	path	tractors.**on**	ruin-**DTR**-PFI-NEARP3sf

'This road has been ruined on (by) tractors.' (Oct–Nov 98 1.2)

c.	*ri*	*haṇejé*	*baál.čhalóo*	*hat-páaoǰ*
	those	eggs	children.of	stool.**on**

pal-iǰ-ií	*rinéy*	*áa~yeṭ*	*uçháčanan*
spread-**DTR**-CONJP	their	mouth.to	they.arrive

'Those eggs, having been spread on (by) the stool (lit. hands feet) of children, reach their mouths.' (Hat-paa 2.11)

d.

ṭiibíi	*khúu*	*ga*	*čhíi~ǰ*	*mútoṭ*	*pal-íiǰ-in*
TB	cough	and	sneeze.**on**	others.to	spread-**DTR**-PRES3sf

'On (by) coughing and sneezing TB is spread to others.' (TB Tape 3.4)

The examples in (25) express a passive voice but with the AGENT not mentioned.

(25) a.

naáe	*çhíile*	*ga*	*búuṭi*
new.PL	cloth.PL	and	shoe.PL

asóokaar	*ǰáa*	*san-íiǰ-anan*
we.for	where	build-**DTR**-PRES3p

'Where are new clothes and shoes made for us? (How can new clothes and shoes be made for us?)' (Chaagun 8.11)

b.

ẓaçé_páačoo	*sinér*	*ǰáalo*	*neé*	*d-íiǰ-an.*
ripe.grapes.of	in.river	raft	not	give-**DTR**-PRES3sm

'A raft is not given (floated) on the river of (in time of) ripe grapes.' (The river is in spate then.) (July 1997 1.6)

c.

reǰistarér	*mey*	*nóom*	*likh-íi-d-un*
register.in	my	name	write-**DTR**-PFI-NEARP3sm

'My name has been written in the register.' (May 1998 1.59)

d.

šudaríi	*šuriyarí*	*ninóǰo*	*luw-íi-d-en*
childhood's	happinesses	them.from	snatch-**DTR**-PFI-NEARP3p

'Childhood happinesses have been snatched away from them.' (Chaagun 13.14)

4.2 Middle voice

In all the examples in (26) the UNDERGOER of the action is the subject and is appropriately in absolutive case. This UNDERGOER can also be said to be controlling the action; no outside controller is implied (Kemmer 1993). These examples reflect the general tendency of middle voice interpretations in perfective aspect to occur more frequently with the valence marker *-íl* than *-d*.

(26) a.

kayáak.khéen.boósang	*baál*	*toóm*	*páaor*
until.the.time	boy	own	feet.on

neé	*kur-**i**-íl-un,*	*ro…*
not	strengthen-**DTR**-PFI-NEARP3sm	he

'Until the time the boy has not become strengthened on his own feet, he …' (Engagement 6.3)

b.

kayáakak	*súuriye*	*gée*	*née*
how.many	suns	go.SIMP3p	and

kayáakak	*ráatiye*	*tar-**i**-íl-e*
how.many	nights	pass-**DTR**-PFI-SIMP3p

'How many days went and how many nights passed?' (Revised Husan 8.1)

c.

ǰaháaz	*se*	*tharí_d-eé*	*d-eé*	*biṣam-**i**-íl-i*
plane	ERG	flights.give-CONJP	give-CONJP	land-**DTR**-PFI-SIMP3sf

'Having flown and flown the plane landed.' (August 99 1.21)

d.

khéenekeǰo	*buyúk*	*raṭh-**íi**-d-i*
after.some.time	back.wind	stop-**DTR**-PFI-SIMP3sf

'After some time the (terrible) wind stopped.' (Hiroshima 10.8)

4.3 ANTIPASSIVE VOICE

An antipassive construction can be thought of as the 'mirror image' of a passive. In a passive construction, the AGENT of a transitive situation is downplayed or omitted while the PATIENT is upgraded to subject status. In an antipassive construction, the PATIENT of a transitive situation is downplayed or omitted, while the AGENT is upgraded from ergative to absolutive status (see, for example, Dixon 1994).

The examples in (27) are all interpreted as antipassive voice, as defined above. The AGENT, in all examples, is in the unmarked absolutive case for the detransitivized verb. In the first three examples, no mention is made of the downplayed UNDERGOERs of the formerly transitive verbs. In the last three examples, the downplayed UNDERGOER remains, but is modified by a suffixal postposition (boldfaced). These examples reflect the general tendency for antipassive interpretations in perfective aspect to occur more frequently with the perfective valence marker *-íl* than *-d*.

(27) a.

mey	*baábo*	*lang-íi-d-un*
my	father	pass.over-**DTR**-PFI-NEARP3sm

'My father has passed over (passed away).' (Finess 1.159)
(No mention of the UNDERGOER of 'pass over'.)

b.

ho	*ek-ek_beé*	*be*	*púure*	*tar-i-íl-es*
then	one-one.become.CONJP	we	all-PL	cross-**DTR**-PFI-SIMP1p

'Then one by one we all crossed.' (Hiroshima 16.8)
(No mention of the UNDERGOER of 'cross'.)

c.

bubá	*wá-t-un*	*loóko*	*samat-íij*
father	come-PFI-NEARP3sm	quickly	gather-**DTR**.IMP2s

'Father has come, quickly be gathered (prepare yourself)!' (Revised Husan 54.8)
(No mention of the object of the transitive verb 'gather'.)

d. *re*	*akheér*	*ṭakálir*	*miṣ-**i**-íl-i*
she	finally	conversation.**in**	mix-**DTR**-PFI-SIMP3sf

'She finally became mixed in (joined) the conversation.' (Revised Husan 13.7)
(Object of transitive verb 'mix' now in oblique case with -r 'in'.)

e. *ro*	*toóm*	*thíito*	*moóreǰ*	*neé*	*yup-**i**-íl-u*
he	own	that.said	word.**on**	not	reconcile-**DTR**-PFI-SIMP3sm

'He did not reconcile on his own words.' (Rainy 5.18)
(Object of transitive verb 'reconcile' occurs in an oblique case, -ǰ 'on'.)

f. *kareé.kareé*	*keé*	*gaaṛíik*	*ané*	*pónier*	*tar-**íiǰ**-iš*
sometimes	which	vehicle.INDEF	this	path.**in**	cross-**DTR**-PIMPFV3sf

'Sometimes some vehicle was crossing in this path.' (Rainy 1.3)
(Object of transitive verb 'cross' occurs in an oblique case, 'in'.)

4.4 AMBIGUOUS CASES

In all the examples in (28) there is no AGENT mentioned, but is there an AGENT really implied? In other words, these sentences could be interpreted as passive with a controller off the scene, or as middle voice with the UNDERGOER subject both undergoing and controlling the action. The interpretation is ambiguous. In the texts from which these examples are extracted, it simply does not matter whether there is or is not an external controller.

(28) a. *née*	*eé*	*haṇeǰé*	*hat-páaesaa~t*
then	those	eggs	with.stool

weéy	*súmer*	*miṣ-**íiǰ**-anan*
having.come	in.dust	mix-**DTR**-PRES3p

'These (parasite) eggs come out with stool (lit. hand-foot) and are mixed in with the soil.' (Hat-paa 2.9)

b. *résey*	*beéne*	*gáaṇe*	*phuṭ-i-íl-en*	*née*
his	both	legs	break-**DTR**-PFI-NEARP3p	and

moṭarsáaykal	*ga*	*kháčik-beé*	*tak*	*bigín*
motorcycle	also	rather.badly	broken	she.has.become

'Both of his legs have broken and the motorcycle has been badly wrecked.' (Road Accident 2.1)

c. *darúm.boósang*	*neé*	*bay-íi-d-un.*
up.till.now	not	decide-**DTR**-PFI-NEARP3sm

'Up till now it has not been decided.' (Nov–Jan 03 1.18)

d. *née*	*čáar*	*poš*	*máazakoǰo*	*aní*	*rupáaye*	*baṛ-íi-d-e*	*to*
then	four	five	from.months	these	rupees	finish-**DTR**-PFI-SIMP3p	so

'Then after four or five months (when) these rupees are finished so ...' (Chaagun 8.3)

4.5 Summary of Section 4

In summary, the detransitivizer *-íiǰ* serves the function of changing the perspective of a transitive verb by downplaying either the controlling participant or the affected participant. The result can be interpreted as passive, antipassive, or middle voice, and sometimes the interpretation is ambiguous. In perfective aspect, it appears that a passive interpretation always occurs with the perfective valence marker *-d*, whereas antipassive and middle voice interpretations occur with both *-d* and *-íl*, but more frequently *-íl*.

5. CONCLUSION

In his 1924 grammar of Gilgiti Shina, Bailey observed irregularities in form and meaning associated with verbs formed with *-izh* (his notation). He noted that some such verbs formed the past with *-ílus*, others with *-ī´dŭs*. Other verbs formed the past with *-ílus*, yet their non-past did not regularly occur with *-izh* (1924: 33, 45ff.). Focusing more on the meaning, he insightfully observed that there was no clear division between plain intransitive, middle voice, or passive voice, and that intransitive verbs sometimes have 'two forms, one the ordinary intrans[itive] and one which is passive in form (if there is such a thing as a true passive)' (1924: 64ff.). Regarding pairing intransitive verbs with their *-izh* counterparts, he commented that 'in the Ṣiṇā mind the two ideas [intransitivity and passivity] are closely allied' (1924: 64).

In this paper we have seen that the picture is greatly simplified by understanding that the primary function of the verb suffix *-íiǰ* 'DTR' is to detransitivize a verb—that is, to reduce its valence. While *-íiǰ* can be suffixed to transitive or intransitive verb stems, this process has different effects in each case. On inherently transitive stems its primary function as a detransitivizer is realized. Voice then becomes a matter of interpretation as either the more AGENT-like participant or the UNDERGOER is downplayed in a given utterance according to context. On stative intransitive stems the effect of *-iij* is to create an inchoative, meaning 'to enter into the state described by the verb'. The detransitivizer does not occur with most active intransitive stems, but when it does it may express inception (begin to do) or other subtle nuances that are particular to individual stems.

TRANSCRIPTION

Vowel length is shown by geminate vowels: *aa*. The accented vowel manifests a higher pitch and is marked with an acute accent´, either on a short vowel: *á* (a higher pitch), on the first mora (part) of a long vowel: *áa* (falling from the high pitch), or on the second mora of a long vowel: *aá* (rising to the high pitch), following Berger (1960) and Buddruss (e.g. 1993, 1996). By convention, the accent is often not marked on monosyllabic words. Nasalized vowels are shown by tilde ~ after the vowel: *a~*, *áa~*, *aá~*, following an *Orientalist* system of transcription described by Masica (1991: xvi). In that same vein, retroflex consonants are marked with a dot below: *ç̣*, *ḍ*, *ṇ*, *ṛ*, *ṣ*, *ṭ*, *ẓ*. Morpheme breaks are shown by a dash: *muláay-e-y* 'girl-OBL-of'. If more than one word is required to gloss a single morpheme, the words of the gloss are separated by full stops, *awaáǰ-in* 'be.necessary-PRES3sf'. Where the grammatical analysis of a word is not in focus, the non-separated morphemes are indicated in the gloss by full stop: *muláayey* 'girl.of'. Syllable divisions between vowels are marked by a full stop *čhami.áako* 'first born'; some speakers pronounce a barely perceptible epenthetic *(y)* at such a point. Phrasal compounds are indicated with underscore characters at the word breaks, and a gloss provided for the whole compound. For example *ek_ek_beé* is a compound meaning 'one by one' (8). If the individual parts were glossed it would be 'one one become.CONV' which would not capture the sense of this compound. Furthermore, some such compounds contain elements which have no independent meaning that can be captured in a gloss.

ABBREVIATIONS

1 = First person
2 = Second person
3 = Third person
CAUS = Causative
CONJP = Conjunctive participle
CONV = Converb
DAT = Dative
DTR = Detransitive
ECHO = Echo formation
EMPH = Emphatic
ERG = Ergative
f = Feminine
FUT = Future
IMP = Imperative
INDEF = Indefinite
JUSS = Jussive
m = Masculine
NEARP = Near Past
OBL = Oblique
p = Plural (in verb morphology)
PAST = Past tense
PFI = Intransitive perfective marker
PFT = Transitive perfective marker
PL = Plural (in nominal morphology)
POL = Polite/Emphatic
PIMPFV = Past imperfective
PRES = Present tense
PRPRF = Present perfect
PSPRF = Past perfect
Q = Question marker
REMP = Remote past
s = Singular
SIMP = Simple (narrative) tense

REFERENCES

Bailey, T. Grahame. 1924. *Grammar of the Shina (Ṣiṇā) Language*. London: The Royal Asiatic Society.

Berger, Hermann. 1960. 'Bericht über sprachliche und volkskundliche Forschungen im Hunzatal'. *Anthropos* 55: 657–64.

Buddruss, Georg. 1996. 'Shina-Rätsel (Shina riddles)'. In *Nā nā vidhaikatā: Festscrift für Hermann Berger,* edited by Dieter B. Kapp. 29–54. Wiesbaden: Harrassowitz Verlag.

——— 1993. 'On artificial glaciers in the Gilgit Karakorum'. In *Studien zur Indologie und Iranistik, Band 18, edited by* Georg Buddruss, Oskar von Hinüber,

Hanns-Peter Schmidt, Albrecht Wezler, and Michael Witzel. 77–90. Reinbek: Verlag für Orientalistische Fachpublikationen.

Chafe, Wallace L. 1970. *Meaning and the Structure of Language*. Chicago: University of Chicago Press.

Comrie, Bernard. 1989. *Language Universals and Linguistic Typology*. 2nd ed. Chicago: University of Chicago Press.

Degener, Almuth. 2008. *Shina-Texte aus Gilgit (Nord-Pakistan): Sprichwörter und Materialien zum Volksglauben, gesammelt von Mohammad Amin Zia*. Wiesbaden: Harrassowitz Verlag.

Dixon, R. M. W. 1994. *Ergativity*. Cambridge: Cambridge University Press. (Cambridge Studies in Linguistics 69).

_______ and Aikhenvald, Alexandra. 2000. *Changing Valency: Case Studies in Transitivity*. Cambridge: Cambridge University Press.

Fillmore, Charles J. 1977. 'The case for case reopened'. *Syntax and Semantics 8: Grammatical Relations*, edited by P. Cole and J. M. Sadock. 59–81 New York: Academic Press.

Kemmer, Suzanne. 1993. *The Middle Voice*. Amsterdam and Philadelphia: John Benjamins. (Typological Studies in Language 23).

Kohistani, Razwal and Schmidt, Ruth Laila. 2006. 'Shina in contemporary Pakistan'. In *Lesser-Known Languages of South Asia: Status and Policies, Case Studies and Applications of Information Technology*, edited by Anju Saxena and Lars Borin. 137–60. Berlin: Mouton de Gruyter.

Liljegren, Henrik. 2008. *Towards a Grammatical Description of Palula: An Indo-Aryan Language of the Hindu Kush*. PhD dissertation. Stockholm: Stockholm University.

Masica, Colin P. 1991. *The Indo-Aryan Languages*. Cambridge: Cambridge University Press.

Payne, Thomas E. 1997. *Describing Morphosyntax*. Cambridge: Cambridge University Press.

Radloff, Carla F. 1999. *Aspects of the Sound System of Gilgiti Shina*. Islamabad: National Institute of Pakistan Studies and Summer Institute of Linguistics.

_______ 1992. 'Dialects of Shina'. In *Sociolinguistic Survey of Northern Pakistan, Volume 2: Languages of the Northern Areas*, edited by Peter C. Backstrom and Carla F. Radloff. 85–203. Islamabad: National Institute of Pakistan Studies and Summer Institute of Linguistics.

_______ and Shakil, Shakil Ahmad. 1998. *Folktales in the Shina of Gilgit (Text, Grammatical Analysis, and Commentary)*. Islamabad: National Insitute of Pakistan Studies and Summer Institute of Linguistics.

Schmidt, Ruth Laila. 2002. 'A grammatical comparison of Shina dialects'. In *Himalayan Languages: Past and Present*, edited by Anju Saxena. New York: Mouton de Gruyter.

_______ 2001. Compound tenses in the Shina of Indus Kohistan. In *Toḥfa-e-Dil: Festschrift Helmut Nespital, edited by* Dirk W. Lönne. Reinbek: Dr. Inge Wezler Verlag für Orientalistische Fachpublikationen.

_______ and Kohistani, Razwal. 2008. *A Grammar of the Shina Language of Indus Kohistan*. Wiesbaden: Harrassowitz Verlag.

Vendler, Theo. 1957. Verbs and times. *The Philosophical Review* 66.2: 143–60.

14

Ideological Imperatives in Urdu Linguistics: A Study of the Works of the Pioneers of Urdu Linguistics

Tariq Rahman

Urdu is the national language of Pakistan and an identity symbol for the Muslims of India. However, it invites analysis from the point of view of both politics and history since it is highly and quite overtly ideologically informed or politicized. In both countries the preoccupation with history is meant to serve ideological, and ultimately political, purposes. In Pakistan it is to prove that Urdu is intimately tied with the areas now in Pakistan and to suggest that it is a 'Muslim' language (see Malik et al. 2006): in India, that Urdu is an 'Indian' language and that it is the fruit of the joint efforts of both Hindus and Muslims, symbol of the Ganga-Jamna civilization (Farouqui 2006: ix–xix).

Unfortunately, the history of Urdu linguistics is ignored partly because most linguists working on Urdu nowadays are not conversant with Persian and Urdu sources, and those who are do not have much interest in the political analysis of the history of Urdu linguistics. This article is a byproduct of my research on the social and political history of Urdu which has been published (Rahman 2011). However, the arguments, as well as much of the material presented here, are being presented in this form for the first time. I believe this article will provide useful insights into some of the linguistic attitudes and assumptions of Pakistanis and north Indians which are encountered by all linguists—especially people like Carla Radloff who spent so much of their lives actually living with language communities in parts of the subcontinent.

This article chooses three pioneers of Urdu linguistics—Insha Allah Khan Insha, Hafiz Mahmud Shirani, and Maulvi Abdul Haq (often called the father of Urdu or *Baba-e-Urdu*)—to illustrate the ideological assumptions of Urdu linguistics. The term Urdu linguistics refers to ideas and assumptions about the Urdu language before the application of Western methods of linguistic scholarship to the language. Moreover, these three pioneers wrote in Persian or Urdu, and not in English, which is the most common language of linguistic writings, after Urdu linguistics underwent a paradigm shift from its native pre-Western methods of understanding to modern ones. Let us take the work of these pioneers one by one and then attempt an analysis of their views with reference to political and historical factors.

INSHA ALLAH KHAN INSHA (1752–1817)

Known mostly as a poet, Insha was the pioneering sociolinguistic historian of Urdu. His pioneering work is a book in Persian entitled *Darya-e-Latafat* in 1802. It was printed by Maulvi Masih Uddin Kakorvi in Murshidabad in 1848. It has two parts: the first, and major part dealing with the notion of *fasahat* 'correctness' in Urdu along with the first grammar of the language written by a native speaker, is by Insha; the second, and minor part dealing with figures of speech, rhetoric, and prosody, is by Mirza Qateel. The book was edited by Abdul Haq in Aurangabad under the auspices of the Anjuman-e-Taraqqi-e-Urdu in May 1916. Then, in 1935, Brajmohan Datari Kaefi translated it into Urdu.

Insha built his whole linguistic theory around the notion of *fasahat* 'correctness'. This notion is based upon a hierarchical, medieval (and colonial) world view. The assumption is that the phenomenal world is a forced entity with an eventual given nature or quality. Thus values and hierarchies within things, including languages, are an immutable given and intrinsic to their nature. Thus some languages—like some people, some religions, some races, etc.—are inferior or superior to others. The modern idea that human beings, or rather groups, give value and determine hierarchies which are, therefore, neither unchangeable, nor objective, nor intrinsic, was not known to Insha and his contemporaries. Indeed, his British contemporaries also did not countenance such a view. They would, of course, have argued for the superiority of Europe and of English while Insha argued for the superiority of Urdu over the other languages of India. But both parties would have agreed with the basic assumption that value (superiority or inferiority) resides in the essential nature of a thing and is not given to it by observers.

Insha develops his notion of *fasahat* on this basic assumption—that there are superior forms of language. He then argues that the standard of correctness lies in the practice of some families of Delhi (which he calls Shahjahanabad).

> The language of Shahjahanabad is that which people attached to the royal court, courtiers themselves, beautiful beloveds, Muslim handicraftsmen, the functionaries of rich and fashionable people—even their very sweepers—speak. Wherever these people go their children are called Dilli *walas* and their *mohalla* is known as the *mohalla* of the Delhites (The present author's translation from Urdu. (Insha 1802: 102)).

This definition is given so late in the book because Insha is preparing the grounds for it in the first 100 pages. First, he excludes the Hindus, arguing that it is well known to refined people that the Hindus learned 'the art of conversation and the etiquette of partaking food and wearing clothes' from the Muslims (Ibid.: 35). Then he goes on to eliminate the working classes of Delhi and such localities as that of Mughalpura and the Syeds of Barah. The working classes, he says, speak Urdu mixed with other languages.

Some localities, such as Mughalpura, are rejected because their Urdu is mixed up with Punjabi. Even the Syeds of Barah, who belonged to a powerful family, have come from outside Delhi and are too proud to learn the correct Urdu language. After this Insha eliminates all outsiders settled in Delhi, be they from Kashmir, Punjab, or the small towns of UP. In the end he is left with a few families of former courtly connections and *ashraf* 'of gentlemanly status'. In short, correctness in Urdu is based upon the membership of an exclusive club which was Muslim, not of working-class status, and belonging to Delhi.

Delhi's language was considered the standard variety of Urdu before 1857. As William Dalrymple puts it:

> The intoxication with the elegance of Delhi's language was common to both men and women—there was a special dialect of Delhi Urdu used only in the women's quarters—and perhaps more surprisingly to all classes. A collection of Urdu poets, *The Garden of Poetry*, contains the names of 540 poets from Delhi alone (Dalrymple 2006: 35).

But here Insha runs into a difficulty. He himself lived in Lucknow and his patron, Nawab Sa'adat Yar Khan, the ruler of Oudh, was from that city and not from Delhi. He therefore praises the correctness of the Urdu of Lucknow in the same rhetorical language as he had earlier praised the language of Delhi. Then he explains that one does not have to be born in Delhi to be correct in Urdu. Indeed, the best *fusaha* 'Urdu-speakers' of that city have migrated to Lucknow. Since the ruler (his patron) encouraged knowledge and the arts, it was in Lucknow that the best form of Urdu flourished (Insha 1802: 97–8). With this stratagem he achieves what he started out with—that correctness resides in the language of the *ashraf* of Delhi—but also placates the egos of Luckhnawis, and especially the Nawab.

Insha's linguistic theory is related to power. First, the hierarchical and value-laden evaluation of languages or linguistic practices in itself confirms the differentiation in society initially created by the powerful. Secondly, Insha clearly states that figures with temporal authority can create linguistic innovations. For instance, the word *rangtara* for *sangtara* by Mohammad Shah is such a neologism. Insha believes that whatever form of language is acceptable to rulers is *ipso facto* 'correct' (Insha 1802: 66). Indeed, Delhi's language is correct precisely because it was the capital of the Mughal Empire for so long.

Given such views about correctness, Insha also believes in purging the language of coarse or inharmonious words. Not all these words are from Hindi, though some—*sarijan, pee, pitam*—are. Indeed, some words are considered *na maqool* 'unreasonable' simply because they belong to a bygone age (*mane* for *maen*; *dasa* for 'seen' or 'that which was seen'; *sati* for *se* etc.). Insha is also in favour of abandoning all words coming from the peripheral areas where Braj Bhasha or (in

Lucknow) Awadhi is spoken (Insha 1802: 62–3). He condemns such words as being unsuitable for Urdu.

The rest of Insha's linguistic theory, as also that of his co-writer Mirza Qateel, is based upon classification. Parts of speech, figurative language, and grammatical categories are classified and categorized. There is no attempt to understand sounds or describe them, or to define the *la langue* 'language system' as Ferdinand de Saussure did later. There is also no interest in describing language families (as philologists and comparative linguists did in Europe) nor in the roots of Urdu (which became an obsession later). Insha's main interest is in defining correctness and establishing that the speech of his own community—basically the urban Muslim elite of the centres of North Indian Mughal culture—is superior to other forms of speech.

The legacy of the social snobbery of eighteenth century linguistics has affected lexicography also. Shamsur Rahman Faruqi, writing about the problems of Urdu lexicography, says 'lexicographers so far have chosen to ignore the living reality of the language and have played strictly according to the book' (Faruqi 1990: 21). He looks at the pronunciation of non-Prakrit words, observing that although the original pronunciation does not agree with the phonological rules of Urdu, the dictionaries insist upon retaining it. For example, three-letter words ending in *ain* (a letter in the Urdu alphabet) and without a vowel after the second consonant, add a short vowel after the consonant as Urdu does not allow such consonantal endings. Instead such words are represented as: *jama, shama, shara,* and *vaza* (Faruqi 1990: 23).

There are numerous other examples illustrating the fact that Urdu linguistics still derives its norms from purist assumptions about language which tend to belittle, denigrate, and dismiss the common people's linguistic usages.

However, although he did set up standards of correctness, he still recognized that Urdu is a language in its own right and not a mixture of languages. Thus he argues that words of foreign origin—whether Arabic, Persian, Turkish, or any other—should be pronounced as they are in Urdu. In his own words:

> 'Because whatever [word] is against Urdu is wrong even if it is true in reality; and that which agrees with Urdu is correct even if it is not correct in reality.' (Insha 1802: 164)

This is a progressive point of view and one with which modern linguists agree. In Insha's time it was a radical position to adopt—as Abdul Haq points out in his preface (Insha 1802: 15)—because people believed in an objective, unalterable, essential 'reality'. This implied that a word from Arabic had to be pronounced and written exactly as in Arabic. But Urdu does not have the sounds of Arabic, so it is impossible to follow the original language. This, however, is what the purists argued. Insha rightly ruled that such purism was wrong. But in reality Insha did set up a new model of purism as we have seen, and this became the new, unalterable reality for others who followed him.

Therefore, as mentioned earlier, even today purism rules the roost in popular Urdu linguistics. The poet Josh Malihabadi, who objected to peoples' pronunciation to their face, might be no more, but the criterion of correctness remains inflexible and refers to the classics or standard, published dictionaries.

Insha was not the first one to set these standards of correctness, but he codified what was agreed upon. Indeed, the number of debates about *fasahat* 'correctness' among Urdu poets is legion. Such debates are found in letters—including those of Ghalib—biographical accounts (Mohammad Husain Azad's *Ab-e-Hayat* comes to mind), and recorded discussions. It is a legacy which remains today in Urdu linguistics where prescriptivism rather than descriptivism still remains a major concern.

HAFIZ MAHMUD SHIRANI

As mentioned in the beginning, apart from correctness, the other major concern of Urdu linguists is the age and ancestry of Urdu. These are, of course, separate themes but are difficult to separate in practice in most cases. Shirani, at any rate, is the major linguistic historian of both these subjects. Let us, therefore, begin with a brief look at his life.

This account of the life of Mahmud Shirani is based on a detailed introduction to the author's work by his son, Mazhar Mahmud Shirani (M. Shirani 1965). In addition to this, some letters of (and to) the author have also been used.

Mahmud Shirani was born on 5 October 1880 'after sunset' as his father, Ismail Khan Shirani, recorded in Persian (M. Shirani 1965: 24). At that time the family was resident in the princely state of

Tonk, though earlier they had lived in Khatu, a *mauza* 'town', in the state of Jodhpur. He had a traditional education, beginning with the learning of the Qur'an by heart (hence the title of *hafiz* i.e. one who has memorized [the Holy Book]). This education comprised the reading of the Persian classics. However, as a concession to modernity, Mahmud also studied English. This was quite an adventurous enterprise because it entailed traveling to Jodhpur. For this he had to travel on camel or bullock carts 60 miles across the semi-desert to Jaipur from where there was a train to Jodhpur. This began in 1897 at the age of seventeen, which is also the year of the youth's marriage. We are not told anything of how the teenager felt about leaving his girl-wife in the first few months of marriage in order to pursue the elusive goal of learning English in a government school. However, in 1898 he had passed middle (eighth class). After this he went to Lahore—surely the dream of all Punjabi youth in those days—where he passed the *Munshi, Munshi Alim,* and *Munshi Fazil* examinations. These examinations were part of preserving and promoting oriental learning and concentrated upon Persian and other 'oriental' subjects.

However, Mahmud and his father both aspired to Western learning also. Thus, not giving up his pursuit of English, he studied for and passed his intermediate examination and then, in 1904, sailed for London. Here, in common with his illustrious predecessor M. A. Jinnah, he was admitted to Lincoln's Inn. In 1906 he appeared in the examination and, his father having died, returned to India. The family being in conflict with each other on account of the distribution of the paternal property, he returned to England to complete his studies. However, his brothers stopped his allowance and Mahmud had to fall back on his own resources to live. These happened to be looking for rare books, research in history, teaching, and editing books. In 1913, without completing his legal studies, but with much experience of research, he returned to India with a job in hand—namely to acquire and send goods of antique value to England. But then World War I intervened and this source of income stopped. However, in 1922 he was appointed lecturer in Islamia College, a post he retained till 1937.

In the next fifteen years Shirani, as he came to be called now, produced that enormous amount of work on Urdu and Persian language and literature for which he is known among Urdu literary circles today (see Annexure 1). During all this period he stayed in Lahore, his favourite city, where he became a lecturer in Urdu at the Punjab University, from which post he retired in 1940. His last years were spent in Tonk indulging in his favourite hobbies—reading, writing, looking after his collection of rare coins and manuscripts, and indulging in melons near a stream—till he died in 1946.

THE WORKS OF SHIRANI

Shirani's essays are available in nine volumes all compiled by Mazhar Mahmud Shirani and published by the Majlis-e-Taraqqi-e-Adab from Lahore. The following volumes are either about Urdu or have a bearing on linguistic history. The others, listed in the bibliography, deal with literature in Persian and Urdu. The contents of the relevant volumes are briefly summed up below:

Volume 1: Seven research articles on Urdu proving that it was used between the eighth to the tenth centuries AH (some given in Annexure 1); some book reviews of Urdu publications

Volume 2: Urdu in north India in the tenth and eleventh centuries AH; Urdu in the Punjab (in Annexure 1); the promotion of Urdu by the Mehdvis and some old Urdu writings

Volume 7: Literary criticism on the poem *Prithi Raj Rasa,* about the adventures of the Rajput ruler Prithvi Raj, proving that this epic is a literary fraud because, contrary to the claim, it was not written in the twelfth century AH by a contemporary of Mu'izz-ud-Din Muhammad ibn Sam, commonly called Muhammad Ghauri, who defeated Prithvi Raj in 1191 at Taraori (Tarain)

Volume 9: Versified primers for children in Urdu, and Persian prosody and works on numismatics

The articles dealing with the ancestry of Urdu were first published in journals and are given in Annexure 1 as mentioned above. Shirani's writings on other subjects, such as Persian literature, are not relevant to this study. Most relevant to it, however, is his book *Punjab Mein Urdu* (1928).

In this article we will pay attention only to his linguistic work in Urdu, thus leaving aside his enormous contribution to literature both in Urdu and Persian.

SHIRANI'S LINGUISTIC THESES

Shirani turned his attention to Urdu when Abdullah Yusuf Ali (1872–1953), then principal of Islamia College, asked him to write something on the origins and age of Urdu. Almost the whole corpus of his writings on linguistic history—for that is how his work would be classified now—addresses these questions directly or indirectly. Of course, while working on these issues he encountered other areas of interest out of which many of his literary and other works were born, but basically these are the mainsprings of his enormous output.

As Shirani was a lecturer in this college between 1921 to 1928, his initial endeavours came to light during these years.

Shirani's magnum opus is *Punjab Mein Urdu* (1928). The central thesis of this work is that Urdu was created in the Punjab and the Muslims took it with them to Delhi when they spread from the western part of India eastwards. A corollary of this hypothesis is that Punjabi and Urdu are very similar even now—Shirani (1928: 8) claims the two languages share 60 per cent of their words, and that words used in old Urdu are still used in Punjabi. However, there are certain distinctive features (morphological [*ka, ki*] and others) which separate Urdu from Braj Bhasha as well as Punjabi/Siraiki (which he calls Multani).

Among other things, Shirani points to the presence of words still used in Punjabi in old Urdu (especially Dakani, the variety of Urdu used in the Deccan) as well as such words in modern Urdu. In the latter case they have no separate meaning but are used idiomatically to supplement and strengthen meaning. Examples are as follows:

sufaed chitta	The word *chitta* is still used in Punjabi whereas modern Urdu uses only *sufaed* for 'white'.
din dehare	The word *din* means 'day' in Urdu. *Dahare* means 'day' in Punjabi even now. In Urdu the latter word is not used in isolation but is used in this idiomatic phrase.
manga tanga	*Manga* is to take as a loan; to beg in Urdu. *Tanga* means the same in Punjabi but has no meaning on its own in modern Urdu (Shirani 1928: 95–7).

Similarly, the possessive markers *ka* and *ke* in Urdu is *da* and *de* in Punjabi nowadays but there are a number of place names in the Punjab with endings *ke* and *ka* such as Murid<u>ke</u>, Sadhuke, etc.

From this evidence Shirani concludes that Urdu is a 'developed'—his term—form of Punjabi. An alternative hypothesis, which Shirani does not even consider, is that Urdu, Hindi, Punjabi, Siraiki, Hindko, etc. could simply be descendants of a language spread over a large area from Peshawar to Benares. That the varieties of such a language would have some vocabulary in common but would also grow and change along different lines is only natural.

The book is not really a thesis from beginning to end because Shirani also makes it a history of the poets of Urdu in the Punjab. This has only an indirect relationship with the main theme of the book, but it takes most of the space in the book.

On the whole, Shirani, whose research on the ancient names, origins, and usages of Urdu is so impressive, is on a weak footing in this book. The reason can only be conjectured. In my view, Shirani was not only a pioneer of certain trends in Urdu's linguistic history, he was also a pioneer of Muslim nationalism in South Asia. He lived at the time of the rise of Muslim nationalism which, as we know, was expressed through the symbols of Islam and Urdu. He witnessed the Urdu-Hindi controversy and was as much concerned with claiming Urdu as part of the Muslim heritage in India as Abdul Haq or other Muslim nationalists. This ideological imperative closed his mind to other hypotheses about the birth of Urdu. His emotional and ideological interests were best served if he associated Urdu with the Muslims and especially those of the Punjab, a major Muslim-majority province of India and one where he had spent almost all his adult life. It is because of this that modern Pakistani nationalists have appropriated Shirani's work—witness Fateh Mohammad Malik's recent statement that Urdu is the language of Punjabi Muslims (Malik et al. 2006 Vol 4: 1–5).

ABDUL HAQ (*BABA-E-URDU*)

The person whose linguistic ideas feed directly into the politics of Pakistan is Abdul Haq (1870–1961), also known as the *Baba-e-Urdu* 'Father of Urdu'. Born in Hapar (UP, India), he was educated at the Mohammedan Anglo Arabic College at Aligarh from where he graduated in 1894. After that he served in several bureaucratic positions as well as educational institutions in the Hyderabad state, retiring as the principal of Osmania College in Aurangabad in 1930. For the next three years he also served as the professor of Urdu at the Osmania University.

By now Abdul Haq had both written and spoken in favour of Urdu being used in the domains of power in India. However, when he became the president of the *Anjuman-e-Taraqqi-e-Urdu* in 1935, he became deeply involved in pro-Urdu activism in India. The rest of Abdul Haq's life was spent in promoting Urdu. In India this meant countering the claims of Hindi as the major language of the people of north India. In Pakistan it meant countering the claims of the indigenous languages of Pakistan—especially Bengali.

Haq's works are linguistic, literary, and activist in nature. Among the first are grammatical and lexicographic works with a few on linguistic history. The *Qavaid-e-Urdu* (1914) is a grammar of Urdu with a preface outlining the history of the writing of grammars of Urdu. This grammar was re-issued in several forms such as *Urdu Sarf-o-Nahv* (1934) and subsequent editions. The main point of Haq's work is to standardize Urdu as a distinct language from Persian and Arabic whose grammatical structures were used to provide the norms of Urdu usage. However, despite calling Urdu the composite language of Muslims and Hindus, Haq neither gives examples from Hindi nor does he refer to the Hindi grammars being written during the same period.

Haq's major lexicographic work is his dictionary which was published in 1937 as the *Standard English Urdu Dictionary*. This was reissued in several forms—*The Student's Standard English-Urdu Dictionary* among them—over many years. Haq's lexicographic principles are flexible in that he includes words of English in the dictionary. He also accepts ordinary Hindi words but stops short of the Sanskrit ones which were being included into the modern Hindi lexicon being prepared by identity-conscious Hindus of the period.

Haq's historical writings are works on old Urdu: *Qadim Urdu* (1996) and *Urdu ki Ibtidai Nash-o-Numa Main Sufia-e-Karam ka Hissa* (1939). The first gives samples of old Urdu from the Deccan, while the latter develops the thesis that the *Sufis* used the ancestor of Urdu, rather than the learned but less accessible Persian, for the dissemination of their ideas.

Another book, *Marhatti Zaban par Farsi ka Asar* (1933), gives passages from writings in Marathi indicating how Persian words entered and came into common use in Marathi.

In all the books mentioned above, Haq's style is historical rather than linguistic. Basically, his focal point is vocabulary. It is with reference to this, rather than phonology or syntax, that he supports his major theses which are that: (i) Urdu is an ancient language which developed in Gujrat and Deccan earlier than it did in north India where it was born; and (ii) Persian influenced the languages of north India, mainly as the ancestor of Urdu but also of other languages such as Marhatti, and is, therefore, now a natural part of the linguistic heritage of north India.

These theses had political implications during the period leading up to the partition of India. These were the Urdu-Hindi controversy days and Abdul Haq wished to promote the idea that Urdu was the common heritage language of the Muslim and Hindu civilizations of India. Therefore, he argued, Urdu—which could be called Hindustani—had to be promoted in all the domains of power in India. The other candidate for this role was modern or sanskritized Hindi, which Abdul Haq (1952) opposed as an artificially constructed and partly incomprehensible language.

The most important aspect of this part of Haq's life is his disagreement with M.K. Gandhi over these issues. These came to a head during the Nagpur session of the Hindi *Sahitya Sammelan* in 1935. During this session, while debating the perennial question of how Hindustani was to be defined, Abdul Haq accused Gandhi of having said:

> 'Urdu is the language of the Muslims. The Holy Qur'an is written in this script. If Muslims want, they can keep it or remove it.'

According to Begum Sultana Hayat, Gandhi denied ever having said these words. She says she had it confirmed by Zakir Hussain, Jawaharlal Nehru, Rajindra Prashad, Kaka Kalekar, and Manshur Wala, who were present there, but none of them confirmed this (Hayat 1993: 19–50). However, Haq and the Muslim League believed that Gandhi had spoken thus and the distances created then contributed to Muslim separatism in South Asia.

After Partition, Abdul Haq migrated to Pakistan where he reversed his earlier position of calling Urdu the joint heritage of Hindus and

Muslims. Now he emphasized the Muslim ownership of Urdu. Indeed, he said:

اردو زبان ہی پاکستان کی بنا کا باعث ہوئی۔ یہ زبان
ہماری زندگی کا جز اور تہذیب وقومیت کی بنیاد ہے۔

> 'The Urdu language is the basis for the creation of Pakistan. This language is the element of our life and the basis of our civilization and nationality.' (Haq n.d.: 20).

He also said that it was Urdu which had disseminated the propaganda of the Muslim League so that it had reached 'in every street and every house' (Haq n.d.: 8).

Abdul Haq's major opponents now were Bengali and English. He looked at the rise of the language movement in East Pakistan with dismay and apprehension. In his view Bengali was a 'Hindu' language:

> 'It does not have Islamic civilization and tradition and even if it appears somewhere it is in a distorted form. In the Urdu language there is a great treasure of religion and Islamic history.' (Haq 1952: 4).

He believed that having a majority of speakers did not qualify Bengali to be a national and state language of Pakistan because nobody understood it outside Bengal (Haq n.d.: Preface). He also believed that the government should not have shown any weakness to the demands for Bengali as these were inspired by Hindu academics of Dacca University, and supported by communists, anti-Pakistan lobbies, and the Hindu press in Calcutta (Haq n.d.: E).

With these right wing views Abdul Haq soon became the bete noire of all supporters of the indigenous languages of Pakistan and those who opposed the centre's domination over the federating units. However, convinced of the correctness of his views, he kept struggling to make Urdu the sole national and official language of Pakistan. In this context two pamphlets (Haq 1952 and n.d.) are important.

Since English was already the official language of the country, he opposed that also. In this context he wanted to create adequate terminology to express scientific and technological ideas in Urdu (Haq 1952b) and also to establish a university with Urdu as the medium of instruction for all subjects, as in Osmania (Haq 1960).

Things came to a head in 1954 when the prime minister, Mohammad Ali Bogra, expressed his willingness to consider Bengali as one of the national languages of Pakistan. In the wake of the *Bhasha Andolon* (the Bengali language movement)—and especially the death of language activists outside Dacca University on 21 February 1952—political expediency demanded that some such compromise, belated though it was, be offered. However, Haq was intransigent and responded by calling for the prime minister's resignation (Haq n.d.: 37–8). He then wrote to the members of the Constituent Assembly on 8 April 1954, giving his point of view. However, on 19 April 1954, the Parliamentary Committee of the League decided in favour of Bengali being one of the national languages of the country. Upon this Abdul Haq declared a strike and organized a protest. Thousands—according to him a hundred thousand—protestors with pro-Urdu and anti-Bengali flags marched towards the Constituent Assembly with Abdul Haq. They stopped just outside the building into which only Abdul Haq was admitted to present his point of view before the assembled delegates. A meeting with the prime minister was promised for the next day and the protesters dispersed peacefully. The next day, according to Abdul Haq, his compromise formula, that Bengali should be the official language of East Pakistan and Urdu that of West Pakistan, was accepted. However, when the bill was presented to the Assembly on 7 May 1954, this proposal was discarded. At last, in December 1955, the declaration to this effect was made and, on 16 February 1956, the new constitution declared that the national languages of Pakistan would be Bengali and Urdu. Moreover, it was also decreed that English would remain the official language of the country for the next fifteen years. In short, as Abdul Haq declared with great bitterness, the government had discarded his ideas.

While English was already firmly entrenched as the official language of British India and was inherited by both India and Pakistan, the other candidate for the official language of Pakistan was Arabic. The candidacy of Arabic was put forward by the Aga Khan on 9 February 1951 in the Motamar Alam Islami—on the grounds that Arabic was the common language of the Islamic civilization and that, among other things, Urdu was a product of the decadent period in Muslim history in India.

Abdul Haq refuted both ideas, calling the first impractical and the other only a half truth. He argued that in practice, since there would be nobody with adequate knowledge of Arabic to carry on the business of the state, it would be English which would remain ascendant for the next half a century or so (*Qaumi Zaban*: 3–6).

Abdul Haq's views have great resonance in the pro-Urdu lobby even now. They feed into the ethnic policies of the country and inform the ideology which creates them. Briefly, the ruling elite uses the symbols of Islam and Urdu to create Pakistani nationalism and an identity which transcends ethnic and sectarian religious identities. The supporters of ethnic identities, which consider Urdu as a tool of the domination of the centrist, Punjabi-dominated ruling elite, consider the views of Abdul Haq as reactionary, right wing, and oppressive. For them, Abdul Haq and others who follow him, are supporters of internal colonialism who are part of the military–bureaucratic establishment of Pakistan.

CONCLUSION

This article has introduced three linguistic historians of Urdu who are not well-known to linguists writing in English either within Pakistan or about it. Insha, Shirani, and Abdul Haq are significant not only because they have written about Urdu, but also because they represent certain linguistic identities which not only inform the ideology of Urdu linguistics in Pakistan, but also remain in consonance with other nationalistic ideologies of the country. Insha, as we have seen, represents the prescriptivist trend which defines the notion of correctness for us. This notion has a privileged place in our linguistic history and also continues to play a part in folk linguistics as well as literary criticism in Urdu. Shirani's work, on the other hand, is about Urdu's antiquity and ancestry—both seminal concerns of Urdu linguists and, again, part of folk linguistics. However, it is Abdul Haq's work which still remains relevant for the activists of Urdu both against Hindi in pre-partition India and the languages of Pakistan after 1947.

All these trends have ideological associations and implications for identity, self-definition, and, ultimately, politics. In Insha's case his concern was to appropriate a certain variety of Urdu for the Muslim aristocracy of Delhi and Lucknow. The notion of correctness he advocated would draw a circle around a politically and economically weakened *shurufa* 'gentlemanly class' whose superiority could no longer be asserted by military or economic power. It could, however, still be underlined and reinforced by what Bourdieu (1982) calls 'linguistic capital', which is a sub-set of cultural capital. Thus language would define identity now that politics and economics were failing to do so in an India in which the East India Company was spreading its tentacles and the Marathas were a formidable force to reckon with.

In Shirani's case, if the ancestry of Urdu could be traced to the Punjab, its significance as a symbol of Muslim identity would be strengthened in an India in which the Muslims were a minority—at places a besieged one, at least in their own perception—but one which was asserting its separate identity.

In the case of Abdul Haq the activist concern with the Muslim identity in India made him a champion of Urdu against Hindi. The same ideology of Urdu being at the core of the Pakistani Muslim identity made him oppose both English as the official language of Pakistan, and the demand for Bengali to be a national language of the country. Such concerns about identity are not dead. Pakistani nationalism still defines itself in terms of difference from the 'other' which is Hindu and Hindi-speaking. Thus, language functions as the identity symbol which complements the primary identity symbol of religion. As for correctness, it has been diluted in Pakistan because the Punjabi Urdu-using educated class which dominates Pakistan itself stands condemned in the eyes of the *ahl-e-zaban* 'guardians' of this notion. However, in India the Urdu-speaking elite still guards the 'purity' of Urdu against what it sees as the transgressions of Hindi. In Pakistan too there is a certain anxiety against the use of Hindi words by the younger generation as Indian TV soap operas and Hindi films are so popular. There is also some apprehension that certain sounds (phonemes) of Urdu (gutturals or, more precisely, velar and uvular stops and fricatives as in Khan and Afghanistan) would be replaced by Hindi sounds (/k/ and /g/ in these cases). In short, the apprehensions about identity in relation to a dominant majority which exercised Muslim minds since the downfall of Mughal power in India, are still valid in some form or the other.

That is another reason why the linguistic views of Insha, Shirani, and Abdul Haq need to be given attention by contemporary social scientists.

ANNEXURE - 1

List of Shirani's Works on Urdu Linguistic History in Journals in Chronological Order

- *Masnavi Laila Majnun az Ahmad Dakani, OCM,* November 1925
- *Rekhtah Oriental College Magazine, OCM,* May 1926
- *Bakat Qissa, OCM,* August 1926
- *Khaliq Bari, OCM,* November 1926
- *Farsi Zaban Ki aik Qadim Farhang Mein Urdu Zaban ka Ansar, Makhzan,* March–April 1929
- *Urdu Zaban our us ke Mukhtalif Nam, OCM,* May 1929
- *Urdu ke Fiqre our Dohe Athwen aur Naveen Sadi Hijri ki Farsi Tasnifat se, OCM,* August 1930
- *Shimali Hind Mein Urdu Daswen aur Giarhween Sadi Hijri Mein, OCM,* May & August 1931
- *Urdu ki Shakh Hariani Zaban, OCM,* November–February 1931–2
- *Bachchon ke Ta'limi Nisab Proceedings of the Mu'arif Islamia,* April 1933, Lahore
- *Sab Ras, OCM,* November 1934
- *Tarikh-e-Gharibi, OCM,* November–February 1938–9
- *Daswin Sadi Hijri ke Baz Jadid dariaft shuda rekhte, OCM,* May 1939
- *Daire ke Mehdaviyon ka Urdu Adab ka Ta 'mir Mein Hissa, OCM,* November 1940–February 1941
- *Urdu-e-Qadeem ke Mutaliq Chand Tasrihat, OCM,* May 1941

REFERENCES

Anderson, Benedict. 1983. *Imagined Communities.* London: Verso. Edition used, revised edition, 1991.

Bhimani, Harish. 1995. *In Search of Lata Mangeshkar.* New Delhi: Indus, an Imprint of Harper Collins Publishers India (Pvt) Ltd.

Bourdieu, Pierre. 1982. *Language and Symbolic Power* Trans. From the French by Gino Raymond and Matthew Adamson. Edited and Introduced by John B. Thompson. Edition used Cambridge: Polity Press, 1992.

Dalrymple, William. 2006. *The Last Mughal: The Fall of a Dynasty, Delhi, 1857.* London: Bloomsbury Publishing Pvt..

Faruqi, Shamsur Rahman. 1990. 'Some Problems of Urdu Lexicography'. *Annual of Urdu Studies* 7: 21–30.

Farouqui, Ather. 2006. *Redefining Urdu Politics in India.* New Delhi: Oxford University Press.

Haq, Abdul. 1960. *Qaumi Zaban* [Karachi] (16 Sept–01 Oct). 7. In Rahman, Syed Mueen ur 1976: 180.

_______ 1952. *Pre-eminence of Urdu as Appraised by Several Distinguished Public Men of East Bengal.* Karachi: Anjuman-e-Taraqqi-e-Urdu.

_______ n.d. *Pakistan Mein Urdu ka Mas'ala [The Problem of Urdu in Pakistan].* Karachi: Majlis-e-Taraqqi-e-Urdu.

Insha, Insha Allah Khan. 1802. *Darya-e-Latafat.* Compiled by Maulvi Abdul Haq. Translated from Persian into Urdu by Pandit Brajmohan Dataria Kaifi. Lahore: Anjuman Taraqqi-e-Urdu, 1988.

Jalibi, Jamil. 1975. *Tarikh-e-Adab-e-Urdu.* Vol. 1. Lahore: Majlis Tarqqi-e-Adab.

Malik, Fateh Mohammad. 2006. *Punjab ki Madri Zaban Urdu Hai [Urdu: The Mother Tongue of the Punjab is Urdu].* In Malik et al. Vol. 4: 1–5.

_______ Pirzada, Syed Sardar Ahmad, and Shah, Tajamal. 2006. *Pakistan Mein Urdu* 5 vols. as given below:

_______ Pirzada, Syed Sardar Ahmad, and Shah, Tajamal. (Comp). 2006. *Pakistan Mein Urdu: Sindh.* Vol. 1. Islamabad: National Language Authority.

_______ Pirzada, Syed Sardar Ahmad, and Shah, Tajamal. (Comp). 2006. *Pakistan Mein Urdu: Balochistan.* Vol. 2. Islamabad: National Language Authority.

_______ Pirzada, Syed Sardar Ahmad, and Shah,Tajamal. (Comp). 2006. *Pakistan Mein Urdu: Abaseen (Sarhad + Shumali Elaqah Jaat).* Vol. 3. Islamabad: National Language Authority.

_______ Pirzada, Syed Sardar Ahmad, and Shah, Tajamal. (Comp). 2006. *Pakistan Mein Urdu: Punjab.* Vol. 4. Islamabad: National Language Authority.

_______ Pirzada, Syed Sardar Ahmad and Shah, Tajamal. (Comp). 2006. *Pakistan Mein Urdu: Kashmir.* Vol. 5. Islamabad: National Language Authority.

Rahman, Tariq. 2011. *From Hindi to Urdu: a Social and Political History.* Karachi: Oxford University Press and Delhi: Orient Blackswan.

_______ 1999. *Language, Education and Culture.* Karachi: Oxford University Press.

Rai, Amrit. 1984. *A House Divided.* Delhi: Oxford University Press, 1991.

Shirani, Hafiz Mahmud. 1928. *Punjab Mein Urdu.* Reprinted. Islamabad: Muqtadara Qaumi Zaban, 1988.

_______ 1965–2002. *Muqalat-e-Hafiz Mahmud Shirani* in 9 volumes. Compiled by Mazhar Mahmud Shirani. Lahore: Majlis-e-Taraqqi in Urdu.

Shirani, Muzhar (Comp). 1965. *Musannif ke Halat-e-Zindagi [Urdu: Events of the Life of the Author].* In Shirani 1: 17–100.

15

Preliminary Notes on the Languages of the Neelam Valley

Khawaja A. Rehman

1. INTRODUCTION

The Neelam Valley is the most linguistically diverse region in all of historic Jammu and Kashmir, with 221,347 people speaking no fewer than seven languages as their mother tongue. This is a preliminary overview of these languages. The aim of this study is to introduce this linguistically rich but undocumented area to the outside world and invite scholars to carry out linguistic research in the region. I also aim to create awareness of language loss among the speakers of these languages.

2. THE LANGUAGES OF THE NEELAM VALLEY

The Neelam District, which is one of the ten districts of Azad Jammu and Kashmir, stretches from Chelhana to Taobat. It covers 3,621 square kilometres and is home to a population of 221,347 people (Population Census 2017). Prior to the 1947 partition of India, the region comprised a part of the Gures Valley and a region known as Drawar or Drawa (Bates 1873: 181). It was collectively known as the Kishanganga Valley after the principal river, the Kishanganga (river of Krishan), which flows through the length of the valley (Bates 1873: 234–6). The name, as with several other places in the region, was officially changed to 'Neelam Valley' and the river's name to 'Neelam' (also spelled Neelum) as a consequence of the 1947 partition. In some cases name changes have occurred twice, as with the village of 'Islampura', originally called Chittan but subsequently becoming Rampur; a name chosen by colonel Beja Singh, the then *zillahdar* of Muzaffarabad, because of the indelicacy of the former appellation (Bates 1873: 320). Subsequently, on ideological grounds, the village was renamed and has remained as Islampura since. The name Neelam was originally derived from the village Neelam, situated above the right bank of the river on a plateau at an elevation of 1,524 metres, 9 kilometres up from Athmuqam, the headquarters of the Neelam District. In addition, there are two other small hamlets known as Neelam in the Neelam Valley.

The elevation of the Neelam Valley along the river and the Neelam Highway ranges from 1,000 metres to 2,200 metres; however, many of the surrounding mountain peaks rise to as much as 5,000 metres. In 2005 the area was upgraded to the position of district and subsequently called District Neelam comprising two *tehsils:* Tehsil Sharda and Tehsil Athmuqam.

The present population of the Neelum Valley has a history of continuous migrations. Most of the population have come from the Kaghan Valley in the Khyber Pakhtunkhwa province. The Kaghan Valley runs parallel to the Neelam Valley. According to oral traditions there are two major causes of migration from the Kaghan Valley: heavy snowfall and the atrocities of the local rulers of the region. *buḍi d̪i ra:t̪* 'Night of the Old Woman' is a popular folk tale about the mass migration from Kaghan. According to the details there was a heavy snowfall in the winter and an old widow who had two sons, slaughtered her bull and kept giving the beef to her two sons who continued removing the snow from the roof of their house till morning. All the other houses of the village were buried under the snow and most of the people had lost their lives. Only the house of the old woman was safe. The incident occured on the night of 18 Phaggan, the eleventh month in the Bikrami calendar. Traditionally, people of the Neelam Valley follow the Bikrami calendar. It is usually expected that there will be heavy snowfall during the night of 18 Phaggan. The night is known as *buḍi d̪i ra:t̪*.

Another major portion of the population migrated from the valley of Kashmir in different phases, mostly in search of pastures to graze their livestock. Apart from these two migrations, a sizeable population also migrated from the adjacent areas of Chilas and Astore, and even from Swat. The emigrants from the different directions also brought a diverse cultural and linguistic heritage along with them,which they are still maintaining. Small pockets of Shina speakers, Pashto speakers, Kundal Shahi speakers, Kashmiri speakers, and Gojri speakers constitute strong evidence of this maintenance. However, modernization is posing a threat to this rich linguistic and cultural heritage.

The languages of the Neelam Valley have mostly remained under-documented or even undocumented in some instances (Rehman 2012). *The Linguistic Survey of India* (Grierson 1915) did not contain substantive information on the languages of the valley, and neither does one find much information about the area in the more recent literature. The fact that the Line of Control runs right through the valley is one obvious reason as to why the area has been inaccessible to researchers in recent times. However, even before Partition, the area was difficult to access due to the absence of a road link. The only document available giving some scant information about the Neelam Valley region is Bates' gazetteer (1873).

In this chapter, I present a brief overview of the languages and language varieties spoken in the Neelam Valley based on recent research as well as my experience as a resident of the area (Rehman 2011, 2012). These varieties include forms of languages that are spoken widely elsewhere, such as Hindko, Gojri, Shina (Guresi and Shina of Phulwei), Kashmiri, and even Pashto, but also the rather distinct language of the village of Kundal Shahi, located near the Neelam district headquarters, Athmuqam (Rehman and Baart 2005).

2.1 Hindko

Most of the Hindko speakers currently living in the Neelam Valley have migrated from the Kaghan Valley as indicated by oral tradition and linguistic affinity. However, there are some people who came from other parts and spoke other languages but shifted to Hindko later.

The Hindko language spoken in the Neelam Valley is usually known as *pa:rmi* by the communities other than the Kashmiris. The Kashmiri community ordinarily calls it *pɨ:rim*, but sometimes also Hindko or Pahaṛi. The word *pa:rmi* or *pɨ:rim* is derived from the Kashmiri word *apɨ:rim* 'from the other side'. Historically speaking, the Hindko speaking communities lived in the highlands of the Kashmir Valley and these highlanders were referred to by the Kashmiris as ɑpɨ:rim '(people) from the other side'. Subsequently, the use of this word has been extended to their language as well. The word *pɨ:rim* for Hindko is also used in Indian-administered Kashmir, as I found the expression in a Kashmiri comedy recorded in Srinagar (Rehman 2012).

The use of Hindko has never been documented before in any part of Kashmir. In traditional literature the Hindko language spoken in the Neelam Valley is referred to as Pahari (Bates 1873, Grierson 1915). In 2004, I recorded a word list, adapted from the Sociolinguistic Survey of Northern Pakistan (O'Leary 1992), at eight different locations in the Neelam Valley. I analysed the word list in collaboration with Dr Joan Baart, who has been working on the languages of northern Pakistan since 1991. The analysis of the word list showed that the variety spoken in the Neelam Valley was closer to the variety of Hindko spoken in the Kaghan Valley than the Pahari spoken in the Murree Hills. This conclusion was also confirmed in informal discussions with the Hindko speakers in the Neelam Valley as well as in the Kaghan Valley and Mansehra.

This proves that the northern dialect of Hindko is also spoken in Azad Kashmir and my hypothesis is that the same variety is also spoken on the other side of the Line of Control. There are many villages in Indian-administered Kashmir along the Line of Control, at a distance of only few yards from the villages of Azad Kashmir. The Line of Control actually divides some villages in the Neelam Valley. Linguistically speaking, it may be interesting to look into the speech differences that have evolved during the last 70 years among adjacent villages lying on either side of the Line of Control.

It is worth distinguishing two populations of native Hindko speakers in the Neelam Valley: ethnic Hindko speakers and the Hindko speakers of other ethnicities. According to the oral histories, Hindko speakers came from Mansehra and the Kaghan Valley, which parallels the Neelam Valley, whereas the non-ethnic Hindko speakers came from either the valley of Kashmir or other parts of South Asia. In spite of the fact that most of the groups originally speaking languages other than Hindko have shifted to Hindko, they retain a strong ethnic consciousness, identifying along ethnic rather than linguistic lines.

The variety of Hindko spoken in the Neelam Valley very interestingly retains, unlike other varieties of Hindko, Pahari, and Punjabi, the old Indo-Aryan voiced aspirated stops /b^h/, /d̪^h/, /ɖ^h/, /g^h/, in word-initial positions. However my present research shows that a shift is going on very rapidly. The shift is quite evident along the roadside and in the main towns, where outsiders visit frequently. In contrast, the settlements away from the main road and further upstream, roughly above Dudnial, show strong retention of this feature. This suggests that frequent contact with speakers of other varieties of Hindko, and with speakers of Punjabi and Pahari, is a major cause of this change. The influence of Punjabi is not restricted to the phonology but also affects syntax. To give an example, the dative and accusative marker *kʊ* of traditional Hindko is being replaced with the form *nu:* of Punjabi.

Hindko is the predominant language of the Neelam Valley. It is the main lingua franca. Speakers of other languages are usually proficient in Hindko, except some women in a few Kashmiri and Shina-speaking villages. It is also encroaching upon the languages of smaller groups.

Virtually all members of the other language communities are bilingual in Hindko. A process of language shift to Hindko is going on in many of these communities. In some of these communities this process started relatively recently, while in others it has been going on much longer.

2.2 Kashmiri

Kashmiri is the second largest language of the area. It is spoken by the ethnic Kashmiris. However, many Kashmiris have switched to Hindko in the last two centuries. The villages where Kashmiri is spoken as the sole mother tongue include: Halmat, Sardari, Shunddas, Tehjian, Malik Seri, and Khawaja Seri. Among these, the former three are adjacent to each other at a distance of about 193 kilometres from Muzaffarabad, the capital city of Azad Kashmir. Further upstream we come to Nekro, where the majority are Kashmiri mother tongue speakers with a few families of Shina speakers. The village of Nekro is adjacent to Karimabad, formerly known as Sutti, where Guresi Shina is spoken as a mother tongue. The residents of these villages are less proficient in Hindko than other Kashmiri speakers of the region. They usually prefer to use Urdu with the Hindko speakers. Malik

Seri and Khawaja Seri are adjacent to each other and are normally known collectively as Khawaja Seri, but the revenue department of the state lists them separately. These villages are about 125 kilometres from Muzaffarabad. Tehjian, another Kashmiri speaking village, is about 7 kilometres further downstream from Khawaja Seri. Almost all individuals of these villages are bilingual in Hindko. Apart from these there are some six other villages where Kashmiri is the majority language.

The variety of Kashmiri spoken in the Neelam Valley is closer to the variety spoken in northern Kashmir, especially that of the Kupwara District of Indian-administered Kashmir, rather than that of Muzaffarabad city. Although the Kashmiri spoken in Muzaffarabad is intelligible to the Kashmiris of the Neelam Valley, they can understand the variety of Srinagar better than that of Muzaffarabad.

The Kashmiri spoken in the Neelam Valley has retained some archaic features. For example, Neelam Valley Kashmiri has *d̪aram mi:j* 'woman' and *d̪aram boj* 'friend', which are hardly found in other varieties of Kashmiri. The word *daram* is probably derived from the Sanskrit word *dharma*. Moreover, my research reveals that the Neelam Valley dialect of Kashmiri retains the third person plural subject agreement suffix *-kh* in ergative constructions more consistently than other dialects (Rehman 2011). Speakers of the Srinagar dialect accept this usage, but it is not in common use, suggesting that it is an archaism. It also shares the retroflex trill /ɽ/ with the variety of Kupwara, which corresponds to an alveolar trill in the variety of Srinagar.

2.3 Kundal Shahi

Kundal Shahi is a village located in the Neelam Valley 74 kilometres upstream from Muzaffarabad, the capital city of Pakistani-administered Kashmir. In 2009, the village had an estimated population of 4,500 (Rehman 2012). The Kundal Shahi language (KS) is spoken in this village.

KS belongs to the North-Western group of the Indo-Aryan languages. It is closely related to Shina and spoken as a native language by some 700 people in the predominantly Hindko-speaking village of Kundal Shahi. Nearly all people whose ancestral language is KS, or who still speak the language, live in the village of Kundal Shahi. I conducted a survey in 2010 which showed that the total population of the KS community was 3,371 living in 537 households scattered throughout eight *mohallas* 'hamlets' namely: Rait, Graan, Gujhaan, Sinji Nakka, Dolur, Frashian/Khujhaani, Gheelan, and Sattra.

The KS community does not have any specific name for their language. Therefore, in our earlier research we chose to name the language after the village, i.e. 'Kundal Shahi'. No other closely related variety of KS is known so far. A word list of 199 items of KS was compared with the word lists of Shina, Hindko, Gojri, and Kashmiri as found in O'Leary (1992). The results show that KS shares 49 per cent lexical similarity with Shina, 47 per cent with Hindko, and 45 per cent with Kashmiri (Rehman and Baart 2005).

Among the languages of the Neelam Valley, KS is the only language which is not spoken anywhere outside the Neelam Valley. The name of KS, with some basic information provided by this author and Joan Baart, first appeared in the 17th Edition of Ethnologue (Lewis et al. 2013). Moreover, at our request, the ISO 639-3 Registration Authority assigned the three letter code *shd* to Kundal Shahi in 2010.

With regard to language research and documentation, this author started working on KS in 2002 with Joan Baart, and as a result of their joint research, a paper on KS appeared in 2005 (Rehman and Baart). This was one of the first descriptions of any language spoken in the Neelam Valley. Later in 2005, this author did a comparative study of ergative marking in Kundal Shahi, Hindko, and Kashmiri (Rehman 2011).

As a part of his PhD research this author described and analysed the status of KS and causes of language shift in the KS community. One of the chapters of the thesis was devoted to linguistic description and analysis including the syntax, morphology, and phonology of KS. Hindko is the dominant language and the main lingua franca of the Neelam Valley. All KS speakers are bilingual in Hindko. A process of language shift to Hindko is going on. Moreover, exchange of firing and shelling across the Line of Control from 1990–2003 between the Pakistani and Indian armies, and the devastating earthquake of 8 October 2005, has aggravated the situation and accelerated language shift. My research establishes the status of KS as a *Severely Endangered Language* (Rehman 2011, 2012). The level of endangerment of KS has been worked out on the basis of the model developed by the UNESCO Ad Hoc Expert Group on Language Vitality and Endangerment (UNESCO 2003).

In addition, the research found that as long as intergenerational transmission was robust, a stable bilingualism existed, and KS was not threatened. The moment parents stopped teaching the language to their children, KS started to decline. Nowadays, there are only two households where the language is, to some extent, actively spoken. KS is rapidly and increasingly being replaced by Hindko (Rehman 2011, 2012).

With only around 700 competent speakers left, KS has no oral or written literary tradition or orthography. It has become completely inactive with regard to emerging domains. Although the community expresses a positive attitude towards the language, unless there is a radical shift in attitude towards speaking it with children, it is doomed. On the UNESCO scale of language endangerment, KS rates near the bottom of the scale. The language is used in fewer and fewer social domains and structures (case markings, etc.) and vocabulary items appear to be eroding (Rehman 2012). Some words recorded from the elderly speakers of the language in 2002 are no longer used and in some instances not even remembered by fluent speakers. Without urgent moves to arrest and reverse its decline, KS is likely to be extinct within less than fifty years (Rehman 2012).

The present situation contrasts sharply with the situation before the construction of the road in the 1960s. At that time, the language was not only actively learnt and used by the KS community, but also by the speakers of neighbouring languages. This small linguistic minority maintained their ancestral language with full vigour and strength for centuries. But with the passage of each day, this linguistic heritage is now being lost, along with its rich indigenous knowledge, culture, and history. Once-fluent speakers are not only losing vocabulary items, but also fluency in KS. Only two or three elderly speakers can recall any songs, and only a few couplets.

In collaboration with the Endangered Language Documentation Programme, School of Oriental African Studies (SOAS), this author collected a range of text materials in audio and video format, translated with annotations (Rehman 2015). The aim of the documentation project was to preserve the dying Linguistic Heritage.

2.4 Gojri

The third largest ethnic group in the Neelam Valley are the Gojar people. Basically there are two types of Gojars: settled Gojars and nomads or Bakarwals.

2.4.1 Settled Gojars

Local folk tales indicate that the settled Gojars are the earliest settlers of the Neelam Valley. They are believed to have migrated to the Neelam Valley to find summer pastures for their goats and sheep, and gradually settled down permanently. These Gojars no longer raise sheep and goats on a large scale. Their villages, Marnat, Kharigam, Kuttan, and Ashkot, are scattered all over the Neelam Valley. The interesting thing about these Gojars is that the majority have abandoned their mother tongue and adopted Hindko. However, there are still a few settlements among the Gojars who speak their mother tongue at least at home. The settled Gojars hardly use Gojri in bazaars and other public places in front of speakers of other languages.

2.4.2 The Bakarwals

The Bakerwals, 'goatherds', are those Gojars who still raise goats and sheep. They are not permanent residents of the Neelam Valley, but come during the summer with their animals, especially goats, sheep, and mules (for carrying loads). They go to high pastures for the summer and sometimes even travel to the northern areas and the Kaghan Valley. These people usually go to the Punjab plains and lower parts of Azad Kashmir during the winters. They use the Gojri language in their daily communication and show a strong tendency for language maintenance, reducing the probability of language shift in the short term. The total population of these nomadic Gojars is not available. However, according to a rough estimate of the Wildlife Department of Azad Kashmir, the summer of 2005 saw a total of 150,000 goats and sheep traveling into the Neelam Valley (personal communication of Manzoor, a local official). Recent research could not collect a Gojri word list for comparison, and only interviews, questionnaires, and personal observations by this author residing in the region were used to determine the status of Gojri.

2.5 Shina

Although the Gojars are the third largest ethnic group in the Neelam Valley, the third most widely spoken language is Shina. Shina is only spoken in three villages, and there are two clearly different varieties of Shina: Guresi Shina and Shina of Phulwei.

2.5.1 Guresi Shina

Guresi Shina is spoken in Taobut, the last village of the Neelam Valley, and its adjacent village, Karimabad (Sutti). Taobut is about 215 kilometres from Muzaffarabad. Both villages are on the right bank of the Neelam River. The language is locally known as Shina and sometimes Dardi. The total population of these two villages was 1,978 in 2017. The majority of the inhabitants belong to the Lone tribe.

Most of the Shina speakers of the area are bilingual in Kashmiri. They use Kashmiri with the neighbouring Kashmiris. They have also borrowed many Kashmiri words. They do not speak Hindko well and prefer to use Urdu with Hindko speakers. Moreover, they do not consider themselves grouped in any way with the Shina speakers of Phulwei. On the other hand, they are culturally closer to the Kashmiri speakers of Halmat and Sardari and associate themselves with these people rather than the Phulweites. There are intermarriages with the neighbouring Kashmiri communities but there is no record of intermarrying with the Shina speakers of Phulwei. According to my informants, there is a low level of mutual intelligibility with the people of Phulwei and their language is different in vocabulary and pronunciation. They claim to have relatives on the other side of the Line of Control and that their variety is similar to the variety spoken in the Gures Valley of Indian-administered Kashmir. However, when I compared some words with the Guresi Shina collected on the other side (Schmidt 2004) I found most of the words quite different. These Shina speakers also claim that their variety is closer to that of Qamri, a town in Gilgit-Baltistan, and they can communicate easily with the people from Qamri.

2.5.2 Shina of Phulwei

Phulwei, a large village with many *mozas* 'hamlets', lies at a distance of 180 kilometres from Muzaffarabad. The total population of the village was 4,500 according to the 2017 census. My current research shows that in the beginning, about two centuries ago, the first group of these Shina speakers settled at *pain seri* 'lower plain'. This group included four brothers who had migrated from Nait, a town in the Chilas area, due to some family feud. The majority of the people claim to belong to the Lone tribe, but have adopted the names of local clans, including Kachray and Nasray. It is very interesting that in Taobut and Karimabad the same tribe is in the majority.

Citing one Sir James Wilson, Grierson (1915) claims that in Nait, Chilas, some people speak Guresi Shina. However, the Shina speakers of Phulwei claim descent from migrants who had come from Nait, and they speak the Chilas dialect, not Guresi. Moreover, recent research (Radloff 1992, 1999; Schmidt 2004) does not report Guresi in the Chilas area.

My respondents belonged to all groups and all claimed to have come from Nait. They report a higher level of mutual intelligibility with speakers from Nait than with the Shina speakers of Taobut and Karimabad/Sutti. They have close relations in Chilas and frequently travel there. However, as the result of a feud, which claimed some lives on either side some nine years ago, intermarriage between the people of Phulwei and Nait has ceased.

The people in the Neelam Valley are normally very peaceful but the people of Phulwei are known all over the region for their feuds and fights. They themselves also admit the fact. One of my informants told me that there are very frequent murders and narrated that his grandfather had committed seven murders, his father three, and even his own son had killed a man.

Locally these people are known as Dard and they themselves call the Hindko speakers Gojars irrespective of their ethnic group. These Dards have no record of intermarrying with the Shina speakers of Karimabad/Sutti or Taobut. However, there are some instances of their intermarrying with the local Hindko speakers. According to the Shina speakers of Phulwei, the Shina or Dardi spoken in Taobut and Karimabad is not the standard variety and they refer to it as *kachi* 'half-baked'.

In the village there are a few Hindko speaking households but they are bilingual in Shina.

2.6 PASHTO

Dhaki and Changnar are two villages in the Neelam Valley where Pashto is the mother tongue of all residents. The speakers of the language refer to their language as Pukhto/Pakhto. The population of these two villages, according to the 2017 census was 1,888 in 255 households. The people claim that some two centuries back their forefathers migrated from Swat, a region in northern Pakistan, and settled in Dhaki. Some others settled in the Kashmir Valley as well. According to the oral history, the main reason for choosing the place was its rich environment, conducive to raising livestock. Dhaki is at about two hours walking distance from the left bank of the river Neelam. Some of these Pashto speakers later shifted to another nearby village, Changnar. Both villages are right on the Line of Control, separating Indian from Pakistani-administered Kashmir.

Almost all male members of the group are bilingual in Hindko. Some of the women can understand Hindko but most of them cannot speak it. The men in these villages have more frequent contact with the Hindko-speaking population than the women, who seldom travel outside these villages and have no Hindko-speaking community nearby.

During the last twenty-nine years, cross border firing between Indian and Pakistani troops has caused a large scale migration from these villages and this migration has led to language loss on a large scale. It will be very interesting to document the degree of this loss.

The Pashto spoken by this population is quite different from other varieties of Pashto and is a dialect in its own right. These Pashto speakers can communicate with other Pashto speakers but they cannot understand them fully. My current research shows that they have assimilated many Hindko words into their Pashto, and also have kept some archaic words of Pashto, which are no longer used by the other Pashto speakers in Pakistan.

No linguistic literature has mentioned the existence of Pashto in any part of Kashmir. To my knowledge, this is the only settlement anywhere in Azad Kashmir where Pashto is spoken.

In the Neelam Valley, apart from these Pashto speakers, there are some other groups who claim to be ethnic Pathans, but apparently shifted to Hindko a long time ago. Locally these groups are still known as Pathans and they also refer to themselves as Pathans.

3. CONCLUSION

Along with an abundant biodiversity, the Neelam Valley also contains a rich linguistic diversity. No other region in Azad Kashmir maintains such linguistic diversity. Over seven local languages and language varieties are spoken in the region, some of which are exclusively spoken in the Neelam Valley, e.g. the Kundal Shahi language.

Apart from these local languages, Urdu and English are also used. These languages are the media of instruction in schools. No indigenous language is taught in schools. No standard orthography is available for these local languages. However, some Kashmiri households retain copies of Kashmiri literature, especially poetry books, published before the 1947 partition. Borrowings from Urdu and English are obvious in all these local languages. Most of these languages are losing speakers and their futures are doomed unless efforts are made to save the rich linguistic heritage.

REFERENCES

Bates, Charles Ellison. 1873. *A Gazetteer of Kashmīr and Adjacent Districts of Kishtwār, Bhadrawār, Jamū, Naoshera, Pūnch and the Valley of Kishen Ganga.* Calcutta: Superintendent of Government Printing, India.

Grierson, George A. (ed.). 1915. *Specimens of the Dardic or Piśāchā Languages (including Kāshmīrī).* Calcutta: Superintendent of Government Printing, India. (Linguistic Survey of India, vol. 8, part 2).

Koul, Omkar N. 2003. 'Kashmiri'. In *The Indo-Aryan Languages*, edited by George Cardona and Dhanesh Jain. 991–1051. London: Rutledge.

Lewis, Paul M., Simons, Gary F., and Fennig, Charles D. (eds.). 2013. *Ethnologue: Languages of the World. (17th Edition.)* Dallas, Texas: SIL International. <http://www.ethnologue.com>

O'Leary, Clare F. (ed.). 1992. *Sociolinguistic Survey of Northern Pakistan*, 5 vols. Islamabad: National Institute of Pakistan Studies and Summer Institute of Linguistics.

Radloff, Carla F. 1999. *Aspects of the Sound System of Gilgiti Shina.* Islamabad: National Institute of Pakistan Studies and Summer Institute of Linguistics.

——— 1992. 'The dialects of Shina'. In *Sociolinguistic Survey of Northern Pakistan, Vol 2,* edited by Clare F. O'Leary. 89–203. Islamabad: National Institute of Pakistan Studies and Summer Institute of Linguistics.

Rehman, Khawaja A. 2015. Documentation of the Kundal Shahi Language, Kundal Shahi, Pakistan. London: SOAS, Endangered Languages Archive, ELAR. URL: http://elar.soas.ac.uk/collection/mp1971104 (accessed on 26 October 2019).

——— 2011. 'Ergativity in Kundal Shahi, Kashmiri, and Hindko'. In *Himalayan Languages and Linguistics: Studies in Phonology, Semantics, Morphology and Syntax,* edited by Mark Turin and Bettina Zeisler. 219–34. Leiden: Brill.

——— and Baart, Joan L. G. 2005. 'A first look at the language of Kundal Shahi in Azad Kashmir'. *SIL Electronic Working Papers 2005-008*. Dallas: SIL International. <http://www.sil.org/SILEWP/2005/silewp2005-008.pdf> accessed 14 October 2016.

Schmidt, Ruth Laila. 2004. 'A grammatical comparison of Shina dialects'. In *Himalayan Languages: Past and Present, edited by Anju* Saxena. 33–55. Berlin: Mouton de Gruyter. *(Trends in Linguistics: Studies and Monographs 149*).

UNESCO. 2003. *Language Vitality and Endangerment*. UNESCO Expert Meeting on Safeguarding Endangered Languages. Paris. <http://www.unesco.org/culture/ich/doc/src/00120-EN.pdf> accessed 27 January 2009.

16

The Phonemes of Gultari Shina

Ruth Laila Schmidt

1. INTRODUCTION

Gultari Shina is spoken in Pakistan on the far side of the Deosai Plains from Skardu, near the Line of Control between India and Pakistan (see map below). The geographically closest Shina dialects are those of Dras and Gures (in India). Radloff (1992: 107–9) groups Gultari in the Eastern cluster of Shina dialects,[1] along with other dialects of Baltistan, and presents a word list of 210 items.

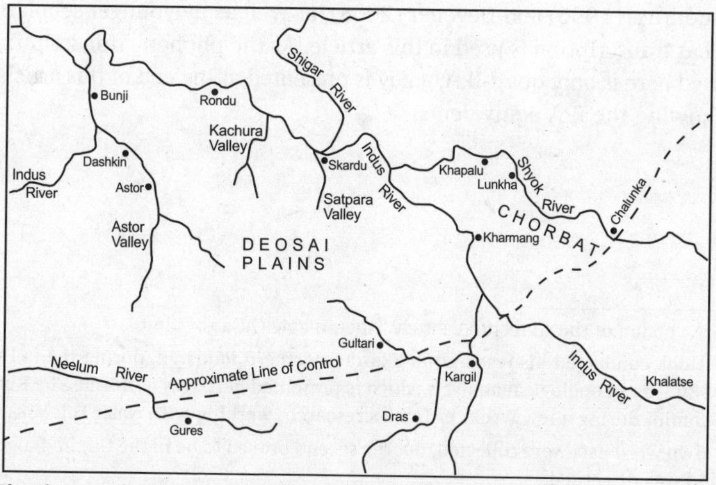

Sketch map of Baltistan and adjacent areas, indicating the location of Gultari.

[1] The other groupings of Shina dialects are the Northern, Diamer, and Kohistan clusters.

Hook (1996) published an annotated text of the Kesar epic[2] narrated in the Shina dialect of Gultari by Nasir Hussain of Babachan[3] village. This text has ample grammatical and etymological notes, but only a partial phonemic representation. This article aims to fill in missing data. The segmental phonemes, vowels, and consonants, are presented with their allophones, and the features of length, nasalization, and pitch accent are discussed. A word list was collected from Nasir Hussain,[4] and is presented below (see Section 4) alongside word lists taken from the Drasi and Guresi dialects.[5] These lists will supplement the data presented by Radloff (1992), which includes Gultari and Drasi, but not Guresi. The word list shows some typical Eastern Shina features, including a tendency to use intervocalic [ŋ] where the other clusters use [g] (Radloff 1992: 144): /aŋaáý/, 'sky'; /síŋal/, 'sand'; preservation of some final [ṣṭ] consonant clusters: /diṣṭ/, 'handspan', /aṣṭ/, 'eight'; and occurrence of some initial plosive + liquid clusters: /krom/, 'work'; /príiẓo/. 'flea'.[6] The similarities between the Gultari list and the Drasi one are quite striking, despite the fact that these dialects now lie on opposite sides of the Line of Control.

Radloff (1999) contributed substantially to the establishment of a now-standard phonemic transcription for Shina, which is also used by Buddruss (1996) and Degener (2008), as well as by younger scholars. That transcription is used in this article. As the phonetic transcription used here is only quasi-IPA, a key is presented at the end of this article, showing the IPA equivalents.

---

2 A version of the sixteenth century Tibetan epic Gesar of Ling.

3 Hook conducted his research in Skardu, northern Pakistan, during the fall of 1989. The phonological analysis which is presented here was performed by Ruth Schmidt during a few weeks of Hook's research, working with Nasir Hussain.

4 Two word lists were collected, but the second proved to be in the Gilgiti dialect, and was discarded.

5 The Drasi and Guresi data is taken from Schmidt and Kaul (2008: 231–82). For a comparable phonological analysis of the Kohistani dialect of Shina, see Schmidt and Kohistani (2008: chapter 2) and Schmidt and Kohistani (1998).

6 See also Schmidt and Kaul (2008: 236–9).

2. PHONEMES OF GULTARI SHINA

Vowels

	Front	**Central**	**Back**
Close	/ i		u
Mid	e		o
Open	æ	a/	

Consonants

	Labial	**Dental**	**Alveopalatal**	**Retroflex**	**Velar**	**Glottal**
Plosives	/ p b	t d		ṭ ḍ	k g	
Fricatives	(f)	s z	š	ṣ ẓ	x	h
Affricates		ʦ	č ǰ	ç		
Nasals	m	n		ṇ	ŋ	
Liquids						
Lateral		l				
Tap			r			
Flap				ṛ		
Approximants	w		y /			

Aspiration: /h/, occurs with / p t ʦ ṭc ç k /

Suprasegmentals (shown above the vowel /a/):

/á/	short, accented vowel
/ã/	nasalized vowel
/aa/	long vowel
/áa/	accent on first mora (high falling pitch)
/aá/	accent on second mora (low rising pitch)

3. PHONETIC REALIZATION, DISTRIBUTION, AND ALLOPHONIC VARIATION

3.1 VOWELS

/ i /, close front vowel

= [ɪ] in the environment (C)iC, except where the final consonant is / ŋ ǰ l /: [sɪn], 'river'; [ɪṣ], 'bear'; [bʌˈrɪṣ], 'year'; [ˈbɪçʊṣ], 'lightning'; [ˈʌsɪlo], 'was'

= [i̯] occurring with nasalization: [ˈbi̯ʌ̃ĩ̯], 'willow'

= [í:ʰ] (breathy vowel) in the environment V́: (with low rising tone): [dí:ʰ], 'daughter'; [kʊˈní:ʰ], 'nineteen'

= [i] elsewhere: [ˈsiŋʌl], 'sand'; [ˈhʌti], 'hands'; [ˈmʊtiǰo], 'shoulder'; [nɪˈril], 'high pasture'; [ˈʌi], 'goat'; [ˈčʰori], 'shady side of mountain'; [nì:lo], 'blue'; [çì:ri̯e], 'day after tomorrow'

/e/, mid front vowel

= [ɛ] in the environment (C)eC (except where C = /y/): [ɛš], 'sheep'; [lɛl], 'blood'; [ˈwʌzɛm], 'I will come down'; [ˈbʊǰɛm], 'I will go'

= [eʰ] (breathy vowel) in the environment Ce (final stressed syllable): [çeʰ], 'walk!'; [ʌˈreʰ], 'bring!'

= [e] elsewhere: [čei̯], 'woman'; [ˈʌǰe], 'mother'; [né:], 'not'; [pè:], 'feet'; [dè:s], 'day'; [ḍé:r], 'stomach'

/æ/, open front vowel

= [æ] in all positions: [kæ̀:ṇ], 'flat rock'; [pǽ:n], 'blunt side of axe'; [mi̯æˈní:], 'my' (f.)

/a/, open central vowel

= [ʌ] in (C)aC and (C)ai: [sʌs], 'sister'; [sʌt], 'seven'; [ʌš], 'today'; [ˈʌi], 'goat'; [ˈčʌi], 'bird'

= [ʌ] in aCV(C) (short a- in di- and polysyllables): [ʌˈreʰ], 'bring!'; [ˈʌsɪlo], 'was'

= [ʌʰ] (breathy vowel) in Ca (final short stressed vowel): [khʌʰ], 'eat!' (sg.); [kʊˈtʌʰ], 'corner (loc.)'; [ṣʌʰ], 'six'

= [ʌ˙] in (C)aw: [ˈgʌ˙u̯], 'he went'; [ˈʌ˙u̯], 'that'; [čʌrˈpʌ˙u̯], 'bed'

= [ʌ˙] in stressed short syllables in disyllabic words: [ˈkʌ˙kʌs], 'a kind of bird'

= [ɑ] in V: (long vowels): [ṣɑ:], 'wish'; [pɑ̀:], 'foot'; [ˈu̯ɑ̀:lo], 'summer'; [bɑ́:r], 'load'; [khɑ̀:], 'eat!' (pl.); [bɑ́:s], 'yesterday'; [bɑ̀:s], 'overnight stay'

/u/, close back vowel

= [ʊ] in (C)uC (except where -C is /z/: [ˈʊtsi], 'springs (of water)'; [ˈmʊto], 'other'; [kʊˈṭo], 'knee'; [ˈo̯ʌtʊs], 'I came'

= [ʊ^{h}] (breathy vowel) in Cu (final short stressed vowel): [tʊ^{h}], 'you' (sg.)

= [ɯ] (unrounded) in the environments uš, šu: [nɯš], 'not'; [pʌˈrɯš], 'listen!' (<[pʌˈrʊǰ-], 'hear, listen'); [ˈʌšɯp], 'horse'

= [u˙] in a short stressed syllable ending in a voiced fricative: [mʌˈnu˙ẓo], 'person'

= [u] elsewhere: [dú:m], 'smoke'; [ˈkù:ṭo], 'deaf'; [sù :], 'needle'; [ˈlúuni], 'salt'; [ruˈbú:], 'wasp'; [ˈmʊsu], 'I' (ag.)

/o/, close-mid back vowel

= [o] in all positions: [čom], 'skin'; [pon], 'road'; [ˈmoto], 'brain'; [ˈò:ṭo], 'lip'; [nò:m], 'name'; [bʌˈzó:no], 'spring (season)'; [koˈkó:], 'chicken'

3.2 Consonants

/p/, voiceless bilabial plosive

= [pϕ ~ p^{h}] with aspiration: [ˈpϕʊŋe], 'moustache'; [pϕiˈli:li], 'ant'; [phi̯ő:li], 'hoe'

= [p] elsewhere: [pon], 'road'; [č^{h}ʌˈpʌru], 'churn'; [ǰɪp], 'tongue'

/b/, voiced bilabial plosive, in initial and medial positions only[7]

= [b] in both environments: [ˈbʌṛo], 'big'; [ˈbʌbo], 'father'

[7] Final [-b] has become voiceless: [i̯ʌp], 'irrigation channel', but [ˈi̯ʌbo ˈu̯ei͜], 'water of the irrigation channel'.

/t/, voiceless dental plosive

= [t] in all environments: [tuʰ], 'you (sg.)'; [ˈnʌto], 'nose'; [sʌt], 'seven'

/d/, voiced dental plosive

= [d] in all environments: [dù:], 'two'; [ʌˈdì:t], 'Sunday'; [bò:d], 'message'; [bʌˈdʌˑm], 'almond'

/ṭ/, voiceless retroflexplosive

= [t̠] initially: [t̠ar], 'break'

= [ṭ] elsewhere: [ˈkù:ṭo], 'deaf'; [ˈkà:ṭo], 'wood'; [dɪṣṭ], 'handspan'; [rò:ṭ], 'road'

/ḍ/, voiced retroflexplosive, in initial and medial positions only

= [d̠] in both environments: [d̠é:r], 'stomach'; [ˈd̠ʌd̠ɛr], 'stony place'

/k/, voiceless velar plosive

= [k] in all environments: [koṇ], 'ear'; [ʌˈkà:ẹ̯], 'eleven'; [muk], 'mouth'

/g/, voiced velar plosive, in initial and medial positions only[8]

= [g ~ g] medially: [tʌˈgʊn], 'box'; [kʌˈgù:no], 'widower'

= [g] initially: [gɪˈtí:ti], 'armpit'; [gʌˈọ̯ó:], 'stream'; [gʌˈọ̯ò:], 'cow'

/ts/, voiceless dental affricate, in initial and medial positions[9]

= [ts] in both environments: [ˈtsʊnmo], 'servant girl'; [tsʰoʰ], 'you (pl.)'; [ˈʊtsi], 'springs (of water)'

/č/, voiceless postalveolar affricate, in initial and medial positions only

= [č] in both environments: [čei̯], 'woman'; [ˈčò:dʌi̯], 'fourteen'; [mʊˈčɛm], 'I will finish'

[8] Final [-g] has become voiceless: [ro:k], 'illness', but [ˈrò:gi], 'illnesses'.

[9] Final [-ts] has become [-s]: [ʊs], 'spring (of water)', but [ˈʊtsi], 'springs'.

/ǰ/, voiced postalveolar affricate, in initial and medial positions only[10]

= [ǰ] varying freely with [ž]: [ǰon] ~ [žon], 'snake'; [ˈbʊǰɛm] ~ [ˈbʊžɛm], 'I will go'

/c̣/, voiceless retroflex affricate, in initial and medial positions only[11]

= [c̣] in both environments: [c̣oṣ], 'loom'; [c̣ʰè :ṣ], 'field'; [ʌˈc̣ʰì:], 'eye'

/f/, voiceless bilabial fricative (in loanwords only)

= [ɸ]: [ˈrʌɸʌl], 'rifle'; [ɸʌˈkì:r], 'itinerant holy man'

/s/, voiceless alveolar fricative

= [s] in all environments: [ˈsà:c̣o], 'dream'; [ˈsù:ri], 'sun'; [ˈmʊsu], 'I (ag.)'; [à:lʊs], 'I came'

/z/, voiced alveolar fricative[12]

= [z] in all environments: [zʌˈmɪn], 'earth'; [dè:zi], 'days'; [ˈkʌrʌz], 'loan'

/š/, voiceless alveopalatal fricative

= [š] in all environments: [šò:], 'white'; [mʊˈšà:], 'man'; [poš], 'five'; [dʌšˈti̯ó:ni], 'to know'

/ṣ/, voiceless retroflex fricative

= [ṣ] in all environments: [ṣí:ṣ], 'head'; [ˈmɪṣṭo], 'sweet'

/ẓ/, voiced retroflex fricative, in initial and medial positions only

= [ẓ] in both environments: [ẓà :], 'brother'; [ˈʌẓo], 'rain'

---

10 Final [-j] has become [-š]: [pʌˈrɯš], 'listen!' (<[pʌˈrʊj-], 'hear, listen').

11 Final [-c̣] has become [ṣ]: [pʊṣ], 'son', but [ˈpʊc̣i], 'sons'.

12 Final [-z] tends to be devoiced and is found only in loanwords: [ˈkʌrʌz] ~ [ˈkʌrʌs], 'loan'.

/x/, voiceless velar fricative

= [x] in occasional loanwords: [bʊˈxà:r], 'fever'

/h/, voiceless glottal fricative, in initial and medial position[13]

= [ʰ] aspirated release in the position Ch: [bʌˈkʰʊni], 'elbow'; [lɪkʰˈyó:ni], 'to write'; [ˈtʰyó:ni], 'to do'; [ˈrʌṭʰʌs], 'demoness'; [pʰʌˈpí:], 'father's sister'; [ˈčʰɪno], 'tore'; [ˈçʰɪle], 'clothes'; [mʌˈçʰì:], 'honey'

= [h] elsewhere: [hʌl], 'plough'; [zʌˈhʌr], 'poison'

/m/, voiced bilabial nasal

= [m] in all environments: [mo], 'I'; [mò:s], 'month'; [lʌˈmoṭo], 'tail'; [čom], 'skin'

/n/, voiced postdental nasal

= [n̠] (alveolar) when followed by a retroflex consonant: [n̠ú:ṣ̌], 'daughter-in-law'

= [n] (dental) elsewhere: [ˈnʌto], 'nose'; [mʌˈnu·ẓo], 'person'; [ˈkʰoǰʌn], 'question'; [kʰò:n], 'they will eat'

/ṇ/, voiced retroflex nasal, in medial and final positions only

= [ṇ] in both environments: [mʌˈṇò:k], 'frog'; [ʊˈrà:ṇ], 'lamb'; [koṇ], 'ear'

/ŋ/, voiced velar nasal, in medial and final positions only

= [ŋ] in both environments: [ˈoŋo], 'sickle'; [dɪ̃́:ŋ], 'leopard'

/l/, voiced postdental to alveolar lateral

= [l] (postdental) intervocalically and after close vowels: [ˈʌsɪle], 'were'; [u̯à:lo], 'summer'; [tʰʊl], 'egg'; [čʰɪˈlɪṣ], 'root'

= [l̠] (alveolar) initially and after open vowels: [l̠ɛl̠], 'blood'; [l̠ʌˈmoṭo], 'tail'; [hʌl̠], 'plough'

---

13 Final [-ʰ] occurs as a conditioned variant after some vowels.

/r/, voiced alveolar tap

= [r] in all environments: [ˈrʌṭʰʌs], 'demoness'; [grom], 'neighbourhood in a village'; [šʌˈruṇ], 'roof'; [nɪˈril], 'high pasture'; [rí:l], 'copper'

/ṛ/, voiced retroflex flap, medial only

= [ṛ]: [ˈbʌṛo], 'big'

/y/, close front approximant

= [e̯] after /a/: [dà:e̯], 'beard'; [ʌˈkà:e̯], 'eleven'

= [i̯] elsewhere: [ˈi̯ó :no], 'winter'; [bɛˈi̯ó :ni], 'to sit'; [ˈʌ̃ṭi̯e], 'bones'; [ˈpʰi̯ő:li], 'hoe'; [čei̯], 'woman'

/w/, close-mid back approximant

= [u̯] ~ [β] initially: [βʌˈgi̯á:], 'ford'; [u̯ʌˈgi̯ù:l], 'river bank'; [ˈu̯à:lo], 'winter'

= [β] in the environment VwV: [ˈṣeβo], 'blind'; [ˈhì:βo], 'heart'

= [o̯] before /e/, /a/: [so̯ɛm], 'I sleep'; [čo̯ʌl], 'morning'; [bo̯à:e̯], 'twelve'

= [u̯] elsewhere: [ku̯i], 'village'; [thʌu̯], 'he did'

3.3 Pitch accent and vowel length

Although syllable stress is marked in the phonetic transcriptions, Gultari Shina is more adequately described as a pitch accent language (Radloff 1999: 57–88). Every word has one accent, as illustrated in (1), and the accent may occur on a long or short vowel. In Gultari, if the word contains a long vowel, that vowel is always accented. All monosyllables are accented, so the accent need not be transcribed on monosyllables.

(1) [ˈṣʌʰ], 'six' /ṣá/
[šʌˈruṇ], 'roof' /šarúṇ/
[ˈbrɛspʌt], 'Thursday' /bréspat/
[gɪˈtì:ti], 'armpit' /gitíiti/
[ǰʌmʌˈçó:], 'son-in-law' /ǰamaçoó/
[ˈkò:rkʊs], 'crow' /kóorkus/

As in Gilgiti and Kohistani Shina, contrasts in pitch (high-falling versus low-rising), see examples in (2), may be described as accent on the vocalic mora. A high-falling pitch occurs when the first part or mora of a long vowel is accented. When the second part or mora is accented, the result is a low-rising pitch. This is because the phenomenon of accent is associated with a high pitch. Concomitant with this, long vowels are written as double vowels (two moras).

(2) [ṣàː], 'king' /ṣáa/ vs [ṣáː], 'wish' /ṣaá/
[mòːs], 'month' /móos/ vs [móːs], 'flesh' /moós/

Pairs like the ones in (3) attest to the two-way contrast in vowel length:

(3) [koṇ], 'ear' /koṇ/ vs [kòːṇ], 'arrow' /kóoṇ/
[sʌt], 'seven' /sat/ vs [sáːt], 'companion' /sáat/

3.4 Word-final approximants

Radloff (1999: 52–6) analyses the Gilgiti vowel approximants [i̯] and [u̯] as consonants: /y/, /w/, citing both a phonological argument (distribution in word-initial, word-medial, and word-final positions) and a morphological one (occurrence with the unshortened form of the agentive case marker). In Hook's (1996) text, [u̯] is represented everywhere as a consonant (*ṭakraaw*, 'meeting'; *walaaw*, 'brought'; *rawaana*, 'departure), while [i̯] is represented sometimes as a consonant: *yaayaa*, 'yeah'; *aziyat*, 'torment'; *pay*, 'cave', and sometimes (word-finally) as a vowel: *angaai* [ʌˈŋáːi̯], 'sky'; *mulaai* [mʊˈlʌi̯], 'daughter'.[14] Gultari Shina does in fact seem to treat word-final [u̯] differently than [i̯], as words which have a non-approximant final vowel [-o] in related dialects have [-u̯o] (phonetically [βo]) in Gultari, as in (4).

(4) ṣéwo, 'blind' (Drasi ṣéeo)
híiwo, 'heart' (Drasi híiu)
But:/čarpáw/, 'bed', /thaw/, 'he did'

[14] Lines 74–76, 91, 114, 129, and 133.

Word-final /i/ can be distinguished from word-final /y/ by treating it as a separate syllable, see (5), and this distinction fits the phonetic transcription of the Gultari data in this paper.

(5) /čái/, 'sparrow'
/ái/, 'goat'
/aŋaáy/, 'sky'
/muláy/, 'daughter'

No analysis of final /w/ and /y/ approximants has been done in Drasi and Guresi, and these are transcribed somewhat subjectively.

4. WORD LISTS

	Gloss	Gultari	Drasi	Guresi
I	Body parts			
	armpit	gitíiti	gikhíiti, khiŋ	gikíiti
	beard	dáay	dáay	dái~
	belly	ḍeér	ḍeér	ḍeér
	blood	lel	léel	léel
	bone	áṭi	áṭi	á~ṭi
	brain	móto	móto	mótu, maġzíi
	breast	mámu (sg.)	mamé~ (pl.)	mámu (sg.)
	ear	koṇ	kon	koṇ
	elbow	bakhúṇi	bakhúni	bakhúnɨ, photuúti
	eye	aċhíi	aċhíi	aċhíi
	face	muk	mukh	muk
	finger	aŋwíi~	aŋwíi~	ãwíi~
	fingernail	nóor	nóor	nóor
	flesh	moós	moóst	moós
	foot	páa	páa	páa
	hair	ǰakúuo	ǰakúu	ǰakúu, báal
	hand	hat	hat	hat
	head	ṣiíṣ	ṣiíṣ	ṣiíṣ
	heart	híiwo	híiu	híi, híiu

Gloss	Gultari	Drasi	Guresi
kidney	ẓuúk	ẓuúk	ẓuúk
knee	kúṭo	kúṭo	kúṭu
lip	óoṭo	óoṭo	óo~ṭi
liver	yúu~	yúu~	yúu~
moustache	phúŋo	phú~ŋo	phúu~ŋɨ (pl.)
mouth	áa~zi	áa~zo	áa~zu
neck	ṣóto	čhágan	šóoṇu, ṣak
nose	nóto	nótu	nóto
skin	čom	čom	čom
shoulder	muṭíǰo	kaṇíi	phíǰo, miṭhíǰ
thumb	aŋú~wo	aŋúu~	oŋúu~to
tongue	ǰip	ǰip	ǰip
tooth	don	don	don
urine	múuṣ	miíko	múuču, myáakul
II Terms for kin and human beings			
brother	ẓáa	ẓáa	ẓáa
brother's wife	ẓawée ǰamáat, kaáki	ǰaǰée	kaáki
child	baál (m.), muláy (f.)	baál	čúnu 'small'
daughter	dií	muláy	mulái, dií
daughter-in-law	nuúṣ	nuúṣ	nuúṣ
father	máalo, bábo	bábo	máalu
father's brother	čuṇ bábo, baṛ bábo,	čuṇo bábo	piçíi
father-in-law	šáyur	šéer	šéer
grand-daughter	póoçi	póoçi	póoçi
grandson	póoço	póoço	póoço
man	mušáa	mušáa	mušáa
mother	áaǰe	áaǰe	máa~, áaǰi
mother's brother	móomo	móomoo	múumu

Gloss	Gultari	Drasi	Guresi
mother-in-law	šaṣ	šaṣ	šaš, ṣaṣ
name	nóom	nóom	nóom
person	manúẓo	manúuẓo	manúuẓu
sister	sas, sah	sas	sas
son	puṣ, baál	baál	baál, puç
son-in-law	ǰamaçoó	ǰamaçoó	ǰaməçoó
wife's brother	šayrí	šayrí	šayrí
woman	čey	čée~y	čey
III Human artefacts			
arrow	kóoṇ	kóon	tíir, kóoṇ
ashes	dáal	dáal	dáal
bed	čarpáw	paláŋ, čaarpáy	khaṭ, čaarpáy
bread	ṭíki	ṭíkki	ṭíki
churn	çhapáru, čhapári	gugúr, čhaparo	çhapáru
curds	múuṭo dut	móṭo dut	čúrko dut, méel, burús
dream	sáaço	sáaço	sáaçu
fertilizer	páaṣ	páaṣ	páaṣ
field	çhéeṣ	çhéeṣ	çhéeç
fire	phúu	phúu, aŋgáaru	phúu
ghee	ǰúuli, gií	daí loǰuúli	gií
grease	míi~	míi~	mií~
handspan	diṣṭ	diṣṭ	driṣṭɨ
honey	maçhíi	maçhíi	maçhíi
house	góoṣ	góoṣ	góoṣ
irrigation channel	íil, yap	yap, íil	yab, íil
loom	çoṣ	luṭhúru, vaán	čoṣ
mattock (hoe)	phyóo~li phyóo~ṛi, ginčí	thokteé,	phyóo~li, genṭí
milk	dut	a~ṇṇá~w, dut	dut
path	pon	pon	pon

	Gloss	Gultari	Drasi	Guresi
	plough	hal	hal	hal
	roof	šarúṇ, tal	šeróon	šarún, tal
	salt	lúuṇi	luúṇi	luúṇi
	sickle	óŋo	óoŋo, yóo léeçi	óŋo, ó~ŋɨ
	smoke	duúm	duúm	duúm
	spinning wheel	çáku 'spindle'	čáku	yo~ṣ
	village	kwi	kwíi, gáa~m	kwíi
	wood	káaṭo	káaṭo	káaṭo
	work	krom	krom	krom
IV	The sky, weather			
	blue sky	béeẓo	—	béẓu
	cloud	áẓo	áẓo	áẓu, kavúu
	lightning	bíçuṣ	bíčuṣ	bíčuṣ, traṭ
	moon	yúun	yúun	yúun
	rain	áẓo	áẓo, me~y	áẓu
	sky	aŋaáy	aŋá~y	aŋgaáy
	snow	hin	hin	hin
	star	—	táaro	táaro
	sun	súuri	súuri	súuri
	water	wey	woy	woy
	wind	óoṣi	óoṣ	óoši, íši
V	Time and space			
	afternoon	šáam	belukhén, bazukhén	peešín
	autumn	šaróo	šaróo	šaróo
	day	dées	dées	dées, čhak
	Saturday	šiŋšér	baṭavaár	baṭaár
	Sunday	adíit	adít	aitvaár
	Monday	tsandraál	tsa~draál	tsa~draár
	Tuesday	aŋgáaro	aŋgáaro	bóŋu vaár
	Wednesday	bóodo	bóodo	bodvaár

	Gloss	Gultari	Drasi	Guresi
	Thursday	bréspat	brésput	brestvaár
	Friday	šukrú	ǰumáa~	ǰumáh
	day after tomorrow	ċiírye, aċíko čhak	ċiírye	ċiíri
	downhill	khári	khári	khári
	east	mašrík	súuri déen warí	mašrík
	evening	baás, šáam	šáam	šáam
	month	móos	móos	móos
	morning	čwal	čal	lóoṣṭ
	night	ráati	ráati	ráati
	sunny side of the mountain	suryóon	suryóon	suréen
	shady side of the mountain	čhóri	čhuryóon	čhóri
	seasonal migration	—	niríl	daróo~ boǰoónu
	spring (season)	bazoóno	uẓáalo	bazoónu
	summer	wáalo	bazoóno	wáalu
	today	aš	aš	aš
	up(hill)	huṇ	aǰá	aǰá
	west	magríb	súuri béen warí	magríb
	winter	yoóno	yoóno	yoónu
	year	sáal, baríš	awéelo	awéelu
VI	<u>Earth</u>			
	earth	zamín	kwíi	zamíin
	earthquake	bu~yál	bu~čáal, tsaŋgúl	mu~yál, buníḷu
	forest	ǰéel, ǰwéel	ǰaŋgál, ǰéel	ǰeél

	Gloss	Gultari	Drasi	Guresi
	highest summer pasture	niríl	šáay	niríl
	hill	brak	thúko	ṭhóku, huç
	mountain	çhíiṣ	šáay	khoṇ, çhíiṣ
	river	sin	sin	sin, gáa
	sand	síŋal	síŋel	síŋil
	spring (of water)	us	uts	uts
	stone	baṭ	baṭ	baṭ
VII	Animals			
	ant	philíili	philíili	pfilíili
	ass	ẓakún	ẓakúṇ	ẓakún
	bear	iṣ	iṣ	iç
	bird	briŋ, čai, trokšát	čǽæi~	ǰaanəwáar
	sparrow	čai	—	čái
	bull	dóono	dóono	dóonu
	bumblebee	bwiyáa~ri	ẓombuú	ẓombuú
	cat *m.*	—	gáǰo, píšu	púšu, gáñǰu
	cat *f.*	púšo	píšu	púši
	crow	kóorkus, káa	kórkuts	káa
	cow	gawóo	gaáo	gaáu
	dog	šúu~	šúu~	šúu~
	egg	thul	ṭhuúl	haṇoó~, ṭhuúl
	feather	páṭo	páṭo	pátu
	fish	čhímo	čhímo	čhímɨ, čhúmo
	flea	príiẓo	príiẓo	príiẓu
	goat *m.*	čanoó	čhatíilo	čhatíilu
	goat *f.*	ái	ái	ái
	hen	kokoó	kokoó	kokói
	horn	šíŋo	ṣíŋo	šíŋu
	horse	ášup	á~šup	a~šp, á~šɨp
	louse	ǰuú	ǰuú	ǰuú~

Gloss	Gultari	Drasi	Guresi
louse (nit)	liçií	liçí *pl.*	liíç
mouse, rat	múẓi	múuẓi	múuẓu
rooster	kokoó	bíiro kokoó	kokoó
sheep	a~i~leé	laṣ	laç
ewe	eš	eš	eš
ram	karaoóṭ	karéelo	karaá, šaróoṭu
snake	ǰon	ǰon	ǰon
tail	lamóṭo	lamúṭi	lamóoṭu, lamṭoó
wasp	rubuú	çaẓáa	bu~yaári
VIII Plants and trees			
apple	paloó	paloó	paloó
apricot	ǰuẓuú	phaṛóor	phaṭóor, ǰaroóṭi
bark (of tree)	dílo	dílo	delú
barley	yóo	yóo	yóo
birch	ǰóoẓi	ǰóoẓi	ǰóoǰi
cedar	čilíi	díiv daár	déva daár, číi
fig (fruit)	—	inǰíir	káa~ á~šɨp, phaṭóoru
grape(s)	—	daṣ	daṣ, dáṣṭom
grass/fodder	kaṣ	kaṣ	kaç
leaf	páṭo	páṭo	páṭu
maize	makáy	makáy	makáy
mulberry tree	maróoṣ	maróoṣ	marúç
pomegranate	daṇoó	anáar	daṇú~
poplar	phras	fras	phra~ts
root	čhilíṣ	čhilíṣ	čhiríṣ
seed	bíi	bíi	bíi
tree	buṣ, tom	byéi~	tom
walnut	açhoó	açhoó	açhoó

	Gloss	Gultari	Drasi	Guresi
	willow	bya~i~	byéi~	béi~
IX	Verbs			
	to beat	kuṭyoóni	kuṭyoóno	kuṭyoónu
	to bite	don dyoóni, čapyoóni	ǰan thyoóno	čapyoónu
	to burn *i.*	daǰoóni	daǰoóno	daǰoónu
	to burn *t.*	dayoóni	dayoóno	dayoónu
	to come	oóni	oóno	oónu, ayoónu
	to cry	roóni	roóno	hívɨ dyoónu, roónu
	to die	miryoóni	miryoóno	miryoónu
	to drink	pyoóni	piyoóno	piyoónu
	to eat	khoóni	khoóno	khoónu
	to fly	talií dyoóni	talwí dyoóno	talée dyoónu
	to give	dyoóni	dyoóno	dyoónu
	to go	buǰoóni	boǰoóno	boǰoónu
	to harvest	leéc̣i thyoóni, lyoóni	lyoóno	lyoónu
	to hear	pariǰyoóni	parǰoóno	parǰoónu
	to kill	maryoóni	maryoóno	maryoónu
	to know	daštyoóni	daṣṭyoóno	daṣṭyoónu
	to laugh	haǰoóni	háaǰi thyoóno	haǰoónu
	to lie (down)	ẓeé~y boóni	dil boóno	ṭam boónu
	to say	raǰoóni	raǰoóno	raǰoónu
	to see	c̣akyoóni	c̣akyoóno	pašoónu, c̣akyoóno
	to sit	beyoóni	biyoóno	byoónu
	to sleep	soóni	soóno	soónu
	to stand	uthyoóni	uthyoóno	cok boónu
	to swim	nóoṣi dyoóni	noošyoóno	núuš dyoónu, tam dyoónu
	to walk	yaǰoóni	yaǰoóno	yaǰoónu
	to wash *tr.*	doyoóni	dowææno	diǰaaryoónu

	Gloss	Gultari	Drasi	Guresi
X	<u>Adjectives</u>			
	all (sārā)	—	búro	básko
	all (sab)	gaŋmá, púure	láa, bučé	búṭɨ, láa
	big	báṛo	báṛo	báṛu
	bitter	čúrko, čurkóo	ċíṭo	ċíṭu
	black	kíṇo	kíṇo	kíṇu
	blind	ṣéwo	ṣéeo	šéeu
	cold	ċaúu~wo	čaamúu~	čaúu~, čawúu~
	dry	šúko	šúko	šúku
	eighteen	aṣṭáay	aṣṭáay	a~ṣṭáa~y
	eleven	akáay	akáay	akáay
	few	ápo	čéek	ǰéek, ápo
	fifteen	paziláy	pazilé~y	pa~zulé~y
	five	poš	po~š	po~š
	forty-one	dubyo-ga ek	dibyu-ga ek	dúbi-gə ek
	four	čáar	čáar	čáar
	fourteen	čóoday	čondé~y	čondé~y
	full	puẓií háa~wik	phúuṇo, puǰí	ṣek
	good	sóo	síi, šabóko	míṣṭhu, siyóo
	green	níilo	níilo	níilu
	hot	táto	tátto	tátu
	hundred	šal	šal	šal
	hungry	unayoóni	niróno	unyaálu, niroṇu
	left (direction)	khábi khiŋ	khaybón	kha, khay
	long	ẓíŋo	ǰíŋo	ẓígu
	many	láa	mága law	tišáar, láa
	new	náawo	náaw	náa~
	nine	naw	na~w	naw
	nineteen	kunií	kuniíh	kunií
	old (person)	ǰáro	ǰáro	ǰáru

Gloss	Gultari	Drasi	Guresi
one	ek	ek	ek
red	loólo	loólo	loólu
right (direction)	dáštini khiŋ	daṣṭibón	daçiṇu
round	gugúuwo	kirkíro	ḍuḍuúro
seven	sat	sat	sat
seventeen	sattáy	sattáay	sattáay
sharp	tíiṇo	tíiṇo	tíiṇu
six	ṣa	ṣa	ṣa
sixteen	ṣó~ŋay	ṣóo~y	ṣóo~y
small	čuṇo	čuṇo	čuṇu
sour	čúrko	číṭo	čúrku
ten	day	day	day
thirteen	ço~y	çóo~y	çoy, çóoy
thirty-nine	bií-ga kunií	bií-ga kuniíh	bi-gə kunií
three	çée	çée	çe
thousand	hazáar	sáas	sáas
twelve	bwáay	bwáay	báay
twenty	bií	bií	bií
twenty-nine	bií-ga naw	—	bi-gə naw
two	dúu	du	dúu
white	šóo	ṣyóo	šóo
yellow	gúuẓo	gúuro	píilu, kumúu~mu
XI Pronouns, etc.			
he	ẓo	ẓo	so, ẓo, aá
I	mo	moh	muʔ, me~y
not	nuš	niš	neʔ, niš
she	ẓe	ẓe	se, ẓe, aá
they*m.* far	ẓe	ẓe, paraá	se, ẓe, aá
they*f.* far	ẓáa	ẓo, paraáo	sǽæ, ẓǽæ
that	aá	paraáo	peraá, paraá
this	aní	anúh, aá	anú, nu

	Gloss	Gultari	Drasi	Guresi
	we	beh	be	beʔ
	what?	ǰiíǰe ga	ǰok	ǰóok
	who?	kói	koói	koóe
	you *sg.*	tuh	tuh	tuʔ
	you *pl.*	tshoh	tsho	tsho~h, tsho~s
XII	Supplementary list			
	camel	u~ṭ	úu~ṭ	úu~ṭ
	chain	šaŋaáli	šaŋaáli	šaŋaáli
	cheese	burús	aí~c̣ɨ	ai~c̣í, burús
	copper	riíl	táam	tráam, zams
	enemy	dušmán	dušmán	dušmán
	fairy	parí	parí	parí
	far	duúr	aščáat	duúr
	fever	buxáar	buxáar, tsat	tap, tat
	flour	áaṭe	áa~ṭe	áaṭe
	foam	pfíiṇ	pfíiṇ	pfíiṇɨ
	fox	loy	loy	loy
	frog	maṇóok	maṇóo~k	maṇóo~k
	gold	sóoṇ	soóṇ	sóoṇ
	gun	ráfal	tumák	tumák, tubák
	hedgehog	ẓúkul	ẓukúl	—
	heel	thúri	thúri	thúri
	lamb	uráaṇ	urán	urán
	leopard	dií~ŋ	dhií~	dií~, dhií~
	Milky Way	laága grup	táaro a ŋá~y	bala~ǰée
	mirror	sisá	šiišá	šiišá
	nut	badám	ac̣hoó, káli	gayáa
	palm of hand	háta táaw	hattáa	hata táa
	rainbow	biẓóon	biẓóon	biǰoóni
	rice (paddy)	bríu~	dayóo~	dayó~
	rice (cooked)	bríu~	brim	bríim, báy
	scorpion	gálthoks	bič	bič

Gloss	Gultari	Drasi	Guresi
shame	laš	šarm, laš	laš
sleep	níiṣ	níi~ṣ	níiṣ
spleen	šóom	šóom	šóom
to write	likhyoóni	likhyoóno	likhyoónu

Key to Phonetic Symbols

Phonetic transcription in this paper	International Phonetic Alphabet (IPA)	Description
a	a	open central unrounded vowel
ʌ	ɜ	open-mid central unrounded vowel
æ	æ	open front unrounded vowel
b	b	voiced bilabial plosive
β	β	voiced bilabial fricative
č	ʧ	voiceless postalveolar affricate
c̣	ʈʂ	voiceless retroflex affricate
d	d	voiced dental plosive
ḍ	ɖ	voiced retroflex plosive
e	e	close-mid front unrounded vowel
e̯	e̯	close-mid front approximant
ɛ	ɛ	open-mid front unrounded vowel
g	g	voiced velar plosive
h	h	voiceless glottal fricative
ʰ	_ʰ or V̤	aspiration; breathy vowel
i	i	close front unrounded vowel
i̯	i̯	close front approximant
ɪ	ɪ	near-close front unrounded vowel
ǰ	ʤ	voiced postalveolar affricate
k	k	voiceless velar plosive
l	l	voiced postdental to alveolar lateral

Phonetic transcription in this paper	International Phonetic Alphabet (IPA)	Description
m	m	voiced bilabial nasal
n	n	voiced dental nasal
ṇ	ɳ	voiced retroflex nasal
ŋ	ŋ	voiced velar nasal
o	o	close-mid back rounded vowel
o̯	o̯	open-mid back approximant
p	p	voiceless bilabial plosive
ɸ	ɸ	voiceless bilabial fricative
r	ɾ	voiced alveolar tap
ṛ	ɽ	voiced retroflex flap
s	s	voiceless alveolar fricative
š	ʃ	voiceless alveopalatal fricative
ṣ	ʂ	voiceless retroflex fricative
t	t	voiceless dental plosive
ṭ	ʈ	voiceless retroflex plosive
ts	ts	voiceless alveolar affricate
u	u	close back rounded vowel
ʊ	ʊ	close-mid back rounded vowel
ɯ	ɯ	close back unrounded vowel
u̯	u̯	close-mid back approximant
x	x	voiceless velar fricative
ž	ʒ	voiced postalveolar fricative
ẓ	ʐ	voiced retroflex fricative
ˇ	ˇ	low-rising pitch
^	^	high-falling pitch
ˈ	ˈ	accented syllable
~	~	nasalization

REFERENCES

Buddruss, Georg. 1996. 'Shina Rätsel'. In *Nānāvidhaikatā: Festschrift für Hermann Berger*, edited by Dieter B. Kapp. 29–54. Wiesbaden: Harrassowitz Verlag.

Degener, Almuth. 2008. *Shina-Texte aus Gilgit (Nord-Pakistan)*. Wiesbaden: Harrassowitz Verlag.

Hook, Peter E. 1996. 'Kesar of Layul: A Central Asian Epic in the Shina of Gultari'. In *Studies in the Popular Cultures of Pakistan*, edited by William Hanaway and Wilma Heston. 121–83. Lahore: Sang-e-Meel.

Radloff, Carla F. 1999. *Aspects of the Sound System of Gilgiti Shina*. Islamabad: National Institute of Pakistan Studies and Summer Institute of Linguistics.

_______ 1992. 'The Dialects of Shina'. In *Sociolinguistic Survey of Northern Pakistan, Vol. 2, Languages of the Northern Areas*, edited by Peter C. Backstrom and Carla F. Radloff. 89–203 and 301–69. Islamabad: National Institute of Pakistan Studies and Summer Institute of Linguistics.

Schmidt, Ruth Laila and Kaul, Vijay Kumar. 2008. 'A Comparative Analysis of Shina and Kashmiri Vocabularies'. *Acta Orientalia 69*: pp. 231–302.

_______ and Kohistani, Razwal. 2008. *A Grammar of the Shina Language of Indus Kohistan*. Wiesbaden: Harrassowitz. (Beiträge zur Kenntnis südasiatischer Sprachen und Literaturen 17).

_______ and Kohistani, Razwal. 1998. 'Páalus /kostyố/ Shina Revisited'. *Acta Orientalia* 59: 106–49.

17

The Jamáal Qháan Story of Alíi Goohár of Ḍomośáal (Hunza)

Hugh van Skyhawk

There is little or no mention of the harsh realities of feudal life in the post-war ethno-romanticism of rosy-cheeked dietary assistants extolling the nutritional virtues of Hunza muesli (cf. Bircher 1952, von Unruh 1955) nor in the perennial reconstructions of the prestigious Alexander descendants of the royal house of Hunza (cf. Sidky 1999).[1] But there can be no doubt that oral tradition in Ḍomaakí, as meagre as it is attested, reveals that wounds had been inflicted on the Ḍóma, the blacksmiths, musicians, and menials of the Burúśo, the scars of which cause pain up to the present day.

Though the following *śilóoku*[2] 'story' begins as a pleasant reminiscence of the benign reign of the well-loved last *mir* 'prince' of Hunza, Muhammad Jamal Khan,[3] the aged narrator soon begins recounting his indelible traumatic childhood impressions of the personality and reign of the last all-powerful *tham* 'ruler' of Hunza, Raja Mir Sir Muhammed Nazim Khan.[4] Through the clarity and richness of detail in Alíi Goohár's[5] account we gain access to the

[1] A notable exception is the work of Anna Schmid (1997) whose study of the culture and self-images of the Ḍoms provides a learned foundation for further studies of the blacksmiths and musicians of Hunza.

[2] From Sanskrit (skt.) *śloka*.

[3] Last monarch of Hunza (1912–76; ruled 1945–74).

[4] The ruler of Hunza during the greater part of the British Raj; born 1867, ruled 1892 until his death in 1938.

[5] To protect the anonymity of the narrator, his clan and lineage ethnonyms, which enable positive identification of the person concerned, have been omitted.

royal audience and assembly ground of that much-feared monarch of Hunza in the final years of his reign, sometime in the years 1930–38.

1. TEXT AND TRANSLATION

1. *Jamáal Qháanan*[1] *apanéi waqtánaaná ko kísei azáa*[2] *ni iráaga ćháaka.*[3] *Ko buṭéċ qhoś iráaga ćháaka. Ko buṭéċ munéega ćháaka: tumée śáa munéegu ćhóot. tumée śáa munéegu ćhóot. ko buṭéċ naaráaz*[4] *ni iráaga ćháaka. Ko buṭéċu ko giyée kísek giḍáaṅe eṅé ta héi déega ćháaka.*

1. Never in his life did Jamáal Qháan make trouble for anyone. He made everyone happy. To everyone he said, 'You speak well. You speak well.' He didn't make trouble for anyone. If people went and asked him for something, he would give it to them.

Notes

[1] Urdu (u.) *xān*
[2] Arabic (a.) and u. *azā*
[3] I am grateful to the doyen of linguistic studies in the Hindu Kush and Karakoram, Prof Dr Dr h.c. Georg Buddruss (Mainz), for his generous help in the initial phases of preparing this Ḍomaakí text for publication (2005). My heartfelt thanks are also due to my dear colleague Prof Dr Almuth Degener (Mainz) and to Prof Dr Tilman Berger (Tübingen) for reading my English translations of the Ḍomaakí text and offering suggestions for their improvement. And certainly not least, I am grateful to Dr Joan Baart of the Summer Institute of Linguistics (SIL) for all he has done to make this volume in memory of Carla Radloff see the light of day. The imperfections that remain in this article are of my own making.
[4] u. *nārāz*

* * * *

2. *aaqhirinanáa*[1] *bap-rajaákiṅ*[2] *eṅ ćhéeka buṭéċ phat irí phat iraaí apanéi qharćás,*[3] *apanéi peesá*[4] *deí, apanéi raakéi kom iráaga ćháaka,apanéi zamíine*[5] *kom iráaga ćháaka, zamíine ta babór*[6] *irí kuyoóćaśu*[7] *deí héi mámu tham*[8] *ćháaka, Jamáal Qháan, nikíne. Puurá*[9] *mámu tham ćháaka.*

2. In the end he did away with all the corvée labour and spent his own money for expenses, had work done on his palace at his own cost, had work done on his fields at his own cost. After he had divided the land equally among his vassals, Jamáal Qháan was a sweet king, wasn't he? A sweet king through and through.

Notes

[1] u. *āxirī*
[2] Burúśaski (bu.) *bap-rajaáki*
[3] u. *xarčah*
[4] u. *paisa*
[5] u. *zamīn*
[6] u. *barābar*
[7] bu. and Shina (sh.) *kuyoóć*
[8] bu. *mámu tham*, 'a milk king', i.e. 'a sweet king'
[9] u. *pūrā*

* * * *

3. *bas.*[1] *Jamáal Qháan muyá. Jamáal Qháane thámkuṣ harinée, Porśée. kísta baaśí kísta huí Jamáal Qháane thámkuṣ śaukulí baadśáaismo*[2] *gaḍinée. gaḍí bas. Jamáal Qháan aaqhirinanáa biimáar*[3] *huí e muyá. muúto*[4] *eséi pué*[5] *ćha. eyán kísta ni śakéega*[6] *ćha. qhaamaqháa*[7] *ćha. e ta ćháśu alóo léega*[8] *ćha govarménṭan. Pówer*[9] *déega*[10] *ćha, eséi púée alóo, leekín*[11] *píye ajáak náa. píye ajáak śaahíi kom náa, e pa. ye bas. guśpúurek iráam ćhóom. amée darúmkuli izát*[12] *iráam ćhóom. éśu guśpúur irí salaamaléek*[13] *juú náa,*[14] *guśpúur śóona ćháai-e séya báan,*[15] *iráam ćhóom, amée. leekín píye ajáak izát eséi púée náa.*

3. What more can I say? Jamáal Qháan is dead. The Burúśos took away his kingdom. They said something, and something happened, and they took away Jamáal Qháan's kingdom, took it away … What more can I say? In the end Jamáal Qháan became sick and died. Now there is his son. But he can't do anything. He's not able. He's just there somehow. The government listens to his words. They give him (some) power, this son. But they don't listen to him as much as they did to his father. He hasn't got as many duties as king as his father had. What more can I say? We say 'Prince' to him. Up to now we honour him. Addressing him as 'Prince', we say '"*as-salām 'alaikum*" ("Peace be unto you!") Are you well, prince?' But we don't show as much honour as we did to his father.

Notes

[1] u. *bas*
[2] u. *bādšāh*
[3] u. *bīmār*
[4] bu. *muúto*

[5] < skt. *putra* ,'son', > '*Rājpūt*', 'King's son'
[6] < skt. *śak-* 'be able', 'have power to do something'
[7] u. *xāmxwā*
[8] Cf. u. *lenā*
[9] English (e.) power
[10] Cf. u. *denā*, skt. *dā-* 'give'
[11] u. *lekin*
[12] u. *'izzat*
[13] u. *'as-salām 'alaikum*
[14] bu. *juú náa* a respectful address such as 'Your Honour', 'My Lord'
[15] bu. *séya báan*, '(people) say'; Latin: *dicunt*

* * * *

4. *píya boót*[1] *śuá*[2] *ćháaka. Jamáal Qháane śáai*[3] *boót śuá ćháaka, boót śuá ćháaka. juaaníinana bulá*[4] *déega ćháaka. juaaníinana, janáabe aalíi,*[5] *kheḍéega ćháaka. buṭ kheḍináak ćháaka. qhupsuuráṭ*[6] *kheḍináak ćháaka. Jamáal Qháan śáa*[7] *śuá ćháaka.*

4. The father was good. Jamáal Qháan's kingdom was very good, very good. In his youth he played polo. In his youth, O worthy Sir, he danced. He danced a lot. He was a beautiful dancer. *Śáa* (king) Jamáal Qháan was good.

Notes

[1] u. *bahūt*
[2] bu. *śuá*
[3] u. *šāhī*
[4] bu. *bulá*
[5] u. *janāb-i-ālī*
[6] u. *xūp sūrat*
[7] u. *šāh*

* * * *

5. *ko kísei azáa ni iráaga ćháaka. kóokiśu*[1] *ḍáanṭ*[2] *ni iréega ćháaka. aazaadí*[3] *denín ćháaka. Jamáal Qháane śáai boót śuá, śuá baadśáa, śuá tham ćháaka. śuá śáai ćháaka, śuá śáai ćháaka e.*

5. He never made trouble for anyone, never threatened anyone. He had given them their freedom. Jamáal Qháan's kingdom was very good. He was a good *baadśáa* 'king', a good *tham* 'prince'. His was a good kingdom, a good kingdom.

Notes

[1] bu. *kóok*
[2] u. *ḍānṭ*
[3] u. *āẓādī*

* * * *

6. *e muyásmo bas mazá*[1] *ni aayá. muúto śaukulíṅe kísta mazá náa. Ye guśpúurek ćha, Ġazanfárek, eséi pué. leekín píye ajáak qáadir*[2] *náa ései śaukulíṅe śáai qáadir ćhíika. ései dáada par dáada*[3] *buṭ*[4] *jabardás*[5] *záalim*[6] *ćhéeka, dáada par dáada. Śáa Silím, Śáa Ġazán, Śáa Safdár Qháan, Śáa Silím Qháan, Ġazán Qháan dáa*[7] *eṅ béesa*[8] *zamaanána*[9] *ćhéeka eṅ buṭ jabardás záalim ćhéeka.*

6. After his death, there wasn't any fun anymore. Now there are no more royal celebrations.[10] There is this prince, one Ġazanfár, who is his son. But he hasn't as much power as his father had. But his ancestors had the power of kings. His grandfather's grandfather was very, very cruel, the great-great-grandfather, Śáa Silím, Śáa Ġazán, Śáa Safdár Qháan, Śáa Silím Qháan, Ġazán Qháan,[11] and others of those times were very cruel.

Notes

[1] bu. *mazá*, u. *mazah*
[2] u. *qadir, qādir*
[3] u. *dādā par dādā*
[4] bu. *buṭ*
[5] u. *zabardast*
[6] u. *zālim*
[7] bu. *dáa*
[8] bu. *béesa*
[9] u. *zamānah*
[10] On Alíi Goohár's ambivalent relationship to the feudal society of Hunza, see my comments on the narrative context of this text at the end of this contribution.
[11] For family trees of the Ayáśo dynasty of Hunza see Müller-Stellrecht (1979).

* * * *

7. *leekín ek óor*[1] *ćáġa*[2] *ćha. Naẓíim Qháanan Ġazán Qháane píya […] Śáa Silím Qháanan raakáanana jéel*[3] *qháana*[4] *irí zindáan qháana irín ćháaka. héi zindáan qhaanana koón śaraarát*[5] *irinée ta koón gaḍbáṭ*[6] *ta zindá*[7] *léi*

jái héyan héi zindáanaśu minéen phal[8] *iréega ćháaka. Héi zindáan ćha, raakananáa muúto qháa*[9] *ćha.*

7. But there is another story. By Nazíim Qháan Ġazán Qháan's father … […]. Śáa Silím Qháan had a jail cell, a dungeon, made in his fortress.[10] In order to take their lives, he cast down those who had committed crimes and those who had made trouble for him into the dungeon. This dungeon is still there. Even now it is there.

Notes

[1] u. *aur*
[2] bu. and Shina (sh.) *ćáġa*
[3] e. jail
[4] u. *xānah*
[5] u. *šarārat*
[6] u. *gaṛbaṛ*
[7] u. *zindah*
[8] bu. and sh. *phal*
[9] bu. *qháa*
[10] Following the lineage given in paragraph 6 (*supra*), Alíi Goohár is probably referring to Śáa Silím Qháan II (1790–1825). But it is not altogether impossible that the dungeon of Baltit fort was originally built by Śáa Silím Qháan I in the late sixteenth century.

* * * *

8. *zindáanaśu bainíaan minéenio kísan ta ćuruṭaaí*[1] *bićaará*[2] *azáapar*[3] *wáau qíu irinée. aná maréega ćháaka. leekín vóo*[4] *ni gaḍéega ćháaka. no koón koón ziaadá*[5] *ésmo ta śaraarát irinée ćhéeka ta eṅ ćaméne*[6] *ráakaa ćháaka. eṅ ćaméne ráakaaśu aná baiáṅo eétoo eṅ kísek ćaćáayo aṅ kísta múndasoṅ*[7] *kísta nikhilí ćuruṭaaí azáap denáṅo ho eṅ gaḍí eṅéću sazáa*[8] *deí ho gaḍéega ćháaka. gaḍí bijaaléega ćháaka. kóoki píye ćaará*[9] *náaka. háai wáqtanana ġalatíi*[10] *karinái*[11] *yáa*[12] *śáaiye qhiláap*[13] *ćáġa iriná kóoki jurát*[14] *náaka.*

8. After (the prisoners) had been thrown down into (the dungeon) and they had been bitten by different (venomous creatures) the poor (fellows) would cry out '*wáau qíu*' (onomatopoeia for howling and whining). They died there. But he (the *tham*) did not take them out. Then there was the 'leather prison'[15] for those who made even more trouble. After he had thrown them into the 'leather prison' and dung beetles and ticks had come out and bitten them and they had been

punished (enough), then he took them out. After he had taken them out, he sent them away. But then (they were so deranged) not even their fathers could help them. In those times no one had the courage to do anything wrong or to go against the kingdom.

Notes

[1] bu. and sh. *ćurúṭ-*
[2] u. be *čārah*, bu. *bećaará*
[3] u. *'azāb*; NB: the Burúśaski dative postposition *-ar* to form a *dativus finalis* 'in order to do something'; cf. Berger (1998: 140 [paragraph 12.33])
[4] u. *voh*
[5] u. *ziyādah* and bu. *ziaadá*
[6] < skt. *carma*; cf. u. *čām, čamār*
[7] bu. *múndas*
[8] u. *sazā*
[9] u, *čārah*, bu. *ćaará*
[10] u. *ġalaṫī* , bu. *ġalát*
[11] < skt. *kṛ-* 'do, make'
[12] bu. *yáa*
[13] u. *xilāf*
[14] u. *jurat*
[15] Two types of 'leather prison' were known in the Karakoram: (i) a variation of the ancient Roman *poena cullei* 'punishment of the sack' and (ii) a pit dug in the earth in which raw animal hides (and certain prisoners) were thrown and left to rot. Alíi Goohár is clearly referring to the second type of 'leather prison' in this context. However, an example of the first type of 'leather prison' can be found in the oral folk epic *Libi Kisar* in the Burúśaski of Nager when Kisar punishes his unfaithful wife Laṅabúṅo by putting her in a leather bag (*gápe butúnulo muwáśimi*), thus making her endure the torture of the unbearable contraction of the leather as it dries (cf. van Skyhawk 1996: 185). Imprisonment in a raw leather bag was a well-known punishment in the Mughal empire, having been used by Shah Jehan (r. 1627–56) to execute one of his elder daughter Jahanara's paramours and, most famously, by Aurangzeb (r. 1656–1707) in his attempt to intimidate the ninth Sikh guru, Guru Tegh Bahadur (1621–75).

* * * *

9. *Nazíim Qháanan*[1] *śuá adaalát*[2] *iréega ćháaka. záalim ćháaka. leekín adaalát jabardás ćháaka. kóokin alúa*[3] *garána alúa raninée ćhe [...]. héi Śáa Nazíim Qháan aśí baláa*[4] *maníśek*[5] *ćháaka. eṅ akaabíre*[6] *aíi marakáanana*[7] *gáṭi*[8] *huinéebelo marakáanana munáaga ćháaka, héi Nazíiman. tée garána kísek raníi ćháai, béesa. tée garána*[9] *kísek raníi ćháai, béesa. tée garána kísek raníi ćháai, béesa. irinée. buṭéċ munáaga*

ćháaka. koón munéṅe ćhéeka amáa garánaana śóoek[10] *raninée ćhéeka, nazéer.*[11] *noó kísek ranéṅeka. mée garánaana śóok raninée ćhe, iráṅo. yaá. tée garána kísek raninée ćhe, iráṅo. aalúare raninée ćhéeka, nazéer. noó mée kísek ranám ta iráṅo. śuá. ekíśu munín ta tée garánaana kísek moós kiskóoṭ aalúa banée ćhéeka, nazéer iráṅo. thaahíi biizát*[12] *irín ćha. óće tu moós ta raníi aalúa ta noó jumúṭiśu kísek ranáaya. óor hal aalúa ranáayaka hal moós ranáayaka irí ayán tháa biizát iráaga ćháaka. ajáp maníśek ćháaka, héi Nazíim Qháan. tu dúi dúi śukáaṅa ek ṭéemas*[13] *kháaya aćimuśulo*[14] *tu ni kháayaka irí biizát iráaga ćháaka, Nazíiman.*

9. Nazíim Qháan held an excellent legal court. He was cruel. But his legal judgement was sharp. If someone had cooked potatoes in his house … […]. This Nazíim Qháan was such a mean man. When the elders were gathered at his assembly ground this Nazíim lashed out at them, 'Hey, you! What have you cooked in your house? Hey, you! What have you cooked in your house? Hey, you! What have you cooked in your house?' (Like that he badgered them all.) One answered, 'In our house we cooked spinach, my Lord. What else should we cook?' 'Is that so?' (Nazíim Qháan replied sarcastically). When he asked another one, 'What have you cooked in your house?' (and the man answered), 'My Lord! We have cooked potatoes in our house. What else should we cook for ourselves?' 'Good!' (Nazíim Qháan replied). But when he asked another one, 'What have you cooked in your house?' (and that man replied), 'We mixed some meat with potatoes, my Lord,' he humiliated that man (before the whole assembly). 'Today you have cooked meat and potatoes too. Then what will you cook tomorrow?' (he asked). 'Either you should have cooked potatoes, or you should have cooked meat.' He was a strange man, this Nazíim Qháan. 'If you eat two dishes at one time, in the end you will have nothing to eat.' Talking (like that in front of the whole assembly) this Nazíim ridiculed (and intimidated) that man.[15]

Notes

[1] Raja Mir Sir Muhammed Nazim Khan, Knight Commander of the Star of India (KCSI), Knight Commander of the Indian Empire (KCIE), whose undeniably self-glorifying autobiography, *The Life of a King of Hunza*, written in 1935 by the royal amanuensis, the young Prince Muhammad Jamal Khan, Nazim Khan's grandson (at the age of 23 years), became part of the literary legacy of the legendary language hunter and political agent of His Britannic Majesty King George V in Gilgit (1920–24), Lt. Col. David Lockhart Robertson Lorimer (1876–1962), who had returned to Hunza as a scholar in 1935 to study Burúśaski and Ḍomaakí.

Nazim Khan's autobiography can be found today in the archives of the library of the School of Oriental and African Studies (London) or in Müller-Stellrecht (1979: 309–76).
[2] u. *'adālat*
[3] u. *ālu*
[4] u. *balā*, bu. *baláa*
[5] < skt. *manuṣya*
[6] u. *'akābir*, bu. *akaabír*
[7] u. *ma'rikah*; bu., sh., Khowar (kh.) *maraká*
[8] bu., sh. *gáṭi*
[9] < skt. *gṛha*
[10] bu. *śóoẏo*, sh. *śóo*
[11] sh. *názur*, bu. *nazéer*
[12] u. be *'izat*
[13] e. time
[14] bu. and sh. *muś*
[15] These words were spoken with palpable contempt for Nazíim Qháan.

* * * *

10. *kóokin śooní kaṭúa*[1] *laíi aphayá ta isléega ćháaka, héi záatas,*[2] *koón kísek huí aayé ćhe ta, koón judá*[3] *boót śooní kaṭúa laíi aayé ćhéeka ta, eṅéċ ar*[4] *iráaga ćháaka. tu atéik śooní laíi aayá ćháai noó aṅée kísek láaṅe. tus dekhíi eṅ buṭée híiṣ*[5] *hóoṅe tu kíje héi iríi laií ćháai irí es thuráak téega ćháaka, Nazíim Qháanan. yáa héi záatas ései adaalát jabardás ćháaka. héi irí isléega ćháaka, marakáaśu aayé. Marakáanana aayé héi irí Nazíim Qháanan isléega ćháaka. koón kísek iréṅe ćhe. koón kísek ni iréṅe ćhe. koón ki huí baaśéṅe ćhe. koón ki ni huí baaśéṅe ćhe. héi irí isléega ćháaka. Taazá*[6] *ni dekhéega ćha irónta irí héi huí beeśéega ćháaka.*

10. If someone wore beautiful clothes, he stared at him like this (demonstrative gesture). If someone looked different or wore very beautiful clothes, he intimidated that man: 'You come looking very smart. But what are they wearing? When they see you they will sigh (in despair). What do you think you are doing? What are you wearing?', and he hit that man with his whip, this Nazíim Qháan. In this way his legal court was very sharp. When they came to the assembly ground he stared like this (demonstrative gesture). When they came to the assembly ground he made gestures like this (threatening gesture) and stared, Nazíim Qháan. Whatever they did, whatever they didn't do, whatever they said, whatever they didn't say, he made gestures like this (threatening gesture). He thought: 'They

think that I am not looking healthy.' That's why he sat like this (i.e. with a rigid upright posture).

Notes

[1] bu. *gaṭú*
[2] u. *ẕāt*, bu. *záat*
[3] u. *judā*
[4] bu. *ar*
[5] bu. *hiṣ, híiṣ*, sh. *hẽẽṣ, hĩĩṣ*
[6] u. *tāzah*

* * * *

11. *koón kísek ġalaṭí irinée ćhéeka ta héi noó hoth*[1] *pharáṭ*[2] *iríi eṅéċ ar iráaga ćháaka. tu héi iríi kíje baaṭháai, tu kóokin aláalana phalaaná*[3] *buráai*[4] *kíje, tu a kíje muníi e kíje muníi. noó eṅ buṭée mée qhiláap hóoṅe. tu mée marakáaśu aíi aćaagí ćaġáana ni irína ćha. śooná ćáġa er. er ta túśu ućáaṅa ta dées, waziiréi ta dées. tu héi huí ni báaś. Aaindá*[5] *huśáar*[6] *ho, śuá-a ni, irí adaalát iréega ćháaka. adaalátaana kaadóq*[7] *maníśek ćháaka. ései garás ćheesá*[8] *eétoo, héi Nazíim Qháan.*

11. If someone had said something wrong, he twisted that man's hand to intimidate him: 'Why did you say that? Who put you up to this? Why did you say this? Why did you say that? Now everyone will be against me. When you come to my assembly ground don't say bad things. Only say friendly words. Do that, and I will give you honour. I will give you a minister's office. Don't say bad words. You'll be smart next time, won't you?' That's how he sat in judgement. In his legal court he was a (very) strange man. May his house disappear from there (heaven), this Nazíim Qháan![9]

Notes

[1] < skt. *hasta*
[2] bu. *pharáṭ*, sh. *pharaáṭ*
[3] u. *fulān, falān*
[4] u. *burā'ī*
[5] u. *ā'inda, āyanda.*
[6] u. *hošyār*, bu. *huśáar.*
[7] Cf. Old Marathi *kādo*, 'marked by a sign'.
[8] < skt. *kṣayaḥ* through Prakrit *ćhayaṁ*; u. *čhay, čha'e, čha' ī.*
[9] This curse is spoken with trembling and intense distortion of the facial expression; cf. bu. *máa háa ćhaí kaḍák maníṣ*; a curse: 'May your house door fall shut (and be locked)!'

2. The Narrative Context

Alíi Goohár of Ḍomośáal was already a very old man when I met him in Lahore and recorded his stories of the Ḍóma of Ḍomośáal from 1–5 August 2004. As vital statistics of the Ḍóma (in contrast to members of the royal house of Hunza) were not kept when Alíi Goohár was born, he did not know when he was born and could only estimate his own age by the fact that as a youth he had witnessed the public audiences of Raja Mir Sir Muhammed Nazim Khan at the *maraká* 'assembly ground' in Baltit (today Karimabad). Thus, Alíi Goohár would have been approximately eighty to ninety years of age when I met him.

While for other forms of linguistic research in Ḍomaakí, Lahore would not have been a proper venue, owing to the fact that the language recorded there could not be checked and verified immediately by other members of the language community *in situ,* for the recording, transcription, and preliminary translation of the foregoing story Lahore, despite (or better because of) its distance to Hunza, proved to be the ideal venue.

This became clear to me when Alíi Goohár told me one afternoon after a recording session that he would not have narrated these stories to me in Ḍomośáal out of fear that the story would have been heard by an eavesdropper and its contents reported to the family of the Mir whose system of spies among the Ḍóma of Ḍomośáal has remained intact even if the feudal system out of which it had developed has long since vanished. Accordingly, Alíi Goohár entreated me not to reveal his identity when the story was published. His son of 30 years, a young, well-educated, upwardly mobile, middle-grade official of the Pakistan International Airlines (PIA), scoffed at his elderly father's fears of reprisals from the Mir's family if their identities were to become known. ('If they make trouble for us we will make trouble for them!') But Alíi Goohár remained firm in his entreaty to me.

Later, at the end of my stay in Lahore, I saw reason to give even more credence to Alíi Goohár's fears than to his son's liberation rhetoric. For the young wife of Alíi Goohár's son is a Burúśin woman and their marriage a forbidden relationship, the stated intention of which would have cost both marriage partners their lives a generation ago and have destroyed the social standing of their extended families and disgraced their lineages. Only through the more egalitarian *farmans* 'decrees' and teachings of Shah Karim, Aga Khan IV, since

1957 could such a marriage have been solemnized in a *jamā'at khāna* 'congregation house' of the Ismaili community. But even today (2004) Alíi Goohár's son and his wife do not travel to Hunza as a married couple. They are visited by their families who come to Lahore from Hunza, though biologically the Ḍóma and the Burúśo had become the major stakeholders in the same gene pool long ago through the frequent irregular unions of Hunza princes with Ḍóma women in feudal times.

But Alíi Goohár's relationship to the feudal society of Hunza is ambivalent (see above paragraphs four to six of the Ḍomaakí text). Like many elderly Ḍóma, he sincerely misses the public festivals in the cycle of the agricultural year which were celebrated with wine, music, and dancing, and functioned as collective fertility rituals (not unlike the often wild Carnival [German: *Fasching*] celebrations in German villages even today) in which the Mir played an indispensable role as guarantor of the fertility of the fields, animals, and humans (not unlike the 'King of Fools' [*Narrenkönig*] whose reign undeniably increases fertility in German villages every year at the time of *Fasching*).[6]

Though the music and dancing (but not the wine drinking) of Ḍóma musicians are being preserved for posterity through the musician training programmes of the Aga Khan Rural Support Program (AKRSP), at the same time, they have been cut off from their functions as parts of Hunza society and lost their *ras* 'taste'. Their conservation in a regimented programme, severed from the feudal society in which they unfolded their meaning and flavour, has given the music of the Ḍóma a museum-like quality. Performances are always a pleasure to listen to and see. But today the music and dancing only give enjoyment to mostly non-interactive audiences, whereas the music and dancing of feudal times put dancers, musicians, and audiences into states of possession.

The similarity to the wild feasts celebrated in honour of the god Dionysus by the men and women of ancient Greece and Bactria

[6] The most important and best-loved festival in the agricultural year in Hunza was the *bóphao* 'seed sowing festival', which took place in February (at about the same time as *Fasching* takes place in southern Germany). For a charming traditional story about wine drinking at the *bóphao*, see Lorimer (1935: 209–13). For an upbeat cultural historical analysis of the *bóphao*, see Müller-Stellrecht (1973: 62–81).

immediately suggests itself. But like other similarities of Hunza culture with Hellenic culture observed by Western scholars and visitors to Hunza from the mid-nineteenth century onward,[7] no direct linkages between the two cultures can be shown. Thus, the seemingly Dionysian rites of the medieval Hunza people, possibly deriving ultimately from Alexander's conquest and colonization of Bactria, will likely remain both a fascinating part of the colourful ethno-romantic Alexander legacy and a cherished part of the romantic heritage of Hunza, and will captivate the interest and imaginations of scholars and other visitors to Hunza for generations to come.

REFERENCES

Berger, Hermann. 1998. *Die Burushaski-Sprache von Hunza und Nager. Teil I. Grammatik*. Wiesbaden: Harrassowitz Verlag. (Neuindische Studien, Band 13).

Bircher, Ralph. 1952. *Hunsa: Das Volk, das keine Krankheit kennt*. Bern: Huber Verlag.

Lorimer, David Lockhart Robertson (Lt. Col.). 1935. *The Burushaski Language, vol. II, Texts and Translations*. Instituttet for Sammenliegende Kulturforskning, Publications, Series B, vol. XXIX, 2. Oslo: H. Aschehoug & Co. (W. Nygaard).

Müller-Stellrecht, Irmtraud. 1979. *Materialien zur Ethnographie von Dardistan (Pakistan). Teil I. Hunza. Aus den nachgelassenen Aufzeichnungen von D. L. R. Lorimer*. Graz: Akademische Druck und Verlagsanstalt. (Bergvölker im Hindukusch und Karakorum, Band 3/1).

——— 1973. *Feste in Dardistan. Darstellung und kulturgeschichtliche Analyse*. Wiesbaden: Franz Steiner Verlag. (Arbeiten aus dem Seminar für Völkerkunde der Johann Wolfgang Goethe-Universität Frankfurt am Main, Band 5).

Schmid, Anna. 1997. *Die Dom zwischen sozialer Ohnmacht und kultureller Macht. Interethnische Beziehungen in Nordpakistan*. Stuttgart: Franz Steiner Verlag. (Beiträge zur Südasien-Forschung 179).

Sidky, H. 1999. 'Alexander the Great, the Graeco-Bactrians, and Hunza: Greek descents in Central Asia'. *Central Asiatic Journal* 43.1: 232–48.

van Skyhawk, Hugh (ed.). 1996. *Libi Kisar. Ein Volksepos im Burushaski von Nager. Mit Beiträgen und Ergänzungen von Hermann Berger und Karl Jettmar*. Wiesbaden: Harrassowitz Verlag. (Asiatische Forschungen, Band 133).

von Unruh, Irene. 1955. *Traumland Hunza. Erlebnisbericht von einer Asienreise*. Mannheim: Verlagsgenossenschaft der Waerland-Bewegung.

[7] Most striking in this connection are three of Alexander's soldiers, who were said to have been left behind in Hunza because of sickness or injury and who are regarded up to the present day as the apical ancestors of the original three clans of Hunza, the Thápkianċ, Husénuċ, and the Hamaćátiṅ. See Müller-Stellrecht (1973: 63).

18

Phonatory Location in the Far North-Western Indo-Âryan Languages

Richard F. Strand

INTRODUCTION: CHARACTERISTIC VOCAL QUALITIES IN THE HINDU KUSH REGION

Carla Radloff must have encountered numerous multilingual conversations in her monumental linguistic quest to elucidate the dialects of the Ṣinâ′ (Shina) language (Radloff 1992). In such situations she must have wondered, as have I, at the variety of vocal qualities that distinguish the native languages of the conversational participants. The question naturally arises: what constitutes these vocal qualities, and how did they evolve out of Old Indo-Âryan?

I discuss this question primarily with reference to my own field research on the Indo-Âryan languages Degân′o (Eastern Paša′î), Gawâr-b′âti, Kal′aṣa-mandr/mun, Khow`ar, the Aćharêtâ′ (Palôlâ′) dialect of Ṣinâ′, Ušuǰ′u, and Bhaṭ′esa-zib. Languages that I have heard but not closely investigated also include Dâmiâ-bâṣa, Torwâli, and Garv′i.

In southern Chitral I became aware of the differing vocal qualities of the many languages spoken there, as I encountered them during numerous multilingual conversations. There the contrast between the vocalism of the Nûristânî and Irânian languages on the one hand and the vocalism of the Indo-Âryan languages on the other, was apparent. Further investigation of the phonatory processes that produce the tonal systems of Khow`ar and the archaic Ṣinâ′ dialect Aćharêtâ′ expanded my awareness of the importance of anterior and posterior phonation in the evolution of Indo-Irânian, and naturally led me to explore the phonologies of the other dialects of Ṣinâ′. Guided by the pioneering research of our colleague and mentor, Ruth Schmidt, it was in the phonatory underpinnngs of Ṣinâ′ dialectology that Carla's and my interests coincided.

I have discerned laryngeal and phonatory activity from acoustic, visual, and proprioceptive observations of speech; but the absence of more sophisticated observational techniques in the difficult field conditions of the region leaves the precise anatomical nature of these speech processes to be determined.

I must also note that the observations reported here are based mostly on the speech of men, as my interaction with female speakers was limited in the stricter Islâmic areas of the Indo-Irânian Frontier region.

1. PHYSIOLOGY: LOCATION AND DEGREE OF GLOTTAL TENSING AND SUPRAGLOTTAL LINKAGES

All researchers who have noticed tones in the region's languages have analysed them acoustically and formulated models based on parameters of high, low, falling, and rising pitch. Perhaps more useful for pedagogy and the understanding of linguistic evolution is an analysis based on the physiology that underlies the production of pitch and tone.

Phonation occurs when the vocal folds are tensed to produce noise or vibration in the exhaled pulmonary airflow. Speakers of the region's languages target differing levels of tension at specific locations along the vocal folds. A comparison of the phonatory types within the region reveals three basic phonatory parameters: (i) the location of glottal tensing along the vocal folds; (ii) the degree of glottal tensing; and (iii) the temporal position of glottal tensing relative to other speech processes.

1.1 Phonatory Target Locations

The target locations for tensing along the vocal folds include: (i) the anterior (or ligamental) portion; (ii) the posterior (or arytenoidal) portion; and (iii) a combination of both.

Anterior and posterior phonation produce respectively a high or low pitch, or a switch in phonatory location during a vowel produces a falling or rising tone on the vowel. In languages with phonemic tonal contrasts, the accent marks ` and ´ respectively indicate the point of transition from anterior to posterior and posterior to anterior voicing.

1.1.1 *Anterior Phonation*

Anterior phonation is produced by tensing the anterior (ligamental) portion of the vocal folds while keeping the arytenoidal portion closed tight (Catford 1977: 102). Speakers of all the region's languages use anterior phonation for accented phonation (*'V* or *`V*). Speakers of the Irânian and Nûristânî languages use anterior phonation for unaccented phonation (*V*) as well.

1.1.2 *Posterior Phonation*

Posterior phonation is produced by tensing the posterior (arytenoidal) portion of the vocal folds while keeping the anterior portion closed (Catford 1977: 103). This process produces a lowered pitch, and it appears to enlarge the laryngeal cavity, producing a slight megaphonic effect. It also restricts the pitch-raising effect of accented anterior phonation, producing a narrow pitch range between accented and unaccented vowels. When strengthened, posterior phonation produces the whispery voice of the traditionally called 'voiced aspirate' consonants (Catford 1977: 101, 106).

Some degree of posterior tensing during phonation occurs in all the Indo-Âryan languages of the Frontier, but posterior phonation is lacking in the Irânian and Nûristânî languages.

Posterior phonation is used for unaccented phonation in Aćharêtâ' (and probably other Ṣinâ' dialects) and Bhaṭ'esa-zib. It is used for one type of accented phonation (*´V*) in Khow`ar, Dâmiâ-bâṣa, Kalkoṭi [?], Garv'i, and Torwâli.

1.1.3 *Mixed Anterior and Posterior Phonation: Indo-Âryan*

Anterior and posterior phonation are not mutually exclusive. The Indo-Âryan languages that border the anterior phonated Irânian and Nûristânî languages have adopted the latter's unaccented anterior phonation, while retaining a degree of simultaneous posterior phonation and supraglottal tension characteristic of their Indo-Âryan origin. Such Irânian-influenced languages include Degân'o (Eastern Paša'î), Kal'aṣa-mandr/mun, Khow`ar, Gawâr-b'âti (and other Peč Valley languages?), Dâmiâ-bâṣa, Garv'i, and Torwâli. In Aćharêtâ' anterior accent is superimposed on default posterior phonation.

For each individual dialect among those with simultaneously mixed phonation, the balance between the acoustic effects of anterior and posterior phonation provides a dialectal signature. But nowhere does the simultaneous mixture or non-mixture of anterior and posterior phonation produce a phonemic contrast, other than one of accent.

1.2 Degrees of Glottal Tensing

Of the range of possible glottal tensing, the following degrees are of importance here, listed in increasing order of tension: (i) default (unaccented) phonation (***V***); (ii) accented phonation (***'V***, including (2a) primary and (2b) secondary accent); (iii) stopped phonation, ending in glottal closure or creak (***Vʔ***); and (iv) whisper, either anterior voiceless or posterior voiced (consonantal ***ph***, ***bɦ***, etc.).

1.2.1 Default (Unaccented) Phonation (V)

Default phonation is that which is normal (unmarked) for the environment in which it occurs. It is used for unaccented phonation of vowels and for unmarked voiced consonants. Its location along the vocal folds is dialect-specific and may also depend on its location in an utterance. For example, in Garv'i and Torwâli the pretonic default phonation of an utterance starts out with low pitch (whether from low-pitched anterior phonation or from posterior phonation is unclear); but it shifts to anterior after the tonic, before laxing into posterior at the utterance's end (Baart 1999: 90 ff., Lunsford 2001: 36–8).

1.2.2 Accented Phonation ('V)

Accented phonation is produced with greater glottal tension than default phonation. The result is a raised pitch for accented anterior phonation and a lowered pitch for accented posterior phonation, relative to the pitch of default phonation.

Two degrees of accented phonation, primary and secondary, have been noted in Khow`ar (Strand 2012), Aćharêtâ′ (Strand 2000/2001), and Bhaṭ′esa-zib (Strand 2001c), and they probably occur in all the region's languages.

1.2.3 Stopped Phonation ('Vʔ)

Stopped phonation, ending in glottal closure (***Vʔ***) or creak, was noted by Baart (1999: 95) on words with 'delayed falling' ('H(L)') tone in Garv′i. Such glottal closure is a consequence of the shift to posterior phonation at the end of an utterance, and therefore non-phonemic.

1.2.4 Whisper ('Aspiration': ph, bɦ)

Whisper is produced with a tensing and narrowing of the glottis, which causes turbulence and noise in the air stream (Catford 1977: 96 ff.). It occurs concurrently with posterior phonation and oral consonants to produce the region's whispery-voiced consonants ('voiced aspirates'). Anterior voiceless whisper concurrent with oral stops apparently produces the 'voiceless aspirated' consonants of the region's languages. With whispery consonants the concurrent tensing of whisper lasts somewhat beyond the closure of the consonant before laxing to normal phonation.

1.3 Supraglottal Effects

All phonation in the region's languages is accompanied by a general tensing of the laryngeal muscles. When strengthened, laryngeal tension may spread upward through the muscles that control the ventricular folds, the epiglottis, the hyoid bone (causing fronting or backing of the tongue), and the jaw (in concert with further fronting of the tongue), as manifested by the phonetic evolution of the region's languages.

1.3.1 Non-Phonemic Glottal–Laryngeal Tensing

Characteristic of the Indo-Âryan languages are degrees of glottal or ventricular noise-producing tensings. Such tensing produces an acoustically 'small' or 'tight' voice when phonation is anterior or an acoustically 'big' or 'open' voice when phonation is posterior. None of these tensings provide phonemic contrasts, but they impart much distinctiveness to the sound of each dialect.

1.3.2 Laryngeal–Lingual Linking

Anterior laryngeal tension may push the tongue forward, and posterior laryngeal tension may pull the tongue backward. Such displacement of the tongue has had consequences in the evolution of the vocalic and consonantal systems of the region's languages, as discussed below (section 2.3).

1.4 Temporal Position

Some languages show phonemic contrasts in the timing of the onset of accentual tensing relative to a vowel (Ṣinâ′, Aćharetâ′) or in the timing of the cessation of accentual tensing relative to the beginning of a word (Garv′i, Torwâli, Kalkoṭi). Details appear below (see sections 2.1.3 and 2.2.2).

2. EVOLUTION: FRONT VS BACK TENSING AS A DETERMINER OF INDO-IRÂNIAN PHYLOGENY

The earliest changes propelling the divergence of the Indo-Irânian languages—the changes that determined the ultimate relationships between the Indo-Âryan, Nûristânî, and Irânian languages—were primarily ones of glottal and lingual fronting and backing. From late Proto-Indo-European the Proto-Indo-Irânian language inherited both anterior and posterior phonation, which persist in the Indo-Âryan languages. In the Irânian and Nûristânî languages anterior phonation apparently became so strongly tensed that it precluded posterior phonation altogether. The effects of strengthened posterior phonation appeared early in the development of Proto-Indo-Âryan, with the rise of the retroflex consonants and the retention of posterior-voiced consonants.

The shift to exclusively anterior phonation in Irânian and Nûristânî became a defining phonological characteristic of those languages. The shift affected the Indo-European so-called 'voiced aspirated' consonants, which were produced with posterior phonation and partially constricted vocal folds. The early Irânian and Nûristânî shift to anterior phonation caused the voiced aspirated consonants to lose their posterior phonation and become anteriorly voiced, thus merging with their counterpart 'unaspirated' voiced consonants.

Coupled with strengthened anterior phonation is an often strong lingual fronting in Irânian and Nûristânî, which had profound consonantal effects. The strong lingual fronting of Nûristânî affected the evolution of the vowel systems of those languages, propelling them from lax–tense to close–open.

Successive waves of tongue fronting have apparently emanated out of the Nûristânî-Irânian-speaking region for over five thousand years. The first two waves encompassed the Indo-Âryan languages during the Indo-Irânian stage of development, so that all the Indo-Irânian languages were affected by them. Waves of tongue fronting emanated even farther through the ancient Indo-European-speaking communities, causing many or all of the same changes that occurred in the Irânian and Nûristâni languages to occur in the Slavic, Romance, and Germanic languages at later times (Strand 2013). The manner in which the latest wave of Irânian fronting has affected the far north-western Indo-Âryan languages is discussed below in section 3.1.

The backing of the tongue in Indo-Âryan likely arose out of the generalization of posterior phonation in the Indo-Âryan languages. As stated above, posterior phonation tends to pull the tongue back. Through certain sound changes a series of tongue-backed ('retroflex') consonants, which contrasted with dental ones, arose in early Indo-Âryan.

Writings of the ancient Hindu grammarians describe the phonation of Old Indo-Âryan, as evidenced by Sanskrit (Whitney 1960: 28 ff., Varma 1961: 161 ff.). These form the source from which we may trace the evolutionary development of posterior phonation in the various modern languages. Old Indo-Âryan source forms that appear in the tables below are mostly from Turner (1966), with associated entry numbers ('Turner #') from that work.

In Sanskrit accented phonation carried a raised pitch (*udâtta-*) that was opposed to the default 'non-raised' (*anudâtta-*) phonation. The existence of a high-falling tone (*svarita-*) on a single vowel points to the abrupt transition from high to non-high pitch that is indicative of a switch from anterior to posterior phonation during the production of the vowel. It is probable that the default phonation in Sanskrit was posterior.

Among the Indo-Âryan languages of the far north-west there is an evolutionary sequence of posterior whispery voicing moving forward from consonants to the following vowel, which resulted in a sequence of default-voiced consonant plus posterior-voiced vowel.

Among some of these languages there was a further evolutionary stage in which the probable OIA default phonation changed from posterior to anterior. This change triggered a further evolutionary stage in some languages, at which point only a default anterior-voiced consonant remained. The evolutionary sequence is summarized as: $\boldsymbol{C^{\text{ɦ}}V > C\acute{}V > CV}$.

Finally, there is a group of languages in which the position of accented phonation may occur contrastively before, during, or after the production of a vowel (see section 1.4).

The distribution of the evolutionary stages of posterior-voiced consonants vs phonation type among the region's languages is summarized in Table 1. The following sections elaborate on the distribution of languages seen in the table.

Table 1: Distribution of Anterior and Posterior Phonation in Far North-Western Indo-Âryan

Accented Phonation	Default Phonation	Phonetic Tone	Evolutionary Development of Whispery Posterior-Voiced Consonants		
			Retention	Posterior Phonation	Anterior Phonation
			$C^{ɦ}V$ remains	$C^{ɦ}V > C'V$	$C^{ɦ}V > CV$
Anterior	Posterior	no	Bhaṭ′esa-zib, Indus-Kôhistâni [?]		
	Anterior + Posterior	no	Kal′aṣa-m., SW Paša′î		Degân′o Paša′î, Gawâr-bâti
Anterior + Position	Posterior	yes	(Sanskrit,) Aćharêtâ′, Ušuj′u	Ṣinâ′: Gilgit, Kôhistyõ	
Anterior or Posterior	Anterior + Posterior	yes		Khow`ar, Dâmiâ-bâṣa	
Anterior or Posterior + Position	Anterior + Posterior	yes		Garv′i, Torwâli, Kalkoṭi [?]	

2.1 Descendant Languages with Inherited Posterior Whispery-Voiced Consonants

Those languages that have retained OIA posterior whispery-voiced consonants ('voiced aspirates') include SW Paša′î (Morgenstierne 1967: 48–9), Kal′aṣa-mandr/mun (Morgenstierne 1973, Strand field notes), Indus-Kôhistâni (Buddruss 1959), Bhaṭ′esa-zib (Strand 2001b, c), Aćharêtâ′ (Strand 2000/2011), and Ušuj′u (Strand field notes).

2.1.1 *Bhaṭ′esa-zib: Default Anterior Phonation without Position: No Tones*

Data on Bhaṭ′esa-zib come from my brief field observations (Strand 2001b, c).

Unaccented phonation is posterior in Bhaṭ′esa-zib; accented phonation is anterior.

There are two levels of accent, normal ′ and strong **′**. Pitch, vowel length, and tenseness apparently are a function of the degree of accent. Unaccented vowels are low-pitched, lax, and short; accented vowels are higher-pitched, tenser, and longer, and strongly accented vowels are even higher-pitched and longer.

The position of accent within words appears to be non-predictable.

The backing of the 'retroflex' (backed apical) consonants appears to be coupled with a backing of the position of phonation in the vocal folds, so that a preceding vowel has a lower pitch than it would if followed by a non-retroflex consonant (e.g. ***ṣ′âṣ*** 'spouse's mother'). Such backing appears to lax the voicing on final voiced-retroflex consonants (e.g. ***p′uJ̣*** 'grandson').

Bhaṭ′esa-zib speakers retain the OIA initial whispery posterior-voiced consonants, including ***ɦ*** (Table 2).

Table 2: Bhaṭ′esa: Retention of Whispery Voice

Bhaṭ′esa: C^{ɦ} = C^{ɦ}, ɦ = ɦ

Form	Gloss	OIA Form	OIA Gloss	Turner #
gh′u˜	big	*g*^{ɦ}*an-′a-*	compact; firm; dense	4424.1
ghi′û	ghee	*g*^{ɦ}*r̥-t′a-*	ghee	4501
gh′ô	horse	*g*^{ɦ}*oṭa-*	horse	4516
ghu′ai	mare	*g*^{ɦ}*oṭ-i-ka-:-*	mare	4516
dh′îr	stomach	*ḍ*^{ɦ}*iḍḍ*^{ɦ}*a-*	belly	5589.1
dh′û˜	smoke	*d*^{ɦ}*û-m′a-*	smoke	6849.1
bhi′o˜	sister	*b*^{ɦ}*ag-in-i-:-*	sister	9349
bhaṭ′era	Bhaṭera	*b*^{ɦ}*aṭṭa-*	lord; noble	9402

Bhaṭ'esa: C^{ɦ} = C^{ɦ}, ɦ = ɦ

Form	Gloss	OIA Form	OIA Gloss	Turner #
bhaṭ'e sa zib	Bhaṭera language	*b*^{ɦ}*aṭṭa-*	lord; noble	9402
bhaṭsi'â xel	name of a lineage	*b*^{ɦ}*aṭṭa-*	lord; noble	9402
bh'eḍe˜	ewe	*b*^{ɦ}*eḍra-*	ewe	9606
bh'iḍ	ram	*b*^{ɦ}*eḍra-*	ram	9606
J̣hâz'e	brother's wife	*b*^{ɦ}*râtr̥-ǰâya-:-**	brother's wife	9660
J̣hâd'i	brother's daughter	*b*^{ɦ}*râtr̥-duɦi-tr̥-**	brother's daughter	
J̣he˜ wal'i	agnate	*b*^{ɦ}*r'âtr̥-*	brother	9661
J̣h'o˜	brother	*b*^{ɦ}*r'âtr̥-*	brother	9661
J̣h'oç	brother's son	*b*^{ɦ}*râtr̥-putra-*	brother's son	9664
hi'u˜	snow	*ɦim'a-*	cold; frost; snow	14096

Posterior whispery voicing of medial consonants and ***ɦ*** was largely anticipated to an initial voiced consonant (Table 3).

Table 3: Bhaṭ'esa: Anticipated Whispery Voice

Bhaṭ'esa: ← ^{ɦ}, ɦ

Form	Gloss	OIA Form	OIA Gloss	Turner #
bhu'âiṭ	son's wife	*vad*^{ɦ}*û-ṭi-:-*	young wife or woman; son's wife	11251
dh'î	daughter	*duɦi-t'r̥-*	daughter	6481
mh'al	father	*maɦa-lla-ka-*	old; feeble	9935
mh'el	mother	*maɦa-ll-i-ka-:-*	old; feeble	9935
mh'eṣ	buffalo (f.)	*maɦi-ṣ'a-*	great; powerful; buffalo	9964

In several words medial whispery posterior-voiced consonants and ***ɦ*** were lost in consonant clusters (Table 4) or under unclear developmental conditions (Table 5).

Table 4: Bhaṭ'esa: Loss of Whispery Voicing in Clusters

Bhaṭ'esa: -CCʱ-, -[Cʱ, ɦ]C- > C

Form	Gloss	OIA Form	OIA Gloss	Turner #
'âru	peach	*arddʱu-*	peach	1103
d'ed	yoghurt	*dadʱi-* *dugdʱa-:-**	curds and milk	6148
s'in	river	*s'indʱu-*	river	13415
k'um	shoulder	*skambʱa-**	shoulder-blade; wing	13640
k'om	shoulders	*skambʱa-**	shoulder-blade; wing	13640
t'i	thee	*tu-bʱyam*	thee [dative]	5889.5
z'îb	tongue; language	*ǰiɦv'a-:-*	tongue	5228.1

Table 5: Bhaṭ'esa: Loss of Whispery Voicing Medially

Bhaṭ'esa: -[Cʱ, ɦ]- > Ø

Form	Gloss	OIA Form	OIA Gloss	Turner #
d'âi	beard	*dâḍʱ-i-ka-:-*	beard	6250
s'um	earth; ground	*s'u-maɦânt-*	very great	13493

A few modern consonants have an unexplained loss of the OIA posterior whispery voicing (Table 6).

Table 6: Bhaṭ'esa: Unexplained Loss of Whispery Voicing

Bhaṭ'esa: Cʱ > C

Form	Gloss	OIA Form	OIA Gloss	Turner #
g'ũḍ	button	*gʱũṭa-*	knot; tag; button	4483
bâri'u	husband	*bʱâr-iyâ-pa-**	husband	9467

2.1.2 Kal'aṣa-mandr/mun: Default Anterior Phonation without Position: No Tones

Observations on Kal'aṣa come from my own unpublished field research on the dialects of Mumuret (Kalm.m) and Urtsun (Kalm.u) and Morgenstierne's (1973) data from the dialects of Rumbur (Kalm.r), Suwir (kalm.s), and Urtsun (Kalm.u).

Default phonation in Kal'aṣa is anterior with a strong posterior component. Kal'aṣa shares with Kâmk'ata-vari, Gawâr-b'âti, and perhaps Dâmiâ-bâṣa a characteristic $^{23}{}_{1}$ intonation on declarative utterances. This intonation pattern may have been adopted from Kâmk'ata-vari.

Characteristically, Kal'aṣa speakers prolong the accented vowel with an accompanying falling pitch as accented phonation returns to default.

Kal'aṣa speakers retain the OIA initial posterior whispery-voiced consonants (Table 7).

Table 7: Kal'aṣa: Retained Whispery Voice

Kal'aṣa: C^{ɦ}- = C^{ɦ}-, *ɦ* = *ɦ*

Form	Gloss	OIA Form	OIA Gloss	Turner #	Dialect
d^{ɦ}r'âus	Drosh	*d^{ɦ}r'â·us**	Drosh		Kalm.u
g^{ɦ}'aṭ-	ask for; want	*g^{ɦ}aṭṭ-a-ti**	decreases; is wanting	4415	Kalm.u
g^{ɦ}'oṇa	big	*g^{ɦ}an-'a-*	compact; firm; dense	4424	Kalm.m
g^{ɦ}'au	ravine; valley	*g^{ɦ}ala-**	stream	4453	Kalm.r
g^{ɦ}er-'	turn around [VT]	*g^{ɦ}er-**	make go round	4474	Kalm.r
g^{ɦ}'er-	turn around [VI]	*g^{ɦ}ir-**	go round	4474	Kalm.r
g^{ɦ}'ořa	horse	*g^{ɦ}oṭa-*	horse	4516	Kalm.u
ǰ^{ɦ}'au	forest	*ǰ^{ɦ}alla-*	bush	5355	Kalm.r
ḍ^{ɦ}'aŋg-	bury	*ḍ^{ɦ}ank-*	cover	5574.2	Kalm.r
ḍ^{ɦ}'ap	wide; broad	*ḍ^{ɦ}appa-**	lump	5580.1	Kalm.r
ḍ^{ɦ}'ak	waist; back	*ḍ^{ɦ}â-kka-**	back; waist	5582	Kalm.r

Kal'aṣa: C^{ɦ}- = C^{ɦ}-, ɦ = ɦ

Form	Gloss	OIA Form	OIA Gloss	Turner #	Dialect
ḍ^{ɦ}'a˜k	waist; back	*ḍ^{ɦ}â-kka-**	back; waist	5582	Kalm.u
ḍ^{ɦ}'uk	meeting	*ḍ^{ɦ}uk-ya-ti*	approaches	5592	Kalm.u
ḍ^{ɦ}'e˜ik	knee	*ḍ^{ɦ}onga-**	projecting part of body	5605	Kalm.u
d^{ɦ}'or	hopper; grain-bin	*d^{ɦ}ar-a-*	holding; supporting	6740	Kalm.r
d^{ɦ}'ar-	keep	*d^{ɦ}âr-'aya-ti*	holds; carries; keeps	6791	Kalm.r
b^{ɦ}and-	order	*b^{ɦ}and-a-ti**	orders	9385	Kalm.r
b^{ɦ}'aira	Bâri	*b^{ɦ}âr-i-ka-*	porter	9464	Kalm.r
b^{ɦ}er'u	husband	*b^{ɦ}âr-iyâ-pa-**	husband	9467	Kalm.m
b^{ɦ}'a-	be able	*b^{ɦ}âv-aya-ti*	causes to be	9477	Kalm.r
b^{ɦ}'as	flame	*b^{ɦ}âs'a-*	light	9480	Kalm.r
b^{ɦ}ř'ia	man from Bhi'oṛi	*b^{ɦ}i'oṛi**	Bhi'oṛi		Kalm.u
b^{ɦ}'ut	demon	*b^{ɦ}û-t'a- ?*	been	9552 ?	Kalm.u
b^{ɦ}'unjeu	earthquake	*b^{ɦ}ûmi-čala-*	earthquake	9560	Kalm.r
b^{ɦ}'umbur	wasp	*b^{ɦ}ramara-*	large black bee	9651	Kalm.r
huň-	kill	*ɦ'an-a-*	strikes; kills	13963	Kalm.r
h'an	house; temple	*ɦand^{ɦ}a-**	place; house	13970	Kalm.r
h'aṇyak	stool	*ɦayana-*	covered palanquin	13977	Kalm.m
har'ila	brass	*ɦ'ari-ta-*	yellow; green	13985.1	Kalm.u
ha˜r'ir	thief; enemy	*ɦar-i-tr̥-*	thief	13989	Kalm.u
h'au	plough	*ɦal'a-*	plough	14000	Kalm.r
hiṇḍ'au	bachelor; unmarried woman	*ɦiṇḍ-âla-**	wandering	14090	Kalm.r
h'uluk	heat	*ɦûlu-kka-**	heat	14148	Kalm.u

Kal'aṣa: C^{ɦ}- = C^{ɦ}-, ɦ = ɦ

Form	Gloss	OIA Form	OIA Gloss	Turner #	Dialect
h'iřa	theft	*ɦr̥-ti-*	seized	14149	Kalm.r
h'eman	winter	*ɦem-a-nt'a-*	winter	14164.1	Kalm.u

Through an unclear initial strengthening process, in a few monosyllables they became whispery voiceless consonants (Table 8).

Table 8: Kal'aṣa: Devoicing of Whispery Voice

Kal'aṣa: C^{ɦ}- > Ch-

Form	Gloss	OIA Form	OIA Gloss	Turner #	Dialect
kh'as	grass	*g^{ɦ}âs'a-*	food; pasture grass	4471	Kalm.r
č'onk	thorn	*ǰ^{ɦ}ank-**	clump; cluster	5323.1	Kalm.r
ç̣h'aṭ	single time; drumbeat	*ǰ^{ɦ}aṭṭ-**	sudden movement	5327.2	Kalm.r
ph'ar	burden	*b^{ɦ}âr-'a-*	burden	9459	Kalm.r
čh'u	daughter	*duɦi-t'r̥-*	daughter	6481	Kalm.m

The initial consonant of ***b^{ɦ}'ava-*** 'become' became ***h***, as in Khow`ar. A few forms have an unexplained loss of the OIA posterior whispery voicing on the modern consonant (Table 9).

Table 9: Kal'aṣa: Loss of Whispery Voice

Kal'aṣa: C^{ɦ}- > C-

Form	Gloss	OIA Form	OIA Gloss	Turner #	Dialect
dr'aus	Drosh	*d^{ɦ}r'â·us**	Drosh		Kalm.r
ḍ'inḍek	[kind of carnivorous animal]	*ḍ^{ɦ}inḍ^{ɦ}a-**	belly	5589.3	Kalm.u
baçh'aň	small ornamental bell	*b^{ɦ}ak-ṣa-ṇa-*	cup	9340	Kalm.r

Kal'aṣa: C^{ɦ}- > C-

Form	Gloss	OIA Form	OIA Gloss	Turner #	Dialect
b'ari	Bâri	*b^{ɦ}âr-i-ka-*	porter	9464	Kalm.r
b'it	roof board	*b^{ɦ}it-ta-*	fragment; split timber	9493	Kalm.u
bunǰeu	earthquake	*b^{ɦ}ûmi-čala-*	earthquake	9560	Kalm.r
b'aya	brother	*b^{ɦ}r'âtr̥-*	brother	9661	Kalm.m
b'ayautr	brother's son	*b^{ɦ}râtr̥-putra-*	brother's son	9664	Kalm.r

Posterior whispery voicing of medial consonants was largely anticipated to an initial (default-) voiced consonant (Table 10).

Table 10: Kal'aṣa: Anticipation of Whispery Voice

Kal'aṣa: ← ^{ɦ}

Form	Gloss	OIA Form	OIA Gloss	Turner #	Dialect
g^{ɦ}'on	stench	*gand^{ɦ}'a-*	stench	4014	Kalm.r
g^{ɦ}amb'uri	flower	*gand^{ɦ}a-pûr-i-ka-:-*	flower	4015	Kalm.r
d^{ɦ}amř'ei	tail	*dumb^{ɦ}a-*	tail	6419	Kalm.r
d^{ɦ}o-	milk	*doɦ-a-ti**	milks	6592.2	Kalm.r
b^{ɦ}'on-	bind	*bad^{ɦ}-n'â-ti*	binds; suppresses	9133	Kalm.r
b^{ɦ}'onyak	skin on which newborn baby is placed	*band^{ɦ}-îya-**	to be bound	9143	Kalm.r
b^{ɦ}'i-	fear	*bi-b^{ɦ}'e-ti*	fears	9241	Kalm.u
b'ahul	name of a constellation (Pleiades?)	*baɦu-la-:-*	Pleiades	9195	Kalm.r
lh'uy	blood	*l'oɦ-i-ta-*	red; blood	11165	Kalm.m

If no such initial consonant existed, the medial consonant retained its posterior whispery voicing (Table 11), but in a few cases the posterior whispery voicing was anticipated to the beginning of a vowel-initial word as ***h*** (Table 12), or the medial consonant became ***h*** (Table 13).

Table 11: Kal'aṣa: Retention of Medial Whispery Voice

Kal'aṣa: -Cʱ- = -Cʱ-

Form	Gloss	OIA Form	OIA Gloss	Turner #	Dialect
'adʱek	smallish	*ardʱ'a-*	half	644	Kalm.r
adʱ'e	half	*ardʱ'a-*	half	644	Kalm.r
'adʱu	day	*ardʱa-divasa-*	noon	654	Kalm.r
idʱ'on	stone andiron; tripod	*ud-dʱâ-na-*	stand; rest	2014	Kalm.m
adʱy'-	run	*ud-dʱâv-aya-ti**	runs away	2020	Kalm.r
udʱun	dust	*ud-dʱûḍi-**	excessive dust	2025	Kalm.s
udʱul'-	tear asunder	*ud-dʱû-ta-*	shaken; shaken off; thrown up	2026	Kalm.r

Table 12: Kal'aṣa: Anticipation of Whispery Voice

Kal'aṣa: ← ʱ; ʱ > *ɦ*

Form	Gloss	OIA Form	OIA Gloss	Turner #	Dialect
haly'a	brought	*'â-labʱ-a-te*	takes hold of; obtains	1362	Kalm.r
h'uṣṭum	yoke	*upa-ṣṭambʱ-a-*	support	2266.2	Kalm.u

Table 13: Kal'aṣa: Lenition of Whispery-Voiced Consonants

Kal'aṣa: -Cʱ- > -ɦ-

Form	Gloss	OIA Form	OIA Gloss	Turner #	Dialect
bah'u	a girl who marries into one's family; SoWi; BrWi	*vadʱ'u-:-*	bride; son's wife	11250	Kalm.m

In a number of words medial whispery posterior-voiced consonants and ***ɦ*** were lost because of minor or unclear developmental conditions or inaccurate etymologies (Table 14).

Table 14: Kal’aṣa: Loss of Whispery Voice

Kal’aṣa: -^{ɦ}-, -*ɦ*- > Ø

Form	Gloss	OIA Form	OIA Gloss	Turner #	Dialect
ajĩnj’ik	near	*ad^{ɦ}y-ant-’ena*	close to	276	Kalm.u
ḉhetr’au	Chitral Town	*kṣetra-’ard^{ɦ}a-*	part; place; country; ‘half a field’	643	Kalm.m
agr’-	get tired	*â-g^{ɦ}râ-p-aya-ti*	causes to smell; get satiated	1062.1	Kalm.r
aẓ’ai	apricot	*âṣâḍ^{ɦ}-îya-*	of the month *âṣâḍ^{ɦ}â*	1474	Kalm.r
indr’e˜	rainbow	*indra-d^{ɦ}an’uṣ-*	rainbow	1577	Kalm.r
ču’ane	snake	*kṣob^{ɦ}a-*	agitation	3751	Kalm.u
gard’okh	donkey	*garda-b^{ɦ}’a-ka-*	donkey	4054	Kalm.r
č’uŋ	beard	*čung^{ɦ}a-**	beard; moustache	5254.2	Kalm.r
prelik	light	*pra-b^{ɦ}â-la-*	light	8711	Kalm.r
b’uǰ-	awaken [VI]	*b’ud^{ɦ}-ya-te*	is awakened	9279	Kalm.r
buǰ-’	awaken [VT]	*b’ud^{ɦ}-ya-te*	is awakened	9279	Kalm.r
maurœ	sweet	*mad^{ɦ}u-r’a-*	sweet	9793	Kalm.r
mr’aç	mulberry	*mad^{ɦ}u-ra-vr̥kṣ’a-**	tree with sweet fruit	9796	Kalm.m
m’oč	middle	*m’ad^{ɦ}-ya-*	middle	9804	Kalm.r
mačhum’ ara dada	father’s middle brother	*mad^{ɦ}-ya-m’a-*	middlemost	9810	Kalm.m
m’eñ	cloud	*meg^{ɦ}’a-*	cloud; rain	10302	Kalm.r

Kal'aṣa: -ᶣ-, -ɦ- > Ø

Form	Gloss	OIA Form	OIA Gloss	Turner #	Dialect
am'eňa	ewe	*menḍᶣa-*	ram	10310.1	Kalm.m
am'eňyak	lamb	*menḍᶣa-*	ram	10310.1	Kalm.m
vad'ok	axe	*vardᶣa-ka-*	cutting	11374	Kalm.m
b'ad-	grow	*v'ardᶣa-te*	grows	11376	Kalm.r
bad'ir	(sledge-[?]) hammer	*vardᶣ-ir-a-*	axe; hammer	11385	Kalm.s
bedark'ar	ill; sick	*vi-dᶣarg-a-**	without movement	11751	Kalm.r
b'itr	clear sky	*vîdᶣriya-**	clear sky	12051.3	Kalm.r
isk'ou	peg	*skabᶣa-**	post; peg	13638	Kalm.r
th'um	tree	*stambᶣa-*	pillar; post	13682	Kalm.r
an'ora	hungry	*an-âɦâra-*	abstaining from food	299	Kalm.r
'a	I	*aɦ-'am*	I	992	Kalm.m
ǰ'ip	tongue	*ǰiɦv'a-:-*	tongue	5228	Kalm.r
ǰur'uk	girl	*duɦit'r̥-*	daughter	6481	Kalm.m
bâz'i gᶣ'al	Bazgal	*baɦi-ra-**	external	9183	Kalm.u
br'u˜ ṣiṣ	precipice	*br̥ɦ-an-t-*	tall; high	9302	Kalm.r
li-	lick	*liɦa-ti*	licks	11069.1	Kalm.r
lo'iṣṭ	male monal pheasant	*loɦ-i-ṣṭha-*	very red	11169	Kalm.m

In summary, Kal'aṣa mostly retains OIA whispery voicing in the face of default anterior phonation, probably through the influence of the strong posterior component of default phonation in that language.

2.1.3 Aćharêtâ': Default Posterior Phonation + Position: Tones

If a language retains whispery posterior-voiced consonants, tonal contrasts may arise from contrasting times in the switch between default and accented phonation during the production of an accented vowel. Aćharêtâ′ exemplifies this situation with its contrasting initiation of anterior-voiced accent at the onset or the offset of a tense (long) vowel (Strand 2000/2001). This was probably the case in early Ṣinâ′, but most dialects have since lost their original whispery-voiced consonants (e.g. Schmidt and Kohistani 2008: 30).

Data from Aćharêtâ′ come from my own observations (Strand 2000/2001; 2000/2011).

The accentual system of Aćharêtâ′ is essentially that of Sanskrit posited above. Default phonation is posterior; accented phonation is anterior. Accented lax (short) vowels only have time to carry the high pitch of anterior phonation, but accented tense (long) vowels are long enough to show a *svarita*-like high-falling tone as phonation switches to its posterior default across the vowel.

The default phonation of vowels in Aćharêtâ′ is produced with posterior phonation and back tensing of the larynx. Throughout the vowel this process produces a fundamental frequency (F_0) that may be more or less progressively lowered, the degree of lowering corresponding to the intensity of the speech. There is also a slight megaphonic effect. Back tensing strengthens slightly over utterance segments, producing a strong step-down lowering of F_0 over the length of an utterance.

Accented phonation is anterior, superimposed on the default posterior phonation. The range of pitch between accented and unaccented vowels is somewhat narrow, because of the restriction of larynx raising caused by the concomitant pull of posterior tensing.

Accented lax (short) vowels are indicated by the accent mark (′) preceding the vowel's symbol.

The position of accent on tense (long) vowels is distinctive. On tense vowels with vowel-onset accent, indicated by the accent mark placed before the vowel, anterior accentual tensing starts at the beginning of the vowel and then drops, producing a falling pitch throughout the vowel. On tense vowels with vowel-offset accent, indicated by the accent mark placed after the vowel, anterior accentual tensing begins toward the end of the vowel, while the entire vowel sustains normal posterior tensing. The result is a level, falling–rising, or rising pitch across the vowel, depending on the intensity of speech. Thus there is a contrast between, e.g. offset accented ***râ′t*** 'night and day (24-hour period)' vs onset accented ***r′ât*** 'blood'.

Almost all long vowels with offset accent occur in the final syllable of a word. In a few forms offset accented long vowels appear penultimately. Most of these contain whispery-voiced consonants which may have influenced their development: ***dhrî'sṭo*** 'seen', ***lhô'ko*** 'little', ***mhô'ro*** 'sweet', ***ghâ'nu*** 'big'. The interrogative pronouns ***kô'ṛo***, ***kô'so***, etc. 'which one' are compounds of ***kô'*** 'who' plus a deictic pronoun. Only ***ǰâ'bli*** 'runny sap' (cf. Pashto ***ž'âwla*** 'resin') is anomalous.

Aćharêtâ' speakers retain the OIA initial posterior whispery-voiced consonants (Table 15).

Table 15: Aćharêtâ': Retention of Initial Whispery Voice

Aćharêtâ': ʱ-and ɦ-Retained

Form	Gloss	OIA Form	OIA Gloss	Turner #
ghâ'nu	big	*gʱan'a-*	compact; dense	4424.1
ghî'ṛ	ghee	*gʱr̥t'a-*	ghee	4501
gh'ûṛo	horse [m.]	*gʱoṭa-*	horse	4516
ghr'ôṇ	stench	*gʱrâṇ'a-*	smelling	4531
ǰhâ'ṭ	hair (generic; animal)	*ǰʱâṭṭha-**	hair	5334.2
-ǰh'uli	on top	*ǰʱulya-ti**	swings	5406
ǰhuṭ'a	adulterated (gold, silk, tila)	*ǰʱûṭṭha-**	false	5407
ḍhê'r	belly	*ḍʱera-**	belly	5589.6
dh'ut	mouth	*dʱutta-**	mouth [contemptuous]	5853.27
dharâ'ṇ	earth	*dʱar'a-ṇi:-*	ground	6744
dhuw-	wash (not textiles or hair)	*dʱuva-ti**	washes	6833.1
dhum'î	smoke	*dʱûmika:-*	smoke	6849.2
dhâtâ'r	hearth	*dʱmâtra-**	fireplace	6888
bh'us	straw	*bʱusa-**	chaff	9293.2
bhak'ulo	fat; thick	*bʱakkha-**	lump	9330.1

Aćharêtâ′: ^{ɦ}-and ɦ-Retained

Form	Gloss	OIA Form	OIA Gloss	Turner #
bhê′ṇ	sister	*b*^{ɦ}*agini:-*	sister	9349
bhûng′êli	hemp	*b*^{ɦ}*ang′a-*	hemp	9354
bhanǰ-	hit (direct contact)	*b*^{ɦ}*anǰa-ti**	breaks	9363
bhâṇ′ôl	stable	*b*^{ɦ}*ânḍa-agâra-*	treasury	9442
bhar′îw	husband	*b*^{ɦ}*âriyâ-pa-**	husband	9467
bh-	be able	*b*^{ɦ}*âv-aya-ti*	causes to be	9477
bhi′ûṛi	Bhi′oṛi	*b*^{ɦ}*i′oṛi**	Bhi′oṛi	
bh′it	board	*b*^{ɦ}*it-ta-*	split timber	9493
bh′oči	vagina	*b*^{ɦ}*očča-**	defective	9524.5
bh-	become [past and nonfinite stem]	*b*^{ɦ}*û-t′a-*	been	9552.1
ghumâ′l	earthquake	*b*^{ɦ}*ûmi-čala*	earthquake	9560
bhr′uǰ	birch	*b*^{ɦ}*ûrǰa-*	birch	9570.1
bh′ûro	deaf	*b*^{ɦ}*ora-**	defective	9633
bhrimboṛ′î	wasp	*b*^{ɦ}*ramar′a-*	large black bee	9651
bhrâǰ′ay	brother's wife; friend's wife	*b*^{ɦ}*râtur-ǰâya-:-*	brother's wife	9660
bhr′o	brother	*b*^{ɦ}*r′âtr̥-*	brother	9661
bhrâp′utr	brother's son	*b*^{ɦ}*râtr̥-putra-*	brother's son	9664
haḍ′ung	bone	*ɦaḍḍa-*	bone	13952
hay′îṇi	native-style chair	*ɦayana-*	covered palanquin	13977
hâ′l	plough	*ɦal′a-*	plough	14000
hîmâ′l	avalanche	*ɦima-čala-**	avalanche	14100
h′uluk	heat	*ɦûlukka-**	heat	14148
haywâ′n	winter	*ɦemant′a-*	winter	14164.1

A paucity of modern words have lost initial whispery voicing (Table 16).

Table 16: Aćharêtâ′: Loss of Initial Whispery Voice

Aćharêtâ′: Cɦ- > C-

Form	Gloss	OIA Form	OIA Gloss	Turner #
g′ir-	go around	*g^{ɦ}ir-**	go round	4474.1
ḍ′ôk	back	*ḍ^{ɦ}âkka-**	back; waist	5582
d′uṛi	dust	*d^{ɦ}ûḍi-**	dust	6835
babâ′y	apple	*b^{ɦ}abba:-**	apple	9387

Posterior whispery voicing of medial consonants was anticipated to the initial consonant (Table 17).

Table 17: Aćharêtâ′: Anticipation of Medial Whispery Voice

Aćharêtâ′: ← ɦ

Form	Gloss	OIA Form	OIA Gloss	Turner #
ghrô′k	worm	*gaved^{ɦ}uka-*	kind of snake	4104
mhô′ro	sweet	*mad^{ɦ}ur′a-*	sweet	9793
mhâr′ôço	mulberry	*mad^{ɦ}ura-vr̥kṣ′a-**	tree with sweet fruit	9796
bh′un-	down (elevation or direction)	*bund^{ɦ}a-*	bottom	9820.1
bh′uṛi	wage	*v′r̥dd^{ɦ}i-*	increase; prosperity	12076

If no such initial consonant existed, the medial consonant retained its posterior whispery voicing (Table 18).

Table 18: Aćharêtâ′: Retention of Medial Whispery Voice

Aćharêtâ′: -Cɦ- = -Cɦ-

Form	Gloss	OIA Form	OIA Gloss	Turner #
oḍh′ôl	flood	*ava-ḍḍ^{ɦ}âl-a-*	falling down	773
uḍh′îw-	flee	*ut-d^{ɦ}âvaya-ti**	runs away	2020.2
urbh-	fly	*ut-b^{ɦ}ara-ti*	raises	2038.1
baḍh′îr	sledgehammer	*vard^{ɦ}ira-**	axe; hammer	11385

Rarely, the posterior whispery voicing was anticipated to the beginning of a vowel-initial word as ***h*** (Table 19).

Table 19: Aćharêtâ′: Anticipation of Medial Whispery Voice

Aćharêtâ′: ← ^{ɦ}; ^{ɦ} > *ɦ*

Form	Gloss	OIA Form	OIA Gloss	Turner #
hû′nḍ-	up (direction)	*ûrd*^{ɦ}*v′a-*	erect; being above	2426

Non-anticipated posterior whispery voicing was lost in medial consonant clusters (Table 20).

Table 20: Aćharêtâ′: Loss of Medial Whispery Voice

Aćharêtâ′: -Cɦ- > -C-

Formula	Form	Gloss	OIA Form	OIA Gloss	Turner #
$C_1C_2^{ɦ} > C_2$	*′ubo*	light (weight)	*ut-b*^{ɦ}*ûta-*	come forth	2046
	bûḍ′ôlo	spider	*buḍḍ*^{ɦ}*a-*	defective	9268.3
	b′ûḍo	old (ani- mate)	*buḍd*^{ɦ}*a-**	old	9271
	b′îḍo	very; much; many	*vi-vr̥dd*^{ɦ}*a-*	grown; large	11929
	b′uḍi	bribe	*v′r̥dd*^{ɦ}*i-*	increase; prosperity	12076
	baḍ′îl	man's name	*vard*^{ɦ}*ira-**	axe; hammer	11385
$C_1{}^{ɦ}\tilde{C}_2 > \tilde{C}_2$	*w′in*	lightning bolt	*vid*^{ɦ}*na-**	pierced	12109
$\tilde{C}_1C_2^{ɦ} > \tilde{C}_1$	*isṭ′um*	yoke	*upa-ṣṭamb*^{ɦ}*a-*	support	2266.2
	ǰ′âmi	jaw (lower)	*ǰ′amb*^{ɦ}*a-*	tooth; jaw(s)	5137
	š′umo	parrot	*šumb*^{ɦ}*a-**	parrot	12503
	ṭ′ombo	trunk	*stamb*^{ɦ}*a-*	pillar; post	13682

Aćharêtâ′: -Cɦ- > -C-

Formula	Form	Gloss	OIA Form	OIA Gloss	Turner #
d^{ɦ}y > ǰ	*aǰ′a-*	up (higher elevation)	*ad^{ɦ}y-ad^{ɦ}i*	on high	274
	-ǰ′e	up in	*ad^{ɦ}y-ad^{ɦ}i*	on high	274
	w′âǰ	stomach; rumen	*′ûbad^{ɦ}ya-*	animal's stomach contents	2417.1
	m′êǰi ang′uṛi	middle finger	*m′ad^{ɦ}ya-*	middle	9804
C^{ɦ}C > CC	*′âbru*	cloud	*ab^{ɦ}r′a-*	rain-cloud	549
	b′îdri	clear sky	*vîd^{ɦ}riya-**	clear sky	12051.3

In a few words medial posterior whispery-voiced consonants and ***ɦ*** were lost because of minor or unclear developmental conditions (Table 21).

Table 21: Aćharêtâ′: Unexplained Loss of Medial Whispery Voice

Aćharêtâ′: -^{ɦ}- > Ø

Form	Gloss	OIA Form	OIA Gloss	Turner #
g′âḍu	big (animate); old	*gâḍ^{ɦ}a-*	dived into	4118
d′êṛi	beard	*dâḍ^{ɦ}ika-:-*	beard	6250
n′êwi	umbilical cord	*n′âb^{ɦ}i-*	navel	7062.1
pr′âl	light	*pra-b^{ɦ}âla-*	light	8711
š′uwo	good	*šub^{ɦ}a-*	bright; good	12532
š′îo	porcupine	*šuvâvid^{ɦ}-**	porcupine	12766.2
s′um	dirt	*s′u-maɦânt-*	very great	13493

Almost all instances of non-etymological whisper, both voiced and voiceless, arose to restrict the airflow of a following continuant, that is, a sibilant, ***r***, or nasal stop.

An OIA cluster of stop + sibilant resulted in a voiceless aspirated affricate (especially ***kṣ*** > ***ḉh***), except in word-final position (Table 22).

Table 22: Aćharêtâ′: Whisper Arising from Sibilants

Aćharêtâ′: Whisper from Sibilants

Formula	Form	Gloss	OIA Form	OIA Gloss	Turner #	Source
kṣ-* > *çh-	*çhâtr′ôl*	Chitral	*kṣetra-′ardʱa-*	part; place; country; ‘half a field’	643	OIA
	çhâtrâl′ûčo	man from Chitral				
	çh′ôṇ	hollyoak (generic)				
	çhâṇm′uṭ	hollyoak tree				
	çhâ′r	waterfall	*kṣar′a-*	flowing; water	3662.1	OIA
	çhâṛ′ôngo	grape stalk				
	çhu˜ç-	straighten	*sû˜kṣa-**	straight	13548	OIA
	çh′udro	thick (liquid)				
	çhup-	wash (textiles or hair)	*kṣup-ya-te*	is pressed	3719	OIA
	çh′iṇ	dark	*kṣîṇ′a-*	worn away	3690	OIA
	çh′îk	faeces; coward				
	çhî′r	milk	*kṣîr′a-*	milk	3696	OIA
	çh′îri	udder	*kṣîr′a-vat-*	furnished with milk	3700.2	OIA
	çh′îtr	field (cultivated)	*kṣ′etra-*	land	3735	OIA
	çhu˜ç-	straighten	*sû˜kṣa-**	straight	13548	OIA

Aćharêtâ′: Whisper from Sibilants

Formula	Form	Gloss	OIA Form	OIA Gloss	Turner #	Source
-kṣ- > -ç̣h-	*aç̣h′âṛi*	walnut tree	*akṣ′oṭa-*	walnut	48	OIA
	âç̣h′âru	fir	*akṣa-dâruka-**	kind of tree	30	OIA
	aç̣h′î	eye	*′akṣi-*	eye	43	OIA
	aç̣hirô′	puffball mush-room				
	aç̣hô′ṛ	walnut	*akṣ′oṭa-*	walnut	48	OIA
	kaç̣hû′l	hard sap				
	daç̣h-	look	*dr̥kṣa-ti**	sees	6507.1	OIA
	dêç̣h′iṇi	right	*d′akṣiṇa-*	right	6119	OIA
	mâç̣hur′î	bee	*mâkṣika-kara-**	bee	9990	OIA
	mêç̣h′i	honey	*mâkṣik′a-*	honey	9989.1	OIA
	paç̣h′î	paddle on mill wheel	*pakṣ′iya-*	pertaining to wings	7640.2	OIA
-kṣ- > -ç̣	*k′âç̣*	grass	*k′akṣa-*	under-growth	2589	OIA
	dhr′âç̣	grape	*dr′âkṣa:-*	vine; grape	6628.1	OIA
	prâwâ′ç̣	waist				
-čč- > Ch…č-	*kh′âču*	bad	*kačča-**	raw; unripe	2613	OIA
	khâč′aṛo	ugly	*kačča-**	raw; unripe	2613	OIA
ts > ćh	*baćhâ′r*	young bull (1 year to maturity)	*vatsa-tar′a-*	young bull before copulation	11241	OIA
ts > ćh > ç̣h	*baç̣h′ûṛo*	calf (to 1 year)	*vatsa-kuḍa-**	calf	11239	OIA

Medial sibilants produced initial whisper (Table 23).

Table 23: Aćharêtâ′: Whisper Arising from Medial Sibilants

Aćharêtâ′: Whisper from Medial Sibilants

Formula	**Form**	**Gloss**	**OIA Form**	**OIA Gloss**	**Turner #**	**Source**
CVS > CS > C*h*	*âghâ′*	sky	*â-kâš′a-*	sky	1008	OIA
CVS > C*h*VS	*aṇabhî′š*	nineteen	*ûn′a-vi˜šati*	nineteen	2411	OIA
	bh′eš-	sit	*′upa-viša-ti*	approaches; sits down	2245.1	OIA
	bhî′š	twenty	*vi˜šat′i*	twenty	11616	OIA
	kh′uši	left	*kuša-*	depraved; crippled	3364	OIA
	dhô′ṛ	yesterday	*doṣ′a:-*	night; evening	6590	OIA
	phuṣ′a	seer	*puṣ′a**	shaman		Kmv
	rhâs′ô	kind of plant	*r′asa-vant-*	juicy; tasty	10657	OIA
	thô′s	back of neck	*tos*	shoulder		Kmv
CṼS > C*h*ṼS	*bhê′˜š*	beam; timber	*v′a˜šya-*	crossbeam	11182	OIA
	mhâ′˜s	meat; flesh	*mâ˜s′a-*	flesh	9982	OIA
	rh′û˜s	musk deer	*r`au˜z*	musk deer		Khow
CVST > C*h*VST	*dhrî′sṭo*	saw [irreg. past]	*dr̥ṣṭ′a-*	seen	6518	OIA
	lhâ′sṭ	plain	*lašt**	plain		EIr
	ghrâ′st	wolf [m.]	*grastr̥-*	swallower	4362	OIA
	ghr′asti	wolf [f.]	*grastr̥-*	swallower	4362	OIA

Aćharêtâ′: Whisper from Medial Sibilants

Formula	Form	Gloss	OIA Form	OIA Gloss	Turner #	Source
CVST > Ch*V*T	*nikh-*	go out	*niḥ-ṣkada-ti**	jumps out	7114	OIA
	baṭh′êri	kind of juniper	*vi-ṣṭara-*	spread-out thing; tree	11987.1	OIA
CV*v* > Ch*V*w	*ghâ′w*	cow	*gav-a-*	cow or bull	4093	OIA
	rhô′	song	*râva-*	yell	10716	OIA
	th′î	thy	*tuv′am*	thou	5889	OIA

Medial ***r*** produced anticipated whisper (Table 24), as did some instances of medial *ṭ* and *ḍ*.

Table 24: Aćharêtâ′: Whisper Arising from *r, ṭ, or ḍ*

Aćharêtâ′: Whisper from *r* and Retroflex Stops

Formula	Form	Gloss	OIA Form	OIA Gloss	Turner #	Source
CV*r* > Ch*V*r	*dh′ûra*	far	*dûr′a-*	distant	6495	OIA
	bhirô′	male	*vîr′a-*	man; male	12056	OIA
	bh′îro	goat [m.]	*vîr′a-*	man; male	12056	OIA
	mhâr-	kill	*mâr′aya-ti*	kills	10066	OIA
	phâ′r-	across; over	*pâr′a-*	bringing across; further side	8100	OIA
	pharaṛ′â	across; over [indefinite]	*pâr′a-*	bringing across; further side	8100	
	sithâ′r	sitar	*sitâr*	sitar		Prs

Aćharêtâ': Whisper from *r* and Retroflex Stops

Formula	Form	Gloss	OIA Form	OIA Gloss	Turner #	Source
CVṬ > Ch*V*Ṭ	*ph'âṭu*	feather	*pâṭ'ü*	feather	7627	Kmv
	dhêṛ'um	pomegran-ate	*dâḍima-*	pomegran-ate tree	6254.1	OIA
	ph'ûṛi	smallpox	*poḍa-**	hollow	8398.1	OIA
	nih'âṛa	near	*nikaṭam*	near	7136	OIA
CV*r*S > Ch*V*S	*khaṣ'î*	hoe	*karṣ'i-*	furrowing	2909	OIA
V*r* > *h*V*r*	*hâraṇ-dhrô'k*	Arandu Valley	*ârand'u*	Arandu		
	hâraṇ'û	Arandu	*ârand'u*	Arandu		
	hâraṇ-'ûčo	man from Arandu	*ârand'u*	Arandu		
	hâ'ṭ	flour	*ârta-**	flour	1338	OIA
	h'êṛi	duck [f. for generic]	*âṭ'i-*	an aquatic bird	1127	OIA
C*r̥*C > CV*r*C > Ch*r*VC	*bhrôk'î*	fat on kidneys	*vr̥kk'a-*	kidneys; heart	12064.1	
	bhr'uk	kidney	*vr̥kk'a-*	kidneys; heart	12064.1	OIA
C*r* > Ch*r*	*dhrak-*	pull	*drakk-**	drag	6613	OIA
	dhrâ'l	markhor hair	*drol*	spiderweb		Kmv
	ghr'ôm	communi-ty; village; town	*gr'âma-*	troop; village	4368	OIA
CV*r* > Ch*r*V	*dhr'ûk*	narrow valley	*dur-g'a-*	impassable	6429	OIA

Medial nasal consonants produced initial whisper (Table 25).

Table 25: Aćharêtâ′: Whisper Arising from Nasals

Aćharêtâ′: Whisper from Nasal Consonants

Formula	Form	Gloss	OIA Form	OIA Gloss	Turner #	Source
(C)VN > (C) *h*VN	*haṇô′*	egg	*ând′a-*	egg; testicle	1111	OIA
	bhâng′i	rooster	*bângi*	cock		Prs
	gh′onǰi	storeroom	*ganǰa-*	treasury; grainstore	3961	OIA
	ǰhâm-atrô′	son-in-law	*ǰâmâ-traka-**	daughter′s husband	5198.2	OIA
	ǰhan′âṭu	intelligent	*ǰân′â-ti*	knows	5193	OIA
	ǰhan-durâ′	snake	*ǰantura-**	offspring; creature; worm	5110.1	OIA
	ǰhangâ′r	liver	*ǰigar* [?]	liver	10394	Prs ?
	ǰh′ôn-	know; recognize	*ǰân′â-ti*	knows	5193	OIA
	ǰhî′˜	louse (large)	*y′ûka:-* [?]	louse	10512	OIA
	ǰh′ûṇi	nettle	*yûniya-*	string-like	10519	OIA
	khangâ′r	sword (native)	*xnğr*	sword		Sogd
	rh′onḍo	mangy (goats only); bad	*runṭa-*	defective	10770.4	OIA
	ṭh′ongi	axe	*ṭanka-*	spade; hoe; chisel	5427.1	OIA
	šâka-ṭhong′i	large axe	*ṭanka-*	spade; hoe; chisel	5427.1	OIA
	ghuweṇ′î	Afghan	*awğân*	Afghan		Psht
	ghwâṇâ′	Pashto	*awğân*	Afghan		Psht

Aćharêtâ′: Whisper from Nasal Consonants

Formula	Form	Gloss	OIA Form	OIA Gloss	Turner #	Source
C... NC > Ch...N	*bhiy′ôṇ*	willow	*veta-danḍa-**	willow stem	12098	OIA
	bhiyâṇ-m′uṭ	willow tree	*veta-danḍa-**	willow stem	12098	OIA
s...˜kṣ- > *ç̣h...˜ç̣-*	*ç̣hu˜ç̣-*	straighten	*sû˜kṣa-**	straight	13548	OIA

In at least one form whisper arose from an unclear source (Table 26).

Table 26: Aćharêtâ′: Unclear Source of Whisper

Aćharêtâ′: Unclear Source of Whisper

Form	Gloss	OIA Form	OIA Gloss	Turner #	Source
yh-	come	*y′â-ti*	comes to	10452	OIA

Contrary to the examples of Table 22, unaspirated **ç̣** appears in a number of words, some of which contrast with words with ***ç̣h***, and some of which appear to have nasalization that somehow precludes whispery voice (Table 27).

Table 27: Aćharêtâ′: No Whisper Arising from Sibilants or Nasals

Aćharêtâ′: Whisperless ç̣

Formula	Form	Gloss	OIA Form	OIA Gloss	Turner #	Source
-kṣ- > -ç̣-	*kaç̣aṭô′p*	haystack	*k′akṣa-*	under-growth	2589	OIA
	ǰuwâ′r-k′âç̣u	threshed maize stalk	*k′akṣa-*	under-growth	2589	OIA

Aćharêtâ′: Whisperless ç̣

Formula	Form	Gloss	OIA Form	OIA Gloss	Turner #	Source
	šêlik′âç̣u	threshed rice stalk	*k′akṣa-*	under-growth	2589	OIA
	t′âç̣-	hew	*t′akṣa-ti*	hews; chisels	5620	OIA
	t′êç̣i	adze	*t′akṣa-*	hew		
	mhâ-r′ôç̣o	mulberry	*mad^{ɦ}ura-vr̥kṣ′a-**	tree with sweet fruit	9796	OIA
č…˜Ç̣ > ç̣…˜Ç̣	*ç̣aṇJ̣′a*	torch	*ç̣anẓ′a*	torch		Khow
	ç̣ô˜ṭ-	write	*ç̣ônṭ-*	write		Shin. Ać
	ç̣′î˜ṭ	fart				
-kṣ…n > -˜ç̣	*′i˜ç̣*	bear	*′r̥kṣa-*	bear	2445	OIA
	′i˜ç̣i	she-bear	*′r̥kṣa-*	bear	2445	OIA
	lîṇç̣î′	nit	*likṣ′a:-*	nit	11045	OIA
nVç̣ > ˜ç̣	*′â˜ç̣u*	raspberry	*ân′o-ç̣uk*	wild strawberry		Kmkt

Almost all offset accented vowels occur in final position. My initial hypothesis was that the origin of vowel-offset accent arose from the accent of a following OIA vowel. An examination of 233 Aćharêtâ′ words with accented tense vowels and accent-indicated reflexes in OIA showed that while 16 per cent of OIA forms with accent not on the initial syllable resulted in vowel-offset accent in Aćharêtâ′, in 27 per cent the accent had been anticipated to the initial syllable with vowel-onset accent (Table 28). The small percentage of the former type seems to rule out my initial hypothesis.

Table 28: Distribution of Accentual Location in OIA vs Aćharêtâ′

n = 233		Accent in Aćharêtâ′	
		Vowel-Offset V̂′	Vowel-Onset ′V̂
Accent in OIA	Non-Initial ˘ ′	16% n = 37	27% n = 63
	Initial ′ ˘	2% n = 4	55% n = 129

As noted above, almost all forms have vowel-offset accent on the final syllable. An examination of 283 such forms showed that at least 180 of them (64 per cent) were loanwords with final accent. A better hypothesis than my initial one would posit that the habit arose of pronouncing loanwords with vowel-offset accent, and that the habit extended to certain accented suffixes (***-â′***, ***-ô′***, etc.) as well.

2.2 Descendant Languages without Inherited Posterior-Voiced Consonants

Languages without inherited posterior-voiced consonants may have tonal contrasts, as in the Ṣinâ′ dialects of Gilgit and Kôhistân, Garv′i, Torwâli, Khow`ar, and Dâmiâ-bâṣa, or they may lack tone altogether, as do the languages of the Kunaṛ Valley.

Kôhistâni Ṣinâ′ (Schmidt and Kohistani 2008) exemplifies a language with default posterior phonation but no inherited whispery-voiced consonants. Tonal contrasts are positional on tense (long) vowels, as in Aćharêtâ′.

2.2.1 Khow`ar: Default Anterior Phonation, Anterior or Posterior Accent without Position: Tones

If a language does not retain posterior whispery-voiced consonants, then it may have retained the posteriorness on the phonation of the following vowel, which if accented may contrast with an accented anterior-phonated vowel.

Data from Khow`ar come from my research on the dialect spoken in Nağar in southern Chitral (Strand 2004/2011, 2012).

The normal unaccented phonation of vowels in Khow`ar is produced with anterior phonation and a concomitant front tensing of the larynx. With many speakers the front tensing produces a somewhat high pitched phonatory register with phonation that tenses into a slight creakiness before a voiceless consonant.

Accented phonation is produced with either tight anterior phonation or posterior phonation, concomitant with the oral articulation of a vowel. There are two levels of accent, primary and secondary, above the level of default phonation. The default accentual level is primary.

Primary accented phonation is indicated by an accent mark (` for anterior phonation or ´ for posterior phonation) written before the accented vowel. The pairs of words in Table 29 demonstrate the contrast between anterior and posterior accented phonation.

Table 29: Accented Phonation Contrasts in Khow`ar

anterior	*g`oḷ* throat	*ḍ`aq* boy	*ḍ`af* frame drum	*ḍ`uk* lump	*š`en* rough
	d`on tooth	*ph`ox* slowly	*b`as* overnight	*b`ol* army	*wez`enote* tonight
posterior	*g´oḷ* gully	*ḍ´ak* hind leg	*ḍ´ap* level area	*ḍ´uk* side peak	*š´en* grape arbor
	d´on ghee	*ph´ox* soft; loose	*b´as* flame	*b´ol* Pleiades	*wez´en* evening

The position of accent within words is distinctive. Accented phonation may occur on the penultimate or the final syllable in a simple, non-compounded word, as in the word pair ***b`eḷu*** 'straw bucket' vs ***beḷ`u*** 'pipe; flute'.

A secondary level of accent appears in multi-word sequences. Secondary accent may be produced by either anterior or posterior phonation. It is indicated by a lighter-faced accent mark: ` or ´. Compared to the normal, primary accent described above, the pitch of secondary accent is not as high for anterior phonation and not as low for posterior phonation. In compound words secondary accent falls on the normally accented vowel of a constituent word.

In the majority of Khow`ar reflexes of OIA words with initial posterior whispery-voiced consonants, the whisper dropped and the posterior voicing remained as accented phonation on the following vowel (Table 30).

Table 30: Khow`ar: Development of OIA Initial Whispery-Voiced Consonants

Khow`ar: ^{ɦ}- > ´ (posterior-phonated accent)

Form	Gloss	OIA Form	OIA Gloss	Turner #
g´oṣ	dough	*g*^{ɦ}*arṣa-*	friction	4448
g´ol	valley with stream	*g*^{ɦ}*ala-**	stream	4453
g´ol´oğ	stream water	*g*^{ɦ}*alodaka-*	river water	14470
ž´al	grove	*ĵ*^{ɦ}*alla-**	bush	5355
ḍ´ap	level area on mountain	*ḍ*^{ɦ}*app-**	cover	5579.1
ḍ´uk	side peak of mountain	*ḍ*^{ɦ}*okka-**	rock	5603.1
d´ol	snare drum	*ḍ*^{ɦ}*ola-*	large drum	5608
d´an	popcorn	*d*^{ɦ}*ân'a:-*	parched grain	6777
g´omdan	popped wheat	*d*^{ɦ}*ân'a:-*	parched grain	6777
d´ey-	run	*d*^{ɦ}*âv'aya-ti*	makes run; drives	6802.2
d´-	drink from a teat	*d*^{ɦ}*îya-te*	is suckled	6816
dr´os	Drosh	*d*^{ɦ}*r'â·us**	Drosh	
b´ot	dinner	*b*^{ɦ}*akt'a-*	food; boiled rice	9331
b´ong	cannabis	*b*^{ɦ}*ang'a-*	hemp	9354
b´os	become!; you [sg.] should become	*b*^{ɦ}*'ava-ti*	becomes	9416
b´ard´oyu	porter	*b*^{ɦ}*ârika-*	porter	9464

Khow`ar: ɦ- > ´ (posterior-phonated accent)

Form	Gloss	OIA Form	OIA Gloss	Turner #
b´ardrozak	porter	*bɦârika-*	porter	9464
b´as	flame	*bɦâs'a-*	light	9480
b´olm`uži	earthquake	*bɦûmi-čala-*	earthquake	9560
b´umbur	hornet	*bɦramara-*	large black bee	9651
b´um	earth; ground	*bɦ'ûmi-*	earth; ground	9557
br´ar	brother; male cousin	*bɦr'âtr̥-*	brother	9661

The posterior whispery voicing of medial consonants also resulted in posterior-phonated accent on an adjacent or resulting vowel, with loss of the medial consonant (Table 31).

Table 31: Khow`ar: Development of OIA Medial Whispery-Voiced Consonants

Khow`ar: -ɦ- > ´ (posterior-voiced accent)

Form	Gloss	OIA Form	OIA Gloss	Turner #
ç̣h´ui	hunger	*kṣudɦika:-* *	hunger	3716.2
ç̣h´uy	hungry	*kṣudɦin-*	hungry	3716.3
gord´oğ	donkey	*gardabɦ'aka-*	donkey	4054
g´oğ-m`aḷi	wormhole	*gavedɦuka-*	kind of snake	4104
d´on	ghee	*dadɦan-v'ant-*	containing coagulated milk	6144
žo´-	copulate	*y'abɦa-ti*	copulates	10418
l´e-	find; get; reap	*l'abɦa-te*	catches; takes	10948
g´an	wind	*gândɦa-*	perfumed	4131
girw´an	collar	*grîva:-bandɦa-**	neck band	4390
sin´oğ	river water	*s'indɦu-*	river	13415

In a couple of instances after a prefix a whispery posterior-voiced consonant was reduced to [ɦ], modern phonemic ***h*** (Table 32).

Table 32: Khow`ar: Development of OIA Medial Whispery-Voiced Consonants after Prefixes

Khow`ar: -ʱ- > *h*

Form	Gloss	OIA Form	OIA Gloss	Turner #
h´o	he became	*'a-bʱava-t*	became	9416
h´anu	cover; sheath	*â-dʱânaka-*	place in which something rests	1163

The development of ***h*** ([ɦ]) paralleled that of the other whispery posterior-voiced consonants, leaving ***h´*** initially and only posterior phonation (´) medially (Table 33).

Table 33: Khow`ar: Development of OIA *h* ([ɦ])

Khow`ar: *ɦ* > *h´* (posterior-voiced accent)

Form	Gloss	OIA Form	OIA Gloss	Turner #
h´on	flood	*ɦanu-*	weapon; death	13965
h´im	snow	*ɦim'a-*	cold; frost; snow	14096
h´imr´oğ	water from melted snow	*ɦimara-udaka-*	snow water	14102
ž´ur	daughter	*duɦit'r̥-*	daughter	6481
b´ol	Pleiades	*baɦulâ-*	Pleiades	9195
m´-	urinate	*m'eɦa-ti*	pisses	10338
l´-	lick	*liɦa-ti*	licks	11069.1

In a significant minority (40 per cent) of words posterior whispery voicing of consonants was lost, replaced with anterior accent, after initial consonants (Table 34) or medially (Table 35).

Table 34: Khow`ar: Loss of OIA Initial Whispery Voicing

Khow`ar: ɦ- > Ø

Form	Gloss	*OIA Form*	OIA Gloss	Turner #
g`az	grass	*gɦâs'a-*	food; pasture grass	4471
gran`iš	morning	*gɦraṇiṣya-**	sun's heat	4530
ḍ`or	hopper	*dɦara- ?*	holding; supporting	6740 ?
dan`u	coriander	*dɦânaka-*	coriander	6776.1
by`oḷi	a community in By´oḷg´ol	*bɦi'oṛi**	Bhi'oṛi	
b`it	board (cut and trimmed)	*bɦitta-*	fragment; split timber	9493
b´olm`uži	earthquake	*bɦûmi-čala-*	earthquake	9560
buḷ`i	birch	*bɦûrǰa-*	birch	9570.1
bḷ`ać	short [animate]	*bɦr̥š-*	fall	
brež`ayu	sister-in-law	*bɦrâtur-ǰâya:-*	brother's wife	9660
br`u	eyebrow	*bɦr'u:-*	eyebrow	9688.1

Table 35: Khow`ar: Loss of OIA Medial Whispery Voicing

Khow`ar: -ɦ- > Ø

Form	Gloss	OIA Form	OIA Gloss	Turner #
`af	down	*adɦ'aḥ*	below; under	246
`ayh	up	*'adɦi*	up; above; on	249
g`oğ	worm; bug	*gavedɦuka-*	kind of snake	4104
duh`u kor-	scold	*d'odɦant-*	fierce; violent	6580
mr`aç	mulberry	*madɦura-vr̥kṣ'a-**	tree with sweet fruit	9796
n`af	umbilical cord; navel	*n'âbɦi-*	navel	7062.1
isk`ow	peg	*skabɦa-**	post; peg	13638
š`u	porcupine	*šuvâvidɦ-**	porcupine	12766.2
phord`u	young plant	*pr'a-vr̥ddɦa-*	grown up	8807

Khow`ar: -^{ɦ}- > Ø

Form	Gloss	OIA Form	OIA Gloss	Turner #
drağ`anẓ s`al	famine	*daur-ârg^{ɦ}ya-**	time of high prices	6426.2
ç̣hetr`ar	Chitral	*kṣetra-'ard^{ɦ}a-*	part; place; country; 'half a field'	643
bard`ox	large axe	*vard^{ɦ}aka-*	cutting	11374
baḍ`ir	sledgehammer	*vard^{ɦ}ira-*	axe; hammer	11385
y`udur	clear sky	*vîd^{ɦ}riya-**	clear sky	12051.3
dr`ung	long; tall [animate]	*drang^{ɦ}a-**	long	6616
gamb`uri	flower	*gand^{ɦ}a-pûrika:-*	flower	4015
b`and	joint	*band^{ɦ}'a-*	bond	9136
s`in	river	*s'ind^{ɦ}u-*	river	13415
m`už	marrow; middle	*m'ad^{ɦ}ya-*	middle	9804

Similarly, the posterior voicing of OIA ***h*** left no trace in some modern forms (Table 36).

Table 36: Khow`ar: Loss of OIA *h*

Khow`ar: *ɦ* > Ø

Form	Gloss	OIA Form	OIA Gloss	Turner #
yom`un	winter	*ɦem-ant'a-*	winter	14164.1
aw`a	I	*aɦ'am*	I	992
b`olu	group of people	*baɦu-l'a-*	large; thick	9194
ber`i	out of	*bâɦirika-*	external	9227
gam`eṣ	female buffalo	*maɦiṣ'a-*	great; powerful; buffalo	9964
l`ey	blood	*loɦi-*	*red; blood	11164
an`us	daytime; day	*aɦnasa-*	day	993

In summary, Khow`ar either transformed the OIA posterior whispery voice of consonants into the posterior phonation of an adjacent vowel, or it lost it altogether.

2.2.2 Garv'i: Default Anterior Phonation, Anterior or Posterior Accent + Position: Tones

In Garv'i (Baart 1999, 2004) and Torwâli (Lunsford 2001) the pitch data allow inferences about their underlying physiology. Both languages have contrasting anterior and posterior accented phonation, which may be contrastively short, medium, or long. Default phonation is anterior, with a posterior component. Its pitch is lower than accented anterior phonation. After accent is released, the pitch of subsequent default phonation falls.

The domain of the accent is the word. Accent starts at the onset of the word and continues until it is released, at which time phonation reverts to its default. The point of release is marked as described above: ` means 'the anterior accentual tensing that started at the beginning of the word is now released'; likewise, ´ means 'the posterior accentual tensing that started at the beginning of the word is now released'.

There are three positions for points of accentual release, corresponding to the three degrees of accentual length measured from the beginning of the accented word (Table 37).

The point of release for short accents is at the onset of the accented vowel; that is, the accentual tensing is instantaneous. Short accent is indicated here by an an accent mark before the accented vowel (Baart's 'HL' and 'LH' tones).

Medium accent (Baart's 'H(L)' tone) is indicated by the accent mark (`) after the accented vowel. Immediately after the accented vowel, phonation returns to its default value, which post-tonically is progressively lower in pitch.

Long accent (Baart's 'H' and 'L' tones) is indicated by an accent mark after the word, indicating that the accentual tensing continues through the word and onto a following syllable before relaxing to default phonation.

Table 37: Accentual contrasts in Garv'i (after Baart 2004)

Duration of Accented Phonation from Beginning of Word	Location of Accented Phonation: Anterior		Location of Accented Phonation: Posterior	
Short	'HL' (22.5%)		'LH' (20.9%)	
	b`a:n	'excuse'	*g´o:r*	'horse'
	š`a:k	'pieces of wood'	*d´atar*	'fireplace'
	b`o:r	'lions'	*bub´ay*	'apple'
	b`aćho:r	'calf'	*luk´uṭor*	'children'
	aŋ`usir	'finger-ring'		
Medium	"H(L)" (25.8%)			
	ba:`l	'hair'		
	dâ:wâ:`l	'wall'		
Long	"H" (22.9%)		'L' (4.9%)	
	dar`	'door'	ba:n´	utensils
	šâ:k`	'piece of wood'	bubay´	apples
	bo:r`	'lion'		
	bire`	'girl'		

Only a few etymologies (Table 38) are available to me from Baart's corpus of reliably marked accent (1999, 2004).

Table 38: Reflexes of OIA Whispery Voice in Garv'i

Formula	Garv'i: Accentual Type	Garv'i: Form	Garv'i: Gloss	OIA Form	OIA Gloss	Turner #
C^{ɦ}V- > C´V	posterior short LH	*g´o:r*	horse	*g^{ɦ}oṭa-*	horse	4516
	posterior short LH	*b´â:g*	place	*b^{ɦ}âga-*	portion; fraction	9430
	posterior short LH	*ǰ´a:*	brother	*b^{ɦ}r'âtr̥-*	brother	9661
	posterior short LH	*d´arin*	land	*d^{ɦ}ar'aṇi:-*	ground (f.)	6744
	posterior short LH	*d´atar*	fireplace	*d^{ɦ}mâtra-*	fireplace	6888

Garv'i

Formula	Accentual Type	Form	Gloss	OIA Form	OIA Gloss	Turner #
C^ɦVC'V- > CVC´V	posterior short LH	*bob´ây*	apple	*b^ɦabba:-**	apple	9387
-C^ɦV- > -'V	posterior short LH	*luk´u-ṭor*	children	*lag^ɦ'ukka-*	light	10896
C^ɦVCV > CV'	posterior long L	*gâ:´*	grass	*g^ɦâs'a-*	food; pasture grass	4471
CVC^ɦV > CVC'	posterior long L	*dut´*	lip	*dudd^ɦa-**	snout; beak; mouth	5853.27
CVC^ɦVCV > CVC´	posterior long L	*go:m´*	wheat	*god^ɦ'ûma-*	wheat	4287
C^ɦVCV > CVCV´	posterior long L	*bobây´*	apple (oblique)	*b^ɦabba:-**	apple	9387
C^ɦVCV > CV`C	anterior medium H(L)	*ḍâ:`g*	back (of body)	*ḍ^ɦâkka- **	back; waist	5582
CVCVC^ɦ-VCV > C`VCVC	anterior short HL	*p`a:ren*	shirt	*pari-d^ɦ'âna-*	garment	7838
CVCVC^ɦV > C`VCV	anterior short HL	*g`edâ*	donkey	*gardab^ɦ'a-*	donkey	4054
CVC^ɦV > CVC`	anterior long H	*tâm`*	tree	*stamb^ɦa-*	pillar; post	13682
?		*ga:n*	big	*g^ɦan'a-*	compact; dense	4424.1

In Garv'i the position of accent appears to have resulted from either the position of accent or of whispery-voiced consonants within the parent word, but the scanty data of Table 38 leave the details unexplained.

2.2.3 Languages with Anterior Accent Only: No Tones

In the dialects of the Kunaṛ Valley, including the Degân'o dialect of Eastern Paša'î and the languages now or formerly spoken in the tributary Peč Valley (G′õgali, Šumâšti, Gawâr-b′âti), whispery voicing has been completely lost. The result is a merging of the whispery-voiced consonants with the default-voiced ones, as in Irânian and Nûristânî. In those languages that I have examined (Degân′o and Gawâr-b′âti), default voicing is anterior with a slight posterior admixture.

2.3 Lingual Consequences of Phonatory Location

The backing of the tongue in Indo-Âryan probably arose out of the generalized Indo-Âryan posterior phonation. As stated above, posterior phonation tends to pull the tongue back. Through certain sound changes a series of tongue-backed ('retroflex') consonants, which contrasted with dental ones, arose early in Indo-Âryan and became ubiquitous in OIA.

Much later ancient consonant clusters consisting of stop + ***r*** underwent distinctive changes in two groups of far north-western IA languages. One group apparently formed in a western, Paša′î-speaking centre and spread eastward to encompass languages of the Peč (Gawâr-b′âti, G′õgali, Šumâšti) and Panjkora (Garv′i). Another group centred among the Ṣinâ′ speakers of the Indus Basin, spreading downriver to encompass the Indus Kôhistâni languages. The panoply of evolutionary outcomes of these ancient clusters in the modern dialects appears in Table 39.

In the first group fronted laminality has replaced backed apicality. This change, the 'Western Fronting', is consistent with a strongly fronted tongue, pressed behind the teeth of a prognathized lower jaw that arises out of default anterior phonation in many of the region's Irânian languages. The sequences of changes for voiceless clusters in, for example, Garv′i, would have been ***tr*** > ***tł*** > ***ł***, ***kr*** > ***kł*** > ***tł*** > ***ł***, and ***pr*** > ***pš*** > ***tš*** = ***č***.

In the second group backed apicality is strengthened and anticipated in the clusters beginning with labials and apicals, producing backed apical affricates, while the backing of ***r*** becomes redundant and lost after the inherently backed velar consonants. Unlike the probable foreign (Irânian) origin of the Western Fronting, these changes, the 'Indus Backing', appear to amplify Indo-Âryan backing. Thus in Gilgit

Ṣinâ′ the sequences of changes for voiceless clusters would have been ***tr*** > *tṣ* > *ṭṣ* = *ç*, ***pr*** > *pṣ* > *ṭṣ* = *ç*, and ***kr*** > ***k***.

This 'Indus Backing' must have happened after the migration of one group of early Ṣinâ′ speakers from Čil′âs to Aćharê′t in the mid 1600's CE (Strand 2001a), because Aćharêtâ′ retains ancient clusters with ***r*** unchanged.

Table 39: Development of Consonant Clusters with -*r*

[Indo-Âryan]	tr	pr	kr	dr-	b/bhr	gr	mr	vr-	šr
(Chitral)									
Khow`ar	*tr*	*pr*	*kr*	*dr*	*br/br´*	*gr*	*br-*	*br-*	*ṣr, ṣ*
Kal′aṣa-mandr/mun	*tr*	*pr*	*kr*	*dr*	*b [?]*	*gr*			*ṣ, š, -s*
(Paša′î)									
Lauṛowân	*tr*	*l*	*l*	*dr*	*l*	*l*	*l*	*ṛ-*	*ṣ-, -yr-*
Iskên	*tr*	*l*	*l*	*dr*	*l*	*l*	*l*	*ṛ-*	*ṣ-, -yr-*
Tagâw (Alasâi)	*tr*	*l*	*l*	*dr*	*l*	*l*	*mṛ*	*ṛ-*	*ṣ-, -yr-*
Nijrâw (Pačağân)	*tr*	*pr*	*pr*	*dr*	*l*	*l*	*mṛ*	*ṛ-*	*ṣ-, -yr-*
Parwân (Gulbahâr)	*tr*	*pṛ*	*kṛ*	*dr*	*bṛ*		*mr*	*r-*	*ṣ-, -yr-*
Čugâni (Kuṛdar)	*tr*	*pl*	*pl*	*dr*	*bl*	*δl*	*bl*	*l*	*ṣ-, -yr-*
Ališang	*tr*	*ṣ*	*ṣ*	*dr*	*l*	*l*		*ṛ-*	*ṣ-, -yr-*
Alingar	*tr*	*s*	*s*	*dr*		*l*		*l*	*ṣ-, -yr-*
Lağmân	*ɫ*	*ɫ*	*ɫ*	*l*	*l*	*l*	*l*	*l*	*ṣ-, -yr-*
Čilas-Kuṛangal	*ɫ*	*ɫ*	*ɫ*	*l*	*l*	*l*	*l*	*l*	*ṣ-, -yr-*
Degân′o (Gorayk)	*ɫ*	*ɫ*	*ɫ*	*l*	*l*	*l*	*-mbr-*	*l*	*š, -r-*
(Peč)									
Šumâšti	*ɫ*	*ɫ*	*ɫ*	*l*	*l*	*l*	*l*	*l*	*ṣ-, -yr-*

[Indo-Âryan]	tr	pr	kr	dr-	b/bhr	gr	mr	vr-	šr
Gawâr-b'âti	*ł*	*pl*	*ł*	*l*	*bl*	*ł*	*bl*	*l*	*ṣ-, š-, -ł-*
G'o˜gali	*ṣl*		*ṣl*						
(Panǰkora)									
Dâmiâ-bâṣa	*tr*	*pr*	*kr*	*dr*	*br*	*gr*	*br*	*br*	*ṣ-, -š-, -štr-*
Garv'i	*ł*	*tš = č*	*ł*	*l*	*dž = ǰ*	*l*			*ṣ, š*
(Kunaṛ)									
Kaṭâr-Qâlâî	*ł*		*k*	*l*	*ṛ*	*g*			*ṣ, š*
(Tirâhi)									
Tirâhi	*tr*		*kr*	*dr*	*br*	*gr*			*x*
(Indus Kohistan)									
Torwâli	*ṭṣ = ç*	*p*	*k*	*ḍẓ = J̣*	*b*	*g*			*ṣ, š*
Chilisso	*ṭṣ = ç*	*ṭṣ = ç*	*k*	*ẓ*	*ẓ*	*g*			
Gowro	*ṭṣ = ç*	*ṭṣ = ç*	*k*	*ẓ*	*ẓ*	*g*			
Indus Kôhistâni	*ṭṣ = ç*	*ṭṣ = ç*	*k*	*ẓ*	*ẓ*	*g*			*ṣ*
Bhaṭ'esa	*ṭṣ- = ç-, -ṭṣh = -çh, či-*	*ṭṣh = çh ?*	*k?*	*ḍẓ- = J̣-*	*dẓh = J̣h*	*g*			*ṣ*
(Ṣinâ')									
Ṣinâ' Kôhistân	*ṭṣ- = ç-*		*k-*		*ẓ-*				
Ṣinâ' Gilgit	*ṭṣ- = ç-*	*ṭṣ = ç*	*k-*	*ḍẓ*	*ẓ-*	*g*			*ṣ*
Ṣinâ' Tilel			*kr-*		*ẓ-*				
Ušuǰ'u	*ṭṣ- = ç-*		*kr-*		*ẓ-*				
Kalkoṭi	*tr-*	*tr-*	*kr-*	*dr-*	*dr-*	*dr-*			

[Indo-Âryan]	tr	pr	kr	dr-	b/bhr	gr	mr	vr-	šr
Aćharêtâ′ (Palôlâ′)	*tr-, -tr-*	*pr-*	*kr-*	*dhr-*	*bhr*	*ghr-*			*ṣ*
(Kašmiri)									
Kə šur	*tr-*	*pr-, p-*	*k-, kr-*	*dr-, d-*	*br-, b-*	*g-*			*h-, -š-*

3. CONCLUSIONS

The data presented here lead to conclusions regarding phylogeny and tonogenesis in the far north-western Indo-Âryan languages.

There are two geographic regions defined by default phonation: one of anterior phonation along the Indo-Irânian frontier, and one of posterior phonation in the upper Indus Valley.

There are two sources of tonogenesis: one arising from a contrast between accented anterior vs posterior phonation, and one arising from positional contrasts in the placement and duration of accented phonation.

3.1 Region of Default Anterior Phonation: Influence from Persian

What is striking is the adoption of anterior phonation as the unaccented default in those Indo-Âryan languages and dialects that lie along the Indo-Irânian frontier, exposed to direct Irânian influence. The location of this frontier has fluctuated over generations, driven by the long-term expansion of Irânian speakers from west to east. A result of adopted anterior phonation is weakened or lost posterior phonation and loss of whispery-voiced consonants, except in Kal′aṣa.

Even before the expansion of Pashto in the region began in the 1500s CE, direct Irânian influence had appeared in the form of Courtly Persian (***Fârsî-i Darî***), used administratively since the Ghaznavî Turks conquered the region in the 1000s CE. Irânian influence emanated from the Turkish-conquered ancient regions of Kâpisâ, Laghmân, Nangarhâr, Peshâwar, Bajǎwïṛ, and Swât.

Khow`ar had direct influence from the Persian of Badakhshân and the Irânian Pâmîr languages, as well as a tradition of courtly Persian since Mughal times.

Likewise, influence from Badakhshân and courtly Persian affected the region of Bajawïṛ, which in the late 1500s CE (16 generations before 1950 [Morgenstierne 1950]) was home to the ancestors of speakers of Gawâr-b'âti (and probably the other Peč Valley languages), Dâmiâ-bâṣa, and Garv'i (at an unclear time). The language names Gawâr, Garv'i, and Gowro derive from Persian ***gabr***, originally, 'Zoroastrian', but later used with much the same contempt toward non-Muslims as Arabic ***kâfir*** 'infidel' is today. All these languages may have originated from a ***Gabaristân*** that once centered on modern Bajawïṛ.

The strong influence of Persian on Degân'o Paša'î is probably more recent, since the imposition of Afghân rule in Laghmân and lower Kunaṛ.

3.2 Region of Default Posterior Phonation

Speakers from the upper Indus Valley region (the Ṣinâ' dialects and Bhaṭ'esa) maintained strong posterior phonation. In the Ṣinâ' dialects Irânian influence manifested itself through the adoption of Persian word-final accent as vowel-offset accent.

3.3 Tonal Contrasts from Posterior-Voiced Consonants

All Indo-Irânian languages have anterior-phonated accent. When the posterior voicing of a consonant moves to an adjacent accented vowel, a tonal contrast arises between anterior- and posterior-accented vowels.

3.4 Tonal Contrasts from Accentual Position

In the Ṣinâ' dialects tonal contrasts apparently arose from loanwords with final-syllable accent, which was borrowed into Ṣinâ' in the vowel-offset position, in contrast with words with 'normal' vowel-onset accent. In Garv'i and Torwâli the position of accent appears to have resulted from both the position of accent and of whispery-voiced consonants within the earlier OIA word.

4. EPILOGUE

Carla's field research and my own spanned a 'golden age' (or opportunity) for linguists to build on the research of our predecessors (Biddulph, Leitner, Baily, Morgenstierne, Buddruss) and gain deeper insight into the languages that span the remote valleys of the Hindu Kush and Karakoram ranges. The years from the late 1960's to the first few years of the twenty-first century provided us foreign scholars with the opportunity for field research and publications; the ensuing years are for native speaker scholars to edify their own linguistic heritages.

REFERENCES

Baart, Joan L. G. 2004. 'Contrastive Tone in Kalam Kohistani'. *Linguistic Discovery* 2.2: 1–20.

_______ 1999. 'Tone Rules in Kalam Kohistani (Garwi, Bashkarik)'. *Bulletin of the School of Oriental and African Studies* 62.1: 88–104.

Buddruss, Georg. 1959. *Kanyawali: Proben eines Maiyẫ-Dialektes aus Tangir (Hindukusch).* Münchener Studien zur Sprachwissenschaft, Beiheft B. München: J. Kitzinger.

Catford, John C. 1977. *Fundamental Problems in Phonetics.* Bloomington, Indiana: Indiana University Press.

Lunsford, Wayne A. 2001. *An Overview of Linguistic Structures in Torwali, a Language of Northern Pakistan.* MA thesis. Texas: University of Texas at Arlington.

Morgenstierne, Georg. 1973. *The Kalasha Language.* Indo-Iranian Frontier Languages, Vol. 4. Oslo: Universitetsforlaget.

_______ 1967. *The Pashai Language, Part 1, Grammar.* Indo-Iranian Frontier Languages, Vol. 3. ISK Serie B: Skrifter 40. Oslo: Universitetsforlaget.

_______ 1950. *Notes on Gawar-Bati.* Skrifter utgitt av Det Norske Videnskaps-Akademi i Oslo II, Hist.-Filos. Klasse, 1950, no. 1. Oslo: Jacob Dybwad.

Radloff, Carla F. 1992. 'The dialects of Shina'. In *Sociolinguistic Survey of Northern Pakistan, Volume 2: Languages of Northern Areas,* edited by Peter C. Backstrom and Carla F. Radloff. 89–203. Islamabad: National Institute of Pakistan Studies and Summer Institute of Linguistics.

Schmidt, Ruth Laila and Kohistani, Razwal. 2008. *A Grammar of the Shina Language of Indus Kohistan.* Wiesbaden: Harrassowitz Verlag.

Strand, Richard F. 2013. *Basic Processes in the Evolution of the Nûristânî Languages.* <http://nuristan.info/Nuristani/BasicEvolutionaryProcesses.html> accessed 6 June 2016.

——— 2012. *The Sound System of Khow`ar.* <http://nuristan.info/IndoAryan/Chitral/Khow/KhowLanguage/Lexicon/phon.html> accessed 6 June 2016.

——— 2004/2011. *Khow`ar Lexicon.* <http://nuristan.info/index.html#TOC> accessed 6 June 2016.

——— 2001a. 'The History of the Açhar'îta'. In *Gates of Peristan: History, Religion and Society in the Hindu Kush,* edited by Alberto M. Cacopardo and Augusto S. Cacopardo. 297–300. Rome: Instituto Italiano per l'Africa e l'Oriente.

——— 2001b. *Bhaṭ'e sa zib Lexicon.* <http://nuristan.info/index.html#TOC> accessed 6 June 2016.

——— 2001c. *The Sound System of Bhaṭ'e sa zib.* <http://nuristan.info/IndoAryan/SwatIndus/Bhatera/BhateraLanguage/Lexicon/phon.html> accessed 6 June 2016.

——— 2000/2011. *Aćharêtâ' Lexicon.* <http://nuristan.info/index.html#TOC> accessed 6 June 2016.

——— 2000/2001. *The Sound System of Aćharêtâ'.* <http://nuristan.info/IndoAryan/Indus/Atsaret/AtsaretLanguage/Lexicon/phon.html> accessed 6 June 2016.

Turner, Ralph L. 1966. *A Comparative Dictionary of the Indo-Aryan Languages.* London: Oxford University Press.

Varma, Siddheshwar. 1961. *Critical Studies in the Observations of Indian Grammarians.* Delhi: Munshi Ram Monohar Lal.

Whitney, William Dwight. 1960. *Sanskrit Grammar: Including both the Classical Language, and the older Dialects, of Veda and Brahmana.* Cambridge, Massachusetts: Harvard University Press.

19

Tonogenesis in Burushaski and Domaki

Bertil Tikkanen

1. BURUSHASKI TONES

In Burushaski[1] only long vowels can carry tone. Following Berger's analysis and transcription of the Hunza and Nager dialects (1998 I: 14–16, 225), the tone system can be summarized as follows.[2] (Unless otherwise stated, the examples are from the Hunza dialect, in most cases identical with the Nager dialect. In the Yasin dialect tones are seldom heard.)

(1) Stress on the first component of a long vowel, *áa* (high-falling tone), e.g. *íi* 'himself', *éemanimi* 'he was able', *zóor* < U. *zōr* 'strength'.

(2) Stress on the second component, *aá* (low-rising tone), e.g. *ií* 'his son', *hiíṣ* 'lots of', *eémanimi* 'he did not become', *saát* 'hour' < U. *sāᶜat* 'hour, time'.

(3) Similar to (2), but due to expressive lengthening of a short vowel, and usually starting at a lower pitch, *āā* [*aá* ~ *àá*], e.g. *jōōṭ* [*joóṭ*] 'smallish'.

---

[1] Burushaski is an unclassified language spoken by some 95,000–100,000 people in Hunza, Nager, Gilgit, and Yasin in northern Pakistan. Of the three major dialects, the Hunza and Nager dialects are fairly similar, but the Yasin dialect differs significantly on all levels. For a thematic survey of research, see Bashir (2000).

[2] Lorimer (1935–88) recorded high and low tones only very sporadically in his dictionary (cf. Morgenstierne 1942: 87–8). However, he referred to Siddheshwar Varma (1931: 259–60), who had found more examples. Also Biddulph (1880) and Leitner (1889) had noted distinctions in accent, length, and intonation in Burushaski vowels. The system was clarified in detail only by Berger (1960: 659), who also introduced the convention of writing long vowels as double vowels with different accents.

As a fourth type one could add unstressed long or double vowels with level tone, e.g. *hiiṣpá* 'mostly', *baaćáa, baa(d)śáa* < U. *bādšāh* 'king'.

The following two diagrams illustrate the pitch contrast in long vowels in Burushaski. I am grateful to Joan Baart for having created these diagrams on the basis of two sound files I sent him.

DIAGRAM 1: BUR. *ÓOMEI BÁAN* 'THEY ARE ABLE' (HIGH-FALLING TONE)

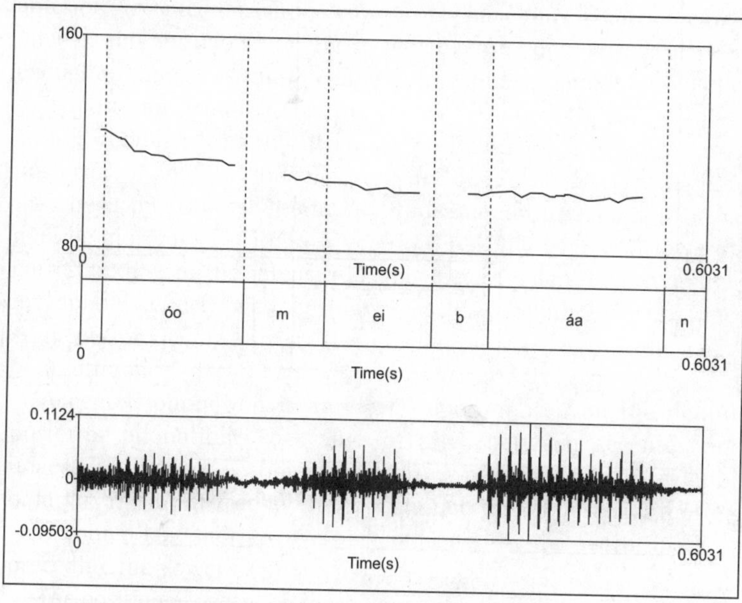

The pitch graph shows how the fundamental frequency (F_0) of the initial long vowel is quite high to start with, then slowly dropping towards the end.

DIAGRAM 2: BUR. *OÓMEI BI* 'THERE IS NOT/IT IS NOT POSSIBLE' (LOW/FALLING-RISING TONE)

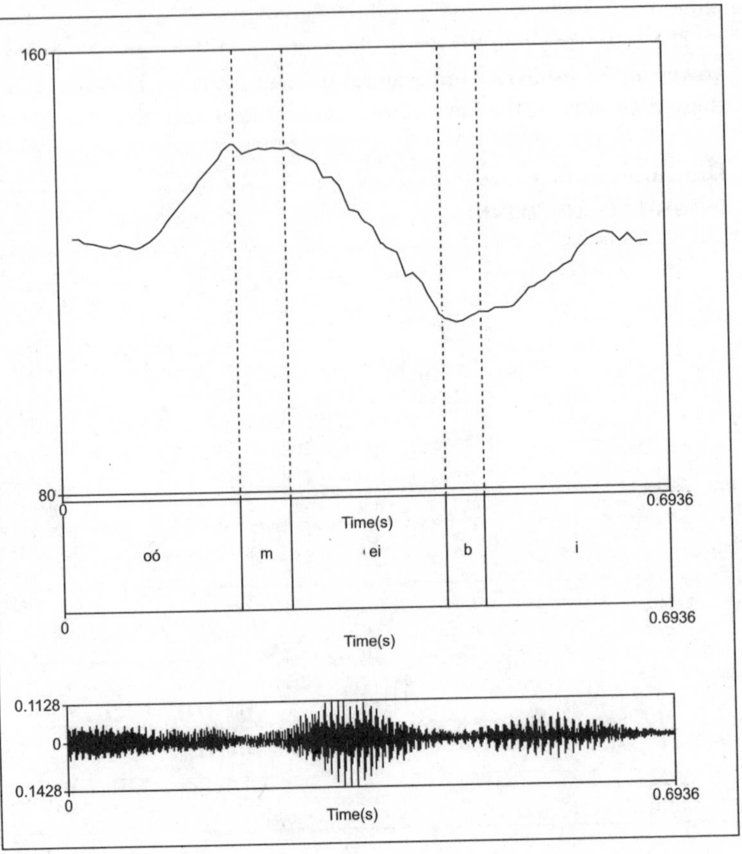

The pitch graph shows how the fundamental frequency (F_0) of the long initial vowel first drops a little then rises.

2. BURUSHASKI STRESS

Stress is distinctive and may fall on any syllable, e.g. *báṭiṅ* 'dusting-flour', *baṭér* 'dried apricot (split and stoned)', *bár-e* 'of the word', *baré* 'look!', *barén-as* 'to look', *amaná* 'then'.

Stress is liable to shift in inflection and then there is a tendency for it to fall on the second syllable, e.g. *bar-íṅ* 'words', *i-ġúyaṅ* 'his hair' < *ġuyáṅ* 'hair' (Berger 1998 I: 19). Inflected words may have two stressed syllables, mostly due to contraction, e.g. *étái* (< **é-t-um bá-i,* cf. Ys. *étum bái*) 'he has done it'.

Short stressed vowels reach the same intensity and almost the same F_0 as long or double vowels with high-falling tone. Unstressed vowels, whether long/double or short, have approximately half the intensity of stressed vowels and are about a third lower in F_0. Stress is therefore primarily dynamic, as confirmed by the reduction of syllables upon paradigmatic accent shift, e.g. *du-kóo-m-a* 'you came', but *a-tú-ku-m-a* 'you did not come' (*g/kóo- ~g/ku-* '2sg').

3. BURUSHASKI TONOGENESIS

Historically the Burushaski tones derive by way of accentual differences in double vowels or by lengthening of short vowels (*a, i, u, e, o*). The following etymological processes can be identified (cf. Berger 2008: 11 – 15).

3.1 Prefixation plus vowel coalescence (with or without elision of intervening segment)

a. The addition of a short pronominal prefix to an unaccented bound stem or morpheme, yielding a double vowel with high-falling tone, e.g.

ú-u(y) (1)[3] 'their father' < *u-* '3hxpl' + *-u(y)* 'father'

í-i (1) 'himself' < *i-* '3mxysg' + *-i* 'self' < **-ya,* cf. Ys. *í-ya* 'id.'

góor (1) 'to you (sg.)' < *gó-* '2sg' + *-ar* 'dat.', cf. Ys. *gó-γa* 'id.'

khúulto (1) 'today' < **khu-búlto* 'this-day' (cf. Yasin *bultú* 'day')

[3] Here and below, the numbers in parentheses refer to the four types of tone on long vowels introduced in section 1.

b. The addition of an accented interrogative or deictic prefix to a bound morpheme, yielding a double vowel with high-falling tone, e.g.

béerum (1) 'how much?' < *bé-urum* (< *bé* 'what?'), cf. Ys. *bérum* 'id.', contrast: Old Ng. *ba-úrum* (< *ba-* 'what?') 'id.'

téerum (1) 'that much', cf. Ng. *téurum* 'id.' < **té-urum* (< **té* 'that', cf. *ité* 'that', Ys. *té* 'id.')

c. The addition of a pronominal prefix to an accented bound stem, yielding a double vowel with low-rising tone, e.g.

i-í (2) 'his son' < *i-* '3mxysg' + *-í* 'son' < **-yé*, cf. Ys. *i-yé* 'id.'

mu-ú$_1$ (2) 'give to her!' < *mu-* '3fsg' + *-ú-* 'to give (hx PAT)'

mu-ú$_2$ (2) 'her tear' < *mu-* '3fsg' + *-ú* 'tear'

mi-íl (2) < *mi-úl* 'our stomach' < *-úl* 'stomach'

gu-ús (2) 'your wife' < **gu-gús* '2sg' + 'woman', cf. Ys. *gus* 'woman; your wife'

oós (2) 'my wife' < **a-ús* < **a-gús* < *a-* '1sg' + *gus* 'woman'

eík ~ *eék* (2) 'my name' < *a-* '1sg' + *-ík* 'name' < **-yék*, cf. Ys. *ayék* 'id.'

d. The addition of an unaccented deictic prefix to a bound morpheme, yielding a double vowel with low-rising tone, e.g.

toórum (2) 'so much' < **ta-úrum* (< **ta-* = **té* 'that'), cf. Ys. *taúrum* 'id.', contrast: *tóorumo* 'ten', Ys. *tórum* 'id.'

teéle (2) '(over) there' < **ta-éle*, cf. *éle* 'there'

toóle (2) '(over) there' < **ta-úle*, cf. Ys. *to*, *tō*, *tóle* 'id.'

e. The addition of the negative prefix *a-´* or conjunctive participle prefix *n-´*, causing a shift of the accent to the second vocalic mora, yielding either high-falling or low-rising tone, e.g. *a-túun* (1) 'don't take hold!' (< *du-ún* (2) 'take hold!'), cf. Ys. *a-tó-hon* 'id.'[4]

eé-man-im-i (2) 'he was not able' < *a-´* 'NEG' + *i-* '3mxysg' + *man-´* 'be(come)' + *-im* 'PFVE' + *-i* '3mxysg (SUBJ)', cf. Ys. *aí-man-i (-mi)* 'id.'	
oó-man-um-an (2) 'they were not able' < *a-´* 'NEG' + *u-* '3hxpl' + *man-´* 'be(come)' + *-um* 'PFVE' + *-an* 'hxpl (SUBJ)', cf. Ng. *oó-umánuman*[5] 'id.'	
eé-u-m-a (2) 'you did not give to him' (in Hz. now often shortened to *ᵉéuma* or just *éuma*) < **a-í-u-m-a* < *a-´* 'NEG' + *i-* '3mxysg (REC)' + *-ú-* 'give (hx PAT)' + *-m* 'PFVE' + *-a* '2sg (SUBJ)', cf. Ys. *aí-u-m-a* 'id.'	
nu-úru(ṭ) (2) 'having sat; sit and...[CP]' < **nu-húruṭ*, cf. Ys. *nuhúruṭ* 'id.' < *hurúṭ-* 'to sit'	

3.2 Suffixation or Compounding plus Vowel Coalescence

a. The addition of a morphological or derivational suffix to a finally accented stem, yielding a double vowel with high-falling tone, e.g.

bayú-ulo (1) 'in(to) salt' < *bayú* 'salt' + *-ulo* 'in(to)', cf. Ys. *bayūle* 'id.'	
bulá-an (1) [1]'a ramchikor [partridge]', [2]'a polo ball' < *bulá* [1]'ramchikor', [2]'polo (ball)'	
háa (1) 'of the house (gen., erg.)' < **há-e*, cf. Ys. *hā*[6]	

N.B. The lengthened pronominal prefixes (*áa-* '1sg', *góo-* '2g', *ée-* '3mxysg', *móo-* '3fsg', *mée-* '1pl', *máa-* '2pl', *óo-* '3pl') in nominals and verbals are all due to suffixation plus vowel coalescence after elision, e.g. *áa-t-* 'to do to/for/on me, to cause me to do (applicative/causative)' < *áar ét-* 'to do it to/for me' < **áa* (< **jáa* < **já-e*) *γaré ét-* (Berger 2008: 68–9, 102).

---

[4] There are some exceptions to this rule, which suggest that double vowels are not counted as fully equivalent with two syllables, e.g. *a-tuús* (2) 'don't come out!' (against expected †*a-túus*) < *du-ús* (2) 'come out!', cf. Ys. *a-tús* (Berger 1998 I: 15, §2.7).

[5] *oó-* has been generalized as a negative prefix or particle for most verbs in the Nager dialect, in Hunza only under certain phonological conditions.

[6] In the Yasin dialect long vowels are usually spelled with a macron. Except for a few minimal pairs such as Ys. *guúru* 'your nail' vs *gúuru* 'mirror', noted by Étienne Tiffou and Jurgen Pesot (1989: 8), the Yasin dialect has no tonal oppositions and even vowel length has been largely neutralized.

b. Suffixation or stem compounding, yielding low-rising tone. Cases like these are hard to identify, but the opaque words *saásaṭ* 'evening' (cf. Ys. *sásaṭ* 'id.') might qualify, if related to *sa* 'sun, day' (+ *asá* 'weak' or *bas-´* 'to fall' + *-(a)ṭ-* 'on, at' [?]). The equally opaque word *saáṭi* 'yesterday' (cf. Ys. *sâṭik* 'id.') might be derived by haplology from the former.

3.3 Vowel lengthening

a. Vowel lengthening in the final syllable in the vocative case and optative mood, yielding a long vowel with high-falling tone, e.g.

Ng. *damáan* (1) vocative '(O) master!' < *damán* 'master'
śée-m (1) 'may he eat' < *śe-* 'to eat (y PAT)'

b. Expressive or spontaneous lengthening of a short stressed vowel, yielding a long vowel with low-rising tone (Hz., Ng.), e.g.[7]

jōōṭ [~ *joóṭ*~ *jòóṭ*] (3) 'smallish' < *joṭ* 'small'
awāāram [~ *awaáram*] (3) 'I got a little tired' < *a-wár-a-m* 'I got tired'
daġāāmi [~ *daġaámi*] (3) 'he hid himself slowly, deliberately' < *daġá-m-i* 'he hid himself'
asiír (2) 'near' < *ˀasír*, cf. Ys. *asúr* 'near'
yoól (2) 'year' < **iól* < **iwél* < **i-bél* < Skt. *véla-* 'limit, boundary, time' (T #12115), cf. Ys. *wel* 'a full year' < **u-bél* (Berger 2008: 69)

3.4 Sporadic phonological processes (mainly in Hunza and Nager)

a. Elision of a 'weak' segment (such as /h/, /g/, or /s/) after the verbal *d*-prefix, yielding a double vowel with low-rising tone, e.g.

[7] Lorimer (1936: 632–5) defined such words as diminutives formed by vowel lengthening and lowering of tone, e.g. *ṭham ɛtas* 'to sweep up' : *ṭha·m ɛ.* 'to sweep up a small quantity, or slowly'; *lukʌn* 'a little': *lu:kʌn* 'a very little, rather little' (cf. also Morgenstierne 1942: 87–8).

du-ún- (2) 'to take hold' < **du-hún* or **du-hón-*, cf. Ng. *doón-*, Ys. *dohón-* 'id.'

du-úśkin- (2) 'to trickle, to dry up' < **du-húśkin-*, cf. Ys. *duhúśkin-* 'id.' < *huśkín-* '(a small amount of water) to trickle' < *huṣ* 'moisture'

du-ús- (2) 'to come out' < **du-gús-*, cf. *du-kóo-gus-* 'to extract or take out on/from you'

di-(s)íl- / di-ċhíl- (2) 'to become wet' < *ċhil* 'water', cf. Ys. *di-híl-* 'id.'

b. Elision of a 'weak' segment (such as /h/, /g/, /y/, /w/, or /l/) between two syllables inside a lexeme, yielding a double vowel with low-rising tone, e.g.

boór (2) 'earth salt' < **bahúr*, cf. Ys. *bahúr* 'id.', Sh. *bahúur*

ċhiír (2) 'goat' < **ċhigír*, cf. Ng. *ċhigír* 'id.', Ys. *ċigír* 'id.'

ċhuúm (2) 'heavy' < **ċhulúm*, cf. Ys. *ċulúm* 'id.'

3.5 External origin (Indo-Aryan loanwords)

e.g.

leél (2) 'known', cf. Ys. *lel* 'id.' < ? Sh. *leél* 'visible, known' (T #11122?)

goór (2) 'waterfall' < **ghara* (cf. T #5343)

awaáji (2) '(is) necessary' < Sh. *awaájei* 3sg.fut. <*awaáj-* 'to be necessary' (T #1197 or #1221)

4. BURUSHASKI DIPHTHONGS

Diphthongs arise in Burushaski in the same way as double vowels. They therefore exhibit analogous contrastive accentual patterns. In an unpublished paper ('Notes on Burushaski (Nagir dialect)', dated 27 October 1996), Prof. J. C. Catford has presented and analysed spectrograms of eleven Nager words. Two of these consist of the same diphthong /ai/ but with different accents: *aí* [ʌ'i] 'my son' <*a-* '1sg' + *-í* 'son' vs *ái* ['ai] 'my daughter' < *á-* '1sg' + *-i* 'daughter'. Already

Leitner (1893 [1985]: 3) was aware of the 'intonational' differences in these words. I quote Catford's description *in toto*:

> In the spectrograms, there is a noticeable difference in duration of the initial **a**-type vowel: in 'my son', about 60 ms. before the formants begin to shift towards their values for [(j)i]. In 'my daughter' the formant shift begins at about 100 ms. after the start of the vowel.
>
> The waveform for 'my son' shows a brief decrease and then increase of amplitude at about where the formants for an **i**-type vowel are established—probably implying weak [j] or [ĭ], followed by a somewhat stressed **i**. The inherent sonority of an **i** is about a third of that of an **a** or ʌ-type vowel, so the smaller amplitude of the **i** in 'my son' does not mean that this vowel is weakly stressed. On the contrary, it is probably more stressed than the initial vowel. In 'my daughter', stress clearly diminishes steadily from beginning to end.
>
> The superimposed frequency curve shows that in 'my son' the frequency is just below 120 Hz during the initial vowel but rises to about 157 Hz during the **i**; in 'my daughter' after a brief rise at the start, frequency drops from just under 140 Hz in the initial **a** vowel to about 120 Hz at the end of the utterance.

This phonetic description of the said words would fit the Hunza dialect pretty well too, with the difference that there the initial vowel in 'my son' tends more towards [ɛ, e]. In the Yasin dialect 'my son' is *ayé* < *a-* + *-yé*. 'My daughter' is the same in all dialects.

5. CONCLUSIONS REGARDING BURUSHASKI TONOGENESIS

The root cause of tones in Burushaski seems to lie in: (i) the existence of unaccented vs accented stems or morphemes and (ii) the occurrence of double vowels in sandhi. Minimal pairs like *múu(y̯)* (1) 'her father' vs *muú* (2) 'give to her!', or 'her tear', or 'now', can arise only because the nominal stem *-u(y̯)* 'father' carries no stress accent, whereas the verbal root *-ú-* 'to give (hx PAT)' and the homophonous nominal stem *-ú* 'tear' carry stress accent, as does the adverb *muú* 'now'.

Similarly, some prefixes are accented, whereas others are not, accounting for tonal differences such as *toórum* (2) 'so much' < **ta-*

úrum (cf. Ys. *taúrum* 'id.') vs *téerum* (1) 'that much' < **té-urum* (cf. Ng. *téurum* 'id.') (Berger 2008: 75 – 6, 12). Phonological changes blurring the triggering environments have enhanced the tonal oppositions as have loanwords from Shina and other Dardic languages.

Nevertheless, Berger (2008: 11) suggested that at some [very early] point in time Burushaski did not have double vowels, seeing that some Shina loanwords with long or double vowels appear in all Burushaski dialects with short vowels, e.g. *del* 'oil', cf. Sh. *teél* < Skt. *tailá-*, *múlo* 'turnip', cf. Sh. *múulo* < Skt. *mûla-* 'root'. However, in most cases the original lengths and tones have been preserved, and there are examples of ancient Indo-Aryan loanwords (obviously predating Shina) retaining long vowels, such as *kiláay* 'curds made from beestings' < *kilāṭ/ḍa-* 'inspissated milk' (T #3181) and *meéṣ* 'bag of skin' < **maiṣya-* 'ovine' (T #10343).

In addition there are, of course, numerous ancient Burushaski lexemes or word forms with long or double vowels, such as *káa* (Ys. *kā*) 'with' (vs Ys. *kà* 'and, if, when'), *dáa* (Ys. *dā*) 'again, more, also' (vs. *darúm* 'still'), *báardum* 'red' (Ys. *bárdum*), *iné-e* (Ys. *nē~ne*) 'his, s/he (erg.)', *báalt* (Ys. *balt*). Many such lexemes have low-rising tone (lost in the Yasin dialect), e.g. *yaári* (Ys. *yári*) 'the first light of morning', *-yaálmun* (Ys. *-hálmun*) 'rib', *muú[to]* (cf. Yasin *[a]mútuk*) 'now'.

In view of these facts, it is hard to reconstruct Proto-Burushaski without long or double vowels. A telling case in point is the comparison Hz./Ng. *gu-ús* 'your wife' = Ys. *gus* 'woman; your wife'. In the Yasin dialect double vowels with low-rising tone are regularly shortened (as are unstressed vowels), which is why Yasin has almost totally lost the tonal distinctions, cf. *leél* 'known' [< Sh. *leél*] = Ys. *lel*, *keér* 'rival' [= Sh. *keér*] = Ys. *ker*, etc. (Berger 1974: 8, Tiffou and Pesot 1989: 7 – 8, Berger 2008: 14 – 15). So, as admitted by Berger (2008: 15), Ys. *gus* 'your wife' must be from **gu-ús*. Otherwise we would have to propose an unlikely haplology from **gu-gús* (pre-Proto-Burushaski). A partly analogous phenomenon I observed in the Hunza dialect in 1994. When a double vowel derived from the coalescence of two prefixes and having low-rising tone is followed by a third vowel belonging to a root, the double vowel is shortened, and the tone fades or is lost, e.g. *eéuma* > *ᵉéuma~éuma* 'you did not give to him' (see section 3.1 e).

6. DOMAKI TONES

As first noted by Georg Buddruss (1983: 8, 1984: 10), Domaki[8] has a similar system of long vowels and tones to Burushaski and Shina. He therefore wrote Domaki long vowels as double vowels, following Berger's convenient model for Burushaski and Shina. Most of the Domaki long or double vowels are stressed on the first mora, e.g. *bée* (1) 'O, hello'. The other type is rarer, occurring chiefly in Shina loanwords, e.g. *peé* (2) 'sons' < *puç̣* 'son'. In addition there are, of course, unstressed long vowels, e.g. *maníś-aare* 'some men, a group of men' < *maníś* 'man'. The functional load of tonal oppositions is much lower in Domaki than in Shina or Burushaski. Minimal pairs like *bée* vs *peé* are very hard to find among native Domaki items.

7. DOMAKI TONOGENESIS

Tonal distinctions in Domaki are mainly due to accent shift in nominal and verbal paradigms (cf. Buddruss 1984: 17, 19, Weinreich 2011: 168ff., Tikkanen 2011: 207ff). External influence is also evident. Unless otherwise stated, the examples are from the Hunza dialect.

7.1 Conditioned accent shift

Forward shift of the stress accent in diphthongal or double vowel stems to the final vowel (or vocalic mora) of the stem, or first vowel of the suffix, yielding low-rising tone, e.g.

kanaáw-ek (2) 'one/a piece of advice' < *kanáu* 'advice' + *-ek* (singulative)
(Contrast: *goowá-ak* (1) 'one/a horse' < *goowá* 'horse' + *-ak* (singulative))

pií-n (2) ~ *pía-n* 'by father' < *pía* (infl. *pií-*) 'father' + *-n* (instr.-erg.sg.)

śunaá-ye (2) 'dog's' < *śunó* (infl. *śunaá-*) 'dog' + *-ye* (gen.sg.)

[8] Domaki is an endangered archaic Central Indo-Aryan language spoken by some 340–400 (?) people in Hunza and Nager in northern Pakistan. The two dialects are rather different, but mutually intelligible (cf. Lorimer 1939; Buddruss 1983; Weinreich 2008, 2010, 2011; Tikkanen 2011).

taá-s (2) 'in(to) the sunlight' < *tóo* (infl. *taá-*) 'sun(-light)' + *-s* (gnl. obl.)

mulaá-ye (2) 'girl's' < *mulaí* 'girl' + *-ye* (gen.sg.)

ḍaá 'run! (2) < *ḍeiná* 'to run' (infl.*ḍaa-*) + *-á* (imp.2pl.)

auúśe (2) 'guests' < *aúśin* 'guest' < Bur. *oóśin* < *aúśin*, pl. *oóśo*, cf. Sh. *õ'õśo*, pl. *õ'õśe*; T #427

Ng. *khaan-e-éŋe* (2) 'of the foods' < *khaane-é-* (infl.pl.) + *-ŋe* (gen. pl.) < *khaané* (nom.pl.) < *khaaná* 'food'; cf. Hz. *khaanéŋe* 'of the foods' < *khaané* 'foods' < *khaaná* 'food'

7.2 Vowel lengthening in the final syllable

In the vocative case, sometimes associated with accent shift or low-rising tone, e.g.

[*bé(e)*] *puúc̣* (2) 'O Son!' < *puc̣* 'son'

[*bé(e)*] *babáa* (1) 'O Father!' < *bába* 'father'
(Contrast: [*ya/wáa*] *mámaa* 'O Mother!' < *máma* 'mother')

7.3 Expressive lengthening of a short vowel

e.g.

buút ~ *buúṭ* (3) 'quite a lot, many, considerably' < *but*~ *buṭ* 'much, many, very'

7.4 External origins (Indo-Aryan and Burushaski loanwords)

More than half of the Domaki vocabulary has been borrowed from Dardic (mainly Shina) or Burushaski. The loanwords mostly retain the respective tones of the donor languages, e.g.

juú (2) 'sir, ma'am' < Bur. / Sh. *juú* (2) (T #5240)

kaáko (2) 'elder brother' < Bur. / Sh. *kaáko* (2) (T #2998)

8. DOMAKI DIPHTHONGS

Short diphthongs may have the stress accent on either one vowel, e.g. *dái* 'ten' vs *daí* 'beard'. Such diphthongs may arise through forward accent shift before a case ending, e.g. *maí-s* 'mother (gnl.obl.sg.)' < *máaya* (infl. *maí-*) 'mother', *śaí-n* 'by the king (instr.-erg.sg.)' < *śáai* (infl. *śaí-*) 'king'.

Long diphthongs are (almost) always stressed, and the accent may be on the first or third vocalic mora, e.g. *aṣáai* (1) 'this one' vs *auúśe* (2) 'guests' (cf. section 7.1).

Certain inflectional and derivational suffixes always carry the stress accent, which may give rise to unstressed long vowels, e.g. *śunaa-íśu* 'to the dog' < *śunó* (infl. *śunaa-*) 'dog', *irwaa-ím* 'I caused to be done/made' < *irwaaná* 'to cause to be done/made' < *iriná* 'to do/make', *daaí* 'grandmother'.

9. TYPOLOGICAL AND REGIONAL PERSPECTIVES

Burushaski and Domaki exemplify scenarios where tones have arisen from mora stress. Of course, one could argue that the Burushaski and Domaki tones are really not tones at all, but just different patterns of accentuation in long or double vowels (*áa* vs *aá*). Historically, that would even be true in most cases. However, acoustically speaking—or, rather, listening—the dynamic stress patterns in long or double vowels in Burushaski and Domaki are not always that conspicuous. The major distinguishing feature between, for instance, Burushaski *íi* 'himself' and *ií* 'his son' is the pitch rather than loudness contour.

Tone systems constitute a fairly widespread areal feature of the northwestern part of the Indian subcontinent. (For a classification of the basic systems, see Baart (2003, 2014).) Burushaski and Domaki tones are similar to those found in the neighbouring Shina language (for a description of Shina tones, see also Bailey (1924: 4, 84), Radloff (1999), Schmidt and Razwal (2008: 24–7), Schmidt and Kaul (2010: 196, 198)). The interesting thing is that the tonal distinctions in these three languages have all arisen through different historical processes involving or yielding long or double vowels: in Burushaski as the result of coalescence of vowels (mostly) at morpheme boundaries or due to conditioned regressive accent shift upon prefixation, in Domaki as the result of conditioned forward accent shift upon suffixation, in Shina as the result of changes in syllable structure upon apocope, conditioned accent shift or other morphophonological processes. It has been found that long vowels and syllables with longer sonorant codas are more likely to bear tone than shorter vowels (Berent 2013: 137). This is natural because it takes some time to switch from one pitch to another.

In other languages of this region voice and aspiration are largely responsible for tones, which are hence not restricted to a certain type of syllable. This is the case in Punjabi and Kalam Kohistani, which has as many as five contrastive surface tones (Baart 2008).

Apparently none of the Indo-Aryan languages of this region had tones from the start (unless perhaps we go back to Vedic Sanskrit, which had a different system). Our eyes then turn to Burushaski, but areal pressure—though evident[9]—is not sufficient for tones to develop. Balti (West Tibetan), neighbouring on Shina and (formerly) Burushaski, has so far not developed tones. If it were to do so, it would probably be independently along the lines of Central Tibetan, where a dual tonal contrast has arisen through a sonorization contrast of syllable-initial consonants and consonant clusters within a previously non-tonal stage (cf. Weidert 1987: 1 – 2). So far Balti has retained those syllable-initial consonants or consonant clusters ('prefixes'), so it has had no need to develop compensatory tones.

9 Areal pressure to conform to a pattern is known to have induced tone in some Mon-Khmer languages that do not have a class node to host them (Kiparsky 1995: 656).

ABBREVIATIONS

Bur. = Burushaski
CP = conjunctive participle
dat. = dative
erg. = ergative
f = feminine (human)
fut. = future
gen. = genitive
gnl.obl. = general oblique
h = human gender
Hz. = Hunza dialect of Burushaski
imp. = imperative
infl. = inflectional base
instr. = instrumental
m = masculine (human)
NEG = negative prefix
Ng. = Nager dialect of Burushaski
nom. = nominative
PAT = patient
PFVE = perfective aspect
pl = plural
REC = recipient
Skt. = Sanskrit
SUBJ = subject/agent
sg = singular
Sh. = Shina
T = Turner 1966 (see bibliography)
U. = Urdu
x = x-class noun
y = y-class noun
Ys. = Yasin dialect of Burushaski

REFERENCES

Baart, Joan L. G. 2014. 'Tone and stress in northwest Indo-Aryan: a survey'. In *Above and Beyond the Segments: Experimental Linguistics and Phonetics*, edited by Johanneke Caspers, Yiya Chen, Willemijn Heeren, Jos Pacilly, Niels O. Schiller, and Ellen van Zanten. 1–13. Amsterdam: John Benjamins Publishing Company.

_______ 2008. 'The tones of Kalam Kohistani (Garwi, Bashkarik)'. In *Proceedings of the Third International Hindu Kush Cultural Conference*, edited by Israr-ud-Din. 263 – 82. Oxford, New York, Karachi: Oxford University Press.

_______ 2003. 'Tonal features in languages of northern Pakistan'. In *Pakistani Languages and Society: Problems and Prospects*, edited by Joan L. G. Baart and Ghulam Hyder Sindhi. 132–44. Islamabad: National Institute of Pakistan Studies and Summer Institute of Linguistics.

Bailey, T. Grahame. 1924. *Grammar of the Shina (Ṣiṇā) Language*. London: The Royal Asiatic Society.

Bashir, Elena. 2000. 'A thematic survey of Burushaski research'. *History of Language* 6.1: 1 – 14.

Berent, Iris. 2013. *The Phonological Mind*. Cambridge, New York, Melbourne, Madrid, Cape Town, Singapore, São Paolo, Delhi, Mexico City: Cambridge University Press.

Berger, Hermann. 2008. *Beiträge zur historischen Laut- und Formenlehre des Burushaski*. Wiesbaden: Harrassowitz Verlag. (Neuindische Studien, Band 15).

_______ 1998. *Die Burushaski-Sprache von Hunza und Nager.* Teil I: *Grammatik*. Teil II: *Texte mit Übersetzungen. Teil III (Unter Mitarbeit von Nasiruddin*

Hunzai): Wörterbuch Burushaski – Deutsch, Deutsch – Burushaski. Wiesbaden: Harrassowitz Verlag. (Neuindische Studien, Band 13).

——— 1974. *Das Yasin-Burushaski (Werchikwar). Grammatik, Texte, Wörterbuch*. Wiesbaden: Otto Harrassowitz. (Neuindische Studien, Band 3).

——— 1960. Bericht über sprachliche und volkskundliche Forschungen im Hunzatal. *Anthropos* 55: 657 – 64.

Biddulph, John. 1880. *Tribes of the Hindoo Koosh*. Calcutta 1880. Reprint 1986. Lahore: Ijaz Ahmad Ali Kamran Publishers.

Buddruss, Georg. 1984. Ḍomaakí-Nachträge zum Atlas der Dardsprachen. *Münchener Studien zur Sprachwissenschaft* 43: 9 – 24.

——— 1983. 'Ḍomáaki *čhot* "Ton". Mit Beiträgen zur historischen Lautlehre'. *Münchener Studien zur Sprachwissenschaft* 42: 5 – 21.

Catford, J. C. 1996. *Notes on Burushaski (Nagir dialect)*, dated 27 October. 4. [unpublished].

Kiparsky, Paul. 1995. 'The phonological basis of sound change'. In *The Handbook of Phonological Theory*, edited by John A. Goldsmith. Cambridge, Massachusetts, Oxford: Basil Blackwell. (Blackwell Handbooks in Linguistics 1).

Leitner, Gottlieb Wilhelm. 1889. *The Hunza and Nagyr Handbook*. Calcutta.

——— 1893 [1985]. *Dardistan in 1866, 1886, and 1893: being an account of the history, religions, customs, legends, fables, and songs of Gilgit, Chilas, Kandia (Gabrial), Dasin, Chitral, Hunsa, Nagyr, and other parts of the Hindukush, as also a supplement to the second edition of the Hunza and Nagyr handbook and an epitome of part III of the author's 'The languages and races of Dardistan'*. First edition 1889. Reprint 1985. Karachi: Indus Publications.

Lorimer, David Lockhart Robertson. 1939. *The Ḍumāki Language. Outlines of the Speech of the Ḍoma or Bērīcho, of Hunza*. Nijmegen: Dekker & van de Vegt N. V. (Comité International Permanent de Linguistes. Publications de la Commission d'Enquête Linguistique IV).

——— 1936. 'Nugae Burushaskicae'. *Bulletin of the School of Oriental Studies* 8: 627 – 36.

——— 1935 – 38. *The Burushaski Language*. Volume I: *Introduction and Grammar; with a preface by G. Morgenstierne*, 1935. Vol. II: *Texts and Translations*, 1935. Vol. III: *Vocabularies and Index*, 1938. (Instituttet for Sammenlignende Kulturforskning, Serie B: Skrifter 29: 1 – 3). Oslo: H. Ashehoug & Co.

Morgenstierne, George. 1942. 'Notes on Burushaski phonology'. *Norsk Tidsskrift for Sprogvidenskap* 13: 61 – 95.

Radloff, Carla F. 1999. *Aspects of the Sound System of Gilgiti Shina*. Islamabad: National Institute of Pakistan Studies and Summer Institute of Linguistics.

Schmidt, Ruth Laila and Kaul, Vijay Kumar. 2010. 'A grammatical sketch of Guresi Shina'. In *Anantaṁ Śāstram. Indological and Linguistic Studies in Honour of Bertil Tikkanen*, edited by Klaus Karttunen. 195 – 214. Helsinki: Finnish Oriental Society. (Studia Orientalia 108).

——— and Kohistani, Razwal (in collaboration with Mohammad Manzar Zarin). 2008. *A Grammar of the Shina Language of Indus Kohistan*. Wiesbaden:

Harrassowitz Verlag. (Beiträge zur Kenntnis südasiatischer Sprachen und Literaturen, Band 17).

T = Turner, Ralph Lilley. 1962. *A Comparative Dictionary of the Indo-Aryan Languages*. London: Oxford University Press. [reference to lemmata as by T #]

Tiffou, Étienne and Pesot, Jurgen. 1989. *Contes du Yasin. Introduction du bourouchaski du Yasin avec grammaire et dictionnaire analytique. Études bourouchaski 1*. Paris: Peeters/Selaf. (Asie et Monde Insulindien, 16).

Tikkanen, Bertil. 2011. 'Domaki noun inflection and case syntax'. In *Pūrvāparaprajñābhinandanam: East and West, Past and Present: Indological and other Essays in Honour of Klaus Karttunen, edited by Bertil Tikkanen and Albion M. Butters*. 205 – 28. Helsinki: Finnish Oriental Socienty. (Studia Orientalia 110).

Varma, Siddheshwar. 1931. 'Burushaski texts'. *Indian Linguistics* 1: 252 – 82.

Weidert, Alfons. 1987. *Tibeto-Burman Tonology. A Comparative Account*. Amsterdam, Philadelphia: John Benjamins Publishing Company. (Amsterdam Studies in the Theory and History of Linguistic Science. Series IV: Current Issues in Linguistic Theory, Volume 54).

Weinreich, Matthias. 2010. 'Language shift in Northern Pakistan: The case of Domaakí and Pashto'. *Iran and the Caucasus* 14: 43 – 56.

_______ 2008. 'Two varieties of Ḍomaakí'. *Zeitschrift der Deutschen Morgenländischen Gesellschaft* 158.2: 299 – 316.

_______ [Вайнрайх, М.] 2011. '*Домааки язык*'. In *Языки мира. Новые индоарийские языки*. 165 – 94. (Ред. колл.: Т.И. Оранская, Ю.В. Мазурова, А.А. Кибрик, Л.И. Куликов, А.Ю. Русаков) Москва: Российская Академия Наук, Институт Языкознания.

20

On Synonym Compounds in Indo-Aryan

Claus Peter Zoller

1. INTRODUCTION

Ferdinand de Saussure analysed the *signe linguistique* as comprising the two aspects of signifié (signified), which refers to an idea, and signifiant (signifier), which he characterized as a sound image. The relationship between the two, according to Saussure, is arbitrary. A certain class of exceptions to this arbitrariness are onomatopoeic expressions which are iconic and do not have an arbitrary character, at least at the time of their formation. Saussure also developed the distinction between the synchronic and diachronic sides of language: under the synchronic perspective, a language is seen as a closed static system—this is also the perspective of the native speaker—whereas under the diachronic perspective successive stages of the historical development of a language are investigated. This is done by the historical linguist. The two conceptual pairs of signifier–signified and synchrony–diachrony constitute the frame of the following study of synonym compounds in Indo-Aryan.

A linguistic compound consists of two or more constituents. However, this also implies that the constituents of a compound are either directly discernible or they are discernible only through a historical analysis by the linguist. Henceforth I treat both manifestations, for which many examples are presented in this article, as 'compounds'. The diachronic process of combining a fixed expression of several words into a new single word—e.g. English 'albeit' from older 'all be it'—is called univerbation. I will extend the meaning of this term and will also call univerbation the diachronic process of former bi- or multi-morphemic compounds having changed into word forms that are now generally interpreted as monomorphemic. In addition I assert that synonym compounds like Hindi *dhan-daulat* 'accumulated wealth' but literally 'wealth–wealth' are more likely to change diachronically through univerbation into monomorphemes than are antonym compounds like Hindi *uṭhnā-baiṭhnā* 'to associate with; association' but literally 'to rise–to sit' or *ulṭā-sīdhā* 'tangled' but literally 'reversed–straight'.

We see that sometimes constituents can be identical as a result of reduplication. In compounds, the signifier (morpheme) and/or the signified (meaning) may be duplicated. In the case of duplicated signifiers, an audible full or partial repetition of the phonetic body of a morpheme (either lexeme or grammeme) takes place, whereas in case of the signified, the concept or idea aspect of a linguistic sign gets duplicated. Sometimes languages combine both strategies and below we will come across a few such examples. However, our emphasis will be on semantic duplications (i.e. compounds consisting of two synonyms).

Studies of phonetic duplication in South Asian languages have been pursued for many decades. According to Colin Masica (1991: 76ff.),[1] strategies for creating expressive forms can be divided into three classes, two of which are relevant here.[2] (i) Onomatopoeia and sound symbolism typically created through reduplication with the form *CVC(V)-CVC(V)* as in Hindi *dhīre-dhīre* 'very slowly' (vs *dhīre* 'slowly') or *jhan-jhan* 'loud or prolonged clashing' (vs *jhan* 'clashing'), but also through certain unusual consonant clusters, like Indus Kohistani *p*- (followed by fluttering of lips), *-ũ̀* 'sound of snorting (as a horse)'. (ii) Echo formations created by changing a consonant or vowel (or both) in the reduplicated word as in Multani *roṭi-moṭi* 'bread and similar eatables'. Both strategies are very similar, because here one may say that each copy of the word modifies the meaning of the whole compound. Moreover, such formations can frequently change into full verbs through verbal suffixes or through conjunct verb-like construction as in Hindi *jhan jhanānā* 'to ring', or into nouns as in Punjabi *ḍugḍugī* 'drum' from *ḍugḍu*gānā 'to beat (a drum)'. These strategies can fulfil a number of functions like 'intensive' or

---

1 More references on this topic are given by Masica and also at the end of this article.

2 Expressive forms employing multiple stems, like Magahi *ghōṛ*, *ghōṛā*, *ghōṛwā* all meaning 'horse' with slight semantic differences are not considered here.

'onomatopoeic' (i.e. imitating sounds and optical or other physical phenomena), or bring about a semantic modification such as '... and the like', etc.

Somewhat deviating from Masica's classification, Anvita Abbi (1992) starts with a differentiation between morphological and lexical reduplications. Morphological reduplications are expressives, like above Hindi *jhan-jhan*. Lexical reduplications are further divided into compounds consisting of semantically and morphologically similar components, like Hindi *aisā-vaisā* 'good for nothing' but literally 'of this sort, of that sort' or Hindi *mol-tol* 'evaluation' but literally 'value–weight', and word reduplications like Hindi *calte-calte* 'while walking' but literally 'walking–walking', or in an absolutive construction like Hindi *rah-rah kar* 'at intervals' but literally 'stay–stay make', or in *andāz apnā-apnā* 'each one's conjecture' but literally 'conjecture own–own'. Within the class of compounds, Abbi distinguishes between paired constructions of semantically identical words like Hindi *kām-kāj* 'work' and paired constructions of words that are connected in different semantic ways like partially similar or antonym formations as in Hindi (quoted already above) *uṭhnā-baiṭhnā* 'to associate with; association' but literally 'to rise, to sit'. In fact, practically all examples discussed in the present article are located somewhere between the two poles of identity and antinomy, although most of the examples are more or less close to the identity pole, reflecting the fact that South Asian languages use much more synonym than antonym compounds. We can see already now that all such compounds—or most of them, as there will also be exceptions—are *dvandvas* 'copulative compounds'. Their components realize a relationship of coordination, not of subordination.

Further below we will see that sometimes such compounds can simultaneously be synonym and antonym in some way or other (e.g. example 2,7,4). With regard to the examples cited by Abbi (1992: 24), she observes that '... each constituent word of a compound has a meaning of its own and hence can be used independently in a sentence. However, when combined in a compound formation, the two constituent words retain their original meaning to some extent. More often than not the paired construction has a new meaning and a new reference.' All this is certainly true for a subclass of synonym compounds, but in many other cases of synonym compounds presented below the situation is more complicated.

Rajendra Singh, in his study on 'redundant' compounds in modern Hindi, presents eight examples of synonym compounds (1982: 346)[3] all of which he translates as 'word etc.' as if they were not 'redundant' constructions but some sort of semantic echo words.[4] Rama Kant Agnihotri (2007: 8) quotes three of Singh's examples, which he also calls redundant compounds, namely (2), (3), and (5). Example (2) he quotes as *śādī-vivāh* which shows that some of the compounds can be reversed.[5] Singh notes that all quoted examples are expressing a ±NATIVE (i.e. inherited vs borrowed words) opposition, but note that the first example *tan* is etymologically ambiguous. In any case, the feature ±NATIVE is certainly not an intrinsic one because synonym compounds are not created on the basis of inherited vs borrowed words.

Against my opinion that the pairing constructions quoted by Singh are actually compounds, he (1982: 345) regards them as adjunctions of two nouns because 'real' compound nouns would allow multiple interpretations (like English 'watermill')[6] and they would be endocentric formations.[7] A similar point of view as Singh's is upheld by John Peterson for Munda languages. He discusses 'lexical juxtapositions as "compounds"' (2011: 118ff.) which he contrasts with

---

3 (1) *tan-badan* 'body etc.', (2) *vivāh-śādi* (sic) 'marriage etc.', (3) *dhan-daulat* 'money etc.', (4) *śāk-sabji* (sic) 'vegetable etc.', (5) *dharm-imān* (sic) 'religion etc.', (6) *sneh-muhabbat* 'love etc.', (7) *lāj-šarm* 'deference etc.', (8) *nāta-rista* (sic) 'relation etc.'

4 Even if in a few cases such a translation may be possible, usually it is not: a *rām-rahīm*, despite the alliteration, surely cannot be translated as 'God etc.' but is an example for a so-called reinforcing synonym compound (see below) and may thus be translated as 'the real and only God'. Note also that inherited *rām* is very frequently repeated in the common and widespread greeting *rām-rām* whereas the borrowed *rahīm* is not used in this way.

5 This may have phonotactic reasons, because the second component in this type of compounds usually has more syllables, or the same number of syllables, but never fewer syllables, than the first component. But this has to be tested with much more data.

6 Singh's little bit far-fetched argument for this assertion (p. 347) is: 'Although the preferred reading of 'watermill' is 'mill powered by water', it can also mean 'mill which produces water', 'mill for analysing the content of water', 'mill where the employees drink water', etc.

7 Needless to say that there are also other types of synonym compounds as we will see below.

'genuine compounds' (2011: 121ff.).[8] The former he further divides into 'equational compounds' like *kheti baṛi* 'field–farm' i.e. 'farms' and 'associative compounds' like *kulam-kulamḍay* 'brother–sister' i.e. 'people' (2011: 119).[9] His first example is a loan from Hindi or another Indo-Aryan language and it demonstrates that the same word combination can have different meanings in different languages. In Hindi *khetī-bāṛī* 'farming-house-and-garden' means 'farming' and is a so-called redundant compound (see below) because *khetī* alone also means 'farming'.[10]

Abbi has pointed out (see above) that in case of reduplicated compounds '... each constituent word can be used independently in a sentence' whereas Peterson takes the same fact to argue that (2011: 119) '... there is little reason to consider them compounds, while there is good reason to consider them simply juxtaposed elements which are closely related to one another semantically.'[11] Indeed, *dhan* and *daulat* are found in lyric lines like Hindi *na dhan cāhie, na daulat cāhie* 'I don't need wealth nor need I riches', but this simply shows that there exist synonym words which sometimes are compounds and sometimes are not. English 'leopard' is a single morpheme for an average English

[8] His distinction between so to say pseudo-compounds and genuine compounds is not really clear to me.

[9] Thus Peterson differentiates between semantically almost identical pairs and semantically somehow associated pairs which resembles Abbi's above-quoted distinction.

[10] There is also e.g. Nepali *kheti-bāri* 'cultivation' where Turner (1931) remarks that *khet* is 'a watered field' as opposed to *bāri* which suggests a basic meaning 'cultivation of watered and non-watered fields'. In addition he quotes *kheti-kisān* 'cultivation', *kheti-pāti* 'cultivation' and *kheti-phal* 'cultivation' which are again redundant compounds as in Hindi. They contrast with Nepali *khet-bāri* 'farm' which is a generalizing synonym compound 'field-garden'.

[11] The deeper issue behind this disagreement seems to be the question of whether the meanings of such compounds are compositional or calculable, or whether they are rather non-compositional. Von Humboldt's famous statement that language is a system that 'makes infinite use of finite means' certainly does not work without problems in the case of synonym compounds. In other words, it is not really possible to deduce the meanings of synonym compounds simply by connecting the meanings of their components without including the existence of a broader (background) knowledge base that provides clues for a contextually appropriate interpretation of synonym compounds. I cannot discuss this issue here in more detail and will therefore stick to a rather descriptive presentation.

speaker, but for the person who knows about etymology, this is basically a bi-morphemic synonym word that was borrowed into English from Greek. Laurence Thompson, in his Vietnamese reference grammar, calls such words pseudo-compounds (1987: 133). They are certainly found in many languages (including Vietnamese, with Chinese as source for such compounds), but they are not a topic of this article. However, the English example demonstrates that whether a paired construction is seen as a compound or not is not only a matter of its syntactic behaviour, but depends also on the background knowledge of the user. A linguistically informed speaker may recognize that a word is originally a compound because it was or is a compound in the donor language; or, if it is not a borrowing, it was originally a compound at a past stage of development of the concerned language. Whereas expressives, echo formations, and word reduplications are, so to say, immune to the ravages of time because over and over they get recreated out of the available elements of a language through a set of rules, compounds on the other hand, being structures like any other words, are subject to history. Probably in every language there exist new and old compounds, inherited or borrowed, and in order to understand also old compounds in modern languages, which is the main topic of this article, Saussure's diachronic perspective is indispensable. Old compounds have more or less completed the way of univerbation that starts with pairing constructions with weak cohesion like *dhan-daulat*.[12] Univerbation can actually go so far that the original compound character cannot be recognized any more. Thus this morphological process goes hand in hand with a gradual loss of semantic transparency. Borgwaldt and Lüttenberg distinguish—from a synchronic point of view—between semantically transparent compounds like 'snowball', semantically opaque compounds like 'pineapple' and partially transparent compounds like 'strawberry'.[13] I transfer this triple scheme to the diachronic perspective of the historical linguist. This means that the examples below belong to the two categories of semantically transparent compounds and partially

---

[12] With 'weak cohesion' I mean that both components can still be used independently.

[13] In case of 'pineapple', the average speaker can still see that the word is a compound, but also this is not always the case, as some of the examples further down will show.

transparent compounds from a historical linguistic perspective. Of course, it would be pointless to present unanalysable opaque forms.

From a synchronic point of view, an example from Hindi for Borgwaldt and Lüttenberg's category of partially transparent compounds is *ḍaṇḍ(a)harā* 'bolt-bolt' i.e. 'door bolt'[14] where *ḍaṇḍ(a)* is used independently but not **harā*.[15] And an example for a semantically opaque compound from a synchronic point of view is found e.g. in Garhwali *phunajhi hoṇu* 'to menstruate':[16] its first component *phun(a)-* is related with OIA *sphāna-* 'swelling, increasing' (13829) from *SPHA* 'increase, turn stout'[17] with a common Outer Languages[18] change of *a* > *u* plus *-(a)jhi* < OIA *rajas* 'the menstrual discharge of a woman' with spontaneous aspiration.[19]

A typical characteristic distinguishing IA compounds from simple morphemes in their historical development is that compounds tend to lose in the course of time more phonological segments and more syllables than simple morphemes. An example is Garhwali *phunajhi* which lost the *-r-* of *rajas*. This would not have happened to this word-medial vibrant had the word been a simple morpheme.[20] An example

---

[14] The compound is not found in the standard Hindi dictionaries but it is found e.g. in Bhishm Sahni's short story *Amr̥tsar ā gayā hai*.

[15] It is, however, used in other Indo-Aryan languages. The second component of the compound belongs (in Hindi in the form of a borrowing from some other IA language because of *-r-* instead of expected *-ṛ-*) to OIA **huḍa-* 'bolt or bar' (14135a). Note that all figures presented here in parentheses, which are sometimes supplemented with further comments, refer to the numbering of the OIA lemmata in Turner (1966). Note also that sometimes the numberings are given without parentheses.

[16] This is to say that most likely a native speaker of Garhwali cannot recognize *phunajhi* as a compound, let alone identify the meanings of its components.

[17] A similar semantic relationship 'swell ~ menstruate' is found in OIA (Suśruta) *púṣpa-* 'the menstrual flux'; *púṣpa* normally means 'flower' and derives from *POṢ* 'thrive, increase'.

[18] The model of Outer and Inner Languages distinguishes between two substantially different sub-branches of Indo-Aryan. The Inner Languages are found in the Ganges Valley, and they are surrounded by the Outer Languages. For more details see Southworth (2005) and Zoller (forthcoming).

[19] Which is also a common Outer Languages change.

[20] However, there are also trends working in the opposite direction with unexpected preservation of phonemes e.g. in the case of onomatopoeic words and pairing constructions with alliterations, as seen in some examples above and

from Munda for irregular loss of syllables in compound formation can be seen in Kharia *baʔ-loʔ* 'paddy land' which is <*baʔ* 'paddy' plus *loʔkha* 'earth' (Peterson 2011: 121).

Besides the various sources quoted above, I want to mention two more authors whose publications—and the notions and terms used by them—are reflected in the classification and linguistic characterizations found in the list of compounds below. Thompson (1987), actually already mentioned, provides a very useful classification of compounds in Vietnamese which is mainly based on morphological–semantic criteria (see his chapter 6). Most important for us is his term 'reinforcing compounds' (1987: 130) which '... are nonsyntactic compounds containing two apparent heads; these two components usually denote identical or very similar items or reality.' We will see in the examples below that in the majority of cases there has been a historical shift from two-head compounds to one-head compounds. Other useful concepts are that of 'generalizing compounds' as Vietnamese *bàn-ghế* 'furniture' ← *bàn* 'table' plus *ghế* 'chair', 'specializing compounds' as Vietnamese *dầ u tầ u* 'locomotive' ← *dầ u* 'head' plus *tầ u* 'large conveyance'. Anders Søgaard's approach to compound structures ('Compounding theories and linguistic diversity') is influenced by semiotic theory and is more abstract than Thompson's classification. But Søgaard also uses several concepts found in Thompson's work. He presents (2005: 326–8) a construction hierarchy of compounding comprising ten construction types. Out of them the following are relevant for us (given here slightly abridged): (i) redundant compounds in which the left or right constituent contains redundant information such as Tagalog *hanging-amihan* 'wind-breeze' i.e. 'breeze';[21] (ii) exocentric compounds with metaphorical left or right constituent modifiers as in English 'shovel head' (here with left modifier).[22]

below. On the potential of onomatopoeic words for perseverance over millennia, see Mallory and Adams (2006: 153).

21 Definition (2005: 327): 'If the union of the denotations of the two constituents is a proper subset of one of the constituents, the compound is redundant.'

22 Explanation (2005: 328): '[A] "shovel head" is not a kind of head, but a sub-species of shark.'

2. SYNONYM COMPOUNDS IN NEW INDO-ARYAN LANGUAGES

Here follow fifty-two examples from New Indo-Aryan languages. This is just a minimal selection, and there certainly exist hundreds of more cases, but the examples will suffice to demonstrate the many differences distinguishing synonym compounds on a closer investigation. Many of the examples are compounds with one-head and one or more modifiers. This looks paradoxical, but is not. All synonym compounds started historically with two or three components (three is the maximum known to me) but in the course of time they became monomorphemic due to different morphonological processes. Historical compounds are not limited to Indo-Aryan. A comparable, yet not exactly identical phenomenon—because it is related to script—is also known from Chinese. Lai and Myers (2012: 41) state: 'In traditional Chinese linguistics, a compound is a word written with two or more characters whether or not they are morphemic. A monomorphemic compound may either be a binding word, written with characters that only appear in this one word, or a non-binding word, written with characters that are chosen for their pronunciation but that also appear in other words' and (pp. 44f.) '... a character is usually regarded by native speakers as a word-level linguistic unit ... and virtually all dictionaries are character-based.' Thus, this phenomenon has a certain similarity with the above-mentioned partially transparent compounds. The authors also introduce the notion of opaque non-binding words (ibid.) which they exemplify with Chinese *han4bao3* 'hamburger' where *han4* actually means 'Chinese' and *bao3* means 'fort'. Thus, *han4bao3* is, though this sounds paradoxical, an opaque monomorphemic compound word.

Unfortunately, for lack of sufficient data, I could not determine in all cases with certainty whether a specific historical compound is presently monomorphemic or bi-morphemic. However, in most cases listed below the status is unambiguous. The following three criteria were applied to identify compounds that, having historically derived from bi- or tri-morphemic compounds, are presently 'monomorphemic compounds': (i) If the compound has, during its history, lost more phonemes and/or syllables, or undergone some other unusual changes in its phonetic shape than would have been expected in the case of a monomorphemic word, then it is bi-morphemic; (ii) In case of

Nuristani and Dardic words:[23] if the term bears one pitch accent it is monomorphemic (if it bears two pitch accents, it is bi-morphemic); and (iii) If a component of a compound is not used independently in the language, even if it is used independently in another language, then it is monomorphemic.

The fifty-two words (alphabetically ordered, as usual, according to usage in Indian languages) have been divided into eight groups on the basis of the above-mentioned different features characterizing compound words.[24] The number of examples is higher than that of the features and feature combinations and it will be seen that most examples are structurally different from each other. Søgaard (2005: 319) comments on this by saying that '[u]nfortunately, the set of compounding relationships is not easily exhausted' quoting Downing (1977) who claimed that the set of compounding relationships is infinite.

2.1 INTERMEDIATE CONSTRUCTION BETWEEN SYNONYM COMPOUND AND PHRASE

Søgaard (2005: 320) argues that the claim found in transformational theories that compounds are derived from relative clauses[25] is probably

---

[23] Thus criterion (ii) does not apply to the data from the other IA languages quoted in the list. The reason is that in most languages of these two groups a free lexeme always bears exactly one pitch accent. One exception is Dardic Kalam Kohistani where a free lexeme always bears one tonal contour consisting of one or two tonemes. (Three of these tonal contours are briefly explained at the end of this article.) So the criterion also does not apply to West Pahāṛī Bangani because only certain Bangani words bear a tonal contour.

[24] Most of the following words have been published by other authors. Restrictions on space, however, do not allow quoting the many dozens of publications from which the data have been taken. Therefore, only authors explicitly mentioned in the article are found in the references. The transcriptions—and sometimes transliterations—coincide largely with Turner's (1966) system, but not all peculiarities have been standardized. In very few cases the transcription had to be slightly simplified due to the limitations of the available fonts. Note that this article does not list explicitly the general historical phonological developments of Indo-Aryan nor the developments peculiar to individual languages. The interested reader is advised to consult the specialized literature.

[25] He gives the example of ignition key as key which causes ignition.

wrong because compounds are acquired earlier than relative clauses. Consequently, also in my data there are no compounds going back to former relative clauses, but only one or two examples which derive from former possessive phrases.[26]

> Ind. *vẽ̀-sʌr* 'water-lake' i.e. 'a big pond, small lake' is ← *vĩ̀* 'water < OIA *udaká-* 'water' (1921) plus *sʌ́r* 'lake' <*sáras-* 'lake' (13254). The nasalization of the first vowel reflects a genitive form and thus a basic meaning 'lake of water'. This seems to be a very rare compound type in NIA (namely a compound with 'internal case ending') but is well-known from OIA. The accent of the second word is subdued in the singular, but clearly audible in the plural, *vẽ̀-sʌrà*^{h}. Thus the singular form is 'more compound' (because of one accent) and the plural is 'more syntagm'.

2.2 Bi-morphemic endocentric transparent reinforcing synonym compounds[27]

2.2.1 Ind. *kùč*^{h}*-ghĩ̀l*, Bhaṭ. *kùč*^{h}*-ghíu*, Dm. *kuč-giŕu* all 'butter-ghee', i.e. 'butter' with first component ← Psht. *kuči* 'butter' plus < OIA *ghr̥tá-* 'ghee' (4501). First component is not used independently in Ind. but second is.[28]

2.2.2 Ash. *ze-tã* 'cult place' and in the Wama dialect of Ash. *ze-tã* 'place for funeral feast' both 'place-place' with first component ← Iranian (cf. Pers. *jā* 'place', Psht. *zāe* 'place') plus < OIA *sthā́na-* 'place' (13753). See footnote 28.

2.2.3 Bng. *dōś-khùṇɔ* 'guilt-guilt', i.e. 'guilt' < OIA *doṣa-* 'fault' (6587) plus <OIA **skupanā-* 'pressing in' (13653) with a modern parallel in G. *khuṇ* 'mark made by pressing'. Both components are also used independently in Bng.

---

[26] For the second example see 2.6.2.

[27] In many of the following examples I cannot say for sure whether one or both (or three) components are used also independently in the respective languages because of scarcity of data. However, in a number of cases it is clear that individual components are used in other Indo-Aryan languages.

[28] This is a ± NATIVE compound. But as pointed out above, I do not regard this as an essential feature.

2.2.4 Kal. *našipáḷi* 'lost-perish', i.e. 'very hard'[29] derives < the two synonym verbs OIA *náśyati* 'is lost, perishes' (7027) plus < OIA *pálayate* 'flees' (7955). Both verbs are also found independently in Kal.

2.2.5 Ku. *but(a)dhāṇ* 'work–work' 'work, business' with first component < OIA *vṛtti-* 'business' (12070) plus second component < OIA *dhā́na-* 'receptacle' (6775) with various meanings in modern languages but in Turner (1985) one finds with question mark Garh. *dhāṇ* 'work, occupation'. Both words are also used independently in Ku.

2.2.6 Ind. *bhirì-māçhírⁱ* 'wasp-bee', i.e. 'wasp' with first component < OIA lex. *varaṭa-* 'wasp' (11330) (cf. there H. *barr* 'wasp') and spontaneous aspiration plus < OIA *mākṣikaraka-* 'bee' (9990). The first component is not used independently, and instead of the second component only related *mʌỹ'çhi* 'bee' (< OIA *mákṣikā-* [9696]) is used independently.

2.2.7 Brj. *marutal* 'desert' < OIA *marú-* 'wilderness' (9876a) plus < *sthála-* 'dry land' (13744).[30]

2.2.8 Ku. *yār-vās* 'friend' and *yār-vāsī* 'friendship' with first component ← Pers. *yār* 'friend' plus < OIA *vayasyà-* 'comrade' (11306). See footnote 28. First word is also used independently, but probably not the second.

2.3 Bi-morphemic Endocentric Partially Transparent Synonym Compounds

Bhaṭ. *čiṭẹe kạrü* 'tiger' and *bhäbär kạrü* 'lion', Gau. *babʌr-síu* 'tiger' and Ind. *síū-kʌ̀rū* 'tiger' contain the following elements: Bhaṭ. *čiṭẹe* is < OIA *citraka-* 'leopard' (4804) which basically means 'variegated' (used as independent word *čītā, čītrā* 'leopard' in Gau.); Bhat. *kạrü* has parallels in Ind. *kʌ̀rū* 'lion; tiger' and Šaṭ. *kʌ́ro* 'leopard'. Note also Ra. *kīri, kīḍi* 'tiger, leopard' (Sharma 1990: 174) with Munda parallels in Pinnow (1959: 142). There are similar sounding words in the area

29 The example given by Trail and Cooper (1999) is about one who works himself almost to death.

30 Brj. *maru* 'desert' and *thal* 'dry ground desert.'

meaning 'sheep', e.g. Wkh. *kar* 'mouton à courtes oreilles' (see Zoller (2005) for further examples), but it is not quite clear whether they are related here. Regarding Bhaṭ. *bhäbär* and Gau. *babʌr* cf. Wkh. *babr* 'tiger' and Klm. *bōr* H 'lion, tiger' the latter of which is same as Psht. *bawr, bōr* 'leopard, panther'. Here perhaps also M. *bib(a)ṭā* 'marked with spots resembling the marking nut, a tiger, leopard, cat'. This component may have either had an original meaning 'variegated' but with unclear origin, or is distantly related with PIE **pers*- 'leopard' (cf. western Mongolian *bars* 'snow leopard; tiger'). The word *síũ̆* is < OIA *siṁhá*- 'lion' (13384). In the first case the different word pairs above may have originally simply had the meaning *'spotted wildcat', but they developed into synonym compounds or into partially transparent compounds. Similar formations seem to be fairly widespread, cf. e.g. also M. *ḍāhaṇyāvāgha* 'a leopard' (literally 'spotted tiger') with second component < OIA *vyāghrá*- 'tiger', and apparently the old Greek word *leopardos* 'leopard' itself is also a comparable compound word.

2.4 Monomorphemic endocentric transparent reinforcing synonym compounds

2.4.1 Mal. *ũ̄dhāval* 'storm-stormy', i.e. 'storm' is < OIA *andhakāra*- 'darkness' (386) with common Outer Languages change of *a* > *u* (regarding meaning cf. e.g. Bhad. *ā̃dharu* 'storm') plus < OIA lex. *vātala*- 'stormy' (11497). The word is monomorphemic because of a reduction from seven to three syllables and loss of several phonological segments.

2.4.2 Bhaṭ. *galgẹ̀rẹ* 'hail–hail', i.e. 'hail' with first syllable < OIA *gala-*[1] 'dripping' (4069)[31] with semantic parallels in Psht. *galaī* 'a hailstone' and P. *gala* 'hail'. Second element is < **gaḍa-*[3] 'dropping' (3969) (cf. under this lemma S. *gaṛo* 'hail'). Note that Turner (1966) suggests, not surprisingly, etymological connection between OIA *GAL* 'drip' and *GAḌ* 'drip', which would suggest here a compound built of two allomorphs of one OIA root.[32] Similarly constructed appears Dravidian Koṇḍa *aṅ-gal* 'hail' (Burrow and Emeneau 1984: 355) whose first component *aṅ*-may also basically mean 'hail' (Burrow and Emeneau 1984: 384). If so, these forms would suggest a Dravidian–Indo-Aryan parallel construction. Despite the reduplication-like structure, the Bhaṭ. word is monomorphemic because of only one pitch accent.

2.4.3 Ko.Kaṇ. *goru-vasrã* 'cattle-wealth', i.e. 'livestock' is < OIA **gorūpá-* 'cow-shaped' (4313), but in NIA frequently meaning 'cattle', plus <OIA lex. *vasura-* 'valuable, rich'. Regarding semantics of second component cf. OIA *vásu-* 'good; wealth' (11446) with modern reflexes in Ash., Kt., Paš., all meaning 'goat(s)'. The nominal compound is built of two former adjectives. It is a generalizing or copulative compound meaning in paraphrase 'the two items of cattle and goats belong to the class of livestock' (see Thompson 1987: 128), i.e. the constituents 'refer to the whole (or more)' (Søgaard 2005: 327).

2.4.4 Ind. *gōṣuíl*[i] 'cowshed' is a triconstituent redundant compound < determinative compound OIA **gośraya-* 'cow refuge' (cf. OIA **gośrayaṇa-* 'cow house' [4335]) plus third constituent < OIA *kula-* 'house, abode' (3330). Only *kúl* is used independently in Ind., however with meaning 'people' and not 'house'. The third constituent provides redundant information (as in English 'palm tree').

[31] The superscript numbers attached to some lemmata from Turner (1966) and Turner and Wright (1985), as in *gala-*[1] 'dripping', are used to distinguish homonyms.

[32] But see also the sceptical remarks in Mayrhofer (1986–2001).

2.4.5 Kal. *čávar* 'human hair' ← *čal* 'mane' which is < OIA **cāla-*[1] 'moving' (4768, see there e.g. Paš. *cāl* 'woman's long hair, mane') plus < OIA *vā́ra-* 'the hair of any animal's tail' which is not used independently in Kal. The word may go back to an older echo word-like form **čarvar* or **calval*. Regarding OIA *vā́ra-*, Mayrhofer (1986–2001) points out that this word is frequently derived < PIE **wel-* 'turn'. Since the predecessor of OIA *CAR* 'move', namely PIE **kʷel-*, means also 'turn', Kal. *čávar* may have originally been an old reinforcing synonym compound 'turn–turn' resembling an echo word.[33]

2.4.6 Kt. *jugũr* 'woman–woman', i.e. 'woman; wife' is < OIA **yuvatí-* 'young woman' (10504) plus *ghariṇī-* 'householder's wife' (4442).

2.4.7 Ind. *ḍhʌṇḍkulṹ* 'pool-pond', i.e. 'a (sometimes artificially made) shallow puddle (for drinking)' is < OIA **ḍhaṇḍha-* 'pool' (5578) plus < OIA *kulyā́* - 'small river' (3352, see there **kūlā-* 'pond, tank'). The first component is used independently as *ḍhã̄ ṇḍ* 'pond, collection of water in field or meadow', but not the second component.

2.4.8 Klm. *täpijä̃l* H(L) 'heat-flame', i.e. 'warm, hot' is < OIA *tapyatí-* 'heat' (5685) plus < OIA *jvālá-* 'flame' (5312). The compound is an adjective built of two nouns.

2.4.9 Kt. *trmir* 'an inflated skin for crossing (a river)' < OIA *dṛ́ti-* 'leather bag' (6511) with word-initial devoicing (for which there are parallels in Outer Languages) plus < OIA **mana*[5] 'skin-bag' (10044). It is unclear whether this word is mono- or bi-morphemic.

2.4.10 Šaṭ. *thʌrčũ̀ ṇḍ* 'woodpecker' is < OIA **thar-* 'tremble' (6092) plus *cúṇṭati* *'strikes' (4857). This is probably a specializing compound.

[33] But *čávar* itself is certainly not an echo word because Kalasha usually uses *m-* in the echo forms.

2.4.11 Garh. *dagaṛi, dagaṛu, dagaṛo* 'friendship–friendship', i.e. 'company, friendship', *dagaṛyā* 'friend' and similar forms in Ku. are < OIA **dutīya-* 'second' (6402) (Pa. *dutiyyatā-* 'friendship') plus OIA **ghāṭa-* 'connection' (Pk. *ghāḍa-* 'friendship' and *ghāḍiya-* 'companion') (4458).

2.4.12 Ind. *dhižū́* 'daughter–daughter', i.e. 'a young daughter'. The two syllables represent two morphologically (and historically?) different derivations from the same original OIA lemma *duhitŕ̥-* 'daughter' (6481, see there for forms beginning with an affricate). Independently used in Ind. is only *dhī́* 'daughter'.

2.4.13 Bng. *nɔnɔ̃ḍi* 'small–young girl' i.e. 'virgin, girl', Deog. *nɔnɔ̃ṇḍ* 'virgin, unmarried woman' are < OIA **ślakṣṇa-* 'small' (12732) plus < OIA **luṇḍī-* 'defective' (see 11076 and there e.g. N. *luṭhi* 'young unmarried woman'). First component is found independently in Bng. *nanɔ̃* 'child', the second component is not used independently. Both words are monomorphemic because of irregular loss of *-l-*.

2.4.14 Klm. '*nīlbot*' 'pigeon' (Biddulph 1971) is a relatively old ± NATIVE type of quasi-synonym compound as it is built < OIA *nī́ la-* 'dark blue' (7563) plus ← Middle Iranian *kabōtar* 'pigeon' which itself is built from Middle Iranian *kabōd* 'grey-blue' and which has a parallel in OIA *kapóta-* 'pigeon'. Many 'pigeon' words in IA are built with initial colour terms like *haritāla-* *'green', 'green pigeon' (13987). The first component Klm. *nīl* H(L) 'blue' is used independently, but not, of course, the second component.

2.4.15 Kv. *phɔnnɔ* 'shoulder' derives < OIA **sphiyá-* *'scapula' (13839) plus < OIA **kandha-* 'shoulder'. See OIA *skandhá-* 'shoulder' (13627) and ibid. Turner's comment on absence of initial *s-* in Nuristani and Dardic allomorphs. Bng. (which is neighbouring Kv.) has the same allomorph *kā̃ dɔ* 'shoulder' also going back to OIA **kandha-*, but neither Bng. nor Kv. have an independent reflex of OIA **sphiyá-*.

2.4.16 Ind. *bʌṭkumā̃r* 'a young (pubescent) girl; a virgin'. Second element (OIA *kumārī́* - 'young girl' [3303]) is not inherited but borrowed from one of the Dardic languages where OIA medial *-m-* has been preserved.[34] First element is < OIA **beṭṭa-* 'defective' (9238, see there e.g. H. *beṭī* 'girl'). The components are not used independently. Similar compounds in IA are: North B. *beṭī chāvā* 'woman' < OIA **beṭṭa-* plus < OIA **chāpa-* 'young one' (5026), Bng. *beṭkuṛi* 'young daughter' with second component < OIA **kuḍī-* 'girl' (3245), Sant. *coṇḍ kuṛi* 'a girl from 8 to 10' with first component related with OIA *cúṇḍati* 'becomes small'; also similar is A. *ji-put* 'child' < OIA *duhitŕ̥-* 'daughter' (6481) and *putrá-*[1] 'son' (8265). Triconstituent synonym compounds are found e.g. in Ash. *istrimalīkuṛā̃* 'girl' < OIA *strī́* - 'woman' (13734) plus *mahallikā-* 'mother' (see 9935) plus **kuḍī-* 'girl', and Kal. *istríža gúdạk* 'young girl' < OIA *strī́* - plus *jāyā́* - 'wife' (5205) plus **kuḍī-* 'girl'.

2.4.17 Klm. *bā̃bäs* HL 'upper arm' is < OIA *bāhú-* 'arm' (9229, regarding second bilabial consonant in Klm. cf. there Ḍ. *baova* 'arm') and second component <*hásta-* 'hand'?[35]

2.4.18 Ind. *bilū̃ṭ*^{h} 'a (bloody) vendetta' and Phal. *biloṣṭ* 'fight (over something)' both are < OIA **vilopa-kuṣṭa-* literally 'destruction-killed' (11912, 3369). This synonym compound is built from a noun and a participle.

[34] This is to say that Indus Kohistani reflects OIA *-m-* normally as a nasalized vowel.

[35] Similar meaning Phal. *bāu'gā̃ṛu* 'arm above the elbow' with second component, according to Turner (see ibid.), < OIA *gāḍha-* 'thick' (4118) is not a synonym compound but has a semantic parallel in West Pahāṛī, e.g. in Kṭg. *bhɔ́mphər* 'that part of the shoulder nearest to the arm' which is < OIA **bāhusphara-* 'arm near shoulder' (9233a).

2.4.19 Sir.dod. *'bullu* 'owl–owl', i.e. 'owl' and probably also New. *bhulūkhā* 'owl' (loanword) contain as second component a reflex < OIA *úlūka-*[1] 'owl' (2359). Regarding double lateral in Sir.dod. cf. e.g. H. *ullū* 'owl'. The first component *b(h)u-* has parallels e.g. in Yid. *bū* 'owl', Kho. *bū, bú* 'owl', Mj. *biū*, and Sang. *bāw* 'owl'. In northwestern South Asia one comes across a bewildering number of different 'owl' words in various combinations with same words sometimes also designating other birds. Yid. *bū* etc. is hardly a borrowing ← Pers. *būm* 'owl' but is an onomatopoeic word that resembles PIE **b(e)u-* 'owl' which is reflected e.g. in Latin *būō* 'owl'.

2.4.20 M.Wār. *belkəḍ* 'crab–crab', i.e. 'crab' is < OIA lex. *bilvaka-* 'crab' plus < OIA *karkaṭa-*[1] 'crab' (2816).

2.4.21 Tor. *lʌgur* 'red–red', i.e. 'red' (Z.) < OIA *lóhita-* 'red' (11165) plus < OIA *gaurá-* 'pale red' (4345). It is unclear whether this word is mono- or bi-morphemic.

2.4.22 K. *vuzmal* and Sir.dod. *uzmuli'ya* 'lightning–lightning', i.e. 'lightning' with first component *(v)uz-* < OIA *vidyút-* 'flashing, lightning' (11742). The second component is probably not used independently in K. and Sir.dod., but has independent parallels in Ḍog. *mɪlk* 'lightning' and variants of Ind. *'mɪli* 'lightning'. Its etymological origin is, however, unclear.

2.4.23 Bng. *śɔgāṛ* and Jaun. *śɔgārɔ* both 'spring of water' are probably < OIA *srótas-* 'stream' (13889) plus < OIA *ghāra-* 'sprinkling' (4468). At least in Bng., the two words are not used as free forms, and therefore the word is monomorphemic.

2.4.24 Deog. *śuĩtāḷu* 'needle of a conifer' is < OIA *sūcī́* - 'needle' (13551) plus < OIA *tū́la-*[1] a.o. 'pencil' (5904) with vowel swapping. First component *śuĩ-* is interesting because Turner (1966) considers under this lemma the possibility of OIA **śūcī́-*; this is supported by the Deog. form and OIA lex. v.l. *śucī̆* - (mentioned by Turner). The palatal sibilants are either due to coronal consonant harmony, or, perhaps more plausible, as argued by Turner, due to an original IA *ś-* because of Ash. *arċū́ċ* 'needle' (with *ar-* < OIA *ā́rā-* 'shoemaker's awl, driver's hook'). Note also the similarity, even though in an inverse order, of the synonym compounds Deog. *śuĩtāḷu* and Ash. *arċū́ċ*.

2.4.25 Mult. (O'Brien 1987) *sangola* 'arrow–arrow', i.e. 'spear' < OIA *śaṅkú-* 'stick; arrow' (12260) plus *bhalla-*[3] 'a kind of arrow' (9409).

2.4.26 Ko. *śempāṭo* 'wing-leaf' i.e. 'fin; wing' with first component deriving < OIA **skambha-*[2] 'shoulder-blade, wing, plumage' (13640, see there Mult. *khambhaṛā* 'fin'[36]) and second component < OIA *páttra-* 'leaf of book' with *-ṭṭ-* extension (see 7733) which is also found in Ko. *puṭ* 'page'.

2.4.27 M. Coch. *sonnarliṅ* 'orange–orange', i.e. 'orange' is < OIA lex. *sugandhaka-* 'orange' plus < OIA *nāraṅgá-* 'orange tree' (7073) but from Pk. onwards also meaning 'orange'. The word probably has an intrusive *-l-*.

2.4.28 Garh. *hilā̃s* 'aquatic bird–aquatic bird', i.e. 'a (type of) bird' is a generalizing compound < OIA lex. *hilla-*[1] 'a kind of aquatic bird' (14117) plus < OIA *haṁsá-* 'goose' (13937).

2.5 Monomorphemic exocentric transparent reinforcing synonym compounds

2.5.1 Bng. *ā̀rul*, Jaun. and Deog. *harul* 'a song which is ravishing–shaking,'[37] i.e. 'type of (mostly: hero) song' is < OIA *hāraka-* 'ravishing; a kind of prose' and second component not directly < OIA *ullalati* 'jumps out' (2373, see there L. *ulraṇ* 'to rush at in a rage') but < OIA *ullala-* 'shaking, trembling'. In Bng. only the second component is used independently as noun *ùlɛ* 'push, shove' and verb *ùlṇɔ*$_1$[38] 'to shoot up', but not the first one which, however, is found in Him., Gaw., Mal., etc., e.g. Him. *hár* 'song'.

[36] The historical change of OIA *sk-* > *(*)c(h)-* > *ś-* instead of *kh-* is typically found in Outer Languages.

[37] Note what, long ago, Oakley and Gairola (1935: 160) wrote about hero songs sung by Garhwali bards: 'Such is the warlike spirit of these songs that the young folk who hear them become hypnotised, as it were, and begin to dance and perform extraordinary feats—such as uprooting trees, carrying huge weights, rushing into the burning fire, eating nettles, earth, etc.'

[38] The falling tone is due to contamination with Bng. *ùlṇɔ*$_2$ 'to be crowded together' which is < OIA **hull-* 'pierce' (14147, see there N. *hulnu* 'to drive in [cattle into a fold]').

2.5.2 Ind. *kʌṭākũl* 'a subject which is swaying–confused', i.e. 'winding, meandering (road, river), coiling (snake)' ← reduplicated *kʌ̀ṭ-kʌṭ^h* 'swaying from side to side' with unclear origin plus < OIA *ākula-* 'confused' (1012) with preservation of *-k-* due to analogical *-kk-* (Turner 1966: 'poss. Muṇḍa origin'). Second component is not used independently.

2.5.3 Mult. *jēṭhā-palēṭhā* 'one who is first–dearest', i.e. 'firstborn' (O'Brien 1987) is a quasi-echo formation < OIA *jyéṣṭha-* 'first, chief' (5286) plus either < OIA *préṣṭha-* 'dearest, most beloved or desired' or < OIA **prathil(l)a-iṣṭa-* 'first-beloved' (see 8652 and 1597).

2.5.4 K. *pōna-bachĕ* 'a woman who is like a vulva-anus,'[39] i.e. '(of a woman) one who has an ill-omened vulva' with first component also found in *pōnuku* 'of, or belonging to, the anus or the vulva' and *pōn* 'anus; female private parts'. This component derives < OIA (Mahābhārata) *apāná-* 'the anus'. Regarding second component cf. Bshk. (same as Klm.) *boč* 'vulva' which Turner derives < OIA **bocca-*[1] 'defective' (9266).

2.5.5 Ind. *šilkʌṇḍà^h* 'hairs which are like spike-thorn', i.e. 'hairs standing on end' < OIA *śū́la-* 'spike' (12575), but with fem. ending as in Pk. *sūlī-* and epenthesis of final vowel, plus < OIA *kaṇṭa-*[1] 'thorn' (2668).

2.6 Monomorphemic Endocentric Partially Transparent Synonym Compounds

2.6.1 Bng. *kɔ̃ ṅgtaḷu* 'palate' with second component < OIA *tā́lu-* 'palate' (5803); first component perhaps morphologically connected with OIA **kakudha-* 'hump' (2583) or *kakubhá-* 'lofty' (2584) but semantically (yet not phonologically) closer is OIA **kākutstha-* 'palate' (2996). Thus, the precise origin and meaning of the first component are unclear. None of the components is used independently.

[39] This is obviously originally a strong invective.

2.6.2 Khaś., Marm., Śeu. *gelhori*, *gəlhoṛi*, Low Rudh. *gəlhoṛa* all 'cheek', and Ind. *mũʌ̀ỹ hargʌỳl*[i] 'cheek' with reverse order of the components found in the West Pahāṛī varieties and with *mũʌ̀ỹ* genitive of *mṹ* 'cheek' which is < OIA *múkha-* 'mouth, face' (10158); here perhaps also Sh. *häróm* 'cheek' if *-m* also derives < OIA *múkha-*.[40] All forms except Sh. contain a component < OIA *galla-* 'cheek' (4089). The origin and meaning of the element *hVr-*, *hVṛ-* *'cheek?' is unclear and the element is not, to my knowledge, used independently. The two accents in Ind. *mũʌ̀ỹ hargʌỳl*[i] show that this is morphologically a genitive syntagm—in this regard it belongs to the first category above of intermediate constructions—but semantically it is a triconstituent compound (see footnote 39).

2.7 'Monomorphemic' exocentric metaphorical transparent synonym compounds

2.7.1 Klm. *kumudīn* (Biddulph 1971) 'wife who is maidenly daughter-like', i.e. 'a wife' is < OIA *kumārī́* - 'young girl' (3303) plus < OIA **duhitājana-* 'daughter's people' (6481).[41] It is, however, somehow unclear whether the modifier is the left or the right constituent, although more likely to me appears as left modifier. The same problem appears in the next example.[42]

---

[40] Cf. also sub 10158 K. *mu-gaṇḍ* 'cheek' with second component < OIA *gaṇḍa-*[3] 'cheek' (3999) which may be etymologically connected with OIA *galla-* 'cheek', and first component being a kind of synecdoche (cheek as part of the face). Semantically similar are Orm. *mux* 'cheek' and Yid. *rūi* 'cheek' both also basically meaning 'face'.

[41] Turner (1966) suggests here alternatively **duhitābhaginī-* 'daughter's young female relative' which fits semantically better with the uses of reflexes of this lemma known to me.

[42] It is quite common in South Asia to describe non-sexual relationships e.g. between gods and goddesses or between non-agnate family members as ones between brothers and sisters, or to designate goddesses without children as mothers, etc. These, and similar phenomena have, to my knowledge, not yet been studied in detail. However, an underlying principle motivating such renaming practices seems to be a form of political correctness for veiling 'critical' social relationships and roles.

2.7.2 Bhaṭ. *dhï-bïȭ* 'a woman who is daughterly sister-like', i.e. 'a woman' < OIA *duhitŕ̥-* 'daughter' (6481) plus < OIA *bhaginī-* 'sister' (9349).

2.7.3 Bhaṭ. *nā̃ k^{w}üṭ˺* 'an (unmarried) girl who is like a (married) woman', i.e. 'a girl' ← *nā̃* 'wife' which is < OIA *nayaná-*^{2} 'eye' (6968, cf. there Kṭg. *naṇi* 'pretty girl') plus < a side-form of OIA **kuḍa-*^{1} 'boy' (3245) (cf. Tam. *kuṭṭi* 'little girl'). Here clearly the left constituent is the modifier.

2.7.4 Bhaṭ. *bh^{i}ɛńdür* 'sister–harlot', i.e. 'a bride' is < OIA *bhaginī-* 'sister' (9349) plus <*dārá-*^{2} 'wife' or, more likely, <*dārikā-* 'girl; harlot' (6481) which in Turner (1985) is suggested to be the same as *dārá-*^{1} 'rent, hole, cleft'. If this interpretation is correct, the compound could be characterized as a ±CONTEMPT synonym compound contrasting the unmarried own sister (–CONTEMPT) with the non-kindred unmarried girl (+CONTEMPT).

2.8 Monomorphemic Synonym Compounds with Unclear Structures

2.8.1 Bng. *dōti* 'tomorrow', Him. *dōt* 'the morning', Chin. *dōte* 'morning hours' are < OIA **doṣā-rātrī-* lit. 'night–night', i.e. < OIA *doṣā́* -^{1} 'night; at dusk' (6590) and *rā́trī-* 'night' (10702) (regarding meaning 'tomorrow' see in the OIA lemma Bshk. (same as Klm.) *rēt, rēd* 'tomorrow' which parallels Bng. *ratti* 'morning' and *ratī-rāt* 'very early in the morning'). The Bng., Him., and Chin. forms may have originally been either antonym compounds 'yesterday-tomorrow' or synonym compounds 'twilight–twilight', but the semantic development from 'night' to 'morning' is unclear.

2.8.2 Ind. *dhúm-dhum* 'a (rising) cloud of dust' looks like a simple reduplicated word deriving < OIA *dhūmá-* 'smoke, vapour, mist' (6849). However, there is related Bur. *duldúm* with exactly same meaning 'sich erhebende Wolke (von Staub, Rauch usw.)' which is a synonym compound with the first part deriving < OIA **dhūḍi-* 'dust, powder' (6835) and the second < OIA *dhūmá-* 'smoke, vapour, mist' (6849). Thus the Ind. word probably dissociated < older **dhúl–dhum* from a synonym compound into a pseudo-reduplicated word. This is supported by the fact that Ind. uses independently only *dhùã* with the same derivation < 6849 but with the different meaning, 'smoke', which thus belongs to a different historical layer. Bur. *dul* 'collyrium' may be the corresponding independent form of the first component derived <**dhūḍi-*, but the second component is not used independently. Both the Ind. and Bur. words are monomorphemic.

2.8.3 Wg. *maǰost-aṭ'i* 'upper arm bone, humerus' is ←*maǰ'ost* 'upper arm' which is, according to Degener (1998), < OIA *mádhya-* 'middle' (9804) plus *ásthi-* 'bone' (982); second element *-aṭ'i* is < OIA *aṣṭhi-** 'bone' (958). Turner (1966) notes that connection of *aṣṭhi-* with *ásthi-* is obscure, and further connection with OIA *haḍḍa-* 'bone' is improbable. Thus it would seem that the Wg. compound is a combination of an earlier with a later form of the same OIA 'bone' lemma which would resemble the entry 2.4.12. But more likely it is a compound similar to Klm. *bắbäs* HL 'upper arm' (see 2.4.17) with second component < OIA *hásta-* 'hand'. If so, this is not a synonym compound.

3. SYNONYM COMPOUNDS IN OLD INDO-ARYAN AND IN OTHER LANGUAGE FAMILIES

In a detailed study of pleonastic compounds in Dravidian, Periannan Chandrasekaran (2011: 1) describes these compounds as '[a] heretofore unidentified word structure … reconstructible to the proto-stage …', i.e. to the level of Proto-Dravidian. All examples discussed by him appear to be perfect reinforcing synonym compounds; for instance, Koṇḍa *uma-gunji* means 'owl' and its two components also mean 'owl' in various Dravidian languages. Among motivations for the use of pleonastic compounds Chandrasekaran (2011: 6) suggests paraphrasing, and he arrives at the following conclusion (p. 48): 'Coming back to the motivations for the Dravidian pleonasm, it is quite likely that this paraphrasing habit started from a speech protocol or convention in the primordial days of Dravidian (Pre-Dravidian?) of a speaker paraphrasing her word in terms of another word hopefully already known to the listener. This might have been necessitated by the extreme diversity in the lexicon'. Even though this may be a factor for the production of synonym compounds, it does not explain its wide spread in South Asia and beyond. The same marked trend for synonym formations is found, e.g. in Southeast Asian languages like Vietnamese and Khmer, and probably also in Tibetan (see LaPolla and Thurgood 2006). It is therefore an ancient areal phenomenon. The same trend is also found in Old Indo-Aryan, even though apparently neither Sanskrit grammarians nor modern Sanskrit scholars devoted much attention to it. Here follows a selection of Old Indo-Aryan synonym compounds. Their evidence is documented from Vedic (note e.g. *ahár-dive* 'day by day' = *ahár-* 'day' + *divá-* 'day'[43]) to later Sanskrit, thus testifying to a long linguistic practice. Note, however, that more than half of the following examples are reconstructed forms found in Turner (1966). Therefore I suggest that the use of synonym compounds in Indo-Aryan was, and is, more typical for informal spoken language than it is for a written and more formal literature style. All of the following examples are bi-morphemic, and I do not know whether 'monomorphemic' compounds can also be discovered in Old Indo-Aryan. But perhaps it is worth a try.

3.1 Endocentric Reinforcing Synonym Compounds

annā́ dya- 'food' (398) = *ánna-* 'food' + *ādyà-* 'food'

**kalaśavarta-* 'circular vessel' (2921) = *kaláśa-* 'water-pot' + **varta-* 'circular object' (11347) but later reflexes typically mean 'cup, bowl'

**gharmoṣma-* 'heat' (4447) = *gharmá-* 'heat' + *ūṣmán-* 'heat'

dīpāloka- 'burning torch' (6357) = *dīpa-* 'light' + *āloka-* 'brightness'

dehīkaṇṭha-* 'wall' (6563) = *dehī́ -* 'surrounding wall' + *kaṇṭhá- 'border' (2680) but meaning 'wall' is found in L. and P.

---

43 This is a kind of narrative or iterative compound. Note also the loss of one accent as in many Dardic examples above.

**phalapaṭṭa-* 'board' (9059) = *phala-* 'gaming board' + *paṭṭa-* 'slab, tablet'

sāmantarāja- *'border chieftain' (13350) = *sāmanta-* 'chief of a district' + *rā́jan-* 'chieftain'

**skambhadaṇḍa-* 'pillar pole' (13642) = *skambhá-* 'pillar' + *daṇḍá-* 'pole, stem'

hambhārava- 'lowing' (13974) = *hambhā-* 'lowing' + *ráva-* 'cry, howl (of animals)'

3.2 Exocentric reinforcing synonym compounds

bālaputra- 'having children' (9220) = *bālá-* 'boy' + *putrá-* 'son'

3.3 Generalizing compounds

**gharāyatana-* 'house and home' (4441) = *ghara-* 'house' + *āyátana-* 'home', but later reflexes typically mean 'good family'[44]

**halasetra-* 'plough and rope' (14011) but the modern reflex means 'whole apparatus of a plough'

3.4 Specializing compounds including semantic narrowing

**dadhidugdhā-* 'curds and milk' (6148) = *dádhi-* 'thick sour milk' + *dugdhá-* 'milk' but the modern reflex means only 'curds'

piṇḍālu- 'a species of Cocculus, Dioscorea globosa' (8173) = *píṇḍa-* 'lump' + *ālu-* 'esculent root'

**śamyāyuga-* 'pin and yoke' (12321) = *śámyā-* 'yoke pin' + *yugá-* 'yoke' but reflexes in West Pahāṛī including Bng. mean only 'yoke'

[44] This compound is actually a *hendiadyoin*, i.e. a set expression like German *in Bausch und Bogen* 'lock, stock and barrel'. Maybe for South and Southeast Asia synonym compounds are more typical than *hendiadyoin*, which, conversely, may be more typical in other parts of the world, but this would need an elaborate investigation. But in any case there is the suspicion that **gharāyatana-* is a relatively late coinage.

3.5 Redundant Compounds

**śilāśānī*- 'whetstone' (12462) = *śilā́* - 'rock' + *śāna*- 'whetstone'

dhvajapaṭa- 'flag' (6899) = *dhvajá*- 'flag' + *paṭa*- '(a painted piece of) cloth'

for H. *pakhauṭā* 'wing' Turner (1966) suggests derivation < OIA **pakṣapaṭṭa*- 'wing' (7630) but semantically better is derivation < OIA *pakṣá*- 'wing' + *páttra*- 'wing' with -*ṭṭ*- extension (see 7733)

**tāḍarukṣa*- 'palmyra palm' (5752a) = *tāḍa*-[3] 'palm tree'+ **rukṣa*- 'tree'

**pūgarukṣa*- 'areca palm' (8314a) = *pūga*- 'Areca catechu'+ **rukṣa*- 'tree'

sphaṭikamaṇi- 'crystal' (13819) = *sphaṭika*- 'crystal' + *maṇí*- 'jewel'

GENERAL SYMBOLS AND ABBREVIATIONS

← = (a) borrowed from another language
(b) deriving from another word class of the same language
< = historically deriving from
> = historically developing into
v̀ = (a) in Dardic languages: pitch accent with falling contour
(b) in West Pahāṛī Bangani: generic sign for several tonemes[45]
v́ = in Dardic languages: pitch accent with rising contour
H = 'high' tone in Klm.
HL = 'high-low' tone in Klm.
H(L) = 'delayed high-low' tone in Klm.
'word' = are words which have been put between inverted commas either because they come from phonologically underspecified sources or in order to indicate a literate meaning
lex. = lexicographic
(Z.) = data from my own field work, especially Bng. and Deog., that has not been published by other authors

[45] In Bangani, v̀ frequently, but not always, indicates historical loss of aspiration of an originally aspirated stop.

LANGUAGE ABBREVIATIONS

A. = Assamese
Ash. = Ashkun (Nuristani)
B. = Bengali
Bhad. = Bhadrawāhī dialect of West Pahāṛī
Bhaṭ. = Bhaṭīse dialect of Indus Kohistani (Ind.) (Dardic)
Bng. = Bangani (West Pahāṛī)
Brj. = Brajbhāṣā
Bur. = Burushaski
Chin. = Chinali dialect of West Pahāṛī
Ḍ = Ḍumāki
Deog. = Deogārī dialect of West Pahāṛī[46]
Dm. = Dameli (Nuristani-Dardic)
Ḍog. = Ḍogrī dialect of Punjabi
G. = Gujarātī
Garh. = Gaṛhwālī
Gau. = Gauro dialect of Indus Kohistani (Ind.)
Gaw. = Gawar-Bati (Dardic)
H. = Hindi
Him. = Himachali
IA = Indo-Aryan
Ind. = Indus Kohistani (Dardic)
Jaun. = Jaunsārī dialect of West Pahāṛī
K. = Kashmiri
Kal. = Kalasha (Dardic)
Khaś. = Khaśālī dialect of West Pahāṛī
Kho. = Khowār (Dardic)
Klm. = Kalami (Dardic)
Ko. = Koṅkaṇī
Ko.Kaṇ. = Kaṇkoṇ dialect of Koṅkaṇī
Kt. = Kati (Nuristani)
Kṭg. = Kōṭgaṛhī dialect of West Pahāṛī
Ku. = Kumaunī
Kv. = Kvārī dialect of West Pahāṛī[47]
L. = Lahndā
Low Rudh. = Low Rudhārī sub-dialect of Khaśālī (Khaś.)
M. = Marāṭhī
M.Coch. = Cochin dialect of Marāṭhī
M.Wār. = Wārlī dialect of Marāṭhī
Mal. = Mālvī dialect of Rājasthānī
Marm. = Marmatī sub-dialect of Khaśālī (Khaś.)
Mj. = Munji (Iranian)
Mult. = Multānī dialect of Lahndā (L.)
N. = Nepāli
New. = Newārī
NIA = New Indo-Aryan
OIA = Old Indo-Aryan
Orm. = Ōrmuṛī (West Iranian)
P. = Punjabi
Pa. = Pali
Paš. = Pashai (Dardic)
Pers. = Persian
Phal. = Phalūṛa (Dardic)
PIE = Proto-Indo-European
Pk. = Prakrit
Psht. = Pashto
Ra. = Raji (spoken in Kumaon and of unclear provenance)
S. = Sindhī
Sang. = Sanglechi (Iranian)
Sant. = Santali (Munda)
Šaṭ. = Šāṭōṭī dialect of Indus Kohistani (Dardic)
Sh. = Shina
Sir.dod. = Sirājī dialect of the Ḍoḍa area of West Pahāṛī
Śeu. = Śeuṭī sub-dialect of Khaśālī (Khaś.)
Tor. = Tōrwālī (Dardic)
Wg. = Waigalī (Nuristani)
Wkh. = Wakhi (Iranian)
Yid. = Yidgha (Iranian)

[46] Spoken south of Bangan.

[47] Spoken north of Bangan.

REFERENCES

Abbi, Anvita. 1992. *Reduplication in South Asian Languages: An Areal, Typological and Historical Study*. New Delhi: Allied Publishers.

_______ 1980. *Semantic Grammar of Hindi: A Study in Reduplication*. New Delhi: Bahri Publications.

Agnihotri, Rama Kant. 2007. *Hindi: An Essential Grammar*. London: Routledge.

Biddulph, John. 1971 (1880). *Tribes of the Hindoo Koosh*. Graz: Akademische Druck-und Verlagsanstalt.

Borgwaldt, Susanne and Lüttenberg, Dina. *Semantic Transparency of Compound Nouns in Native and Non-Native Speakers*. <http://www.nytud.hu/imm14/abs/borgwaldt_luttenberg.pdf> accessed 16 October 2016.

Burrow, Thomas and Emeneau, Murray Barnson. 1984. *A Dravidian Etymological Dictionary*. 2nd edn. Oxford: Clarendon Press.

Chandrasekaran, Periannan. 2011. 'Pleonastic compounding: An ancient Dravidian word structure'. *Electronic Journal of Vedic Studies* 18.1: 1–58. <http://www.laurasianacademy.com/pleonastic.pdf> accessed 16 October 2016.

Degener, Almuth. 1998. *Die Sprache von Nisheygram im afghanischen Hindukusch*. Wiesbaden: Harrassowitz.

Downing, Pamela. 1977. 'On the creation and use of English compound nouns'. *Language* 53.4: 810–42.

Emeneau, Murray Barnson. 1980. *Language and Linguistic Area*. Stanford: Stanford University Press.

Haiman, John and Ourn, Noeurng. *Coordinate compounds and Khmer phrase structure*. <http://sealang.net/sala/archives/pdf4/haiman2002coordinate.pdf> accessed 17 October 2016.

Lai, Yu-da and Myers, James. 2012. 'The recognition of spoken mono-morphemic compounds in Chinese'. *Taiwan Journal of Linguistics* 10: 41–88.

LaPolla, Randy, J. and Thurgood, Graham (eds.). 2006. *The Sino-Tibetan Languages*. London: Routledge. (Routledge Language Family Series 3).

Mallory, James Patrick and Adams, Douglas Quentin. 2006. *The Oxford Introduction to Proto-Indo-European and the Proto-Indo-European World*. Oxford: Oxford University Press.

Mayrhofer, Manfred. 1986–2001. *Etymologisches* Wörterbuch des Altindoarischen. 3 vols. Heidelberg: Carl Winter.

McGregor, Ronald Stuart. 1993. *Oxford Hindi–English Dictionary*. Oxford: Oxford University Press.

Oakley, E. Sherman and Gairola, Tara Dutt. 1988 (1935). *Himalayan Folklore*. Gurgaon: Vintage Books.

O'Brien, Edward. 1987 (1881). *Glossary of the Multani Language Compared with Punjabi and Sindhi*. Lahore: The Panjab Government Civil Secretariat Press.

Peterson, John. 2011. *A Grammar of Kharia: A South Munda Language*. Leiden: Brill.

Pinnow, Heinz-Jürgen. 1959. *Versuch einer historischen Lautlehre der Kharia-Sprache*. Wiesbaden: Harrassowitz.

Sandell, Ryan. 2011. *Reduplication and Grammaticalization in Vedic Sanskrit.* <http://www.academia.edu/1693673/Reduplication_and_Grammaticalization_in_Vedic_Sanskrit> accessed 17 October 2016.

Sharma, Devi D. 1990. *Tibeto-Himalayan Languages of Uttarakhand.* Part two. New Delhi: Mittal Publications. (Studies in Tibeto-Himalayan Languages 3).

Singh, Rajendra. 1982. 'On some "redundant compounds" in modern Hindi'. *Lingua* 56: 345–51.

Southworth, Franklin C. 2005. *Linguistic Archaeology of South Asia.* London: Routledge-Curzon.

Søgaard, Anders. 2005. 'Compounding theories and linguistic diversity'. In *Linguistic Diversity and Language Theories*, edited by Zygmunt Frajzyngier, Adam Hodges, and David S. Rood. 319–37. Amsterdam: John Benjamins. (Studies in Language Companion Series 72).

Thompson, Laurence C. 1987. *A Vietnamese Reference Grammar.* Honolulu: University of Hawai'i Press.

Trail, Ronald L. and Cooper, Gregory R. 1999. *Kalasha Dictionary—with English and Urdu.* Islamabad: National Institute of Pakistan Studies and Summer Institute of Linguistics. (Studies in Languages of Northern Pakistan 7).

Turner, Ralph Lilley. 1966. *A Comparative Dictionary of the Indo-Aryan Languages.* London: School of Oriental and African Studies.

——— 1931. *A Comparative and Etymological Dictionary of the Nepali Language.* London: Kegan Paul, Trench, Trubner & Co.

——— and Wright, Jack Clifford (ed.). 1985. *A Comparative Dictionary of the Indo-Aryan Languages. Addenda and Corrigenda.* London: School of Oriental and African Studies.

Zoller, Claus Peter. (forthcoming). Indo-Aryan and the Linguistic History and Pre-history of North India *(working title).*

——— 2005. *A Grammar and Dictionary of Indus Kohistani. Volume 1: Dictionary.* Berlin: Mouton de Gruyter.

Contributors

ALEXEI KOCHETOV, Department of Linguistics, University of Toronto, Canada
ALMUTH DEGENER, University of Mainz
BEATE LUBBERGER, SIL International
BERTIL TIKKANEN, University of Helsinki
CARLA F. RADLOFF, SIL International
CLAUS PETER ZOLLER, University of Oslo
ELENA BASHIR, University of Chicago
FAZAL AMIN BEG, Quaid-i-Azam University, Islamabad and Karakoram International University, Gilgit
GEORG BUDDRUSS, University of Mainz
GREGORY D.S. ANDERSON, Living Tongues Institute for Endangered Languages and University of South Africa (UNISA)
HENRIK LILJEGREN, Stockholm University
HUGH VAN SKYHAWK, Seminar for the Science of Religion, University of Basel, Switzerland
JAN HEEGÅRD, University of Copenhagen
JEREMY HAWBAKER, Forman Christian College, Lahore
JOAN L.G. BAART, SIL International
JOHN MOCK, American Institute of Afghanistan Studies and University of California, Santa Cruz
KHAWAJA A. REHMAN, University of Management Sciences and Information Technology Kotli, Azad Kashmir
MIR ALI WAKHANI, Ministry of Education, Islamic Republic of Afghanistan
NABAIG, independent lawyer, Chitral
PAUL ARSENAULT, Tyndale University College, Toronto, Canada
PETER E. HOOK, University of Michigan/University of Virginia
RICHARD F. STRAND, Cottonwood, Arizona, USA
RUTH LAILA SCHMIDT, University of Oslo
TARIQ RAHMAN, Beaconhouse National University
THOMAS E. PAYNE, SIL International and University of Oregon
WAYNE E. LOSEY, SIL International

About

Carla Faye Radloff

12 December 1949–15 April 2012

On Sunday, 15 April 2012, our esteemed colleague and dear friend Carla Radloff passed away in a car accident. Carla was driving home to Loveland, Colorado from a speaking engagement in Wyoming when an oncoming car lost control and hit her head-on. Carla was 62 years old at the time of her death and was survived by three sisters, two brothers-in-law, seven nieces and nephews, and five great-nieces and nephews. Carla's life touched many others around the world through her many years of overseas service. She was an accomplished linguist, an effective leader, and an irreplaceable friend.

Carla was born in 1949 in Cozad, Nebraska. She graduated from Fort Morgan High School in 1967, and received a bachelor's degree from Colorado State University and a master's degree from the University of Wisconsin at Madison. She worked as a speech therapist in elementary schools in Delta, Colorado and Thermopolis, Wyoming.

In 1980, Carla felt called to work overseas, though not immediately sure where that would be. The people of Western Asia were placed on her heart in 1981 and she had been serving there since 1982. Her affiliation with SIL International started in 1986, first as a short-term assistant, and from 1994 as a career member.

Carla made invaluable contributions to dialect survey and the study of bilingualism and language use in Pakistan, to the methodology of sociolinguistic survey in general, and also to the linguistic study and documentation of the Shina language of Gilgit, Pakistan. Having already published on several aspects of the language, she was recently working on a more extensive grammatical description of the language. She encouraged and facilitated work on the development and standardization of a writing system for Shina and on the publication of folk tales and other materials in the language, and enthusiastically supported initiatives to introduce mother tongue-based multilingual education in the Gilgit area. In addition to her language work, she also very competently served as SIL's team leader in northern Pakistan between 1999 and 2006.

Carla Faye Radloff
12 December 1949–15 April 2012

One of our colleagues commented: 'I always enjoyed talking with Carla and appreciated her wit and humor, as well as her smile that made life appear so much more valuable.' Many of us share that experience, and sorely miss that wit, that humour, and that smile.

EDUCATION

- BSc from Colorado State University, Fort Collins, Colorado, USA, 1971; major: Speech and Hearing Disorders.
- MSc from University of Wisconsin at Madison, Madison, Wisconsin, USA, 1972; major: Communicative Disorders.
- Graduate linguistic studies, Summer Institute of Linguistics, University of Washington, Seattle, Washington, USA, 1980.
- Graduate linguistic studies, Summer Institute of Linguistics, University of Texas at Arlington, Arlington, Texas, USA, 1981.
- Graduate linguistic studies, Summer Institute of Linguistics, University of Oklahoma, Norman, Oklahoma, USA, 1984.

SERVICE

- Language Disorders and Development Specialist and Consultant, Colorado and Wyoming, USA, 1972–9.
- Urdu language and cultural study and experience, South Asia, 1982–3.
- Several terms as Short-Term Assistant with SIL International, 1986–94.
- Sociolinguistic Survey of Northern Pakistan, based in Peshawar, Pakistan, 1986–92. Field research in rural areas of northern Pakistan, conducting interviews and comprehension and bilingualism tests with speakers from different language groups. Coordinated and wrote report on the survey of the Shina language (Northern Areas).
- Member of SIL International from 1994.
- Supervisor of the Sociolinguistic Survey of Punjab, Pakistan, and co-author of the report, 2003–11.
- Field linguistics, language research studies on the Shina language of Gilgit, 1993–2012.

PUBLICATIONS

2011. With Lars O. Dyrud. *Sociolinguistic Survey of Punjab, Pakistan.* Islamabad: National Institute of Pakistan Studies and Summer Institute of Linguistics, 397 pages.

2008. 'Indicators of language attitudes toward Shina dialects'. In *Proceedings of the Third International Hindu Kush Cultural Conference*, edited by Israr-ud-Din. Karachi: Oxford University Press, 235–49.

2003. 'The solution to a linguistic mystery: the absence of diphthongs in the Shina language of Gilgit'. In *Pakistani Languages and Society: Problems and Prospects*, edited by Joan Baart and Ghulam Hyder Sindhi. Islamabad: National Institute of Pakistan Studies and Summer Institute of Linguistics, 145–53.

2002. With Shakil Ahmad Shakil, Talib Jan Khan, and Muhammad Zaman Sagar. *An Outline for Cultural Research [Urdu: Saqafati Tahqiqi Ainah]*. Islamabad: National Institute of Pakistan Studies and Summer Institute of Linguistics, 112 pages.

1999. *Aspects of the Sound System of Gilgiti Shina*. Islamabad: National Institute of Pakistan Studies and Summer Institute of Linguistics, 128 pages.

1998. *Folktales in the Shina of Gilgit*. Islamabad: National Institute of Pakistan Studies and Summer Institute of Linguistics, 197 pages.

1997. 'An example of reduplication in Gilgit Shina (with notes on "compound" verbs)'. *North Pakistan Newsletter NIPS-SIL* 21: 3–11.

1997. 'Analysis of Gilgiti Shina noun classes, revisited'. *North Pakistan Newsletter NIPS-SIL* 19: 14–21.

1997. 'Social aspects of the languages of Northern Pakistan'. *North Pakistan Newsletter NIPS-SIL* 19: 3–14.

1997. 'An exercise in areal linguistics: the place of Gilgiti Shina in the South and Central Asian linguistic areas'. *North Pakistan Newsletter NIPS-SIL* 17: 3–11.

1996. 'A preliminary analysis of Gilgiti Shina noun classes'. *North Pakistan Newsletter NIPS-SIL* 14: 3–8.

1992. *Sociolinguistic Survey of Northern Pakistan, Volume 2, Languages of Northern Areas*, edited with Peter C. Backstrom. Islamabad: National Institute of Pakistan Studies and Summer Institute of Linguistics.

1992. 'Sentence repetition testing for studies of community bilingualism: an introduction'. *Notes on Linguistics* 56: 19–25.

1991. *Sentence Repetition Testing for Studies of Community Bilingualism*. Dallas: Summer Institute of Linguistics and University of Texas at Arlington, 194 pages.

1991. 'Avenues of acquisition of Urdu proficiency for Hindko-speaking women of Hazara Division (Pakistan)'. In *Proceedings of the Summer Institute of Linguistics International Language Assessment Conference, Horsleys Green, 23–31 May 1989*, edited by Gloria E. Kindell. Dallas: Summer Institute of Linguistics, 235–42.

Index

N

O

P

Q

R

S

Y

Z